AF473772

A Singular Man

A Documented Life of the Artist
Frederick Sandys: 1829-1904

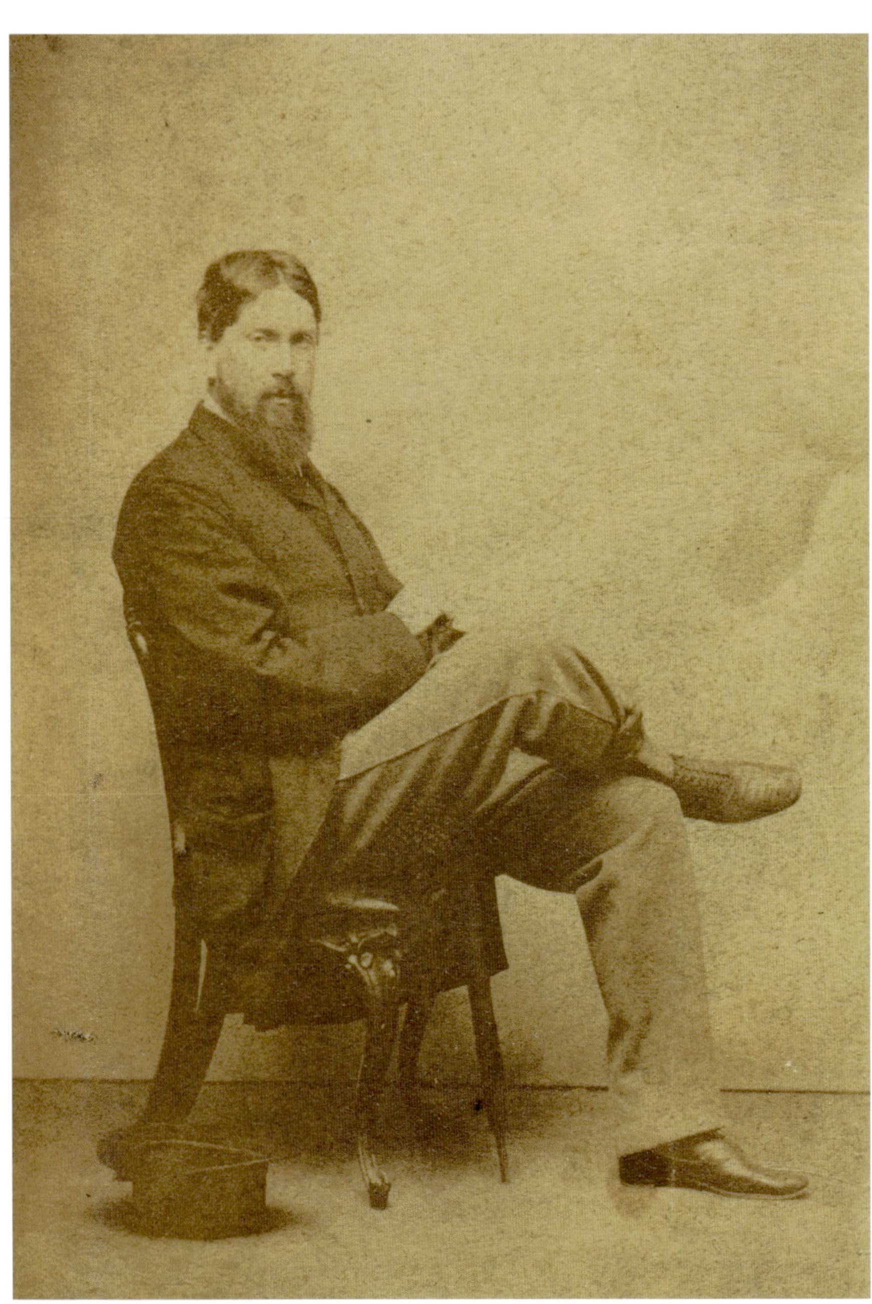

A Singular Man

A Documented Life of the Artist Frederick Sandys: 1829-1904

Betty Elzea

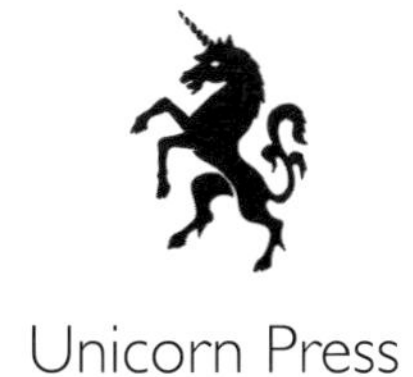

Unicorn Press

To Andrew Wilton

First published in 2023 by
Unicorn Press
60 Bracondale
Norwich NR1 2AS
UK

tradfordhugh@gmail.com
www.unicornpublishing.org

The publication of this book has
been made possible with a grant from
The Albert Dawson Educational Trust

A CIP record of this book can be obtained from the British Library

ISBN 978 1 838395 39 1

Designed by Karen Wilks

Printed in the UK by Swallowtail Print,
Norwich

Frontispiece: Frederick Sandys, photograph taken in Norwich by William Boswell Jr (1840–1889), 1860s. Sandys Family Archive. Word and Image Department, Victoria and Albert Museum.

CONTENTS

The work of Frederick Sandys first captured my interest when, in the early 1960s, I found an unfinished, unframed and unsigned oil painting in a second-hand furniture and general house clearance shop in the London Road, Norbury, in South West London. How it came to be there still baffles me. It depicted the head and shoulders of a young woman in profile with luxuriant hair, sulkily chewing a lock of it, against a background of apple blossom (which was the only part of the picture painted to any degree of finish, the face and head being left in outline as a strong but delicate drawing in rust-coloured paint). The painting was on a wood panel and was soiled and marked with tea stains where a cup had been plonked down on it, but the quality of the work shone through the dirt.

In my ignorance, I had a hazy idea that it might have been by that rather famous Pre-Raphaelite, Dante Gabriel Rossetti. Excitedly, I paid 30 shillings for it (£1.50 in today's money). It seems little enough money now, but it was a large chunk from my 1960s pocket.

I worked then in a lowly position at the Victoria and Albert Museum (V&A) and, soon after finding it, took the painting in to show my colleagues in the Circulation Department (the now defunct travelling exhibition service of the V&A). One of them, the late Harold Barkley, a Prints and Drawings man, recognised it straight away as a familiar subject by Frederick Sandys, *Proud Maisie*, of which several versions on paper are in the V&A's Prints and Drawings Department. Thanks to Harold, I was put on the right track. *Proud Maisie* turned out to be perhaps Frederick Sandys's most successful image. It embodies his appreciation of women's beauty and the love of one particular woman, as we shall see later. In total, he had produced eleven versions after the original drawing, along with two replications with his youngest daughter Gertrude's head, and one, mysteriously, unfinished painting.

Frederick Sandys was only known to me as one of the 'Sixties' illustrators, a group of artists, many of them the Pre-Raphaelites, who designed outstanding illustrations for the new family magazines being published in the 1860s. In fact, this was how his name stayed in the public memory after his death in 1904. During this period Victorian painting began to be thought old fashioned, but the wood-engraved prints of the 'Sixties' artists and illustrators were being 'discovered' by a new generation. By this time, the old, illustrated magazines and books were in dusty attics and in bins outside second-hand bookshops.

The opportunity to extend my knowledge about Frederick Sandys came at last with the project of organising a comprehensive exhibition of his work, after my move in 1971 to Brighton Museum and Art Gallery to be Exhibitions

Organiser. My acquaintance with Sandys and his milieu improved by leaps and bounds in the nine months of research prior to the opening of the exhibition in May 1974 but, due to the time limitation, many facts about this elusive man escaped me still, and the catalogue of that exhibition is flawed. However, connecting with Frederick Sandys's grandson Anthony Crane, the keeper of the family papers, and having his cooperation, was vital to my project to study the man and his work.

As facts unravelled, it gradually appeared to me that Sandys had managed to live two lives, one as an unattached gentleman and an artist, and the other as the father of an illegitimate family. (In fact, he was the father of two illegitimate families, as I was to discover.) It was no surprise that this part of his life was kept under cover to all but his intimate acquaintances.

Sandys seems to have confided nothing about his first family of four with Keomi Gray, the gypsy, to his second, later partially acknowledged, family of eight surviving children. Nevertheless, Mary Emma Jones, their mother, must have known something about his earlier liaison, but presumably it was in her interest to avoid the subject, and certainly not to pass on anything about it to her children.

Following my research in public records and other documentary sources, which opened up many facts (particularly since the advent of the internet), I realised that very little of the earlier part of Sandys's family's history had been passed down to his grandson. Anthony Crane was unaware of the facts about his grandfather's relationship with Keomi Gray, as well as the truth about his grandfather's first daughters with Mary Emma Jones who were fostered but are made evident in Sandys's bankruptcy papers of 1876. Anthony simply knew of them as (unexplained) distant relatives.

There had been factual errors about Sandys more or less from the beginning when art journalists and critics first began to write about him, even during his lifetime. Many of the errors were copied, uncorrected, again and again through the ensuing years. Sandys himself does not seem to have been bothered by such inaccuracies, a fault perhaps of his upbringing. His father, Anthony, had ambitions to be an artist himself and to gain some status in a city which had a historic and still active art tradition. Unfortunately, his artistic efforts turned out to be nothing more than third rate. The son, our subject, was genuinely talented, but was disorganised, impulsive, and financially incompetent, but was above all concerned with maintaining his dignity and the precarious foothold he had managed to achieve at the centre of artistic society in London.

Respectability was in fact a necessity for an artist hoping to make a living from portrait painting. In his case, his patrons were rarely from the aristocracy, but generally came from the wealthy middle class who had made their money in business, industry or the professions.

In defence of his dissembling act, one could also say that he was the victim of the social *mores* of the time, by which he was constrained to present himself at large as a dignified and socially acceptable bachelor artist. In truth, we find that he was the largely absentee father of two families of illegitimate children who, as a result, were brought up in extremely difficult financial circumstances. Very few people must have known the facts of his life and, as it turns out, not even his family knew the whole of it.

First of all, little is known about his early childless marriage to a young Norwich woman except what can be gleaned from the records of his unsuccessful attempt at a divorce. Next, his gypsy model Keomi gave birth to four of his children before disappearing with them back into the semi-obscurity of her East Anglian family background in tents and caravans. His subsequent children with the young actress Mary Emma Jones seem to have been unaware of their three older sisters, who were fostered from birth; indeed, it was a shock for his grandson, Anthony Crane, to learn about them.

His third and final liaison with Mary Emma Jones, his 'little girl', became a permanent one. She had to endure an undercover role for most of her life – a socially and financially precarious life under the assumed name of 'Mrs Neville' in a separate establishment, and with an ever-increasing family to care for. For me, the name of 'Mrs Neville' was a mystery for a long time until the recorded facts of the death and burial of the first of their children gave the clue to this name.

Mary Emma was one of the five daughters of Justice Jones, a customs official in the seaport of Hull in Yorkshire, who moved to London, in retirement, after the death of his wife Rosanna. Mary Emma took to the stage to earn a living, as did two of her sisters, Augusta Maria and Emily Eyre. The Jones sisters supplemented their income with modelling for artists in London, and they can be seen in several artists' works from the 1860s and 1870s.

Augusta Maria, the eldest of the three, married Frederick Vincent Hart, an artist and designer, in 1871. Emilie Eyre, the youngest, married Frederick H. Robson Jr, an actor, in 1870. Mary Emma captured her man (Frederick Sandys) in 1866, but they never married because Sandys was not divorced from his first wife, Georgiana Creed of Norwich.

The importance of maintaining status and respectability, combined with the creation of a large, illegitimate family, meant that Sandys wove a curtain of mystery about his actual private life. The artist and art dealer Charles Fairfax Murray (1849–1919), who was one of the few who knew Sandys well, recognised the problem in a letter of 1897 to the American collector Samuel Bancroft Jr in which he wrote: 'There is, as you say, no good account of Sandys and there's never likely to be one. He won't supply much information about himself, but the inaccuracies of Gray's article are so terrible that he was obliged to correct them. Still the information he gives is very meagre. I suppose I know more about him than any outsider, but it's a difficult subject to handle, the more so that he has several children.' Murray was in a good position to understand, for not only had he known Sandys since the mid-1860s when he began to be a part of the Pre-Raphaelite circle (with which Sandys was then associated) but also in the late 1890s Murray employed Sandys's former housekeeper who must have given him some rare insights. Unfortunately, Murray did not give us the benefit of any further knowledge. We now know, too, that Murray had fathered two illegitimate families himself.

It was frustrating to run out of research time when the 1974 exhibition catalogue had to go to press, but the idea stayed with me to try to excavate further facts about this enigmatic man. Shortly afterwards I moved to Wilmington, Delaware, in the USA, where eventually I had the time to tackle research in depth using the unique Pre-Raphaelite Archive in the library of the Delaware Art Museum where there are papers generated by the collector Samuel Bancroft Jr's correspondence with the Sandys family, and much else. The facilities of the University of Delaware's Morris Library were also invaluable to me. I benefited too from several travel and research grants enabling me to visit many museums and libraries in North America and Britain. But none of this I could have accomplished without the support and expertise of my husband Rowland Elzea.

I began writing a catalogue raisonné of all Sandys's work, to which I added any biographical information which came to light. After several years of research and writing, and the valuable help of Douglas Schoenherr, then of the Prints and Drawings Department of the National Gallery of Canada, it finally came together. It might have remained a manuscript but for the initiative of Andrew Moore, then Keeper of Art at Norwich Castle Museum, and his fundraising abilities. The Museum sponsored the publication, together with the Antique Collectors' Club, who produced it, and organised an exhibition, 'Frederick Sandys and the Pre-Raphaelites' to coincide with the book's launch in 2001. Unfortunately, the writing and organising of the catalogue and the publishing deadline meant that I was not able to complete a biographical note to accompany it. My attempt then, to make good that deficiency, was to include a documented chronology of Sandys's life. Douglas contributed an excellent critical overview of Sandys's career to the catalogue.

The catalogue raisonné having been accomplished, I went on to acquire more documentary information and turned my attention again to a biography. I have pieced the narrative together quoting extensively from Sandys's contemporaries from a variety of sources, and interlaced them with documented facts from public records which were once troublesome to access, but which are now of easy access through the internet.

Over the years working on his life, I have learned to be cautious with information, published or unpublished, and I have tried to substantiate every fact before setting it down. It has been difficult to truly understand the man. He seems to have been of ordinary, not outstanding, intelligence, though reasonably well-educated for his time, but his disorganised habits resulted in the chaotic and irresponsible management of his financial affairs. He had an undoubted eye for feminine beauty (as did his friend Rossetti) to which his pictures bear witness and his numerous offspring prove, but he seems to have had little thought for the financial consequences of his actions – a serious matter in those days before a welfare state was established.

In his correspondence he wrote as if he were talking, virtually dispensing with punctuation. I have therefore added this where I have made quotations. His dating of letters was hardly ever complete, merely giving the day of the week in which he was writing.

Sandys was tall, and proud, even probably vain, of his appearance, fastidious in his dress (to the extent that his lack of funds would allow), conventional in outward ways yet highly unconventional in his habits. He was sociable and witty, attracting many friends in his heyday in the 1860s, but quick to take offence. Despite his poor record as a breadwinner, and possibly as a father, his children continued to be devoted to him as they grew up.

[1] The name Crane entered this family history when Sandys's youngest child Gertrude married Lionel Francis Crane, the eldest son of Walter Crane. Their only child, Anthony Charles Walter Crane, inherited papers and relics from both families (in the case of Sandys, this is noted as the *Sandys Family Archive* throughout this text).

[2] The first biographical note about Sandys is to be found in Henry Ottley's *Biographical and Critical Dictionary of Recent and Living Painters and Engravers*, forming a supplement to *Bryan's Dictionary of Painters and Engravers* as edited by G. Stanley. London, 1866. Continuing in the 19th century, there were articles about his work in 1878, 1884, 1888, 1896, 1897, 1899, and a picture book in 1896. All are comparatively superficial.

[3] Anthony Crane often seemed apprehensive as to what I might find when I started research.

[4] Rowland Elzea (ed.), *The Correspondence between Samuel Bancroft Jr. and Charles Fairfax Murray*, 1892–1916. Delaware Art Museum. Occasional Paper no. 2, February 1980. Letter 79, dated 27th December 1897.

[5] J.M. Gray, 'Frederick Sandys' in *Art Journal*, March 1884. This was the first article on Sandys and his work. Gray wrote again on Sandys in 1888: 'Frederick Sandys and the Woodcut Designers of Thirty Years Ago' in *Century Guild Hobby Horse*, vol. 3, April 1888. I have found Gray to be the most careful, and relatively accurate of all the early writers on Sandys, contrary to C.F. Murray's statement in the letter quoted above. Gray (1850–1894) was the Curator of the Scottish National Portrait Gallery.

[6] Perhaps he mistakenly refers on this occasion to Esther Wood's statement that Sandys assisted her in the preparation of her 1896 monograph: *A Consideration of the Art of Frederick Sandys*. I have found Wood's monograph to be full of errors.

[7] Rowland Elzea, op.cit., Letter 54, dated 16th June 1896.

[8] Murray had one family in Florence and one in London. David Elliott, *Charles Fairfax Murray* (Oak Knoll Press, New Castle, 2000).

overleaf: *Interior of an Academy: the Critics*. detail. see page 26

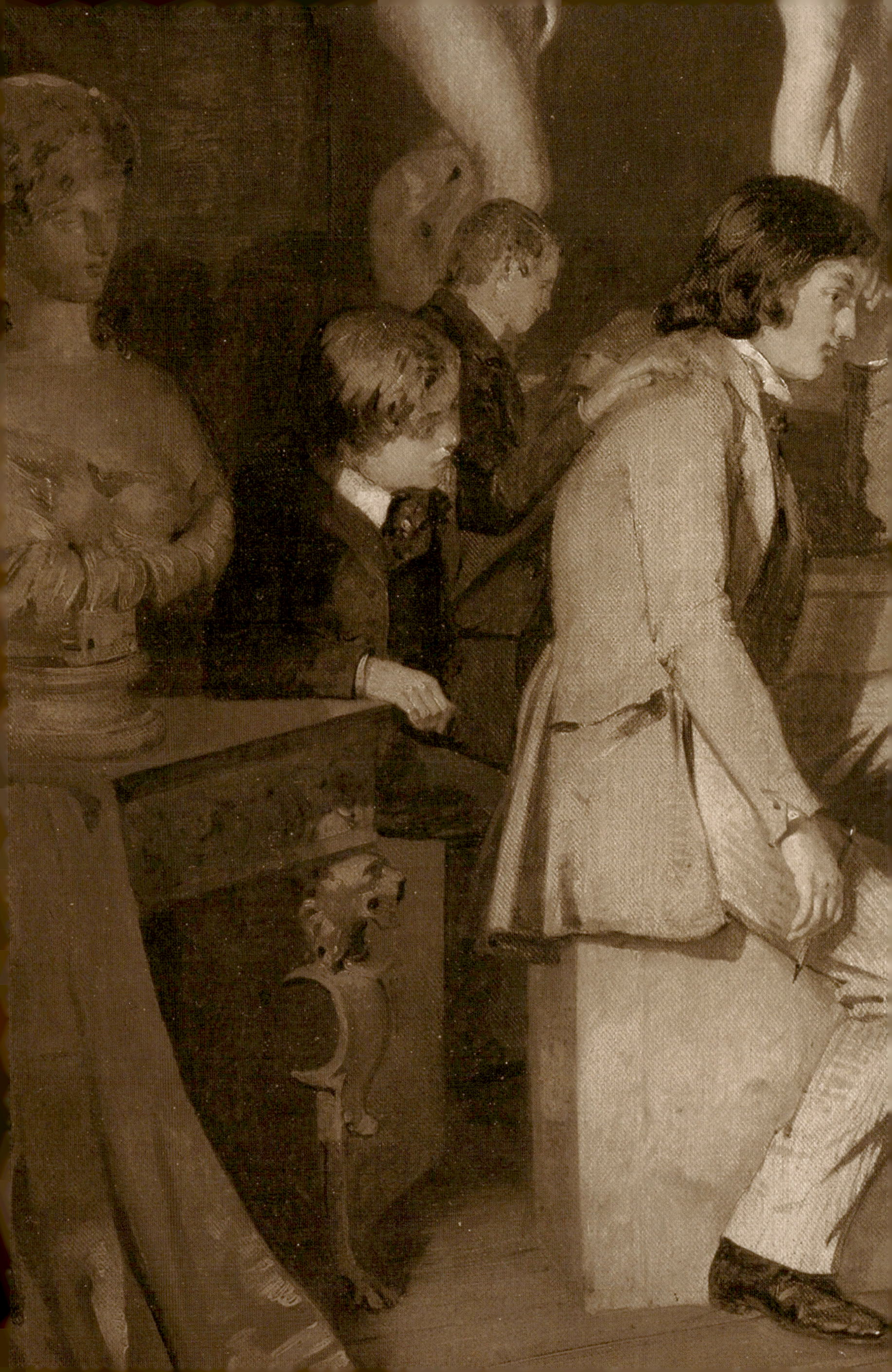

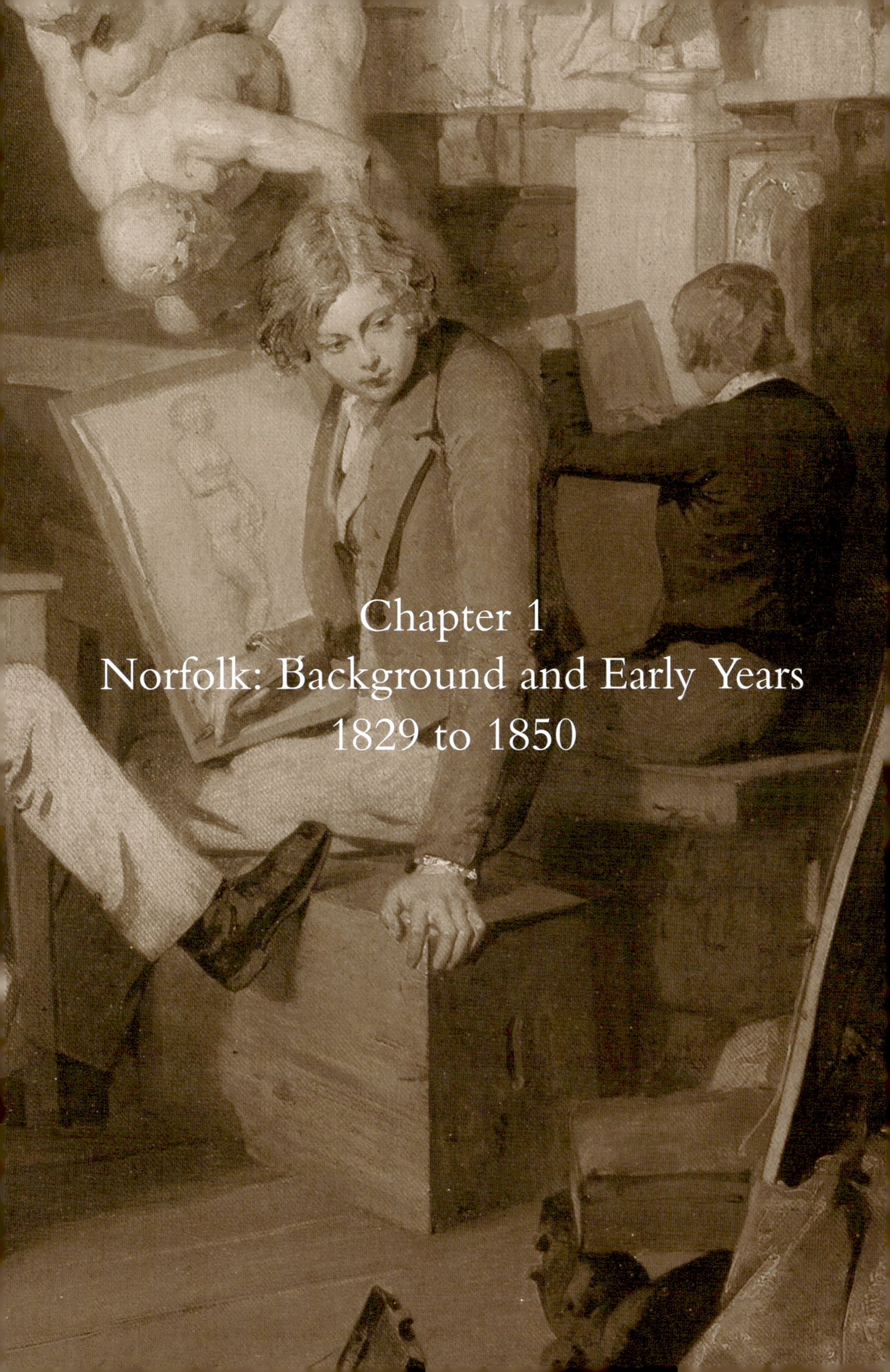

Chapter 1
Norfolk: Background and Early Years
1829 to 1850

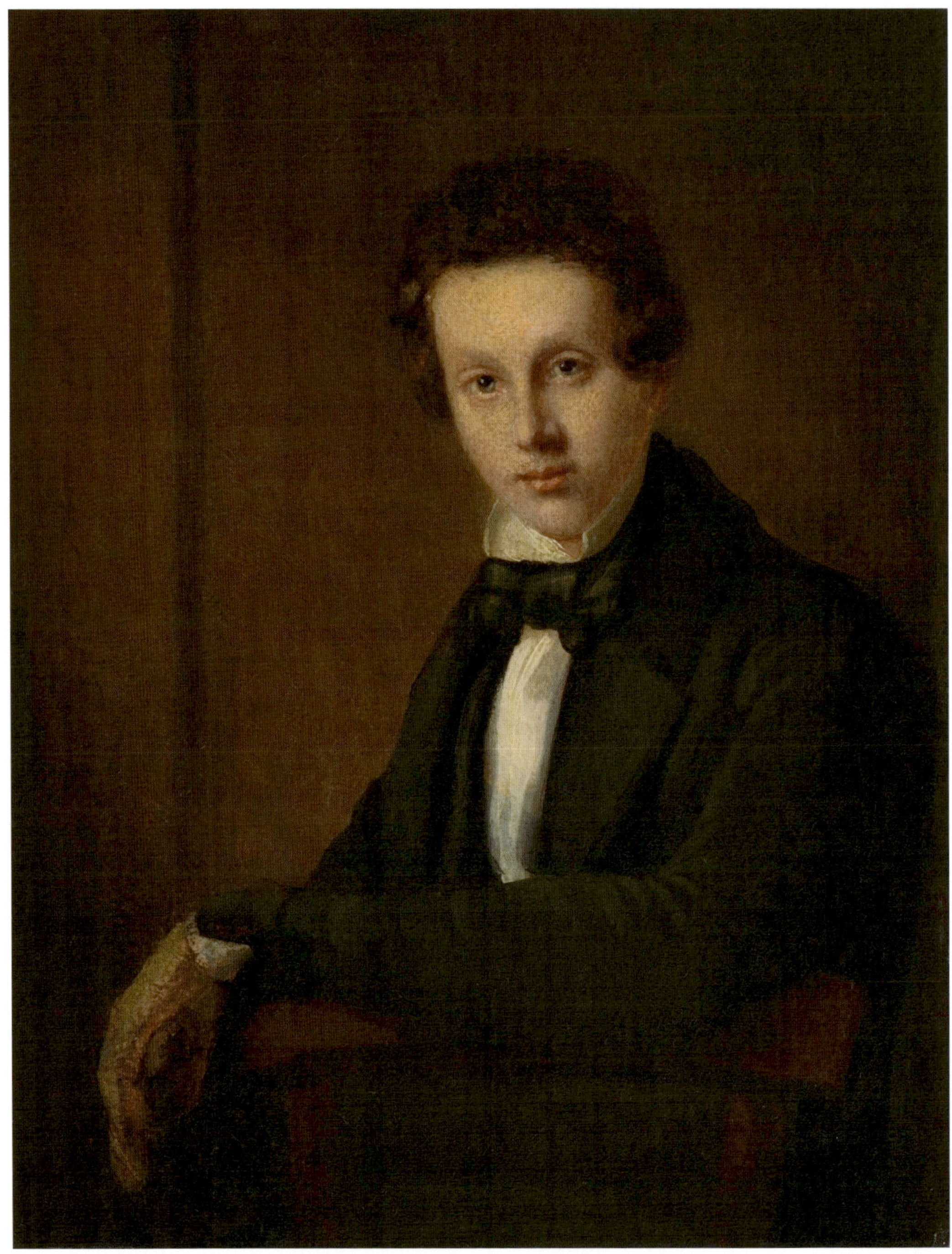

Anthony Frederick Augustus Sands at the age of 19, by his father Anthony Sands. Oil. 1848.

Frederick Sandys was a Norfolk man by birth and ancestry. Although his exceptional artistic talent led him eventually to study and seek his fortune in London, where he had found a foothold in lodgings by 1848 at the age of nineteen, his Norfolk origins and connections had an enduring effect on his life.

He was born on 1st May 1829 in the parish of St Stephen's Norwich, being the first born and only son of Anthony (1804–1883) and Mary Ann Sands (1809–1883).[1] His baptism was recorded in the parish register on 3rd May with the entry, 'Antonio Frederic Augustus Sands, son of Antonio and Mary Ann'. The Italian spelling of the name Anthony seems to reveal the fanciful, aspirational character of the father. However, the record of the parental marriage (on 22nd December 1828 at St John's and All Saints' Church, Lakenham, a village on the southern outskirts of Norwich) gives their names as plain Anthony Sands and Mary Ann Brown.[2] A similar impulse apparently, occurring some twenty-four years later, prompted both father and son to add a 'y' to their name, thus hinting at a more distinguished ancestral origin than they, in reality, could claim. At the time of their marriage, Anthony was aged twenty-four, and Mary Ann nineteen. It seems that Mary Ann was already pregnant, for their son was born only four months and nine days later.

Anthony Sands was born in 1804 at Hindringham, a small village in North Norfolk, the son of Sampson Sands and Mary Read. Sampson Sands was born about 1768 in the rather larger village of North Elmham, about nine miles due south of Hindringham, and was the son of John Sands and his wife Mary. This John Sands, the great grandfather of our subject, and father of a large family, was probably the John Sands whose baptism was recorded in 1690 at North Elmham as the son of Thomas and Elizabeth Sands who were married in 1682. The family name of Sands was not uncommon in Norfolk. The offspring of these rustic ancestors from North Norfolk seem generally to have been artisans and small tradesmen by the beginning of the nineteenth century.[3]

Anthony must have migrated to Norwich in his teens to learn the trade of a dyer. We know that he became a dyer from the record of his son's baptism in 1829, which also places the young parents as residents of the parish of St Stephen's Church, in the southern part of the city centre, and not too distant from Lakenham, the weavers' district from which Mary Ann came. It should be remembered that Norwich was still an important wool and silk manufacturing centre, which encompassed a wide range of textile processes including spinning, dyeing, weaving, and finishing, including the famous 'Norwich Shawls', so fashionable in the nineteenth century.

By the later 1830s the family had moved to 7 St Giles' Hill (sometimes known as Grapes Hill after the local public house), a street now partly demolished by the cutting through of the modern Ring Road which is roughly on the site of the old city wall around the city of Norwich.[4] It bordered the parish of St Giles' Church, which is in the north-western part of the city, and the adjoining village of Heigham, which was outside the old city walls. There, at the same address, Anthony Sands was listed in a new role in Blyth's *Norwich Guide and Directory* of 1843, under 'Artists', as a 'Drawing Master'.

It would be an interesting social study to follow the actual development of Anthony from dyer to artist, but a glimpse of it can be obtained from an anecdote which was published in the *Eastern Daily Press* in 1923. It was extracted from a manuscript memoir (which, sadly, has since disappeared) written by the artist Frederick Bacon Barwell (1831–1922), a Norwich-born contemporary of Frederick Sandys who was born to a higher social station in life (which Barwell took care to make obvious).[5]

Barwell recalled that Anthony came to speak with his father John Barwell:'… knowing that [my father] was an excellent amateur and a good judge, [he] called upon him to ask his advice regarding a small painting of a head by the aid of a looking-glass and wishing to know whether my father considered the thing of sufficient merit to warrant his throwing up his employment and taking to painting as a means of livelihood. "What is your employment?" asked my father. "Well, sir, I am a journeyman dyer." "What wages do you earn?" The sum named was I think some 28s a week. "If that be the case, I would advise you to stick to the trade and paint in your leisure." The man looked disappointed, and then said, "Well, sir, I would rather be a poor artist than a rich dyer." "Oh," said my father, "in that case there is nothing further to be said, but I am afraid that you will remain a poor artist," and so he did. I am at a loss to know how he lived, but I have seen many a head from himself in a smoking cap, and I believe these were put up in lotteries in public houses.'[6]

Against such advice Anthony, perhaps foolishly, persevered and, furthermore, with more reason, encouraged his son to become an artist also. We find early evidence of paternal pride in his promoting the young Fred's work in 1839 when he was only ten, exhibiting a drawing by him of *Minerva* in the First Exhibition of the Norfolk and Norwich Art Union. Although this drawing has disappeared (it was probably copied from a print), a spirited drawing of a leaping horse done by Frederick (also probably a copy from a print) in the same year has survived.

Anthony Sands. Oil. *c*.1850. The father of Frederick Sands . He was born at Hindringham, Norfolk, and moved to Norwich in the early 1820s. He became a dyer for Stark & Mills dyeworks on the River Wensum.

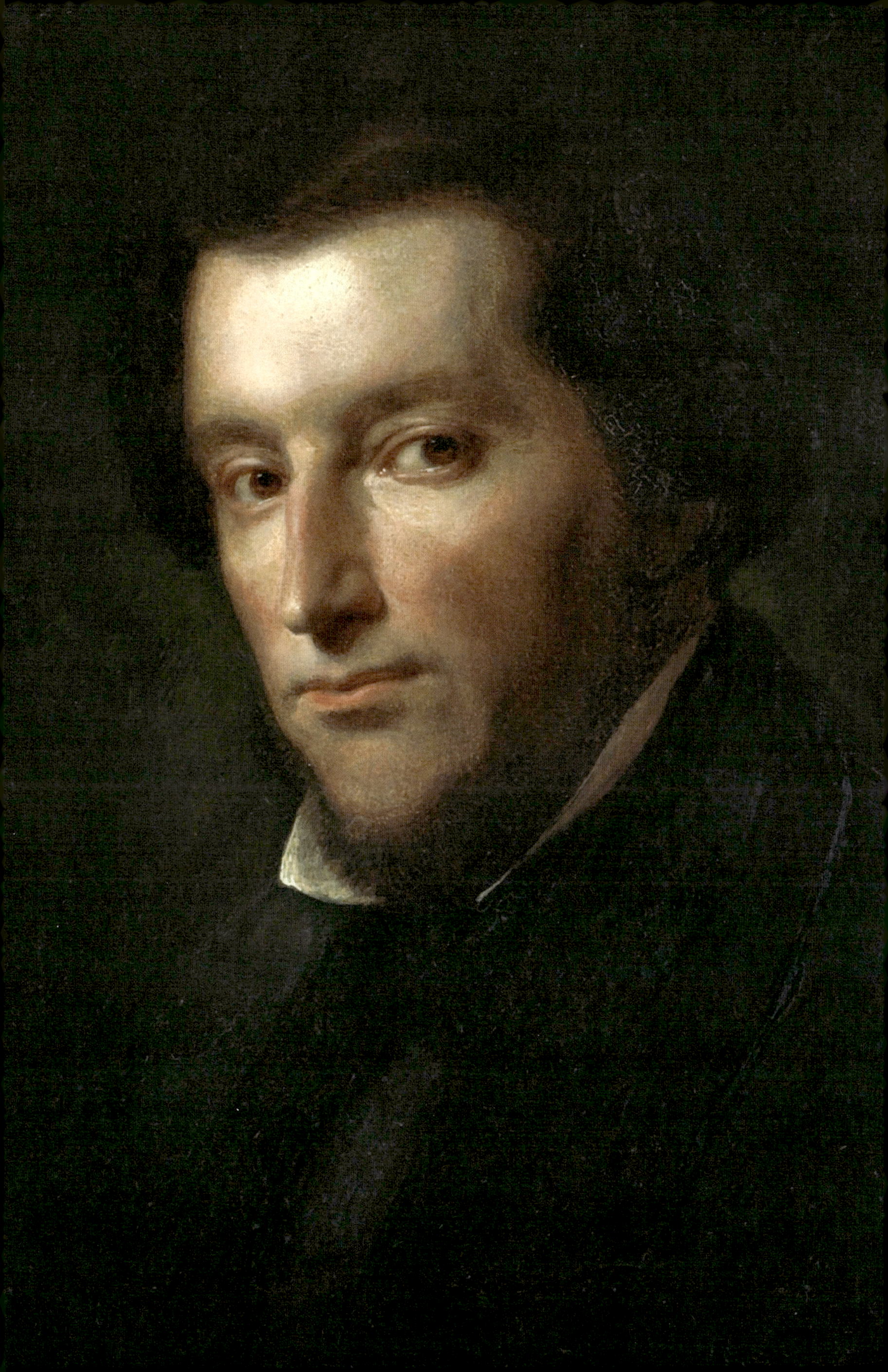

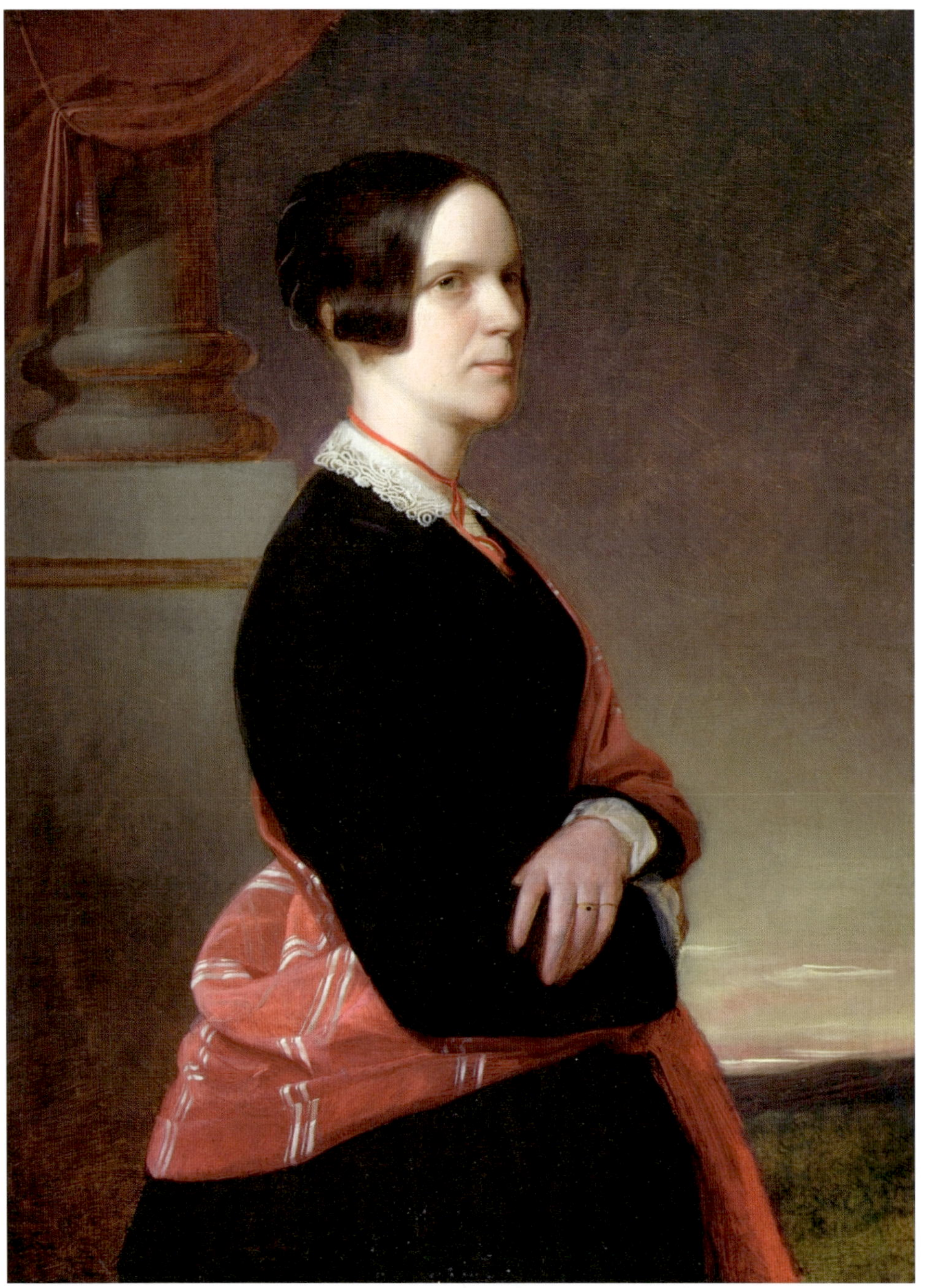

Mary Ann Sands. Oil. *c*.1850. The mother of Frederick Sands. She came from Lakenham, a village just outside Norwich where weaving was the chief occupation. The young Frederick was attempting to produce a formal portrait in the style of the 1840s, hoping thereby to attract commissions.

Not surprisingly therefore, Anthony and Mary's only other child, Emma, was also to become an artist. She was born in 1843 (but, oddly, was not baptised until 1862 at the rather grand church of St Peter Mancroft in the centre of Norwich). Her baptismal record gives her name as Mary Ann Emma Negus Sandys.[7] Endowed with far less talent than her brother, through diligent application and the guidance of her father, and more particularly of her brother, whose style and technique she strove to imitate, she eventually became a creditable portrait artist and a painter of saleable 'fancy heads'. She worked in London as well as in Norwich, and was particularly successful in her portraits of children. She died at the early age of thirty-four.[8]

Sandys's early education was at the St John Maddermarket School in Norwich, a small private academy run by the brothers James and Thomas Farnell. Some writing exercise books dating from 1837 and 1838, kept and handed down in the Sandys family, attest to these years being spent there. His exercises in calligraphy in these books show an unusual skill, calling to mind a similar instance in the case of the young John Constable, another East Anglian, at school in Dedham. According to Constable's biographer '… the only thing he excelled in [was] penmanship'.[9] Although they were roughly two generations apart, this shows that primary education had not changed much in the intervening time.

Evidently then the young Frederick came to the notice of the Norwich City Charity Trustees for, when he reached the suitable age, he became one of the twenty-four or so Norwich boys, usually sons of local tradesmen, who were accepted for a free place at the grammar school attached to the cathedral.[10]

According to the sardonic Barwell, '…Frederick was put to the Grammar School in the Cathedral Close by a Governor, and had to get on as he could'.[11] Since the age of induction was usually ten or eleven (the schooling normally lasting until the age of eighteen), Sandys probably entered in September 1839, during the regime 1834 to 1849 of the Rev. Henry Banfather. There he would have had a typical classical education for a middle-class boy of his time. He would later put this to use when he lived in London as an adult, where he was accepted into educated society and was generally regarded as being excellent company and something of a wit.

A surprising and unexplained revelation from this period in Sandys's life is that, according to the catalogue of the Norfolk Polytechnic Exhibition in December 1841, 'Master A. Sands lent Australian bows and arrows, and war clubs'. Clearly, he was an unusual child.

It must have been when he was still a schoolboy, at the age of thirteen in 1842, that he was noticed and given his first commission as an artist. His patron was the wealthy banker[12] and ornithologist John Henry Gurney Sr (1819–1890) who set Sandys to making drawings of birds in pencil and watercolours. Sandys completed with reasonable competence seventy-two large sheets of watercolours (mainly) and drawings ranging over a period of time from 1842 to about 1848.[13] These were eventually bound together by Gurney in an album titled *Drawings of Birds*, which came to light in 1978 in the hands of an Eastbourne dealer.[14] The subjects include East Anglian as well as North American birds, drawn from stuffed and mounted specimens, or 'skins'. Some sheets are copies of the hand-coloured engraved plates in J.J. Audubon's *The Birds of America* (1827–1838) to which Gurney's father Joseph John (1788–1847) was an early subscriber.

However, regarding this first commission, in 1888 a trail of misconception began in the literature on Sandys and his work. In the first serious article on him as an artist by the Scottish curator and art critic John Miller Gray (1850–1894), the facts were muddied by his stating: 'Among Sandys's first drawings was a series of illustrations of the birds of Norfolk.'[15] This led on in 1896 to the misunderstanding by Esther Wood of the nature of Gurney's commission in her monograph on Sandys: '… almost his first professional work was to illustrate some local handbooks to the *Birds of Norfolk*.'[16] It should be noted that, by 1896, Sandys was remembered as an illustrator for his fine magazine illustrations of the 1860s, and Wood's statement carried the implication that these early drawings for Gurney were actually book illustrations. Admittedly, two of his bird watercolours appear to have been loosely copied by the jobbing wood-engraver who made illustrations for the long and sparsely illustrated 1846 article by Gurney on Norfolk birds.[17] There seems to have been no attempt by Sandys to clarify this. The true circumstances were finally understood by the present writer when the Gurney album surfaced in Eastbourne after an interval of over one hundred years, and the Gurney commission could be seen in its original form as a bound album of original watercolours and drawings by the young Sandys.

There is an anecdote about him which is also connected with the Gurney family and must refer to an incident at about this time. It has his meeting 'in early boyhood' with the legendary Norwich poet, author and linguist, George Borrow 'under the roof of one of the Miss Gurneys of Earlham'. It continues, 'it was here he heard the manuscript of Lavengro read by the author, and was powerfully impressed by the personality of Borrow, whose

Mary Ann Sands. Oil. *c.*1850. Unfinished portrait of Mary Ann Sands, showing Sandys's early technique of stippling to tone the surface of the support.

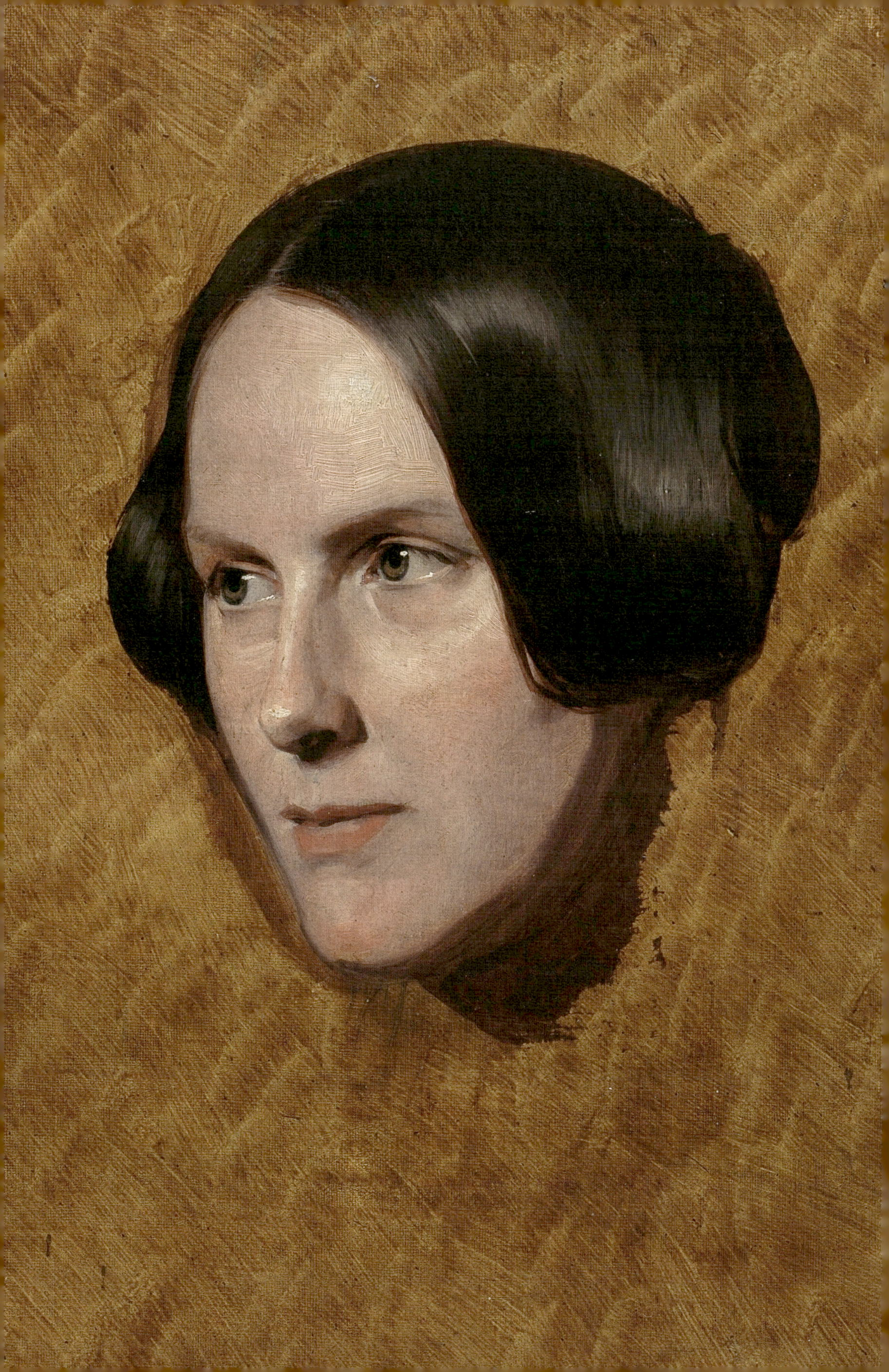

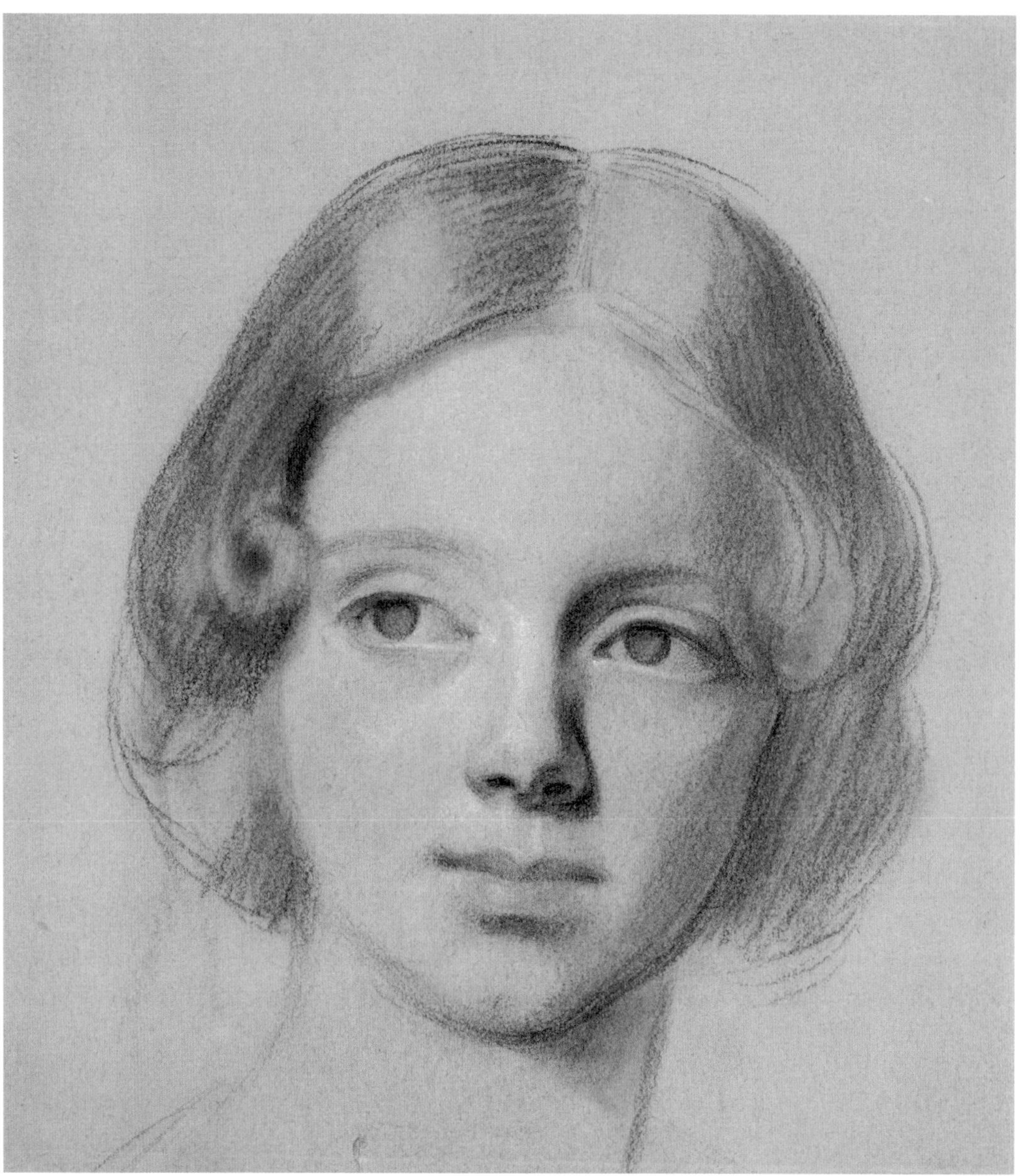

Mary Anne Emma Negus Sands. Chalk drawing. *c*.1850. The sister of Frederick Sands born in 1843. Following in her brother's footsteps, she too became an artist and evidently owed much to his teaching. At first her work was crudely naïve, but by the 1870s her skill had developed to the extent that it is sometimes difficult to distinguish her work from her brother's. Unfortunately she died early, in 1877.

black eyes had a glow of fire in their depths, their effect being enhanced by a tossing mane of prematurely whitened hair'.[18] This is one among the several legends faithfully preserved by Sandys's family, which probably have a basis in fact but were undoubtedly improved upon. Such an encounter no doubt originally awakened a romantic awareness in Sandys of the gypsy people, later manifested in his attraction to Keomi Gray who was his model and mistress in the 1860s. The 'Miss Gurneys' would have been the sisters of Joseph John Gurney (1788–1847), and the aunts of John Henry Gurney, the banker-ornithologist. The Gurneys were part of a cultured and philanthropic group of Quaker families who flourished in Norfolk during the eighteenth and early nineteenth centuries, Elizabeth Fry (née Gurney, 1780–1845), Louisa Hoare (née Gurney) and their friend Amelia Alderson (1769–1853) who married the artist John Opie (1761–1807).

Several years later, in 1862, Sandys was to illustrate *Harald Harfagr*, one of George Borrow's poetic translations from Scandinavian legend, using Keomi Gray as his model. Another anecdote from Sandys recalls his visiting Earlham, the Norfolk home of the Gurneys, in the lifetime of Joseph John Gurney (1788–1847) and hearing Mrs Opie sing there.[19]

His other early patron, the most important by far, was an antiquarian parson from Aylsham, the Rev. James Bulwer (1794–1879). The young Sandys would contribute over two hundred careful depictions of local antiquities between 1845 and 1858 to Bulwer's immense *Norfolk Collection*[20] which he formed to augment Francis Blomefield's *Essay Towards a Topographical History of the County of Norfolk* (1805–1810), a comprehensive work in the wake of several standard county histories then being researched and published in the eighteenth and early nineteenth centuries.[21] Bulwer, who was a keen and experienced artist himself, and a frequent sketching companion of professional artists such as John Sell Cotman (1782–1842) and William J. Müller (1812–1845), became personally concerned in helping the young Sandys in his artistic development. This included a time in which Sandys was retreating from his 1853 marriage to Georgiana Creed, and seems to have found a refuge with the Bulwer family at Hunworth Rectory. Sandys remained close to the Bulwer family until the death of James Bulwer's eldest son, his friend James Redfoord Bulwer (b.1820) in 1899.

J.R. Bulwer appears to have been an enthusiastic mountaineer in his youth and wrote a journal of his alpine climb in 1852. This he asked Sandys to illustrate with etchings. Without ever having seen the Alps, Sandys made a creditable job of it from Bulwer's sketches. It was published privately as *Extracts from my Journal MDCCCLII*, by Charles Muskett of Norwich in 1853.[22]

On 21st January, 1846, the new Norwich School of Design (one of the earliest of the government art schools established in manufacturing centres all over Great Britain under the Board of Trade) was opened in the Royal Norfolk and Norwich Bazaar building in St Andrew's, Broad Street.[23] Sandys must have been one of the first students to enter it and to benefit from the instruction and facilities under William Stewart (1823–1906), the first headmaster. The origin of these government-supported art schools had been the alarming realisation in the second quarter of the nineteenth century by both the British government and leading industrialists from those industries reliant on the work of designers, such as in textiles, metalwork, and ceramics, that Britain was losing trade to its European competitors (particularly the French) for the lack of well-trained British designers. Comprehensive training in art and design already existed in the educationally more progressive France and Germany.

From 1837 to 1852, twenty-two art schools were either newly established or were given government support and direction for the first time. The new system established a 'Head School' in London with satellites in the manufacturing towns, such as Norwich with its old-established textile industry.[24] The Head School's small but increasing collection of historic and contemporary artefacts, collected as worthy examples to inspire and be copied

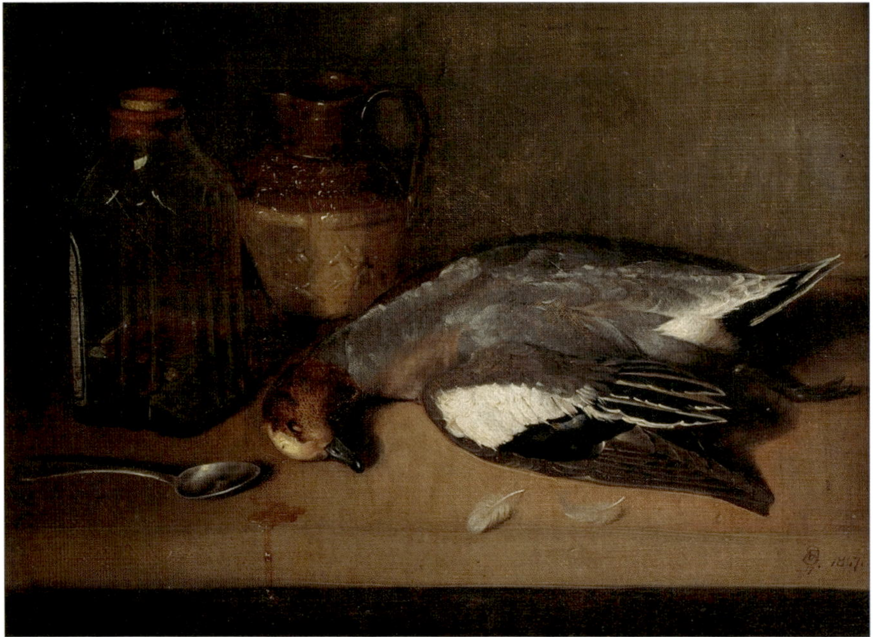

Still Life with Wild Duck (wigeon). Oil. 1847. Inscribed with his monogram 'AFAS', '1847', and '17' (proudly displaying his age). Undoubtedly done for a competition held by the Royal Society of Arts in London in that year, in which he won a silver medal.

by students, was the origin and nucleus of today's Victoria and Albert Museum in South Kensington and its now vast collection of applied (or decorative) art. In parallel, the Head School metamorphosed into the South Kensington School of Art which is today the Royal College of Art, still teaching art and design.

The new Norwich art school was properly equipped, in the prescribed manner for an art academy, to include plaster casts made from classical sculpture and architectural details for the students to copy to develop their draughtsmanship skills and feeling for design and proportion and, at the same time, to inculcate in them the highest aesthetic standards of the day. One of Sandys's surviving early drawings, dated January 1846, which must have been drawn very soon after he arrived at the school, is a monochrome watercolour of one of the school's plaster casts. There exists also a rare contemporary view into the antique sculpture studio at the Norwich School of Design in a painting dated 1848 by William Stewart, the headmaster himself. It is tempting to think that the fair-haired student on the right is Sandys, as the figure bears a decided resemblance to him as a boy.

As a student, he was encouraged to enter the competitions organised by the Society of Arts in London (which had been an active player in founding the new Schools of Design), and he won their silver 'Isis' medal for a portrait drawing in 1846.

At this time, his journey to London may have been by the new railways, which were beginning to spread rapidly over the country, for the examinations in March or April, and again to receive his medal on 12th June.[25] Travellers from Norwich to London in 1846 would probably have had to travel via Brandon, Suffolk, to Ely and Cambridge, terminating at Shoreditch in London. Norwich had to wait until 1849 for a more direct rail connection with the capital, through Ipswich and Colchester. The present Liverpool Street terminus in London did not open until 1875.

The next year he again won a Society of Arts silver 'Isis' medal, this time for an oil painting of 'Wild ducks from nature'.[26] Many years later, Sandys recalled that he and John Everett Millais sat together in the same room being tested at the Society of Arts.[27] Each had to execute a painting on the spot as proof that he was the genuine executant of the work. He remembered that Millais attracted a lot of attention on the occasion, being pronounced by onlookers (*sotto voce* but overheard by Sandys) to be an 'astounding genius', while Sandys went unnoticed. His task was to paint a pigeon procured from a nearby market, and he was feeling nervous and uncomfortable while Millais

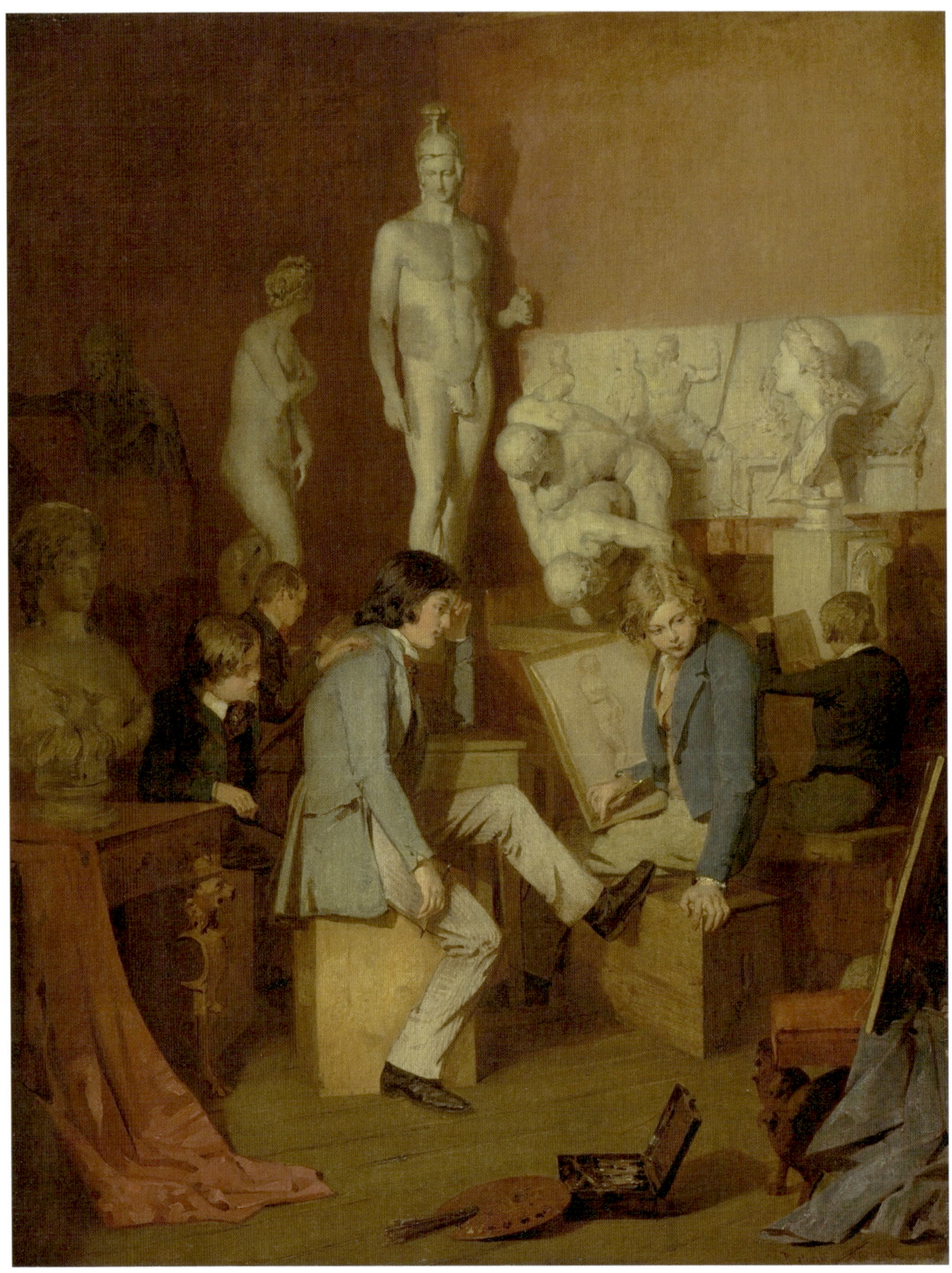

Interior of an Academy: the Critics (the Norwich School of Design), by William Stewart (1823-1906) the first headmaster. Oil. 1848. Sandys was one of the first students there, after its opening in 1846 in the Bazaar Building, Norwich. Sandys is possibly the boy on the right.

was self-confident. Millais advised him to pay attention to the feet of the bird as the most difficult part, an insight which impressed Sandys, which is evident from his telling the story to Elizabeth Pennell in 1898.[28] An oil painting of a still life with a wigeon (not pigeon) that came to light in recent years may be the actual test piece. This painting is remarkable for its accurate realism and its delicate handling of paint in the prevalent low-key style. It is signed with his monogram, the date 1847, and his age, seventeen.

In the years 1848 through the early 1850s, Sandys was occupied with drawing and painting watercolours of archaeological finds and medieval relics for James Bulwer, carrying out commissions for portrait drawings locally in Norfolk, and trying his hand at portraits in oil (mainly of his own family), as well as learning the technique of etching. He and his father did reproductive work together for the Norwich bookseller and publisher Charles Muskett at about this time. Muskett was compiling a folio of plates of Norfolk worthies of past centuries, which he published as *Norfolk Portraits* in about 1850. As was common practice in the days before photo-mechanical reproduction, father and son would make pencil drawings of the original oil portraits wherever they happened to be hanging, which they and other local jobbing artists and engravers would translate into etched or engraved plates for the folios. This work is mechanical and uninspired, and it is almost impossible, in the surviving examples, to be sure who made the drawing or the etching, or vice versa, except on the basis of quality, the son being a markedly better draughtsman than the father. In the event, none of the Sandys etchings seem to have been used for *Norfolk Portraits* as the etchings of the same subjects which were published by Muskett are by other hands.[29] However, one of the Sandys engravings was printed by Muskett as a frontispiece to his *Notices and Illustrations of the Costume, Processions, Pageantry, etc. … of Norwich* (1850). Experience of this sort was to be valuable to the young Sandys in supporting himself when he moved to London. His work for the London printsellers Hogarth, Graves, and others, probably began at about this time.

Sandys also provided etched illustrations to one of James Bulwer's articles in 1849 in *Norfolk Archaeology*, possibly another in 1852, and for another correspondent to the same journal in 1859. A small, rather different group of his etchings, which have been preserved, are of landscapes and can be associated with his friendship with the Bulwers.[30] They are sketches of scenery (probably drawn directly on the plate itself) in North Norfolk in and around Hunworth or within easy reach, and must have been made while staying at Hunworth Rectory, the Bulwer home. Sandys stayed at the rectory for long periods from the late 1840s to about 1858. The latest of these landscape studies is dated 1858.

The suggestion made by J.M. Gray in the first article devoted to Sandys in the art periodicals[31] that he studied under the portrait artists George Richmond (1809–1896) and Samuel Laurence (1812–1884) was denied by Sandys, as stated in Esther Wood's monograph of 1896.[32] All the same, his early drawings give proof of the influence of these older, established, and skilful portrait artists, especially Richmond. The latter was '... an old family friend' of the Sandys family, according to another statement he made to Esther Wood.[33] Richmond is known to have had several Norfolk patrons and was a frequent visitor to Norwich.[34] Perhaps there is some truth in Frederick Barwell's statement that ' ... the late George Richmond RA, got to hear of Sandys, and for a long time employed him to make copies of the chalk heads of ecclesiastics, for which that artist was at one time celebrated. Replicas were always desired by the friends of the sitter, and Sandys became very expert in the use of chalk for such work, beginning presently to do such portraits on his own account, and later on by exhibiting some in a print-seller's window he got a good deal to do of that kind'.[35] Another recollection of George Richmond's portrait work in Norfolk can be found in Verily Anderson's *The Northrepps Grandchildren* (1968) in which she states that Richmond painted over fifty portraits of the Hoare family (and related families) and that he usually made three or four copies of each portrait so that each member of the family could have one. Could these have been the copies by Sandys mentioned by Barwell?[36]

Sandys, however, did acknowledge as a teacher the local artist John Joseph Cotman (1814–1878) who was the talented, but professionally unsuccessful, younger son of John Sell Cotman, and continued his father's teaching practice for the most part in Norwich. In 1854 Sandys wrote a letter of recommendation on behalf of J.J. Cotman who was applying for the post of Professor of Drawing at King's College, London, which had been held earlier by his father and elder brother. Sandys wrote: 'I speak from experience being intimately acquainted with many of his pupils and having received great benefit from his drawing myself.'[37] Sandys must have been taught by him in the mid-1840s, very likely at the Norwich School of Design, the founding of which Cotman had much to do with.

Sandys's father Anthony, who Sandys often referred to as 'the guv'nor' remained an important part of his son's life. Anthony often visited Sandys in London and there are amusing references to the father by the son's London friends. Such visits were often connected to selling art, which Anthony would acquire, probably cheaply in Norfolk, for his son to sell in London.

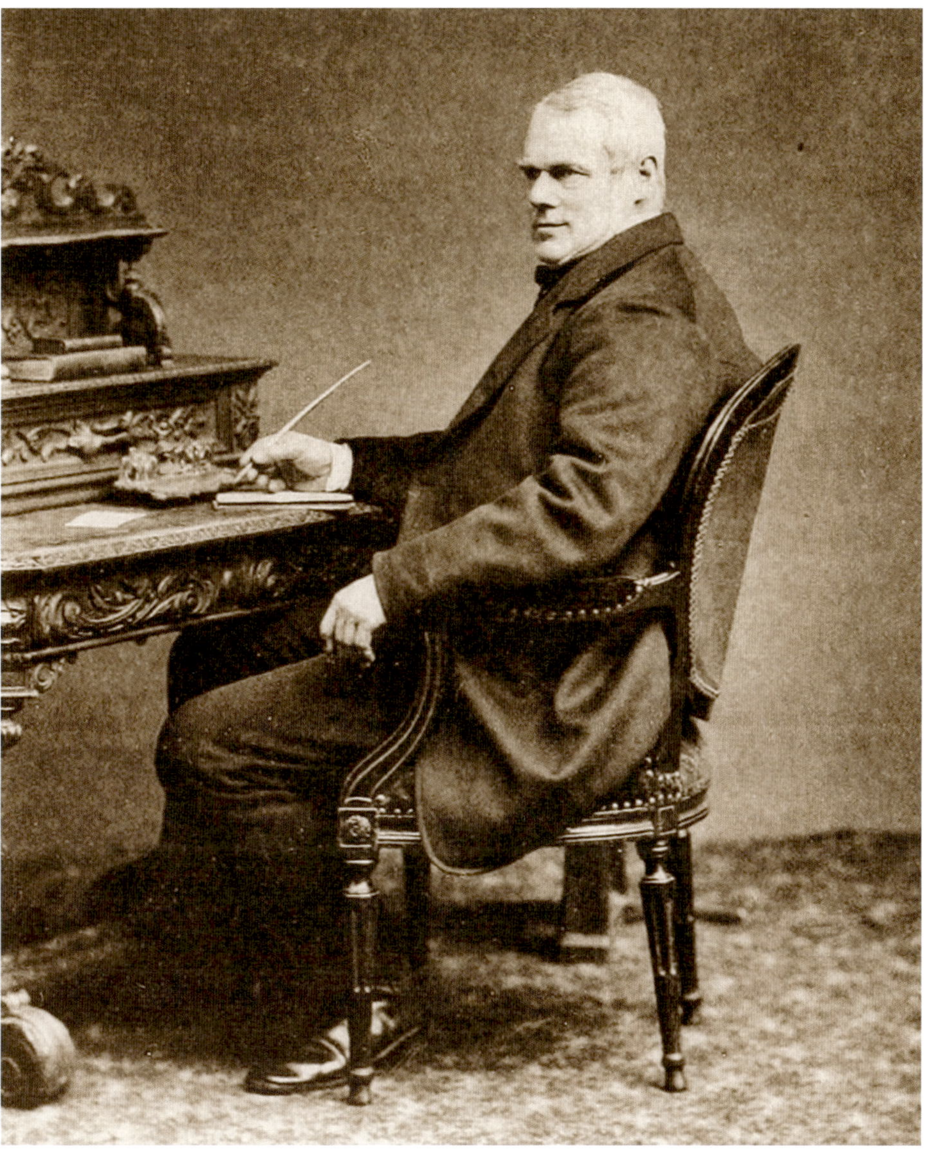

John Henry Gurney Sr (1819-1890), Norwich banker, *c.*1865. Gurney, an ornithologist, was on the founding committee of the Norwich School of Design, and gave the young Sands a commission to make watercolours and drawings of his collection of bird specimens.

[1] However, Sandys told the census recorder in 1881 that he had been born at Heigham, which was just outside the walls of the old city but is now part of modern Norwich. He also stated that he was 48, which gave him a birth date of 1832. He stuck to the latter all his life, but the records say 1829.

[2] I have found the spelling Anthony to have been used by the father throughout his life, but both spellings, Antony and Anthony, even Antonio, seem to have been used on the few occasions where his whole name appears. In the case of Frederick, again there was no regularity of spelling – Frederic occasionally being used. I have chosen to use the more normal Frederick throughout.

[3] This information has been extracted from the *International Genealogical Index*, and with the help of Dr J.H. Pound of the University of East Anglia. White's 1845 *Norfolk Directory* has also been consulted.

[4] The Sands family appear in local trade directories at 7 St Giles' Hill between *c.*1836 and *c.*1842. I quote from a response to my enquiry dated 16th October 1981 from C. Wilkins-Jones, County Local Studies Librarian, Norwich.

[5] 'Mr Barwell's Reminiscences', 'A Norwich Dyer Artist [*sic*]. Frederick Sandys', from *The Eastern Daily Press*, Norwich, 23rd August 1923.

[6] John Barwell (1798–1896). Wine merchant, prominent in the cultural life of Norwich, was one of the founders of the Norwich School of Design. His son Frederick Bacon Barwell became a genre painter and friend of Millais and Bell Scott. He became an Inspector of the Schools of Design, at the Science and Art Department, South Kensington. Marjorie Allthorpe-Guyton in *A Happy Eye, a School of Art in Norwich* (1982) gives more information about Barwell, pp. 53–56.

[7] The name Negus originates in Mary Ann Brown's family. Her mother Sarah was born a Negus. Her grandfather Josiah and great grandfather John were Neguses. The name Negus was also given to Frederick's eldest son Hugh who was sceptical of it because of its historic connections, according to his nephew Anthony Crane. However public records show that it was truly part of his ancestry.

[8] Emma Sandys died in Norwich on 21st November 1877 of 'congestion of lungs', according to the death certificate. She exhibited at the Royal Academy from 1868 to 1874.

[9] C.R. Leslie, RA, *Memoirs of the Life of John Constable* (ed.) Jonathan Mayne, 1951, p. 3.

[10] 'The (Norwich) City Charity Trustees nominated 24 of the sons of the inhabitants to this school, between the ages of 10 and 18 years, to be taught Latin and Greek, free of expense; but for writing and arithmetic, each pays two guineas a year. The Rev. Henry Banfather, the head master, and Mr. Thos. Hodgson, the second master, do not take any other pupils besides the 24 on the foundation.' William White, *History, Gazetteer,* and *Directory of Norfolk,* Second edition, 1845, p. 124.

[11] F.B. Barwell, op. cit., no. 5.

[12] At Overend, Gurney & Co.

[13] The paper sizes vary, but average about 20 x 16 ins.

[14] Harold Day. The album was later acquired by Norwich Castle Museum with the help of the National Art Collections Fund in 1995.

[15] J.M. Gray, 'Frederick Sandys', *Art Journal*, vol. XLVI (March 1884), pp. 73–78.

[16] Wood, Esther, Special Winter Number of *The Artist*. London: Constable, 1896.

[17] This was published in *The Zoologist*, vol. 4, pp. 1300–1393. It was simultaneously issued in bound form as a book.

[18] These are the words of the artist E. Borough Johnson (1867–1949) in his Introduction to Mary Sandys's *Reproductions of Woodcuts by F. Sandys, 1860–1866*, London: Carl Hentschel for Mrs. Sandys, nd (1910); Borrow, George. *Lavengro, the Scholar, the Gypsy, the Priest*, London, 1851.

[19] This is contained in a note written after 1909 from Mary Buxton to her friend Prince Frederick Duleep Singh, the Norfolk squire and art historian. It quotes Sandys's visit as 'a white haired old man' reminiscing to an elderly female. Norfolk Record Office: MC109/7, Duleep Singh. This was an unacknowledged quotation from Eliza Brightwen's *The Life and Thoughts of a Naturalist*. (ed.). W.H. Chesson, 1909, pp. 107-108.

[20] As with Sandys's work for Gurney, Esther Wood misrepresented his work for Bulwer.

[21] For example, Edward Hasted's *A History of the County of Kent*, 1778–1799.

[22] Sandys purchased copper plates from Roberson in 1853 and hired a lay figure from them also – perhaps for help with his drawing of J.R. Bulwer in the etching *Dressed for the Glacier.* Cambridge, Hamilton Kerr Institute, Roberson Archive, 1820–1939.

[23] Marjorie Allthorpe-Guyton, op. cit., no. 6.

[24] Quentin Bell, *The Schools of Design*, 1963, pp. 66, 101–2.

[25] Unidentified press cutting from a Norwich newspaper dated 3rd July 1847, preserved in a scrap album originating from the Sandys family in Norwich, in the Print Room of the Fitzwilliam Museum, Cambridge (Album PD 865). Also, Society of Arts, Printed Premium Lists, 1846–1853. I am indebted to D.G.C. Allan, Curator-Historian of the Royal Society of Arts, as well as his successor Evelyn Watson for information.

[26] Society of Arts, no. 35, ibid.

[27] Millais (1829–1896) was the same age as Sandys but was more advanced in ability, having already won a gold medal for an ambitious subject picture.

[28] E. and J. Pennell, *The Whistler Journal*, 1921, p. 23. Sandys's story was recorded by Elizabeth Pennell after his visit to their chambers in Buckingham Street on 3rd October 1898. Her story is slightly flawed in that she thought that Sandys's silver medal was for 'watercolours of birds', confusing it with the Gurney commission. Sandys must have also mentioned it, but had not made the two unrelated endeavours sufficiently clear to her. RSA records merely state that the 1847 silver medal was for 'oil painting of birds from nature'.

[29] However, it is likely that their preliminary graphic transcriptions were used by the published engravers.

[30] James Bulwer dabbled with etching himself. Some etched as well as blank copper plates were listed in the catalogue of the sale of the contents of Hunworth Rectory after his death (Norwich, Spelman's, 25-26 September 1879, lots 267-269) showing his active interest. A small etching by Bulwer can also be found in the Bulwer Collection at the National Gallery of Canada, Ottawa.

[31] J.M. Gray, 1884, op. cit., no. 15, p. 74.

[32] Esther Wood, 1896, op. cit., no. 16, p. 8.

[33] Esther Wood, 1896, op. cit., no. 16, p. 8.

[34] Raymond Lister, *George Richmond, A Critical Biography*. 1981.

[35] F.B. Barwell, 1923, op. cit., no. 5.

[36] Verily Anderson's statement is on p. 106 of her memoir, The Northrepps Grandchildren (1968). Verily Anderson (1915-2010) was related to the Gurney, and the Hoare families.

[37] Letter from F.S. to the Council of King's College, London, on behalf of John Joseph Cotman, dated 11th September 1854. A copy of the original (in the possession of the Cotman family, Norwich) is in the Archives of the Art Department of the Norwich Castle Museum.

opposite: *Rev. James Bulwer.* detail. see page 41

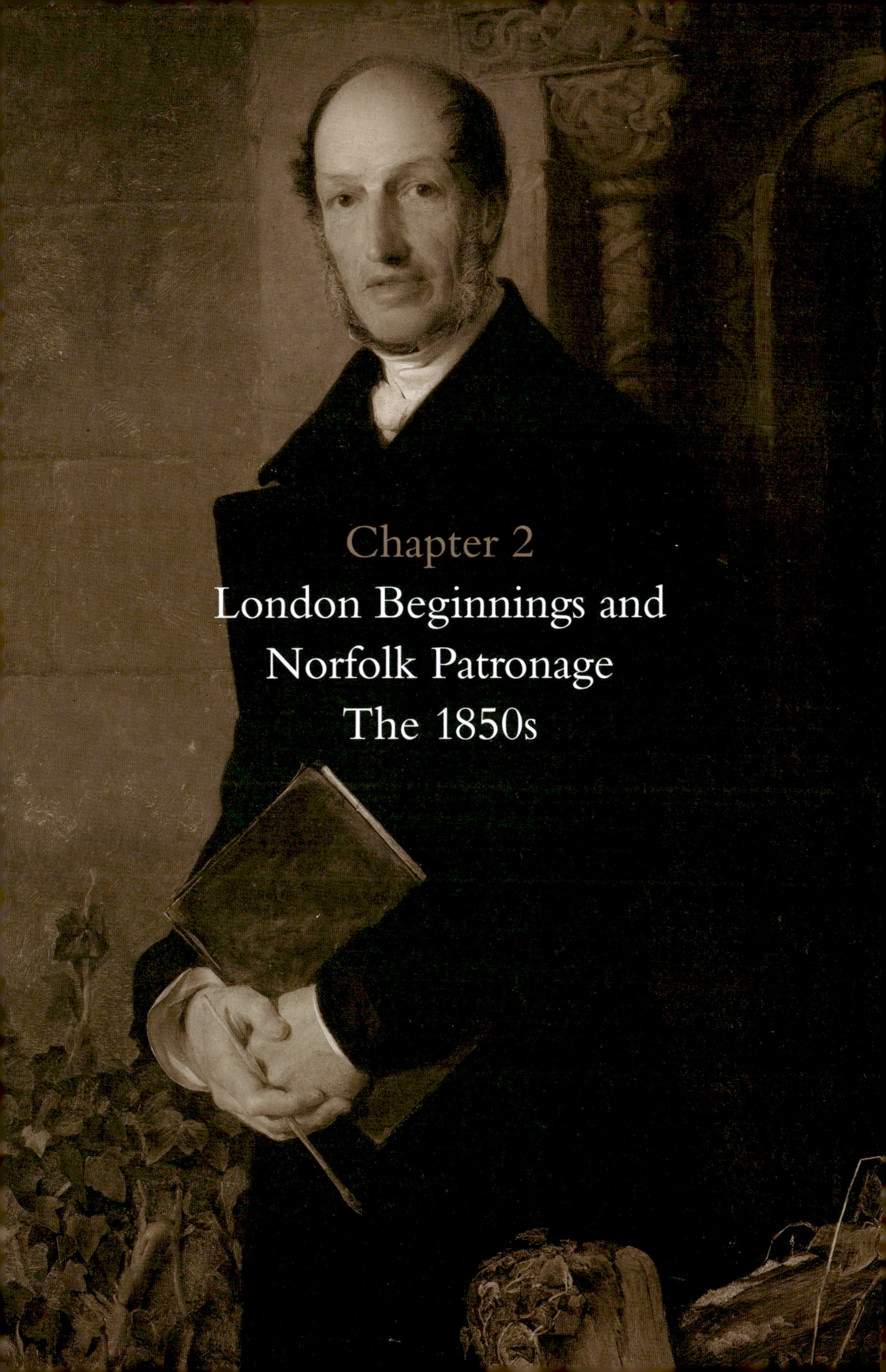

Chapter 2
London Beginnings and Norfolk Patronage
The 1850s

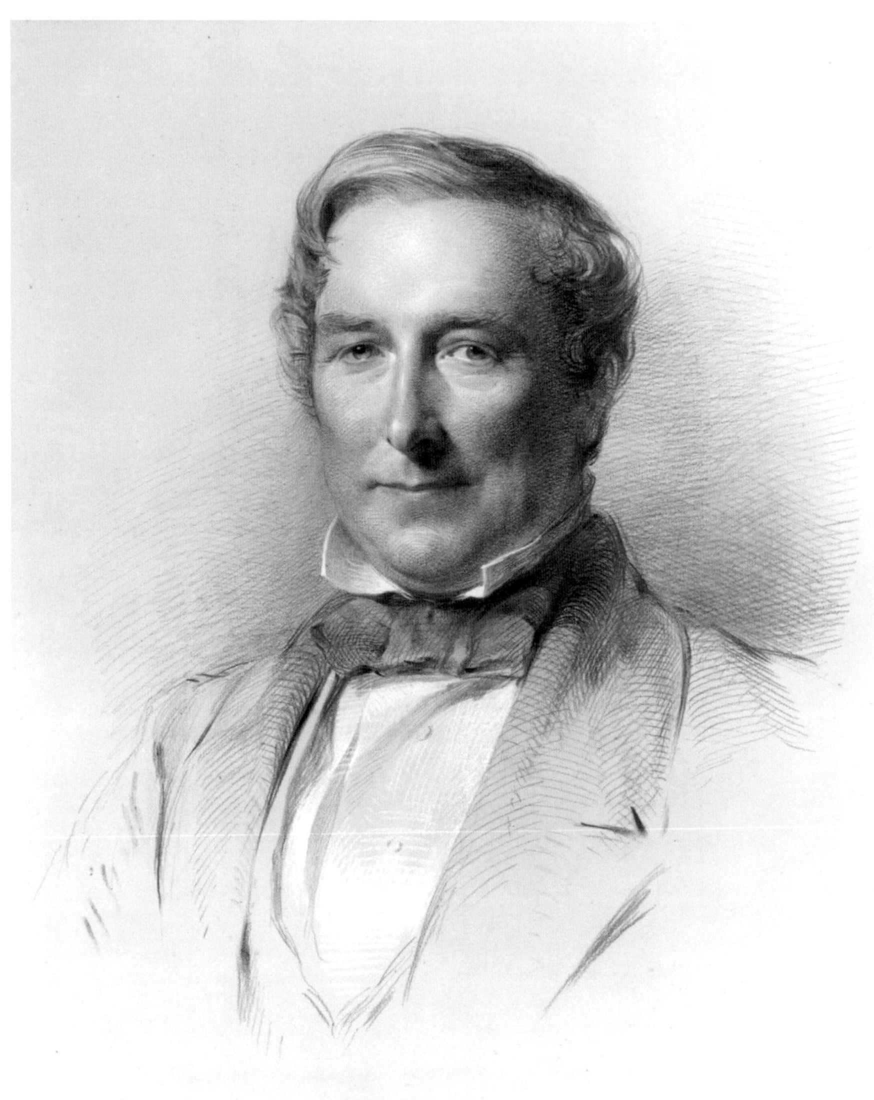

Henry Graves (1806-1892), the London printseller. Chalk drawing. *c.*1855.

Already in 1848, from the evidence of the catalogue of a Norwich exhibition,[1] Sandys must have found lodgings in London, but it is likely that he still divided his time between the two places. The address given in the catalogue was 2 Osnaburgh Street, which is just north of the Euston Road near Regent's Park.[2] Sandys was to be found at the same address when the 1851 census was taken.[3]

His portrait drawing of *Lord Henry Loftus* was accepted for the Royal Academy exhibition of that year, the catalogue giving his address as 21 Wigmore Street, which probably was his work room. The Royal Academy Summer Exhibition catalogues continued to list him at Wigmore Street until 1856. Five portrait drawings were exhibited at the Royal Academy exhibitions in the 1850s but unfortunately none of these have been identified. It was not until 1861 that his first oil paintings were shown there. However, he had exhibited two oils, *Mary Magdalen* (*c.*1859) and *Queen Eleanor* (1858) at the British Institution gallery in 1860, which must be regarded as his London debut as a painter. *Queen Eleanor*, his first essay in medieval Pre-Raphaelite style, was bought by James Anderson Rose, the art loving lawyer. The attributes to the legendary subject show the cord which led the wicked queen to 'Fair Rosamund' hidden in her bower, and the chalice containing poison. Her coronet and cloak are decorated with Celtic style ornament. It was painted in Norwich from an unidentified model.

From 1851 to 1855, 21 Wigmore Street was occupied, according to Kelly's Directories, by the booksellers John Mortimer and Charles Haselden, and from 1856 by John Lee Benham and Sons, ironmongers. One assumes that these businesses were at street level and some of the upper floors were let as apartments or work rooms.

In 1853, Sandys embarked on what he was later to describe as 'a most foolish marriage'.[4] The bride's name was Georgiana Creed and she came from a Norwich family. From the few facts I have found, it is difficult to conjure up any sense of her, other than of her reputed good looks. Something of the circumstances was reported by Frederick Barwell in his *Reminiscences*: 'There were in Norwich two exceedingly handsome girls, the daughters of a respectable tradesman.[5] Sandys married one and a young man of fair position the other, but neither marriage turned out a success.'[6] Georgiana Creed, in fact, had three sisters, Emma Jane, Harriet, and Emily. Emily married the Rev. Henry Farebrother and moved to London, and it was he who conducted the marriage ceremony on 28th May 1853 at St Pancras Church, between 'Antonio Frederick Augustus Sands' and Georgiana Creed, the certificate noting that Georgiana was then a spinster of the parish of St Marylebone, and Antonio an artist of the parish of St Pancras. George Smith and Emily Farebrother were recorded as being the witnesses.[7] A slight landscape sketch in black and white chalks inscribed 'Nailstone Leicestershire May 53', in the collection of Birmingham City Art Gallery, is a mystery but perhaps records a honeymoon visit at this time.

The Creed sisters were the daughters of Jonathan Creed and Emma Freeman of Norwich.[8] Creed family tradition has it that Jonathan Creed was an 'Irish glee singer'. He was Irish but glee-singing was no doubt a hobby.[9] His main occupation, as already noted, was as an ornamental painter and grainer. Although the Creed name goes back to the seventeenth century in Norfolk parish registers, censuses indicate that Jonathan was born in Ireland.[10]

The 'most foolish marriage' lasted until 1856, when Sandys left Georgiana.[11] We next hear about her when Sandys (foolishly) petitioned for a divorce in September 1863. This petition was easily demolished by the evidence that Georgiana gave as respondent. Sandys petitioned '...that on divers occasions since the said 28th day of May 1853 [the date of their marriage] the said Georgiana Sands has committed Adultery' and 'That from the month of November 1863 the said Georgiana Sands cohabited and habitually committed Adultery with Michael McHaffie at a house situate in Upper Montague Street, Bryanston Square in the County of Middlesex'. Far from Georgiana committing adultery (it seems to be the case that McHaffie was acting as a supporter, not a lover), it can be seen from Georgiana's response that it was Sandys who was the adulterer.

Her responding statement was dated 7th November 1863: '... [she] denies that she committed Adultery with Michael McHaffie as set forth ... [she] further saith that in and during the years 1858, 1859, 1860, 1861, 1862, and 1863, up to the date of the said Petition, the Petitioner has had a woman living under his protection[12] and has during such time frequently committed adultery with her. This Respondent further saith that the said Petitioner has on divers occasions since this marriage been guilty of cruelty to this Respondent, to wit in the years 1853 and 1854 at 2 Osnaburgh Street, Regent's Park by several times striking her with great violence and knocking her down, in the year 1855 by frequently striking her, knocking her down and abusing her at 21 Wigmore Street, Cavendish Square, and again on a certain occasion in the month of July 1856 by striking her on the face with a book he had in his hand at 21 Wigmore Street aforesaid. ... the Respondent further saith that in and since the year 1856 the Petitioner has deserted and wilfully separated himself without reasonable excuse ... this Respondent further saith that since the year 1855 the said Petitioner has left this Respondent without any means

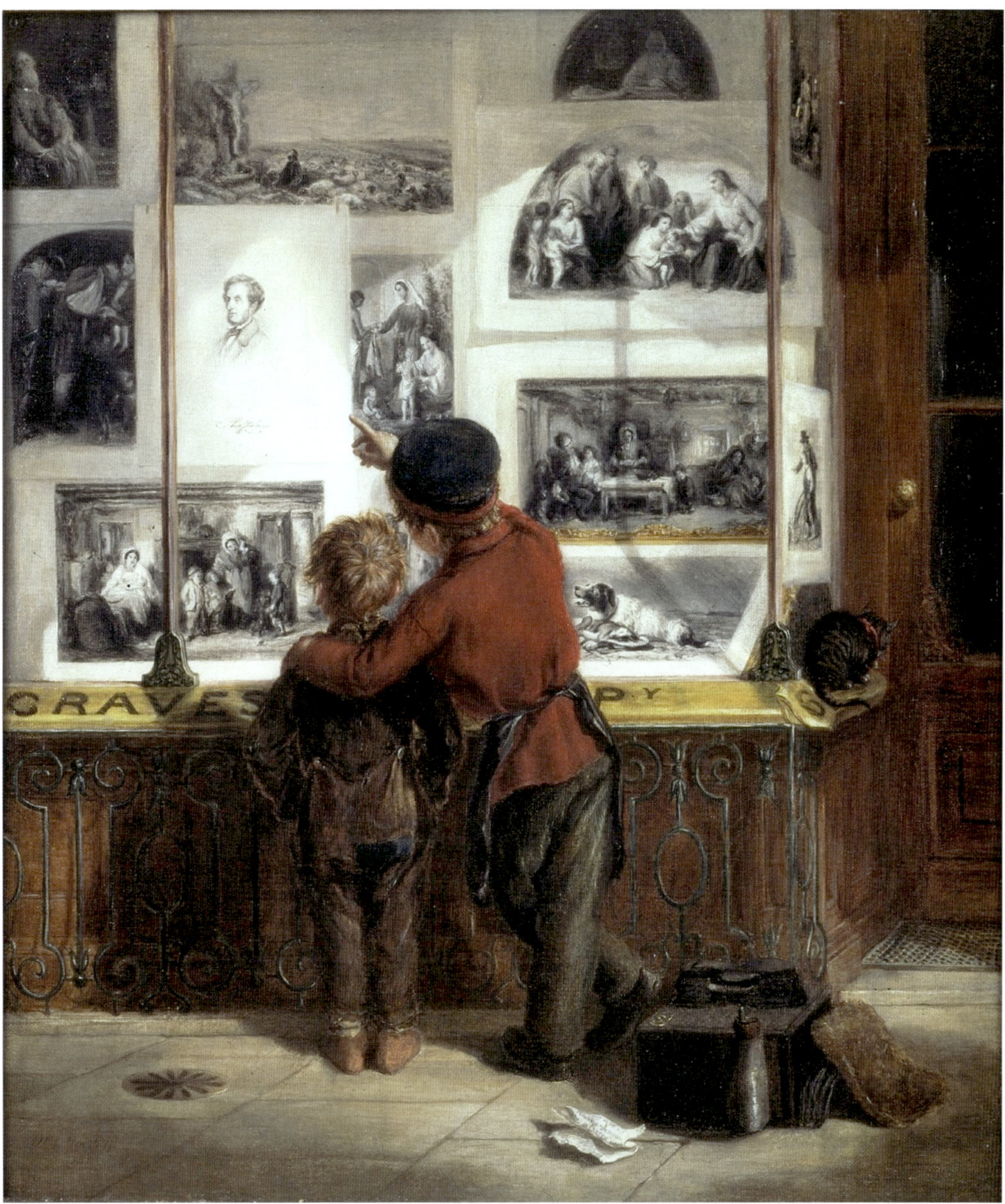

The print shop of Henry Graves, at 6 Pall Mall, with the Sandys portrait of Lord Shaftesbury displayed in the window. *Shaftesbury* or *Lost and Found*. Oil, 1862. By William MacDuff (1824-1881).

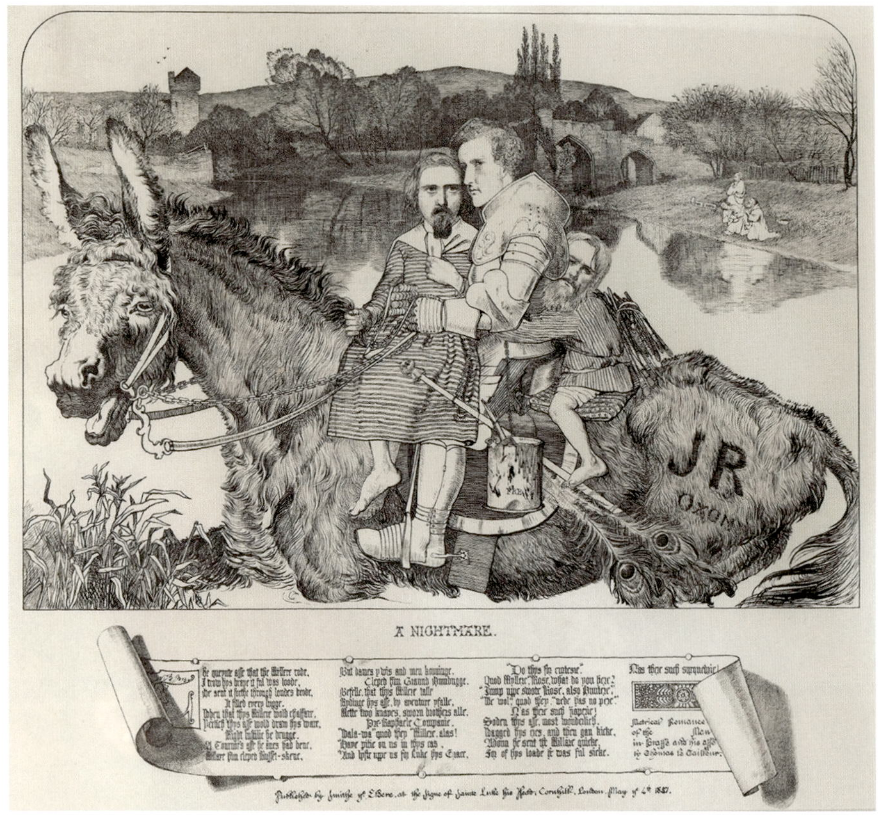

A Nightmare. Lithograph. 1857. The anonymous print which brought Sandys into the limelight in the London art world. By means of a satirical cartoon drawing based on a painting by Millais currently being shown at the Royal Academy, his cartoon lampooned the critic John Ruskin and his promotion of the Pre-Raphaelite artists.

of support. … Therefore this Respondent humbly prays that this Honorable Court will be pleased to reject the prayer of the said Petition.'

Sandys, the Petitioner, through his solicitor James Anderson Rose, denied all these charges.[13] It should be noted that the principal figures do not seem to speak in court but are spoken for by their lawyers – in the case of Georgiana, William Smith of Arlington Square.

The Court Minutes record the final judgement of Judge James Wilde during the hearings from 16th January to 22nd March 1864. The Petitioner – Antonio Frederick Augustus Sands – was ordered to pay Georgiana Sands alimony at the rate of £31 per annum to be paid monthly, and Sand[y]s was to pay the costs and expenses incurred by Georgiana. He had lost his case and was liable to pay out regularly large sums (in terms of monetary values of the 1860s). A search in the Central Index of Decrees Absolute finds no trace of a Decree Absolute given in this case. No children appear to have resulted from the marriage. A portrait of Georgiana once existed but it has not been traced.[14]

It was in the year of his marriage, 1853, that Frederick Sands altered the spelling of his name to Sandys. The former spelling is recorded on his marriage certificate and on a letter written by him in July. The letter 'y' appears on a second letter written to the same correspondent in September.[15] His parents apparently followed suit. However, in the divorce proceedings in 1863–1864, his legal birth name is reverted to.

There is another early instance of Sandys's name spelt with a 'y' in 1853. This was when he was elected an Associate of the British Archaeological Association. This event surely must have been a result of his friendship with James Bulwer who probably nominated him for election having aroused in Sandys an interest in archaeology while he was working on Bulwer's antiquarian collection.[16]

At the end of the marriage, Sandys 'was in great trouble', and I quote his own words recalling this time, as they are so revealing:

'Consulting with Mr Bulwer [his friend James Redford Bulwer] he advised me to go abroad – but I had not the money. He could not help me but he offered to be security [for a loan]. But I knew of no means [of going abroad] in those days, and the idea passed away, and I went down to Hunworth Rectory and stayed two or three months with the Revd. James Bulwer. There the idea of Italy started again, and I went to John Henry Gurney[17] who I had known for years and asked him for the money. He laughed over the whole matter and eventually Mr Bulwer's name being mentioned, he asked me if he would be security. I said I thought so. He said I will write to him and communicate with you. The sum [lent] was £100 or £150. I neglected one year or possibly two to pay the interest. The next time I saw Mr Bulwer about 1858 or 59, he had been called to pay it. I repaid Mr Bulwer in 1862 or 63.'

There is no evidence that Sandys ever went to Italy. The only trip abroad he made for which we do have evidence was a short trip to the Netherlands at Easter in 1862 with James Anderson Rose, and this, perhaps, is how the loan was spent.

What he saw there gave him a new inspiration for his painting style and technique, a change from the Reynolds tradition still prevailing in the early nineteenth century to the pure, bright, colours and the methodical and craftsman-like techniques of the early masters of Northern Europe. Whether he lacked the money or the will to travel to Italy we do not know, but Italy must have lost its pull because Sandys was enchanted by what he saw in Amsterdam, Rotterdam and The Hague, in churches, cathedrals, and state and municipal collections.

His new sources of inspiration were the pictures of van Eyck, Memling, Gerard David, van der Weyden, Dürer, Holbein, and Rubens. Two leaves from a notebook which he kept during this trip have been fortunately preserved. On one is a sketch of Hans Holbein the Younger's portrait of *The Man with the Hawk* (1542) in the former Dutch Royal Collection at the Mauritshuis. The sketch is surrounded by notes about details and colours, including the comment: 'A most wonderful picture. The finish and beauty of the hand, nails, velvet dress and hair miraculous – face, beard, and whole is too.'[18]

The other leaf contains a sketch of Rubens's portrait of Helena Fourment (1630–1631) which Sandys must have seen in Amsterdam. It was part of the Collection of Adriaan van der Hoop (1778–1854) which had been bequeathed to the city of Amsterdam in 1854. It was first shown to the public in the former *Oudemmanenhuis* (almshouse), which was opened as a public gallery.[19] His tonal sketch of the composition is surrounded by colour notes, and he was clearly impressed by Rubens's masterly depiction of the rich textiles of the dress, commenting on the ribbed white satin ribbon around her waist.[20] Although only these two sketches remain, giving evidence of his studies of paintings on this excursion, the visit was clearly crucial to the broadening of his experience of art.

Esther Wood in her monograph of 1896 perceptively touched on the difference in Sandys's aesthetic orientation with that of the Pre-Raphaelites (with whom Sandys is frequently associated), stating: 'His inclinations turned strongly towards the early Flemish styles. … From these he learnt that loyal regard for truthful expression, in subject and detail, which the Pre-Raphaelites [on the other hand] found blended with more spiritual qualities in fourteenth century Florentine art.'[21]

Sandys's early years in London seem to have been occupied with bread-and-butter reproductive work on portraits for the London printsellers, such as Henry Graves.[22] His work for Muskett in Norwich had given him some experience for this, in making copies of portraits to be etched or engraved on metal or drawn on stone for lithography – for multiple reproduction by professional engravers and printers. Sometimes a journey of some distance would have to be made to copy a portrait. For instance, Sandys must have

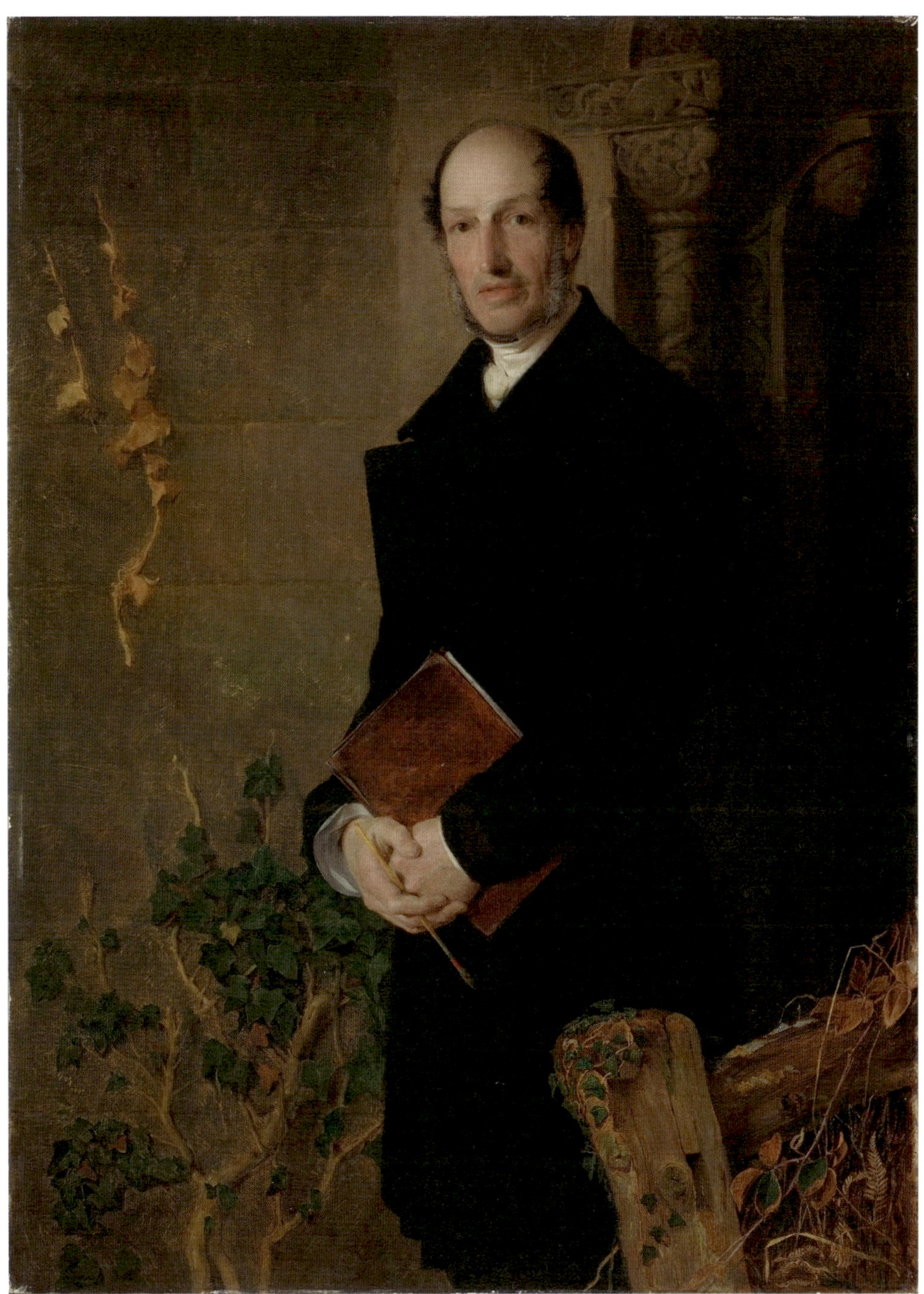

Rev. James Bulwer (1794-1879). Oil. 1858. The rector of Hunworth and Stody, Norfolk. He was an important early supporter of Sandys. Bulwer himself was a keen artist and antiquarian, and recognised Sandys's unusual talent. In the Bulwer household he was introduced to a more educated and cultured society.

travelled to Salisbury in 1854 to copy a portrait of the recently deceased Bishop of Salisbury.

The copy drawing would translate the original painting into graphic form which could be copied line for line by a professional engraver. Photographs, too, which were coming into use for portraits, needed to be translated in the same way, and there are examples in Sandys's work which can be recognised as such. An important part of the printsellers' trade was in portraits of contemporary 'celebrities'. One such notability, whose portrait was drawn by Sandys, probably from an oil portrait, was the philanthropist Lord Shaftesbury (1801–1885). What lends this unexceptional print, which was published in 1855, a particular interest was that an artist named William Macduff (1824–1881) painted an engaging picture titled *Shaftesbury*, or *Lost and Found* (1862),[23] which shows the Pall Mall shop window of Henry Graves and two small urchins, one a boot-black boy, pointing at the print made from Sandys's drawing which is prominently displayed. Several such portrait prints were engraved after Sandys's copy drawings.[24]

Sandys also spent time improving his skills by copying Old Master paintings in the National Gallery which had moved into its present building in Trafalgar Square in 1837.[25] In this early period of its history the National Gallery's then comparatively small collection included such great works as Jan van Eyck's *Arnolfini Marriage Portrait*, Tintoretto's *St George and the Dragon*, and Rubens's *Rape of the Sabine Women*. One can see influences from these particular works in his oil painting of the little dog *Darby* (*c.*1859–1860), his illustrations *The Portent* (early 1860) and *The King at the Gate* (*c.*late 1861). Also, we know that he made a copy of the Rubens, for his copy, now lost, was listed in the house-clearance sale in Norwich after the death of his parents in 1883.[26]

At Hunworth, he had the great benefit of being able to copy a portrait by Rogier van der Weyden, which was owned by James Bulwer. Also, at nearby Blickling Hall, where Bulwer was Librarian, in 1858, Sandys made a copy of the fine sixteenth century replica of Holbein's small portrait of the head of Henry VIII.[27]

Other opportunities for studying and copying paintings were at the British Institution where his own work was exhibited.[28] Later, in the 1860s, there were three major loan exhibitions of National Portraits held at South Kensington from which Sandys undoubtedly benefitted. For instance, the first, in 1866, showed portraits by Holbein, Petrus Christus, Clouet, Mabuse, and Antonis Mor.[29]

The British Museum was another source of inspiration and knowledge and, as to be expected, the Elgin Marbles made a big impression on an artist whose work contained a number of classically draped figures. There is evidence from his notebooks,[30] now alas fragmented and with pages lost, of his having studied medieval illuminated manuscripts, prints from the sixteenth and seventeenth centuries, and books of historic costume and armour. Yet, perhaps surprisingly, although many references in his notes relate to the manuscript originals in the British Museum, it is likely that many of these studies (which were traced and on tracing paper) would have been made at Hunworth Rectory in James Bulwer's extensive library, from published illustrated books showing medieval art and ornament, illustrating some examples at the British Museum. For example, there are twenty-nine tracings from plates in Camille Bonnard's *Costume Historique* (Paris, 1829–1830) among his many copies and tracings of historic reference material. Several antiquarian books with engraved plates were being published at this time, such as Frederic Madden and Henry Shaw's *Illuminated Ornaments selected from Manuscripts* (1833), and Henry Shaw's *Dresses and Decorations of the Middle Ages* (1843), W.Y. Ottley's *An Enquiry into the Origin and Early History of Engraving* (1816), and Samuel Meyrick's *A Critical Enquiry into Antient Armour* (1824), and others, from which plates and wood-engravings were probably copied or traced by Sandys.

It appears that Sandys joined a London sketch club, where he could draw from the figure. This must have been the Artists' Society, which from 1838 had used premises at 29 Clipstone Street, Fitzroy Square. It moved in about 1854 to the newly built Langham Chambers, in Langham Place, and became known thereafter as the 'Langham Sketching Club'. This was an important resource for professional artists: there was no teaching offered, and the necessary studio and model facilities were run on a cooperative basis, the members of the management committee taking it in turn to pose the model for a week at a time, either nude or in 'costume'. In addition, it served as a meeting ground for many artists living in London, several of whom, such as John Everett Millais, and Lowes Dickinson, had their own painting rooms in the building.[31] It appears also that George Price Boyce, Ford Madox Brown, and Rossetti also attended there.[32] A few of Sandys's 'life' studies have survived and are probably from this period.

A record of his attendance there in an anonymous newspaper cutting (which may be unreliable) has been preserved by the Sandys family. It dates from early 1904 and it relates to an incident in late 1857: '… this cartoon [*A Nightmare*] was published anonymously in 1857, and it was not until six months later that its author's name transpired. Shortly afterwards, at the Langham Sketch Club, Sandys heard someone who was standing behind him address him with the words, "Young man are you the author of that impudent cartoon of the Pre-Raphaelite Brotherhood?" "I am," acknowledged the young artist." "And a [damned] clever thing it is," retorted the other. "My name is Rossetti, come and dine with me." From that day, Sandys and Rossetti were the closest of friends.[33]

The target of this unique caricature was the large painting by Millais, *Sir Isumbras at the Ford,* which was hung at the Royal Academy Summer Exhibition that year. It is a large and impressive work, somewhat touched with sentimentality (to which Millais was prone in his work, in my opinion), showing an elderly knight in armour mounted on his steed, crossing a wide river. Clinging to the back of the veteran warrior are two small children being thus carried across the water. Unfortunately, Millais had overdone the proportions of the horse in relation to the rest of the picture. However, the monster-horse did not escape public notice, and inevitably it provoked much ridicule. Sandys's print *A Nightmare* (punningly derived from knightmare?) was a brilliant gesture to caricature the painting and make it a vehicle to 'send up' the Pre-Raphaelite artists and their advocate, the art critic, John Ruskin.

A subtle detail worth noting in the print are the figures on the far riverbank, of Titian, Michelangelo, and Raphael in attitudes of prayer, with a common speech bubble in black letters stating '*orate pro nobis*'.[34]

Joseph Pennell later observed in his praise of Sandys as an illustrator in his article *A Golden Decade in English Art*[35] that it was due to this caricature, in which the large jackass (instead of the horse in the painting) bore the initials 'J.R. OXON' branded on its side, was an obvious gibe at Ruskin. It is significant that nowhere in the copious writings of Ruskin is Sandys referred to.

There is a mock-medieval poem printed below the cartoon (as there were verses below the 1857 Royal Academy Exhibition catalogue entry for the Millais painting), titled *Metrical Romance of the Man in Brasse and his Asse by Thomas le Tailleur,* from which one might assume that Tom Taylor was the author.[36] However, since Tom Taylor had written the original verses attached to the Millais painting, it may have been written by another in an attempt to satirise Tom Taylor also.

A story connected with *A Nightmare*, with slight variations from two different sources,[37] we are told originated from Sandys himself. In essence, to get a

Queen Eleanor. Oil on canvas. 1858. Painted in Norfolk, it was first shown in London in 1860 and was bought by the art-loving solicitor James Anderson Rose (1819-1894), who became Sandys's London patron and friend.

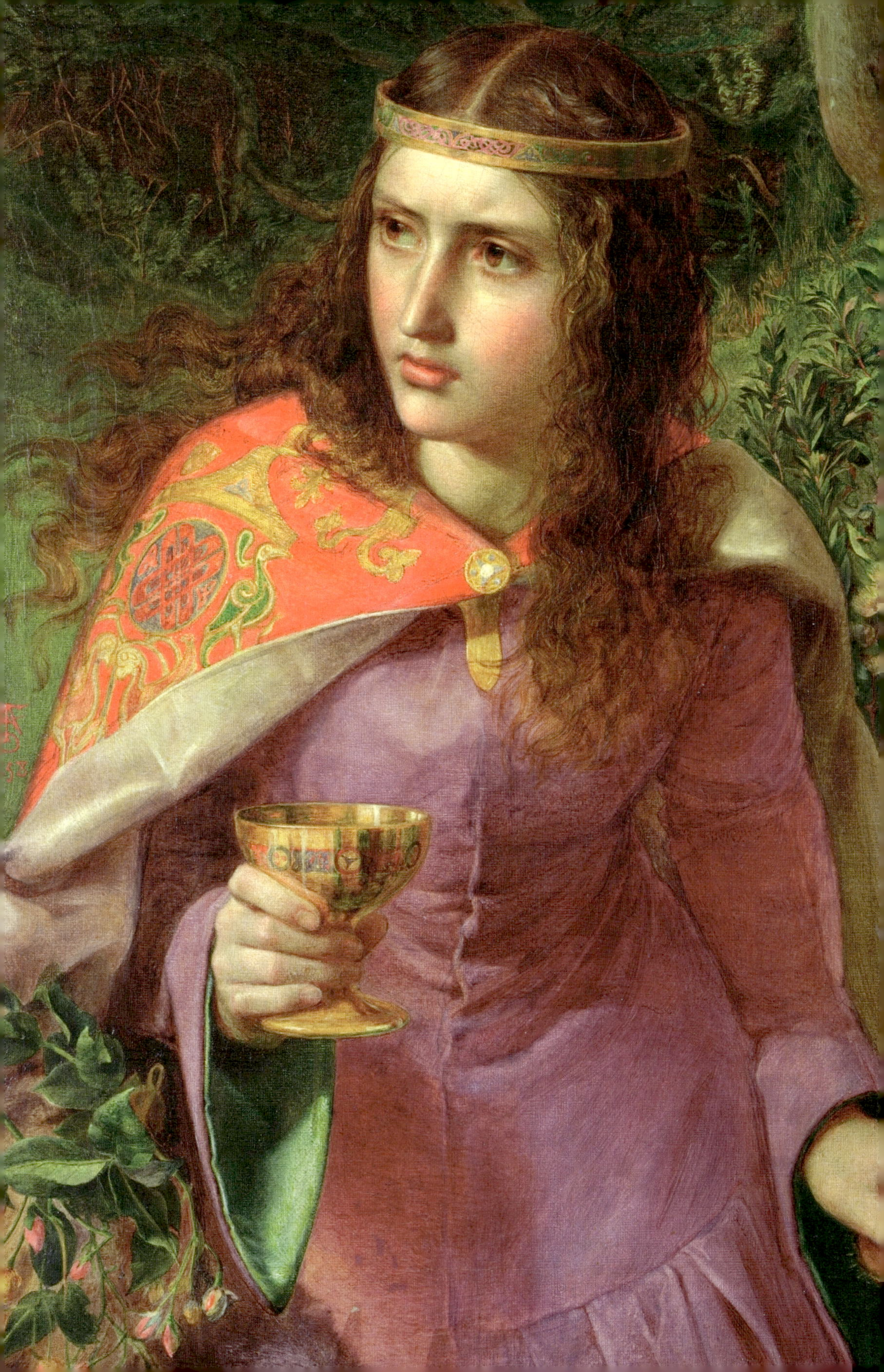

likeness of Rossetti for the caricature, Sandys (who was not yet a friend) called on him at his rooms at Chatham Place '…on some pretence, and from that brief glimpse was able to capture a likeness'.

Walter Crane remembered seeing it in the printseller Colnaghi's window when it appeared.[38] Once it was realised Sandys was the artist responsible, he emerged from his comparative obscurity in the London art world.

The ensuing friendship with Rossetti was to be of great importance for both Sandys's life and for his work, as it proved to be for many others.[39] Rossetti, a poet as well as a painter, was the hub of a sociable group of artists and writers in the late 1850s and 1860s, some of whom had been part of the original Pre-Raphaelite Brotherhood of the 1840s. There was a change in painting style largely due to Rossetti's influence – a looser, more romantic vision, inspired by Italian Renaissance art – and particularly celebrating feminine beauty. Unfortunately, posterity has inextricably confused the two phases which succeeded one another by the use of the single term to encompass both. The new Rossetti circle included William Morris, Edward Burne-Jones, Simeon Solomon, William Bell Scott, Arthur Hughes, George Boyce, Sandys, the writer George Meredith, the dealer Charles Augustus Howell, the lawyer James Anderson Rose, and the poet Algernon Charles Swinburne. The expatriate American James McNeill Whistler (by nature an independent and in possession of a considerable ego) flitted in and out of the group at this time, but he had his own group of admiring followers, and also had his own aesthetic agenda.

Through his friendship with Rossetti, Sandys was able to meet the glamorous actress Ruth Herbert and he made a drawing of her in the late 1850s.[40] Rossetti had obtained an introduction in about June 1858 through Tom Taylor. Sandys was later to benefit from several portrait commissions from Ruth Herbert and her friends. In the later 1860s, he was to have a more personal connection with the theatrical world through his 'little girl' and her two sisters, who with varying degrees of success combined acting careers with modelling for artists.

When in London, Sandys evidently began his entry into the bohemian, convivial night life of the day, a world in which no women played a part. Drinking, talking, smoking, and singing, were the relaxations and amusements.

The first record of Sandys in this context comes from the reminiscences of Rossetti's brother William who wrote that the first time he met Sandys was at the musical parties of William Vaux, the antiquary, in his rooms at Gate

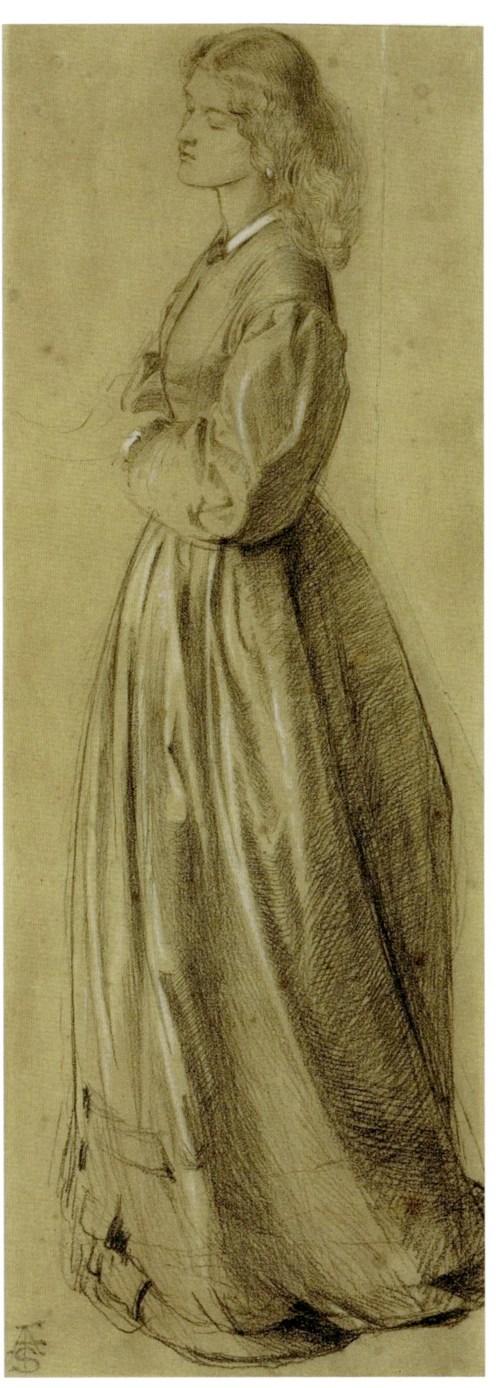

Louisa Ruth Herbert (1831-1921). Chalk drawing. *c.*1858. She was an actress and great beauty. Sandys's opportunity to make this study was undoubtedly due to Dante Gabriel Rossetti's first making her acquaintance.

Street, Lincoln's Inn Fields.[41] As he recalled, this was in 1857 or 1858. Sandys also became a member of the Arundel Club, at a site south of the Strand which overlooked the Thames. From 1865, he was elected to the socially desirable Garrick Club (which exists to this day).

Perhaps not surprisingly, Sandys does not seem to have enrolled in the Artists' Rifle Corps, a part of the large National Volunteer Association formed in the winter of 1859, in the real fear of a French invasion, considering that most of his London acquaintances did so at the time, with the greatest of enthusiasm and camaraderie at the outset, camping, drilling and practising rifle marksmanship in parks and on commons. Those who joined were Leighton, Millais, Holman Hunt, William Morris, Rossetti, Burne-Jones, Watts, Charles Keene, Ford Madox Brown, and of course many others. However, except for an enthusiastic few, their patriotic fervour does not seem to have lasted for long.[42] Sandys's absence may be explained by his lack of money and time, and also for being largely in Norwich, preoccupied with a major picture, *Autumn*, for William Clabburn.

In spite of increasing involvement in London professional and social activities, Sandys seems to have spent a good deal of time from 1858 to 1864 in Norfolk. The greater part of 1858 was spent there, perhaps on account of the break-up of his marriage (which had taken place in London). He may have quit London completely for a while.

A revelation of some of his movements in London and Norfolk comes from a report of his first summons for insolvency that appeared in May 1859. It records his varied addresses from Wigmore Street to Duke Street, Westminster, then to Kelling Hall, Norfolk (the seat of the Girdlestone family), the Royal Hotel, Norwich, the family home at 9 St Giles' Hill, the Norfolk Hotel, and lastly the Norwich suburb of Thorpe where he settled in lodgings for a while.[43]

In March 1858, he painted a portrait of James Bulwer, at Hunworth. He kept a diary while working on it from 9th March to 6th April 1858, and several titled or dated drawings and studies show that he was at Hunworth, Kelling, or in the vicinity, in April, May, June, July, and October, November and December 1858.[44] In the latter month also, Sandys worked on a watercolour for Bulwer's *Norfolk Collection*, which is dated, showing that he was continuing to supply Bulwer with drawings and watercolours for this extensive project, to which he had first contributed a decade before.

At this time in Norfolk, he made many studies from nature, and from books and prints, many of which he utilised later in paintings, drawings, and illustrations for a decade or so, until his work changed to portraiture almost exclusively. These and other reference studies, using Bulwer's extensive library, remained in Norwich until the clearance of the Sandys family home on the deaths of both his parents in 1883. This material soon after passed, via local dealers, into the hands of Charles Fairfax Murray, and eventually came to rest, with other of his studies on paper, at the Birmingham City Art Gallery.[45]

Bulwer was accumulating prints, drawings, and manuscripts, and copies of historic material for his 'extra-illustrated' or 'grangerised' collection, which was to illustrate the volumes on Norfolk history by the Rev. Francis Blomefield's *An Essay towards a topographical History of the County of Norfolk*, published (posthumously) 1805–1810. Bulwer employed Sandys and other local artists to make watercolour copies of medieval paintings in churches and a variety of other historic artefacts, and Bulwer himself executed many also. At Bulwer's death in 1879, this collection comprised hundreds of items.[46]

1858 was the year of Sandys's first dated subject painting in medievalist Pre-Raphaelite style, his *Queen Eleanor*. Another dating from about this time is his *Mary Magdalene* or *The Magdalen*, both of which he showed in London at the British Institution in 1860. The British Institution was a private but philanthropic gallery under royal patronage in Pall Mall. It was founded in 1805 before the establishment of the National Gallery. Two exhibitions a year were held, one in spring of modern works for sale, and in the autumn, of old master paintings on loan. It closed in 1867.

In 1858 we also have the first evidence, from the Royal Academy Exhibition catalogue of that year, that he was living in lodgings at Thorpe across the River Wensum from the city of Norwich.[47] Thorpe was once a separate hamlet where some of the wealthier Norwich citizens were building villas. At Thorpe, the River Wensum joins the River Yare, which flows on to Yarmouth, giving Thorpe a picturesque riverside character that had already attracted local artists to it. It is no surprise that, when Sandys listed his favourite outdoor recreations for *Who's Who*, they were the water sports of rowing and sailing.[48]

We now find Sandys's interest turning to riverside landscapes. The first dated work of this nature was a study of 7th November 1859 of a broken-down jetty at Whitlingham. Whitlingham was the site of a ferry across the River Yare opposite the Thorpe bank. An ambitious 'subject' picture, *Autumn* was occupying his mind at this time – a river landscape with figures. In fact, one might describe it as a *dejeuner sur l'herbe* with a man and his wife and their baby – a relaxed scene in an imaginary riverside landscape. The landscape

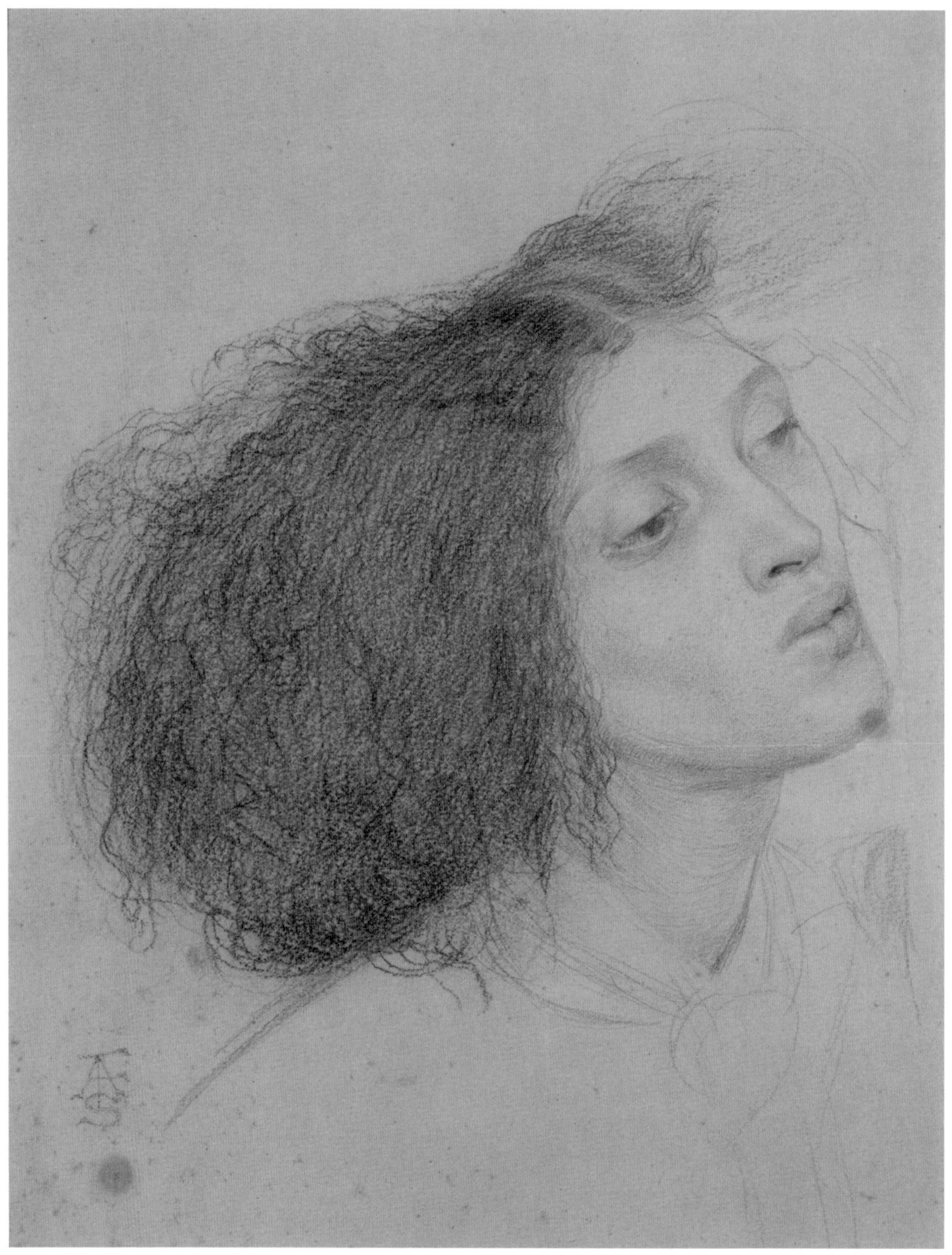

Fanny Eaton, the model (1835-1924). Chalk drawing. 1859. This study was later used by Sandys for his *Morgan le Fay* (1863). The mixed race Mrs Eaton was drawn by several artists at this time and was probably a frequent model at the Langham Sketch Club in London.

is not quite imaginary because the details are real Norwich fixtures such as the medieval Bishop's Bridge, but it is showing its opposite face to the general view as seen in the picture. A descendant has convincingly identified the figures as Sergeant Faux, his wife Mary Ann and their son Robert. The sergeant was a discharged veteran from service in India.[49] Why they were chosen as models is unknown, but they were neighbours of Sandys's parents, living at Pottergate Street, at St Giles' Hill. Somehow, they fit the autumnal, somewhat melancholy, scene.

For this, Sandys produced a large preliminary drawing (or cartoon) in black and white, dated 1860, which he showed at the Royal Academy in 1862. Gaining the interest of local buyers, he painted two versions in oil, one full scale, the other smaller. Generally, a small version of a large painting is a preliminary colour sketch, but this is a detailed picture, presumably painted for his client, Canon Edward Bulmer who lived in Norwich Cathedral Close and who probably did not have space for a large picture on his walls. The musician and collector William Dixon, who bought the full-sized version and lived in the newly developed Mount Pleasant area of Norwich, clearly had a great deal of space, as can be seen from the sale of the contents of his house at his death.[50]

Autumn marked a high point in Sandys's capabilities, and it is regrettable that he failed to put together more landscapes of this calibre.

Another river landscape, *Whitlingham, Autumn*, dated 1860, is purely a landscape painting. It came into the hands of the Norwich shopkeeper Theodore Rossi. The Rossi family business, founded by Theodore's father George Rossi (*c.*1795–1865), had a prominent establishment opposite the marketplace.[51] They were makers and sellers of clocks and scientific instruments, opticians, jewellers, gold and silversmiths, as well as art and antique dealers. The Rossis were good patrons of Sandys for several family portraits, and were the source of many a loan in times of crisis. This painting may have remained with the family in lieu of an unredeemed loan.[52]

Meandering river landscapes are also seen in two of his magazine illustrations of the early 1860s: *The Old Chartist*, and *Until her Death*. Another illustration titled *Sleep*, shows a view from his window, we are told, over Thorpe rooftops to the Yare which would have been busy with river traffic passing between Norwich and Great Yarmouth, the seaport.[53] The 1861 census shows that his lodgings were at 35 Thorpe Street, consistent with a view of the River Yare.

It was probably in about 1855 that he began his association with his important

Norwich patron, the shawl manufacturer William Houghton Clabburn (1820–1889). Shawls were an important article of women's clothing in the first half of the nineteenth century and Clabburn, Son and Crisp were highly successful award-winning manufacturers of shawls as well as other high-quality textiles such as silk 'mourning crape'. Clabburn and his young family lived at Thorpe where he had built himself a handsome villa named Sunny Hill. It was appropriately named, as it was built on a south-facing hillside overlooking the River Yare.

Although the first ownership of *Autumn*, the large cartoon drawing for the oil painting, is unknown, it is possible that it started as a commission from Clabburn, who certainly was behind the associated *Spring* (*c.*1861), in which all five of Clabburn's children appear.

Clabburn was probably aware of the talented young Sandys from his student days, since he, as a manufacturer of products in which design was fundamental, was on the founding committee of the Norwich School of Design; but the earliest clear evidence of Clabburn's interest in Sandys is the portrait drawing he commissioned of his father Thomas Clabburn in about 1855. In 1859 or 1860 Clabburn commissioned a stunning oil portrait of his young wife Hannah Louisa. According to J.M. Gray this portrait was seen by Rossetti, when it was shown at the 1861 Royal Academy Summer Exhibition, and admired it so much that he sought him out and he became a friend.[54]

The portrait of Hannah Louisa was followed by one of Mrs Thomas Clabburn, William Clabburn's mother, dressed up, inexplicably, in seventeenth century historicist costume. These were followed by seven other portraits of himself, another of his wife, and his children.[55] Of all Sandys's patrons, Clabburn formed the most important collection of his work, most of which he bought directly from him. *Oriana*, dated 1861, from an unidentified Norwich model, was one of those which must have been largely painted in 1860, since it was entered and hung in the Royal Academy Exhibition of 1861.

Through Sandys's introduction, Clabburn also became interested in the work of Rossetti and Edward Burne-Jones. In fact, he commissioned in 1863 a replica from Rossetti of his *Mary Magdalene Leaving the House of Simon the Pharisee* (1858)[56] which, several years later in 1869, was the cause of complaint by Rossetti of plagiarism by Sandys, which he saw in Sandys's *Mary Magdalen* (*c.*1859–60) and two other works. These two other works, *Vivien* (1863), and *Helen of Troy* (1869) might better deserve Rossetti's complaint.

Jeremiah James Colman (1830-1898). Chalk drawing. *c.*1858. The miller of flour and mustard seed at Norwich. He was an important Norfolk patron

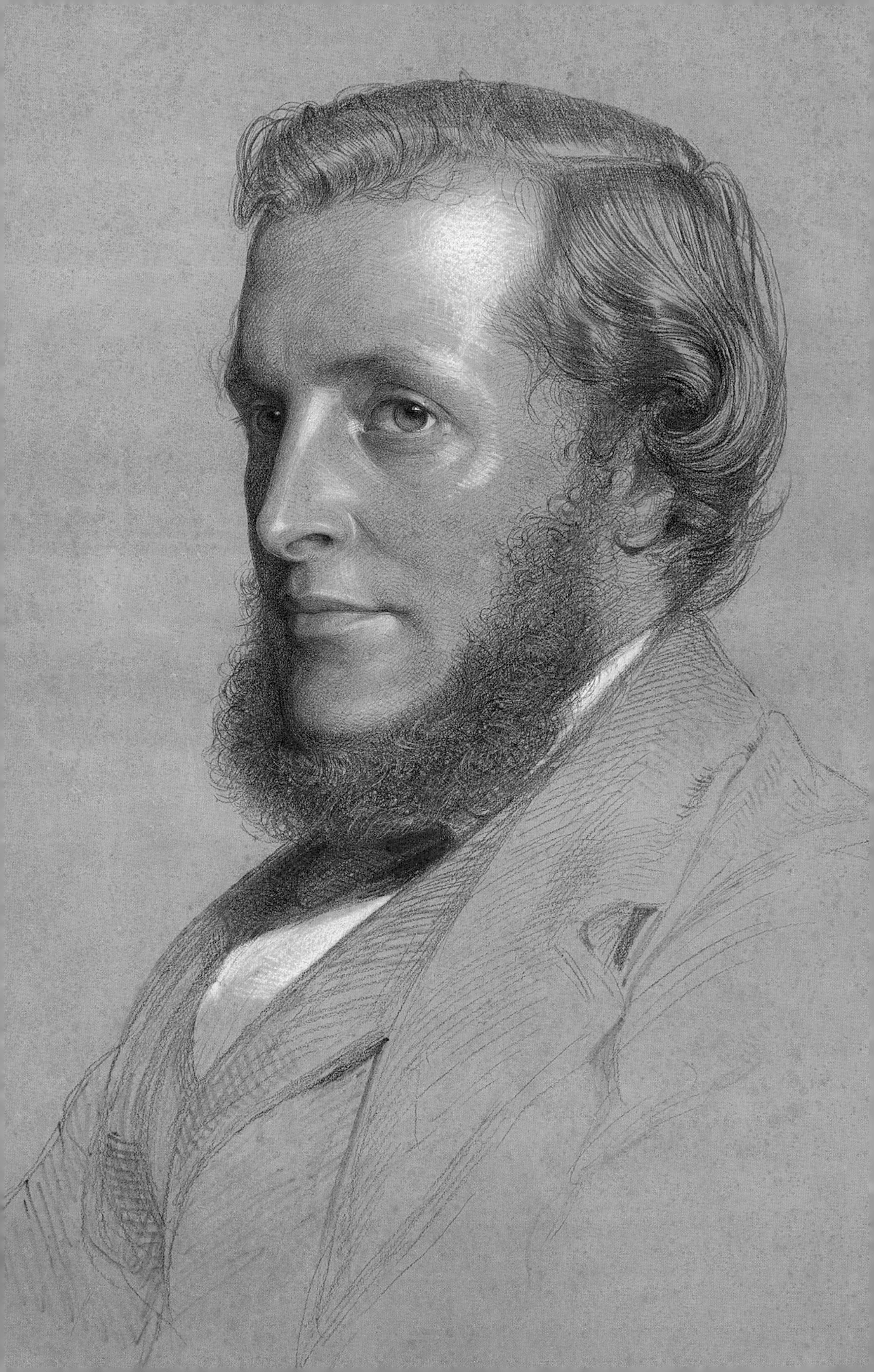

Another important Norwich patron was the miller Jeremiah James Colman (1830–1898). Colman had succeeded in 1854 to the management of his father's and great-uncle's business, Jeremiah and James Colman, millers of flour and mustard, at the village of Stoke Holy Cross (about four miles south of Norwich). Between 1856 and 1862 he transferred the whole operation to Norwich, to have access to a navigable river and to the site of a new railway, and it was he who built up the business into the internationally known company of recent times. Sandys made a fine portrait drawing of the young Colman which unfortunately is not dated, but must belong to the late 1850s, from family information and judging from Colman's youthful appearance.[57] Jeremiah James, and later his son Russell, were to commission a total of at least ten family portrait drawings, and later acquired other works by Sandys – mostly from the Clabburn collection after William Clabburn's death in 1889 – which were eventually given to Norwich Castle Museum.

In Norfolk, Sandys's reputation as a portrait artist spread out from the Norwich group of these prosperous tradesmen and professional men, and men such as Samuel Bignold, the son of the founder of the Norwich Union Insurance company, and Jacob Tillett, newspaperman (*The Eastern Daily Press*) and politician, into the Norfolk county landed families and gentry. Of the latter, portraits of Bedingfelds, a Reeve, a Jary, Buxtons, and Hoares have come to light. Known but still untraced are portraits of the Freemans, and a Frere, while others may still remain in obscurity with the descendants of the sitters.

[1] Norwich, *First Exhibition of the Norfolk and Norwich Association for the Promotion of the Fine Arts*, 1848. There were five exhibits by F. Sands.

[2] The Euston Road was then called the New Road. Was it a coincidence that the architect of the first building to house the Norwich School of Art, the 'Bazaar' building (in 1846–1847), Samuel Lovick, had his office at 3 Osnaburgh Place, New Road? The Bazaar Building had been built in 1831.

[3] It was a lodging house, and the householders were Thomas and Jane Ellwood.

[4] Letter of 20th December 1899 from Sandys to an anonymous correspondent, probably the executor of J.R. Bulwer's estate. (National Portrait Gallery Archive). This was published with some minor errors of transcription, but with many erroneous conclusions derived from it by R.L. Ormond in 'Another Bulwer Portrait by Sandys' in the *Burlington Magazine*, April 1966, pp. 194–197. In this letter Sandys was having to account for his debts to J.R. Bulwer.

[5] Jonathan Creed, originally from Carlow in Ireland, is variously described in the censuses as: 'painter' (1841), 'ornamental painter' (1851), 'painter and grainer', in St Helen's Workhouse, Norwich (1871 and 1881 censuses).

[6] *Eastern Daily Press*, Norwich, 23rd August 1923, 'Mr Barwell's Reminiscences, no. 6. A Norwich Dyer Artist [*sic*]. Frederick Sandys'.

[7] George Smith was probably the genre painter of that name (1829–1901). I have found no other connection between him and Sandys, so perhaps the friendship did not last.

[8] I am indebted to Mrs Margaret Oxbury, a descendant of the third sister, Emma Jane Creed (who married Thomas Bulwer Butler of Norwich), for Creed family information.

[9] Glee, or unaccompanied part singing, was a popular male recreation of the day.

[10] According to the International Genealogical Index. Furthermore, a variant spelling Crede, can be traced back to the 16th century.

[11] In this letter Sandys remembers the date of the break-up of the marriage as 1856. This is confirmed by Georgiana's statement to the Divorce Court in 1863.

[12] This certainly refers to the gypsy Keomi Gray.

[13] A fellow member of the Arundel Club. Founded in 1859 in Arundel Street which ran between the Strand and the Thames riverbank. It moved in 1861 to Salisbury Street, nearby, retaining its original name. Its members were drawn from the fields of journalism, drama and art, and was deemed to be 'bohemian'.

[14] Christie's sale of 23rd February 1925, the property of the Misses Jackson of 138 Goldhurst Terrace, NW6, lot 3, 'Portrait of Miss Read [*sic*], afterwards Mrs Sandys, oval, chalk, 8 x 6 ½ in.' Bought by Carey for £2/18/0.

[15] Two letters from F.S. to an unnamed correspondent, perhaps a London frame-maker: the first dated 'July/53' and the other dated 'Sept/53'. They seem to have been dated by the recipient. Gordon N. Ray Collection, New York Public Library.

[16] *Journal of the British Archaeological Association*, vol. 10 (1855), p. 118. List of Associates elected in 1853. No. 65. Frederick Sandys Esq., 2 Osnaburgh Street. I am indebted to the late Ray Watkinson for this reference.

[17] His former patron, the Norwich banker and ornithologist, John Henry Gurney Senior.

[18] Cambridge, Fitzwilliam Museum. P&D Dept. no. 865.53.

[19] I am indebted to Dr P.J.J. van Thiel of the Rijksmuseum (where it is now located) for this information.

[20] Cambridge, Fitzwilliam Museum, as above.

[21] Esther Wood, (1896).

[22] Henry Graves (1806–1892) evidently recognised a higher talent in Sandys when he had him draw a portrait of himself (*c.*1855). National Portrait Gallery, London.

[23] Museum of London. no. 93.165.

[24] F.S.'s work for the London printsellers is corroborated in F.B. Barwell's account. See footnote 5, p. 30.

[25] The new building, by William Wilkins (1778–1839), was shared also by the Royal Academy and its school, which had moved from Somerset House.

[26] Spelman's, Norwich, 16th October 1883, lot 119, *The Rape of the Sabines* from the original [framed oil painting]. Sold for 7s 7d.

[27] This is one of several contemporary copies of a lost original. Sandys's copy remains with Bulwer descendants in Canada. His copy of the van der Weyden is at the Fitzwilliam Museum (the original is now in the Bearsted Collection at Upton House, National Trust).

[28] The British Institution exhibitions alternated loans of privately-owned 'old masters', with contemporary works.

[29] Exhibition of National Portraits, from Wikipedia.

[30] Numerous small sketches on small sheets, originally notebook pages, which were sold at the 1883 Norwich sale. They came into the hands of a Mr Jackson of Bethel Street, Norwich, who sold them on to Charles Fairfax Murray. They are now in the Birmingham Art Gallery collection.

[31] George Somes Layard, *The Life and Letters of Charles Samuel Keene* (Sampson Low, Marston, 1892), pp. 34–36, 60. Layard lists, besides Keene, Tenniel, the Dalziel brothers, Arthur Lewis, Carl Haag, P.H. Calderon, E.J. Poynter, H.T. Wells, Fred Walker, attending. It appears also that Millais, Boyce, Lowes Dickinson, Rossetti and Sandys attended. Also see Mary Lutyens (ed.) *Letters from Sir J.E. Millais and William Holman Hunt in The Huntington Library*, in *The Walpole Society*, xliv, 1972–1974, p. 16, no. 33.

[32] See Virginia Surtees, (ed.), *The Diary of Ford Madox Brown*, (1981), p. 116, note 10.

[33] This is part of a review of the Sandys exhibition held at the Leicester Galleries, London, in February and March 1904. The anecdote, probably emanating from the family, is somewhat simplistic and probably inaccurate. For one thing, Rossetti

was only one year older than Sandys. Sandys Family Archive.

[34] A frequent text, 'pray for us', seen on medieval memorial brasses in parish churches with which Sandys had become familiar when working for James Bulwer.

[35] *The Savoy*, no. 1, January 1896, p. 121.

[36] Tom Taylor (1817–1880) was a journalist and playwright of burlesques. He was editor of the humorous magazine *Punch* from 1874–1880. He studied at Cambridge and was no doubt aware of Frederic Madden's work on medieval manuscripts there.

[37] Elizabeth and Joseph Pennell in the *Whistler Journal* (1921), p. 23. Robert Ponsonby Staples in an unpublished letter of 24th May 1930, to the National Portrait Gallery (NPG Archives).

[38] Walter Crane. *An Artist's Reminiscences* (1907), pp. 38–39.

[39] Dante Gabriel's brother William, however, gives 1861 as the beginning of the intimate friendship between the two, and also with the writer George Meredith. W.M. Rossetti, *Dante Gabriel Rossetti, his family letters*, 1895, p. 210.

[40] Louisa Ruth Herbert, Mrs Edward Crabbe (*c.*1831–1921) was a leading actress at the Olympic Theatre at this time. Later she was manager of her own company at the St James's Theatre. Besides her husband, from whom she was estranged, she had several aristocratic and rich admirers, one of whom became the great-grandfather of the late Virginia Surtees, author of the *Paintings and Drawings of Dante Gabriel Rossetti*, Oxford, 1958.

[41] W.M. Rossetti, *Some Reminiscences*, 1906, vol. 1, p. 269; vol .2, p. 321. W.S.W. Vaux (1818–1885) was Keeper of Coins and Medals at the British Museum.

[42] There is an amusing commentary in A.M.W. Stirling, *The Richmond Papers* (1916), pp. 164–167.

[43] *The London Gazette*, 24th May, 1859. p. 2095.

[44] This diary is merely a piece of folded paper, inscribed in pencil, which Bulwer kept (Bulwer Collection, Ottawa, National Gallery of Canada). This habit of diary-keeping while working on a picture was repeated when Sandys painted two other pictures, one in 1880, and one in 1887. There may have been other diaries which are now lost.

[45] A large batch of some 269 works on paper entered the Birmingham collection in 1906, and another batch of 47 arrived in 1927 (45 of the latter wrongly attributed to Ford Madox Brown). All of these came from C.F. Murray's large collection of Pre-Raphaelite drawings.

[46] This collection is described at length in Appendix 2 in my *Frederick Sandys, a Catalogue Raisonné* (2001).

[47] His address in RA catalogues was given as Thorpe from 1858 to 1864, after which London addresses are given.

[48] This was noted in *Who was Who*, 1897–1916, p. 626.

[49] Correspondence with Dr David Faux of Hagersville, Ontario. March 1988.

[50] William Dixon (1813–1882). According to the 1871 census he lived at Albion Terrace, Mount Pleasant, in the parish of Eaton, near Norwich.

[51] George Rossi had emigrated from northern Italy in about 1820 as a refugee from the political and military upheavals there.

[52] It is now at the Yale Center for British Art, New Haven, CT.

[53] According to Borough Johnson in his introduction to *Reproductions of Woodcuts* by F. Sandys, (ed.), Mary Sandys, 1910, the view through the window shows 'the river Yare, as it appeared from the painter's own window'. This fact undoubtably came from Mary Sandys.

[54] J.M. Gray in *Art Journal*, March 1884, p. 75.

[55] Lucy and Mary (*c.*1861–1862); Hannah Louisa (1866, 1869); William H. Clabburn (1870, 1871); Walter (1871); Henry (1871–1872).

[56] Clabburn was dissatisfied with the replica, however, and it was then bought by Charles Augustus Howell who sold it on to Heaton and Brayshay, Manchester art dealers and decorators. Clabburn was the provider of a pair of peacocks to patrol Rossetti's garden at Chelsea and, perhaps rather regrettably, a bull which probably ended in a butcher's shop.

[57] A letter dated 1st October 1938, from his daughter Helen C. Colman to his daughter-in-law Edith (Mrs Russell Colman) which suggests that it was drawn 'about 1858'. Colman Collection Records, Art Department. Norwich Castle Museum.

opposite: *Elizabeth Clabburn.* detail. see page 66

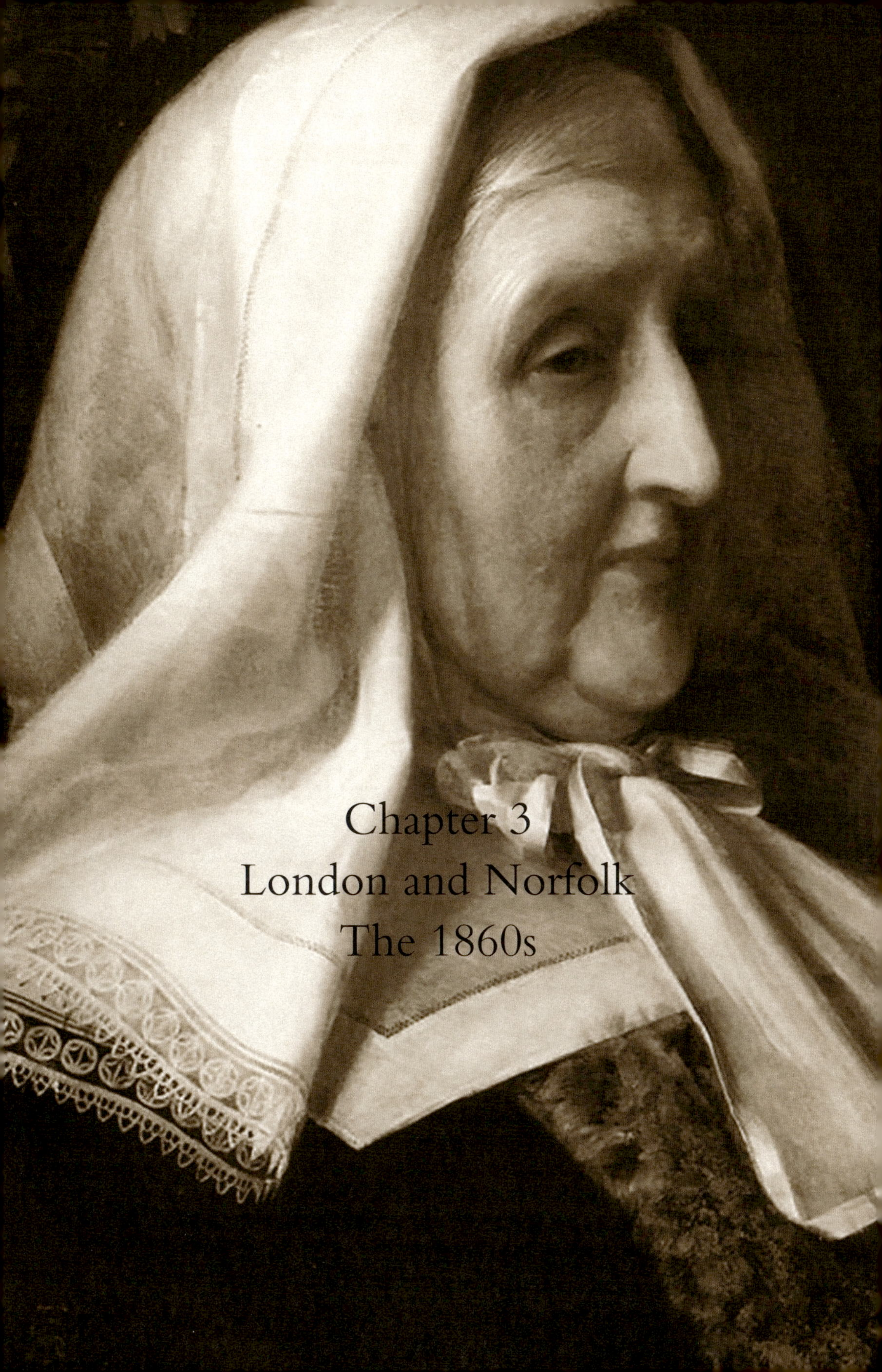

Chapter 3
London and Norfolk
The 1860s

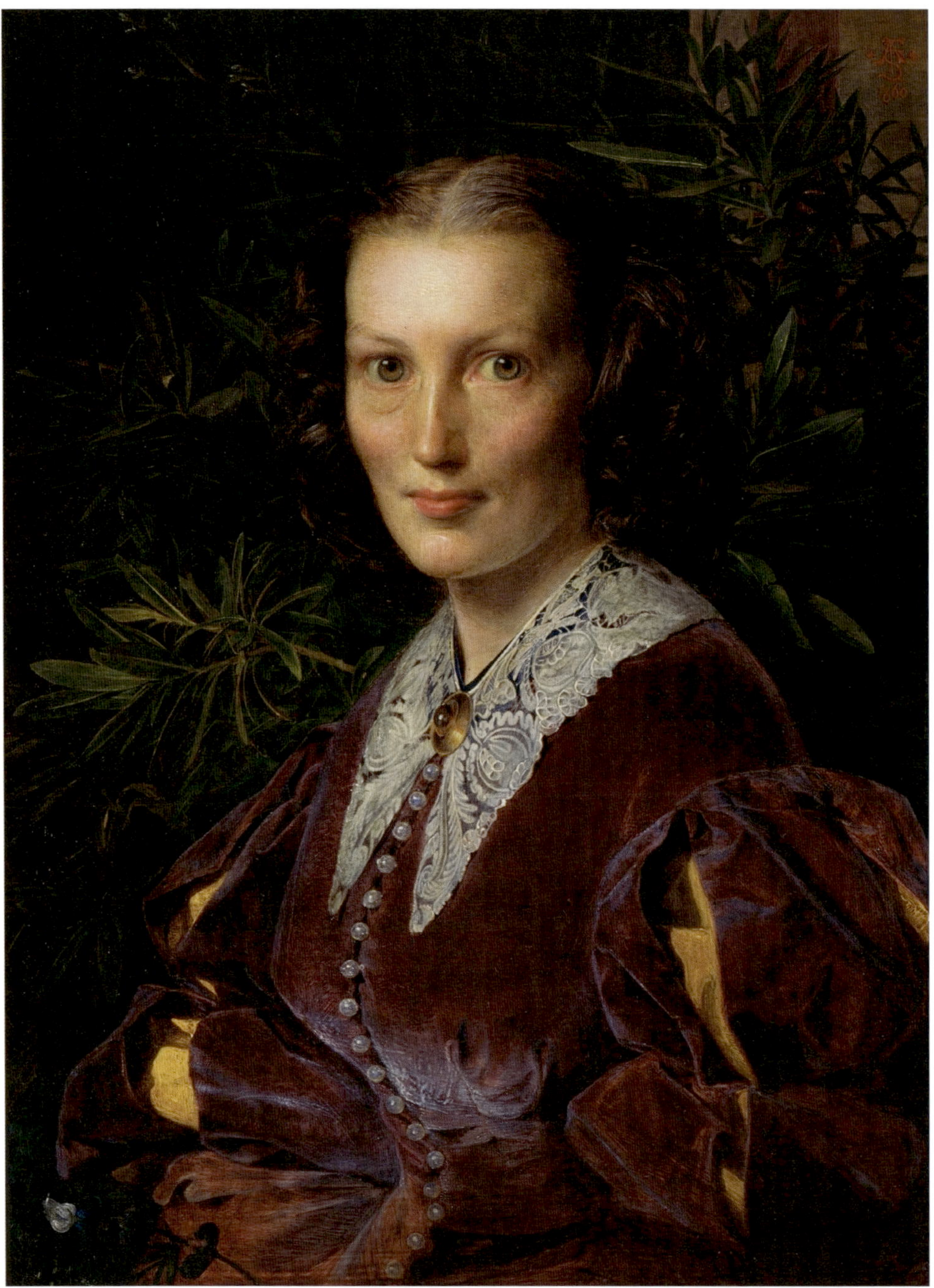

Hannah Louisa Clabburn (Mrs William Clabburn, b.1825). Oil on panel. 1860. The first of many commissions from an important Norwich patron who was a leading textile manufacturer in Norwich. This portrait was shown at the RA in 1861 where it was noticed by Dante Gabriel Rossetti, leading to their friendship.

The decade of the 1860s, when Sandys was in his thirties and his career in the ascendant, was without doubt the most fruitful of his life. Although he had a foothold in London, in lodgings, in fact he was still spending a good deal of time attending to his Norfolk commitments until about 1864. There survives a letter from Thorpe, dated 27th January 1863, to one of his new London friends, the wealthy and sociable silk merchant Arthur Lewis.[1] Thereafter we find him increasingly drawn to London.

In Norfolk, however, there was still much lucrative work to be done. He was based at Thorpe and engaged in several commitments for William Clabburn who was voracious for Sandys's work and, in retrospect, it appears that a large proportion of Sandys's finest work was done for him. Probably many of his pictures were executed in a rented painting room at The Bazaar, 24–26, Broad Street, St Andrew's, Norwich, in the borrowed Thorpe studio of his friend Herbert Roberts,[2] or at Clabburn's house Sunny Hill, Thorpe, for the portraits of the Clabburn family.

The Bazaar had recently housed the School of Design (1846–1857) which Sandys himself had attended, but in 1857 the School had moved to more commodious premises nearby above the newly built Free Library (where it was to remain until 1901). The Bazaar building, having been vacated, would have had space available for painting in or for exhibitions. An undated letter (probably written in the early months of 1861) from Sandys to the Headmaster of Norwich School, the Rev. Dr Augustus Jessopp, addressed from The Bazaar, St Andrew's, invites Jessopp and his wife to look at a recently finished picture which he was about to send away. This was probably the portrait of the young Mrs Clabburn, which was to be shown at the Royal Academy in 1861. He wrote: 'Do not be disappointed when you see my picture to find it a portrait and consequently without much interest ... I have three or four others which (also) will leave me next week ... my rooms are to the left by some benches immediately on ascending the first flight of stairs.'[3]

Clabburn provided the patronage for the above-mentioned *Portrait of Mrs Hannah Clabburn* (1860), probably *Autumn* (1860), *Oriana* (1860–1861),[4] *Portrait of Mrs Elizabeth Clabburn* (1861),[5] *At Vespers* (probably December 1861), *Spring* (*c.*1861–1862),[6] *La Belle Ysoude* (1862), *Mary Magdalen* (1862), *Vivien* (1863), *Deborah* (1863), *Morgan le Fay* (1863–1864), *Medea* (1866), *Red Rose and White* (1867), *Love's Shadow* (1867), *Berenice* (1867), *Portrait of Mrs Hannah Clabburn* (1869), *Ysoude with the Love Potion* (1870), *Portrait of William H. Clabburn* (1870), *Portrait of Walter Clabburn* (1871), and *Portrait of Henry Clabburn* (1871–1872).

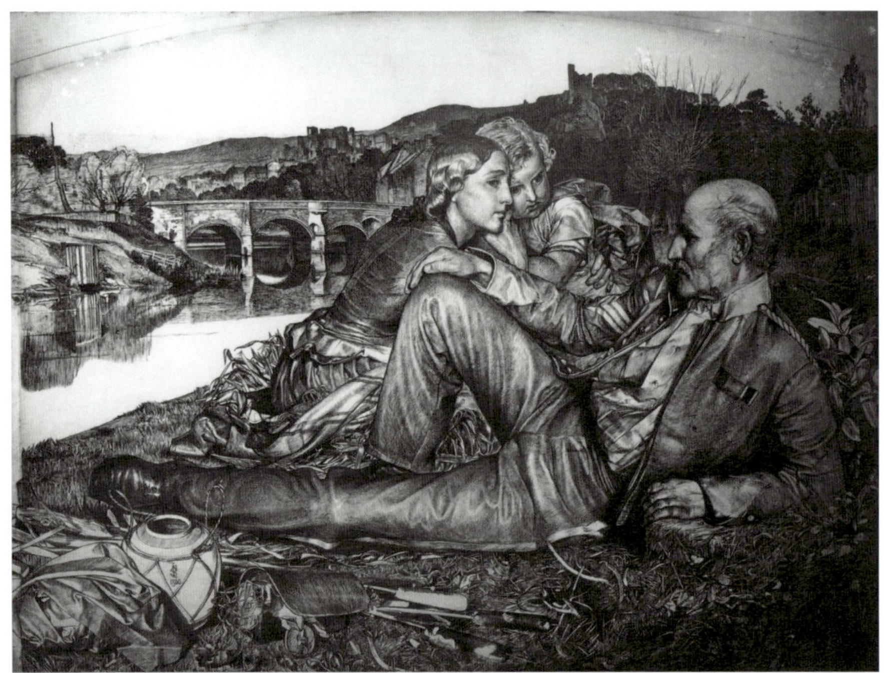

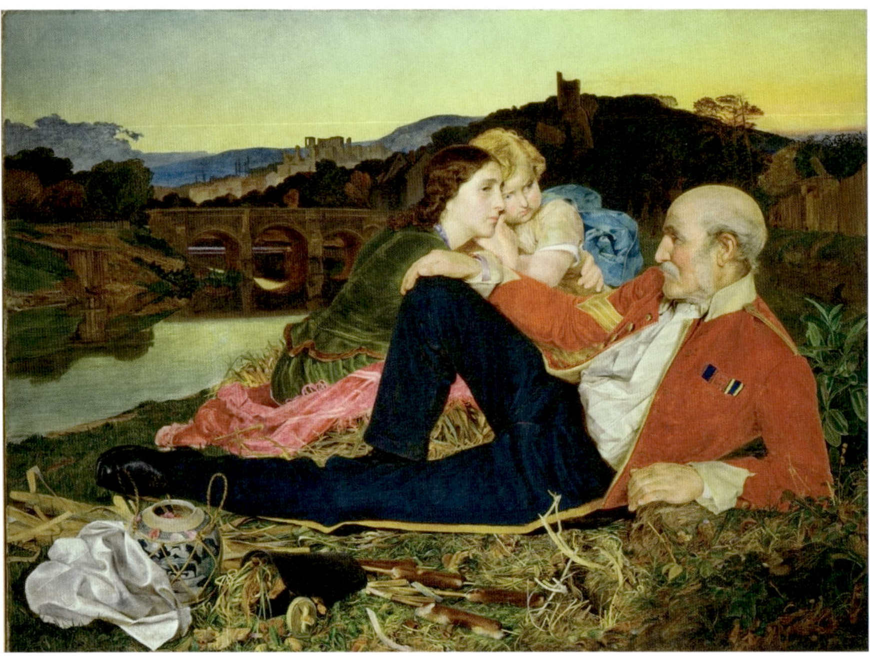

Autumn. Ink drawing. 1860. The phenomenal draughtsmanship in this drawing, later translated into a painting, was noted by Walter Sickert (1860-1942) in his review of the 'Loan Exhibition. Paintings and Drawings of the 1860 Period' at the Tate Gallery in 1923. Sandys's models were the Faux family who lived in Pottergate, Norwich.

In the winter of 1861, we find Sandys on a visit to London.[7] Given that as a young artist he was full of promise, and as a social being he was soon welcomed into the artistic and bohemian circles in the metropolis. He seems to have been valued for his wit, and respected for his talent, by many of his contemporaries. As his later friend and patron, Harold Hartley wrote: 'Frederick Sandys impressed me more than any other as a unique personality. I had the privilege of knowing him intimately during the latter portion of his life. He seems to have known all his contemporary celebrities. He was the most entertaining talker I ever met.'[8]

His life-long friend George Meredith was later to write of him: 'Sandys beats me amazingly as a humourist.'[9] Rossetti's studio assistant Henry Treffry Dunn thought him a 'a splendid raconteur', adding that, at Rossetti's dinner parties, he and their friend and business agent Charles Augustus Howell 'between them would keep us all listening and set us all laughing until long past midnight'.[10] He was no less of a talker at the end of his life, when Elizabeth Pennell recorded in 1898 that Sandys 'talked steadily the whole afternoon. It was like listening to, instead of reading, a book of memoirs. He told one story after another, so that it would be hopeless to try and remember them all'.[11] Sadly, this entertaining side of his personality is lost to us except by repute.

A sense of the congeniality of these parties can be got from a letter from Rossetti to Ford Madox Brown dating from late 1861: 'A few blokes and coves are coming at 8.00 or so on Friday evening to participate in oysters and obloquy. Will you identify yourself with them and their habits? The names of them may probably be [Alexander] Gilchrist, [James Anderson] Rose, Sandys, Meredith, Val [Prinsep], W.M. [Morris] and D.G. Rossetti.'[12]

Another assessment of Sandys's character comes from the haughty Frederick Barwell who, as we have seen, knew him from early days in Norwich: 'His acquaintance began to be cultivated by several of the younger men till some of them became alarmed at his efforts to get them to accept bills of exchange, in slang parlance "to help him to fly kites", and to borrow money off some of them. He had the peculiar faculty of making people who could be useful to him to believe that he was a man of extraordinary genius whose ill-fortune had kept him back, and that he only needed encouragement and help to astonish the world. In the long run they found him an expensive protégé, and that it were better to keep clear of him.'[13]

Established in London's bohemian society, he also became a frequenter of the renowned Saturday evening parties of Arthur Lewis[14] which first began in his rooms in Jermyn Street, just south of Piccadilly. They had begun in

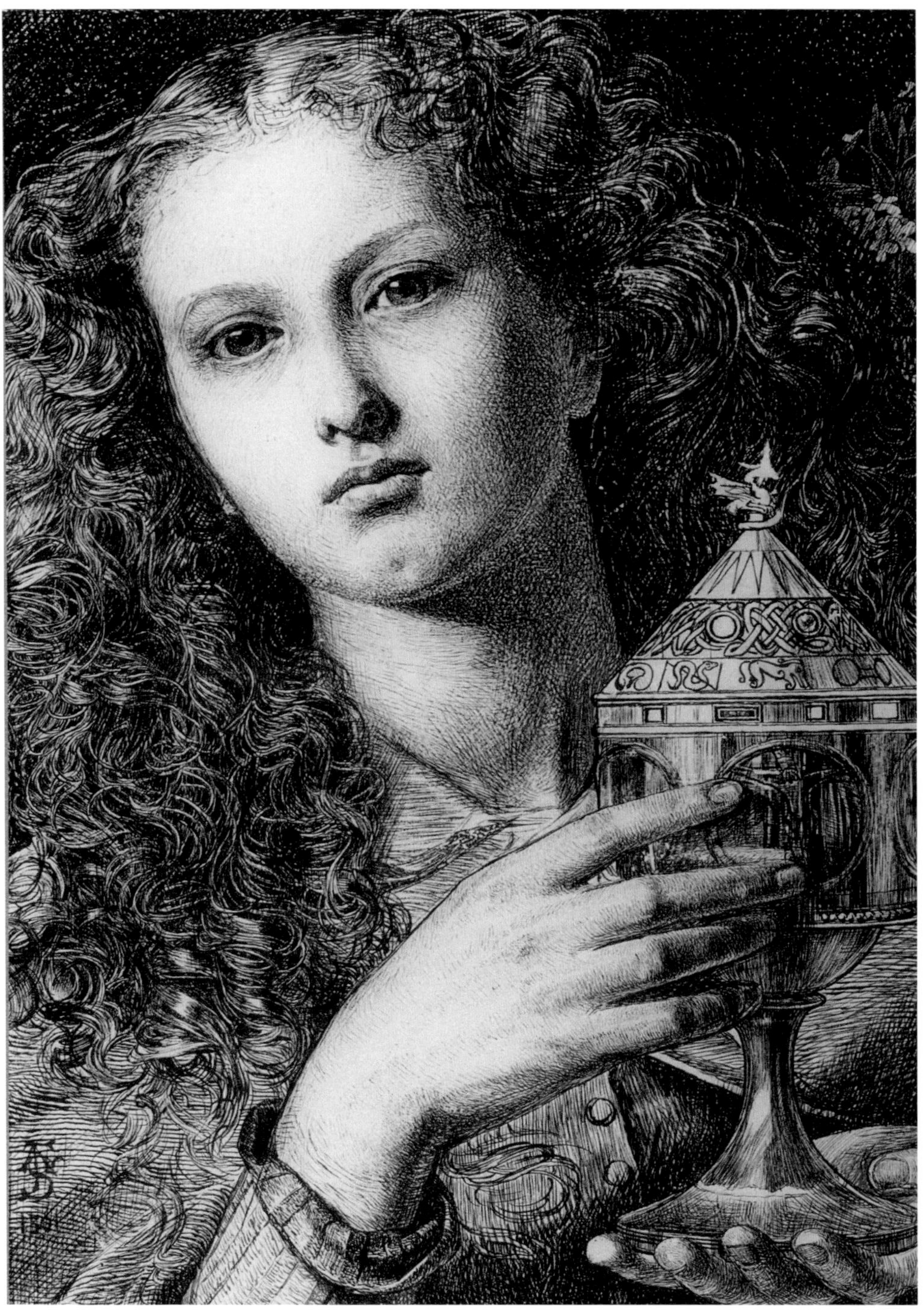

King Pelles' Daughter bearing the vessel of the Sangrael. Ink drawing. 1861. Another 'cartoon' which became the basis of an oil painting.

1858 when Lewis formed from among his friends an amateur choir known as the 'Jermyn Band', which progressed to 'smoking concerts' at which artists, writers and musicians gathered to imbibe champagne with oysters, at the expense of their jovial host. A list of those who attended them would amount to a 'Who's Who' in the arts in Victorian London.

In 1862, when Arthur Lewis moved to more spacious quarters at Moray Lodge on Campden Hill, Kensington, the parties moved there, and they have been immortalised in the memoirs and correspondence of many who attended them and their biographers.[15] To these songs and amateur performances can be traced the origin of the comic operettas of W.S. Gilbert and Arthur Sullivan, both of whom regularly attended. Fortunately, also, the watercolourist Frederick Walker, who was one of the regulars, has left us a delightful cartoon of 'Dear Arthur's Round Table' which shows some of their number seated around a table at Moray Lodge in 1866, playing cards with others standing by and watching. The bearded Sandys seen here is identified by Walker amongst the latter. Some of the curiosities in Arthur Lewis's collection, castings of a pair of bronze busts of a North African man and woman,[16] and an ostrich egg suspended in an ornamental net bag, can also be spotted in the background of the cartoon. Besides being a perceptive collector, Arthur Lewis was a talented amateur painter and, such was his energy, he was an active volunteer in the Artists' Rifle Corps, and also the founder in March 1863 of the Arts Club at 17 Hanover Square.[17]

A letter of January 1862 from George du Maurier to his friend Tom Armstrong gives a sense of the popularity of Lewis and his parties: '… you must feel the want of artistic entourage, which keeps the pot of enthusiasm boiling. I think you would much like to come to one of Lewis's evenings and meet all the fellows; there have been already two, and Lewis has given me carte blanche to bring my friends … the first Saturday was wonderfully jolly, and I fraternised with Leech and Sandys who were both deuced jolly; Sandys has just gone back to Norfolk but [I] saw a great deal of him, and never met a fellow who took art in a better spirit. He showed me his crayon portraits he is doing, the finest things of the sort I ever saw, and as for his studies they are wonderful. If he has a patch of grass to do in a [wood] cut, an inch square, he makes a large and highly finished study from nature for it first … he has work on hand for 2 years, after which he will go abroad [which he didn't]. His painting tickles me not quite so much. Gave me lots of very good advice which I intend to follow … You can't fancy anything jollier than Lewises. As [Stacy] Marks says, the artists make a noble appearance there, and so they do; lots of professional glee singing and comic ditto.'[18] Again, in July 1862, 'Sandys and I are great pals; the Rossetti clique awfully droll, full of the strangest and most childish irrepressible affectations'.[19]

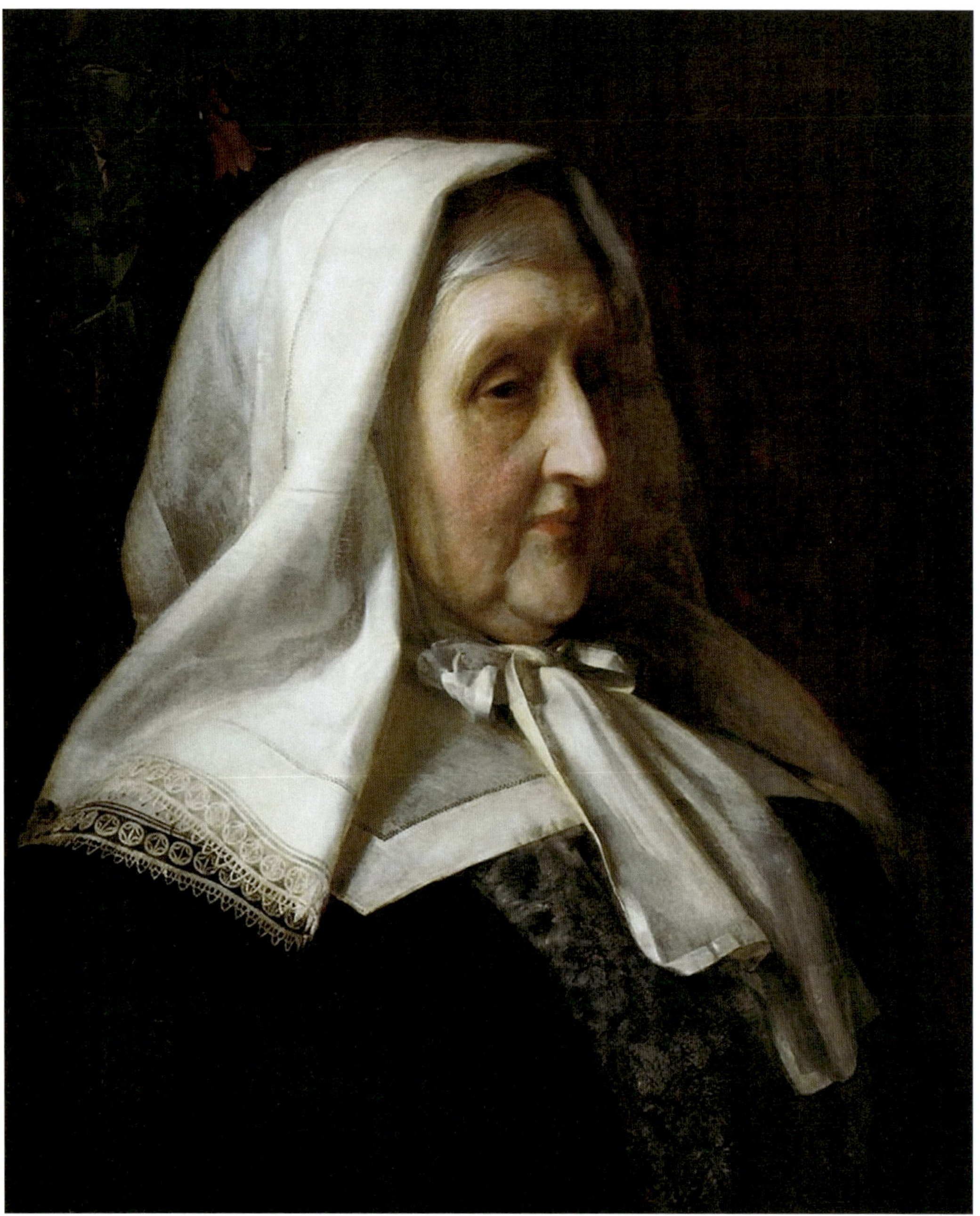

Elizabeth Clabburn (1786-1862). Oil on panel. 1861. She was the wife of Thomas Clabburn of Norwich, a manufacturer of the Jacquard loom-woven shawls which were immensely fashionable in the nineteenth century. William Clabburn was her eldest son. She is depicted in the style of a Dutch seventeenth century portrait

In January of 1863, writing from his lodgings at Thorpe, after Lewis had evidently asked Sandys to paint a portrait for him, Sandys replied with a curiously off-putting letter: 'I do not make it a custom to paint portraits. I refuse all – Mrs Clabburn and Mrs Rose are quite exceptions. Your note is so flattering, it seems to require in some shape a fit acknowledgement. But how to do this, I know not. I am at work on pictures which will occupy me fully till next June twelve months. It would be unfair to you to make any engagement for a time so distant – and I think I should be better pleased to be left free, so that, if I desired at the conclusion of my present engagements, I might at once quit England. Apart from these considerations I know nothing that would give me greater pleasure than undertaking this work for you. Believe me. Yours very truly, Fredk Sandys. Remember me kindly please to Jopling.'[20]

Nevertheless, the portrait of Lewis's mother was begun, and it turned out to be, arguably, his finest and most interesting portrait, in which he approached nearest to his ideal in portraiture – Hans Holbein. It was the third of his masterly portrait paintings of elderly ladies, starting with the mother of his Norwich friend and patron, Mrs Thomas Clabburn (1861), continuing with the mother of his London friend James Anderson Rose, Mrs Susanna Rose (1862) and, as his reputation grew to encompass a wider circle, other such commissions came to him. Of these, Mrs Thomas Barstow (1868) and Mrs William Brand (*c.*1875) are comparable achievements.

The portrait of Mrs Stephen Lewis is elaborately staged in an interior setting (undoubtably at Moray Lodge, Campden Hill) with objects carefully placed to lead one's eye around the picture plane and through to its 'depths'. It is particularly engaging because a large mirror over the mantelpiece in the adjoining room, seen behind the sitter, adds an element of mystery by its multiple reflections, by which the spectator feels drawn to try and identify what is 'reality' and what is reflection. In the furthest 'depth', we see the back of Sandys's canvas on the easel and, opposing the front of the easel, a large plate-glass window showing the view outside, through which daylight provides the light falling on the sitter. The chain of events connect as in a circle. His friend Holman Hunt had already tackled the mirror theme as a simple reflection in 1853 in his *The Awakening Conscience*. However, in his intimate scene of a woman and a man, the full circle with the artist/spectator included was not appropriate. Hunt was to use the mirror device again in a later portrait of his first wife Fanny of 1867–1868. The French painter Ingres had also effectively used large plate glass mirrors, in his *Madame de Senonnes* (1814), *Vicomtesse d'Haussonville* (1845) and, latterly, his magnificent *Madame Moitessier* (1856). Perhaps inspired by such pictures, or the prevalence of plate glass, Lewis Carroll's ingenious mind was led to create the metaphor of another world existing behind the mirror in his story book *Alice Through the Looking Glass* (1871). As interpreted by his illustrator John Tenniel, we see Alice literally stepping through the mirror over the drawing-room mantelpiece into an imaginary world in reverse. In practical terms, these pictorial ideas could have only arisen through technical developments in plate glass manufacture in the nineteenth century, in making large plates of flawlessly flat glass, allowing for much larger mirrors and windows in the new houses of the rich.

In Sandys's portrait of Mrs Jane Lewis, in the distance, to the right of her head, the bust of Cordier's *La Vénus Africaine* can be identified, and to the left of Mrs Lewis dangles a beautifully netted and tasselled ostrich egg.[21] On the left of the mirror in the adjoining room can just be discerned a likely replica of Ingres's *La Source* (*c.*1830–1856), the original of which Arthur Lewis must have seen on show at the International Exhibition at South Kensington in the summer of 1862. The inclusion of these disparate items must have been important to Arthur Lewis and were an inspiration to Sandys to create this highly original construction.

In 1867 Lewis married the actress Kate Terry,[22] who retired from the stage to start a family. The parties at Moray Lodge therefore inevitably changed in character, and the Moray Minstrels carried on their bachelor 'smoking concerts' elsewhere until 1879.[23]

At Easter 1862, Sandys went on a short holiday to the Netherlands to look at art collections, with James Anderson Rose, a solicitor and keen art collector,[24] whom Sandys probably first met at the Arundel Club in 1860 or 1861. Rose commissioned portraits of himself, his wife, and his mother, and no doubt recommended Sandys to his brother William Anderson Rose (1820–1881) who was a wealthy London merchant. William was Lord Mayor of London from 1862 to 1863 and was knighted in 1867.

The portrait of old Mrs Rose aroused a good deal of attention when it was exhibited at the Royal Academy in 1863. According to the memoirs of Jerome K. Jerome, the humourist and playwright, writing in the 1880s of the time when he was a junior in James Anderson Rose's office: 'Sandys's portrait of Mrs Anderson Rose, his mother, made a sensation when it was first exhibited; and it is still famous.'[25] Robert Ross, Sandys's biographer in the *Dictionary of National Biography*, wrote that the portraits of Mrs Lewis (and Mrs Rose) '… deserve a place among the great achievements of English painting'. Arthur B. Chamberlain (1859–1931) of the Birmingham Art Gallery wrote: '… His likeness of elderly ladies … will always rank among the great portraits of the nineteenth century.'[26] It was rightly said that the quality of the portraits owed

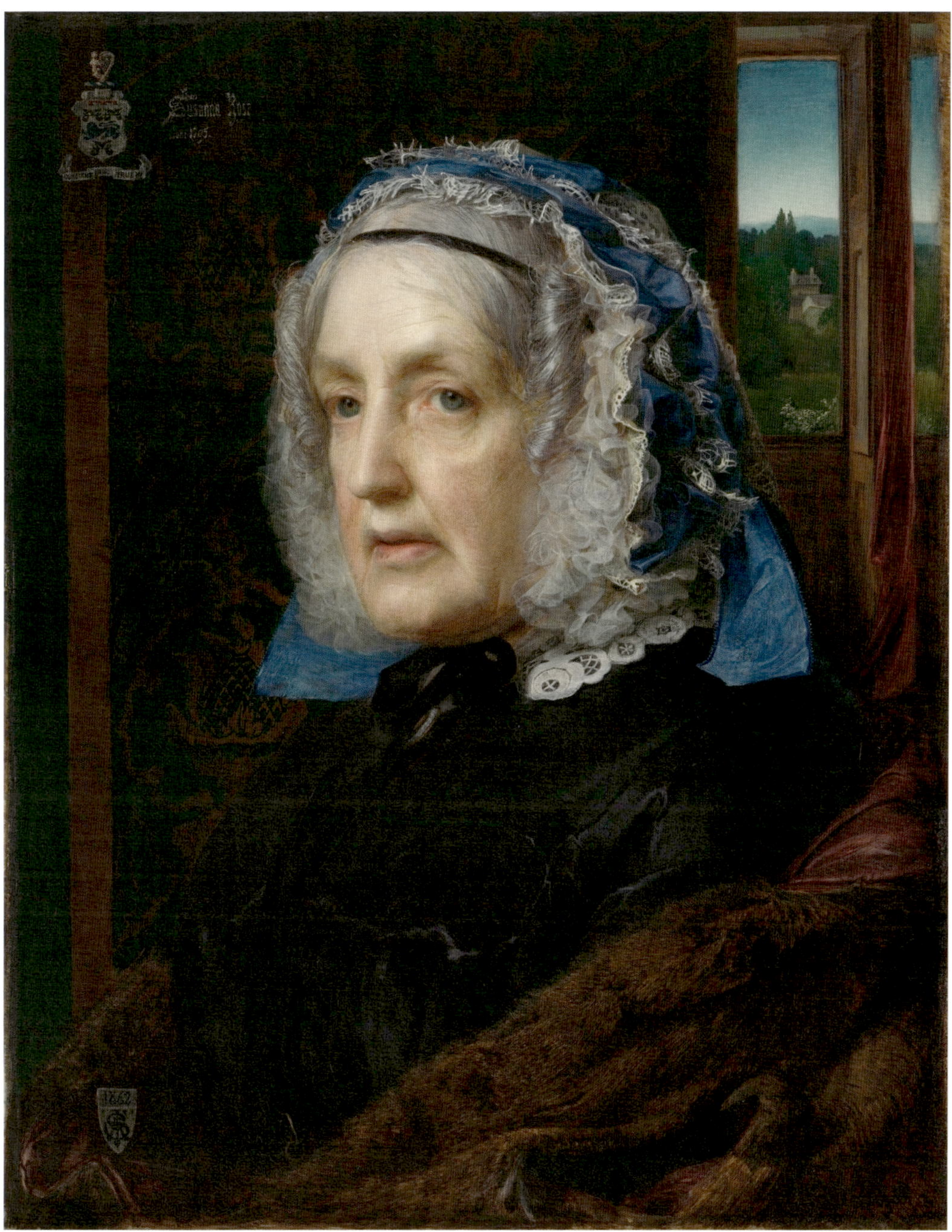

Susanna Rose (1795-1870). Oil on panel. 1861-1862. The mother of Sandys's friend the lawyer, James Anderson Rose. When first exhibited at The Royal Academy in 1863, it attracted much attention and was the start of Sandys's reputation as an artist.

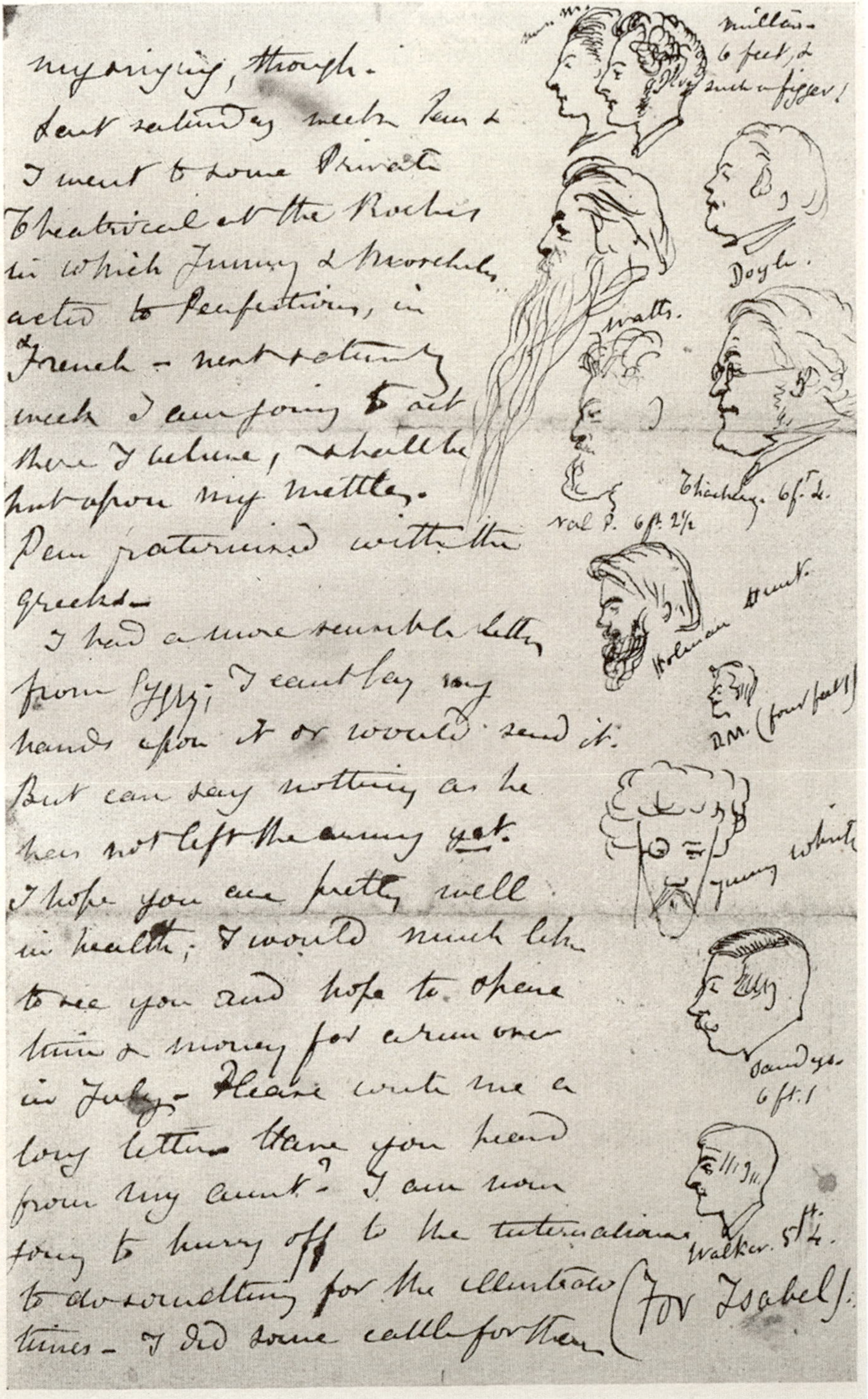

my origin, though.
Last saturday week Pen &
I went to some Private
Theatricals at the Rookes
in which Jimmy & Moscheles
acted to perfection, in
French - next saturday
week I am going to act
there I believe, & shall be
put upon my mettle.
Pen fraternised with the
greeks -
I had a more sensible letter
from Lizzy; I cant lay my
hands upon it or would send it.
But can say nothing as he
has not left the army yet.
I hope you are pretty well
in health; I would much like
to see you and hope to spare
time & money for a run over
in July - Please write me a
long letter. Have you heard
from my aunt? I am now
going to hurry off to the International
to do something for the Illustrated
times - I did some cattle for them

Millais.
6 feet, &
such a figger!

Doyle.

Watts.

Thackeray. 6 ft. 2.

Val P. 6 ft. 2½

Holman Hunt.

D.M. (four feet)

Jimmy White

Sandys.
6 ft. 1

Walker. 5 ft. 4.

(For Isabel).

much to the experience of the trip which Sandys and Rose made together in 1862 to the Netherlands.

James Anderson Rose also bought two 'subject' pictures from Sandys: *Queen Eleanor* (1858) and *The Magdalen* (*c.*1859–1860) which, as already noted, had been exhibited together at the British Institution, Pall Mall, in 1860. He also possessed two elaborate ink drawings, *King Pelles' Daughter* (1861), and *Judith and Holofernes* (1864), the chalk drawing of *Oriana* (1861) and two studies (on one sheet) for the *Weeping Magdalen* (1862), of which the Norwich collector William Clabburn had the oil version, besides having several studies and designs for illustrations. Rose also acted for Sandys in his professional capacity of principal in the firm of Rose and Thomas, solicitors, of Salisbury Street, Strand, a role in which Rose appears again and again in the several legal cases in which Sandys was embroiled, starting with his petition for a divorce from his wife Georgiana in September 1863.

Other commissions came through James Anderson Rose: from his brother William Anderson Rose, and James's friend the potter Henry Doulton (1820–1897). In due course, these led to commissions from other wealthy mercantile families such as those of Philip Flower (1810–1872) and James Brand the younger (1833–1893), all of whom lived in large villas in the then semi-rural Wandsworth and Tooting area of south London (then part of Surrey), having moved outwards from central London. It was this chain of neighbourhood acquaintances which led to the important patronage of Sandys by Cyril Flower (1843–1907).

It is likely that the caricature print *A Nightmare* which he drew in 1857 led to Sandys's employment for illustration work for the new concept of family magazines of the 1860s, and it was these illustrations, all produced within that decade, which kept his name alive long after the main body of his work had lost its appeal and had sunk into a long period of oblivion. The excellent draughtsmanship of the caricature must have made an impression on George Smith, its publisher. He was the principal of Smith, Elder & Co., of 65 Cornhill, the publishers of *The Cornhill Magazine*.

In 1859 George Smith proposed starting this new monthly magazine, to appear the next year under his aegis, and when it was time to engage illustrators, it was likely to have been Smith who suggested Sandys. In any event, in 1859, his editor J.M. Thackeray asked Sandys for an illustration to a story by George MacDonald entitled *The Legend of the Portent* which appeared in the first issue

Caricatures by George du Maurier (1834-1896) from a letter dated 16th July 1862, to his mother. It shows the artists he had met at Little Holland House. Profiles are of Millais and his wife, Richard Doyle, Watts, Val Prinsep, Thackeray, Holman Hunt, du Maurier, Whistler, Sandys, and Frederick Walker.

of *The Cornhill Magazine* in May 1860. It is recorded that Sandys was paid the relatively large sum of 40 guineas for this design,[27] indicating Sandys's growing reputation, and which must have added to his sense of his own worth. Tom Armstrong in his *Reminiscences of du Maurier* wrote that Sandys was the most highly-paid of the artists, after Millais, for the contemporary magazine *Once a Week* ' … and something of his lordly ways and of his attitude towards the engraver of those days may be gathered by his remark to the editor, when he complained of his work having been ruined by the engraver: 'If the small sum you give me for the drawing would serve as an inducement to the engraver to take more pains you had better hand it over to him.'[28]

This was the first of twenty-five highly acclaimed designs for wood-engraved illustrations that Sandys produced. The last, and one of the finest, was *Danae in the Brazen Chamber* (early 1866) made for *Once a Week* to illustrate a poem by Swinburne but, in the event, the poem was published without this stunning illustration due to the Victorian prudishness of William Bradbury the publisher. Surprisingly for this period (he ought to have known better) Sandys had carefully drawn the genitalia of the god Zeus in prominent detail. It is related that Bradbury stamped his foot and said, 'I will have no poultry displayed in Once a Week'.[29] This illustration shows an early appearance of Mary Emma Jones as the model for the seductive Danae.

Although he was already versed in the techniques of both etching and lithography, it appears that this commission was the first time he had to make designs for wood engraving. Percy Bate, in quoting Sandys's own words, described how he tackled this reproductive medium: 'He told me that his first box-wood block was a puzzle to him when he received it, with a request from Thackeray that he would supply an illustration to a story of George Macdonald's for *The Cornhill*. He knew nothing of the correct method of preparing it; it was impossible to work on its smooth surface with either pencil or pen, and he finally drew *The Portent* line by line with a brush and Indian ink, and found the process so simple and the result so satisfactory that he always thereafter employed the same method.'[30] As a confirmation of Sandys's method of drawing on the polished surface of an end-grain boxwood block, this statement is interesting but it is hard to believe that he was so ignorant about the process of wood engraving, which was a well-known medium introduced and perfected some seventy years before. However, Sandys was apt to dramatise things. At any rate, he evidently devised a satisfactory technique for himself, and it is my opinion that there is a link here with the characteristic brush drawing with black ink which he also employed for larger black-and-white works at this time, such as the cartoons for *Autumn* (1860), and *Spring* (*c.*1861), in spite of Percy Bate's statement (which was repeated by others) that he used a pen for these.[31]

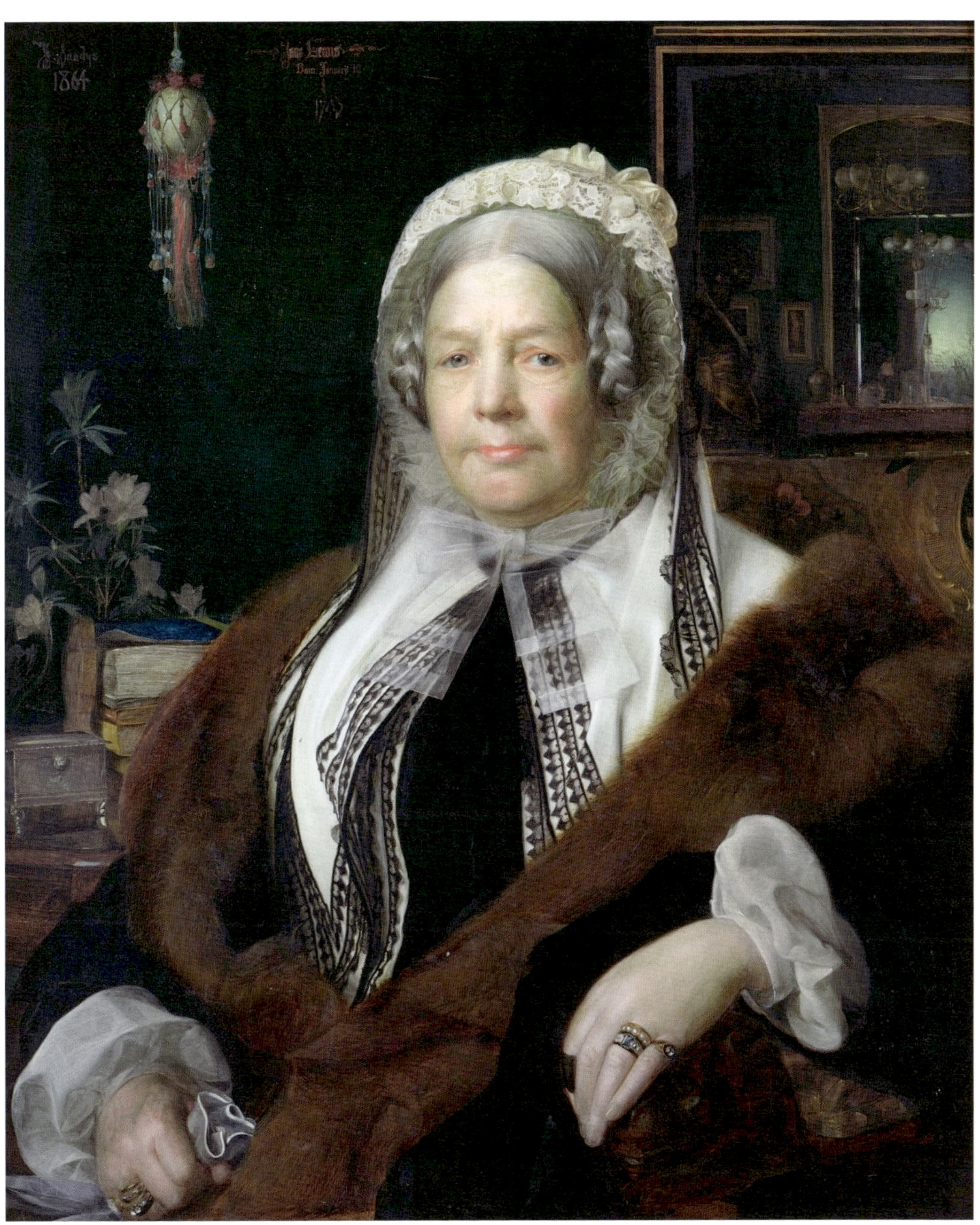

Jane Lewis (1793-1873). Oil on panel. 1864. The mother of Arthur Lewis (1824-1901), and widow of Stephen Lewis who founded the fashionable West End haberdashers and silk merchants, Lewis & Allenby. Arthur Lewis was an amateur artist and generous host, giving regular musical parties open to his friends.

The veteran wood engraver W.J. Linton (1812–1898) was the engraver of *The Portent*, and it was Sandys's first published wood-engraved illustration in 1859. The older engravers such as Linton were used to interpreting in line the original sketches on the woodblock by the artist (which sometimes included wash drawings). The next development in this very active 'industry' saw the younger artists drawing on the block with linear precision, to which the engravers could respond by cutting an exact facsimile of the drawing. Sandys was praised for his precise drawings which suited the technique perfectly. However, Linton's habitual interpretative hand is evident in *The Portent*. The young Walter Crane (he was only fourteen in 1859) was a pupil in Linton's workshop at the time and commented on Sandys's 'remarkable' work coming into the shop.[32]

Two more commissions for illustrations came in 1860, from *The Cornhill's* rival magazine *Once a Week*. As noted, the latter had been started in 1859 and was the first of the new family magazines in which illustrations played an important part. Samuel Lucas was the editor, and Bradbury and Evans (who were also the publishers of the immensely successful *Punch*) included it in the issue of 23rd March 1861. It was Sandys's second published illustration, to accompany a translation of a Scandinavian ballad by Johann Uhland (1787–1862) titled *Yet Once More on the Organ Play*, and it was followed by an illustration to a poem *The Sailor's Bride*, by Marion E. James, in the next issue of 13th April 1861. There is a study for the latter at the Fitzwilliam Museum with the added inscription (in the hand of Charles Fairfax Murray, once the owner) 'original drawing for the second block ever done by F.S.'.[33] Thus it is possible that the design for *The Sailor's Bride* illustration preceded the other in actual fact. We also know that Sandys was working on *The Sailor's Bride* in December 1860, for there is a dated study for it (in Sandys's handwriting) in the extensive holdings of Sandys material (again from Fairfax Murray's collection) at the Birmingham City Art Gallery.[34] *Once a Week*, or more precisely, Joseph Swain[35] the engraver, whose firm had the art direction of this magazine, seemed almost to monopolise Sandys's time. Swain also engraved a Sandys design for *The Argosy* magazine and one for *The Cornhill*. Of the eight other known Sandys illustrations, the Dalziel brothers' workshop engraved two for *Good Words* and two for *English Sacred Poetry*, one each for *The Shilling Magazine*, *The Quiver*, and their ill-fated *Illustrated Bible*, and W. Thomas engraved one for *The Churchman's Family Magazine*.

In his discussion on the illustration movement for magazines and books of the 1860s, the art critic Joseph Comyns Carr was later to comment in his memories of the time: 'The one man of all the group who showed, perhaps, the surest hold of the essential qualities of design was Fred Sandys. Though

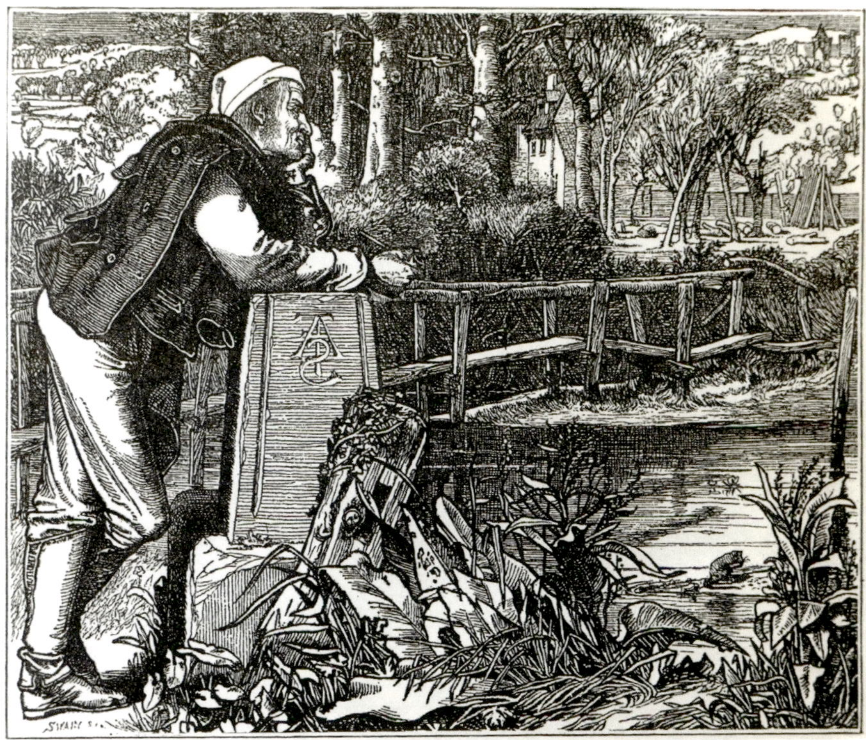

The Old Chartist. The printed illustration. Late 1861.

not of the body, he was closely associated with the Pre-Raphaelite movement, and already in *Once a Week*, in such drawings as his illustration to Meredith's poem of *The Old Chartist*, he had exhibited a complete command of technical resources.'[36] This interesting illustration shows the Chartist having returned from 'transportation' lovingly looking over his old home landscape again. Many of the details are derived from studies made at Hunworth in 1858. It would have made an excellent easel picture if Sandys had attempted it. According to Percy Bate it was Sandys's favourite illustration.[37]

It should be noted that in Sandys's work 'design' predominates, and not all his illustrations strictly 'illustrate' the subject. They have a quality in which they could stand alone as works of art. In fact, in two cases Sandys turned an illustration into a full-sized picture: *Harald Hafagr* (1862) became the oil *Valkyrie* (1868–1873) which was bought by Frederick Leyland; *Danaë in the Brazen Chamber* (early 1866) became the large unfinished drawing *Danaë*.

1860 was the year of the completion of Sandys's most ambitious painting, *Autumn*, which is very much in the manner of Millais, who was then still working in his Pre-Raphaelite style. Alas, it is the only oil painting of any compositional complexity which Sandys seems to have undertaken. There is a full-scale cartoon for another multiple-figure subject, titled *Spring*, but this idea seems to have foundered before being made into an oil picture.[38] W.H. Clabburn provided the patronage for these two works, and in fact his children are depicted in the latter, but there is no evidence that pictures based upon the two other seasons of the year were ever embarked upon. It is sad that Sandys did not complete such a series which would have been an impressive exercise in the Pre-Raphaelite manner. 'Might have been' is a theme which was to characterise his life.

In April 1862, as noted already, Sandys made a trip to the Netherlands with his friend James Anderson Rose, the art-loving lawyer. Rose was in the habit of taking a short holiday abroad at this time of year to see European art collections and, on this occasion, he evidently invited Sandys to accompany him. Having entered five works for the Royal Academy Exhibition[39] in March, Sandys naturally felt free to take a holiday. Some interesting relics remain from this journey in the form of five pages torn from a notebook kept by Sandys. From these we know that they set forth from London on *The Leo* on Saturday 19th April, bound for Rotterdam.[40] They were in Amsterdam from Sunday to Tuesday, and they also made a trip to The Hague.

Sandys seems to have spent most, if not all, of the summer of 1862 in London. Some of the time must have been spent in completing the portrait of Rose's mother, which he had started in 1861, but there were unmissable social events opening up new circles to the promising young man from Norwich. Notably, he was to enjoy the hospitality of the Prinsep family[41] at Little Holland House, Kensington (situated not far from Arthur Lewis's Moray Lodge). The hostess was Mrs Sarah Prinsep (1816–1887). She was one of the now famed Pattle sisters, the eldest being the amateur photographer Julia Margaret Cameron, and another the handsome Virginia who became the third Countess Somers. Mrs Prinsep presided over literary and artistic 'at homes' on Sunday afternoons in the summer, to which several of the young Pre-Raphaelites were invited to mingle with their more established confrères in the contemporary art world. Here Sandys would have encountered G.F. Watts[42] (the close friend of the Prinsep family who lived with them for twenty-five years), the Prinsep's son Valentine, Frederic Leighton, Holman Hunt, Millais, Rossetti, Burne-Jones, William Morris, Whistler, George du Maurier, Ruskin, Tennyson, Thackeray, Browning, Carlyle, and many others. That Sandys was a guest there in the summer of 1862 is recorded in a letter written by the young George du Maurier to his mother which he illustrated with sketches of the guests he saw at a Little Holland House supper party in mid-July. The caricatured profile heads were drawn in the margins of the letter and included

Millais and his wife Effie, Watts, Richard 'Dicky' Doyle, Thackeray, Val Prinsep, Holman Hunt, Sandys, Fred Walker, du Maurier himself, and a full-face of the monocled Whistler. He noted the stature of some of the more extreme, such as the tall Thackeray, Prinsep, and Sandys '6 ft. 1"', (depicted with a moustache and without a beard), contrasting with Fred Walker's '5 ft. 4"', and the height that he felt himself to be, 'four feet', compared with these giants of the art world.[43]

The artist George Boyce (1826–1897) noted Sandys at Swinburne's house-warming gathering on 11th July at 77 Newman Street, in the company of Rossetti, Rose, Clabburn, George Meredith and Alexander Munro, the sculptor.[44] Again at Swinburne's on 28th July, he was there with Rossetti, Boyce, Whistler, Prinsep, and Burne-Jones.[45]

Rossetti sought distraction through companionship all summer after his bereavement in March of 1862, when his wife Elizabeth (Lizzie) Siddal died from an overdose of laudanum,[46] and in his disheartened state he decided that he could no longer stay in the riverside apartment at Chatham Place where they had lived together. William Rossetti in his memoir doubted that Rossetti ever slept there again after the funeral.[47] I suggest also that the dust and clamour resulting from the demolition of the old, and the building of the new, Blackfriars Bridge, which Chatham Place overlooked, probably was another factor in driving Rossetti away.

A plan took shape to share a house with Swinburne, whom Rossetti had known since 1857 when Swinburne was still up at Oxford, and Rossetti was lodging there to take part in the group effort of decorating the interior of the new Oxford Union Society debating chamber. Their friendship became closer after Swinburne came to live in London in 1861, and it extended particularly to include Lizzie Siddal who enjoyed his high spirits and playfulness. Swinburne was dining out with Gabriel Rossetti and Lizzie the night that she took the fatal overdose of laudanum in February 1862.

Accordingly, when the time came to find a paying companion with whom to share living quarters, the moneyed Swinburne would seem a natural choice to Rossetti. The property he settled upon to lease was a large early eighteenth century house at 16 Cheyne Walk, on the riverbank at Chelsea. Rossetti took on the tenancy (negotiated by James Anderson Rose) from the Cadogan estate, and the sub-tenants, besides Swinburne, were his brother William Rossetti, and George Meredith. Swinburne was to live in the house full-time. William, who wished to continue living with his mother and sisters at Albany Street, had a bedroom there for his use on three nights a week, probably anticipating late dinner parties and also, privately, to keep a brotherly eye on the practical aspects of the establishment.

Meredith, who was living at Esher in Surrey, required a London room for one night a week for attending to his journalism work and as a publisher's 'reader'. At the end of September 1862, he had just placed his motherless boy, Arthur,[48] as a boarder at Norwich School where his friend the Rev. Dr Augustus Jessopp was headmaster. Meredith's tenancy at Cheyne Walk lasted about six months until August 1863, he not being suited to the irregularities of the household, as it turned out.[49]

At the inauguration of the Rossetti ménage at Cheyne Walk, in late October 1862,[50] Sandys was probably absent in Norwich, for Rossetti wrote to him that he longed to show him the new house.[51] We know that he was in Norwich in November because George Meredith, in a gossipy letter to his son at Norwich School, asked if he had seen him.[52] Jessopp and his wife were acquainted with the Clabburns, and thus Sandys would have been known to the Jessopps, besides being an 'old boy' of the school himself.

Sandys and Clabburn, as noted, were close at this period. On 19th December 1862, Clabburn knowing Sandys's unbusinesslike character, entered into an informal, handwritten contract with him for some pictures which Clabburn wanted. This is inscribed on a double-sided sheet of paper which was annotated and receipted by Sandys as he received instalments from Clabburn. He received the first payment in cash of £60 towards the £300 which Clabburn agreed to pay for three oil paintings, a chalk drawing and an ink drawing ('all the above framed and glazed'). The subjects were *Morgan le Fay*, and the ink cartoon drawing for it, *Vivien* and its preliminary chalk drawing, and *La Belle Ysoude*. One item from Clabburn was in kind ('silk dress and India goods' in February 1862) and the rest was either in cash, or by cheque to pay off named creditors (G.B. Eyston, possibly a lawyer, and James Anderson Rose).[53] *La Belle Ysoude*, dated 1862, must have been already well-advanced, if not finished, and was certainly complete by the sending-in date of the Royal Academy Summer Exhibition where it was hung.[54] *Vivien*, dated 1863, was also shown in 1863,[55] but was undoubtedly begun in 1862. The drawing *Morgan le Fay* no doubt was begun in 1862, and perhaps was completed by the end of the year. It is in the style of the 1862 illustration *Cleopatra Dissolving the Pearl*. I would infer from the fact that *Morgan le Fay* (both oil and ink versions) which head the list in the contract, for works 'bought of Fred Sandys', that the oil had been started by the end of 1862, and probably finished in 1863.

The item, which was paid in kind by Clabburn, as we see from the description, 'silk dress and India goods - £23.15', may account for the accessories seen in the oil *Vivien*, such as the rich brocade (also seen in the drawing *Morgan le Fay*) and the ornate ivory and ebony panelling which appears in front of the figure of *Vivien*. The peacock feathers probably came from Clabburn himself since he kept peacocks in his Thorpe garden.[56] The last of Clabburn's payments towards the agreed £300 was received on 26th March 1863.

Excepting possibly in the case of *La Belle Ysoude*, Sandys seems to have used the gypsy Keomi as a model in these pictures. Although his style was realistic (or representational), especially compared to Rossetti's looser way of painting, it is difficult in some cases to be able to positively identify the model in some of Sandys's subject pictures because portraiture was not his intention. The sitter's beauty would be enhanced, or idealised. Besides, as for instance in the case of *Morgan le Fay*, he would sometimes make use of an earlier study from another model, probably having Keomi in front of him when the time came to paint and finish the picture.

At the bottom of the contract sheet mentioned above are notes about future works which Clabburn was interested in having. Among these were the proposed *Deborah* or *The Prophetess*, for which he wanted the option of buying, for not more than £200 both the preliminary chalk drawing and the oil painting. This subject has never surfaced and did not appear in the two sales of Clabburn's property in Norwich in 1879 and 1889. However, *Deborah* was lent by Clabburn to a Norwich exhibition in 1867[57] and my feeling is that, in context, this was a drawing. The projected oil of *Deborah* for Clabburn may not have been attempted. However, it is possible that the oil known as *Cassandra* started its life as *The Prophetess*. Until *Deborah* in either medium surfaces, we shall not know the answer to this. *Cassandra* was certainly painted from Keomi and the inspiration for this dramatic rendering of the subject is likely to have come from George Meredith's poem.[58] Although it is untitled, undated and unsigned, we know its title through its being shown at the Royal Academy in 1865,[59] where the Yorkshire collector Edward Salt acquired it.

Listed below this, on the same contract between Clabburn and Sandys, are the two portraits Clabburn also desired: one of his wife, to be painted in the autumn of 1863, and one of himself, to be painted in spring 1864. These were to be 'size of life with hands', for £200, to include the preliminary chalk drawings as well as the replicating oils. On the reverse of the sheet of paper, we find the disbursements at £10 a fortnight toward a total of £175 for the oil painting and chalk study of *Deborah*, ending on 25th December 1863.

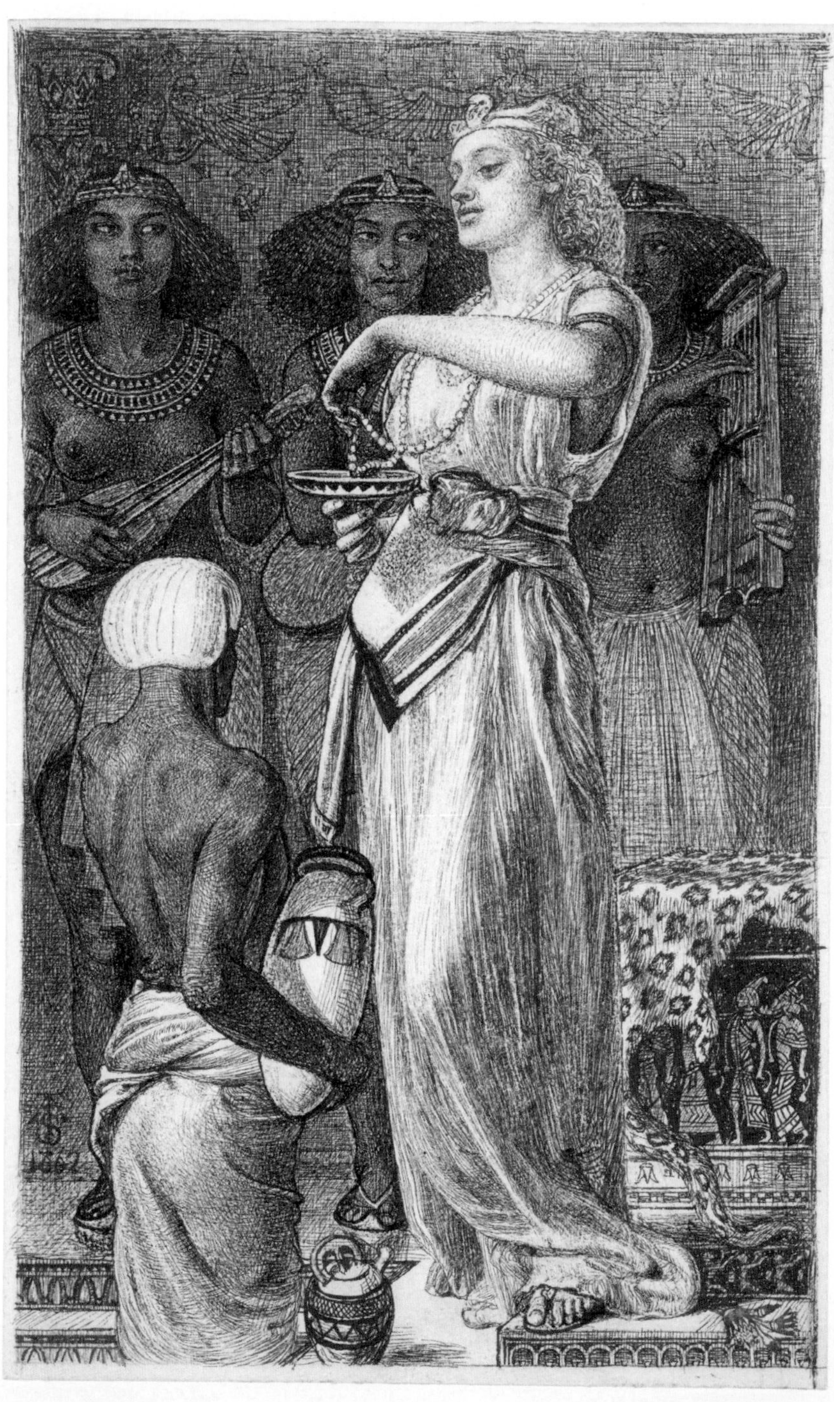

Cleopatra Dissolving the Pearl. The finished design (prior to transfer to the woodblock). 1862.

From April to October, 1863, while receiving the payments, we may assume that Sandys was mostly in Norwich or Thorpe, getting on with the work. In fact, in the summer of 1863, he was asking Whistler to come to Norwich to do some yachting on the river with him (undoubtedly with the friendly Clabburn who probably owned a boat). Whistler replied that he was busy completing some commissions but wished to send his regards to 'Tom Gecky' (Thomas Jeckell the architect who was from Norfolk).[60] In October Sandys was still at Thorpe making a portrait of one of Isaac Coaks's daughters, and possibly others, although only one, of Ella, has been identified.[61] In December he also made a portrait drawing of a pair of Jeremiah James Colman's children, Russell James and Laura Elizabeth.

Some time was spent in London, however, and on such occasions at this period it seems that he introduced his friend Clabburn to his London friends Rossetti and Burne-Jones,[62] Charles Howell,[63] and also to Arthur Lewis.[64] The meeting with Rossetti promised to be fruitful, for Clabburn commissioned a replica of his *Mary Magdalene*.[65]

It is likely that Sandys first met Meredith through the Rossetti circle in 1861. Meredith was already well acquainted with Rossetti and Swinburne through their literary activities, and a personal friendship with both had developed by the end of 1861. Sandys spent most of 1861 in Norwich but, from correspondence, it appears that he was in London in November and December of that year and, in fact, an invitation to dinner from Rossetti to Ford Madox Brown mentions, by way of enticement, that Sandys and Meredith, amongst others, would be his dinner companions on 22nd November.

Unlikely as it may seem, the friendship between these two proved to be a life-long one. On the one hand, Meredith, an intellectual, was conventional and methodical in his ways, but had a playful sense of humour. On the other, Sandys was literate but in no way literary (judging from his unpunctuated and laconic letters) and he led a disordered life, striving always to maintain a dignified appearance to hide the reality of his perpetually fragile financial state. There is no hint from Meredith's extensive correspondence that he knew about Sandys's sexual liaisons, but no doubt he was aware of them. For instance, in his novel *Harry Richmond* (1870) he introduced a strong gypsy character named Keomi who was clearly based on Sandys's model (and mistress) Keomi Gray.[66]

In his inimitable style, Meredith wrote about Sandys to Augustus Jessopp: 'Sandys has some fine conceptions for pictures. Altogether, he is one of the most remarkable of the "brushes" of our day, with the quaintest stolid Briton way of looking at general things … [also] … Sandys has a romantic turn that lets me feed on him.'[67]

The tone of Meredith's letters to Sandys, and about Sandys to others, indicates that he was genuinely fond of him, enjoying his companionship, which gives credibility to the anecdotes about Sandys's wit in the writings and memoirs of his contemporaries. As for Meredith's wit, as Sandys told the Pennells many years later, it could be personally wounding, and he attributed Meredith's departure from the Cheyne Walk ménage to an occasion during a dinner party, which Rossetti was giving to entertain some of his patrons, at which Meredith made some remarks apparently ridiculing his rather vulnerable host.[68]

Throughout his life, if Sandys's patron or sitter lived out of town, he would usually stay at their house for the duration of the work. Instances of this were at the houses of Alexander Macmillan, Alfred Tennyson, Josiah Caldwell, George Donaldson, Mrs Oliphant, and others; the length of stay sometimes adding to the discomfiture of the host. Mrs Oliphant had something to say about this in 1881.

In the case of his friend Meredith, Sandys instead stayed to paint spring flowers in his garden at Esher, for *Gentle Spring*. He stayed from 30th April to late June 1864. Meredith wrote to his friend William Hardman in May 1864: 'I have been that busy … and besides, here's a man staying with me, Sandys, the artist, painting a great picture of Spring. He came down here when I came. He will remain probably two weeks longer. Dear Sir, may I bring him over on Sunday? … I am very anxious to see you … You will like Sandys. He is a fine painter and a good fellow.'[69] Again, this time writing to Jessopp in Norwich on 18th May: 'Sandys will have been with me next Friday just three weeks. He is painting country for background of a picture of the maiden Spring … with heaps of flowers at her feet and immense periwigs of apple blossom about her poll. She with a look of unconsciousness and a rainbow over her head and such larks in the sky: a nice girl. We walk hard, though Sandys is not much of a leg at it and develops groaning feet, etc. At 7 ½ we dine and are uproarious, and I wish, and he wishes you were with us. Tom Taylor speaks well of his work in the Academy. I suppose he will be here about a month longer, he has so much to do. He is going to give me a drawing of Arthur, and also of – what's the name? I've forgotten the name of the person but am not the less grateful for his kindness. This latter in the time to come. I ask him whether he has a message for you, and he says (or tries to say) that one never knows what message to send to those one cares for, except that he'd be glad if you were here.'[70]

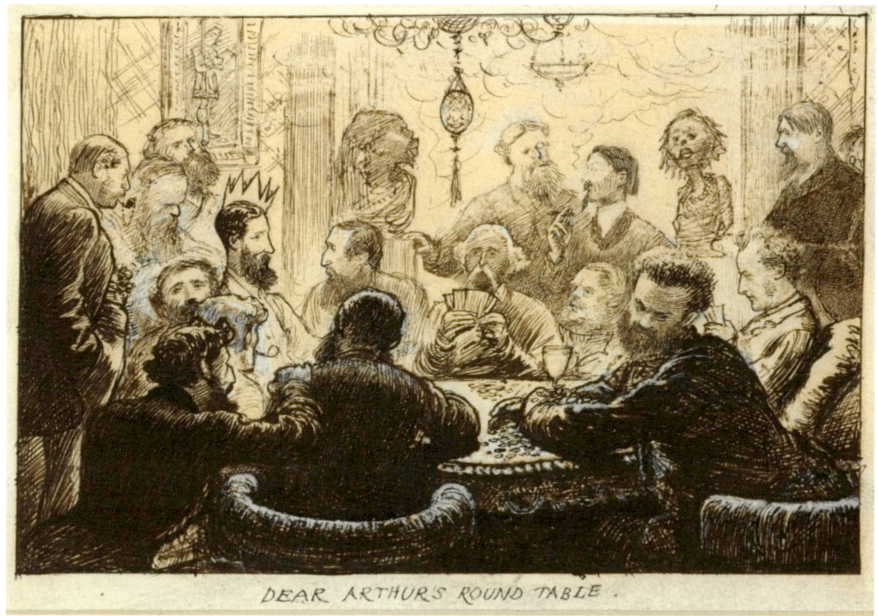

Dear Arthur's Round Table. Ink drawing by Frederick Walker (1840-1875). 1866. An evening at Arthur Lewis's house, Moray Lodge, Kensington. Arthur Lewis is seen at the table wearing a crown. The now-bearded Sandys is on the far right above the seated Millais. Also seen are the Charles Cordier (1827-1905) busts and the netted ostrich egg which appear in the portrait of Jane Lewis.

Meredith's modest budget ran to commissioning from Sandys four portrait drawings of his family.[71] Late in their lives (1894), Meredith also commissioned a watercolour unique in Sandys's oeuvre, as a gift to his friend and patroness Lady Jean Palmer,[72] and as a financial help to Sandys. This was a copy in watercolour of Sandys's monochrome engraved illustration of an oriental dancing girl for the second edition (1865) of Meredith's story *The Shaving of Shagpat*.

For the magazines which published Meredith's writing, Sandys illustrated Meredith's poem, *The Old Chartist* in 1861,[73] one of the best of Sandys's designs. In 1864 Meredith wrote a poem to accompany an existing Sandys drawing, *Cleopatra* of 1862 (*Cleopatra Dissolving the Pearl*).[74] For a reason unknown, Meredith's poem was rejected by the editorial board of *The Cornhill* and one by Swinburne was substituted. The genesis of Sandys's subject matter is that he probably knew Joshua Reynolds's painting Kitty Fisher as *Cleopatra Dissolving the Pearl* (*c.*1759). It was shown at the International Exhibition of 1862, held at South Kensington, where it was lent by the Earl of Morley. Although Sandys's design does not in the least resemble Reynolds's design, the subject probably attracted him. Having interpreted the subject in his own way, he may have offered it to *The Cornhill* as a possible future illustration, which set in train Meredith's verse. Swinburne's poem with this illustration was eventually published in 1866.[75]

Whistler came into the Rossetti circle on Swinburne's introduction in 1863. He was, in contrast to Meredith, a true bohemian, and there are many points in common between Whistler and Sandys, although they do not seem to have formed a close relationship. Sandys must have seemed a provincial to the cosmopolitan Whistler. However, they appear to have enjoyed an acquaintance for several years, and there is no evidence of their having fallen out, unless it were to do with Whistler's notorious 'vandalism' (1876-1877) of the decorative scheme of Frederick Leyland's dining room at 49 Prince's Gate, which had just been designed and installed by Sandys's friend Thomas Jeckell. A friendly letter from Whistler to Sandys, when both were old men, testifies to this.[76]

Sandys around this time brought the gypsy Keomi Gray to London, where he must have set her up in lodgings. This dark-haired woman of striking beauty seems to have generated a good deal of interest among his brother artists. She appears in several diaries and memoirs of this time as 'Sandys's gypsy girl', implying that she was his mistress (which turned out to be right) as well as his model. The Pennells wrote of Whistler's reminiscences about Sandys's 'love affairs' with the gypsy as well as the 'little girl'[77] which (as we shall see later) followed closely one after the other.

Keomi can be recognised in several of Sandys's inspired subject pictures from 1861 to 1866, which increasingly took a turn for the dramatic: *La Belle Ysoude* (1862), *Vivien* (1863), *Morgan le Fay* (1863–1864), *Judith and Holofernes* (1863–1864), *Cassandra* (1863–1864), *Medea* (1866), and his illustrations *Rosamund, Queen of the Lombards* (1861), *The Waiting Time* (1863), and in several untitled studies. There is a story of her posing for the lost *Deborah* (1863), '... keeping her eyes fixed for hours on one point as he drew ...'[78] and she undoubtedly sat for other works in which she is less easily identified. William Michael Rossetti wrote that she modelled for one of the figures in his brother's *The Beloved* (1865–1866)[79] and one can see the resemblance, allowing for Rossetti's romanticising style. She fired the imagination of George Meredith, as well as Theodore Watts-Dunton, for she appears in books by both of them: under her own name as a figure in Meredith's *The Adventures of Harry Richmond* (1871). She also contributed something to Watts-Dunton's character Sinfi Lovell in his novel *Aylwin* (1898).

Keomi Gray[80] was born in 1841 at Wisbech, the daughter of Oseri (or Ozray) Gray, a travelling musician[81] and Eliza Heron, both from well-known East

Anglian gypsy families. Sandys must have met her in Norfolk, where he returned after the failure of his marriage in London to Georgiana Creed. He was first at Hunworth with the Bulwer family, then in lodgings at Thorpe, from March 1858 to about November 1861. Thorpe Common, nearby, was traditionally used by gypsies as a camping ground. He may have lived with Keomi at Thorpe and then in London, where Keomi gave birth to three of his children: Ethel (Athela) Maud Gray in January 1864, Frederick Cyril Gray in June 1865, and Madeline Mabel Gray in about 1867. Their last child Henry Herbert Gray was born in Heigham, Norwich, in February 1870. Although Heigham is close to Sandys's paternal family house, the relationship ended and Keomi had returned to her itinerant family with the children.[82]

Keomi seems to have been a 'character' and an earthy one at that, a guarantee of finding favour with the Rossetti circle. Rossetti used some of her bon mots with relish in a letter of 24th July 1873 to Charles Augustus Howell. To characterise a couple of points he was making, he wrote that she replied when asked why she had stoned a raven to death, that it was to 'amuse the mind', and that 'a toad wasn't made for a side-pocket'.[83] This may have had some relevance to the prominent toads in the foreground of *Medea* (1866–1868), for which she had been the model. She may even have provided the toads. There was also a story (now lost) of a fight she got into with a rival over Sandys.

From reading between the lines of a fragmentary anecdote, it is possible that Sandys knew Mary Emma Jones, his 'little girl', his eventual common-law wife and mother of the majority of his children, as early as 1862, probably first meeting her in Norwich when she was an actress in a travelling theatre company. The story is from the memoirs of Herbert H. Roberts, a comfortably-off amateur artist who would frequently lend Sandys his studio at Thorpe. He wrote: 'I remember one of the pictures which Sandys painted in my studio was a Magdalen,[84] with the tears trembling on her eyelids and rolling down her cheek. His model was a pretty girl, whose father he abused, though he knew nothing of him, in order to cause her to shed the tears which he wanted to represent in his picture. I remember the track of the tear down the cheek – a most difficult effect to produce – was beautifully suggested.'[85]

Mary Emma Jones, known on the stage as 'Miss Clive', is easily recognisable in this, the second of his versions of the subject of Mary Magdalene which he painted for William Clabburn, finishing it in the early months of 1862. The sitter herself, late in life, stated that she had been the model, although she was unaware that the picture being discussed on this occasion was an earlier picture for which Sandys had used another unidentified model from Norwich.[86] In this picture of 1862 Sandys seems to show a change to a rather more sensuous painting style, which also probably indicates a greater technical confidence. Undoubtedly, Rossetti's influence played a part, but, above all, it shows inspiration from the personal charms of the sitter and her beautiful hair. Sandys shows here a preoccupation with depicting curling, twining, luxuriant hair, forecasting, as art invariably does, the fashion for abundant hair worn by both women and men (if one can also include men's facial hair) in the later 1860s.

Another anecdote about Sandys, with feminine hair as its topic, is attributed to Bosworth Harcourt, the nineteenth century Norwich drama critic who 'knew Sandys well. [He] was invited to the artist's house then on Bracondale[87] to meet the leading lady of a touring Shakespearean company. After supper, the lady let fall her abundant hair and gave the sleep-walking scene of Lady Macbeth, to the admiration of the two men'.[88] The description 'leading lady' seems unlikely to apply to 'the little girl' as she appears never to have achieved any notable rank as an actress. In Norwich, for instance, she is recorded in June 1873 as appearing in a minor role in the play *Twixt Axe and Crown* on tour with Mr and Mrs Rousby's company. Her first appearance in theatre records was in London in 1869, as the Maid in the farce *Lover by Proxy* at the Queen's Theatre, Long Acre.

'Miss Clive' continued there in *Lover by Proxy* in 1870, to which was added to the repertory in the same year as the first production of Tom Taylor's *Twixt Axe and Crown*, playing on alternate dates. In this piece *Twixt Axe and Crown*, she was joined by her sister 'Miss Jones'. They continued to play the same roles there intermittently until 1878.

It is difficult to disentangle the reality from Bosworth Harcourt's Norwich anecdote. However, Sandys and his 'little girl' were united as early as the summer of 1866, their first child Maura being born in January 1867, probably in London.[89] This was the start of a life-long illegitimate attachment, since Sandys had failed to divorce his legally married wife Georgiana.

The Jones family were from Hull, an important seaport on the east coast of Yorkshire, but they migrated to London approximately between 1862 and 1863, probably on the retirement of the father, Justice Jones (b.1807), a customs inspector at Hull docks. He and his wife Rosanna (b.1812) had a large family which included five daughters. The eldest, Equity Ann (b.1835), appeared in the census of 1861 as an 'artist de modes' (presumably a dressmaker), but two of the others who were of working age, Anne Maria and Mary Emma, were listed as actresses. The youngest, Emily Eyre, was still a child at the time of the census.

Mary Emma Jones's sister, Emelie Eyre 'Milly' Jones (1850–1920), proved to be a more regular actress than her sister, perhaps being less burdened with childbearing and also having married an established actor. She married in May 1870[90] Frederick Henry Robson (1843–1919), the son of the famous burlesque actor Frederick Robson,[91] and they had a daughter.[92] She, like her sisters, worked as an artists' model. In the second half of the sixties, Milly sat for Whistler and appeared in *Symphony in White, No.3* (1867–1868),[93] and for Albert Moore, Simeon Solomon, and Frederic Leighton, probably giving up that aspect of her work after marriage but continuing her acting career.

A third sister, 'Augusta' (originally listed in records as Anne Maria) Jones (1843–1902)[94], was a particularly admired model, appearing in works by Burne-Jones, Simeon Solomon, Charles Hallé, Henry Holliday, and Rossetti, in the sixties and early seventies. She was personally linked with Arthur May,[95] who was part of Edward Godwin's circle of friends and associates. However, she married Frederick Vincent Hart (1843–1915) in December 1871. Hart was a freelance designer, supplying designs for stained glass for Edward Godwin, Daniel Cottier, and George Edward Cook.[96]

Confirmation that Sandys was part of the 'Rossetti lot' appears in a letter of October 1863 from George du Maurier to his friend Thomas Armstrong, which also reveals the French artist Alphonse Legros (1837–1911) to be a part of it,[97] alongside Swinburne and Whistler. The group was already in the grip of 'Japanese mania', as reported by William Rossetti,[98] who recalled that this was towards the middle of 1863, although one imagines that their first sight of Japanese art was the large exhibit from Japan at the 1862 International Exhibition held at South Kensington.[99] This 'mania' could be seen as a development of the earlier craze for collecting Chinese blue and white porcelain, and one can see the evidence of Sandys's interest already in 1860, in *Autumn* which, inexplicably, has a large Chinese blue and white ginger jar placed prominently in the foreground of the picture. An illustration of his of 1862, *Until her Death*, has a Chinese or Japanese ceramic vessel, again, in the foreground.

As stated in Chapter 2, ten years after his marriage of 1853 (he had parted from Georgiana in 1856),[100] Sandys was taking steps to obtain a divorce.[101] The evidence of this is in a letter (which is datable to July 1867) from Sandys to James Anderson Rose (in the role of his solicitor) in which he complains of Rose's negligence, in that his divorce was to be settled three and a half years before, and Rose had not acted on it.[102] However, in examining the actual divorce records of 1868, it seems that Sandys was attempting to blame his wife Georgiana for committing adultery with Michael McHaffie. This she denied. Instead, Georgiana turned the case against him by accusing Sandys of

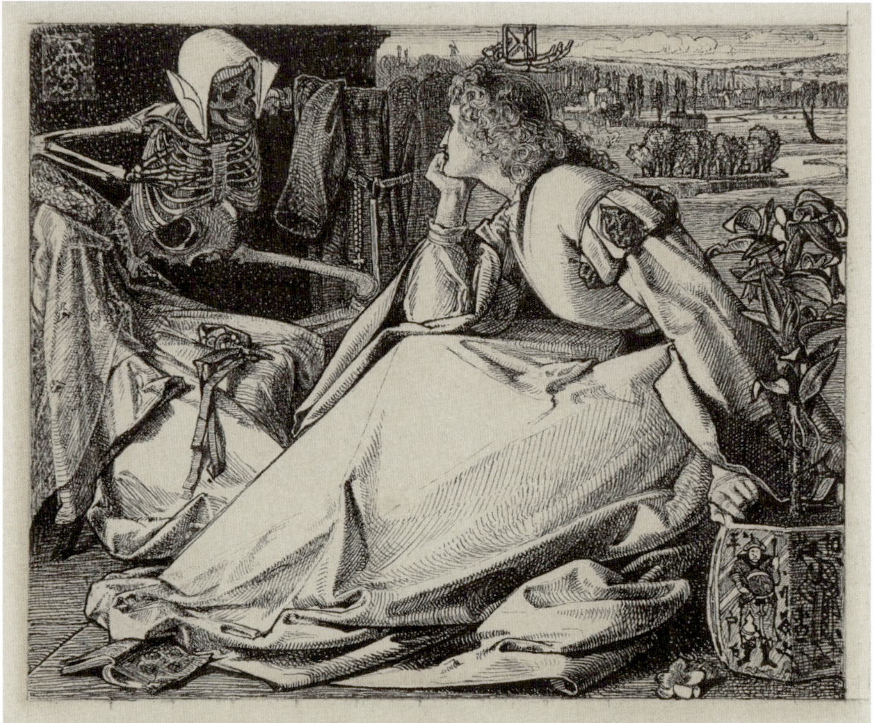

Until her Death. Late 1862.

adultery, cruelty, desertion, and leaving her without any means of support. The judge saw through Sandys's petition attempt, and in 1864 he was ordered to pay Georgiana alimony of £31 per annum and to pay the court the costs and expenses of the counter-petitioner Georgiana. So that put an end to it. It is not known whether Sandys fulfilled these obligations, but it is doubtful.

Turning again to his social life, a report of a Sunday breakfast on 7th February 1864 establishes Sandys as a friend of Frederic Leighton, who had a reputation at this period for his breakfast parties at his house in Orme Square, Bayswater. George Boyce (1826–1897) wrote in his diary that Wells, Prinsep, and Poynter, were also there.[103] There was a discussion afterwards as to the comparative artistic merits of Rossetti and Burne-Jones in which Sandys sided with Boyce in preferring Rossetti. They then had talk about the treatment of flesh in painting. In the latter, Sandys again sided with Boyce as to the importance of rendering it as *flesh* (not unexpectedly), against merely treating it as a piece of colour in the composition.

In March, an emergency arose when Sandys crushed the top part of the middle finger of his right hand, and in a friendly act Holman Hunt finished the painting of certain small details[104] in the portrait of Arthur Lewis's mother which he was still working on, so that it could be sent in time to the Royal Academy Summer Exhibition. He wrote about this accident to the Dalziel brothers by way of excusing himself for not having some illustrations ready for them. These were for the projected *Biblical Life of Joseph* which he had agreed to work on in 1861. He wrote: 'I have two of "Joseph" nearly ready and have been for some month or more.'[105] In spite of good intentions, in the event, only one was ever forthcoming, as the Dalziels ruefully wrote forty years later, which they eventually used for their *Bible Gallery* issued in 1881.

Meredith wanted Sandys to illustrate 'a series of wayside pieces for *The Cornhill*' which he planned to write to 'ultimately form a volume special and I hope popular'.[106] As C.L. Cline, the editor of Meredith's correspondence, noted, 'the wayside pieces apparently never materialised',[107] but two collaborations did take place in 1864.While on his honeymoon with Marie Vuilliamy in October 1864,[108] Meredith wrote a poem on *Cleopatra* to be published by *The Cornhill* to accompany a design for illustration which Sandys had completed in 1862. The original reason for the design has never been explained. Also unexplained is why *The Cornhill* magazine published a poem by Swinburne to accompany it when eventually it was printed in 1866.[109] The other collaboration resulted in a drawing to be engraved as a frontispiece for the second edition of Meredith's story *The Shaving of Shagpat* which came out in 1865.

My guess, at some time in the early 1860s, is that he was commissioned to make portraits of William Quilter (1808–1888) and his wife Elizabeth Harriet, née Cuthbert (d.1874). William Quilter, of Norfolk Street, Park Lane, and Lower Norwood, was a very successful accountant specialising in insolvencies. He designed new methods of accounting, particularly with respect to railway development which was fraught with disputes over land acquisition. He was the founder of the Institute of Chartered Accountants and formed a notable collection of English watercolours which he sold at Christie's in 1875. His eldest son William Cuthbert Quilter (1841–1911) continued his interest in art and would also commission family portraits from Sandys in the 1880s. Harry Quilter (1851–1907), his third son, became an art critic. He wrote an appreciation of Sandys at his death.[110]

In the autumn of 1864, Rossetti and Sandys made a plan to visit Astley's Amphitheatre,[111] just south of Westminster Bridge in Lambeth. Rose was also invited and probably joined them. From the date of Rossetti's letter of invitation,[112] this will have been to witness Adah Menken (1835–1868), the American actress-poet, in a new production of the sensational equestrian drama *Mazeppa*, in which she performed to packed houses wearing a flesh-coloured bodystocking, tied to the back of a 'wild' horse.[113] Menken became immensely celebrated for a short time in the sixties and used her fame to attract and cultivate a circle of literary and artistic friends rather than to bestow her favours on wealthy admirers in which she had no interest; she had no need of gaining wealth from an admirer, for she was making an unprecedented amount herself from box-office receipts.

Rossetti was soon welcomed into Menken's circle of acquaintances and was offered the use of her box at Astley's. Swinburne accompanied him on an occasion at the end of November, and this was the start of a friendship which three years later took a foolish turn that brought unwelcome ridicule. It appears that Adah, urged on by Rossetti and Richard Burton,[114] was to attempt to 'make a man' of Swinburne who was known for his erotic verse but was allegedly impotent and a masochist into the bargain. On her part, Menken was hoping for help with editing and publishing her own poetry. Swinburne had photographs taken of the two of them together in an amorous pose, and circulated copies amongst his group of friends. Copies eventually reached a wider public and were the cause of scandal and deep embarrassment to the aristocratic Swinburne family.

At the height of this period of her London fame, according to Bernard Falk in his biography of Menken,[115] she and Rossetti, sometimes joined by Sandys, would visit the oyster bars, which were then a feature of West End London, in particular one near Leicester Square in which a portrait of Menken was prominently displayed. No doubt Sandys would have also been invited to the lavish dinners and champagne suppers she gave at her London residence, the Westminster Palace Hotel.[116] Sadly, poor Adah died in 1868, in Paris, probably of cancer.

Back in Norfolk in the autumn of 1864, Sandys seems to have been unwell and out of sorts with the world, as we understand from a letter written to him by Rossetti, '… I fear from the tone of your letter that you love not the face of man for the time being … when you hate your kind less, write and tell me'. The reason for this is not clear, and it seems likely that he remained in Norfolk for the rest of the year. His first child by Keomi, Ethel Maud, had been born in January 1864 at 4 Barossa Place, Chelsea.[117]

Sandys may have brought about William Clabburn's second visit to Rossetti at Cheyne Walk, with his wife, on 4th December 1864. This time Rossetti must have been disappointed that Clabburn bought a picture by Alphonse Legros (1837–1911)[118] and not one of his own. Legros now appears in the letters and the diaries of the circle. It was Whistler who encouraged Legros to come to

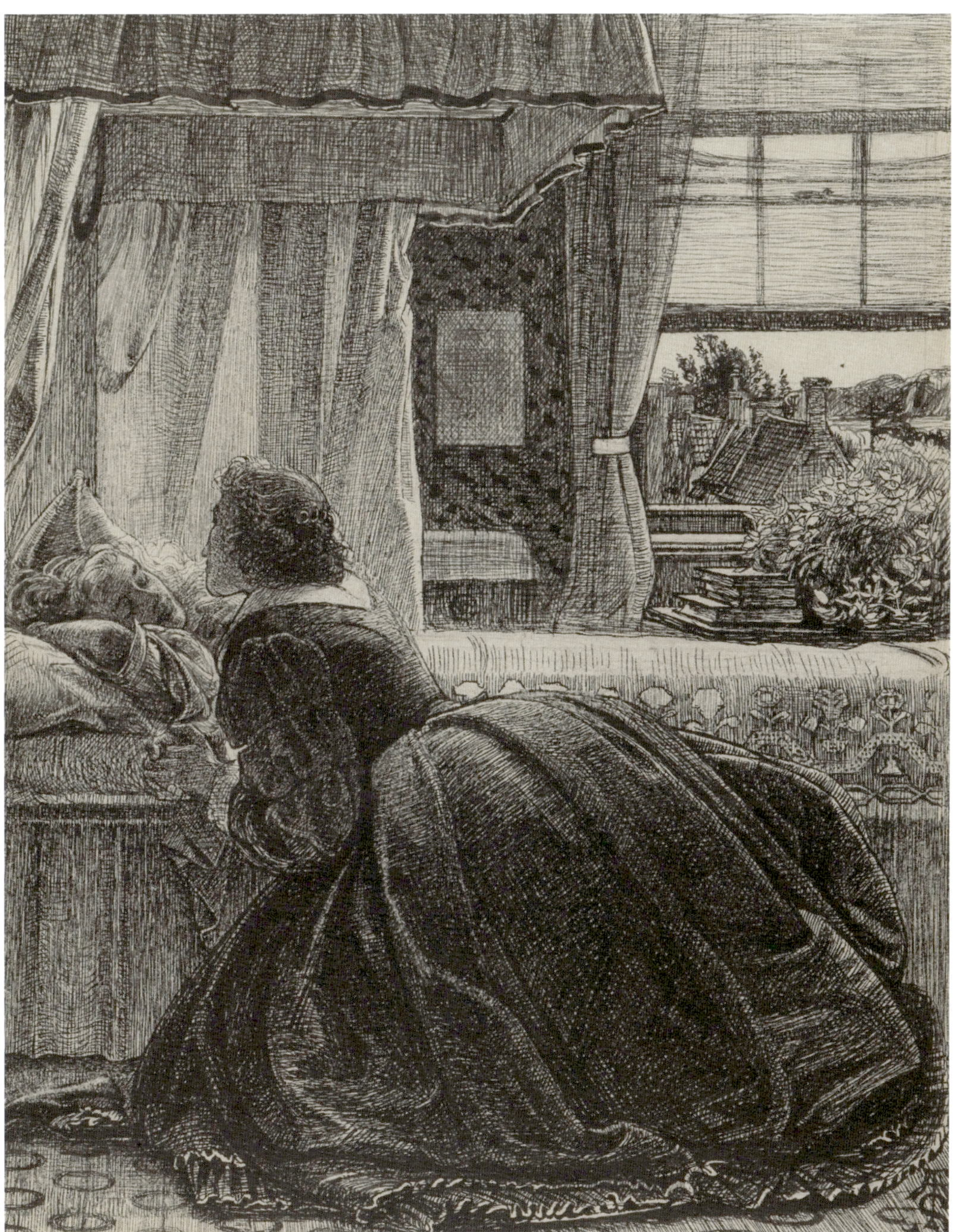

Sleep. 1863.

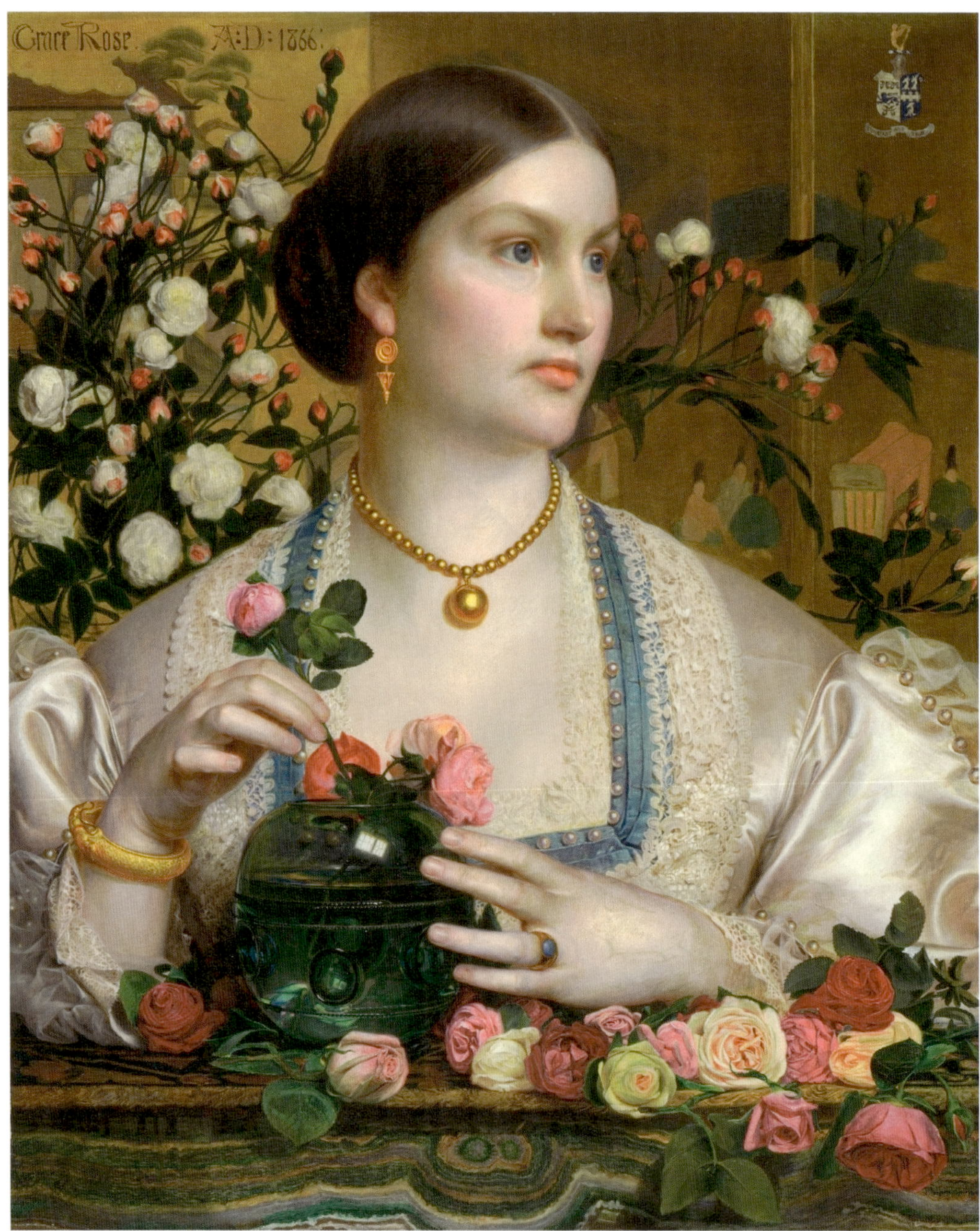

Grace Rose. Oil on panel. 1866. The second wife of William Anderson Rose (1820-1881), the brother of James Anderson Rose. Probably started in June, she is appropriately surrounded by roses. She is fashionably and expensively dressed and bejewelled. She became Lady Grace Rose when her husband was knighted in 1867.

England in 1863 and introduced him to his friends. Legros settled in England, marrying an Englishwoman in 1864, and became a highly esteemed teacher, first at South Kensington then at the Slade School. His close friendships were presumably confined to those who spoke French, for it seems that he never learned English, and thus his direct intercourse with Sandys would have been minimal.

The clubs of which Sandys was a member should not be overlooked, for this was a regular part of his everyday social life. Almost to the end he lived outwardly as a bachelor, whereas his covert families seemed to live from hand-to-mouth. Sandys lived this way also but managed to maintain his gentleman bachelor persona until ill health in his last years drove him to ground in Earl's Court to live with Mary and their large family together. They lovingly and reverentially tended to his needs as best they could towards the end.

In the late 1850s and 1860s he was a member of the informal Arundel Club in Salisbury Street,[119] just south of the Strand and near The Adelphi, a street which disappeared with the building of the mammoth Cecil Hotel in the late 1880s. In July 1864 he was proposed for membership in the Garrick Club, a more established club, but with much the same membership, drawn from the arts, the stage, and letters. He was proposed by Frederick Maxse, the friend of George Meredith, and seconded by Millais, but still felt he needed further support. 'I know so few men' he wrote to Samuel Lucas,[120] the editor of *Once a Week*, 'may I ask you for your influence in getting me in?' He was elected in February 1865.[121]

At the time of Sandys's joining, the Garrick Club was newly established in a grand Italianate building designed by Frederick Marrable in Garrick Street. An inveterate clubman all his life, Sandys, even at the very end, and penniless, was regularly to be found at the Punch Bowl Club.

At some time in 1864, Sandys moved to 8 Victoria Road, Kensington, which was the house and studio of the landscape painter Frederick Lee Bridell who had recently died.[122] Bridell's widow, Eliza Florance Fox, also an artist, was his landlady.

Sandys apologised to Samuel Lucas to whom he wished to show a picture he was 'just finishing', that Kensington was 'so far to ask anyone to come out to'.[123] This sense of concern over the possibility of losing custom must have understandably motivated Sandys to seek a more central painting room, and by my reckoning, it was by early 1865 that he was negotiating for a studio at 47 Leicester Square with the owners, the auctioneers Puttick and Simpson, but this did not materialise until about 1868 or 1869 due to his insolvency. Meanwhile he seems to have carried on working, and perhaps also living, at Victoria Road until he moved into Rossetti's house in Cheyne Walk in May 1866, and we know from a letter of November 1866 that he left owing Mrs Bridell money.[124] Apparently, she impounded some Rembrandt etchings belonging to Sandys as security for his debt.[125] This reveals Sandys's occasional side-line as a dealer in collaboration with his father, and is documented in his bankruptcy papers in 1876. However, he was to deny being a dealer. Taking him in at Cheyne Walk shows Rossetti's essentially kind-hearted and friendly nature.

Other accommodation was considered but probably came to nothing because of high rent or Sandys's precarious financial state at the time. One suggestion was for Tor Villa on Campden Hill, Kensington, owned by J.C. Hook, RA, which Holman Hunt was vacating on the expiry of his lease. Hunt wrote to Sandys offering it to him.[126]

An interesting impression of Sandys while he was living at Cheyne Walk has been given by William Allingham, the poet and customs inspector then living at Lymington, Hampshire, who met him for the first time while visiting Cheyne Walk. He wrote in his diary: 'Sandys, painter, large heavy man with short yellowish hair parted in the middle. Tells me he wants "a dreary moor to paint – is there such a thing in the New Forest?"'[127]

The friendship between Sandys and Rossetti was probably at its best in October 1866 when they set off together on a walking tour in East Sussex and Kent. They must have taken a train from London, on the Hastings line, to Winchelsea. There they stayed for the best part of a week, walking out in the environs, and watching an ancient civic ceremony in the town. Rossetti was delighted by the quiet and 'old world character' of the place. They took a dog-cart to Northiam, where Rossetti was much impressed by the topiary at Brickwall House, the seat of the Frewen family, well-known for its ancient topiary garden. He bought a curious example from a villager, a retired gardener, in the form of an armchair, which he had dug up and sent up to London for his servant to plant in his Chelsea garden. We have Rossetti's record of these events;[128] Sandys's thoughts are not known. The short holiday ended with visits to Cranbrook and Tenterden, and the two were back in London on 23rd October.

Interestingly, William Rossetti noted in his diary on 5th November 1866, that Edward Burne-Jones disliked Sandys because of his gossiping tendencies. Clearly, the two were very different in character and had little to do with each other throughout their lives.

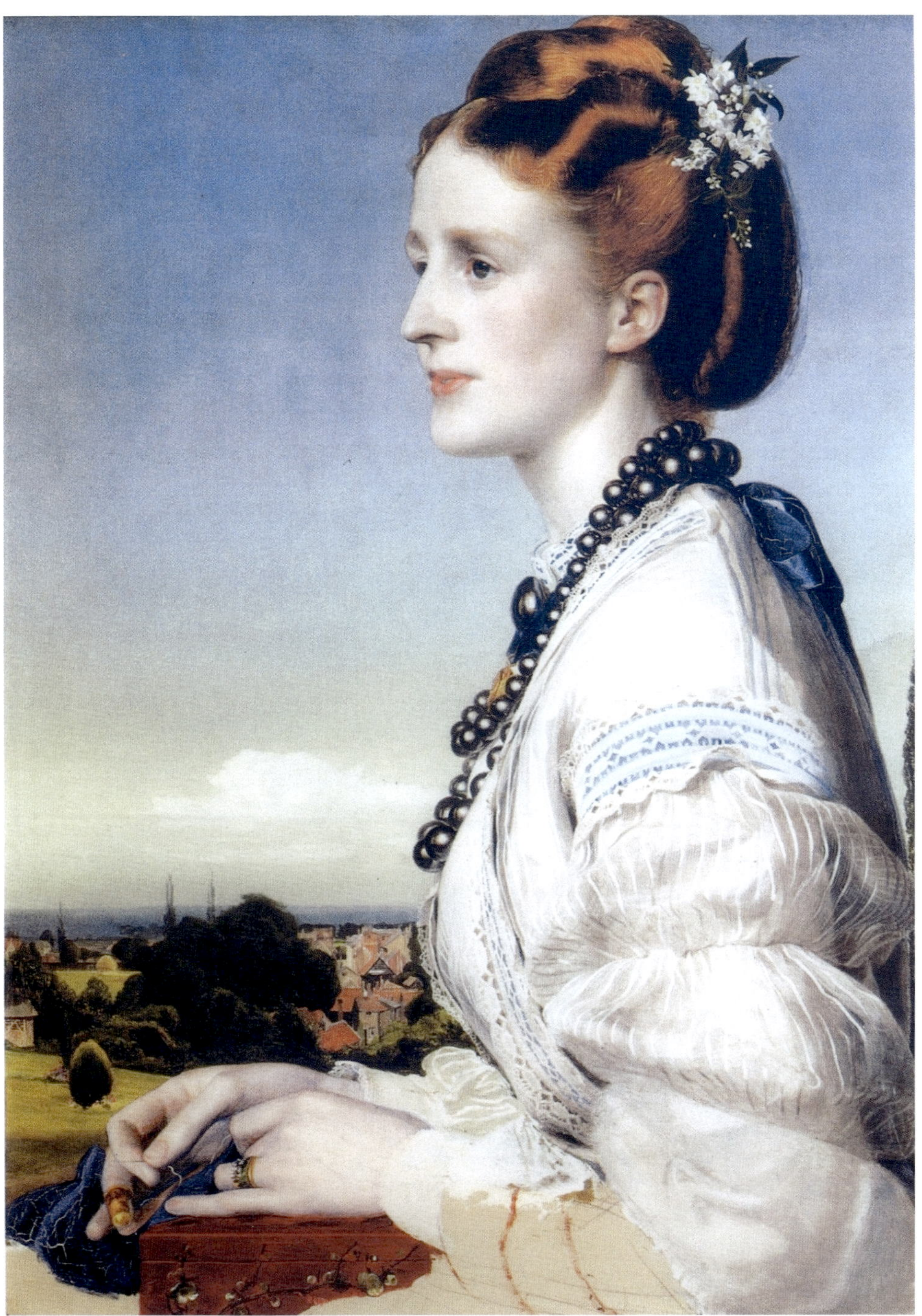

Mary Elizabeth Barstow. (d.1919). Oil on panel. *c*.1867. One of Sandys's most successful portraits. Painted in his studio in Leicester Square. Barstow family history explains the reason for its being unfinished: it was hastily removed by the family from the studio, fearing its impoundment by bailiffs.

By 1st November, Sandys was writing in some distress to James Anderson Rose, saying that he was penniless, and offering for sale, in advance of being able to let it go, a drawing of the head and hands of *Medea* for fifteen guineas. He couldn't yet part with it because he needed it for reference while working on the oil painting. Alternatively, if Rose would pay his bill at Winsor's, the colourman, he could have the drawing in due course.[129] Around this time, Sandys seems to have entered into business arrangements with Charles Augustus Howell,[130] and we find that Howell had in his possession Sandys's detailed study of the foliage of a sycamore tree (no doubt to sell for him)[131] which Rossetti wanted to borrow in order to paint a tree into his current picture *Fiametta*, it being winter at the time.[132]

Charles Augustus Howell (1840–1890) came into the Rossetti circle in about 1865. During his teens, in about 1856, he was sent by his family to England from Portugal, to further his education and to find suitable employment. He had an English father, who was involved in the wine trade in Oporto, and a Portuguese mother. This enterprising and apparently well-educated young man with an unusual and somewhat colourful background soon developed a consuming interest in art, but, owing to various escapades, not relevant enough to outline here, he had to return to Portugal in 1858 and did not go back to England until 1864. In 1865, having established himself in London, he was taken on by John Ruskin as a trusted secretary and general factotum, which would soon put him at the heart of the London art world. There is a possibility that the wine trade made a link between the two families: Ruskin's father was a prosperous London wine importer and, as we have noted, Howell's father was in the wine trade at Oporto. There is no factual evidence that this was the case, but his biographer Helen Rossetti Angeli alludes to it as a possibility.[133]

Howell, or 'the Owl',[134] was a born entrepreneur with a tendency to favour his own pocket in the many transactions which he handled on behalf of Ruskin, Rossetti and others. He evidently lost Ruskin's trust by 1870 and their association was terminated. Cast adrift on his own, he lost no time in furthering his career as a dealer in art, art objects, and of interior decoration at a time when fashionable tastes were changing.

In January 1867, the birth of a baby girl, Maura, confirmed the intimate relationship between Sandys and Mary Emma Jones, who as we have noted, had been a model for him as early as 1862. It is the first child of theirs of which we know and, sadly, she is chiefly known by her accidental death on Christmas Eve 1868, from 'violent shock and scalds'.[135] The records disagree on her age at death: the death certificate states that she was one year old, but the burial record states that on her burial on 31st December 1868 she was aged one year and eleven months.[136] She died at 22 Kingsbridge Place, Millwall, where she had been placed with a 'baby farmer'. The other new fact which emerges from documentary research is that baby Maura was recorded as the daughter of Frederick Neville, gentleman, of Draycott Lodge, Sloane Street, Chelsea, who bought the burial plot in Brompton Cemetery on 30th December 1868. One has to assume that Sandys had taken this name for the purposes of this relationship in order to preserve his separate bachelor and professional identity to the world at large. Probably at the same time, Mary Emma Jones would have assumed the name of 'Mrs Neville'. On the stage, of course, she was 'Miss Clive' and her career on the boards must explain why Maura was placed with a baby-minder, but why so far afield is a mystery. Further investigation into the dwellers at 22 Kingsbridge Place has shown that it was occupied by Edward and Elizabeth Smith, a police constable and his wife. In 1871 they were looking after their own one-year-old grandson and two more Neville children, Cissily and Dorothy, aged two and one, respectively, with the help of a young servant girl. Seemingly, Frederick and Mary were not put off this ménage by the nasty accident in 1868,[137] and perhaps were chosen in the first place by a perception of the respectability and good management which a policeman's household might offer. Both Cissily and Dorothy were born in Brompton in about 1869 and 1870.[138] We shall hear more about them later in the 1870s.

Sandys and the architect Thomas Jeckell (1827–1881),[139] without doubt, were already known to each other through their common Norfolk origin. Jeckell was active in Norwich and Thorpe, sometimes working for the same clients as Sandys. Also, in London they had many friends and acquaintances in common, especially among Rossetti's circle. At the end of January 1867, on returning from Norwich to London, Jeckell brought a message to Sandys from Jeremiah James Colman that he wanted Sandys to paint a picture which would include his little daughter. Sandys replied to Colman that he would rather paint a portrait of her as well as paint an ambitious subject which he had in mind, namely Judith.[140] As oil paintings they remain a mystery and perhaps were never undertaken.[141] However, Sandys did make portrait drawings of all J.J. Colman's children, as double portraits, in 1863, 1870, and 1872.

Meanwhile, at Cheyne Walk, Sandys was reported in February 1867 to be working on his major painting *Medea*, commissioned by William Clabburn.[142] Brewing up was another financial crisis, and in May and June Jeckell provided a refuge for Sandys from his creditors at his lodgings at 11 Gloucester Road, Kensington. This is known from Sandys's letters to James Anderson Rose in May, June, and July 1867. Rose was trying to manage the situation for Sandys. Among his debts was one to Charles Roberson, the artists' colourman of Long Acre, and one to an unidentified Mr Jones.[143] Sandys wrote: 'My dear Rose, You may tell Mr Jones he may have one hundred in a month and the whole before the end of the summer. About Roberson's matter, I scarce know what to do for the best. I do not see I can pay it under a fortnight … I have at least a thousand pounds worth of work by me – and I ought not to be in this frightful mess. Manage the best in Roberson's matter – make the best terms so that my expences [*sic*] may be as small as possible.'[144]

Clabburn became alarmed that bailiffs might seize the pictures he had commissioned from Sandys, which Sandys was working on at Rossetti's house, and took them away. This was a serious matter for Clabburn because he virtually owned them already, having paid large advances to Sandys. Clabburn wrote in a letter of 20th June 1867 to Rose: 'It is quite true, as I told you when I last saw you, that *Medea* is mine. It was by Sandys special request that I forwarded to you £50, the sum he asked for. Having already advanced more than agreed, I must decline paying any more till I get the *Children* or *Berenice* when I shall be only too glad to pay that which will then be due to Sandys.'[145]

In spite of all of these financial uncertainties, Sandys was still planning to move into a studio in Leicester Square.[146] Rossetti was quite naturally irritated as can be seen from his letter to Sandys of 8th July (1867) because of two summonses of Sandys for petty amounts coming to his house, wasting the time of his servant Loader. He also reported the visit of Clabburn to take away his pictures in case of impoundment.[147] His brother, William, commenting on Sandys's behaviour in his diary, noting that: 'Sandys is persecuted with writs. He scarcely stays in Cheyne Walk any part of the day, and has only done some six weeks' steady work since he has been staying here, now about three-quarters of a year. … His debts continue a source of trouble to the inmates. It is believed that Lowder's [*sic*] leaving is partly due to this cause.'[148]

The year 1867 ends with Rossetti trying to reconcile Sandys to Howell after Sandys had perceived that he had been slighted by him while dining at the Solferino restaurant.[149] The cause of the misunderstanding was concerned in some way with John Camden Hotten, the opportunistic publisher and bookseller who, through the agency of Howell, was to take on the publication of Swinburne's *Poems and Ballads* and Swinburne's future literary work.[150]

Forty-seven Leicester Fields (later Square) had been Sir Joshua Reynolds's London house, an adapted large late seventeenth century house with many rooms and a large studio which Reynolds had built in the garden.

The distinguished historic associations later entered into the Sandys family mythology, to be described by Sandys's daughter Winifred in a letter to Samuel Bancroft Jr as 'Sir Joshua Reynolds' old studio'.[151] However, the house contained many capacious rooms, and it would seem likely that the original studio was used by the auctioneers, Puttick and Simpson, who were the landlords.

Still strapped for cash, Sandys was writing from Leicester Square in January 1868 to Rose for a loan for a week, until Clabburn paid him £20 for three drawings,[152] and £50 owed on *Berenice*, which, perhaps he would have finished by then.[153]

With *Medea*, for Clabburn, completed at last (having taken two years), Sandys had high hopes for a great success; the painting having been highly praised by his friends. When he submitted it to the Royal Academy for the Summer Exhibition, however, there was another setback: it was rejected! Evidently, it was Thomas Sydney Cooper, RA, and Philip Calderon, RA, who were on the hanging committee, who were responsible for the rejection. William Rossetti, our source of information, wondered if 'some personal considerations have intervened'.[154] However, not mentioned were the two copulating toads in the foreground which most probably was the objectionable factor. William thought, aesthetically considered, the rejection was shameful, as did his brother Gabriel, Swinburne, and the journalist and art critic George Augustus Sala (and no doubt others of the circle such as Whistler). The art critics, Tom Taylor, Burnell Payne, and others also came to see the rejected *Medea* at the studio in Leicester Square.[155]

Victorian prudery now cast aside; this picture is considered an undoubted masterpiece today. The beautiful woman, her angry expression, the archaic and exotic jewellery ornamenting her, and the inventive way of telling the story in a two-dimensional frieze behind the three-dimensional figure of Medea, and the curious objects with which she was casting her deadly spell. In this way, Sandys encapsulated the Greek legend of Jason and the Argonauts, the quest for the Golden Fleece (a symbol of kingship), Medea's help in finding the Fleece, Jason's betrayal of Medea, and her revenge. The painting is packed full of narrative and symbolic detail, exemplifying and, perhaps, forecasting the European Symbolist movement of some thirty years later.

In defence of Sandys, Swinburne and William Rossetti collaborated on a pamphlet which they based on the format of John Ruskin's annual critical review, *Academy Notes*, which Hotten published.[156] William Rossetti took his characteristic cautious and moderate line, hinting that there were currently two styles of painting which were causing a division among the hanging committee '... and that judicial equity in adjusting these interests may sometimes be in default ...'. Swinburne, however, took the opportunity to sing out the praise of his friend Sandys's two accepted exhibits: a portrait drawing of the distinguished ophthalmic surgeon George Critchett (1817–1882) and the drawing we know as *Proud Maisie*. He brought attention to the rejected painting and wrote that 'beyond all doubt *Medea* is as yet his masterpiece' and proceeded to rhapsodise upon its abundant symbolic details. He couldn't resist the impulse to praise the work of two of his other 'outsider' friends: 'The present year has other pictures to be proud of, not submitted to the loose and slippery judgment of an academy. Of one or two such as I am here permitted to make mention ...' (they were by Whistler and Rossetti).

This was the summer in which Rossetti had a marquee set up in his garden at Cheyne Walk, and had a large dinner party for his friends, at which Sandys was present.[157]

Probably at some time in November 1868, Sandys wrote to Rossetti (who was unwell at the time) asking for the return of his white and gold 'Algerine' dress, which he wanted to put into a picture. This exotic textile is probably identifiable as the one he used in *Miranda*. Both Sandys and Rossetti gloried in rich and colourful fabrics and striking oriental accessories, which (incidentally) were to bring about new styles in female dress and adornment for a later generation.

After leaving Cheyne Walk, Sandys shared Swinburne's rooms at 22A Dorset Street, Portman Square, until sometime in 1869. However, on the last day of 1868, Sandys was entered in the records of the Brompton Cemetery as Frederick Neville, of Draycott Lodge, Sloane Street, Chelsea.[158] This was the revelation which provided the author with the fact that Frederick Neville was one and the same as Frederick Sandys and provided the window into Sandys's new family life with Mary Emma Jones, who thus became 'Mrs Neville' in her outward (and maternal) role.

The history of the picture *Medea* continued in 1869 with the publication of a lengthy poem inspired by it. Handsomely produced and bound, it was written by one of Sandys's friends, Alfred Bate Richards.[159] Richards had earlier written a poem to accompany Sandys's design *Helen and Cassandra* which was published in the magazine *Once a Week*.[160] He was, unfortunately, a third-rate poet, but was certainly well-versed in classical literature.

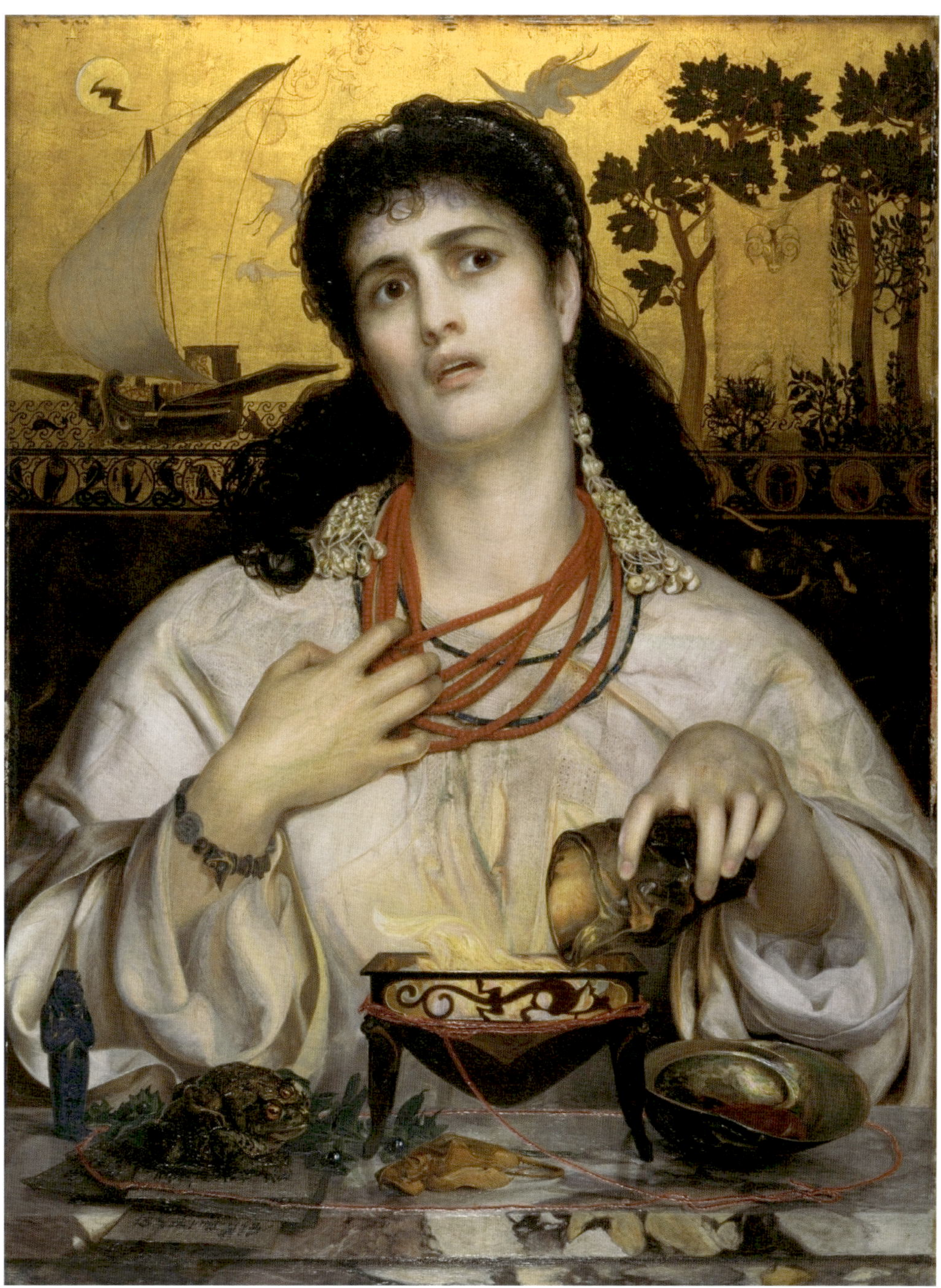

Medea. Oil on panel. 1866-68. One of Sandys's major pictures. Innovatory was the landscape background treated as a two-dimensional frieze which is full of suggestive and symbolic references to the Greek legend. It was entered for the RA Summer Exhibition in 1868, but was rejected. After protests, it was accepted by the RA in 1869 and hung 'on the line'. No doubt the rejection was because of the copulating toads in the foreground. The gypsy Keomi was the inspiring model.

Richards wrote in his introduction to the volume: 'A portion of this Poem was written towards the latter end of 1867, soon after I first saw the Picture, then in an unfinished state. I may, indeed, say that my admiration of it grew with its growth on the canvass. … If enthusiasm could always command ability, my part would not be unworthily executed, for I certainly began to write *con amore*, but without the slightest idea that a few occasional lines would ever expand themselves into matter for a separate publication.' In fact, the poem ran to sixty-two pages, and was published by Chapman & Hall with a photograph of the painting inserted as a frontispiece. The ivory linen-covered boards were gold-stamped with the title in Greek letters and two curious Egypto-oriental devices. The design was undoubtedly by Sandys.

Medea was submitted again to the Royal Academy Summer Exhibition in 1869, and this time it was accepted. His friend Sala had written a brief review for the *Daily Telegraph* and wanted to call on Sandys to discuss further remarks Sandys might wish him to make about the picture. He wanted to make up a dinner party with Sandys, Rossetti and Whistler at his house in Putney, 'no dress or ceremony' as his wife was abroad.[161]

In early 1869 Sandys was suffering with 'boils' as William Rossetti noted and, sympathetically, his brother Gabriel was asking advice from Alice Boyd, a friend of the Rossettis, about possible cures for this which Sandys might be able to afford.[162]

Rossetti and Sandys became estranged at about this time. The accusation by Rossetti of Sandys's plagiarism of his work has long been documented in Pre-Raphaelite literature. In general, it seems that Rossetti was right to feel aggrieved because Sandys was choosing similar, sometimes identical, subjects or, more rightly, the same titles for pictures Rossetti was using for his. However, in practice, the particular strengths of their talents were completely distinct, with the result that (in any case) Sandys's pictures looked rather different from Rossetti's. Furthermore, these poetic, mythical and dramatic subjects were common currency amongst the new generation of artists who were ushering in the new romantic aestheticism. Evidently Rossetti did not see it that way.

The circumstances were that Rossetti was extremely upset to hear from Howell that Sandys was contemplating painting the subject *Lucretia Borgia*.[163] He felt unable to speak to Sandys directly about the matter and was therefore writing to him about it. He wrote that from the description he had received (from Howell), he was angered to find that it resembled his own picture of the subject.

'It is described to me as Lucrezia Borgia mixing poisons, with her husband & the Pope (or a Cardinal) seen in a mirror behind her. This so nearly resembles a design of my own that you must pardon my writing you a word about it. I should much prefer speaking but should feel so awkward in doing so that I must confess sheer cowardice in tackling the question [that it] causes me to write instead.'

Furthermore, he wanted to say that in the past he had noticed two other pictures by Sandys in which he felt, as well as some (un-named) others, had been too close to his own designs, namely *The Magdalene at the House of Simon*, and *Helen of Troy*. As both of these works, he said, were preparatory designs yet to be 'realised', and because of his treatment of the subjects, which he considered original and his own property, he felt somewhat 'injured' by Sandys. The letter was couched in Rossetti's best diplomatic manner, explaining that he wanted to be frank about these matters that were troubling him 'lest friendship itself should suffer'.[164] He might well have anticipated, given Sandys's volatile nature, that Sandys would take offence. From what one can gather from scanty evidence, Sandys's *Lucrezia Borgia* subject, if completed, would not at all have resembled Rossetti's picture.[165]

Sandys's (uncharacteristically) long reply might be summarised by one sentence: '… I give up these subjects – and with them your friendship.'[166]

Rossetti could also be characterised as over-sensitive and vulnerable at this period in his life. He was under a severe emotional strain with a borderline psychosis, frustrated by his unfortunate love-obsession with Jane, his friend William Morris's wife. This could have been consummated only rarely (if at all), and there could be no future for it. Physical symptoms developed, such as temporary blindness and insomnia, for which Rossetti resorted to drugs and alcohol.

At any rate, Rossetti's accusation about the *Mary Magdalene* subject is not difficult to follow when comparing his picture, a watercolour drawing dated 1857, with the Sandys oil picture (of *c.*1859–60): the pose of the head is similar, with the model holding the jar of aromatic ointment close to her throat, but shows just the head, hand, and shoulders of a single figure with nothing but a flat, patterned background, whereas Rossetti's full-length figure has a fully worked-out architectural setting.

Sandys's *Magdalen* shows a bland, rather contemplative, realistically-painted young woman, somewhat in Millais's early style. Rossetti's *Magdalen* shows a dramatic scene of frozen action. However, it must be conceded that

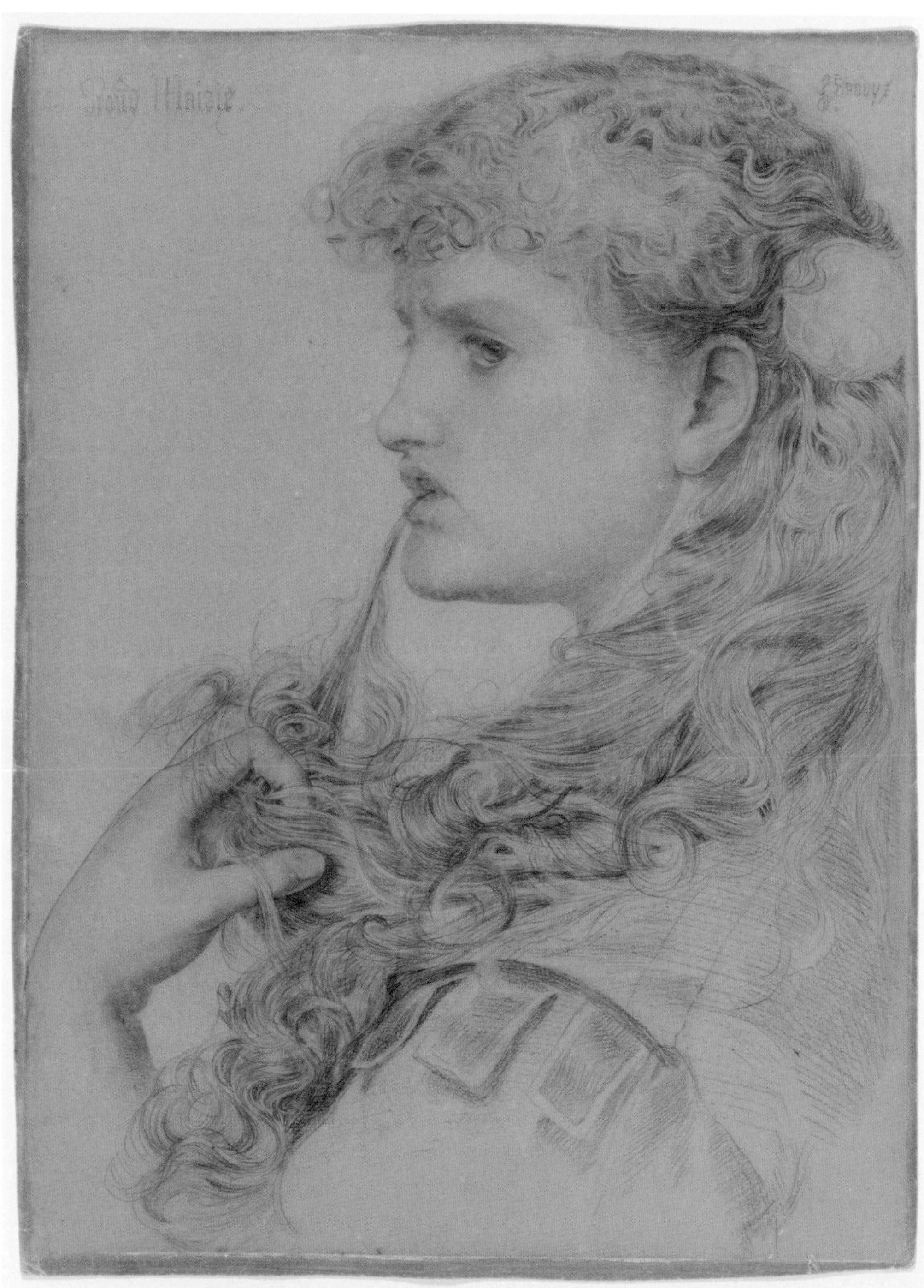

Proud Maisie. Chalk drawing. 1868. Probably the first version of this very popular image, of which Sandys was to produce at least 13 versions in chalks and an unfinished painting. It shows the young Mary Emma Jones as the model.

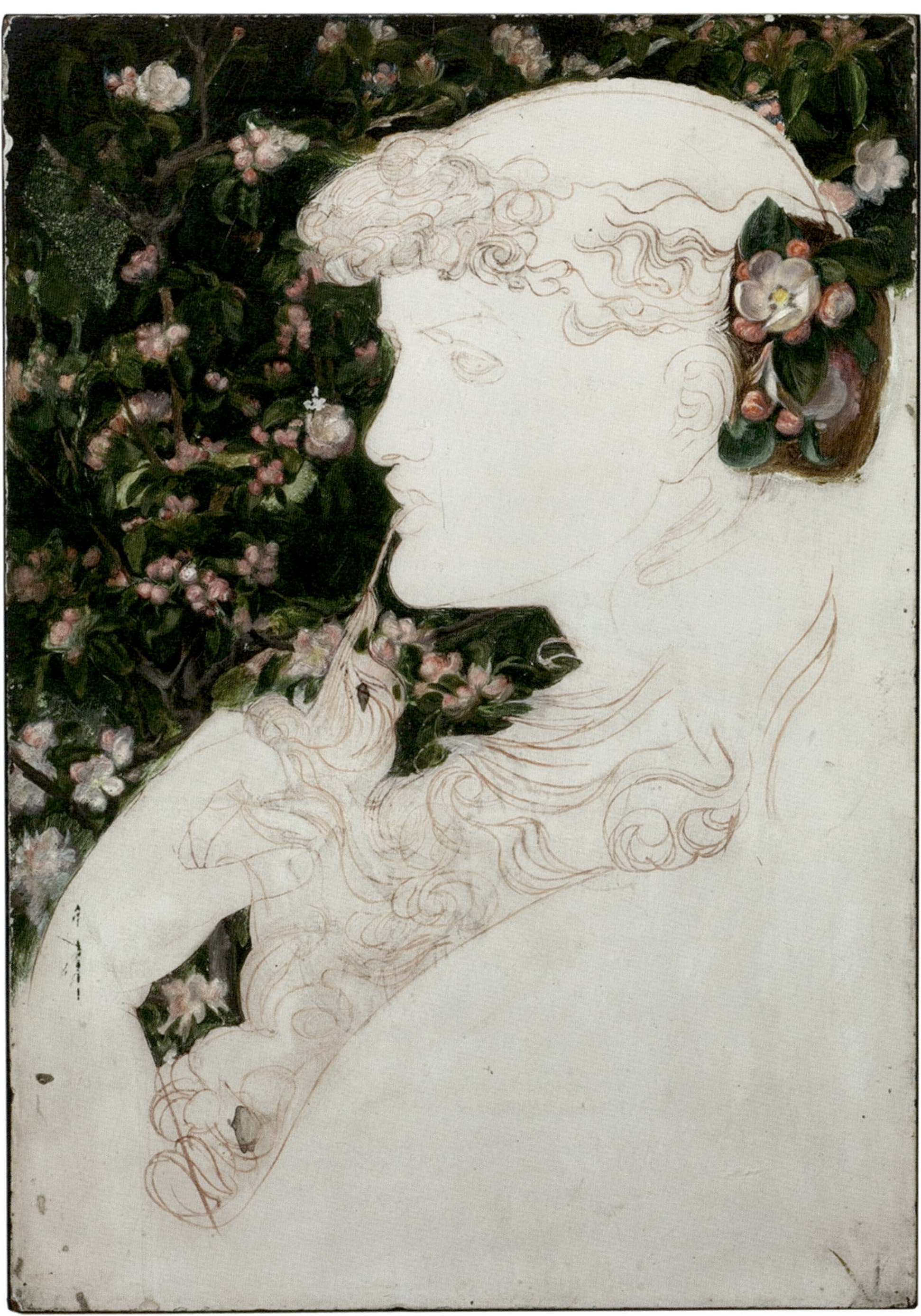

*Proud Maisie. c.*1868. An oil on panel version of Sandys's image. It was based on his drawing of Mary Emma Jones. It was never finished but shows his method of painting.

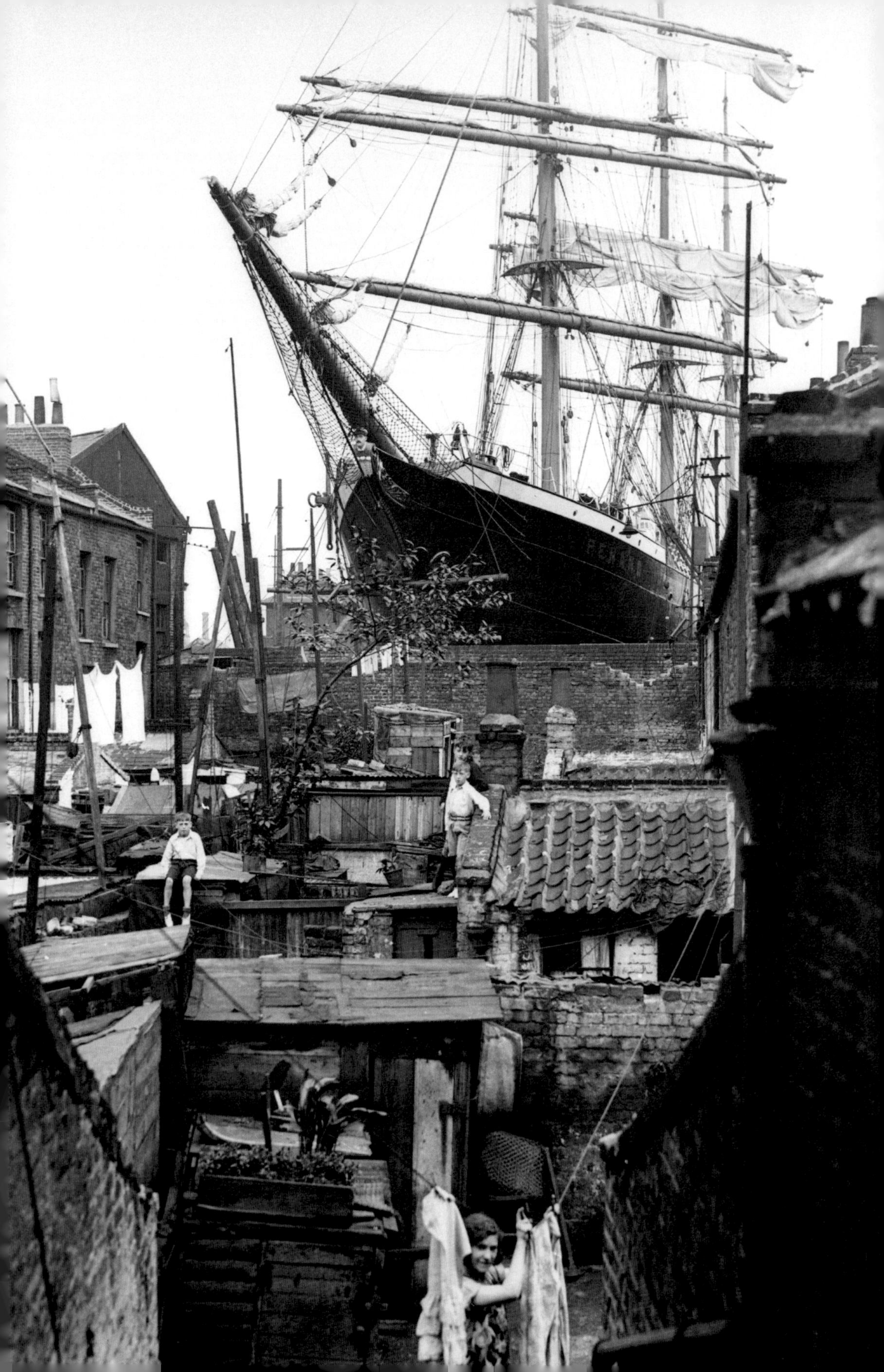

there are similarities in the pose in both cases. Sandys might have seen the Rossetti watercolour at Cheyne Walk. Whether he carried Rossetti's image subconsciously in his mind or made a deliberate copy, it is impossible to know. My understanding of Sandys's somewhat naïve, character convinces me that it was the former.

Identifiable also is the subject of Rossetti's complaint about *Helen of Troy*. Rossetti's picture of 1863 shows, frontally, the head and shoulders of a pouting beauty (the model Annie Miller) with both her hands held to her throat, fingering her necklace. The background shows a burning city on the horizon.

In the case of Sandys, there is an untitled, undated (*c.*1869) painting of another sulky beauty (this time Mary Emma Jones) in a similar pose, with her hands up to her throat but, instead, clutching her long curling hair which cascades down, covering her shoulders and breast. The painting is unfinished and the background to the figure has not been attempted. However, the unfinished preliminary drawing shows what appear to be flames above and behind the head. This must be the offending *Helen of Troy* as it fulfils Rossetti's accusation so closely and must account for the fact that Sandys left it unfinished.

As for a third disputed picture, *Lucretia Borgia*, no painting by Sandys has surfaced, but there exists an unfinished pencil study from the head of Mary Emma Jones, which includes, on the same sheet, unconnected sketches of two doves that must have been the start of this subject.[167]

Sandys wrote to Rossetti: 'I was about to paint two pictures of Lucretia Borgia, one standing, the other sitting. The motive in both pictures being the same – Lucretia in her chamber testing her poison on one of two pet turtle doves; one lying dead at her feet, the other sitting up behind her. You must say how far this is your idea – how far it is the motive of your picture, which by the way I have never seen – only the photograph. *I say it is not.*'

He continued by saying that he had been inspired by seeing 'the little girl' posing in emulation of what she had seen after a visit the previous autumn to the opera.[168] This idea must have been for the abandoned *Lucretia Borgia* – although, by his description, Sandys's image would have been quite different from Rossetti's. Rossetti's *Lucretia Borgia* is a watercolour of 1860–1861, which shows a full-length figure of a woman washing her hands over a hand basin to the right of the picture, with her head glancing backwards towards some dimly realised figures in the background.

View of the neighbourhood at Kingsbridge Place (now West Ferry Road), Millwall, where Mary and Frederick's children were boarded from January 1867 until the mid-1870s. Although the photo was taken in 1932, conditions probably had not much changed.

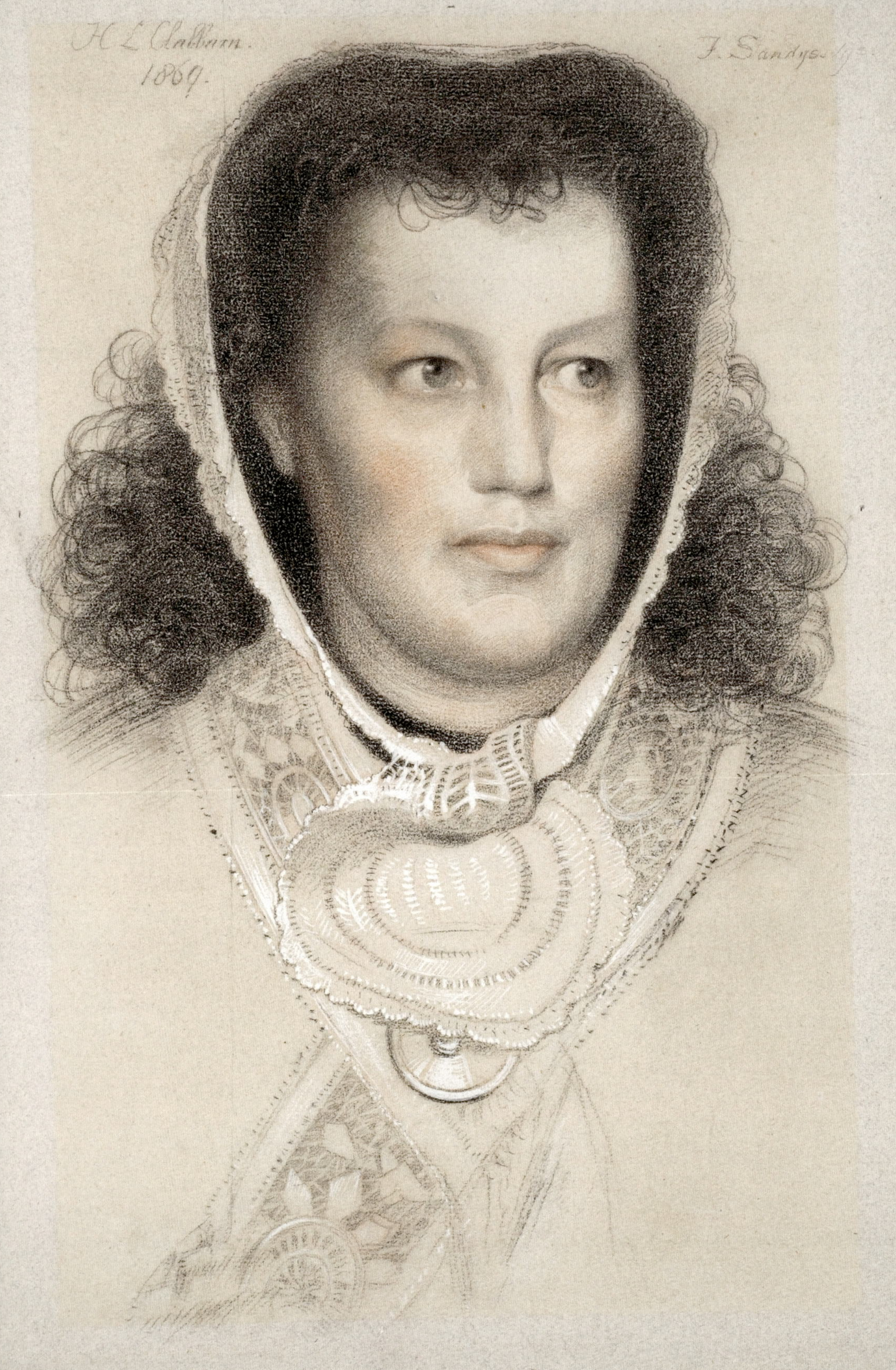
1869
F. Sandys

The history of these so-called plagiarisms is difficult to piece together at this distance in time with the evidence that remains. My feeling is that there is much truth in Rossetti's accusation, but that Sandys, who was rather lacking in pictorial invention, was repeating poses unconsciously.[169] One can recall other cross-fertilisations between contemporaries.[170]

In the same letter of 15th May, Sandys reminded Rossetti that he told him 'some five or six years back' that he was about to paint a Perdita. He wrote that not knowing that Rossetti was about to paint such a picture, but having heard this, he gave up the idea, and gratuitously gave Rossetti 'a long account of all I had gathered of Perdita', although he felt he had a perfect right to the subject. No Perdita by Rossetti has been recorded, but the oil by Sandys (*c.*1866), a fine portrait head of 'the little girl' certainly was not abandoned by him.

Another conflicting subject was brought up at the end of Sandys's defensive letter: 'I mentioned to you some short time since I intended to paint *Merlin and Nimue*. You said you were going to paint such a picture. I had never heard this. I never saw a line of your design – but I gave it up. So much for simple repetition. Another circumstance of the same occurred, the particulars of which I now forget, and it is too much like the others to be worth remembering.'[171] 'Simple repetition': what he meant by this remains unclear. Neither seems to have tackled the *Merlin and Nimue* subject, although Burne-Jones had produced a very fine one in 1861.[172]

The facts were that they were all competing on the same turf, in a manner of speaking. Sandys and Rossetti were both engaged in the production of pictures of 'stunners': single figures, often half-length or bust-length only, of beautiful women well-endowed with hair ('a woman's crowning glory'), dressed in rich and exotic clothing and jewellery.[173] Rossetti had the more creative imagination, but Sandys was a better draughtsman, and craftsman in paint. Rossetti had a more direct painting method, whereas Sandys was slow and painstaking to an extreme degree, using a historical technique. With their varied and attractive confections, they were both competing for the same clients – who were, largely, newly rich industrialists and professionals who were then buying pictures for their walls.

Sandys thus ended their friendship with a payment of his debts (probably rent) to Rossetti, but his brother Michael later pointed out that the £50 (sent by Sandys with a rueful note) was probably only half what was actually owed.[174]

In May and June 1869 Sandys was at Knowlmere Manor, near Clitheroe,

Hannah Louisa Clabburn. Chalk drawing. 1869. A fine Holbeinesque portrait.

drawing the portrait of Jonathan Peel[175] who was a member of the Lancashire family whose fortune was made originally in the eighteenth century from manufacturing and printing on cotton textiles. It seems that Sandys was there for about two weeks completing the preliminary drawing, returning at the end of the year to complete the oil, which he had no doubt started in his Leicester Square studio from the drawing.[176] The fact that Peel had been a barrister in the south of England before retiring to Lancashire may have made the connection for this commission.[177]

Sandys must also have been in Norwich in 1869, executing the fine Holbeinesque portrait drawing of *Mrs Hannah Clabburn* (1869), and his oil *La Belle Jaune Giroflée*, a 'fancy head' for which the sitter was a young Norwich woman Marianne Shingles, a silk weaver. The Shingles family lived across Grapes Hill from the Sandys family house, and it seems that Emma Sandys discovered her as a potential model in about 1869. She sat again for Sandys for his *Hero* in 1871 and continued to sit for Emma until Emma's death in 1877.[178] The Holbeinesque portrait drawing of Hannah Clabburn is a masterpiece and, to my mind, it is likely that Sandys knew of the portrait drawings by Holbein in the Royal Collection, though perhaps it was through the fine stipple-etched reproductions of them made by Francesco Bartolozzi (1727–1815).

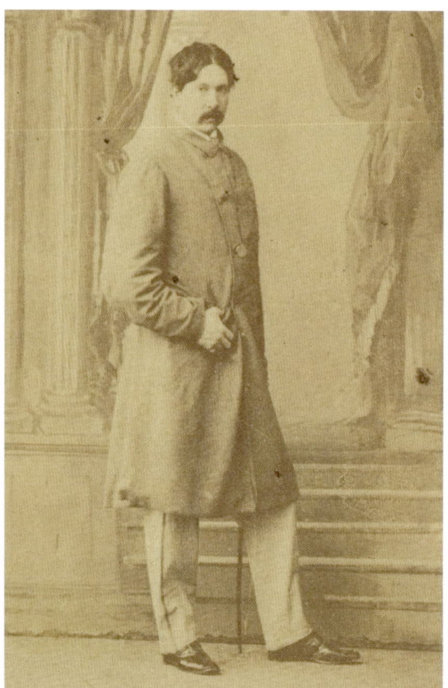

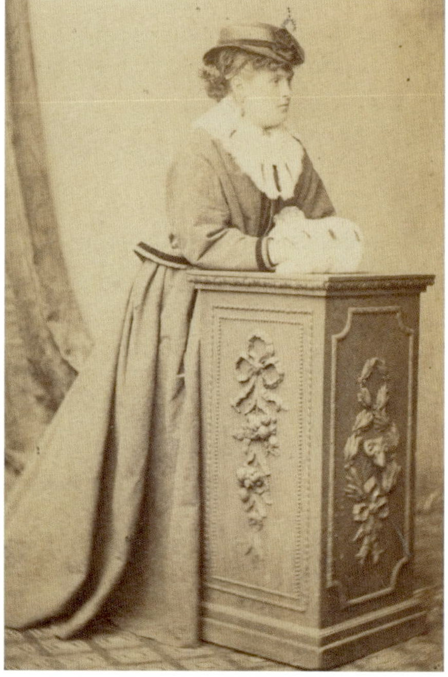

Left: Frederick Sandys from a carte de visite by Caldesi, Blanford & Co., 13 Pall Mall East, London. Late 1860s. Right: Mary Emma Jones (1845–1920) from a carte de visite by S. Ayling, Oxford Street, W.C., London. Late 1860s.

[1] Letter from F.S. to Arthur Lewis in London from Thorpe (Norwich) dated Tuesday 27th January 1863. Author's collection.

[2] H.H. Roberts, *Memories of Fourscore Years* (1920).

[3] Undated letter from The Bazaar, St Andrew's, from F.S. to Augustus Jessopp. Probably February–March 1861. Author's collection.

[4] Shown at the RA in 1861 were *Mrs W. Clabburn* (178) and *Oriana* (639).

[5] The young daughters of William and Hannah Clabburn: Mary Louisa and Lucy.

[6] The five elder children of William and Hannah Clabburn.

[7] Letters from Rossetti to Ford Madox Brown in November and December 1861. W.M. Rossetti, *Dante Gabriel Rossetti, Family Letters...* vol. 1, 1895, p. 210; C.L. Cline, *The Letters of George Meredith*, 1970, vol. 1, p. 85. Rossetti had just met Meredith in May 1861. Meredith met Sandys at one of Rossetti's parties held at Chatham Place in November 1861; Lionel Stevenson, *The Ordeal of George Meredith.* (1953), p. 102.

[8] Harold Hartley, *Eighty-Eight Not Out: A Record of Happy Memories* (1939), p. 240.

[9] Letter from Meredith to Weldon, dated 24th May 1876; C.L. Cline, (ed.) *The Letters of George Meredith* (1970), no. 565. Cline tentatively identifies Weldon as Walter Weldon (1832–1885), publisher of *Weldon's Register*, but it is my strong belief that it was William Henry Weldon (1837–1919), an officer of the College of Arms, and friend of Sandys, of whom Sandys drew a portrait in 1875.

[10] H.T. Dunn quoted by Gale Pedrick in *Life with Rossetti* (1964), p. 97.

[11] Of course, by the age of 69, Sandys had much to tell. Elizabeth Pennell's comment is tantalising. Alas, voice recorders had not yet been invented. E.R. and J. Pennell, *The Whistler Journal* (1921), p. 22.

[12] Ford Madox Hueffer, *The Life of Ford Madox Brown* (1896), p. 182.

[13] F.B. Barwell, (1923).

[14] Arthur J. Lewis (1824–1901) was the son of Stephen Lewis, one of the founders of Lewis and Allenby, haberdashery and silk retailers of 195 Regent Street, a leading shop in its day.

[15] Amongst these were: George Somes Layard, *The Life and Letters of Charles Samuel Keene* (1892); L.M. Lamont, (ed.) *Thomas Armstrong, a Memoir* (1912); J.G. Marks, *The Life and Letters of Frederick Walker* (1896); A.M.W. Stirling, (ed.) *The Richmond Papers* (1926); Elizabeth R. and J. Pennell, *The Whistler Journal* (1921); C.C. Hoyer Millar, *George du Maurier and others* (1937); Kate Terry Gielgud, *An Autobiography* (1953); Leonée Ormond, *George du Maurier* (1969).

[16] Copies of the well-known pair of anthropological bronze busts by Charles Cordier (1827–1905): *Said Abdallah de la tribu du Darfour* and *La Vénus Africaine*, which were a popular and critical success at the London Great Exhibition of 1851, and were purchased by Queen Victoria.

[17] G.A.F. Rogers, *The Arts Club and its Members* (1920), p. 2.

[18] Daphne du Maurier, (ed.) *The Young George du Maurier* (1951), pp. 98-99.

[19] Daphne du Maurier, *The Young George du Maurier* (1951), p. 161.

[20] Letter from F.S. to Arthur Lewis dated 27th January 1863. Author's collection. Joseph Jopling (1831–1884), was a caricaturist for *Vanity Fair*, and Lewis's intimate friend.

[21] In a letter to the author dated 24th January 1981, the actor John Gielgud recalled seeing the same suspended ostrich egg in his grandmother Kate Lewis's house, in West Cromwell Road in the 1920s. The Lewises had moved there after the downfall of Arthur's business in the 1890s.

[22] Kate was the elder sister of Ellen Terry, who had a much longer theatrical career and ultimately was more celebrated. Kate became the grandmother of John Gielgud.

[23] J.G. Marks (1986). According to Marks, the last venue was at 44 Maddox Street. Marks was the brother-in-law of the illustrator, Frederick Walker.

[24] Rose also formed a large collection of engravings of historical portraits which he catalogued. It was published in two volumes in 1874 and 1894.

[25] Jerome K. Jerome, *My Life and Times*, (Hodder and Stoughton, London, 1926), p. 85. The portrait is dated 1862.

[26] Arthur B. Chamberlain, Works by Frederick Sandys in the Birmingham Art Gallery, *Apollo*, November 1925, p. 258.

[27] Forrest Reid, *Illustrators of the Sixties* (1928) p. 56. I have not discovered Reid's source for this information.

[28] Included in Thomas Armstrong, C.B., (ed.) L.M. Lamont, *A Memoir 1832-1911*, (M. Secker, London, 1912), p. 155.

[29] J.B. Swain, *Memoir of Joseph Swain* (1820–-1909). Unpublished typescript in Hartley Collection, Museum of Fine Arts, Boston. The engraving has the Swain signature.

[30] *The Studio*, vol. 33, October 1904, p. 7.

[31] Ibid. It was simply not practical to use a pen on a hard, shiny surface such as on a woodblock.

[32] W. Crane, *The Hazelford Sketchbook* (The John Barnard Associates, Cambridge, Mass., 1937), p. 13.

[33] Cambridge, Fitzwilliam Museum, Album PD. 865, p. 3.

[34] Inscribed *Bottom of Dress*. Decr.1 – 1860, Birmingham City Art Gallery, 877'06.

[35] Joseph Swain (1820–1909) was also manager of the engraving department for *Punch*, the humorous magazine.

[36] J. Comyns Carr, *Some Eminent Victorians. Personal Recollections in the World of Art and Letters* (London, 1908), p. 115.

[37] Percy Bate, *The Studio*, 1904, p. 7.

[38] This picture, if it ever existed, is yet an unsolved mystery, as outlined in the author's Catalogue Raisonné (2001) under nos. 2.A.37 and 2.A.71.

[39] 1862 RA catalogue numbers: (350) *Portrait of Mrs Clabburn*, oil; (361) *King Pelles' Daughter*, oil; (789) *Portrait of Mrs Doulton*, chalk; (805) *Autumn*, ink drawing; (809) *Portrait of Mrs Rose*, ink drawing.

[40] His application for a passport was

recorded on 17th April 1862. National Archives. Index to Register of Passport Applications, 1851–1903.

[41] The art-loving family of the retired East India Company administrator, Henry Thoby Prinsep (1793–1878).

[42] Incidentally, Watts died in the same year as Sandys (1904), and their retrospective memorial exhibitions were shown concurrently at the Royal Academy in 1905.

[43] Daphne du Maurier, (ed.), *The Young George du Maurier, A Selection of his Letters* (1951), pl. opp. p. 224. The caricatures were depicted in the margin of a letter of 16th July 1862, from George to his mother, pp. 157-159.

[44] *The Diaries of George Price Boyce*, (ed.), Virginia Surtees (1980), p. 35.

[45] As above, entry for 28th July 1862, p. 35.

[46] Tincture of opium, to which she was addicted.

[47] W.M. Rossetti, *Dante Gabriel Rossetti, his Family-Letters, with a Memoir* (1895), vol. 1, pp. 227–229.

[48] Arthur's mother was Mary Ellen Peacock. She married Meredith in 1849 but left him in 1858 to live with the artist Henry Wallis (1830–1916). She died in 1861. Arthur was born in 1853, dying of tuberculosis in 1890.

[49] The circumstances are enlarged upon in Lionel Stevenson, (1953), pp. 224–225.

[50] The move to the Chelsea house took place on 24th and 25th October 1862.

[51] Letter from Rossetti to F.S., dated 28th December 1862, sent from Newcastle. HRC at U. of Texas, Austin.

[52] Letter from Meredith to Arthur dated 12th November (1862), sent from Copsham Cottage, Esher. C.L. Cline, (ed.) *The Collected Letters of George Meredith* (1970), no. 190.

[53] Manuscript contract between Clabburn and Sandys. Dated variously from Dec. 19th until Dec 25th 1863. Wilmington, Delaware Art Museum Library,

[54] London, RA Summer Exhibition, 1863, no. 606.

[55] London, RA Summer Exhibition, 1863, no. 707.

[56] Clabburn gave Rossetti a pair of peacocks in about 1863 or 1864. They were in his garden in the summer of 1864, according to Doughty. Oswald Doughty, *Dante Gabriel Rossetti: A Victorian Romantic.* (Frederick Muller, 1949) pp. 317–318.

[57] St Andrew's Hall, Norwich. *Norwich and Eastern Counties Working Classes Industrial Exhibition*, 14th August 1867, no. 827.

[58] Written *c.*1850–51, but first published in *Modern Love*, and *Poems of the English Roadside*, 1862.

[59] London, RA Summer Exhibition, 1865, no. 503.

[60] University of Glasgow Library. Correspondence of J. McN. Whistler. No. 09455.

[61] Isaac Bugg Coaks (*c.*1830-1909) of Fern Hill, Thorpe, was a creditor of Sandys, commissioning at least one family portrait drawing from Sandys, and possessing four other works by him. He must have had a hand in

the development of the hamlet of Thorpe, for four streets there were named after his daughters there: Ella, Marion, Florence, and Beatrice. He was a wealthy lawyer and had a connection with the Norwich Union insurance business.

[62] H.J. Clabburn, 'Some Relics of Rossetti' in *Pall Mall Budget*, 22nd January 1891, pp. 14-15. H.J.C. (W.H.C.'s son) wrote: 'Early in 1863 my father was introduced to Rossetti by Frederick Sandys. …' Also, letter from Burne Jones to Clabburn, dated 20th January 1863, saying that he hopes to see Clabburn and Sandys in the spring.

[63] C.L. Cline, (ed.), *The Owl and the Rossettis* (Pennsylvania State University Press, University Park, 1978), p. 147.

[64] George Meredith wrote to his Norwich friend Augustus Jessopp that he had encountered Sandys and Clabburn at one of Arthur Lewis's 'evenings'. Meredith to Jessopp, dated 'Monday night' (7th March 1864). Cline, (1970) no. 270.

[65] However, Clabburn later resold it (as he thought it was an unsatisfactory replica) either attributable to Charles Fairfax Murray or Howell. See Surtees (1971), no. 109, R.2, and Cline (1978), nos. 155, 159.

[66] S.M. Ellis, *George Meredith, His Life and Friends in Relation to His Work* (Grant Richards, London, 1919), pp. 224–225.

[67] Letter from Meredith to Jessopp, nd. (early 1864), *Letters of George Meredith, Collected by his Son*, vol. 1 (1844–1881), (1912) p. 136. This was published by his second son William Maxse Meredith (1865–1937).

[68] E.R. and J. Pennell, *The Whistler Journal* (1921), pp. 24–25.

[69] Letter from Meredith dated May 1864, to William Hardman (1828–1890). William Maxse Meredith (1912), p. 141.

[70] Letter from Meredith to Augustus Jessopp dated 18th May 1864. William Maxse Meredith (1912), pp. 143–144.

[71] Mrs George Meredith (1864), Mrs George Meredith and daughter (1872), Miss Meredith (1890), Miss Marie Meredith (1894–95).

[72] The wife of Sir Walter Palmer, MP, of the family of the Reading biscuit manufacturers, Huntley & Palmer. Sandys, through Meredith's friendship, also produced a pair of chalk portraits of the Palmers.

[73] *Once a Week*, vol. 6, 8th February 1862, p. 183.

[74] Illustrating the legend of Cleopatra, who invited Julius Caesar, Mark Antony and Pompey to a sumptuous feast, after which she dissolved a pearl in strong liquor and drank it, boasting that her draught was more valuable than the whole feast. This story originated in Pliny the Elder's *Naturalis Historia*, Book XXXV.

[75] *The Cornhill Magazine*, vol. 14, September 1866, p. 331.

[76] Letter from Whistler to F.S., nd. (1896, probably March or April). Washington, Library of Congress, Pennell Collection, LC1/469–472. For its content see Chap. 6, and note 801.

[77] Elizabeth and Joseph Pennell, *The Whistler Journal*, (1921), p. 171. Whistler and Sandys probably first

met in the summer of 1862.

[78] Alfred Munnings, *An Artist's Life* (1950), p. 65.

[79] W.M. Rossetti (ed.), *Dante Gabriel Rossetti: His Family Letters with a Memoir* (1895), p. 242.

[80] The date of her baptism was 31st March 1841 at St Peter's Church, Wisbech. At this date Ozray is described as a 'tinker'. For most of this biographical information I am much indebted to Sharon Heppell, editor of the Romany and Traveller Family History Society, who has generously shared her research with me.

[81] Ozray Gray was a well-known harpist and fiddle player in the gypsy community, according to *Anglo-Romany Gleanings from East Anglian Gypsies* by T.W. Thompson, in *The Journal of the Gypsy Lore Society*, vol. 8, no. 3, Third Series (1929), pp. 116–117. Four of his sons became musicians, and Keomi his daughter was also described as a 'travelling musician' in the 1871 census. It should be noted that the spelling of gypsy names can vary through illiteracy. When transcribed they were written down according to the best ability of the transcriber.

[82] The census of 1871 finds 'Keona Gray' and four of her children by Sandys, stated as aged 8, 6, 3 and 1, living in tents on Thorpe Common, with her parents and four brothers and sisters, as 'travelling musicians'.

[83] C.L. Cline (ed.), *The Owl and the Rossettis*, (1978). Letter 273.

[84] Roberts used a common euphemism for a 'fallen woman'.

[85] Herbert Henry Roberts, *Memories of Four-Score Years* (1920), pp. 61–62.

[86] In a letter dated 15th July 1908 from her daughter Winifred to the American collector Samuel Bancroft Jr, Winifred wrote, '… the *Proud Maisie*, the *Mary Magdalene* and the *May Margaret* were all done from my Mother. She is very happy to think you admire them so'. Delaware Art Museum Library, Bancroft Archive. The family undoubtedly had never seen or were not aware of the earlier *Mary Magdalene* (*c.*1859) which had been bought early on by Rose for his collection and was owned by him at his death in 1891. Bancroft bought it in 1894.

[87] From 1872 to 1874, Sandys wrote letters from 4 Queen's Road, St Catherine's Plain, which adjoins Bracondale.

[88] This comes from a review by Horace Tuck of an exhibition of Sandys's work at the Castle Museum, Norwich, in the *Eastern Daily Press*, 22nd January 1944. Bosworth Harcourt (1836–1914), by profession a dentist, was closely involved with the musical and theatrical life of Norwich and had a reputation as a Shakespearean expert.

[89] Public Records. Death certificate of Maura Neville, who died 24th December 1868 in Millwall, East London, at the house of a baby-minder.

[90] The marriage was at St James's, Norland Square; her elder sister Augusta was present.

[91] The elder Robson (1821–1864) popularised the song *Vilikins and his Dinah*, and played Jem Baggs in the *Wandering Minstrel* and the *Yellow Dwarf* (Robson was extremely short) in the play of that name. I am

indebted to the late Mollie Sands for information about the Robsons through correspondence in 1984 and from her book, *Robson of the Olympic*, (1979).

[92] A 'Miss Eyre Robson', on the stage in the 1890s, was most probably their only daughter.

[93] Milly is the figure on the right.

[94] Ann Maria evidently preferred to use the name Augusta, also being known as Gussie.

[95] Arthur Dampier May, a genre and portrait painter, fl. 1872–1900.

[96] He described himself as an architect on Augusta's death certificate in 1902. See Max Donnelly, 'Daniel Cottier, Pioneer of Aestheticism' in *Decorative Arts Society Journal*, 23, (1999), p. 40.

[97] Letter from du Maurier to Armstrong dated 11th October (1863). Daphne du Maurier, *The Young George du Maurier*, (1951), p. 216.

[98] W.M. Rossetti, *Some Reminiscences*, (1906), p. 276.

[99] On the exhibition's closure, a large proportion of the Japanese exhibits were bought by Farmer & Rogers' 'Great Shawl and Cloak Emporium' in Regent Street, who then opened an 'Oriental Warehouse' next to their main shop. This was the start of Arthur Lasenby Liberty's famed career, when he was deputed from the main firm to work in the new department. In 1864, aged 21, he became its manager.

[100] United Kingdom. Civil Divorce Records (1858–1911), via Ancestry.co.uk.

[101] After the passing of the Divorce Act of 1857, it was possible for the first time to obtain a divorce in a court of law instead of, as before, having to obtain a private Act of Parliament (at considerable expense), which took it beyond the reach of all but a few. I am greatly indebted to Robin Hopkins for explaining to me the legal proceedings in the records of this case.

[102] Washington, Library of Congress, Pennell-Whistler papers, box 23.

[103] The Diaries of George Price Boyce, (ed.) Virginia Surtees (1980). Diary entry of 7th February 1864, p. 39.

[104] According to Otto von Schleinitz in his 1907 biography of Holman Hunt (p. 70), the details which he completed were of her jewellery. I am grateful to Judith Bronkhurst for help with the translation.

[105] George and Edward Dalziel, *The Brothers Dalziel, A Record of Fifty Years' Work,* (1901), p. 258.

[106] C.L. Cline, vol.1 (1970) p. 263, no. 287 . Letter from Meredith to Jessopp, 6th June 1864, Cline, no. 287.

[107] C.L. Cline, idem. (1970) p. 264, no. 288, note 1. Letter from Meredith to Frederick Maxse.

[108] Marie Vulliamy (1840–1885), George Meredith's second wife, was the youngest daughter of Justin Theodore Vulliamy (1787–1870). Their children were William Maxse Meredith (1865–1937) and Marie Eveleen (1871–1933).

[109] *The Cornhill Magazine*, September 1866, p. 331.

[110] *The Times*, 5th July 1904.

[111] Founded by Philip Astley (1742–1814), his Amphitheatre is considered to be the ancestor of the circus ring and was designed for live equestrian displays. It was approximately on the site of St Thomas's Hospital.

[112] Letter from Rossetti to James Anderson Rose dated 17th October 1864. The first night of *Mazeppa* was on 3rd October.

[113] This spectacle, based on a narrative poem (published 1819) by Lord Byron, was adapted first in 1831 for the London stage. The part of *Mazeppa* (actually a man in the original Ukrainian legend on which the poem was based) was first played by a woman in 1859. Adah Menken had played it in the USA before appearing at Astley's Amphitheatre in London.

[114] Richard Francis Burton (1821-1890). Explorer and writer.

[115] Bernard Falk, *The Naked Lady*, (1934), p. 125.

[116] The hotel was across the Thames from Astley's.

[117] Renamed South Parade in 1912.

[118] W.H. Clabburn, deceased, Spelman's, Norwich, sale 25th November 1889, lot 151, *The Death of St Francis* (12 x 7 in.)

[119] Originally founded in Arundel Street in 1859 and moved to Salisbury Street in 1861.

[120] Letter from F.S. to Samuel Lucas dated 'Wednesday' from 8 Victoria Road, Kensington. This must date from after 27th July 1864 (when he was proposed by Frederick Maxse), and before 18th February 1865 (when he was elected). Ian Hodgkins, Catalogue no. 79 (Winter-Spring 1995), item 340.

[121] Garrick Club records. His membership was still active in 1875.

[122] Frederick Lee Bridell (1830–1863). His wife Eliza (1823–1903) exhibited portraits and figure subjects at the RA, 1859–1871.

[123] Letter from F.S. to Samuel Lucas, dated Wednesday (early 1865). Ian Hodgkins, Catalogue no. 79 (Winter-Spring 1995). No. 340.

[124] Letter from F.S. to James Anderson Rose, as above. Washington, Library of Congress, Manuscripts Division, Pennell Collection.

[125] Letter from F.S. to James Anderson Rose, as above. Washington, Library of Congress, Manuscripts Division, Pennell Collection.

[126] Letter from Holman Hunt to F.S., from Tor Villa, dated 7th June 1866. San Marino, California, Henry E. Huntington Library, HM. 12968.

[127] H. Allingham and D. Radford, (eds.) *William Allingham, A Diary* (1907), p. 139, 31 July 1866.

[128] Letter from Rossetti to his mother, written in Tenterden, dated Friday night (12th October 1866). *Dante Gabriel Rossetti. His Family Letters, with a Memoir by William Michael Rossetti* (1895), vol. 2, pp. 189-192. The topiary chair did not survive for long after its transplanting in Chelsea.

[129] Letter from F.S. to James Anderson Rose, dated by Rose to 1st November 1866. Washington, Library of Congress, Manuscript Division, Pennell Collection.

[130] Two bills dated 21st December

1866, one for £59 and the other, £57.10.0 (the latter cancelled) in which Howell is to pay 'after sale' of an un-named item, have been preserved by Charles Fairfax Murray. Howell papers. Manchester, John Rylands University Library, Eng. Ms.1279/164, 165.

[131] Sandys had used this drawing, dating from the late 1850s, in his illustration *Life's Journey* of 1861.

[132] Letter from Rossetti to Howell dated 21st November 1866. University of Texas at Austin, HRC.

[133] Helen Rossetti Angeli, *Pre-Raphaelite Twilight. The Story of Charles Howell*, (1954), p. 155. Mrs Angeli was the daughter of William Michael Rossetti.

[134] Ruskin's nickname for Howell.

[135] Death registration at Poplar, Middlesex, on 5th January 1869 (no. 496). General Register Office.

[136] Brompton Cemetery Records (Department of National Heritage). The plot, termed as a 'private grove', and marked as 'AJ' on the cemetery map, is located at the south end of the cemetery, nearest the Fulham Road entrance. However, when the author visited the plot several years ago, there was nothing to be seen of any marker.

[137] Perhaps an upset kettle full of scalding water.

[138] 1871 Census report, and information from the Local History Librarian, Tower Hamlets, Local History Archive.

[139] Curiously, Jeckell changed the spelling of his name to Jeckyll, adding the 'y', as Sandys did to his own name.

[140] Letter from F.S. to J.J. Colman from 16 Cheyne Walk, dated 4th February 1867. Colman Papers, Norfolk Record Office.

[141] Sandys's elaborate drawing of *Judith and Holofernes* (Keomi was the model) was shown at the RA in 1864 and was bought by James Anderson Rose. His oil of *Judith*, which one could hardly describe as ambitious was also of about that date.

[142] William Michael Rossetti, (ed.), *Rossetti Papers 1862–1870* (1903), pp. 224–225.

[143] Roberson Records. University of Cambridge, Hamilton Kerr Institute.

[144] This undated letter was dated by Rose to 14th May 1867. Pennell Papers, Manuscripts Division, Library of Congress, Washington DC. Roberson was the supplier of artists' materials.

[145] Letter from Clabburn to Rose, dated 20th June 1867. Washington, Library of Congress, Manuscript Division, Pennell Papers. Presumably 'the Children' referred to the oil *At Vespers*, which remains unfinished.

[146] Undated letters from Sandys to Rose, dated by Rose to 14th May 1867, 1st June 1867, and (undated) July 1867. Washington, Library of Congress, as above.

[147] Letter dated 8th July 1867, from Rossetti to F.S. University of Texas at Austin, Harry Ransom Center.

[148] Helen R. Angeli, *Dante Gabriel Rossetti*, (1949), p. 35 (quoting from William Rossetti's diary).

[149] Letter from Rossetti to F.S. dated Friday 27th December 1867. University of Texas at Austin,

HRC. Solferino's restaurant was part of the Hotel de Solferino at 7-8 Rupert Street. It seems to have been a favourite resort of Swinburne, Sandys, Godwin, W.G. Wills, and their friends in the late 1860s to the late 1870s.

[150] The publisher Edward Moxon eventually declined publishing *Poems and Ballads* as too controversial. Hotten was a publisher who would take on anything which would sell well, but some of Swinburne's sado-masochistic effusions might have been problematic.

[151] Letter from Winifred Sandys to Samuel Bancroft Jr dated 4th August 1911. Bancroft Archive, Library, Wilmington, Delaware, USA.

[152] These must have been studies for illustrations, of which Clabburn had many in his collection.

[153] Letter from F.S. to Rose dated Monday 6th January 1868, added by Rose. Washington, Library of Congress, Manuscript Division, Pennell Collection.

[154] William Michael Rossetti, (ed.), *Rossetti Papers 1862–1870* (1903). William Rossetti's diary, 1868, p. 306.

[155] William Michael Rossetti (1903), pp. 306–307. We know from a letter from Sala to D.G. Rossetti, dated 15th May 1868, that he was painting at his studio in Leicester Square (information from the late Dr W.E. Fredeman).

[156] *Notes on the Royal Academy Exhibition, 1868. Part I*, by William Michael Rossetti; Part II, by C. Algernon Swinburne, (J.C Hotten 1868).

[157] Letter from F.S. to Rossetti, dated Thursday (*c.* November 1868) as from 47 Leicester Square. Special Collections, University of British Columbia Library.

[158] Brompton Cemetery Records (Department of National Heritage), on the purchase of a burial plot for the interment of Maura Neville.

[159] Alfred Bate Richards (1820-1876), originally a lawyer, was a journalist (he was the first editor of the *Daily Telegraph*), dramatist, and one of the founders of the military Volunteer Movement in 1859.

[160] *Once a Week*. vol, 1, series 2, 28th April 1866, pp. 454-455.

[161] Letter from George Augustus Sala to Sandys, dated Saturday (early March 1869). Manchester, John Rylands University Library. Eng. Ms.1279/160.

[162] W.M. Rossetti, *Rossetti Papers* (1903), p. 385. Rossetti's diary entry for 6th March 1869. Letter from D.G. Rossetti to Alice Boyd, dated Tuesday (March 1869). Doughty and Wahl, (eds.), *The Letters of Dante Gabriel Rossetti*, 1965, 822. Alice Boyd had sent some information leaflets to Gabriel Rossetti, and he replied that, of the cures described, he thought that sulphur baths would be the more affordable option.

[163] C.L. Cline, (ed.), *The Owl and the Rossettis* (1978). Letter 99.

[164] Letter from D.G. Rossetti to F.S. dated 10th May 1869 from 16 Cheyne Walk. University of Texas, Austin, HRC.

[165] Rossetti's *Lucretia Borgia*: Original watercolour begun 1860–61, figure repainted 1868. Tate Britain.

Replica watercolour started by Charles Fairfax Murray, 1871. Fogg Art Museum, Harvard University. Winthrop Bequest.

[166] Letter from F.S. to D.G. Rossetti, dated Saturday May 15th, 1869. Vancouver, University of British Columbia Library, Special Collections.

[167] See Maas Gallery, *Pre-Raphaelitism*, Spring 2013, no. 4, *Study for Girl with Doves*.

[168] The visit would have been in 1868. Letter of 15th May 1869 from Sandys to Rossetti. University of British Columbia Library, Special Collections. Sandys never bothered with punctuation. He wrote as he spoke. Where a pause was needed, he used a dash. I have added punctuation where I have thought it necessary.

[169] William Michael Rossetti gave Sandys some credit when he wrote in his diary (27th May 1869) that, in the case of *Lucretia Borgia*, Sandys's version 'cannot be called a plagiarism', but in general he thought there was some truth in his brother's accusation of plagiarisation but he was not sure if Sandys was plagiarising consciously or unconsciously. W.M. Rosetti, *Rossetti Papers* (1903), p. 394.

[170] For instance, in Whistler's oil of *c.*1868, *Variations in Blue and Green* (one of his 'Six Projects'), is featured a woman in the same pose as in Sandys's illustration *The Advent of Winter* (1865). Whistler used this pose again in his chalk *Annabel Lee* (1885–1887). New York, Freer Gallery of Art.

[171] Letter from F.S. to D.G. Rossetti. Dated Saturday 15th May 1869, from 47 Leicester Square. Vancouver, University of British Columbia Library, Special Collections.

[172] Edward Burne-Jones, *Merlin and Nimue*, watercolour and body colour (1861), V&A Museum, no. 257-1896.

[173] They even lent each other these expensive accessories.

[174] The squabble continued and can be followed in the published literature. Doughty and Wahl, (eds.) *The Letters of Dante Gabriel Rossetti* (1965), vol. 2, pp. 697–699. Also, *Rossetti Papers* (1903), p. 395.

[175] Jonathan Peel, MA, JP (1806–1885) was Deputy Lieutenant of Lancashire. He was the great grandson of Robert 'Parsley' Peel (1723–1795), the founder of the cotton manufacture and printing industry in Lancashire.

[176] Letters (in sequence) from F.S. to Rossetti were from Leicester Square, 15th May 1869, but he was no longer there on the 25th; F.S. to Rossetti from Knowlmere, undated; F.S. to William Rossetti from Knowlmere, 2nd June, indicating that he would be at Knowlmere until 9th June. Vancouver, University of British Columbia Library, Special Collections.

[177] Letter from Walter M. Peel to the author, 15th January 1984.

[178] Correspondence between the elderly daughter of Marianne Shingles (Miss Mary Warren) and the author, October 1977 to September 1978.

opposite: *Penelope*. detail. see page 156

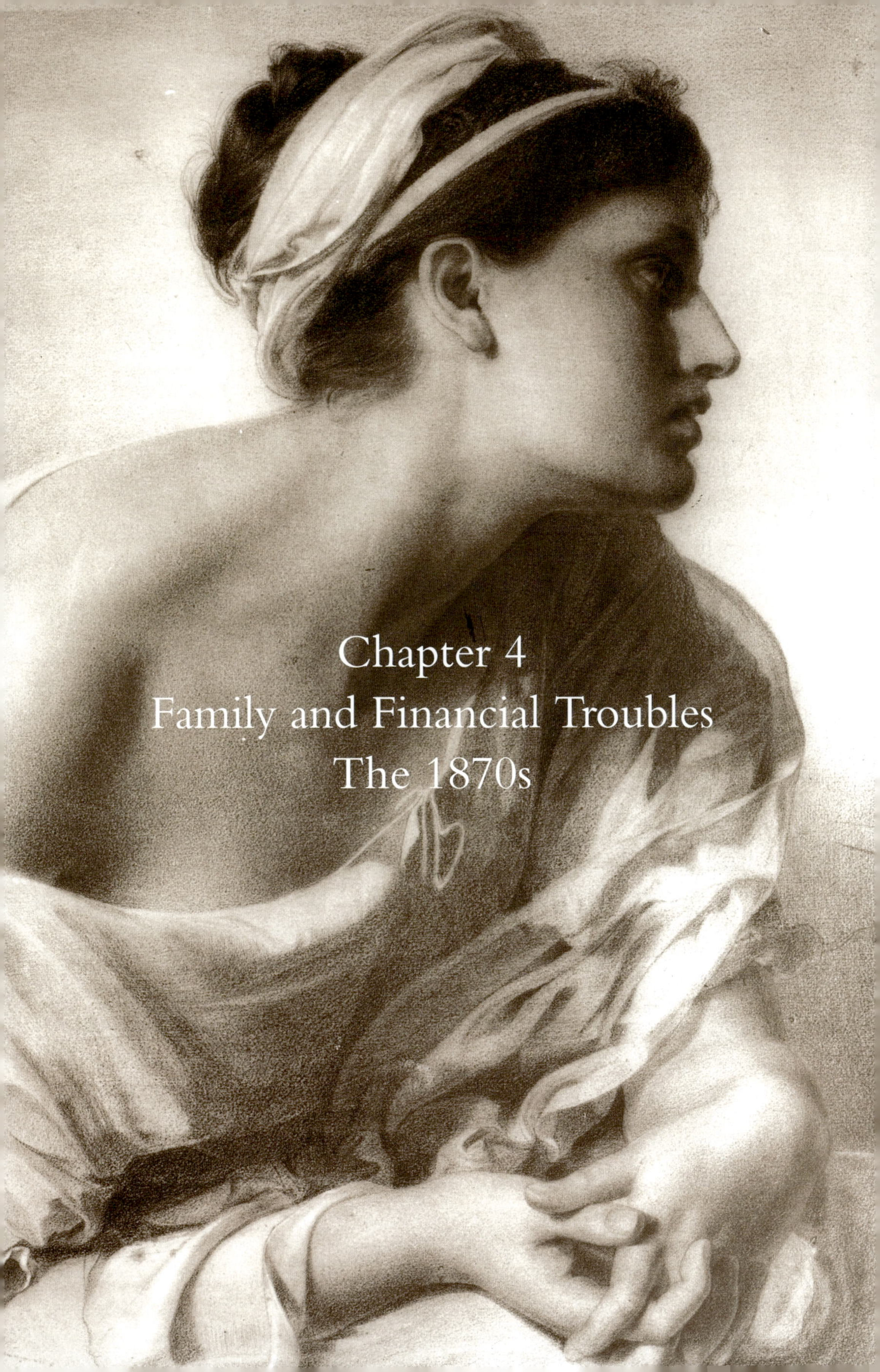

Chapter 4
Family and Financial Troubles
The 1870s

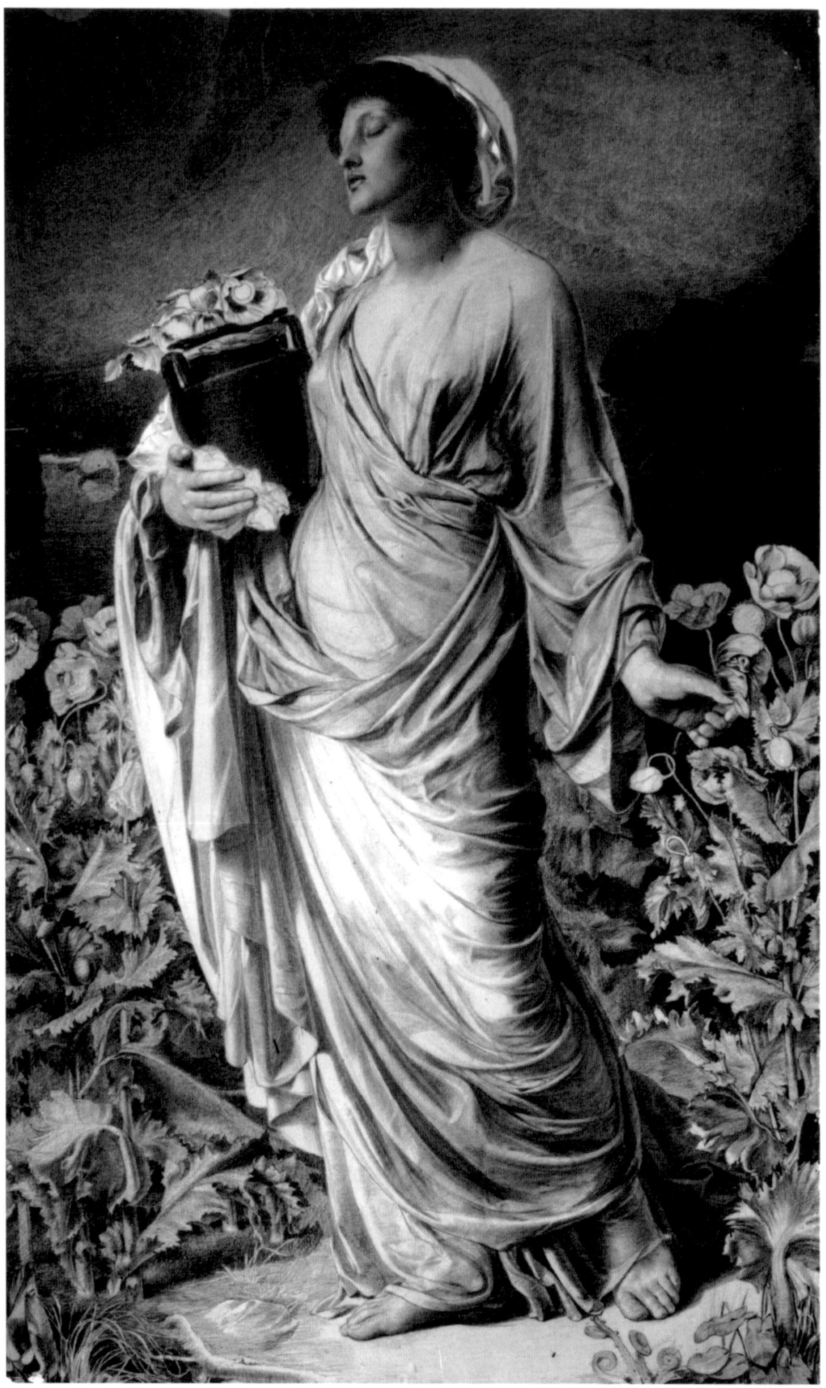

Lethe. Chalk drawing. 1870-1874. The model was Emma Sandys (1843-1877), the artist's sister. The plant studies were made at Fairlight, near Hastings.

Presumably, Mary Emma Jones ('Mrs Neville') had recovered from the birth, in 1869, of Cissily (Cecilia) to be able to work again in December, when 'Miss Clive' (her stage name) had an engagement for a minor part in the farce *Lover by Proxy* at the Queen's Theatre, Long Acre. She was still playing this role in February 1870.[1] In January and February of 1870, 'Miss Clive' was joined by her sister Emelie Eyre Jones (known as Miss Jones) in minor parts in *Twixt Axe and Crown* at the same theatre, and again from April to June, and in August. Mary was evidently known to Sandys's intimates as his established mistress at least by 1869.[2]

Another daughter, Dorothy, was born in 1870. Since the death in 1868 of their (presumed) first born Maura, Cissily and Dorothy were the eldest surviving children of the new relationship between Sandys and Mary Emma Jones. They too were sent to Poplar, to be looked after by Edward and Elizabeth Smith, where they were recorded in the 1871 census.

A family secret, apparently not known to their younger children, and certainly not known to their grandson Anthony Crane, unravelled when the author was able to search into Sandys's 1876 bankruptcy in the Pennell-Whistler Collection at the Library of Congress in Washington DC. This collection contains the papers of James Anderson Rose (who served as solicitor to both Whistler and Sandys). Contained within are the bankruptcy papers of Sandys, which reveal that he owed T.J.M. McManus, a builder, of 29 Upper Phillimore Place, Kensington, for '2 Years (of) Board and lodgings for (2) children, Wardrobes & education' amounting to £250 in 1876.[3] After babyhood in Poplar, they must have been moved to the McManus household in Kensington, where the family seem to have been willing to take responsibility for the two little sisters.

In 1980 I corresponded with, and later visited, Peter Eaton, the bookseller, who had at that time owned several Sandys items. In his words to me: 'I bought this (a replica by Sandys of his drawing *Proud Maisie*) about 1953–54 from a house near Hammersmith Broadway. It was one of three streets which all look very much alike, but I could probably still point it out. The old lady I bought it from sold me books belonging to Frederick Sandys, which I have since sold, but I can remember some drawings. I believe she was a family connection of the Sandys's.'[4] After I reported this to Anthony Crane, he recalled 'the McManuses were never specifically labelled as any particular relations – they merely appeared, as I remember them as a child, to have something approaching "family status"'. He also remembered them as spinster-like and dressed in black, and older than his aunts Connie and Ruth. Assembling all these clues made it clear that the ladies were in fact also

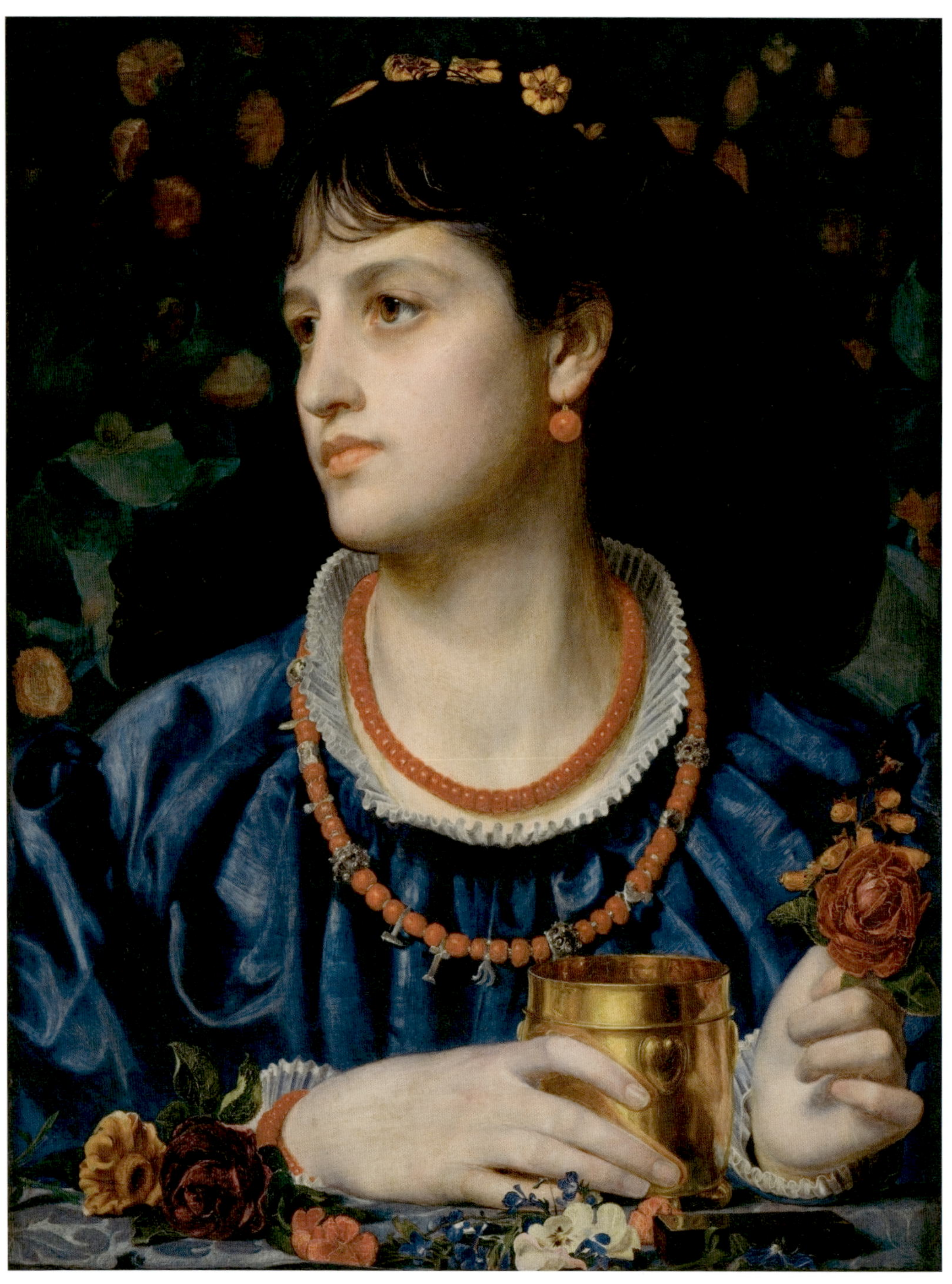

Ysoude with the Love Philtre. Oil on panel, 1870. *The Blue Picture,* painted at Norwich while staying with William Clabburn.

Anthony's aunts, and were the unacknowledged eldest surviving children of his grandfather and grandmother: Frederick Sandys and Mary Emma Jones. Further research in public records revealed that a few years earlier, prior to the 1876 bankruptcy, in 1871, 'Cissily Neville' and 'Dorothy Neville' were being cared for by a baby-minder in Poplar.[5] This was at the same address where the one-year-old Maura Neville had died of an accidental scalding on Christmas Eve in 1868.[6]

Verifying Peter Eaton's memory of his 1954 visit and acquisitions, the 1901 and the 1911 census reports indeed reveal that both Cecilia and Dorothy McManus lived at 'South Hammersmith, including Starch Green'. Cecilia died in 1937 and Dorothy lived on until 1955, leaving £1,748 worth of effects to Mary Frances Morris, a spinster. Her address had been 5 Caithness Road, Brook Green. Evidently, she and her sister had been comfortably supported by James McManus who seems to have, possibly unofficially, adopted the two sisters, probably having accepted that Sandys was unable to support them.

While the Jones sisters were in London, Sandys was away at Hastings in Sussex making studies from nature in nearby Fairlight. He needed something for the background of *Fading Light* which '[he was] about to paint … and to put it on a block for Sala – for twenty guineas'. This title has not been identified, but the drawings he made were used in *Lethe* (1870–1874),[7] and *Fate*, or *The Tangled Skein* (begun about 1870, finished after 1890), which he must have started at this time. Once there, he was appealing in the most desperately worded letters to Charles Howell, by now his agent and intimate friend, to send him money, as he had 'exhausted [his] supply' and later, needing to pay his landlady and return to London since his 'absence has been construed into a desire to keep away…'. One might hazard a guess from this that 'Mrs Neville' was also short of funds and burdened with domestic cares. From the gist of his letters, it seems that Sandys was not merely making landscape studies but had a picture[8] down in Hastings which he was working on – although, a few days later, he wrote: 'My drawing is a good one and I have too much work and trouble to be ever repaid for it – one hundred pounds would not pay my time alone.'[9]

A still unsolved mystery is the fate of the oil portrait that he made some time in late 1870 of Jane, the wife of William Morris, known only through its sale by auction in 1935.[10] The catalogue describes her as wearing a white embroidered dress and a pearl rope. Immediately comes to mind Edmund Gosse's recollection of his first meeting with Swinburne (whose biography he was writing) and his first sight of Jane Morris at an evening party held at the home of the Ford Madox Browns in Fitzroy Square 'towards the end of

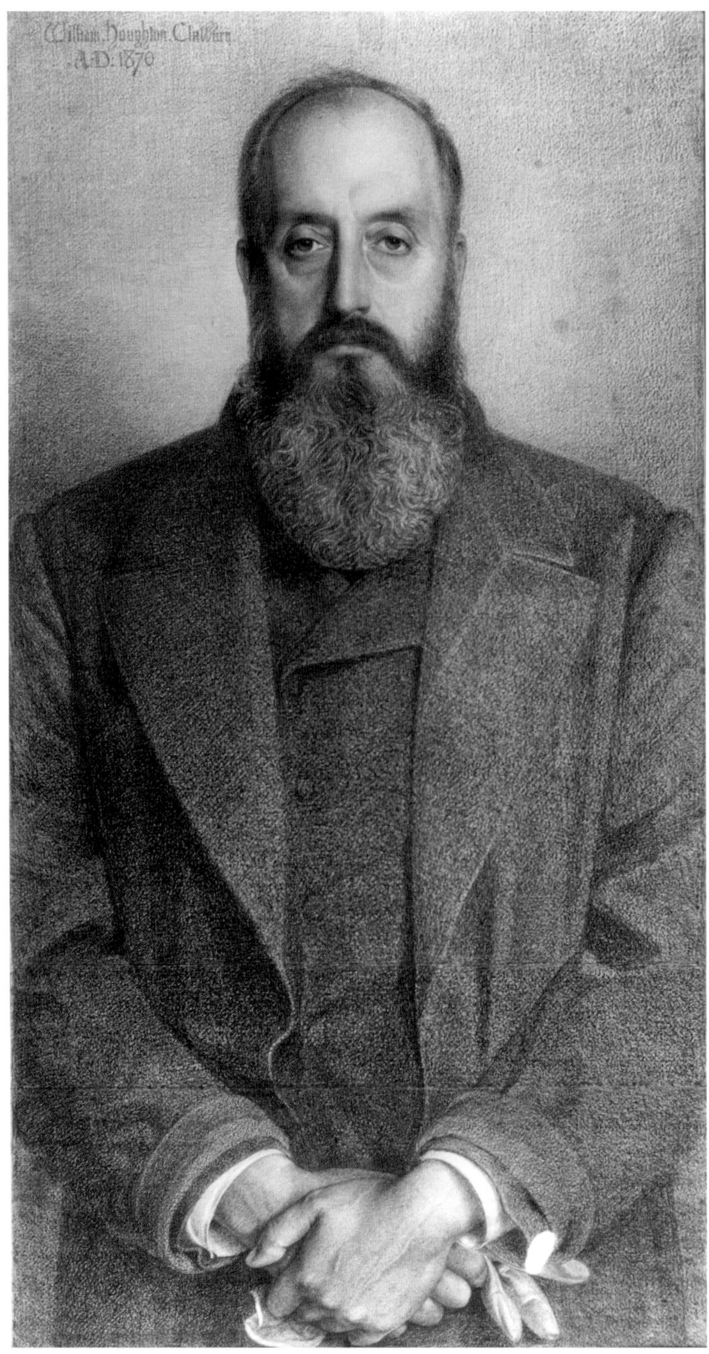

William Clabburn (1820–1889). Chalk drawing. 1870. An important Norwich patron for whom Sandys drew and painted portraits of his family and embarked upon two unique landscape pictures, *Autumn*, and *Spring*.

December 1870 or the beginning of January 1871'. He described her: 'Mrs William Morris, in her ripest beauty, and dressed in a long unfashionable gown of ivory velvet, occupied the painting throne …' (and Rossetti was sitting on a hassock at her feet).[11] This was at the time of Rossetti's infatuation with Jane Morris.

After these events, Sandys was to be found in Norwich or, more precisely, at the Clabburn villa at Thorpe, where he seems to have been based until about May 1872, probably living as a guest of the family. No doubt his living expenses were insupportable in London. The Clabburns were hospitable, and Sandys relayed an invitation to Howell 'for a sail – and some business'. Clabburn, having experienced a recent financial setback, wished to sell some pictures from his collection, including *Medea*.[12]

There were occasional brief visits to London and elsewhere to exhibit or to carry out portrait commissions. For instance, he showed a painting at the 1871 London International Exhibition, the catalogue giving his address as 'North End Grove, Fulham' which was Howell's current address.[13] At Thorpe he was working on his picture *Ysoude with the Love Philtre* from a local model, as well as a portrait of Clabburn, and portraits of Clabburn's sons Walter and Henry. He wrote to Howell in October, saying that he was about to finish the painting *Ysoude* and planned to send it to him 'in time for Friday' for exhibition with *Perdita* (which Howell had just sold to Philip Henry Rathbone of Liverpool) at the Dudley Gallery.[14] He continued: 'I intend to remain here till I have the money to come back and paint uninterruptedly. Of course, I must come to town for reasons you may guess in about a fortnight for ten days or so – and if you hear of any place where I could paint for that time I should be tremendously glad. Every day is important to me and I must come inconvenient as it is for the sake of the dear little girl.' The needs of the latter probably were occasioned by the imminent birth of Dorothy, who was born at Brompton in 1870.[15] He thanked Howell for attending to his overdue rent to Puttick and Simpson for the Leicester Square studio.[16] On 13th October he sent *Ysoude with the Love Philtre* to Foord & Dickinson's, the framers, and wrote to Howell that he thought it 'very striking, altogether a picture to "hit up" the picture buying public. The price ought to be £250 or £300 at least'.[17] Further letters to Howell in November from Sunny Hill show his intense frustration with Howell's lack of response to his entreaties for money. He owed £50 to an unnamed person and £60 to the landlord (Simpson of Puttick & Simpson) of the Leicester Square studio, who had served him with a writ. Evidently Howell had not attended to this, after all.[18]

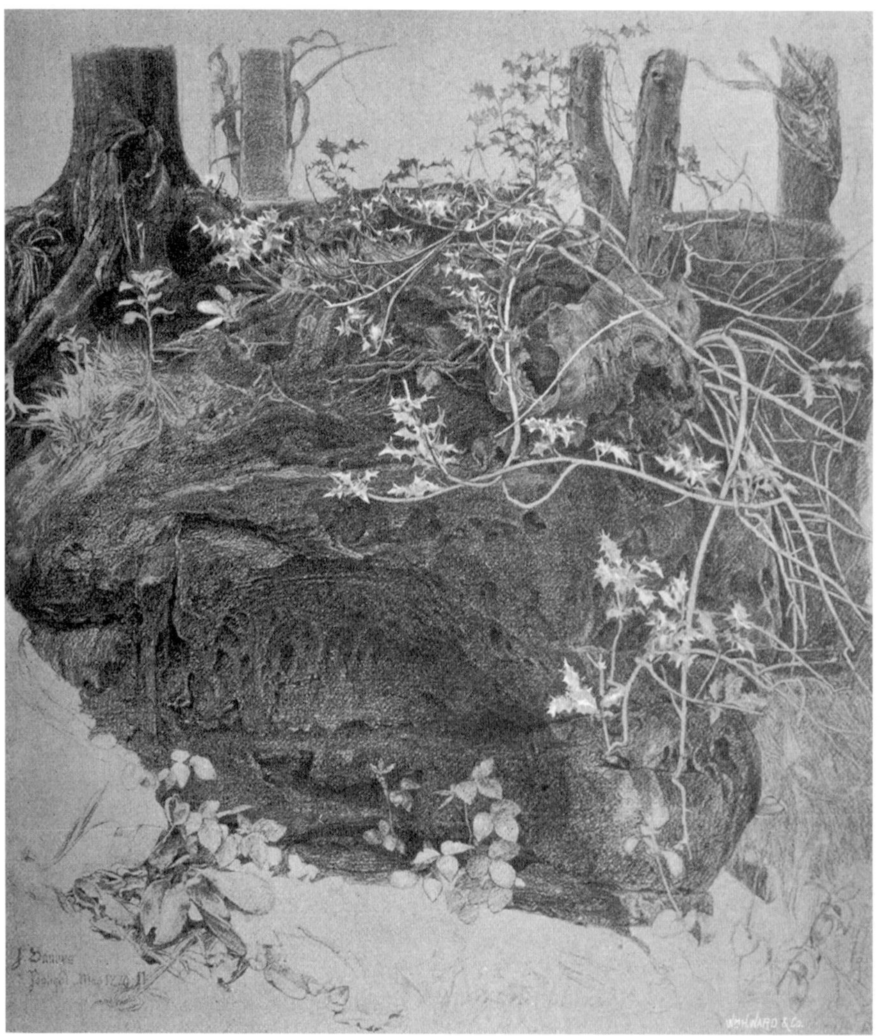

Study of undergrowth made at Fairlight, Sussex. Chalk drawing. May 1870 (from *The Artist* Special Winter Number, vol. xviii, November 1896).

He sent Howell a telegram entreating him to go to 'Mrs Neville' immediately and 'get her a hundred on account if you can' as he wanted her to come to Norwich.[19] Evidently Howell complied, for in November Sandys wrote to him saying that the 'little girl' had arrived in Norwich (supposedly his family already knew her). Probably at this time he took a house at 4 Queen's Road, St Catherine's Plain (where he is recorded as living from 1872 to 1874) because in a later letter to Howell he states that he has to pay a rent of £53 besides having another debt of £50. He was also appealing to Howell to send him some apple green velvet: 'a piece of rich old Genoa with a good pattern'[20] for a background to the Clabburn portrait. Evidently, he did not use it, perhaps because it never came. Sandys seems to have been entirely dependent on Howell's support as agent and factotum, but Howell was not responding to all his demands. For example, Sandys wrote: 'I have been in the most awful suspense and in a terrible fix through your silence … I am in fearful want of money instantly. I have had nothing since the little girl came down' and, later, 'I must have the money to send to my sister so she may get home by Xmas.'[21]

The 'little girl' gave birth to their next daughter, Winifred, in Norwich in January 1871, which we know from the 1891 census. She became the eldest acknowledged child of Sandys and Mary Emma Jones.

Writing to Howell, Sandys was fulsome in his praise for their mutual friend Rossetti: 'I read Gabriel's last thing in the *Fortnightly* – how splendid it is. Upon my soul it is the finest piece of writing and the finest and noblest thought I have ever read. He is indeed a mighty fellow.'[22] However, Sandys's distraction seems to have been total at this time, and his old friend Meredith was writing to their mutual friend the Rev. Augustus Jessopp in Norwich: 'Have you seen Sandys? He will not answer my letters.'[23]

On the positive side, there were several achievements in 1870: The double portrait of another pair of Jeremiah James Colman's children, executed in December, which he showed at the Royal Academy in 1871, together with the portraits of Clabburn and his son Walter. The oil *Hero*, and its chalk version, drawn from the Norwich model Marianne Shingles, must have been completed before April 1871 when the oil painting was handed over as security for a loan from a Knightsbridge jeweller named Shout.[24] Later in July he 'sold it' to Shout, who then cancelled his debt.[25]

Sandys had wished to show the portrait of Clabburn at the International Exhibition at South Kensington in 1871, though it was not accepted.[26] There was still time, however, to submit it to the Royal Academy Summer

Exhibition. Sandys showed it at Graves' gallery prior to this and wrote to William Rossetti (in his capacity as an art critic) to ask him to look at the portrait, which he believed was 'an advance upon anything I have done'. Thanking him later for his 'long account [of it]' in his review, he gave an excuse for the painting of the surface of the coat which Rossetti had criticised: 'The coat was unfortunately painted in a great hurry and on a day when I was full of trouble for me even …', and ended the letter by writing that he had hoped to submit a painting, *Penelope*, to the Academy, but could not finish it in time.[27] Next, he appealed to Howell to find out if it had been accepted: 'Watts or Leighton – or any of these mighty swells could tell. It is so important it should be accepted and above all in a good place – no such luck I am afraid.'[28] Fortunately it was accepted, as well as the portrait of Walter Clabburn, and the portrait of the two Colman children. Tellingly, he was concerned to hear Watts's opinion of the W.H. Clabburn oil,[29] because, uniquely amongst Sandys's portrait paintings, this one comes close to one of Watts's frontal portraits like that of Alfred Tennyson (of *c.*1863–64).[30]

Eighteen seventy-one was a productive year. He was commissioned to paint a full-length portrait of the MP for Norwich, *Jacob Henry Tillett*, resulting from a subscription raised by the citizens of Norwich. It hangs today in St Andrew's Hall, part of the historic collection known as the *Civic Portraits*. Although finely composed, it suffers from the unsuitability of Sandys's flat glazing technique in large canvases where, as in this case, there are extensive areas of black gentleman's suiting and empty areas of gloomy and indistinct background – dull in effect and worsened by the ageing of the paint layers. The oil portrait alone earned him £800 which ought to have put Sandys's finances in order. There was also income to come from the preliminary chalk drawing of Tillett, and another of Tillet's wife, Jane Elizabeth.

It is my belief that his 1871 landscape subject *Breydon Water* must have been a commission, as it is untypical of his work. Although it is far from being as stunning as his few early landscapes such as *Autumn* and *Whitlingham*, it is an interesting, atmospheric picture showing a change in style from his early Cotman-inspired landscapes. Noticeable, too, is that out of his four known landscapes in oil, including the early ones, all have vivid skies, either at dawn or sunset. Edward Trafford of Wroxham Hall was certainly the first owner of the (preliminary) drawing for *Breydon Water* which is dated September 1871. It was shown at the Dudley Gallery in June 1875 and elicited high praise from William Rossetti, writing for *The Academy*: '… one of the really fine things in the gallery; a simple and beautiful drawing of a flat shore and its buildings.'[31] One has to agree that Sandys had handled a difficult subject well in an accurate and uncompromising way. An oil version followed, probably first owned by

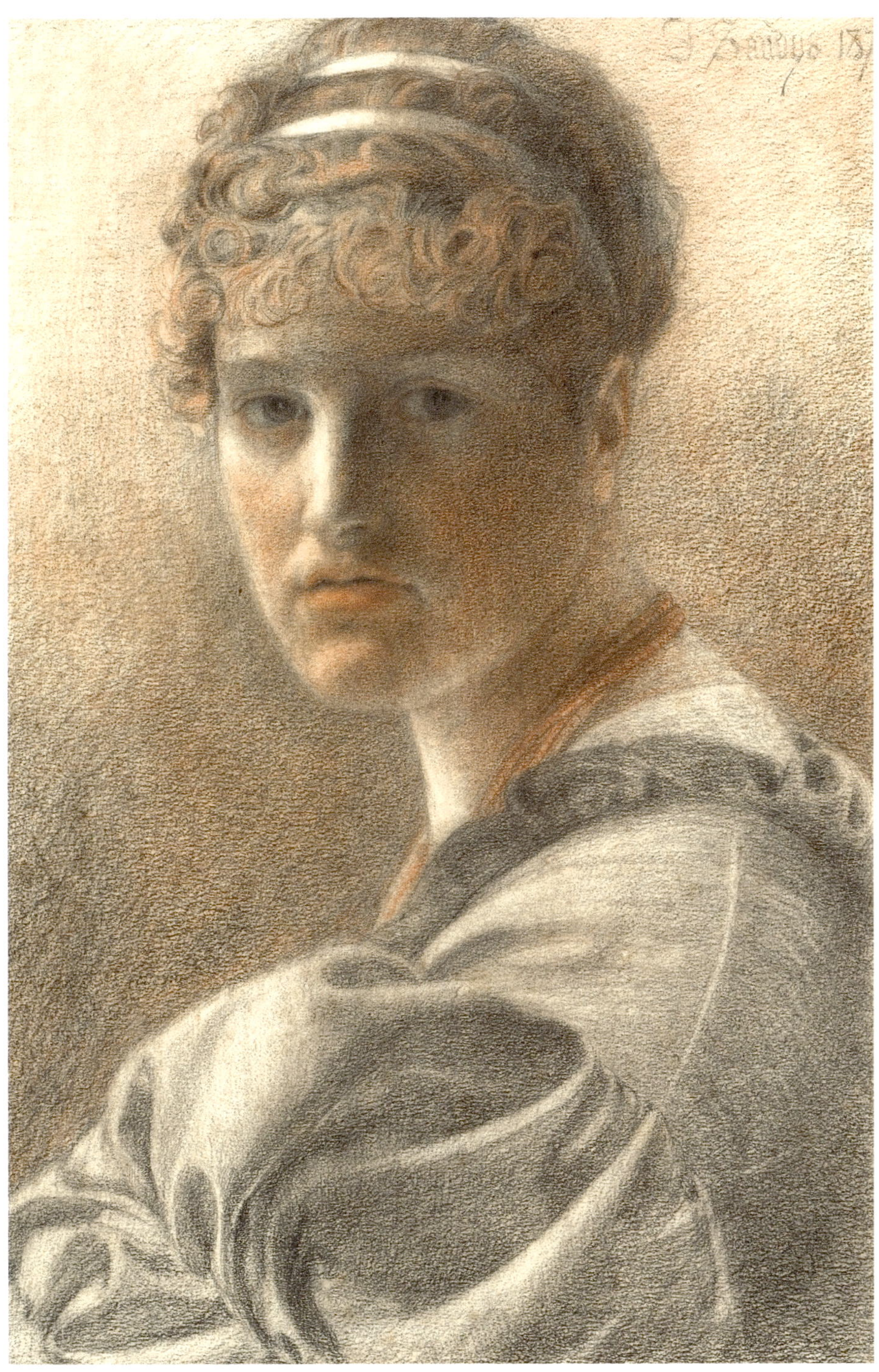

Reflection. Chalk drawing. 1871. Mary Emma Jones. An innovative drawing on textured paper.

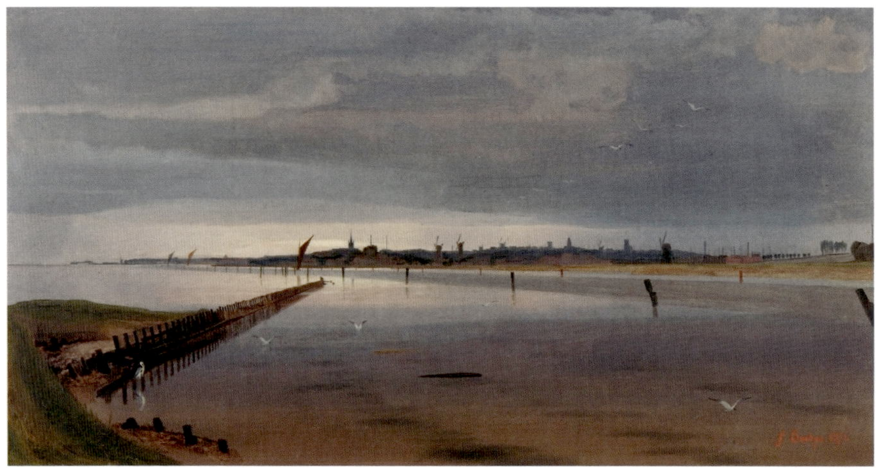

Breydon Water with Yarmouth in the distance. Oil on board. 1871. A panoramic view of a very flat landscape with the familiar Yarmouth landmarks outlined in the distance. A rare landscape in Sandys's oeuvre.

Canon Edward Bulmer of Norwich (1851–1900) who had a good collection of Norwich School landscapes.[32] Such was the interest in the motif that an oil replica (untraced) was made for Cyril Flower, and an untraced 'pencil' version was made for Benjamin Edgington Fletcher of Marlingford Hall, Norfolk.

With 'Mrs Neville' on hand in Norwich, Sandys produced a series of four beautiful drawings of her head on coarsely textured paper, all dated 1871, which were given the fancy titles of *Reflection*, *Rose*, *The Coral Necklace*, and *Azaleas*. These remained together as a group until 1964, their earliest traced provenance being J. Beecroft of Bradford.[33] It is probable, therefore, that they were disposed of together by Howell to this Yorkshire collector. Sandys's use of this textured paper for chalk drawings (often in sanguine-coloured chalk) seems to have been favoured by several artists of the fraternity at this period, such as Rossetti, Brown, and Burne-Jones.

It is clear that Norwich was thought of as only a temporary refuge from London and, as Sandys wrote to Howell, he yearned for: '… a thorough good studio with sitting room and bedroom for myself[34] – a good large studio – … I could never go back to Leicester Square again – it is so wretched noisy and filthy. I would give as high as £130 – if the studio was really a very fine large room.' He added: 'Could you help me to this?'[35]

However, there were protestations of poverty in 1871 which kept him Norwich-bound: 'I have no money. I have not had one sixpence for two months.'[36] Even so in July 1872 Sandys did manage a brief visit to London, when he was overheard at the Solferino restaurant in Rupert Street gossiping with Swinburne about Rossetti's recent attempt at suicide,[37] but he was still based in Norwich at 4 Queen's Road, St Catherine's Plain.[38]

Commissions were not lacking in 1872. Colman had him produce another double portrait, of his daughters Ethel Mary and Florence Esther, which is dated April 1872. He was at Wroxham Hall shortly after that, to work on *Breydon Water* for Edward Trafford. One of his least successful portraits, that of the Norfolk dignitary Edward Howes was another public commission. Since Howes had died in March 1871, Sandys must have had to resort to painting from a photograph – and lifeless it is.

By October he was at Weir Bank, Teddington, staying with his London patron, Thomas Chappell, to draw a double portrait of his young second wife and son. Thomas Patey Chappell (1819–1902) was a music publisher and maker and seller of musical instruments, with premises at 50 New Bond Street.[39] He was one of the original directors of the Royal College of Music, and was instrumental in founding a concert hall, the St James's Hall, Piccadilly in 1858. He was later a governor of the Royal Albert Hall and helped to finance the beginnings of the D'Oyly Carte enterprise.

Letters from Sandys to Howell in October ask him to pay a debt to 'Rossi' from the proceeds of the sale of the *Magdalen* drawing to Clarence E. Fry (the partner of Joseph Elliott in the portrait photography business of Elliott and Fry of 55–56 Baker Street), whose current idea was to enhance his studio and reception rooms with original works of art. 'Rossi' was Theodore Rossi, the son of George Rossi, who was now the head of the Norwich clocks and antiques business.

Howell may not have attended to Sandys's request, for it appears that he still owed Rossi £700 in 1873. A London solicitor's letter dated 5th November 1873 remains with the Rossi family. It shows that Sandys was trying to arrange an agreement with the Rossis to pay only £400, waiving the remainder, if paid at once. The solicitor was asking them to itemise the bills of debt, 'as Mr Sandys does not recollect the dates and amounts of them'.[40] Clearly, Sandys was in the habit, when in Norwich, of using the Rossis as money lenders. His debts were sometimes redeemed by the acceptance of his works, such as a painting and two drawings in lieu,[41] or a family portrait was undertaken, such as the portraits of Theodore's half-brother, Father Gregory Rossi (*c.*1850, and 1875). In another kind of involvement, Sandys would buy (or borrow?) art and antiques from the Rossis to sell on in London at a profit.

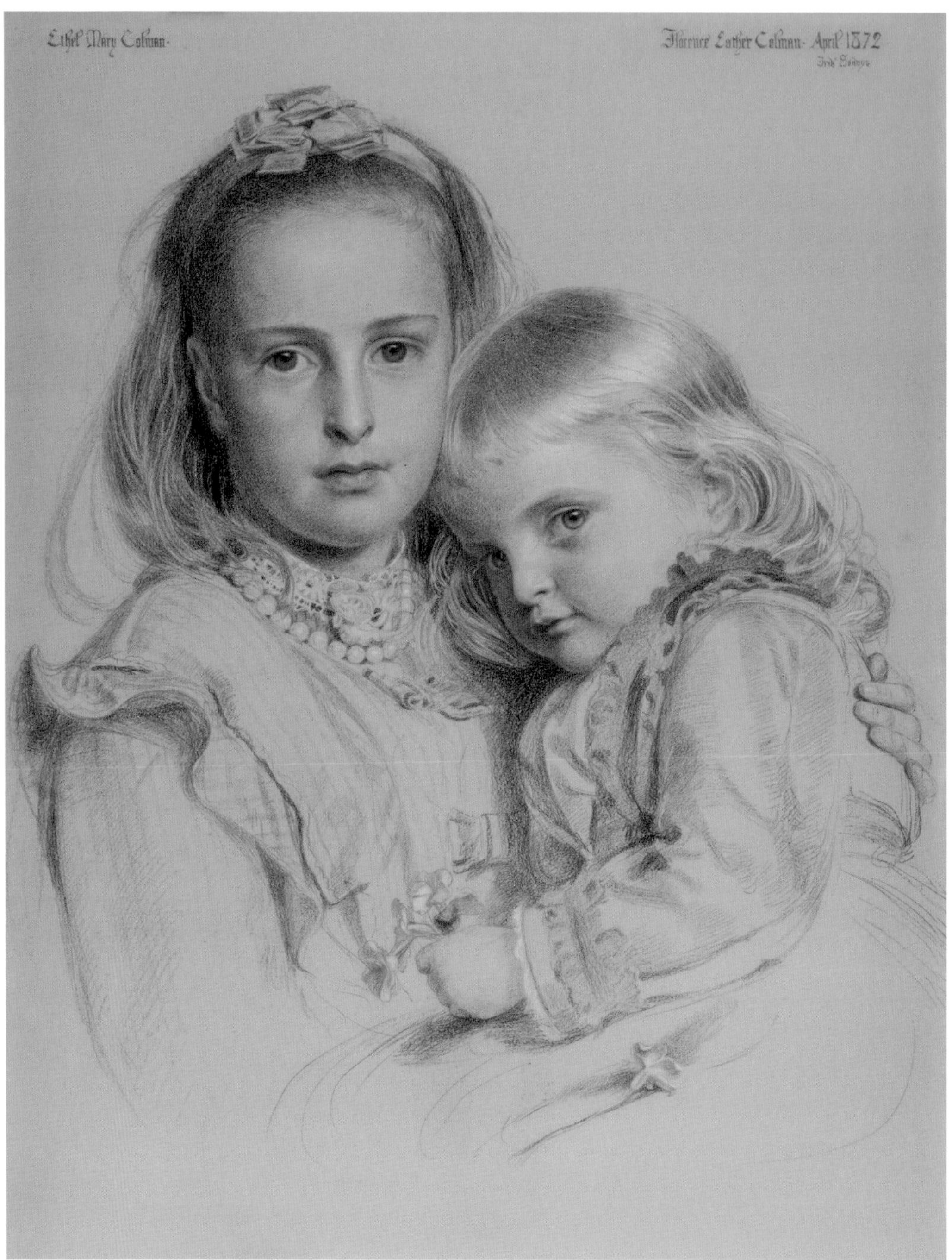

Ethel and Florence Colman. Chalk drawing. April 1872. Two daughters of Jeremiah James Colman and Caroline Cozens-Hardy Colman. One of the many children's portraits which Sandys made. It originally hung in the Colman residence, Carrow Abbey, Norwich.

Other portrait commissions at this time necessitated travel to Yorkshire to a house named Ferniehurst near Shipley, where he made a portrait of Edward Salt's second wife Amelia. Edward Salt's wealth was inherited from his father, Sir Titus Salt (1803–1876), the woollen manufacturer and philanthropist who built the model factory village of Saltaire. His son Edward Salt had a notable collection of orchids which surround Amelia in the portrait. Also in Yorkshire, Sandys completed a portrait of *Frederick A. Milbank* (1820–1898), of Barningham Park, Richmond, who was Liberal MP for the North Riding of Yorkshire. This was followed in early 1873 by a portrait of his wife Alexina Don.

On another occasion, Sandys went to Mickleham in Surrey to stay with his friends, the Merediths, to draw a double portrait of Marie Meredith with her little daughter Marie Eveleen.

The first instance of the important patronage of the Flower family came in 1872 when, almost certainly, it was Cyril Flower (1843–1907) who commissioned a chalk portrait of his favourite sister Clara who was about to be married to William T. Brand.[42] There followed in 1872 portraits of Cyril Flower himself, and his Cambridge University friend Leopold de Rothschild, and Leopold's cousin Constance de Rothschild (who was later to marry Cyril Flower in 1877). To end a busy year, Sandys's daughter Mildred Emma was born in Norwich on 10th December 1872. She was his ninth child (the fifth by Mary Emma Jones).

Not surprisingly, in January 1873, he was to be found in Norwich afflicted with rheumatism and 'bothers',[43] probably brought about by financial distress and related difficulties. However, he was in London in February and March to finish the portrait of Mrs Milbank[44] and, staying this time at Morley's Hotel in Trafalgar Square, he was able to keep in touch with London friends and acquaintances. Thus, on 11th March, he was at dinner with Howell at his villa at North End Grove, Fulham, with Frederic Burton (who was shortly to be appointed the Director of the National Gallery, 1874–1894) and William Rossetti.[45] Burton, Sandys, Howell, and Rossetti together, in 1866, had been actively supportive of Swinburne in the controversy over the publication of Swinburne's *Poems and Ballads*, then thought to be too risqué to be publishable.

In April Sandys supported Henry Irving for membership of the Garrick Club. Irving had failed to be accepted at the first ballot and Sandys wrote to him encouragingly. The second attempt was successful, and it became a favourite haunt of Irving's.[46]

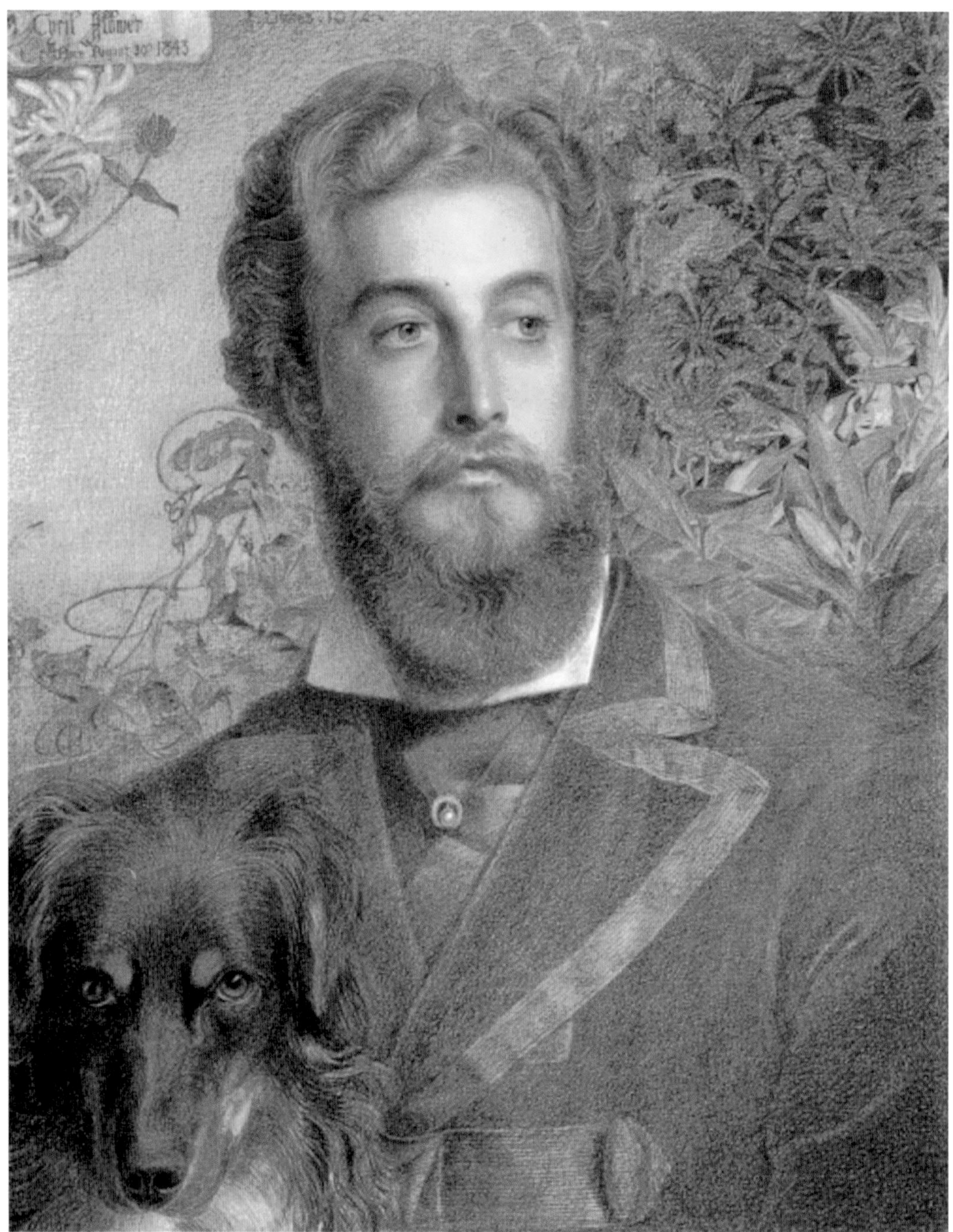

Cyril Flower (1843-1907). Chalk drawing. 1872. The eldest son of Philip Flower, a merchant in Australia and developer of land in Westminster and South London. In the 1870s and 1880s, as a most loyal patron of Sandys, Flower tried to rectify Sandys's chronic financial liabilities. He was a prominent member of the Liberal Party and became a peer as Lord Battersea.

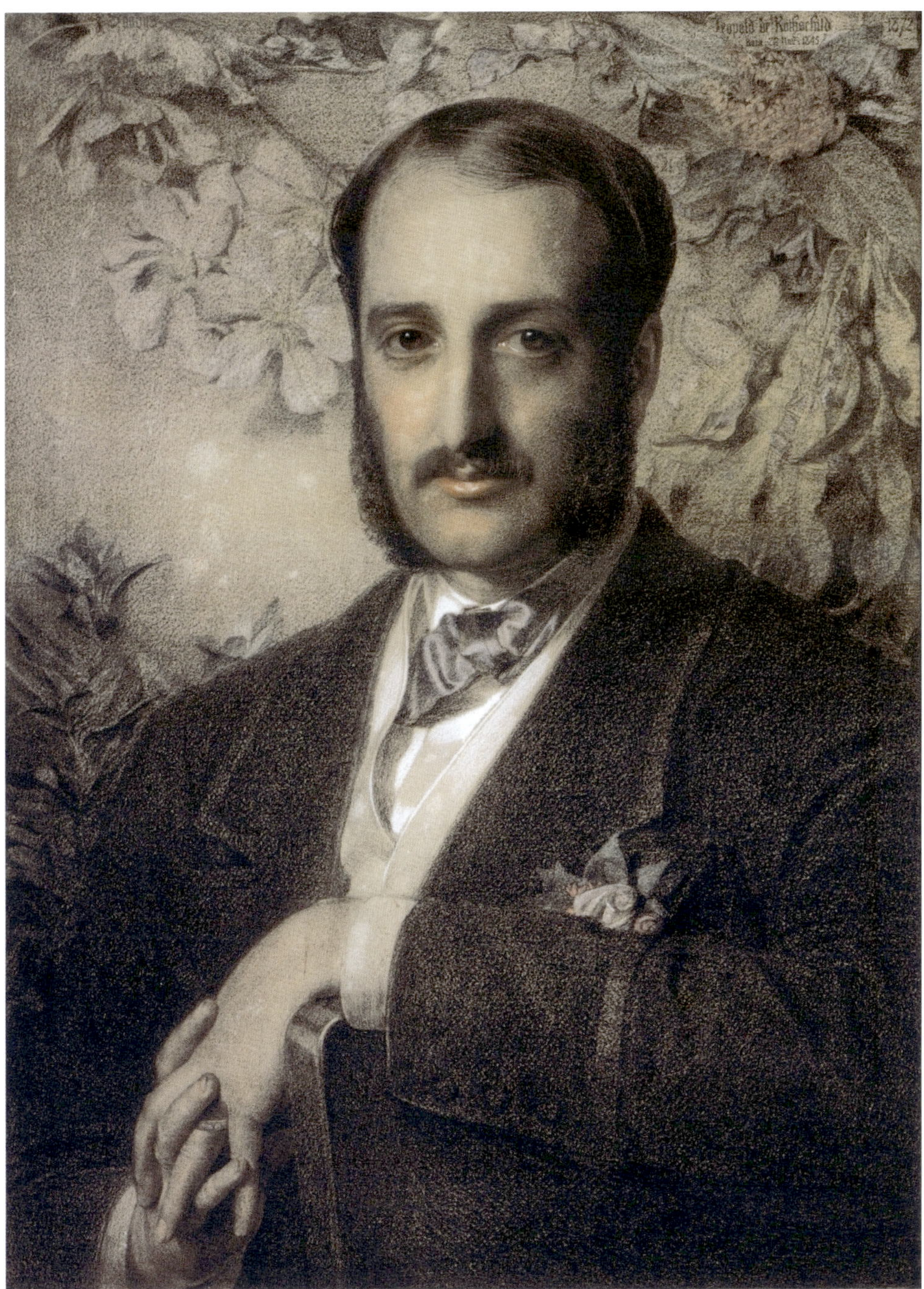

Leopold de Rothschild (1845-1917). Chalk drawing. 1872. He was the grandson of Nathaniel Meyer de Rothschild (1777-1836) the head of the English branch of the banking family. He met Cyril Flower at Cambridge University, and introduced his cousin Constance who, in 1877, married Flower.

In April or May a fortunate opportunity came along for a portrait to be made of the actress Ruth Herbert, commissioned by herself. The circumstances, one assumes, of the friendship of the Milbanks and Ruth Herbert lies in the fact that they were neighbours in London. The Milbanks, besides Barningham Park in County Durham, had a house in Kensington close to the rather grand Sidmouth Lodge, which was the home of Ruth Herbert.[47]

As already noted, Sandys had made an earlier study of her in the late 1850s, when she was modelling for Rossetti, but this introduction does not appear to have led to anything further at that time.

There is a letter from Sandys to Mrs Crabbe (Ruth Herbert's married name) dated 3rd May (1873) in which he apologised for his delay in finishing the portrait, and proposed a new appointment for the following week.[48] Although this portrait has since disappeared, there is evidence of its once existence: it was Ruth Herbert's gift to Mrs Milbank on her fiftieth birthday in February 1876. This fact is recorded, and something of its appearance can be seen on a large hand-painted Minton creamware dish, which is inscribed on the reverse by the painter:

'Mrs Crabbe as "Cleopatra"/ From the picture by Fk Sandys given by her to Mrs F.A. Milbank on her birthday Feby 1876' and 'J.D. Rochfort p(inxi)t 40 Eaton Place London 15 Feby 1877.'[49]

The painting on the dish shows a plump blonde woman in a muslin gown, reclining on a tiger skin, holding a writhing snake up to her face. The image is in full colour, but the Sandys original may not have been an oil painting; it may have been one of his large, detailed drawings using coloured chalks.

During the 1870s there was a fashionable craze for pottery painting among leisured amateur artists. Inspiration came from the spectacular new ceramic architectural decorations at the South Kensington Museum in the new galleries to display ceramics. Also, in a new suite of dining rooms there, two were faced with pictorial painted tiles (these are still to be seen). They were painted from 1867 to 1870 by students from the South Kensington art schools on tiles made by Minton's, the Stoke-on-Trent factory. A wide range of ceramic colours was newly available, developed by the Staffordshire-based industry which had made tremendous technical progress in the nineteenth century. With these newer ceramic colours it was possible to achieve a high degree of pictorial realism.

For the hobbyists, such as John Rochfort, Minton's initially supplied the materials including tiles, and flat dishes (which offered a suitably large area for painting on). Popular subjects for decoration were landscapes, floral arrangements and fancy heads, or scenes from history and mythology. Minton's, furthermore, in 1871, established an 'Art Pottery Studio' on Kensington Gore, equipped with a kiln for the convenience of the amateurs. Exhibitions were held at the high-class showrooms of Thomas Goode & Co., in Mayfair. Unfortunately, a fire ended the life of the studio in 1875, but alternative kiln facilities must have been arranged, judging by the inscribed date of 1877 on the Rochfort dish.[50]

The circumstances surrounding the portrait of 1873, and the Minton dish of 1877, take on an added piquancy with the knowledge that both Frederick Milbank (*c*.1861) and later, John Rochfort (from 1862), were lovers of Ruth Herbert.[51] She had a daughter, Madeleine Augusta 'Midge', by the former, and a son by the latter.[52] She eventually took the name Rochfort.

Having received the gift of the portrait by Sandys from Ruth Herbert: '… the exquisite drawing of herself as Cleopatra by Sandys …', Mrs Milbank's diary[53] shows her to be distressed, as if past, long suppressed, memories had risen to the surface to haunt her: '… I spent a wretched day, ill in mind and body, and disappointed in my 50th birthday!'

The third piece of evidence of the portrait's existence lies in a postcard of 1940 from Midge to her grand-daughter Virginia. She wrote: 'He [Sandys] did a wonderful picture of my mother – a Cleopatra – full life size & he insisted Cleopatra was fair not dark as always said. Where the picture is I know not.'[54]

June 1873 brought Mary Emma Jones ('Miss Clive') into the limelight. She had secured an engagement at the Queen's Theatre, Long Acre,[55] with a production managed by Marie Litton, to play Constance in Shakespeare's *King John*. The first reference to this can be found in a letter of about 10th June from Howell to D.G. Rossetti: 'Have you heard about Sandys's "little girl"[?] Theatrical London (after some private shows) has gone clean mad about her, and Robertson[56] and Marie Litton have engaged her for three years at £30 a week and three benefits and all expenses and dresses found. She is coming out in *King John* and Robertson is trying to get the best theatre in London and engaging a whole company for her. I am told that the whole affair is unparalleled in the annals of the English stage as a start. She comes here to consult me about everything and is going to fund all the tin except £5 a week for the kids. Sandys is in a state and ill with excitement.'[57] The 'kids' referred to would have been Cissily (b.1869), Dorothy (b.1870), Winifred (b.1871), and

Mildred (b.1872), all of whom would have been in the hands of a child minder. Further comments were made by Shirley Brooks[58] in his diary on 11th June: 'A new actress is coming out in Constance, she is to be called "Clive" and is a mistress of Sands [*sic*] the artist. Tom Taylor declares there has been nothing like her since Siddons, but he is lavish in praise of those he likes. Not educated. And as she is a magdalen, only not repentant, she will not be taken into drawing rooms and made a fool of like some of 'em.' Therein lies the clue to why Sandys presented himself to 'society' as a bachelor, and why Mary Emma Jones was to bring up her family in obscurity as 'Mrs Neville'. Shirley Brooks later added a note to the diary page: 'She was an utter failure, and vanished.'

An undated cutting (early June 1873) from an undocumented newspaper preserved by the Sandys family provides more details under: 'AT THE PLAY. Rumour insists that we are very shortly to see a new actress and, what is more to the point, an actress of very considerable merit. "Miss Clive" – for this is the name of the lady – is advertised to appear at the Queen's Theatre on Saturday week, in the character of Constance in *King John*. The Queen's Theatre has been taken for a summer season by Miss Litton purely for the sake of introducing Miss Clive to the London public, and Shakespeare will have full justice done him on this occasion by Mr Hermann Vezin,[59] Mr George Rignold, and Mr John Ryder. It would be unfair to the future of the lady to state at this moment how warm is the praise bestowed upon her talent. We are assured that Miss Clive has received no stage instruction whatever; that she has never yet appeared in public; and that she has been engaged for a long period, and very liberal terms, entirely owing to her marvellous power of recitation, which has enthralled those who have been privileged to hear her declaim in private various well-known speeches from Shakespeare. … If Miss Litton has made a discovery, she will have done the stage great service.'

The critic of the *Athenaeum* also reviewed the performance in a sympathetic vein: '… In Miss Clive we have some eminent gifts, unaided, if unembarrassed, by cultivation from without. A nature ripe and rich, passionate impulse, and artistic instinct, are marred by no stage convention or artifice. Whatever Miss Clive does upon the stage is fresh, original, and crude … Miss Clive has distinct gifts of perception and has the means of rendering dramatically effective the views she adopts.'[60]

In retrospect, it appears that Clive was vastly over-publicised, and expectations were raised too high to be fair to her, as some of the kinder reviews of the performance observed. More truthfully, the reviewer in *The Observer* stated: 'The actress was dreadfully, often painfully nervous. She lost her lines, she

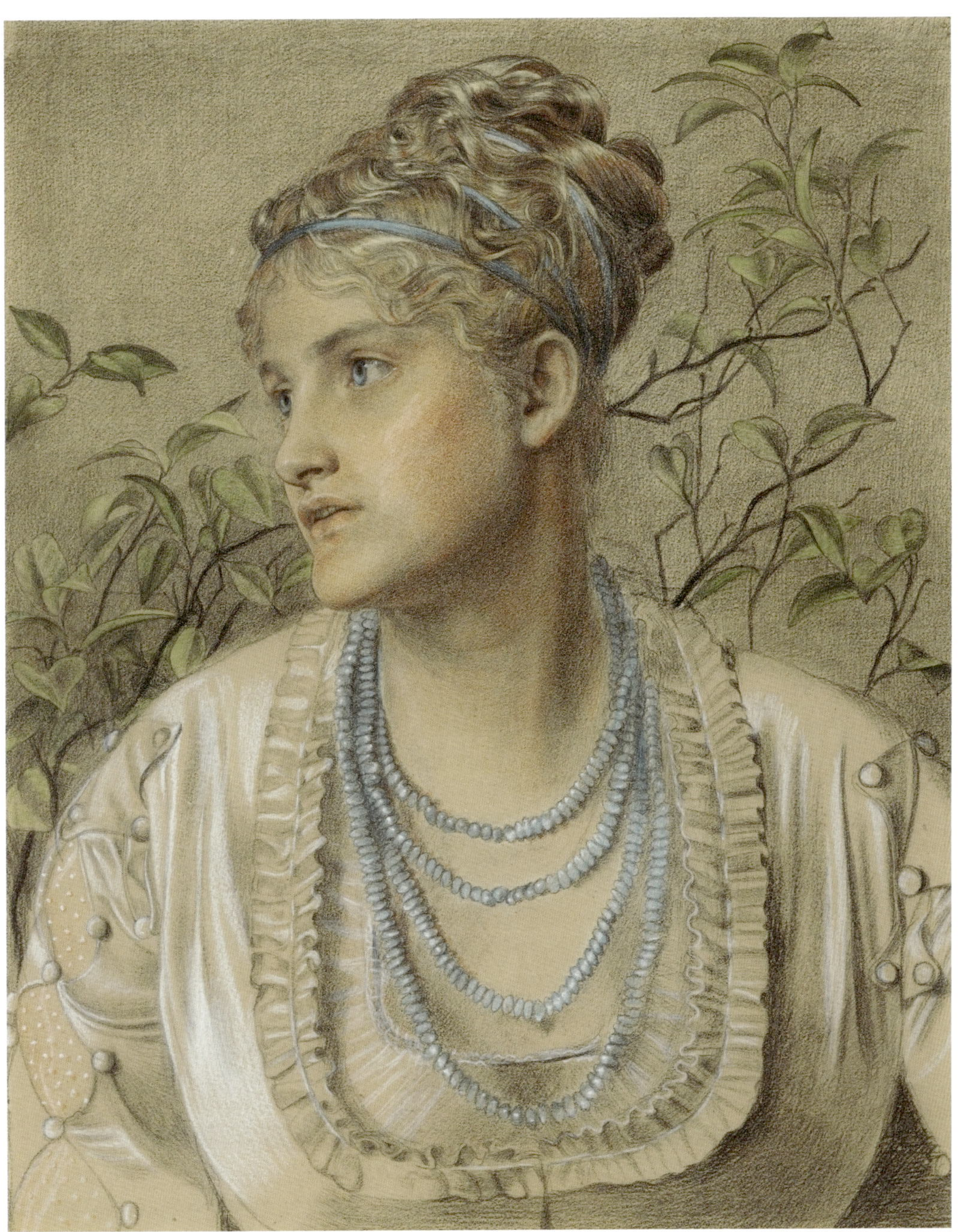

Mary Emma Jones. Chalk drawing, *c.*1873. Sandys's 'Little Girl', who bore him twelve children. Born in Hull, she started her working life as an actress and as an artists' model, eventually giving up to look after her family, under the pseudonym of Mrs Neville.

broke in at the wrong places; her command over her voice was gone from time to time, mainly owing to this stage fright, which must have been as painful to the actress as it is distressing to the audience. Unquestionably the voice of Miss Clive last evening was altogether beyond control. Sometimes it was inaudible, often it went entirely. Only in one speech she really felt her audience. … With a voice out of control, with an inability to reach a sublime point, either in passion or tenderness, it will be asked, then, how she managed to force her acting into the notice which it certainly obtained? … On the other hand the success of the actress was an unconventionality of business,[61] and a force of action very rare on the stage. There was not a trace of the amateur in walk, pose, or movement. When the hand, arm, or fingers, were pointed out, the actress was spirited and effective. When the arms were uplifted, the picture was admirable. As a picture, tearing and gnawing at her hair,[62] as a picture, fondling her child; as a picture, rocking on the ground, and clasping her knee, Miss Clive was altogether admirable. It is strange she would have succeeded in the very things which come last to the amateur – grace, ease, suppleness, natural movement – and have failed in the effective reading of a character so brimming over with effect. The thorough want of practice and knowledge of the stage was most shown in the over-prolonged bursts of grief and the tame and ineffective exits. … In our opinion by far the best speech delivered by Miss Clive, the point at which one could tell best her instinct and her talent, the lines which best developed her poetical aspirations and fancy was the address to death, "Death! Death! O amiable and lovely death!" Here there was a dreamy and delightful thought running through the lines, which showed how thoroughly the poet was understood by the artist. Such readings as these are delightfully unconventional, and to get an artist who can offer them is a great gain. But then, how disappointing it was to get the strained and occasionally painful delivery of the speech.

'… To deny the existence in Miss Clive of rare material for stage purposes would be very foolish in our opinion, but it would be equally foolish to say that such a performance as that shown last evening is one of the highest kind. … The cheering and applause, the bouquets and the enthusiasm after the third act might mean that the audience recognised in Miss Clive an artist of extraordinary merit. They might, on the other hand, mean a "*succes d'estime!*"'[63]

A laconic summary of 'Miss Clive' and her performance is recorded in an anonymous scribbled marginal note in a programme which has been preserved in the Enthoven Theatre Collection:[64] '… a short dumpy lady – *néz retroussé* – wants power – should not have played such a part.'

Rossetti, holed up in the country in the old house, Kelmscott Manor, with which he shared the lease with William Morris and his family, read a complimentary notice in the *Daily News* and wrote to Howell, his agent and factotum: 'I have seen about Miss Clive in *Daily News*, and she has no friend better pleased than I am. I always thought her a great-hearted girl, and always said she was a genius.'[65]

In Howell's reply, dated 30th June 1873, came the distressing news that she had been taken ill: 'Yesterday I called on poor Clive with your flowers and found the poor thing down with rheumatic fever. She was taken ill on Saturday morning.[66] They are truly unfortunate and poor £500[67] is in a dreadful state. I told him all you said, and he is going to write to you … do make it up, one has such few friends.'[68]

Rossetti's concern is evident in his reply of 2nd July: 'Your news of Sandys and poor Mary grieves me most deeply, and I have written – enclosed – to him which please send or deliver. It is a sad letter indeed, and I fear such a misadventure is enough to cancel the engagement, is it not? That she will not recover I cannot bring myself to fear.'[69]

Howell's reply to this was interspersed with much about business matters concerning the sale of Rossetti's pictures: 'This is a beautiful letter for poor old Sandys and I will take it tonight. He too is very ill, not only anxiety, but yesterday lifting her by himself from the floor on to the bed, he nearly broke his back, and it is so strained that he is in great pain cannot sleep or lie on it so that you must not expect an answer for some days.

'… Poor things! I am so sorry for them, the fever has left her, but the pain is dreadful, up to the present there seems to be no fear of Miss Litton withdrawing the engagement. I saw a very kind letter from her to Clive last night, but who knows what will come, as the illness drags on and they have to keep up the Queen's with a most expensive company and empty houses! They keep advertising Clive every night and this I think is a very bad plan. It draws the people and then they have to listen to an excuse and a lot of sticks.'[70]

It seems that 'Miss Clive' was well enough to perform again by 8th July, having been seen by Ford Madox Brown in performance, as reported in another letter from Rossetti at Kelmscott to Howell.[71] However, she had a relapse soon after, according to Rossetti's note to Howell dated 5th July: 'How sad about poor Clive! Will it really end badly?'[72]

In another letter to Rossetti, Howell wrote: 'Poor Clive is much better, and £500 also, he is delighted with your letter and is going to write, only I told him never mind about writing now, I have told Rossetti all about it, and he knows you are much too worried to do anything. Poor chap has been nearly half cracked and lives on brandy – *entre nous* – I am going to stop it if I can, and last Saturday, I spoke very strongly to him on the subject. Of course, nothing can make him drunk and that is just the Devil of it, for it is enough to kill any one to fly at the bottle every moment. When I am worried, I cannot drink, only when I am jolly.'[73]

Sandys replied to Rossetti's friendly letter. It was dated 'Tuesday' (probably 8th July 1873), from a new address, 30 Stanford Road, Victoria Road, Kensington – a wide street of newish villas in the area between Kensington Square and Gloucester Road.[74] He wrote: 'The poor little girl has been so ill (I have allowed days in consequence to pass without answering your letter. Otherwise, I should have not delayed an hour). First let me say I shall be delighted to see you as soon as you will give me an opportunity – pray let it be quickly. Next let me ask that we should be absolutely as we were and meet up. I have never felt otherwise than yours entirely – never had a mean or unworthy thought towards you – never said an unkind word of you. However, it is not of this I wish to write, but simply to say I long to see and talk to you. I unfortunately have had no opportunity to do any work I care about, so think no more of that and when I have seen your drawings and paintings done lately, they [will] make me feverish with desire to change my life or end it. The little girl is out of bed today for the first time since Friday week. She is quite delighted with all your kind feeling towards her and is quite as anxious to see you as I am. Yours affectionately, Frederick Sandys.'[75]

On the back of this letter, later possessed by William Rossetti, is a note by him: '... It shows that Rossetti must have taken the first step towards repairing the breach which had taken place, in 1869, in the intimacy between himself & Mr Sandys. Tho' both of them were now very willing to meet again, I rather question whether they ever did so.'[76] They may not have met again but it was not the end of their friendship.

In another letter, from Rossetti, still in Oxfordshire, writing on 16th July to his studio assistant Henry Treffry Dunn who was attending to domestic matters in Chelsea, we find words of concern: 'I am very glad poor "Miss Clive" is better. I wrote to Sandys lately and received an affectionate answer. I fear Miss C's engagement must be sadly thrown out by her illness. It seems she had somehow secured unheard of terms – £30 a week (Howell says) besides other advantages.'[77]

However, the troubles continued. In Rossetti's letter of 20th July to George Hake, one of his companions at this period, he wrote that: '... [Howell] is cluttered up at home at present with the unlucky Sandys and poor Miss Clive. The latter, as you know, had an attack of rheumatic fever, got somewhat better, and (prematurely no doubt) came to dine with the Howells. The result was her being taken bad again during dinner, since which it has been impossible to remove her from the house, and her present attack is worse than the first, two doctors having to visit her daily.'[78]

At the end of July, when the 'little girl' was well enough to have left the care of the Howells,[79] Sandys wrote to Howell wishing to set up a time for working on a portrait of Kitty Howell, probably in gratitude for the Howells's kindness, although it seems that Howell had advanced some money for it.[80] He was now writing from 1 Spenser Street, just off Victoria Street.[81] This was the studio that Sandys had long desired and which his new patron and friend, Cyril Flower, was able to offer him to rent.

Cyril Flower was a wealthy young barrister, with a boundless interest in art and architecture who, from 1872, after his father Philip William Flower's death, took on with his brothers their father's building developments in Westminster and South London. Philip William Flower had made his wealth by trading in Australia. Already, in 1872, Sandys had completed a series of portrait drawings of Flower's family and close friends: Clara Flower, Cyril's sister,[82] Constance de Rothschild his future wife, her cousin Leopold de Rothschild who had been Cyril's Cambridge University friend, and Cyril himself. In due course of time, Sandys was commissioned to portray eleven more Flowers and their close connections.

In August, Sandys wrote to Howell announcing that he had finished his portrait of Mrs Murray Marks.[83] Murray Marks (*c.*1840–1918) was a London art and antiques dealer whose shop at 399 Oxford Street had become a honeypot for artists such as Rossetti, Burne-Jones, Whistler and, among others, the prominent surgeon Sir Henry Thompson (1820–1904), who were early into the appreciation of Chinese blue-and-white porcelain and Japanese artefacts, in the 1860s and 1870s, and formed collections largely through Murray Marks. According to Marks's biographer G.C. Williamson,[84] it was Rossetti who first introduced him to Sandys. Marks much admired Sandys's skilful draughtsmanship and was helpful in getting him portrait commissions. Marks also bought and sold work for him. Besides the portrait of Marks's wife, Louisa, of 1873, in 1875 he made a drawing of her pug dog Sambo which Marks liked so much that he had it engraved as a print for the then large sum of £80. Sandys's original drawing of the dog remains lost but copies of the reproductive print – in fact an etching titled *Mischief*, by Leopold Flameng (1831–1911) are known, though rare.[85] Later in 1882, there is mention of portrait commissions of Marks's children, but nothing appears to have come of this.[86]

In spite of being busy with portrait work, in a letter to Rossetti of 2nd September (1873)[87] Sandys complains of being set back by 'bothers', a characteristic word of his indicating trouble, usually financial. In confirmation of the situation, Howell in a letter of 5th September to Rossetti wrote: 'Sandys is worried as usual, and Clive goes on limping, and so fat that I cannot see how she can go on the stage next month.'[88] Relief might well have come in the form of a cheque from Frederick Leyland (1831–1892), the wealthy owner of a Liverpool shipping company, for the painting *Valkyrie* in early October 1873, except, as was often the case, Sandys had received the money in advance and had already spent it. In fact, according to William Rossetti, Leyland had bought it from Sandys in April 1868 for £200. Leyland wrote to William's brother Gabriel on 2nd October: 'I have just this moment received Sandys' *Valkyrie* after some years of weary waiting. He has however made a very fine thing of it – by far the best I have seen of his.'[89] He had it hung above the principal staircase at his London house, at 49 Prince's Gate.

In November, Sandys was continuing to have financial difficulties partly connected with his debt to the Rossi family, and with the furnishing of his new studio. He chided Howell for not collecting from the docks some imported chairs (for which probably customs fees had to be paid), and for not selling a small drawing for him for £25, which, according to Sandys, might have saved the current situation.[90] A letter sent to the Rossis by London solicitors on 5th November 1873 has been preserved by the Rossi family: in it Sandys seeks to clarify what was probably a verbal agreement he made with the Rossis in order to cancel his debt to them (of about £700) by paying them £400 immediately.[91] To Howell, he added that he was about to leave for Norwich for a month which, undoubtedly, was to undertake the commission for a portrait of Sir Samuel Bignold, of the Norwich Union Insurance company. Samuel Bignold (1791–1875), who was the son of the founder of the company (in 1792), succeeded his father in 1818, and presided over the increase of the wealth and importance of the enterprise which soon became nationwide in its coverage. Bignold was one of the outstanding citizens of Norwich, becoming mayor four times, in 1833, 1848, 1853, and 1872, and receiving a knighthood in 1854. He was Conservative MP for Norwich from 1854 to 1857. The portrait was funded by a subscription raised by the board of the proprietors of the company to honour Bignold on his eightieth birthday on 13th October in 1871. Sandys was in Norwich at 4 Queen's Road, St Catherine's Plain, from 5th December 1873 to at least the end of February 1874, according to his correspondence, and probably was occupied with the preliminary drawing and the oil portrait during this time.[92]

Writing from Norwich to Howell on 11th December, he continues to be concerned with furnishing the Spenser Street studio and living quarters. These seem to have been quite capacious, as described in *Modern Society* in 1907 on the death of Cyril Flower: 'It is said that the house in Spenser Street, Victoria Street, in which Sandys once lived was built for him by the recently deceased peer. The house was afterwards the residence of Sir William Orchardson, RA, and is now tenanted by two or three well known artists, as it contains several painting rooms.'[93]

Sandys wrote: '... You see I cannot spend much – and I have a good deal to do – and what I really want I had better confine myself to – a sideboard I must have and I want a good one – no half and half sort of a thing – and one that all people will envy.

'I have bought an immense blue and white Nankin bowl – dragons inside and out – fiends. It is the finest and biggest bowl I ever saw – with the blue on the dragons is in places a fine gold hue – is a very rich dark blue [*sic*] – the dragons in their fight seem to have kicked the clouds to atoms – for there are patches of clouds all over the dish inside and out. There is a slight crack but the ring is perfect – it is I should think two feet across. What do you suppose it is worth? I have given a large price for it – I have given £17 for that and three other beautiful pieces of blue and white.'[94]

If his source for this bowl was in Norwich, it was probably from Theodore Rossi. That Sandys was well aware of the beauty of Chinese export wares was evident as early as the beginning of the 1860s. Among other acquisitions which we know about was a fireplace fender designed by his friend Thomas Jeckell and made by the Norwich metalworking firm Barnard, Bishop and Barnard. This we know about because it caught the eye of Edward Godwin in 1878 when he made a quick drawing of it in a sketchbook.[95] It appears also that around this time Godwin designed him an overmantel and made colour schemes for his rooms.[96]

The Jeckell designs for Barnard, Bishop and Barnard were highly thought of at the time, winning awards at exhibitions. The firm had their main London showrooms at 91–95 Victoria Street, and from here it is likely that they were involved in equipping the new building developments there with the necessary ironmongery.

Another furnishing piece, probably from Sandys's studio, was handed down in the Sandys family, who assumed that it had been designed by Sandys himself, but it is now recognised as a Jeckell design. This is a brass ash pan or trough, patented in 1876 and made by Barnard, Bishop and Barnard.[97]

It was around this time that artists' 'painting rooms' began to evolve into the rather grander 'studios', as the wealth and status of artists rose. These purpose-built rooms took on the additional function of showrooms, or reception rooms, and their occupants had to pay attention to their furnishings to impress their clients, or at least provide civilised surroundings in which to receive them or have them sit for their portraits.

Sandys's new studio, which included living accommodation, was purpose-built on a short access road to a piece of land on which stables were to be built to serve the tenants of the new blocks of high-class apartments and shops in Victoria Street, all of which were being developed from *c.*1867 by James Knowles (1806–1884) and his son, also named James Knowles (1831–1908), who were the Flower family's architects for their extensive building developments in Westminster, Pimlico, and Battersea.[98] The connection between the Knowles family, and the wealthy Flowers who were involved in land development among their other business enterprises, was as neighbours in South London.[99] The elder Knowles had already built for himself, in 1846, a villa named Friday Grove on undeveloped farmland just south of Clapham Common, and in the early sixties he was enlarging an existing late eighteenth century villa, further south, named Furzedown, for Philip Flower (1810–1872) and his large family. By this time, the younger James Knowles became active in partnership with his father. They were both involved in the Westminster developments and other projects such as the Cedars Estate which stretched northward from Clapham Common to the then fields of Battersea.

Meanwhile, Sandys spent the early months of 1874 in Norwich, ill with bronchitis and liver problems, during the time he was finishing the portraits of Samuel Bignold. His mother's sister had just died, for in March he purchased a plot in the new Rosary Cemetery at Thorpe where, later, he buried his sister and his parents also.[100] A portrait drawing he probably undertook at this time, in return for the loan of his studio at Thorpe, was of Herbert Roberts. Herbert Harrington Roberts (1837–early 1920s) was a Colonel in the 1st Warwickshire Militia. He had studied art at Norwich and at the Royal Academy Schools in the early 1860s, and was a comfortably off amateur painter. In his autobiography *Memories of Fourscore Years* (1920) he records Sandys's regular use of his studio when he was in Norwich.

Sandys wrote to Howell in February of 1874, promising that, on his return to London, he would finish his portrait of Kitty Howell and would start on a portrait of Howell himself which he would try and do in the evenings by gaslight. Writing from Norwich, he was still anxious about the new London studio which he was furnishing with the help of Howell, with chairs, a sideboard and 'a wardrobe, and an "old-fashioned" washing stand for [the] bedroom. I am so anxious to get that sitting room more or less furnished by my return ... [else] it will show the state of my exchequer so distinctly that I know not what to do – what way to conceal it'.[101] He was wondering if the Howells had yet moved out of North End Grove.[102] The evidence is that they had moved, for Howell was writing from Norris's Hotel, Elsham Road, Kensington by 6th February 1874.[103] The planned move to Chaldon House, Fulham, a mid-eighteenth century villa, near to the old wooden bridge from Fulham to Putney, was not complete until the first week in April.[104] These moves in Fulham were no doubt prompted by Howell's strategy to be in a position for compensation from the Metropolitan District Railway Company when it was extending its lines south-westwards to North End, Fulham, and Hammersmith [in the case of North End Grove]. It consequently had to buy land and demolish buildings along the route. Chaldon House also would be directly on the route when the proposed railway branched off southwards across the Thames towards Putney in the late 1870s. He had successfully tussled with the railway company in 1869 over compensation for being turned out of North End Grove, having been assisted by E.W. Godwin as a professional witness.[105] He again won compensation for his loss of Chaldon House with Godwin's help in 1879.[106]

Charles Fèret, the historian of Fulham, wrote an account of the transfer in 1874 of Howell's 'elegant furniture' from North End Grove to Chaldon House: 'The transfer was effected by means of a procession of twelve cabs wending to and fro for over a week. Every room became, in the hands of this celebrated connoisseur, a picture. The firehearths were paved with the costliest of tiles, Portuguese and Japanese. One window was designed by Burne-Jones and another by Rossetti. The house was speedily turned into a house of aestheticism. The rooms of this "Paradise of Beauty," as it was termed, were "arrangements" in blue and gold, and other colours.'[107]

By April 1874, Sandys was in London at Spenser Street,[108] and was presumably getting his house in order to receive patrons and sitters. He started a portrait at about this time of the matriarch of the wealthy Brand family, Jane Wilson Brand (1804–*c.*1881). The Brands were neighbours and close friends of the Flowers in the as yet undeveloped land in the Streatham and Tooting area, the Flowers, as noted, being at Furzedown House, and the Brands at Bedford

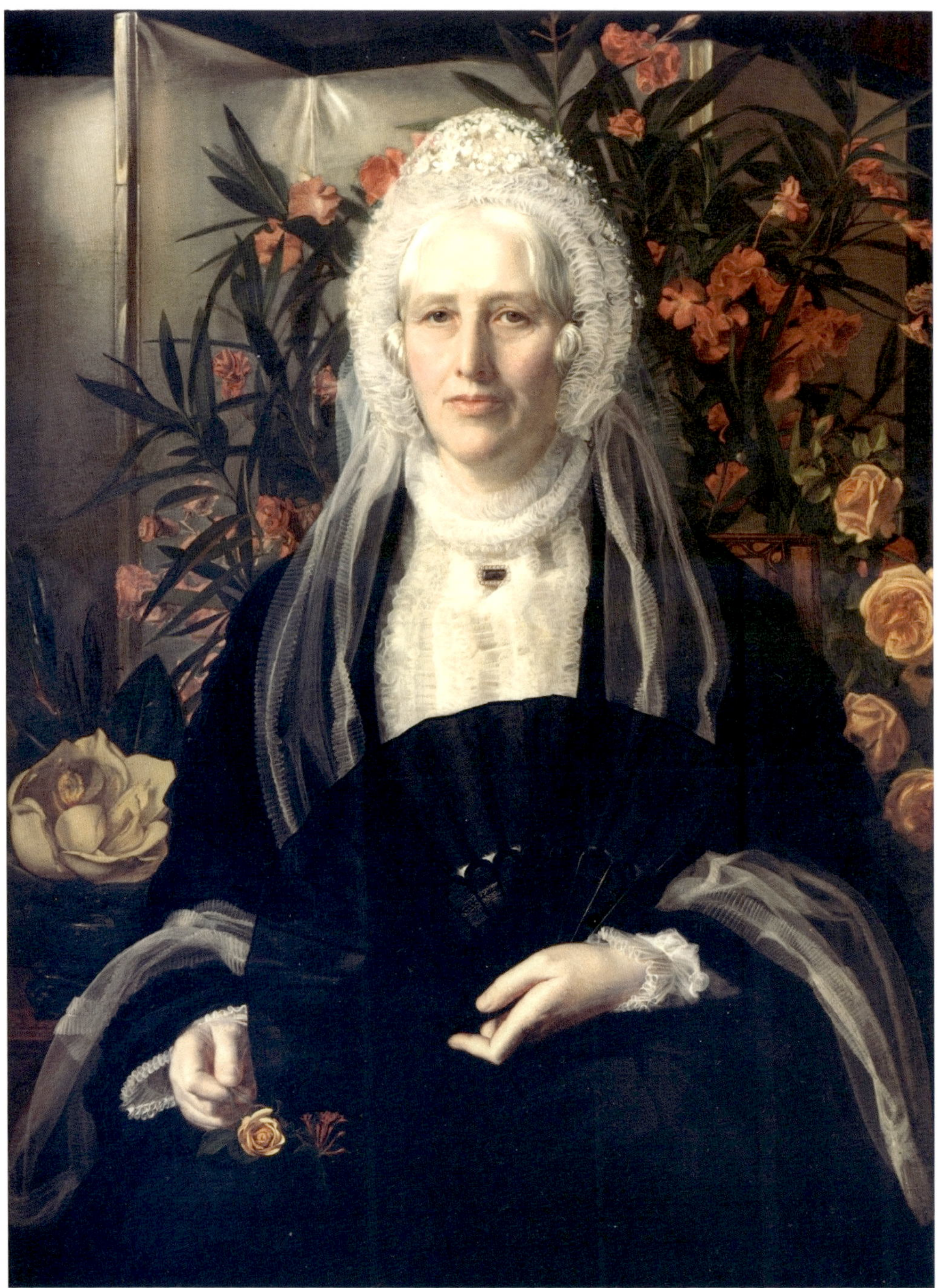

Jane Brand (1804 – *c.*1881). Oil on canvas. 1874. The last of the five known outstanding oil portraits of elderly ladies by Sandys. She was the wife of James Brand, a China and East India merchant who lived at Bedford Hill House, Streatham. They were neighbours of the Flower family at Furzedown House.

Hill House. By 1874, the head of this large family, James Brand (1798–1860), had died, leaving his widow Jane and nine children. The eldest child, Jane (b.1830), had married the artist William Dyce in 1850 and they lived close by, near St Leonard's Church in Streatham. The eldest son James (1832–1893), listed as an 'East India and China Merchant' and a Justice of the Peace in the 1871 census of Bedford Hill House, succeeded as head. James was a widower by about 1870, with six children. It was he who commissioned at least eight family portraits from Sandys, starting with his mother Jane.

There was to be a large chalk portrait of Jane in 1874, and an oil version was completed in 1875. It was in July 1874 that Sandys wrote to William Rossetti asking to be put in touch with his brother Gabriel whom he wanted to see his current portrait 'of a fearful old woman ... There is an awful lot of work in the picture in fact it consists entirely of cap – cap strings and white stomacher. Do come (yourself) and communicate my most earnest desires to Gabriel. My place is a new red brick house, by [beside] Large and Ivall – coachbuilders'.[109] The oil portrait of Jane Brand was shown at the Royal Academy in 1875.

In the summer of 1874 correspondence between Dante Gabriel Rossetti and Howell, and William Rossetti and Sandys, reveals Rossetti's desire to have Howell and Sandys come down to Kelmscott to stay with him.[110] Following letters show that Sandys did not go after all, but Howell did from 4th to 6th July,[111] after which Rossetti left Kelmscott for London, never to return.

At the end of July, we find that Sandys's sister Emma is in London sitting for her brother,[112] and it is my belief that this was the beginning of his work on the large chalk drawing *Persephone*: a young woman in classical costume carrying an urn filled with pomegranates in one hand and a sheaf of wheat in the other. Just behind her figure is a hedge of evergreen foliage and, in the distance, the misty silhouette of a mountain. The symbolism carries the attributes of the Greek goddess Persephone, who was daughter of Demeter and the wife of Pluto, the god of Hades. It was eventually in the possession of Cyril Flower and was hung at his seaside house, The Pleasaunce, at Cromer.[113] The writer Esther Wood illustrated this drawing and gave it the date 1878[114] but it must have been largely worked on much earlier, for Emma died in Norwich at the family home in November 1877.

Later in the year Sandys was having trouble extracting money owed from Howell. It seems that his father Anthony had in his possession a painting by John Crome (1768–1821), the Norwich artist, and was hoping to make some money from it through Howell. Sandys wrote to him in August: 'It is most important I should have for my governor – the £20 or £25 for the

Crome, Saturday, by three o'clock – if not the picture by that time. He then leaves town – I quite expected you yesterday and I have been expecting you today.'[115] Howell must have been going through a financial crisis, evident from two more letters written by Sandys in September and October. From the Garrick Club, probably in September (although it is not dated), he wrote: 'Daily now for one month I have been expecting to see you with the £20 for the Crome. Do pray let me have [it] if not tomorrow – at latest on Monday.'[116] In early October, Sandys was insisting: 'I must ask you to let me have tomorrow either the Crome picture – the money – or the address of the gentleman who bought it, so that I may write to him.' Perhaps regarding an unrelated issue, he added: 'I suppose you are aware I have a County Court Summons for the eighteen pounds due by you to the Loan Office.'[117]

In happier circumstances in September, Sandys's old friend George Meredith wrote to him inviting him to dine at Box Hill, and to bring W.G. Wills with him. William Gorman Wills (1828–1891), an artist and playwright, became one of Sandys's intimates. He was also a member of the Garrick Club.[118]

In October, Swinburne wrote to Sandys asking if he were still intending to portray him, as he had finished some writing and would be free to sit.[119] The proposal was raised again over a year later, in December 1875, but it seems that the opportunity for sitting was not acted upon, as no portrait of Swinburne by Sandys has come to light.[120]

Eighteen seventy-five appears to have been a good year for Sandys. In May he won the Garrick Club sweepstake on the Derby and, also in May, he was invited by George Augustus Sala to dinner at home at 68 Thistle Grove, Chelsea. Sala was the energetic and prolific journalist who, amongst many other activities, served as art critic on the *Daily Telegraph*, and in his letter of invitation he was excusing himself for the brief mention he had made of Sandys's work currently showing at the Royal Academy Summer Exhibition. Sandys showed two chalk portraits and the large oil portrait of Mrs Jane Brand, which cannot have failed to impress. He wrote, 'I gave you (mainly as a mention) the most honourable place I could find, the "wind-up". ... 'He promised that he would write more fully 'very soon'.[121]

His old friend George Meredith, congratulated him on winning the sweepstake: 'It is evident that you have now an Income for life ... I expect a dinner ... [and] lots of treats mind.' He proposed coming up from Box Hill to stay with Sandys over the weekend, having a quiet dinner together on Saturday, and possibly even staying over on the Monday to be at the opening night of *Hamlet* at the Drury Lane Theatre, starring the actor Salvini,

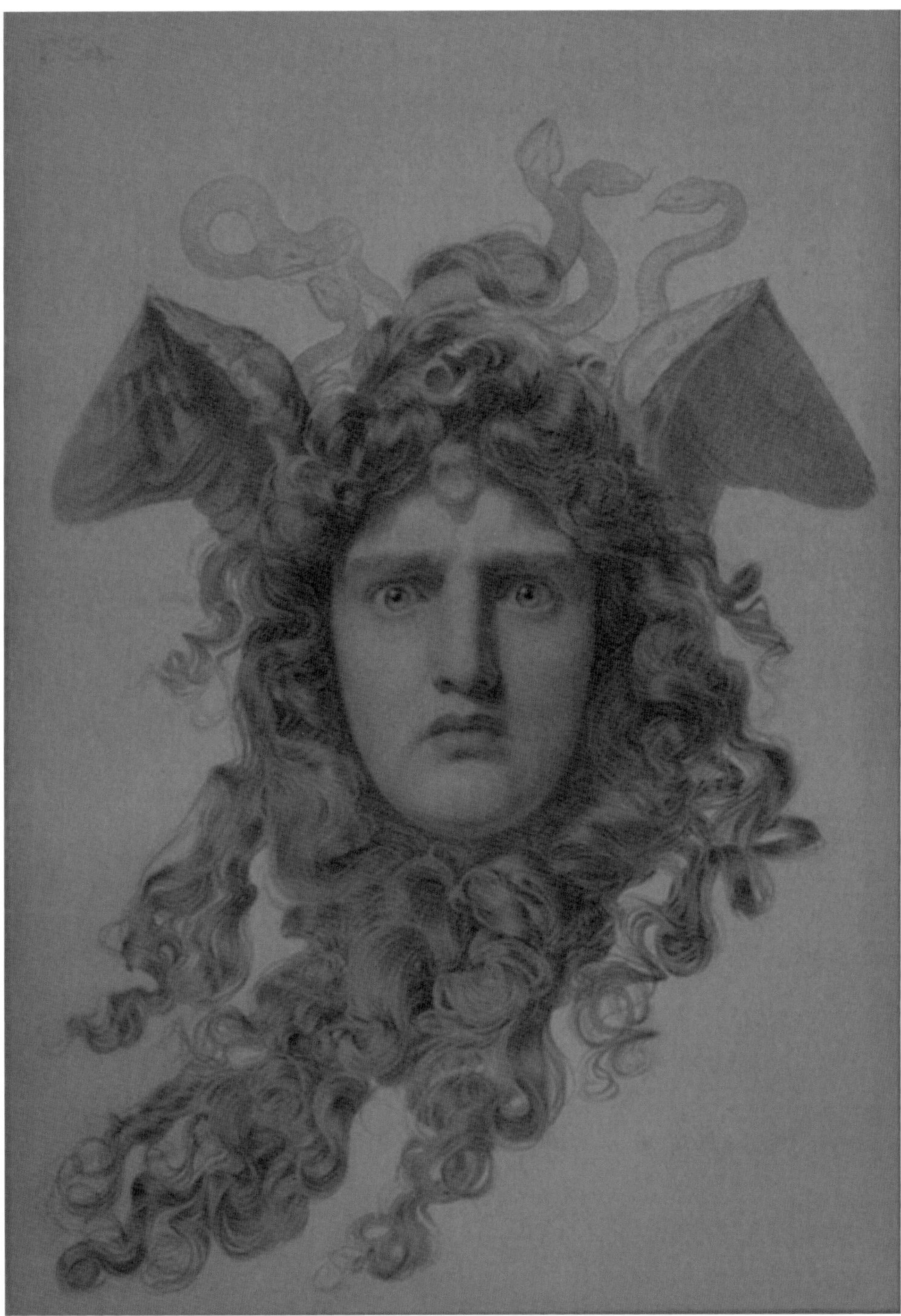

Medusa Head. Chalk drawing. *c.*1875. The femme fatale theme has here been carried to its extreme. The model is recognisable as Emelie Eyre Jones, the actress sister of Sandys's 'little girl'.

although he doubted that Salvini would be a satisfactory Hamlet.[122] There were few times in Sandys's life when he was able to provide accommodation for his friends, in the short time he could enjoy living [before his bankruptcy] at the Spenser Street studio. Perhaps even then he couldn't always play the host, as the 'little girl' would be in residence, and though Meredith probably knew of the liaison, there is no evidence for it in any existing records of their friendship.

Records vary, but his eldest surviving (and acknowledged) son Hugh was born in Belgravia in about 1876,[123] and from that one assumes that the birth was at Spenser Street. The 'little girl', after a period of recovery, was on the boards again in October with her sister Miss Jones in a benefit performance of Tom Taylor's *Twixt Axe and Crown* at the Queen's Theatre, in a repetition of the roles they played in 1870.

In November 1875 there is evidence of Sandys giving Rosa Corder, Howell's protégée (and sometime mistress), lessons in drawing at Chaldon House. Howell reported to Rossetti that Sandys thought her: 'The most remarkable girl he ever met … and a very fine nature. He has given her two lessons in drawing, i.e., had her to see his work and to teach her to be careful, he has been to her twice and given her capital lectures as to care and trouble on the ground that she must do everything with all the pains in the world. He has only tackled her on drawing and outline – no colour … or anything else of the kind. He says that if she is backed and helped for two years, she will be able to do anything.'[124]

Rosa Corder (1853–1893) was born in Hackney, the youngest daughter of a wharfinger, granary keeper, and lighterman[125] named Micah Corder (1808–1888), a man who was engaged in the loading and unloading of goods in the London docks, and was in charge of a team of labourers. The family may have been 'working class' but they were comfortably off, employing servants at home, and Rosa was enabled to study portrait painting with Felix Moscheles (1833–1917). She soon became part of the bohemian group of the 1870s, perhaps introduced through working as a model. According to various sources, she also studied with Rossetti in 1874, and probably Whistler, besides Sandys. Whistler painted a full-length portrait of her in riding habit around this time, commissioned by Howell. She must have had some success with her own painting as it appears also that Edward Godwin, who was designing studios for the new building developments in Tite Street, Chelsea, for Whistler and others at that time, designed a small 'cottage' studio for her in 1879. Godwin's 1879 diary reveals that on 25th September, he showed her his design and instructed her on finding a plot of land for it in the area.[126]

This was never built – saddening for the aspirations of people such as these (including Godwin himself). So much in their lives remained unfulfilled due to the chronic shortage of money common to them all (and they associated with people of great wealth).

In the same month, November, 1875, Howell gossiped to Rossetti that he had sold a picture by Sandys for £1,000. Sandys had made it a condition 'that [he] should have £200 [of the sum] paid [him, at once in cash]'. Howell opined 'that I find that being firm we remain much better friends than if I had followed the old way of saying "Oh never mind" and got nothing not even thanks'.[127] Possibly this was intended as a subtle warning to Rossetti as well as Sandys with both of whom he was feeling aggrieved, as Rossetti also took a somewhat relaxed attitude to financial affairs, and Howell felt that they were both selfish and ungrateful for his efforts, failing to recognise that he, Howell, had also to make a living. The buyer of the Sandys picture from Howell was the photographer Clarence Fry, and the picture was one of the versions of *Penelope*, a powerful, three-quarter length drawing of a model in classical drapery.[128] Rossetti was also working on a picture for Fry, his *Astarte Syriaca*, commissioned by Fry for £2,100, which was eventually finished in 1877. In December 1875, Howell boasted in a letter to Rossetti that he had sold, besides *Penelope*, three more works (portraits) for Sandys, at £1,000 each.[129] The sum of £1,000 for Sandys comes up again later in a letter dated 16th March 1876, from Clarence Fry to Rossetti, written in an endeavour to clarify Howell's complex financial dealings with him in respect of Fry's purchases of works by Rossetti. Fry wrote: 'Howell's conduct is such as to render me uneasy – he interests me extremely – but after all this, it's strange to say the least. I have said nothing about £1,000 he prevailed upon me to advance to Sandys.'[130] Fry's unfortunate dealings with Howell show him to be a willing buyer and altogether too trusting of Howell, who it seems was going through a low point in his fortunes.

Sandys produced several portraits in 1875. With Norfolk connections, these were a second portrait of Father Gregory Rossi,[131] the elder brother of Theodore Rossi, and, amongst the gentry, Lady Catherine Buxton, née Gurney (1814–1911), wife of the Liberal politician Sir Edward North Buxton (1812–1858), and their son Charles Louis Buxton (1846–1906). With London connections, there was William Henry Weldon (1837–1919), a member of the Garrick Club and good friend of Sandys who, at the time of his portrait was Rouge Dragon of the College of Arms. Weldon's head was cleverly set in front of a panel of Chinese embroidery depicting red scaly dragons flying about in the sky. Another was the younger brother of his friend James Anderson Rose, William Anderson Rose (1820–1881) who was

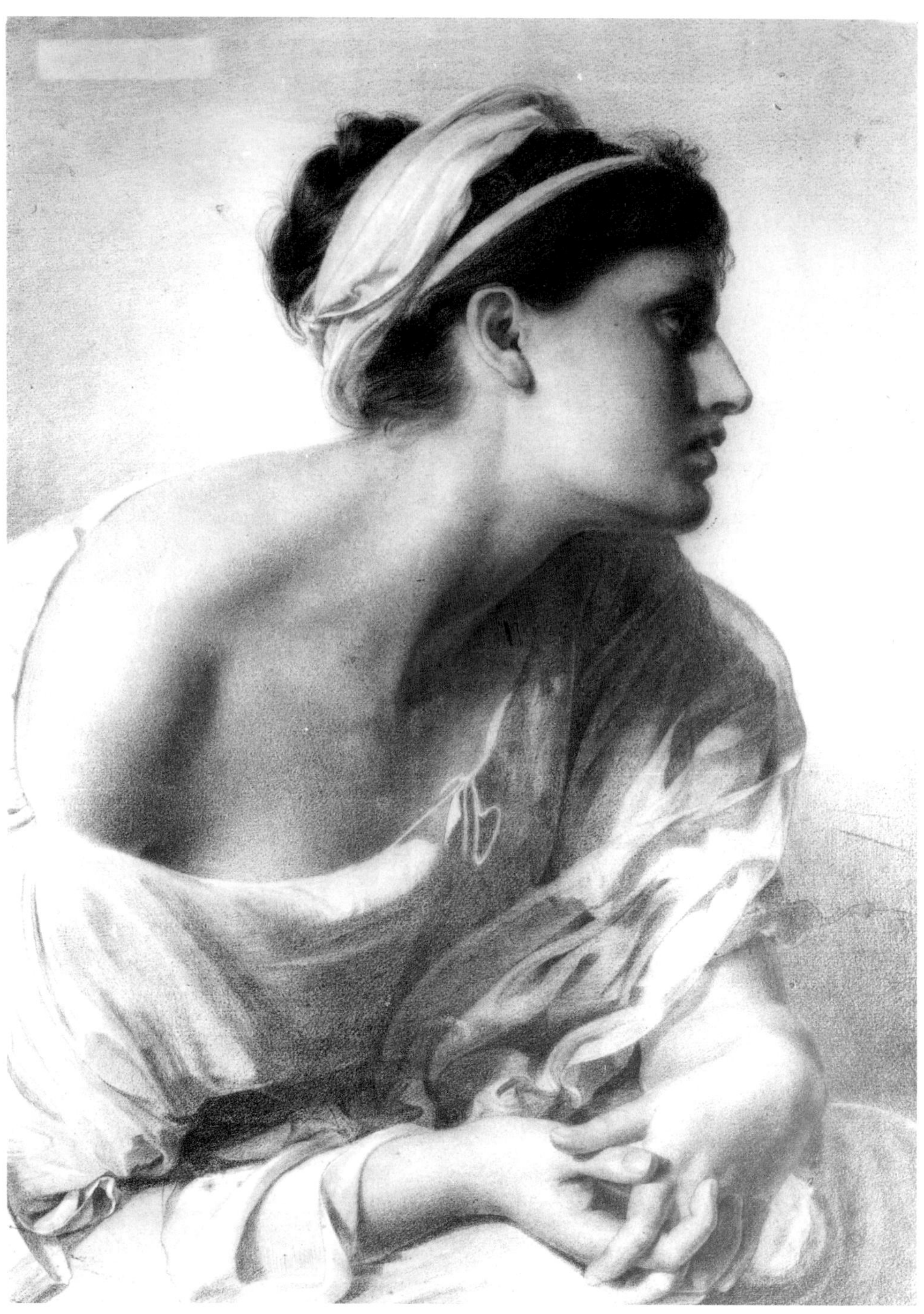

Penelope. Chalk drawing. *c*.1875. A powerful neo-classical drawing which Sandys's friend Edward Godwin (1833-1886) admired. Sandys's draughtsmanship was still at its finest.

a prominent businessman in the City of London, being made Lord Mayor in 1862 and knighted in 1867. The portrait is titled *Col. Sir William Anderson Rose*, showing his pride in being Colonel in the Royal London (Volunteer) Rifles. The hanging of a Japanese textile immediately behind his head in the portrait might have been to show the sitter's aesthetic sophistication, and certainly showed Sandys's.

In 1875 also, Sandys devised a highly dramatic vision of Medusa, one of the three Gorgon sisters from Greek mythology. It was another exercise in the dramatic or femme fatale subject to which Sandys frequently returned. Medusa, in Greek legend, was a beautiful woman who, as a punishment, was turned by the goddess Pallas Athene into a terrifying creature with a headful of writhing snakes instead of hair. At the sight of her, the spectator was immediately turned into stone. The hero Perseus was charged with beheading this unfortunate creature, and was helped by Athene who armed him with a polished shield by which he could see her indirectly by her reflection. He thus safely beheaded her and used her frightful head as a weapon by showing it and turning his adversaries to stone. As a model for *Medusa*, of which he made two, possibly three, versions, Sandys used Milly Jones (Mrs Robson from 1870) who, as an actress, was capable of producing dramatically heightened expressions. Sandys's *Medusa* has luxuriant curling locks which seem partly to be turning into writhing snakes on the crown of her head, from which bird wings spring from either side. This femme fatale, in common with Sandys's many others of that kind forecasted the turn-of-the-century pan-European Symbolist movement. One of the versions had been given to the Victoria and Albert Museum in 1909.[132] The dealer George Donaldson acquired the second, but less complete version, and no doubt displayed it at his New Bond Street gallery.[133]

Eighteen seventy-six was an unfortunate year for Sandys. However, it began well. In January he was working on the portrait of Mrs Temple Soanes and a fancy picture named *Forgive Me*.[134] Neither of these works has yet been discovered, but we know that the portrait was of a lady in a blue dress with bright red flowers (carnations and roses) and that it was later exhibited at the Royal Academy in 1879. F.G. Stephens, who reviewed the exhibition in *The Athenaeum*, described it as: '… brilliant in lighting, and coloured to a high key; sharp and hard in its definition of form … the local colours are too distinct for the harmony of the picture.'[135] In short, he did not regard it with much favour. Temple Soanes (born *c.*1822) and his wife Alice (born *c.*1843) lived with their daughter Florence and a governess in a large house in Frant, near Tunbridge Wells, in Kent. He was a 'Russia Merchant' according to the census of 1881. Soanes evidently had a fine appreciation of art, for he owned Henry Wallis's painting *The Stone Breaker* (1857), avant-garde in its time for its social realism.[136]

Busy with work in-hand in his studio at Spenser Street, Sandys wrote on 8th January to Howell, who was asking him for more work which he could sell. Sandys replied: 'If you like I will paint for you for two thousand five hundred pounds per annum for two years' … (not counting the two pictures he had presently in-hand, mentioned above), 'but you must understand that I shall have to draw on you freely for my necessities within or up to the two thousand five hundred pounds during the year as it might suit me. I know and you know how this would pay you from a commercial point of view, but two strong reasons induce me to make this proposal to you, first the confidence I have in your judgement and friendship, next the desire I have to carry out my plans and designs peacefully and un-intruded on by strangers.' In the same letter he refers to a portrait of 'Mr Elliot's children'. 'I will do you the four little Elliots for 200 guineas, though you know how much Buxton, etc. etc. have paid me.'[137] One may speculate whether these were the children of John Elliott, Clarence Fry's partner in the photographic business, but there is no proof that such a portrait was undertaken, nor that Sandys's proposal to Howell ever materialised, given the impecuniosity of both parties.

Likewise in March, Howell appears to be in trouble with Clarence Fry who was buying Rossetti pictures through Howell. Although this is not the place to elaborate upon these problems, which are detailed in Helen Rossetti Angeli's *Pre-Raphaelite Twilight*, Fry wrote to Rossetti complaining about Howell's confusing transactions, referring, incidentally, to the £1,000 which Howell 'prevailed upon me [Fry] to advance to Sandys'.[138] It is unclear what this large sum of money represented or was intended for, and still a mystery is Howell's reference to '… my fine Sandys which has been strangled in Mr Fry's hands ever since as security for the lot'.[139] The latter perhaps refers to drawings by Rossetti sold on to Fry without Rossetti's knowledge, which were at the heart of Rossetti's complaint with Howell and which virtually ended his connection with Howell as his agent in 1876. As for 'my fine Sandys', the only Sandys work in Fry's hands at this time would seem to be his *Mary Magdalene* drawing of 1872.

Meanwhile, Swinburne had just had his poem *Erechtheus* published by Chatto. Andrew Chatto (1841–1913) had taken over John Camden Hotten's business after his death in 1873. Swinburne asked Chatto to send copies to a list of his friends which included Sandys.[140]

On 24th March 1876, Sandys was writing anxiously from the Garrick Club to Howell to deliver his portrait of Kitty Howell either to him, or to the framers

Foord & Dickinson, as it was the last day for receiving pictures for the Royal Academy Summer Exhibition.[141] Foord & Dickinson had an arrangement with the artists for whom they made frames, for delivering their pictures to exhibition venues. Sandys had three portraits ready to show: *Lady Buxton* (1875), *Father Gregorius Rossi* (1875), and that of Kitty Howell. Following this, a letter from Sandys to Howell shows some confusion over the delivery of the pictures to the Royal Academy, resulting in the *Kitty Howell* portrait being the only one shown. It seems that Howell had taken his wife's portrait directly to the Academy but the other two portraits which Sandys was hoping to show, although already sent to Foord & Dickinson, were, unknown to Sandys, too late for delivery to the Academy because of a change in the receiving hours there. Sandys berated Howell for failing to tell him about this.[142]

In June he was at Knapdale, Upper Tooting, at Alexander Macmillan's suburban villa drawing a portrait of his wife Emma and their daughter Mary.[143] It is a picture of great charm, showing his wife and their little girl enjoying a Walter Crane picture book together. While at Knapdale Sandys wrote to the engraver Joseph Swain asking him to send proofs of his 1860s illustrations *The Old Chartist*, *The Old Sea King* (*The Death of King Warwolf*), and 'the illustration … made to a poem of Miss Rossetti' (*Amor Mundi*) to Alexander Macmillan. He wrote: 'I ask you to do this with reference to his seeing your work in connexion with book illustration.'[144]

A reference to Sandys, at the time of the Epsom Derby in 1876, in a book of memoirs connected with *The Sporting Times*, *The Pink 'Un'*, confirms several hints of his gambling habit. The author, the journalist J.B. Booth, wrote: '"Ballyhooley" Martin came within an ace of having his fortune made by poor Fred Sandys. … In 1876 Sandys wanted to back the treble event on the strength of a dream: *Thunder* for the "City", *Petrarch*, for the "Two Thousand", and *Kisber* for the "Derby". He wanted to take 8,000 to 10 but being short of the necessary tenner asked Ballyhooley to find it and go halves in the bet. Ballyhooley either couldn't or wouldn't, so Sandys borrowed a sovereign, and took eight hundred pounds to a sovereign. And when the treble event came off, a broken Irishman kicked a hole in his hat and retired to his native morass.'[145] Lucky as Sandys sometimes was, dreams and omens are not a reliable guide for betting, and there is no doubt that he suffered many losses. However, such a windfall at this time must have helped to pay off at least some of his debts, if he were so inclined.

By July, the dark clouds of accumulated debts had gathered above Sandys when his creditors began to lose their patience. The deluge began with a letter dated 13th July 1876 from the solicitors acting for the executors of 'the late Sir John Sutton and the Reverend Aimé Boone of Bruges', to whose fund he owed £909 4s 3p including 'costs'. This amount was demanded by the following Saturday (15th June) and if defaulted upon, they would serve him with a notice of bankruptcy. Sir John Sutton (1820–1873) was a wealthy convert to Roman Catholicism who moved to Bruges after his conversion, dying there.

Sandys's response of the 16th resulted in their solicitors' reply: 'We have waited so long on the faith of repeated promises from you which have never been fulfilled or apparently any attempt made to do so that we altogether decline to delay proceedings for a single day.' This was probably a long-standing loan in the form of a bond carrying an interest rate of four per cent. I have been unable to find Sutton's connection with Sandys other than this fund being a source of a loan.

James Anderson Rose came on the scene at this time, to sort out Sandys's financial problems, calling for his creditors to present statements of Sandys's debts, and there was a court-ordered meeting of creditors on 16th August. Sandys was described as an artist and dealer in pictures (the latter being later denied by him). Rose stated: 'Mr Sandys is an artist and of course never kept any books nor any accounts and the statement of his affairs must be prepared by an accountant; Mr Sandys is entirely without funds.'[146]

Sandys was judged to be bankrupt on 29th July 1876, and a 'Trustee of his Estate' was appointed to supervise a settlement of his affairs. The Trustee was Sydney Smith, an accountant of Basinghall Street. Smith announced a meeting of creditors in his office on 5th April 1877, and then made an offer of payment to the creditors of £925 to cover all the expenses of the case, with the balance being divided up to pay the creditors.

A list was shortly drawn up by Rose's clerk.[147] It showed nine creditors:

Frederic Arthur, furniture maker, of Motcomb St., Belgravia.
Furniture to Studio and house, 1 Spenser St. £650.0.0
Sir John Sutton's Executors
Judgement on Bond carrying interest at 4% £875.0.0
Mr MacManus, builder, 29 Upper Phillimore Place
Board and maintenance of 2 children[148] £250.0.0
J. Coaks, Solicitor, Bank Plain, Norwich[149]
Money Lent £100.0.0

J.C. Chittock, Solicitor, Bank Plain, Norwich
Money Lent £90.0.0
(Baruch Joseph) Meyer, wine merchant, Frankfort on Main
Wine, and costs £60.0.0
W. Slo(w)man, Chancery Lane, corner of Southampton Buildings
Costs of bankruptcy £53.17.6
Dr Whistler, 80a Brook Street[150]
(Loan) and costs £32.0.0
Farmer & Rogers, Regent St. W.
Carpets and rugs £22.0.0
Mrs Bateman[151]
Money lent £25.0.0

Total £2,157.17.6

Among the Rose papers in the Library of Congress[152] is a brief dated 1st August: 'To apply to the Registrar to postpone insertion of advertisement in Gazette.'[153] Another brief of 2nd August states: 'On the adjudication being annulled and the petition taken off the file Mr Rose is to pay £25 for agreed costs and guarantee the payment by the Debtor of the Petitioning Creditors debt within 2 months.'

From Rose's (or his deputy's) notes dated 15th August, prior to a meeting of creditors, various facts can be gleaned, such as that Sandys said he was unaware that the notice of bankruptcy was served, being away as he was 'staying with a Mr Macmillan making a drawing of his wife and child'.

From the notes, the list of debts follows:

> 'Mr MacManus £250 for board and lodging and money lent. Two of Mr Sandys's children are with Mr McManus – two girls for five years. The debt for board and lodging.
>
> Mr Arthur – there ought to be a committee of managements and he ought to insure his life.[154]
>
> Question, how far back to go with the account (?).
>
> Had £1,000 for a picture (not touched). Is he to be entered as a Br [bankrupt]?

£400 had as a wager. Qz [query] any other moneys.

£400 was to have the bkcy annulled.

Probably offer £200 a year.

Flowers[155] bill of sale [invoice] £2,500. Amt of rent he pays. Amt he owed.

Mr Roses a/c. Costs never dec'd. Money lent and money paid.'[156]

At the first meeting of the creditors on 16th August, Rose proposed that Sandys should accept the payment of the full twenty shillings in the pound, in instalments of £400 a year until all debts were paid with the condition that the bankruptcy court case be annulled. There were some adjustments (upwards) to the sums on the list of creditors.

If Sandys signed an agreement to do this, but failed to follow up, he risked his creditors applying for his imprisonment.

There were ill feelings at the end of August between Sandys and Rose, with Rose writing to Sandys: 'Nobody could be more anxious or willing to serve but there are limits to forbearance. The contents of your letter of Friday evening [25th August] are intolerable after the pain and trouble I have been taking in your affairs. Being so annoyed I have taken 24 hours to think what I should do & have determined to accept your letter as your decision that you will at once relieve me from all thought or anxiety about you. I shall therefore take no further steps in the matter of your bankruptcy nor will Messrs Harding[157] whose charges I will pay to the present time as I guaranteed them.'[158]

It seems that a further complication entered the case which is outlined in a note to Rose in which Sandys repudiates it: 'I called with a note which I received from Harding and Co – in which is this statement, "We are informed that Mr Sydney Smith, acting under your instructions has sent out a circular note calling a meeting of your creditors to be held tomorrow. Under these circumstances we shall not be able to act for you". You know well this is false.[159] I have spoken to Sydney Smith. Nor have I rec'd a note nor communication either direct or indirect from him. I must ask you at once to write to Mr Smith from your own knowledge and not from my statement that the extract of his letter copied above is utterly false.' Another matter is revealed in a letter from Sydney Smith to Rose, 'I am in receipt of your letter of the 31st ultimo informing me of your claim to a certain drawing made by the Bankrupt known as *Danae*. I know nothing about it at present, but will enquire into it. Do you happen to be a Creditor?'[160] From this it is clear that Rose had been interested in acquiring the large drawing *Danae* of 1866–1867[161] and probably advanced some money but, as it was never quite finished, it probably remained all those years with Sandys for completion. I have found no record of Rose ever having possessed it.

It was during this period that the irrepressible and self-centred Whistler was painting over the recently installed dining room of his patron Frederick Leyland's London house, to match the colour scheme of his own painting *La Princesse du Pays de la Porcelaine* which was to be hung over the mantelpiece. The designer of the dining room scheme was Sandys's Norfolk friend, the architect Thomas Jeckell, who was deeply upset by this abuse of his work. Whistler had painted over Jeckell's antique leather-mounted walls, elaborate panelling, and even the specially designed furniture. Leyland naturally was annoyed. He had not been consulted, and had been away in Liverpool attending to his shipping business, while all this was happening.[162]

Understandably, Sandys's friendship with Whistler came to an end with this outrage, although there was a brief revival in their old age through the Americans Joseph and Elizabeth Pennell, who were then resident in London, and interviewed both Whistler and Sandys in the 1890s.[163]

At the end of the year, in November 1876, another daughter, Maud Mary, was born to Mary Emma Jones ('Mrs Neville').[164]

In January 1877, Sandys was officially declared bankrupt, owing £4,948, assets nil. Little is known about his activities that year except through four dated portraits which he completed. The first from mid-June, is of the two children of Arthur and Isabel Flower. Arthur was the second son of Philip Flower and was the brother of Sandys's landlord and patron Cyril Flower. He was listed as an 'East India merchant, as was his father, in the 1871 census taken at the family home, Furzedown, Streatham, before his marriage in 1873. Following the portrait of the children, in July, Sandys produced a fine portrait of Isabel, their mother, in a lace dress, holding a fan, and another, at the end of July, of Arthur himself. The Flowers lived at The Hyde, a large estate near Luton in Bedfordshire.[165]

Another portrait, from July, for George Donaldson, was of his wife Alice, swathed in classical draperies, which Sandys titled *Alcestis* (in Greek letters). The subject of Alcestis had already been treated in 1870–1871 by Frederic Leighton, and the name perhaps caught Sandys's attention but there is otherwise no resemblance between their pictures. In Sandys's fine portrait of Mrs Donaldson, the pose and costume seem to have set him thinking about another version of *Alcestis*, this time using a model. This led to two more drawings, using similar draperies and the same model, one in the same pose which Mrs Donaldson took, and the other in exactly the same pose but drawn from a different angle. The latter he titled *Penelope*.[166] They formed an attractive pair and were evidently admired at the time, and it appears from correspondence that his friend Godwin had *Alcestis* and *Penelope* hanging in his rooms for a year or so, either on loan or as surety for a loan, at a time when they were close friends (from 1879 to 1880). They must have been returned, for in July 1880 Sandys wrote to Howell: 'Now sell the two big drawings that Godwin had. I think you might manage to get £250 for them. ...'[167] He wrote again anxiously: 'Allingham[168] has the drawings. Now do pray sell them at once – that is the completed drawings *Penelope* and *Alcestis*. You can I am sure easily get £250 for the two possibly £300.'[169] There is something of a resemblance between these drawings and some of Rossetti's images of ten years earlier, especially those for which Jane Morris sat, such as *Reverie* (1868) and *Study for La Pia de' Tolomei* (1868) and also, from a different model, *Penelope* (1869), all of which show similarly sibyl-like, brooding women. However, although Rossetti may have been, possibly, the original inspiration for the images, they are very different in effect and execution. There is nothing of earthy seductiveness in Sandys's women, but they are tours de force of 'finished' draughtsmanship, and have a static, monumental quality. George Donaldson, much later, bought one of these versions of *Alcestis* at the first owner's sale in 1904.[170]

George Donaldson (1845–1925) was a remarkable man: a dealer, collector, connoisseur, and philanthropist. Son of an Edinburgh merchant and importer of furniture, after early travels on the Continent and a period in Paris, he established a gallery[171] at 64 New Bond Street, in London, selling art and antiques to such notable nineteenth century collectors as George Salting and John Jones, and to the South Kensington Museum. He was an admirer of Sandys's work, judging from his commissioning portraits of himself and his family, and of exhibiting Sandys's work at his gallery.

From 1867 Donaldson was also involved with international exhibitions either as organiser or as juror. At the Paris exhibition in 1900 he was so impressed with the new style of 'art nouveau', which had developed on the Continent, that he bought a collection of examples to present to the South Kensington Museum. Unfortunately, the contemporary curatorial attitude at South Kensington was not appreciative of the 'new art' and so the collection was circulated round the provinces for a few years and then relegated to the

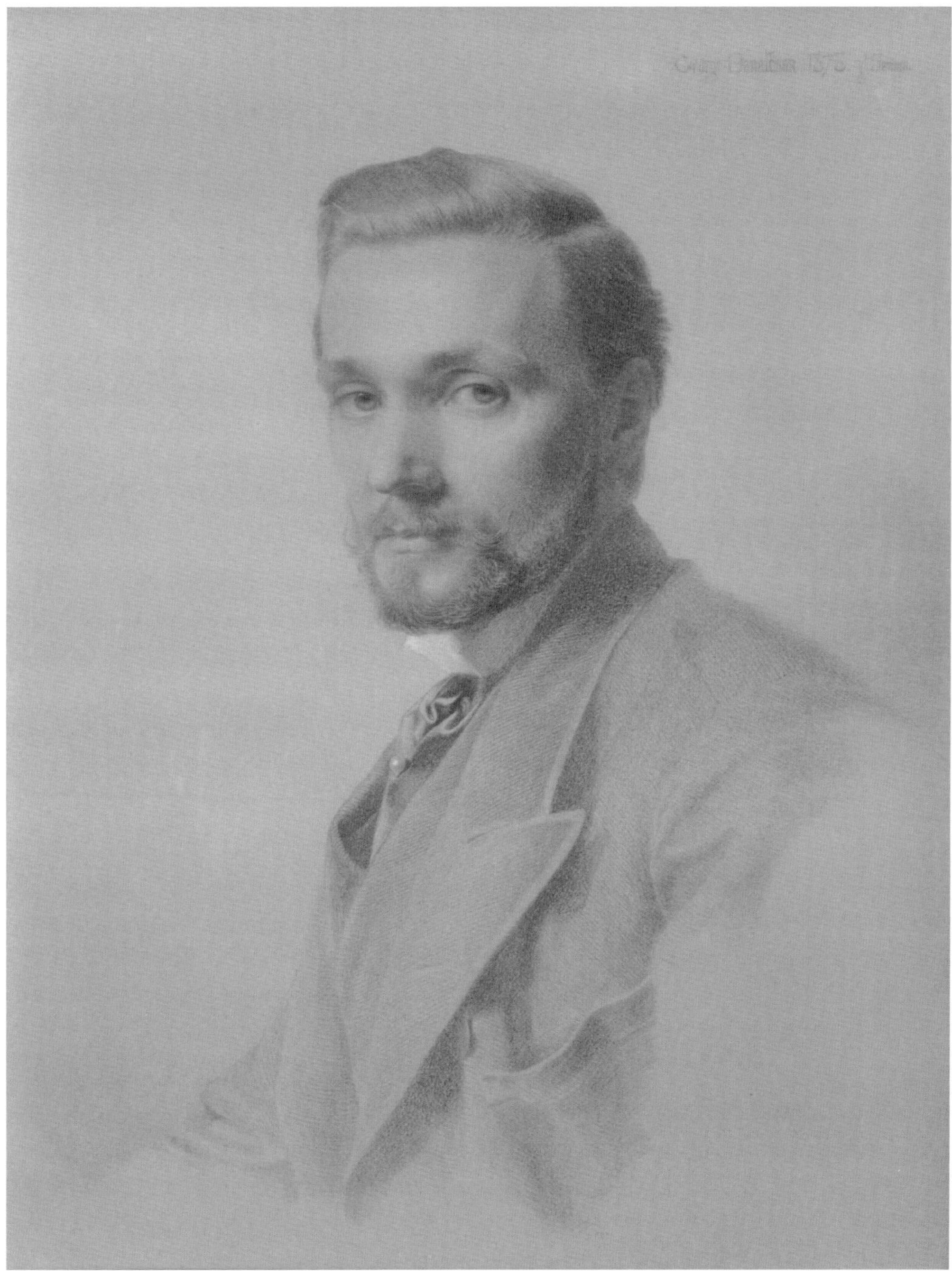

George Donaldson (1845-1925). Chalk drawing. 1878. The Edinburgh-born George Donaldson set up in business as an art dealer in New Bond Street in the mid-1870s. He commissioned several family portraits from Sandys and exhibited his work in his gallery. He was actively involved with international and London exhibitions and with the foundation of the Royal College of Music.

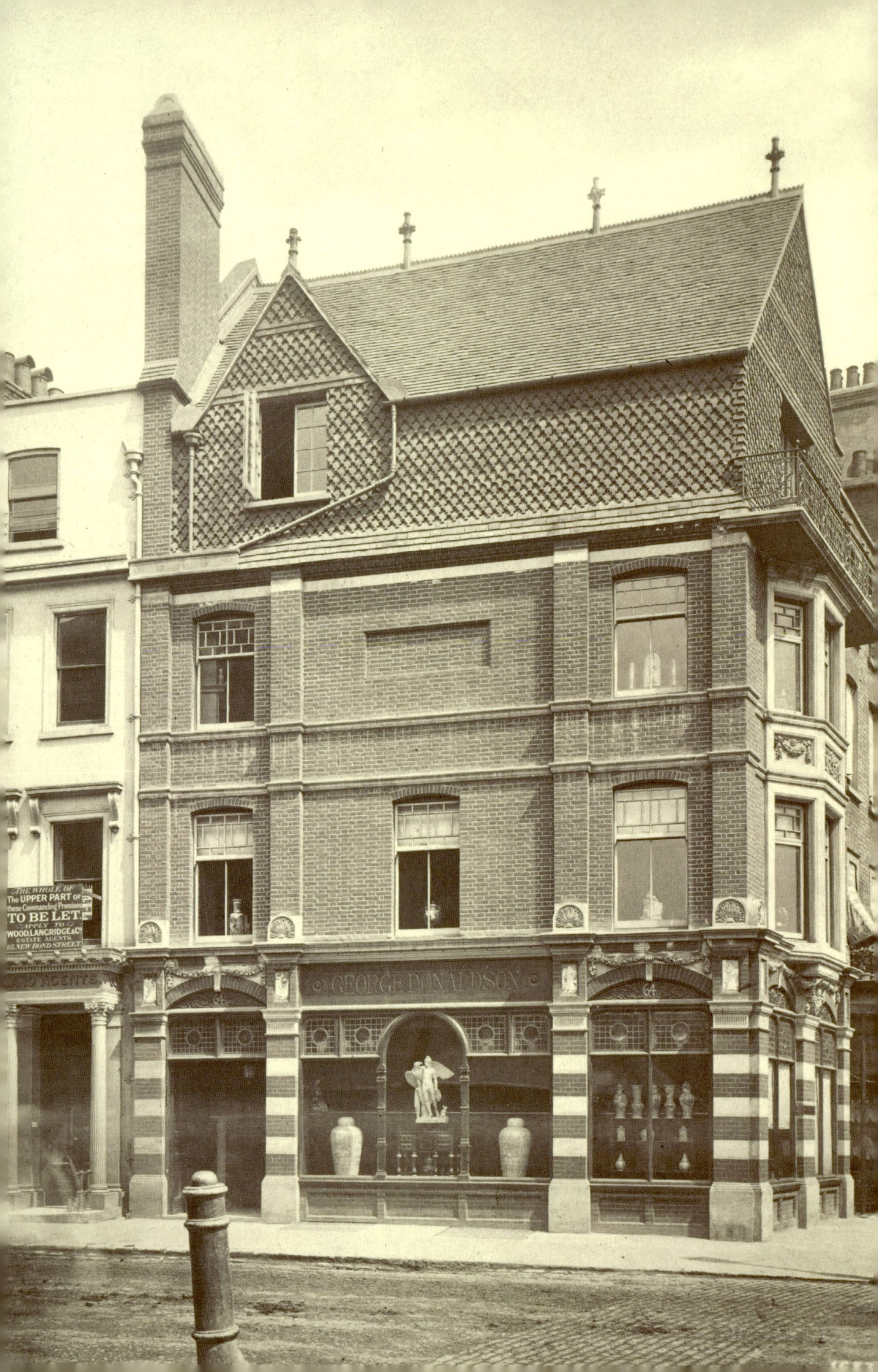
THE WHOLE OF
The UPPER PART OF
these Commanding Premises
TO BE LET.
APPLY TO
WOOD.LANGRIDGE &Co
ESTATE AGENTS.
63, NEW BOND STREET
AGENTS.
GEORGE DONALDSON
64
64

museum's outstation at Bethnal Green in the east end of London.[172] It had to wait to be rediscovered sixty years later by a young generation of curators.[173] Donaldson was rather more appreciated when he gave his collection of historic musical instruments to the Royal College of Music,[174] together with funds to house them in a handsomely designed and furnished gallery in their building in Kensington which opened in 1894.[175] He was knighted for this and other philanthropies in 1904.

A new and spectacular exhibition gallery opened in the summer of 1877, the Grosvenor Gallery at 135–137 New Bond Street. It was the creation of Sir Coutts Lindsay (1824–1913) a wealthy amateur artist and his wife Blanche, née Rothschild. Lindsay's motivation was to provide an elegant showing space for a group of artists who were not served well by the Royal Academy. Instead of choosing pictures by a 'hanging committee', as at the Academy, Lindsay and his associate Charles Hallé[176] would make the selections themselves for the twice-yearly exhibitions. The featured artists from the first exhibition at the Gallery were Edward Burne-Jones, Walter Crane, Albert Moore, and James McNeill Whistler, thereby establishing a new romantic and poetic mood in art which became popularised by name as the Aesthetic Movement. It drew much ridicule at first from the journals of the establishment. In fact, the first exhibition in the summer of 1877 made history when Whistler's near-abstract painting *Nocturne in Black and Gold: The Falling Rocket* drew the slanderous criticism of John Ruskin in his pamphlet *Fors Clavigera.*[177] Whistler hotly responded with a lawsuit for libel which eventually resulted in his bankruptcy and the loss of his new studio-house.[178] Sandys's remarks on this event have not been recorded, but his detailed and 'finished' painting style embodied the very opposite of Whistler's.

Sandys's work was not presented until the third Grosvenor Gallery Summer exhibition in 1879. There were two pictures, *Perdita* and the portrait of *Sir Thomas G.F. Hesketh*, and his address was given as Spenser Street, Victoria Street. In 1880, at the Gallery's Winter exhibition he had a bumper representation of seven works owned or commissioned by Cyril Flower. Again, the address was Spenser Street, but he had to move out shortly afterwards, in August 1881.[179]

At some time in November 1877, Cyril Flower sat for his portrait, whether it was at Aston Clinton, or in London is not known. Aston Clinton, Bedfordshire, was the family home of Sir Anthony de Rothschild (1810–1876), and when in the country, Cyril Flower lived there with his wife Constance and her

George Donaldson's gallery at 64 New Bond Street was designed in 1876 by Robert W. Edis (1839-1924), a leading architect and designer in the eclectic new 'Queen Anne' style. Edis lectured and published books on progressive household furnishings and decoration, and served as a colonel in the Volunteer regiment, the Artists' Rifles.

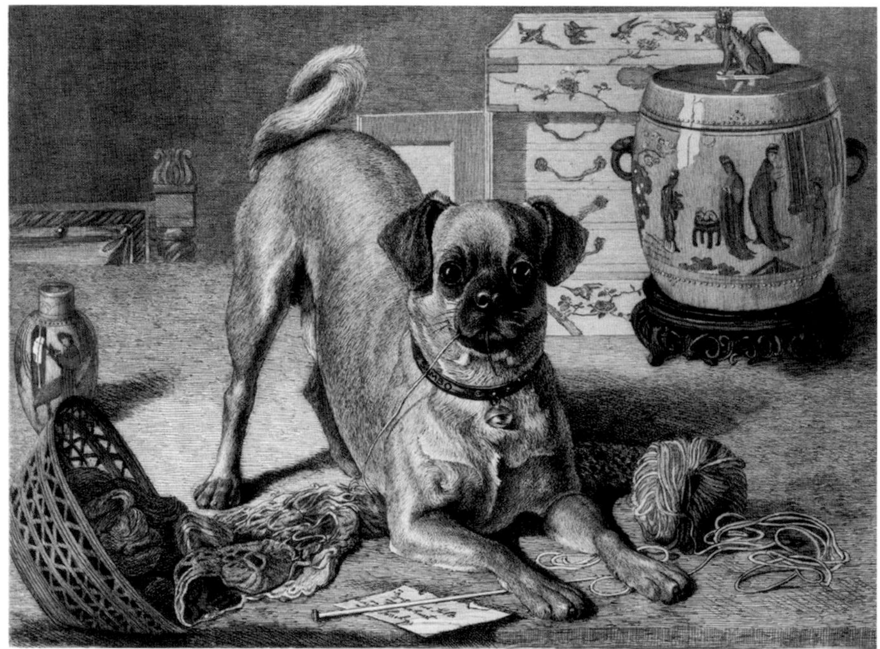

Mischief. Etching by Léopold Flameng (1831-1911) reproducing Sandys's portrait of the art dealer Murray Marks's pug dog Sambo. 1876

recently widowed mother. For this fine three-quarter length portrait, Flower, it seems, was originally wearing a shirt, but in 1880, he asked Sandys to alter it to show him wearing a tweed riding jacket, gloves and a riding crop, skilfully extending the dimensions as well.

In November also, Sandys's sister Emma died at the early age of thirty-four. She died of 'congestion of lungs' at the family house at Grapes Hill. She was buried in the new Rosary Cemetery at Thorpe in a plot which had been purchased by Sandys in 1874 after the death of his mother's relative, Maria Negus Browne.[180] Emma, after a weak start as an artist, after some years of perseverance and the influence and help of her brother, developed considerable skill in her portraiture.

In 1878 Sandys embarked on a near replica of the drawing *Penelope* which was never quite finished. Even so, it was bought by the photographer Clarence Fry, apparently to furnish his business premises. He eventually sold it in 1891. In later hands it was reduced in size, removing the unfinished area. The three related drawings (*Alcestis* and the two *Penelopes*) were originally each subtitled *Study for an oil painting* revealing Sandys's frequent hope that a buyer would commission one. No oil versions have been found.

In February 1878, 'Miss Clive' and her sister Miss Jones were back again on the boards at the Queen's Theatre in Tom Taylor's *Twixt Axe and Crown* which they had first performed in 1870, this time with the distinguished leads Hermann Vezin and Mrs Rousby. This may have been 'Miss Clive's' last engagement.

In March 1878, Sandys was at Aston Clinton with Cyril Flower and his wife Constance. He, perhaps, was beginning work on the portrait of Constance which was finished and dated December 1879.[181]

In the summer of 1878, through the patronage of William Clabburn, Sandys had a singular breakthrough to a wider audience with his picture *Medea* (1866–1868) which was being exhibited at the Exposition Universelle of that year in Paris. This, no doubt, came about because Clabburn, its owner, as a prominent English textile manufacturer, was one of the jurors of the textile section of the exhibition. Edmond Duranty in the *Gazette des Beaux Arts*[182] noted in a review that, in common with Leighton, Sandys used extreme realism to depict the unreal world of Hellenic mythology. Sandys was thus dipping into the current trend in art of Neo-Classicism. To be specific, this was a late manifestation in the 1860s and 1870s. Following the initial late eighteenth and early nineteenth century phase that was inspired by the archaeological discoveries in Italy and Greece, it completely transformed European architecture, sculpture and painting styles. This was at its extreme in France under the regime of Napoleon I who used it to enhance his status as Emperor.

In this later Neo-Classical revival of the second half of the nineteenth century, sometimes known as the Second Empire of Napoleon III, the arts in Europe developed comprehensively from Mediterranean travel and a deeper knowledge of the cultural legacy of Greece and Italy. In England, artists who were inspired by this 'antique' world, besides Sandys, were principally Frederic Leighton (1830–1896), Albert Moore (1841–1893), Edward J. Poynter (1836–1919) and Laurence Alma-Tadema (1836–1912). Admittedly, Sandys never travelled to these faraway places in the Mediterranean, but Classical art and artifacts were accumulating at home, notably at the British Museum (such as the Elgin Marbles from Greece). Illustrated travel books and engravings proliferated and served to spread the knowledge.

At the end of 1878, Howell won a substantial compensation (£3,650) from the Metropolitan District Railway Company for the loss and demolition of Chaldon House in Fulham which lay in the path of the extension of the railway across the Thames. E.W. Godwin stood for Howell again as his principal professional witness.

There is scant evidence of Sandys's activities in the early months of 1879 but preserved by chance are some letters to him from two solicitous lady friends[183] which inform us that he was unwell in February and March, and that he had a painting, a 'great work' in hand, and also a 'crayon head'. He submitted an oil portrait of *Mrs Temple Soanes* to the Royal Academy,[184] the work already referred to, which probably occupied most of his time during these months before the sending-in day at the end of March.

It was Gertrude Blood who wrote in February expressing her sorrow that he was unable to come to dine with her father and herself in Bryanston Place, but if he was not fond of music 'it is perhaps as well you were not here' since she had to sing 'the whole evening'. She hoped that she and her father might call to see the 'great work' and the 'crayon head' and wished to have proofs of each when they were photographed. Gertrude Blood (1857–1911) became Lady Colin Campbell in 1881 and was painted by Whistler in 1886 as *Harmony in White and Ivory*. The other correspondent was Beatrice May Butt, a writer, who left some spring flowers for him in March 'to remind you that summer is on its way'. Revealingly, but not revealing much, she wrote: 'Your retainer gave me a short but careful analysis of your character. From her account I fear that it is Faith that is wanting – at least so she seems to think.' Perhaps the 'retainer' was the same woman who was later also housekeeper to Charles Fairfax Murray.[185] Murray and Sandys were neighbours in Holland Park Road from the beginning of 1887 to 1888, which was when Sandys left The Cottage, Holland Park Road, undoubtedly for financial reasons. This may have been when Murray took on Sandys's housekeeper.

Another portrait was commissioned by Cyril Flower for himself. It was a second portrait of his sister Clara, now *Mrs William Brand* (dated 1879). It was shown in 1880 at the Grosvenor Gallery Winter Exhibition. Around this time, Sandys was probably also working on the double portrait of Ethel and Mary Brand, the younger sisters of James Brand, since it and his portrait of James were shown at the RA Summer Exhibition in 1880.

From May 1879 onwards, much is revealed through the diaries of Edward Godwin. It was probably sometime in 1876 when Sandys and Godwin became close friends. They must have known each other from soon after 1865 when Godwin moved his practice from Bristol to London, but there is no evidence of any particular link between them in those days even though their paths must have crossed. Godwin's world included his fellow-architect William Burges[186] who was also on friendly terms with the Rossetti group, Whistler, and Howell.

The first clear evidence we have of their direct relationship occurs in 1878 when it appears that Godwin designed a colour scheme and chimney-piece for Sandys's studio-residence at Spenser Street.[187] Godwin's diary for 1879 shows that from May 1879, at least, their friendship grew – possibly through their mutual friend the artist and playwright W.G. Wills.[188]

In 1879, Godwin was much occupied in building developments in Chelsea, including a studio-house for Oscar Wilde's friend Frank Miles,[189] and Godwin took his wife Beatrice[190] and Sandys to look over their progress on one of the many occasions in May and June which they spent together. In the seventies there was an extraordinary spate of studio building in London, a direct effect of a period of growing prosperity for the English upper and upper-middle classes. There was spare money to spend on pictures, and artists, particularly portrait artists, benefited financially. Geographically, the more prosperous Royal Academicians preferred to settle in Hampstead, or the former Holland estate in Kensington. Another development began in Chelsea along the newly built Thames Embankment and in Tite Street, which is at a right angle to the Embankment. Tite Street offered smaller plots for the artists and aesthetes of a younger generation and the less wealthy. It was with these Chelsea developments that Godwin was largely involved.[191]

Among them, Godwin designed and built for Whistler in 1877–1878 a small studio-residence in Tite Street. It was named The White House for its façade of pale stock bricks (which, later, were covered in whitewash). Whistler's notorious bankruptcy prevented him from living there for long, as it had to be sold to pay his debts, and it pained him that his beloved new house was bought by the wealthy dilettante and art critic Harry Quilter, who vociferously opposed all manifestations of the new art movement of which Whistler was at the heart.

In June 1879, Godwin and Sandys were together in either one or the other's houses on at least ten occasions. They were living conveniently near to one another at either end of the new Victoria Street development in Westminster. Other friends whom they saw together in May and June were Wills, and Wills's secretary Alfred Calmour,[192] George Lefanu,[193] and Johnston Forbes-Robertson.[194] On 11th June, Sandys in an affectionate gesture gave Godwin's wife Beatrice a copy of the published book of Alfred B. Richards's poem *Medea*,[195] which had been inspired by the Sandys painting (1866–1868). Lefanu had dined with the Godwins and the three of them afterwards went over to Sandys's house in Spenser Street that evening. On another occasion Sandys and Godwin had dinner with Wills at the Solferino restaurant in Rupert Street. In July, on one of their three occasions together, Sandys and

Godwin went to see the Royal Agricultural Society's Show which was being held in London that year. It is abundantly evident that they were enjoying each other's company.

In August, Sandys dined at the Godwin's on four Sundays out of five (there is no indication that 'Mrs Neville' was ever included). Other guests at these parties included Wills (who, with Burges, seems to have been Godwin's closest friends), Horace Green,[196] Arthur May,[197] Thomas Marwick,[198] Isaac Barrable,[199] Frank O'Donnell,[200] Willie Wilde,[201] and his younger brother Oscar (recently down from Oxford), and Herman Vezin. On another occasion, Wills took the Godwins and Sandys out to dinner at the Criterion restaurant,[202] coffee at Monico's,[203] and afterwards they all shared a box at a Promenade concert.[204] Wills was at the height of his career as a playwright and was consequently prosperous but was in any case a generous and hospitable man. He had recently concluded a successful season with his play *Ellen*, at the Haymarket Theatre.

In September Sandys and Godwin were together on fifteen occasions, which may be regarded as the height of their friendship, but in Godwin's diary ominous notes began to appear of small loans of money to Sandys, sowing the seeds of disillusionment in Godwin's mind and leading to the ending of the friendship.

On 9th September, Godwin noted that he met the wealthy James Brand at Sandys's studio-house, and that he met him again there on four other occasions. It seems he discussed some architectural plans with him. Brand was sitting at the time to Sandys for his portrait, which was shown at the Royal Academy in 1880.[205] Sandys and Godwin dined together on the 22nd and again on the 25th at the Café Royal in Regent Street, and on the latter occasion Godwin noted that he paid Sandys £200, which perhaps, had some connection with the two large chalk drawings of *Penelope*[206] and *Alcestis*[207] to which Godwin seems to have become attracted and had on loan.[208]

On September 26th, Godwin was at the British Museum, perhaps for some study purpose of his own, but while he was there he 'made sketches of pots for Sandys'. One may infer from this that Sandys used a Godwin sketch as reference for the pottery vessel in his large drawing *Persephone*.[209] This together with the similar, but earlier, full-length classical figure *Waters of Lethe*[210] was probably bought by Cyril Flower soon afterwards.

The next day, 27th September, Sandys and Godwin lunched at a City dining room, The Ship and Turtle,[211] before Sandys departed from Liverpool Street

Station for a short visit to Norwich, probably to see his parents. Godwin recorded that on 1st October they dined together again at the Garrick Club, and played billiards afterwards at the Arundel Club.

Sandys and Godwin met only three times in November, but during the second half of December they were together nearly every day, often in the company of their mutual friend Wills. Sandys sent the Godwins a present of a Norfolk turkey which arrived on 23rd December, and he spent Boxing Day with them, and then dined with them on New Year's Eve, staying on to see in the New Year, 1880.

One cannot help but wonder where Sandys's own increasing family fitted into this kind of life since, besides his more public life which was concerned with socialising with friends and patrons, not forgetting his work hours, he seems to have spent a large amount of the remaining time with Godwin and his wife, either at their home at 8 Victoria Chambers, Westminster, or going out with them on various occasions. Godwin's diaries never mention Sandys's Mary although he surely would have known of her, since Howell, known to them both, certainly did. She had, after all, been Sandys's 'little girl' for at least ten years and probably more. By 1879 he had seven living children by Mary: Cissily, Dorothy, Winifred, Mildred, Hugh, Maud, and Constance. Ruth arrived in 1880. Born after that were Guy Edwyn in 1882, and Edwin Myles in 1884 (who died at two weeks), and lastly Gertrude in 1886. They must have been like baby chicks in a nest with their beaks open, needing sustenance. I have found no evidence of any family life going on at Sandys's studio-residence in Spenser Street, Westminster, except perhaps in the births of Hugh (1875) and Maud (1876) who, according to the census, were born in Belgravia (Spenser Street?). Constance, however, was born in Hammersmith in 1878. The next child, Ruth was born in Kensington.[212] Besides being a mother of so many small children, it appears that Mary was still acting as 'Miss Clive' in small parts until the end of February 1878.[213]

[1] Programme collection, Theatre Collection, V&A Museum.

[2] Letter from Rossetti to F.S., dated 5th June 1869, mentions 'Marie' as if she were an established part of Sandys's life. Doughty and Wahl. (1965), p. 699.

[3] Washington, Library of Congress, Manuscript Division, Pennell-Whistler Collection.

[4] Peter Eaton (d.1993), a well-known bookseller who had premises at 80 Holland Park Avenue and, later, at Lilies, Weedon, Bucks.

[5] Census return of 1871 for 22 Kingsbridge St., Poplar, Borough of Tower Hamlets.

[6] Death Certificate of Maura Neville registered in Poplar, 5th January 1869.

[7] Esther Wood, (1896), p. 39. She dates it as *c.*1874, which probably was the date of its completion. Emma, his sister, seems to have been his model.

[8] By 'picture', he probably meant 'drawing' in this case.

[9] Letters from F.S. to Howell with dates such as 'Saturday', 'Friday evg', 'Monday', 'Sunday May 16th' (actually 15th), 'Tuesday', all concerning his stay in Hastings in May 1870. Manchester, John Rylands University Library. Eng.Ms.1279/10, /146, /13, /12, /11.

[10] Christie's sale of 13th May 1935, lot 135, S. Morris, vendor, *Portrait of Mrs William Morris – in white embroidered dress with pearl rope*'. Dated 1870, Oil, 13 ½ in x 11 ½ in., bought by L. Burr for Morris (or Pearson?) for 8 gns.

[11] Edmund Gosse, *The Life of Algernon Charles Swinburne* (Macmillan, New York, 1917), pp. 199–200.

[12] There was a crisis at Harvey & Hudson's bank, the Crown Bank, at Norwich, precipitated by the death of Sir Robert Harvey on 19th July 1870, coinciding with a large claim from creditors. Although the debts were honoured promptly, a Chancery Suit followed which must have delayed the bank's recovery. Clabburn was probably one of the bank's silent guarantors and had to produce cash quickly to honour his share of the debt. *Medea* however, stayed in the Clabburn collection, passing to his daughter in 1879. Manchester, John Rylands University Library. Eng.Ms. 1279/15.

[13] Sandys showed the oil painting *Mary Magdalene*, 1862 (109). The 1871 exhibition buildings were on the yet to be developed plot of land south of the Albert Hall and to the west of Exhibition Road.

[14] The Dudley Gallery, housed in the Egyptian Hall, Piccadilly, opened in 1865. I have found no evidence of Sandys having exhibited there, so perhaps his plan was not realised.

[15] 1871 census return for 22 Kingsbridge St., Poplar.

[16] Letter from F.S. at Sunny Hill dated 'Sunday' (before 13th October 1870) to Howell at North End, Fulham. Manchester, John Rylands University Library. Eng.Ms.1279/18.

[17] Letter from F.S. to Howell, nd. (dated by Howell). Manchester, John Rylands University Library, Eng.Ms. 1279/19.

[18] Manchester, John Rylands University Library. Eng.Ms.1279/21/22/16,/23.

[19] Princeton University Library, Special

Collections. Troxell Collection, Box 29, folder 4. Date indecipherable, but November 1870.

[20] Manchester, John Rylands University Library. Eng.Ms.1279/28/30. nd. (November 1870).

[21] Manchester, John Rylands University Library. Eng.Ms.1279/26. Dated 'Thursday' and (by Howell '8 Dec.1870').

[22] Manchester, John Rylands University Library. Eng.Ms.1279/24. nd, but mid-December 1870. *The Fortnightly Review* printed Rossetti's 'Hand and Soul' (1850) in December 1870, pp. 692–702.

[23] Meredith to Augustus Jessopp, dated 22nd December 1870. Cline, *The Collected Letters of George Meredith*, no. 464.

[24] James Tagus Shout of 22 Parkside, Knightsbridge. Originally a pawnbroker of 123 Shadwell High Street in the 1840s, he had moved to Knightsbridge by 1871. He was a contact of Howell's and probably supplied jewellery to Sandys, for in March 1871 Sandys owed him £75 and handed him *Hero* as security. It is no surprise that Shout kept the picture in July 1871 as Sandys could not redeem it.

[25] Note from F.S. to Howell, dated 6th July 1871, written on a sheet of memorandum paper headed 'From Jas Tagus Shout/22 Parkside, Knightsbridge SW'. Manchester, John Rylands University Library. Eng. Ms.1279/39.

[26] His *Mary Magdalen* (1862), owned by Clabburn, was accepted.

[27] Letter from F.S. to W.M. Rossetti, dated 'Sunday' (12th February 1871), 'Thursday' (16th February 1871), 1 March' (1871). Vancouver, University of British Columbia, Library, Special Collections.

[28] Letter from F.S. at Sunny Hill, Thorpe, to Howell, dated Monday (March 1871). Manchester, John Rylands University Library.Eng. Ms.1279/36.

[29] Letter from F.S. to Howell, dated 21st April (1871). The RA catalogue of the 1871 exhibition gives his address as North End Grove, Fulham, which was Howell's address. Manchester, John Rylands University Library. Eng.Ms.1279/37.

[30] Watts's *Tennyson* was one of the earlier portraits in the large group he depicted of Victorian 'Worthies', the latest was painted in 1900.

[31] *The Academy*, 26th June 1875, pp. 668–669. Quoted by Martin Hopkinson, 'Drawings in the Dudley Gallery's "Black and White" Exhibitions' in *The British Art Journal*, vol. XV, no. 1, p. 21.

[32] Spelman's, Norwich, sale of 27th and 28th February 1900, Vendors: the executors of Rev. Canon Bulmer, lot 475. He is listed in John Venn, *Alumni Cantabrigiensis*, vol. 2 (2011).

[33] His sale was at Christie's 21st February 1927, lots 67–70. His address was given as Thorpe Chambers, Hustlergate, in the centre of Bradford.

[34] This is evidence of Sandys's habitual way of living: alone as a bachelor.

[35] Letter from F.S. to Howell from Sunny Hill 'Thursday', dated by Howell to 27th April 1871. Manchester, John Rylands University Library. Eng.Ms.1279/38.

[36] Letter from F.S. to Howell, dated 21st April (1871). Manchester, John Rylands University Library. Eng. Ms.1279/37.

[37] Letter from H. Treffry Dunn to W.M. Rossetti dated 22nd July 1872. Gale Pedrick, *Life with Rossetti*, 1964, pp. 116–117.

[38] Letters from F.S. to Howell (1st, 3rd May 1872). Manchester, John Rylands University Library, Eng.Ms. 1279/43-44.

[39] The original showroom was still there, though somewhat run-down, when I visited in May 1999. Much of this information is derived from Carlene Mair's *The Chappell Story*, 1811–1961, Chappell & Co. Limited, 1961.

[40] Letter from W. and W. Cower & Nussey, 1 & 2, Gt. Winchester St. Buildings, London E.C., dated 5th November 1873. Family papers of the late Nigel Rossi.

[41] These were *Whitlingham*, and *Autumn* (1860), an unidentified 'pen and ink sketch', and '*Head of Antigone*' (*c.*1880). These were sold on to other buyers by Theodore Rossi.

[42] Described in the 1871 census return as an 'East India and China merchant'.

[43] Letters from F.S. to Howell (12th 16th January 1873). Manchester, John Rylands University Library, Eng. Ms.1279/48.

[44] Dated February 1873.

[45] O. Bornand, (ed). *The Diary of W.M. Rossetti*, 1870–1873. (1977), p. 246.

[46] Letter from F.S. to Irving (April 1873), in Laurence Irving, *Henry Irving*. (1952), p. 233.

[47] The two houses were near to the new development of The Boltons, Kensington.

[48] Letter from F.S. to Mrs Crabbe dated Saturday 3rd May (1873). Papers of Virginia Surtees. Durham County Record Office, D/X 772.

[49] Author's collection.

[50] Much of this information has been derived from the catalogue of the exhibition, *Minton 1798–1910*, V&A Museum, 1976, p. 67.

[51] John Downes Rochfort (1825–1885). A wealthy barrister with estates in Ireland. He was a keen traveller and collector of photographs bought on his travels. He was a watercolourist and ceramicist, owning a villa at Monte Carlo, and London houses at Eaton Place and The Boltons.

[52] Information from the late Virginia Surtees, the grand-daughter of Madeleine Augusta, nicknamed 'Midge', the child of the Milbank liaison.

[53] Monday, 7th February 1876. A copy of the page was kindly sent to me by Mrs Surtees. The original diaries are in the Milbank family's possession at Barningham Park, Co. Durham.

[54] Postcard dated 8th July 1940 from Ruth Herbert's daughter Madeleine to her grand-daughter Virginia Surtees, kindly passed on to the author.

[55] Newly built in 1867, it was the largest of the London theatres except Drury Lane and the opera houses. It closed in 1878.

[56] William Wybrow Robertson (1831–1908), theatrical manager. Marie Litton (Mary Jessie Lowe,

1847–1884), actress and manager. She married him as his second wife in 1879.

[57] Transcribed in C.L. Cline's *The Owl and the Rossettis*, (1978), no. 246.

[58] Shirley Brooks (1816–1874), journalist, novelist and playwright, was editor of *Punch* from 1871–1874. I am indebted to Virginia Surtees for sending me this reference from the Shirley Brooks diaries at the London Library.

[59] Hermann Vezin (1829–1910), who was to play King John was a Shakespeare specialist. Wisely perhaps, he dropped out and was replaced by William Creswick (1813–1888). Born in Philadelphia, Vezin came to London in 1850 where he became a leading actor-manager. He was a close friend of Godwin and Wills. An undated portrait of him by Sandys was probably done at about this time. Clearly a sympathetic man, he was supportive of the Sandys family beyond Sandys's death in 1904.

[60] *The Athenaeum*, 28th June 1873. Drama, *The Week*. p. 862.

[61] Stage business: the way an actor conducts himself or herself physically on the stage.

[62] Was this piece of 'business' inspired by her pose for the *Proud Maisie* of 1868?

[63] In other words, a polite reception.

[64] Now part of the Theatre Collection, V&A Museum.

[65] Letter from D.G. Rossetti to C.A. Howell (24th June 1873), no. 253 in C.L. Cline, *The Owl and the Rossettis*, (1978).

[66] 28th June 1873.

[67] Howell's nickname for Sandys. Also see p. 152, footnote 785.

[68] This refers to the rift between Sandys and Rossetti from 1869, when Rossetti complains of Sandys's plagiarism of his work. C.L. Cline, op. cit., no. 254.

[69] C.L. Cline, (1978), op. cit., no. 256.

[70] C.L. Cline, (1978), op. cit., no. 257.

[71] C.L. Cline, (1978), op. cit., no. 258.

[72] C.L. Cline, (1978), op. cit., no. 260.

[73] C.L. Cline, (1978), op. cit., no. 261, dated 7th July 1873.

[74] These houses had been built in the early 1850s.

[75] This seems that she was well enough to get out of bed on the 8th July.

[76] Letter from F.S. to Rossetti, dated 'Tuesday', probably 8th July 1873. Vancouver, University of British Columbia Library, Special Collections.

[77] Doughty and Wahl. *The Letters of Dante Gabriel Rossetti*, vol. 3 (1871–1876), no. 1376.

[78] Ibid., no. 1382.

[79] F.S. writing to Rossetti on 2nd September 1873, wrote that she was recovering but still far from well. Vancouver, University of British Columbia Library, op. cit..

[80] C.L. Cline, (1978), op. cit., no. 436. Sandys finished this portrait in November 1875.

[81] Manchester, John Rylands University Library. Eng.Ms.1279/50. 29 July 1873.

[82] She married William Brand of the neighbouring Brand family. Her portrait of 1872 was exhibited at the RA in 1873 as '*Mrs. William Brand*'.

[83] London, V&A Museum, no. P.41–1939.

[84] G.C. Williamson. *Murray Marks and his Friends*, London, nd (1919), p. 108, 111–112.

[85] Ibid. pp. 111–112. At least two impressions are known. They are dated 1876. One is at the Fitzwilliam Museum (given by Charles Fairfax Murray), and one is in the author's possession.

[86] Manchester, John Rylands University Library. Eng.Ms.1279/ 94. Dated 20th August 1882 by Howell.

[87] Vancouver, University of British Columbia Library, Special Collections.

[88] C.L. Cline, (1978), op cit., no. 295, dated 5th September 1873.

[89] Francis Fennell Jr, (ed.) *The Rossetti-Leyland Letters*, 1978, no. 54.

[90] Letter from F.S. to Howell. Manchester, John Rylands University Library. Eng.Ms. 1279/53.

[91] Collection of the late Anthony Rossi, RIBA.

[92] The oil portrait was hanging in the board room of the Norwich Union building in Norwich in 2001. The preliminary drawing has recently been discovered (in 2017) and is in the author's collection.

[93] *Modern Society*. 7 December 1907, p. 22. 'Art Gossip'. Albert Moore was another tenant. Sandys Family Archive.

[94] Letter from F.S. from 4 Queen's Road, St Catherine's Plain, to Howell, dated by Howell to 11th December 1873. Manchester, John Rylands University Library. Eng.Ms. 1279/54.

[95] London, V&A Museum, no. E.248-1963:12.

[96] Edward William Godwin Jr (1833–1886), architect and designer, writer on art, architecture, theatre, and dress reform. He was a respected figure in advanced art circles in the 1870s and 1880s. He lived with the actress Ellen Terry from 1868 to 1875, by whom he had two children: Edith Craig and Edward Gordon Craig. He married Beatrice Birnie Phillip in 1876, by whom he had one child, Edward Godwin. The majority of my facts I have gleaned from Godwin's diaries (spanning the years 1873–1883) which are in the V&A Museum, Archive of Art and Design, No. AAD19, the gift of Edward Godwin junior. I am grateful to the late Elizabeth Aslin for first drawing this source to my attention. A travel grant from the Delaware Humanities Forum in 1984 enabled me to study the diaries.

[97] Susan Weber Soros and Catherine Arbuthnott, *Thomas Jeckyll*. Yale University Press, (2003), pp. 222–223).

[98] Priscilla Metcalf, *James Knowles, Victorian Editor and Architect*. Oxford University Press, (1980). A major source of information, and through personal correspondence with the late Miss Metcalfe.

[99] Then part of the County of Surrey. The Doulton family, the James Anderson Rose family, and the Brand family were also neighbours of the Flowers.

[100] Maria Negus Browne of the parish of Easton, Suffolk, the apparently unmarried sister of Mary Ann Sandys (née Browne). Square-holder's certificate for No.J.1547, dated 31st March 1874. Sandys Family Archive.

[101] Letter from F.S. to Howell dated Sunday (22nd February 1874). Manchester, John Rylands University Library. Eng.Ms. 1279/58.

[102] Letter from F.S. to Howell dated 1st February (1874). Manchester, John Rylands University Library. Eng.Ms. 1279/57.

[103] Letter from Howell to D.G. Rossetti dated 7th February 1874. C.L. Cline, (ed.) *The Owl and the Rossettis*, 1978, no. 331.

[104] Howell to D.G. Rossetti dated 9th April 1874. C.L. Cline, ibid, no. 351.

[105] Dudley Harbron, *The Conscious Stone*, 1949, p. 130.

[106] Howell argued that he had a 21-year lease on the house and had spent at least £2,000 on repairs and redecorations, making it fit to be a showroom where he could invite his clients to view the works of art he had for sale. He won £3,650 from the Metropolitan District Railway Company. Dudley Harbron, op. cit., no. 104. pp. 132–133.

[107] Charles Fèret, *Fulham Old and New,* Vol. 2, 1900, p. 61.

[108] Manchester, John Rylands University Library. Eng.Ms.1279/62.

[109] Letter from F.S. to W.M. Rossetti, dated Friday (17th July 1874). Vancouver, University of British Columbia Library, Special Collections.

[110] Inter alia, C.L. Cline, op. cit., Letter from Rossetti to Howell, 21st June 1874; D.G. Rossetti to F.S., 21st June (1874), University of Texas at Austin, HRC.

[111] Rossetti to F.S., 25th June (1874); University of Texas at Austin, HRC; C.L. Cline, op. cit., no. 360, n. 2; Rossetti to Howell, 15th July 1874; C.L. Cline. op. cit., no. 368,

[112] Letter from F.S. to Howell dated 24th July 1874. Manchester, John Rylands University Library. Eng. Ms.1279/59.

[113] A.D. Mackintosh & Co., Sale of the contents of The Pleasaunce, 4th February 1935, lot 1627.

[114] Esther Wood, (1896). pp. 39, 45, repr.

[115] Letter from F.S. to Howell. Manchester, John Rylands University Library. Eng.Ms. 1279/60.

[116] Ibid. Eng.Ms.1279/116.

[117] Ibid. Eng.Ms.1279/61.

[118] C.L. Cline, (ed.), *The Collected Letters of George Meredith*, 1970. No.532. Dated 10th September 1874.

[119] C.Y. Lang, (ed.), *The Swinburne Letters*, 1959-62. No. 563, dated 18th October (1874).

[120] Ibid. Vol.3, p.95. Letter from Swinburne to W.M. Rossetti, dated 14th December (1875).

[121] Letter from Sala to F.S. Manchester, John Rylands University Library. Eng.Ms.1279/161.

[122] Letter from Meredith to F.S., 'Derby Day' (26th May 1875). C.L. Cline, op. cit., no. 542. Tommaso Salvini (1829–1915) was better known for playing the part of Othello.

[123] 1891 census report for 28 Maude Grove, Chelsea.

[124] Letter from Howell to Rossetti, dated 5th November 1875. C.L. Cline, *The Owl and the Rossettis*, 1978, no. 434.

[125] According to the censuses of 1881, 1871, and 1861, respectively.

[126] E.W. Godwin Diaries. Victoria and Albert Museum, AAD 4/4 -1980.

[127] C.L. Cline, *The Owl and the Rossettis*, 1978, no. 436, Letter from Howell to Rossetti, dated 14th November 1875.

[128] Ibid, no. 436, n.1. It is tempting to suggest that the model was Rosa Corder. This drawing, once 29 ½ x 21 ½ was reduced in size sometime after 1940 to 16 ¾ x 13 in. Fry lived at The Little Elms, Watford, in 1876.

[129] C.L. Cline, op. cit., no. 433, dated 10th December 1875. This is corroborated in a letter from Rossetti to Treffry Dunn, his studio assistant, at Cheyne Walk, published in Gale Pedrick's *Life with Rossetti*, (1964), p. 187. Pedrick has mistaken the source of the letter, which is from Bognor, Sunday (December) 1875.

[130] Helen Rossetti Angeli, *The Pre-Raphaelite Twilight* (1954), p. 111.

[131] An earlier portrait of c.1850 is known only from a single impression of the lithograph made from it at the National Portrait Gallery.

[132] V&A Museum, P. 18–1909. Presented by George A. Macmillan in 1909.

[133] In my opinion, Brighton Art Gallery has this version which lacks details of provenance. Donaldson (1845–1925) was a Hove resident at the end of his life.

[134] Letter from F.S. to Howell, Saturday, 8th January 1876. Manchester, John Rylands University Library. Eng. Ms.1279/65.

[135] *Athenaeum*, vol. 1 (1879), 7th June. p. 734.

[136] Stephen Wildman, *Visions of Love and Life, Pre-Raphaelite Art from Birmingham Museums and Art Gallery*, Art Services International, Alexandria, VA, 1995. no. 40.

[137] Letter from F.S. to Howell. Manchester, John Rylands University Library. Eng.Ms.1279/65.

[138] H.R. Angeli, *Pre-Raphaelite Twilight, the story of Charles Augustus Howell*, (1954), pp. 110–111.

[139] C.L. Cline, *The Owl and the Rossettis*, (1978), no. 461, n. 1. Was this Penelope?

[140] Cecil Y. Lang (ed.) *The Swinburne Letters*, (1959–1962). Swinburne to Chatto, dated 8th January (1876).

[141] Letter from F.S. to Howell. Manchester, John Rylands University Library, Eng.Ms.1279/67.

[142] Letter from F.S. to Howell, dated by Howell to 2nd April 1876. Manchester, John Rylands University Library, Eng.Ms. 1279/68.

143 Emma Pignatel married Alexander Macmillan (1817–1896) as his second wife in 1872; their daughter Mary (*c.*1873–1960) married James MacLehose (1863–1943).

144 Letter dated 'Wednesday' from F.S. to Joseph Swain. Cambridge, MA, Harvard University, Houghton Library. Hartley Collection. bMS Eng. 745. The portrait is dated 10th June 1876.

145 John Bennion Booth (b.1880-1961), *The Pink 'Un Days* (1925), p. 137. Booth and Bob 'Ballyhooley' Martin were both on the staff of *The Sporting Times.*

146 Washington, Library of Congress, Manuscript Division, Pennell/Whistler papers.

147 Washington, Library of Congress, vide supra.

148 The children were Cissily (b.1869) and Dorothy (b.1870), the second and third children born to Sandys and Mary Emma Jones.

149 A solicitor, a Norwich patron.

150 Dr William Whistler, brother of James McNeill Whistler, was a friend.

151 Sidney Frances Cowell Bateman (1823–1881). Born in America, she became a successful London actor-manager and was a lessee of the Lyceum Theatre in 1878, and afterwards Sadler's Wells Theatre. Rose's notes to the list show that Sandys had borrowed £30 from her, repaid it, then borrowed £20 or £30 afterwards. She probably knew Sandys through 'Miss Clive'.

152 Washington, Library of Congress, Manuscript Division. Vide supra.

153 *The London Gazette*. The official newspaper of record in the UK. It carries government, military, and legal news. An announcement here would make public the fact that Sandys was a bankrupt.

154 Presumably, this was Mr Arthur, the furniture provider, offering advice. He was owed £650.

155 Cyril Flower, Sandys's patron and his landlord at Spenser Street. The bill of sale probably represented the sale of Sandys's books, furnishings, etc.

156 Washington, Library of Congress, Manuscript Division. Vide supra.

157 Harding & Co appear to be solicitors acting for Sydney Smith & Co.

158 Washington, Library of Congress, Manuscript Division. Vide supra. Sandys's letter of the 25th is missing. Sydney Smith & Co were accountants and auditors at Basinghall Street, London.

159 Washington, Library of Congress. Manuscript Division. Vide supra. Sandys's letter has been dated by Rose to 29th August and may actually precede Rose's letter of resignation above.

160 Washington, Library of Congress. Manuscript Division. Vide supra. The letter is dated 1st September 1876.

161 Mary Emma Jones was the model for *Danae.*

162 Whistler finished his work on the room, now famous as 'The Peacock Room', in February 1877. After Leyland's death in 1892 the room was dismantled and sold to Charles Lang Freer. It is now reassembled in the Freer Gallery, Washington DC.

[163] According to the Pennells, Sandys had 'remonstrated with Whistler about what he had done in The Peacock Room and that Whistler had resented it'. E. and J. Pennell, *The Whistler Journal*, 1921, p. 22.

[164] 1891 census. She was born in 'Belgravia', presumably at Spenser Street.

[165] 1881 census.

[166] *Alcestis* (1877), Arwas Collection, and *Penelope* (*c.*1877), with Maas Gallery from 27th March 1973, untraced. These two were probably designed as a pair. A second, unfinished, replica of *Penelope*, later cut down in size, is now at the Cecil Higgins Art Gallery, Bedford. This latter *Penelope* can be identified with one of the illustrations in Wood (1896), p. 39. I note a resemblance of the model to Rosa Corder.

[167] Letter from F.S. to Howell dated 'Saturday' (10th July 1880). Manchester, John Rylands University Library. Eng.Ms.1279/75.

[168] Theodore Frederick Allingham (b.1845), solicitor. He appears often in Sandys's letters.

[169] Letter from F.S. to Howell dated 'Thursday eveg' (30th July 1880). Manchester, vide supra. Eng.Ms. 1279/76. Allingham still had them in September 1880 and Sandys was still pleading for Howell to sell them. Manchester op. cit., Eng.Ms. 1279/82, 83.

[170] C.H.T. Hawkins, deceased, of 10 Portland Place, sold at Christie's 26th March 1904, lot 108, bought by Donaldson for £33.12.0. Christopher Henry Thomas Hawkins (1820–1903) was a wealthy landowner in Cornwall and collector of bijouterie, miniatures, etc. His sale was at Christie's, 22–26 March 1904, and realised £185,008.

[171] A most original building, now demolished. The architect was Robert Edis (1839–1927).

[172] Elizabeth Aslin, 'Sir George Donaldson and 'Art Nouveau' at South Kensington' in *Journal of the Decorative Arts Society*, vol. 7 (1982), pp. 9–14.

[173] Elizabeth Aslin, one of the group of young art-school trained curators recruited by Peter Floud for the Circulation Department (travelling exhibitions) at the reopening of the Victoria and Albert Museum after the Second World War.

[174] The architect of the Royal College of Music was Sir Arthur Blomfield (1829–1899), designed in 1882, opened in 1894.

[175] Elizabeth Wells, 'The Donaldson Collection in the Royal College of Music Museum of Instruments', London, in *Musique. Images. Instruments, Revue Francaise d'organologie et d'iconographie musicale.* 9 (2007), pp. 103–125.

[176] Charles Edward Hallé (1846–1919) artist. Eldest son of Sir Charles Hallé (1819–1893) pianist and founder of the Hallé Orchestra, Manchester.

[177] *Fors Clavigera*, no. 79 (June 1877).

[178] Fully treated in Linda Merrill's *A Pot of Paint. Aesthetics on Trial in Whistler v. Ruskin*. 1992.

[179] A letter from F.S. to Cyril Flower dated 24th August 1881: Having been locked out of the Spenser Street premises, Sandys was petitioning Flower not to sell his books. Collection of Professor Allen Staley.

[180] Mary Ann (née Browne) was Frederick and Emma's mother. My guess is that the 1874 burial was for Mary Ann's unmarried sister in Suffolk.

[181] I am grateful to Virginia Surtees, from Suffolk, for this information from Constance Flower's diaries.

[182] *Gazette des Beaux-Arts*. 1878. p. 310.

[183] Letter from Gertrude E. Blood (1857–1911) to F.S., 5th February 1879; letter from Beatrice May Butt (1853–1918) to F.S., nd (19th March 1879). Manchester, John Rylands University Library, Eng.Ms.1279/159 and 158.

[184] London, RA, 1879, no. 429.

[185] 'Talk about Sandys must stand over (for the present). I know a good deal about him naturally. My housekeeper was his for years.' Rowland Elzea (ed.), *The Correspondence between Samuel Bancroft Jr. and Charles Fairfax Murray, 1892–1916*. Letter no. 55. CFM to SB Jr, 16th June 1895, Delaware Art Museum Occasional Paper, 2. (February 1980).

[186] William Burges (1827–1881). Neo-gothic architect, designer, writer, antiquarian. Noted for his extraordinary medieval-style painted furniture and decorations at Cardiff Castle and Castell Coch for the wealthy Marquis of Bute, and for his own house in Melbury Road, Kensington. Godwin collaborated with him in their unsuccessful designs for the new Law Courts in 1866.

[187] Susan Weber Soros (ed.), *E.W. Godwin* (1999), p. 370.

[188] William Gorman Wills (1828–1891). Irish artist and verse playwright. Lived in London from 1862. Wills, a particularly kind and sociable man, knew the Sandys/Neville family well, as evidenced by his dedication to the 16-year-old Winifred of a copy of his book *Noon* (1887). He wrote many plays now forgotten, but which were successful in their day, for the actor-managers Herman Vezin, H.L. Bateman, and Henry Irving.

[189] George Francis Miles (1852–1891). Minor artist of portraits and landscapes. Diagnosed as insane in 1887.

[190] Beatrice (or Beatrix) Birnie Philip (1857–1896). Daughter of the sculptor John Birnie Philip, she married Edward Godwin on 4th January 1876. They had one son, Edward. After Godwin's early death, she married Whistler in 1888.

[191] For further information about the Chelsea studio developments, see Mark Girouard, *Sweetness and Light* (1977), pp. 177–185.

[192] Alfred C. Calmour (1857? –d.1912) became Wills's secretary in the early 1870s. Actor and, later, dramatist, he came into prominence with his *The Amber Heart* (Lyceum Theatre, 1887–1888) in which Ellen Terry played Ellaline.

[193] Perhaps George B. Lefanu. London landscape painter, exhibitor at the RA, RBA, and RI, 1881–1885.

[194] Johnston Forbes-Robertson (1853–1937). Modelled for Rossetti as a child, and encouraged by him to study art, he started life as a painter. From 1874 he embarked on a stage career for which he was eventually knighted in 1913.

[195] Alfred Bate Richards, *Medea: A Poem*, with a photograph of the painting of *Medea*, by Frederick

Sandys. London, Chapman and Hall, 1869.

196 Possibly Green, a contractor whom Godwin employed.

197 Arthur Dampier May (1857–1916). London portrait and landscape painter, and friend of both Godwin and Oscar Wilde in the 1870s and 1880s.

198 Thomas Purves Marwick (1854–1927), architect.

199 Isaac Barrable (1845–1892), architect.

200 Possibly Frank Hugh Macdonald O'Donnell (1848–1916) Liberal MP from 1874–1885. Radical politician, an Irish Nationalist and advocate for self-government for India. Co-founder of the National Democratic League in 1899.

201 William Charles Kingsbury Wilde (1852–1891). Elder brother of Oscar Wilde, he studied law but became a successful journalist instead.

202 The Criterion Restaurant, Piccadilly Circus, had been opened in 1876 with much fanfare. It was in a very large building (taking up the entire south-eastern side of the Circus) and was lavishly decorated in high style by W.B. Simpson & Sons. *Baedecker* (1887) stated that the table d'hôte was accompanied by glees and songs performed by a choir of men and boys.

203 Monico's, both a café and a restaurant, was in Shaftesbury Avenue, on the north side of Piccadilly Circus. *Baedecker* (1887).

204 At this time, Promenade concerts (which later became a tradition at the Queen's Hall, and later still, at the Royal Albert Hall), were held from August to November, after the opera season. *Baedecker* (1887).

205 London, RA, 1880, no. 1233.

206 *Penelope*, *c*.1878. Black, white and red chalks on green-tinted paper. 30 x 21 in.

207 *Alcestis*, *c*.1878. Black, white and red chalks on green-tinted paper, as above. 30 x 21 in.

208 These two drawings are mentioned repeatedly in F.S.'s letters to Howell in July and August 1880, Sandys appealing to Howell to 'sell the two big drawings that Godwin had,' and again, 'do pray sell them at once – that is the two completed drawings of *Penelope* and *Alcestis* …'. Manchester, John Rylands University Library. Eng.Ms. 1279/75,76.

209 *Persephone*, 1878–1879. Black, white, red, and blue chalks on buff-tinted paper. 47 x 33 in.

210 *Lethe*, or *The Waters of Lethe*, about 1874. Black, white, and red chalks on buff-tinted paper. 47 ¼ x 29 in. Probably started in 1874, the model being his sister Emma, confirmed from his correspondence.

211 The Ship and Turtle at 129 Leadenhall Street, was noted for its turtle dishes, according to *Baedecker* (1887).

212 Her birthplace as recorded in the 1881 and 1891 census reports.

213 Queen's Theatre, *Twixt Axe and Crown* (by Tom Taylor). V&A Theatre Collection.

opposite: *Julia Caldwell*. detail. see page 241

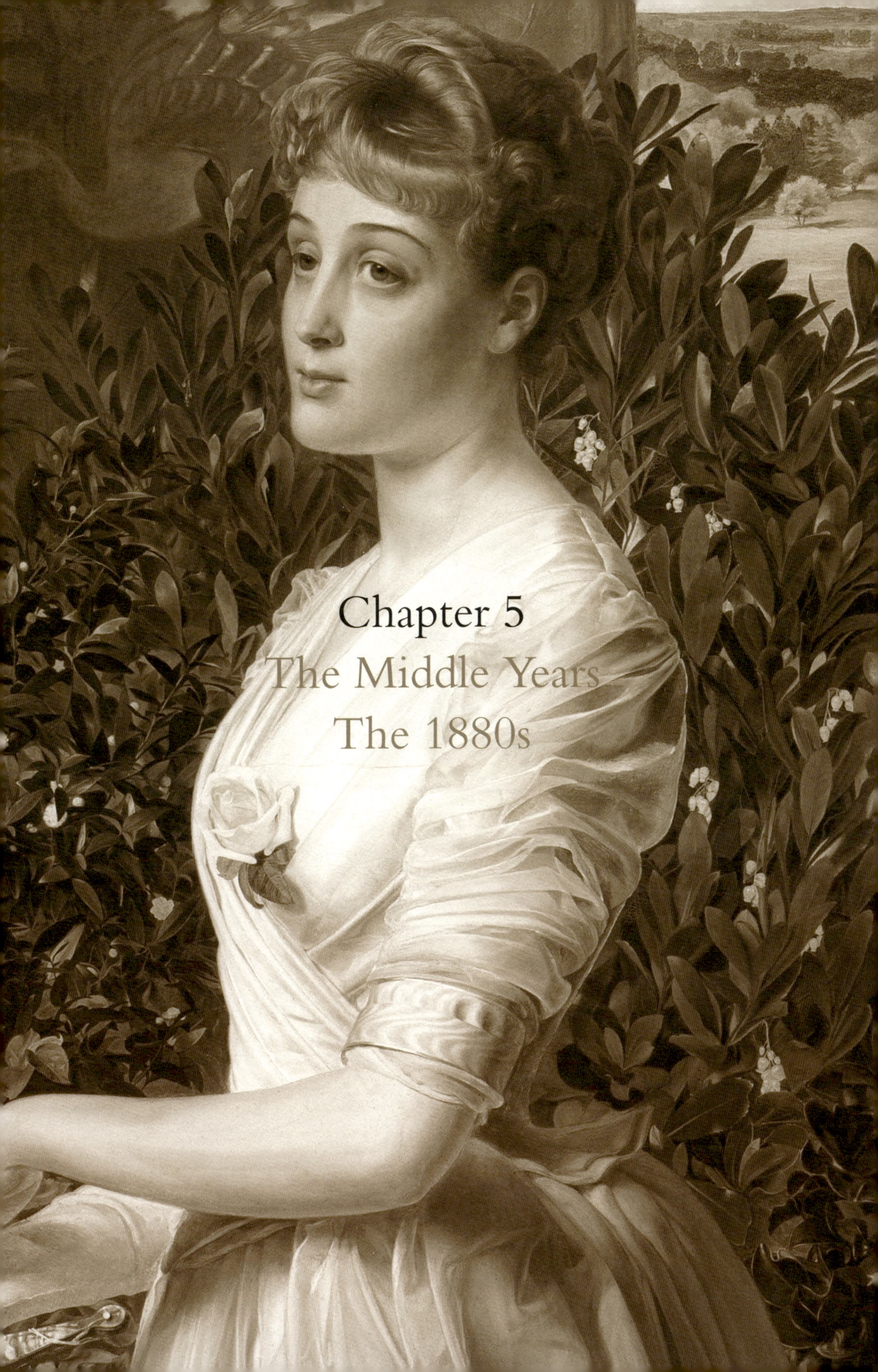

Chapter 5
The Middle Years
The 1880s

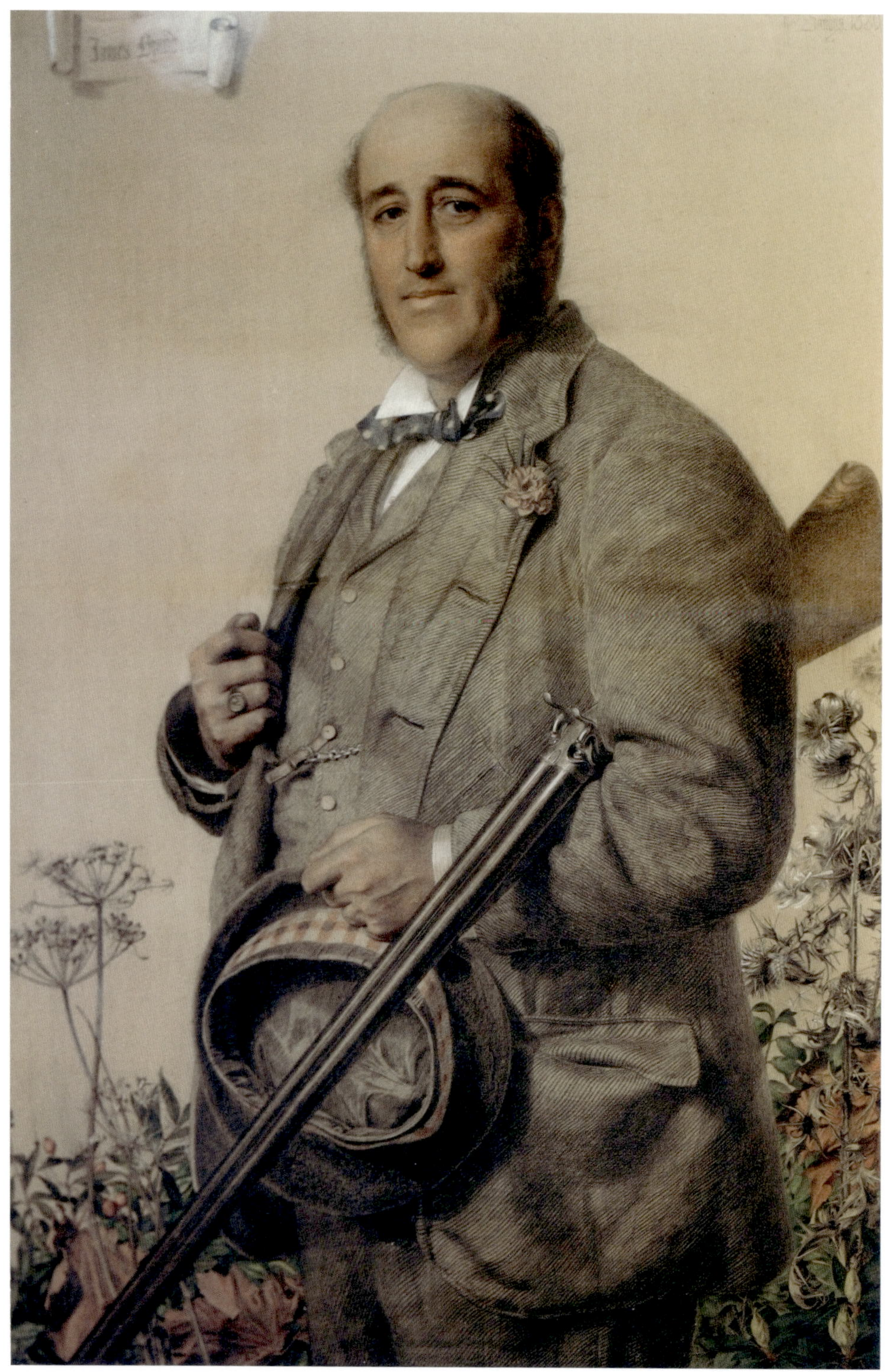

As an artist, Sandys, who was fifty-one in May 1880, should have been at the top of his powers. Instead, one sees a lack of progress and innovation, and a kind of slow stagnation in his work, with frequent complaints in his correspondence of feeling unwell.

He had a major showing of seven chalk drawings at the Grosvenor Gallery Winter 1880 Exhibition, which opened in January. This should have given him some self-confidence and satisfaction.[1] Generally, selection would have been made in November 1879 when Coutts Lindsay and Charles Hallé made the rounds of the studios. In this case the pictures were owned by Cyril Flower. For instance, *Mrs William Brand* was Flower's sister, Clara, of whom he was particularly fond. The portrait of Flower's wife, Constance, had only recently been completed in December 1879. The only uncertainty is the *Study for an Oil Picture*, which is difficult to identify. It could have been the drawing *Gypsy Head* which was in Flower's collection but it remains untraced or unidentified. Work that occupied Sandys in the early months of 1880 must have included the large chalk portrait of James Brand which, although probably started in 1879, would have been completed in the early months of 1880 ready for submission to the Royal Academy Summer Exhibition in March.[2] James was William Brand's elder brother. It was paid for in two halves: £40 in April and £35 in May. A double portrait of James Brand's teenage daughters was also shown.[3]

In a new development, Mary was to be found in June 1880 with some of her children at 28 Maude Grove, Chelsea, in a relatively new row of houses near the boundary of Chelsea and Fulham, just to the north of the former Cremorne pleasure gardens which had closed in 1877, eventually to be built over.[4] The situation was less simple than it might seem. In referring to the 1881 census for 28 Maude Grove, we find that Mary was listed as Mrs Mary Neville, the head of one of three households at that address. Mary's household consisted of two small children and a servant. There were, besides Mary, Constance Neville aged two, Ruth Neville aged eleven months, and the servant Helen Langland. There was no Mr Neville (Sandys) present at that time, nor were their three older children, Winifred, Hugh, and Maude, present. They must have been elsewhere at the time of the census-taking, as were the eldest of all, Cissily and Dorothy, who we know were being fostered.

According to the census of 1881, Sandys at this time was staying across the river in South London (then Surrey). He was listed as single and as a visitor,

James Brand (1833-1893). Chalk drawing. 1880. The Brands were a Scottish family domiciled in London. James and his father (also James) were prosperous China and East India merchants. From the 1860s they were living at Bedford Hill House, Streatham. James's sister Jane married William Dyce (1806-1864) the artist.

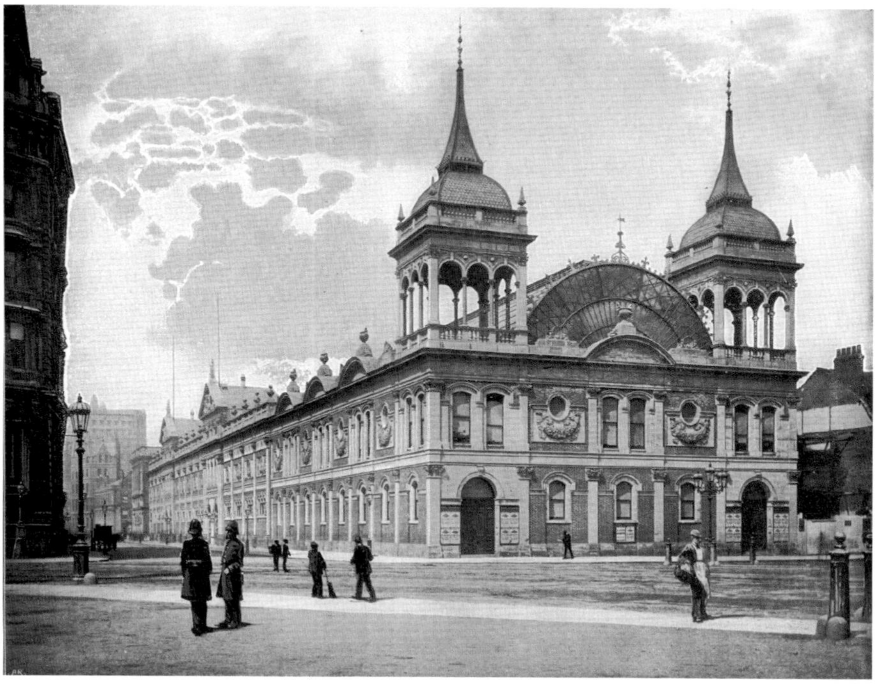

The Royal Aquarium and Winter Garden. Opened in 1876 on a site of former slums on Tothill Street, Westminster, opposite Westminster Abbey. Ambitiously, it included a promenade, an exhibition gallery (guided by Millais), a library, a reading room, and an ice rink. Music was provided by an orchestra and an organ, guided by Arthur Sullivan. Theatrical entertainments there later descended into freak shows. Its original high class reputation gradually deteriorated and it was demolished in 1902. The (Methodist) Central Hall now occupies the site.

staying at Alexander Macmillan's residence, Knapdale, in Upper Tooting. Perhaps he was there to finish his portrait of Emma, Macmillan's second wife, and their young daughter Mary (b.1876), or to discuss the series of portraits of authors he was to undertake for Macmillan in the 1880s. He would shortly have to leave Spenser Street for rent arrears and bankruptcy, writing of Maude Grove as 'home' in his diary entry of 5th October 1880.

The friendship between Sandys and Edward Godwin continued, with Godwin calling on him in his Spenser Street studio on 15th January, afterwards walking out with him in Victoria Street to the Royal Aquarium where he 'dined him'.[5] Sandys returned with Godwin to his Westminster apartment to 'talk about art till late', Godwin noting that 'wife sang'.[6] Later, on the evening of the 27th, Godwin came home after dining with Archibald Stuart Wortley to find Sandys already there, waiting for him.[7] Godwin's diary entry evokes a miserably foggy day, probably as bad as any endured by nineteenth century Londoners, with 'office fires smoking, dull fog, place unendurable'.[8]

The next morning, a cold and frosty one, Sandys set off for Wales from Paddington Station with Hugh, his small son, to begin the picture *St George for Merrie England*, commissioned by Cyril Flower. Hugh was to be the juvenile model and the picture was to be painted at Ffrwdgrech, a house near Brecon in South Wales that Flower, the parliamentary candidate for the borough of Brecon, was renting. It was Flower's political debut, as the Liberal candidate for Brecon, against the Conservative incumbent Gwynne Holford. Flower won the seat in April 1880.

The house was empty a good deal of the time and its seclusion ensured that Sandys would have few distractions or excuses for not getting on with the job. This was Flower's strategy to get him to complete a picture, knowing Sandys's dilatory nature. Besides, both Sandys and the child could be looked after by the servants in the house, allowing him freedom from most practical and even parental responsibilities.

Sandys, it seems, applied himself assiduously to the task daily, seven days a week, but nearly six months were to pass before he finished the picture. This may seem incredible, but it can be explained by his excessively slow and laborious method of working. Granted, the four-and-a-half-year-old boy was a difficult model to work from, but Sandys had the use of a lay figure[9] and a local small boy who could be hired when necessary. We know Sandys's methods, his thoughts, his worries, and how he spent his time, because he kept a detailed diary[10] between 28th January and 12th March, and then from 9th June to 20th October, covering the days he worked – rather as he once did – but in infinitely more detail than when working, over twenty years before, on the portrait of James Bulwer in Norfolk. The difference between these diaries was that in the 1880 diary, in the absence of anyone he could talk to, he confided his thoughts to it. The earlier diary was the briefest notation on a single sheet of paper of what he did every day, covering just a week, accounting for his hours of work on the James Bulwer portrait. From 1880 there are many letters preserved also, between Sandys and Howell who continued to act as his agent.[11]

During the days from January to mid-March 1880, Sandys made a detailed full-sized charcoal and chalk drawing of the figure of the boy, alternately fussing and despairing over every inch of it, while contending with his bored and fidgety model. The completed painting (most unfortunately now lost), which was based on it, shows a rather defiant-looking little boy wearing Tudor fancy-dress, with a feathered cap and silk sash, standing with his legs akimbo on a wolf-skin rug,[12] holding in front of him a sword almost as big as himself. The source of this kind of imagery is the iconic Holbein portrait

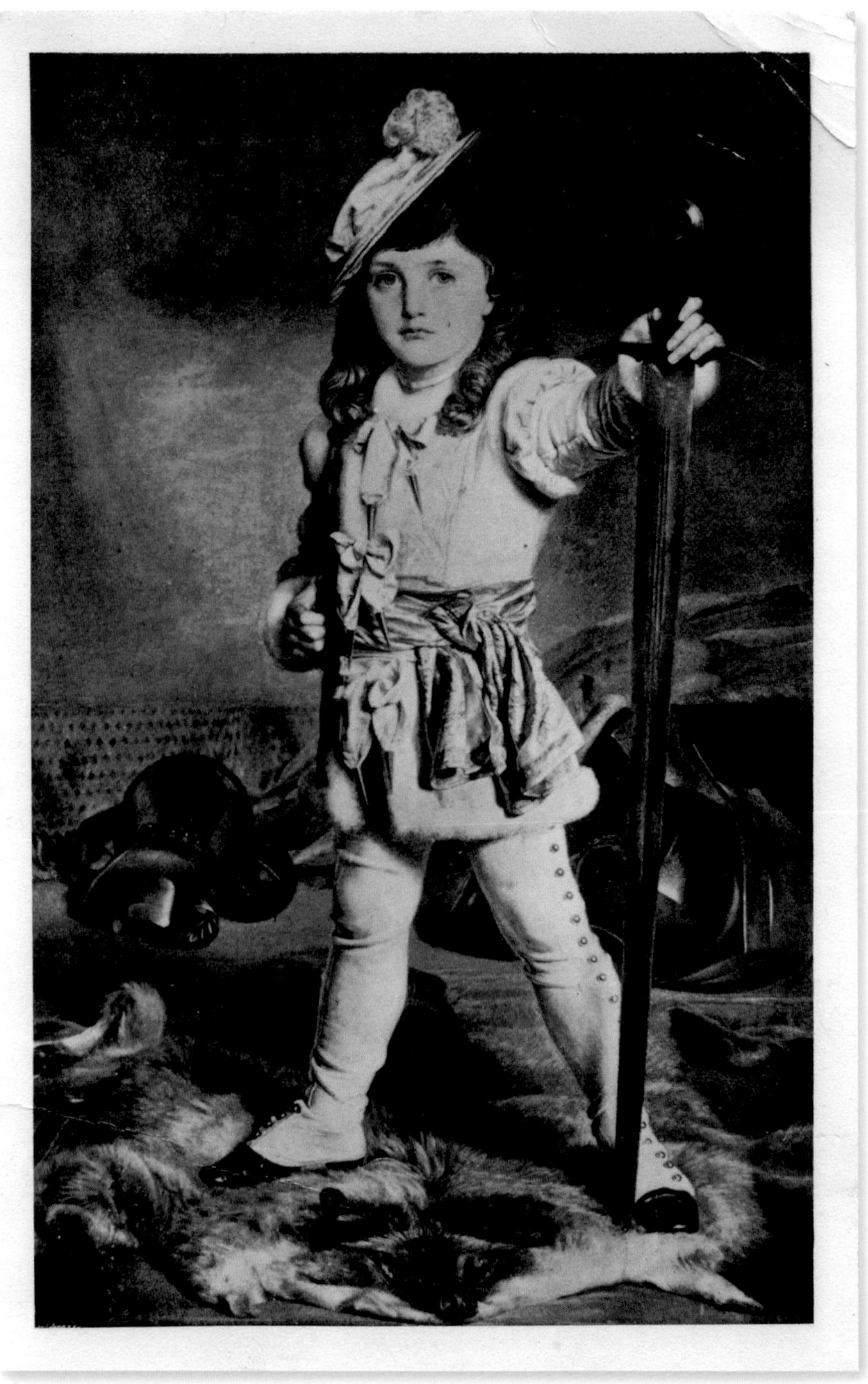

St George for Merrie England. Oil on canvas. 1880. This major Sandys picture has not been traced. It owed its existence to Cyril Flower who sequestered Sandys and his small son Hugh in a rented house in Wales for Sandys to be able to work without distraction.

of Henry VIII, which inspired some juvenile versions, notably Reynolds's *Master Crewe as Henry VIII* (1776), and Holman Hunt's *The King of Hearts* (1862).

To obtain the sword, as well as some armour as accessories in the picture, Sandys had appealed for help from Godwin[13] with his antiquarian and theatrical connections. Sandys next wrote in his diary on 14th February that a case had arrived containing a sword, a helmet, and a pair of armour gauntlets, 'borrowed by Godwin'.[14] Sandys did not think much of them ('not worth the carriage'), but nevertheless made use of them. They can be seen in the picture, randomly placed in the background, and the sword in the hand of the child. Compared to the size of the child, they appear to be the armour of a giant, but perhaps this added to the fanciful notion.

The facts were that Godwin had contacted his friend Frederick Weekes,[15] an artist specialising in battle scenes and genre subjects, who had some reproductions of historic armour, and thus was able to provide some pieces. By October, Weekes seems to have been having trouble in getting his armour back, as shown in a letter from himself to Godwin in which he wrote: 'I am very much obliged to you indeed for the trouble you have taken to recover the armour. I would when Sandys turns up (which he is bound through his profession to do at some time) make him pay the expenses. … However, you will I know be very glad (as I am, and you must I beg take no offence) to know that I have through Mr Allingham extracted the greater part of the armour, viz. the salade[16] and the gauntlets. I did this by saying that if the things were not returned by this Saturday (they were promised eight days ago) I should proceed against you. This of course was bosh on my part, and I repeat that I hope that you will in no way feel hurt or offended over what was only a ruse to try and get back these things, when all other efforts had failed. I thought and perhaps was right, though as you know, I don't think much of Mr Sandys as regards character, that still he might have sufficient honour to prevent you (who did him the kindness to borrow from a stranger to him) suffering. I do most firmly believe that except for this I should never have got the things returned. So please again take no offence, over what certainly I never intended to have done. When I said I should place the matter in the hands of a solicitor it was because I know Mr Webb is or was somewhat mixed up with business with Sandys, he might not like to do altogether what I wanted done. I'd [have] if possible, a Detective set on and a Warrant – perhaps however this could not have been done, it might have been considered a breach of trust! There's no knowing with the humbugging Law. However, the greater part of the things are back, and the remainder is all right, I have Mr Allingham's promise which is quite sufficient.'[17]

It is much to be regretted that neither the preliminary drawing (or cartoon) nor the final painting have surfaced to this day. Two studies, one of each of the boy's hands, are to be found at Birmingham City Art Gallery.[18] We know the painting only from a black and white reproduction, but from reading Sandys's diary, where he mentions the pigments he was using, it must have been colourful. The figure in the painting, of course, would have exactly replicated the figure in the preliminary drawing, as was Sandys's custom.

It seems that, soon, Sandys and the boy had to rapidly decamp and return to London to make way for the imminent arrival of Flower and his wife, and their train of retainers, on 10th and 11th March 1880. Parliament had dissolved and Flower had to be on-hand for electioneering towards polling day on 1st April (on which he won the seat from the sitting Conservative MP).

Back in London, Sandys resumed his intimacy with the Godwins (presumably all the contentious armour and weaponry had been returned to Weekes), and Godwin's diary records a visit by Sandys on 14th March, when he called in after dinner and spent the evening with them and their friend Barrable,[19] who had also dropped in. On 4th April, Sandys called to see Godwin and paid him six shillings, but then (strangely) he lent Godwin £1, which Godwin recorded that he returned on the 16th. Apparently, they both suffered from cash shortages.

On 5th April, it appears from other evidence, since there are no clues to this event in Sandys's 1880 diary, that another daughter, Ruth, was born to the 'little girl' in Kensington.[20] The steadily growing 'Neville family' now numbered six children,[21] not counting the eldest two girls who continued to be fostered. Coincidentally, Godwin also recorded the visit of a Mr MacManus on the 16th March. Was this the same man to whom Sandys owed money in 1876 for two years' child-care, as revealed in the records of his bankruptcy?[22] Since MacManus (or McManus) was a builder by trade, Godwin might well have had dealings with him.

Work on the *St George* picture was to resume in June 1880, and in order for Sandys and the boy to return to Brecon, Flower advanced him £20. In addition he had to borrow a further £30 from the solicitor Theodore Allingham. This was probably to fund the family at Maude Grove. Sandys also noted a payment of £10 via the 'little girl' to 'Frost' who was very likely the housekeeper Sandys had at the studio house in Spenser Street, and later at The Cottage in Holland Park Road.

The father and son arrived in Wales again on Thursday 10th June, and Sandys spent a couple of days acclimatising himself and the boy to the rural environment and the chilly temperatures compared to London. He unpacked his drawing on the Sunday, and on Monday started work by tracing the drawing, which took him all day. On the 14th, he wrote to Howell to send him etching materials: 'I commenced working on my picture of the boy today, but I wish I could have done two or three etchings first, and a large landscape ...', but he later wrote on the 25th that 'the plates must stand over – it has been raining ever since I came, so could not use them'.[23] He also urged Howell to attend to selling the two drawings he had on hand[24] so that he could pay his debt to George Webb.[25] On Tuesday the 15th he transferred his tracing of the completed drawing of the boy on to the canvas and oiled the outline to fix it.

What is so characteristic of Sandys's invariable painting technique is that having transferred the composition from the preliminary drawing, he started the picture on Wednesday the 16th by painting a minor detail in the centre of the picture, the 'upper bow and tags', and on the next day he painted the second bow, working on it from 10.30 in the morning to 7 at night. Altogether the bow and the tags took him five full days of work, his usual day of work (according to the diary) being from 10.30 am to 7.30 pm, but sometimes he went on till considerably later. Nothing in the diary suggests that anything other than natural light was his light source. The days were frequently rainy and overcast, and there are many complaints about bad light in the diary.

On Monday 21st June 1880, he started to paint the boy's right arm, and so it went on, separately, part by part, through June, July, August, September, and most of October, which totalled one hundred and nineteen days of painting. The diary contains abundant technical notes, about, for instance, his modification of the mixture of the important grounding white, so as not to be 'pulled up' by the application of the following layer of paint, and the colours he used for grounding and glazing in each discrete part of the composition, giving one an inkling of his piecemeal procedure and why it hardly seemed to matter where he started on the picture (except, perhaps, for a technical reason).

Otherwise, Sandys noted his walks with the boy, and reading to him at bedtime. A local farmer's daughter was hired to look after Hugh while Sandys was working but not requiring him as a model. Occasionally, the boy stubbornly refused to pose – his spirit having been tested beyond endurance.

As June progressed, Sandys complained that his financial worries were affecting his work, for evidently he was now in bad grace with Flower, probably for several reasons such as his rent arrears for Spenser Street. He confided to Howell on June 24th: 'Never was man so worried as I am. It is with the greatest effort I can keep my thoughts on my work – yesterday and today I think I have done very bad work, but I am so distressed in mind I know no longer good work from bad. Flower since I have been here has, I believe, rounded on me – but I cannot tell for certain. I wrote him a very strong letter in which I said it was almost madness his conduct to me – first so kind and considerate – next capricious and tyrannical[;] never the same two days consecutively. I have received no answer at present. I should not be surprised if Webb's damned conduct has lost me my studio at Spencer Street. From one point of view I should be sorry, from another I should be glad, for it would end this tyranny of Flower's and I should be my own master again even if in an empty room somewhere.'[26] Bailiffs or creditors had already made an embarrassing scene at Spenser Street and he was anxious to prevent it happening again.[27]

His frustration comes through again in his letter to Howell of 21st June: 'I am bound up here and the little girl is terribly pushed for money.'[28]

On 7th July, he watched the (hitherto unmentioned) *Head of Medusa* drawing and painting being packed, to be sent to Webb in London.[29] The three known versions of *Medusa*, dating from about 1875, are all drawings. No painting of the subject has come to light.

Sandys also wrote to Cyril Flower, to Theodore Allingham (the solicitor from whom he had borrowed £30 in June), and to the 'little girl'. Sandys had written to Howell around this time too: 'Now sell the two big drawings that Godwin had. I think you might manage to get £250 for them[30] – then there are three heads besides, I remember now could be sold I believe immediately after – one a drawing of the *Proud Maisie* for £30 or £35 – one of *Faustine* and one of *Antigone*. These two[,] more or less incomplete as they are[,] ought to bring more than £100 – they are the two best drawings I have ever done'. Again he wrote: ' …two more I could sell – the study of some trees done at Hastings – the little girl knows which.'[31] Worth noting is that Sandys was perfectly willing to part with unfinished works (and they remain unfinished to this day), and studies, as is his frequent resort to superlatives, as in 'the two best drawings I have ever done', a questionable statement, in his effort to press Howell into action.[32]

On 25th June he wrote: 'It is I am certain all important to me to clear off the Webbs – this by Allingham – I have a thing I must pay on Tuesday about £27 or £28. This is imperative. I want also by the sale of these drawings to pay Benjamin £52.10 and some expenses. I shall make myself stand so much better with Flower.'[33]

Evidently Howell did not bestir himself, because we find Sandys still entreating him in July: 'Surely you might have tried something before this. These Webbs will ruin and bedevil me ... if you care to help me, do so at once, for if something be not done by Wednesday – or Tuesday I believe is the last day – I shall lose the studio. To do me the utmost harm seems to be the purpose of Webb. They have already written to Flower and there [are] enemies in this world who would be glad to see me out of the studio.'[34]

It appears on 8th July that Howell advanced £30 in cash to Sandys, charged him £4.19.1 in interest, and sent £5 to Mary.[35] In his letter of 10th July, Sandys was concerned about the disruption of his work in a month's time by the next arrival at Ffrwdgrech of the Flowers and Mrs Flower's mother, Lady de Rothschild. He wrote that he had been 'working very closely, from 10 or 10.30 till 8 and even 8.30, but the scarf round the waist has occupied me rather over a fortnight'. He continued woefully: 'I am so distressed in mind it is with the greatest difficulty I can keep my thoughts on my work. Sometimes I find myself going on mechanically and suddenly become conscious I am painting. I have never been in such a state in my life. I am doing my best to make the picture a good one – so much depends on it. I have not as yet tackled the face or hands. I trust to get this matter of the Webbs and the two other matters settled first.[36]

'I want to be prepared to start [to return to London] at any moment. I do not know how soon I shall leave. I should think about the end of next week that is to say in about a fortnight – but it may be this week. Of course I shall bring all my things with me. I have made another drawing of the boy's head twenty times as good I think, and I am now painting it. Whether it be good or bad I cannot say. I have not got on sufficiently far. I have painted the hair and nearly finished the hands. Tomorrow I commence painting the cap so that I may have all the surroundings done before I finish the head. The lower half of the picture I have not commenced yet – it seems little to show for two months work – but I have worked like the devil on it. On Thursday last I commenced cleaning my brushes at 7.30 [and] with the exception of the time occupied by breakfast and lunch I went on till eight o'clock and had not finished cleaning palette etc till 8.20. Of course I work very nervously[,] so much depends on the success of the picture and again, I paint so little.[37]

I also forget how the paints go, and I have been worried to death here. I am sure a picture was never painted under such circumstances[;] another reason why I am anxious to make the picture[,] if I can[,] a friend of mine calls a "snorter". I return Allingham's letter – now surely you will try and get rid of those two infernal drawings at once. What light is the big room of yours at Fulham,[38] North South or East? Can you get a frame made like the one for your portrait,[39] if I said the size?'

It seems that Howell bestirred himself and sent down a locket, stockings, and neckties as gifts to the servants at Ffrwdgrech, for Sandys acknowledges these and asks him to do his utmost to sell the new drawing – probably the one of the boy's head referred to in his letter of 8th August, which was one of the studies for the *St George* painting.

These letters were written while there was an interruption in his work caused by having to clear out of the room in which he was working for the decorators. After three days' loss of working time, being prevented from using the room in which the lighting conditions played an important part in the picture, he had to set up in another room – and then another – complaining in his diary of noise and interruptions.

He was having trouble with the drawing of the boy's head for, on Sunday 25th July, he made a tracing of the head, presumably from the original drawing, and transferred it to a piece of paper 'to draw it again afresh'. After a couple of days' more work on the painting, he 'commenced … drawing from Hugh [and] worked at nose, could not find out the blunder', complaining that 'he sits so badly, is never still for one second, it is impossible to compare one part with the other, impossible to do otherwise than trust one's eye, piece by piece, trusting to get the whole right' (another revealing statement confirming his adherence to his rigid technique, which did not adapt at all to the impossibility of a child to keep still).

His financial affairs were a constant distraction. In one of his letters to Howell he said: 'Howell I do not ask you for money. You say what can you do? All I ask of you is sell these drawings of mine, as quick as possible, for as much as possible. So much depends upon this being done at once. I am in constant dread of some devilry.'[40]

Inevitably, the child's inability to endure the demands made on him by his father came to a point of crisis: 'Nothing will induce him to sit, kindness or cruelty – worn out, I had to give up at 5.30 having done my best and hardest. The time I could get between rests, scolding, and kindness, [I] went on with hair and hat, having marked in a little from him.' A couple of days later, on the 30th, he was still drawing the boy's head: 'He sat a little better ... (from 10.30 to 5.20). If I can but complete the drawing as satisfactorily, I think my patience ought to be rewarded. Work[ed] on without boy from the first drawing and memory till 7.30.'[41] He wrote that evening to Howell, urging him again to sell the drawings: 'Allingham has the drawings. Now do pray sell them at once – that is the two completed drawings *Penelope* and *Alcestis* – you can I am sure easily get £250 for the two possibly £300.' He wanted to return to London around 10th August, but added: 'I cannot move for the want of coin – and I depend on your selling these drawings to get back – and I cannot let it be till the last day. Now let me Howell for once ask you to do this immediately. I am so crazed here I hardly know what I am about or what my painting is like.'

He hoped to finish all but the legs and wolf-skin before returning and was 'working hard on the hands and face. 'My boy is without exception, not only the perfect idea, but the absolute realisation of a fiend as a sitter, and in spite of his wretchedness at sitting he seems to gloat like a goule *[sic]* at my misery distraction and hopelessness.[42] Hugh's behaviour is hardly surprising given that he was scarcely five years old!

Sandys had evidently allowed himself a week to complete the revised drawing of the head, for on Saturday the 31st he was writing: 'Worked on the boy's face all day, hoped to have finished it. Could not get the off-side of the face right, the modelling of the cheeks also trouble me. Worked from 10.30 till 8. Left off much disappointed I could not commence painting the face on Monday.'[43] Putting aside the difficulty of working from a fidgety small child, Sandys's incredible slowness as a professional artist was, throughout his life, a major handicap.

He was finishing up the drawing on Tuesday 3rd August with dissatisfaction: 'I have done too much, and the last part not good. The shaded side of the face wrong somewhere, not drawn. At 3.30[,] traced it to the canvas – this occupied me till 8, so dark then I could not see.'[44] Feeling unwell and despondent several days later, he wrote: 'Sad I was that I should be in such a position, with such a man.'[45] This is one of two signs of his growing aversion to Cyril Flower.

He wrote to Howell on Sunday 8th August, pointing out that, besides needing his fare to London, he would need to tip four servants for attendance over something more than three months, and to give the housekeeper a present (no doubt an inconvenient problem for the chronically penniless Sandys who felt obliged to maintain his social status towards servants). The latter had been kind to the boy and he wanted some little thing that the boy could give to her. He suggested that it could be a small piece of jewellery '... either a brooch or a bracelet[,] and though not to cost much[,] I want one that she would like as uncommon. She asserts herself as a lady, travelled, etc.'[46]

Some more trouble seems to have been stirred up in his relations with Flower, for in the same letter he wrote: 'I suppose the little girl has been (a thing not uncommon with her) talking a good deal of that which she knows nothing – Flower has written to me two kind letters since I have been here. I then had to write to him a very strong letter, in consequence of notes written by the little girl. It was unfortunate, but had she written and posted her note as she ought, the last unpleasant incident in connection with Flower would not have occurred. Since this last letter, now more than a month since, I have not heard from him.'

There is a sense of Flower's waning patience with Sandys and his financial affairs, although other members of his family continued to commission portraits, and Flower himself bought another drawing in 1885. Incidentally, in Flower's wife's memoirs Sandys receives only the briefest passing reference.[47] This hints at disapproval!

In conclusion to the letter of 8th August to Howell, Sandys wrote: 'I have made another drawing of the boy's head twenty times as good I think – and I am now painting it. Whether it will be good or bad I cannot say. I have not got on sufficiently far. I have painted the hair and nearly finished the hands.'[48] Occasional intrusions such as on 13th August, when he received a welcome cheque for £15 from Allingham, and on the 18th when he was 'much upset by a note from Frost', were more reminders of London affairs.[49]

On 14th August he: 'Worked all day on the feather [in Hugh's cap], tried hard to get it to come right – the colour and sheen - but could not. Eventually worked into it all over, distinct tints of red, green and blue. I suppose it will do sufficiently well. It seems a long time to paint on a small feather – two whole days.'[50]

From the 15th to the 20th, he painted the cap and different parts of the face. Feeling 'worn out', he took a break on Saturday the 21st and, after walking with Hugh to Brecon, they took a train to Tal-y-Llyn, where they walked to the lake and hired a boatman to take them out. It was a fine afternoon and Sandys noted the wild birds they saw. He frequently complained to his diary about his feet giving him trouble around this time,[51] and yet he had to walk for exercise, walk to fill his off-duty time and to occupy Hugh, as well as walking to the nearest town, Brecon, when necessary. One wonders also how the small boy managed the distances they covered together. Sunday was another 'rest' day and he took Hugh for a walk towards the Brecon Beacons, southwards from Ffrwdgrech.

From the 23rd until the 25th he painted the face and the hair and then fell into another fit of despondency: 'I feel nervous about my work, at the same time with the strongest conviction over my ultimate victory over art – bothers ruin me. I am aghast at the damnable drawing I made after great efforts' and 'it is strange how uncertain, how little to be depended on I feel my eye [is]. I cannot but think it is in consequence of my having done so little but draw, and that I see form (at the expense of colour) now more than all besides.' Another aspect of this problem he was having with painting can be found in a previously quoted letter to Howell: 'I paint so little [that] I also forget how the paints go.'[52] It seems clear that Sandys never developed an efficient or economically viable method of painting. His slow, myopic way of working was adequate when he was doing a drawing, but the additional factors of colour and the slow process of painting which he espoused combined to make it almost impossible for a sitter to sit (or stand) for him long enough, and for him to complete a painting without an unfortunate loss of primary vision and inspiration. He attempted probably four more oil pictures in his lifetime: those of Mary and William Gilillan in 1885 and 1886, Julia Caldwell in 1889, and James Redfoord Bulwer in 1894.

On Thursday 26th August, he felt 'worn to death', but went into the garden after breakfast and 'saw a most beautiful cloud and mist effect on the Beacons' and was moved to make an oil sketch of it.[53] On the 27th and 28th, Hugh had a toothache and swollen face, and so instead Sandys worked on the background of the painting. A note from Flower arrived, and on Sunday the 29th he spent much time 'bothered' as to how to reply. After having replied to the note on Monday morning (and he gives no clue to the contents but continues to be troubled by it throughout the following week), he made a late start in painting the boy's left hand, using an extraordinary number of different pigments – five, not counting white, and then 'became aware for the first time I had made both hands far too big. I think my drawing now damnable!'[54] He wrote to Howell on the 29th asking him to make arrangements to send him a frame 'for the picture of the boy'. He was expecting the Flowers to arrive in about ten days and wanted to make a trip to London in the meantime, and he was uncertain as to whether he should return to Brecon: '… and if I should decide to return, I should be glad to leave the picture in a frame for these people to see. Should I decide not to return here to paint, I should want to pack it, and a frame would be about the only way I can see to pack it without injury.'[55]

There are four more letters from Brecon written in continuing frustration with Howell over the now familiar themes: entreating him to sell the drawings 'held by Allingham', the drawing of Hugh's head, and to send him a big frame suitable for the painting of *St George*. As an incentive he offered to make 'a drawing of little Blanche – a clinker'.[56] The last letter on 14th October stated that he intended to leave Brecon in a few days.[57]

For the first six days in September, he worked on various parts of the picture, and on Tuesday the 7th, the Flowers were to arrive at Ffrwdgrech, and Sandys and Hugh transferred to the Castle Hotel in Brecon. Items of clothing for them were bought in the town and excursions made to the Llangorse Lake and to Aberedw on the 9th to see Llewellyn's Cave. On the 10th, Flower appeared at the hotel and Sandys noted that they 'had a wrangle' with the result that Sandys was to take the child back to London and return alone on Monday the 13th to work on the picture.[58]

On the following day, Saturday, Hugh and his father accordingly set off and were met at Paddington station, in London, by the boy's mother, and they took a cab to Maude Grove. The "little girl's" brother John [was] there, waiting'[59] and Sandys felt so 'worn out' that he stayed at Maude Grove all Sunday.

On Monday, 13th September, Sandys alone returned to Brecon where he was met by Flower and they walked together to Ffrwdgrech, where he and Mrs Flower were 'gracious'.[60]

On the 18th, in a letter to Howell, Sandys was still desperately urging on the selling of the 'two drawings held by Allingham' because 'the little girl cannot go on', as well as the drawing of the boy's head (which had been taken to London after he had finished with it). He carried on, painting accessories such as the armour gauntlets, and put in the wolf skin, when on the 30th, news came from Maude Grove that Hugh had a high fever. He discussed with Flower the idea of making a 'flying visit to town' on the following Monday to see Hugh; Flower's reaction to this can be guessed by Sandys's bitter remark in his diary: 'Flower is certainly the most heartless and cruel man I have yet met.' There was no satisfaction either from Howell, who had not sold the drawings nor sent the desired frame by the 29th.[61]

Hugh was better by the time Sandys arrived back in London on Monday 4th October, but as Sandys noted, was physically altered by his illness. Financial affairs seem to have come to another crisis, and Sandys took advantage of a few days in London to seek help. Accordingly, the next day he called on Jephson (a friend he shared with Godwin) who seems to have been an intimate at this period, for he spent much time with him during the next three days.[62] He had a long talk with him before going to see Hastings, a lawyer, at 18 Bennet's Hill.[63] Hastings was out all day and so an appointment was made for noon the following day. Sandys reported a long talk with him, saying that Hastings 'behaved wonderfully well'. There was another appointment with Hastings the next day, on the 7th, after which Sandys was left in 'a terrible agony fully expecting to have had some money, knowing not what to do'. It appears that Hastings gave Sandys some advice and assurance in the matter of his outstanding debts, but was not forthcoming with a loan as Sandys had probably hoped. Sandys wrote that he felt 'never more miserable'.[64]

On 8th October he returned to Brecon and, on arriving at the station, no doubt to his great dismay, a young man came up to him and served him with a bankruptcy notice.[65]

He started work again on the painting on Saturday the 9th, as usual at 10.30 am, working till dusk on the subject's left gaitered leg, presumably from the hired local lad. Flower came to him and told him that he had had an offer of £200 from the artist Orchardson[66] for the studio in Spenser Street, unfurnished, and asked if he should accept this. In fact, there was no alternative, and Sandys's only proviso was that he should be able to remove his books and painting things, 'furniture and trinkets'. On Sunday he worked on the other gaitered leg, but it was a 'dark dull heavy day [and he] could hardly see,' so gave up at 4.45, fearing that what he had done was 'bad'. On Monday from 10 am till dusk he worked on the lower part of the same leg, confiding to the diary: 'I am so worried. I cannot work well,' and complaining of pain in his groin. The latter seems to have resulted from crouching or sitting low on the ground for long hours while painting the wolf skin lying on the floor. His bitter comments about Flower's character are revealing: 'He [is] delighted to get out of the expense of [renting] Frwdgrech – has cunningly thrown the onus of it on Smith and Evans.[67] Has shewn *[sic]* himself to me a thorough hypocrite. Can his transparent cunning deceive anyone?'[68]

On Tuesday the 12th, the Flowers went up to town for a funeral and Sandys worked at Ffrwdgrech from 10.30 to about 5, when it became too dark to work. He accomplished the painting of the buttons on one gaiter (four of which are visible) and four on the other. The next day he finished painting these buttons and worked a little on the wolf skin, putting his brushes aside to write a letter to Hastings about his financial affairs, which he had put off doing 'because I could not think what to say'. After 5, he walked out and started a pencil sketch of a landscape, giving up after it became dark. On Thursday and Friday, he worked on the shoes and the surrounding wolf skin, but his financial affairs again obtruded in the form of a Mr Thomas who came at 3.30 and served him with a summons 'for £10 odd' from George Webb, one of his creditors.[69] On Saturday 16th October, he continued to work from 10.30 am till dark on one of the shoes and the adjacent parts of the wolf skin.

The same evening, Flower returned from London so that Sandys could work on the alteration of his portrait. This was the second of the two known portrait drawings by Sandys of Cyril Flower, of 1872 and 1877. The latter had just recently been shown at the Winter Exhibition at the Grosvenor Gallery, and the showing might have given Flower thoughts of improving it. Sandys spent Sunday rubbing out the shirt Flower was depicted wearing, and re-drawing him wearing a coat, which pleased him better. He paid Sandys £15 for doing this. The 1877 portrait now shows Flower in a double-breasted coat with a hood, and there is evidence of a strip added to the base of the picture to lengthen it.

On Monday 18th October Sandys was working again, as usual, on *St George*, this time on the sword blade. The picture must have been nearly finished, which gave rise to reflective thoughts on his daily walk: 'Walked in the wood really feeling sad, in spite of the misery I have endured, that I should have to leave it [Ffrwdgrech]. I have so revelled in delight with Hugh here, he is so winsome and loving, although a little temper – and a fearful sitter.' On the 19th he continued, working on the wolf skin, and with Flower sitting and talking with him for a while.[70]

Wednesday 20th October was the last day on which there was a full entry in the 1880 diary. Sandys started painting as usual, but halfway through the morning Flower came into the room and discussed business. Flower had devised a programme to enable Sandys to work off his debts. In this plan Sandys would use the payment he was getting from Flower for the *St George* painting to cover the debts, first reimbursing Flower the money he had already advanced to enable him to paint. He was then to paint a proposed new picture to be entitled *Samuel* from Hugh, and to finish the picture he had started of the *Head of Medusa*, during which time Flower would pay him £12 a week. Sandys could keep his drawings and studies for himself, but the pictures (oil paintings) were to be sold to reimburse Flower, and then other creditors. On the same terms he was to continue painting further pictures until his debts were all paid. For present needs, Flower gave Sandys a cheque for £200, and one for £5 'to get away with, and to pay Webb, Woodruffe, and some of Mrs Parfitt's bill'.[71] Clearly, Flower was above all a businessman. Flower left for London by the 2 o'clock train and Sandys accompanied him to the station, and on his return to the house put the cheque for £200 in an envelope with 'directions about Allingham'[72] and addressed it to the 'little girl'. He also noted that he sent £5 to his parents in Norwich. He did a little more work on the picture but was 'too excited to do much'. He may have worked some more and done some packing on Thursday and Friday, and on Saturday 23rd October he left Ffrwdgrech for London for good. There are no more diary entries except three notes of the weekly cheque from Flower for £12, the last one being on 22nd November.

In the back of the diary on pages headed 'Cash Account' for each month, there are entries from January to November showing receipts from Flower and expenditures. They show that Sandys, or Flower, was sending the 'little girl' small sums, from £5 to occasionally as much as £25. Flower's regular contributions to the 'little girl' were £5 weekly from February to the end of October.[73] These pages also show how these sums and others added up to a total of £420, which Sandys owed Flower at the time of the financial discussion on 20th October.

After the diary entries end, feast becomes famine in terms of documented information of Sandys's movements in 1880. However, Godwin's diary on 26th October supplies the fact that 'Sandys sent old man with envelope containing £2 lent but no note, he still owes me £10.10.0 for services'. The latter probably accounts for his work on the Spenser Street studio.[74]

Of the unfortunate story of *St George for Merrie England* there remains a letter from Sandys to Rossetti dated Saturday,[75] which reveals his continuing anxiety over the picture. He was writing from Spenser Street, and so it seems that he had not yet left his studio: 'I have called so many times long since without being admitted. I do not know if even now I should be otherwise than a most unwelcome visitor.[76] However I write because you can if you like render me a great service. I have been painting for six months on a painting in Wales. I worked like the devil on it and have looked so long and am so nervous. I no longer know what it is like, and I must finish and sell it within the next fortnight. The service I want you to render me is to come and look at it and tell me what to do to make it better. It is the first time in my life I have been able to make a start for a picture *[sic]*.[77] I have painted it in Wales in a very small room with very bad light and getting it into a large room and seeing it as a whole for the first time, I find I have failed in getting what I desired. If you will come, will you say when, or shall I come and speak more fully of what I want you to do? I am induced to ask you to do this because so much depends upon my making this a success. Should I be fortunate enough to do so, I am right for life.'

Sadly, Rossetti by this time had become a recluse. He replied, however, with a friendly letter: '… in spite of the sincere pleasure I should have felt in being of any use. The fact is, I have been for some time more out of health than usual & this compels me to say that I cannot comply with your wish. … Yours as ever, DG Rossetti.'[78]

In the end, Sandys did bring *St George* to a satisfactory completion. We know this from the illustration in Esther Wood's 1896 monograph,[79] published when it was still in the possession of Cyril Flower, but neither it, nor the preliminary cartoon drawing,[80] nor the study (or studies) of the head of the boy, have been discovered at the time of writing. Studies of the boy's hands have been at the Birmingham City Art Gallery since 1906, coming from the Fairfax Murray collection.[81] An early reproductive photograph (by Frederick Hollyer, perhaps) of one of the studies of the boy's head surfaced in recent years with a dedication in pencil on it to 'Charles A. Howell from his friend Fredk. Sandys, April 9th, 1885'. This is not in Sandys's characteristic handwriting which suggests it is a forgery, perhaps by a member of the Howell family.[82]

Perplexingly, the caption under the illustration of *St George* in Esther Wood's book states that it shows a drawing. However, from the 1880 diary, we know that an oil painting was being worked on.

While Sandys had been sequestered for so many months in Wales, Godwin had been on trips to Paris in June with W.G. Wills, and to Antwerp in September with a friend named Smith, but after Sandys's return to London, as already noted, Godwin's friendship with Sandys had cooled. Thereafter, Sandys's name appears twice only in Godwin's diaries: not at all in 1881, and in 1882 on 28th January, when he noted briefly, 'sent registered letter to Sandys', and then on 21st March, 'Sandys pd. Webb debt and cash'.[83] This seems to mark the conclusion of the friendship.

The American actor Hermann Vezin, who was a friend of Godwin, W.G. Wills, and Henry Irving, sat for a Sandys portrait around this time. Vezin, an intelligent and sociable man, continued to be a friend to Sandys and was sympathetic and supportive to the family beyond Sandys's death. The Vezin portrait is undated, but the use of greenish blue paper and the details of the framer's label on the backboard of the original frame indicate a date from about 1879 to the early 1880s.

In the early 1870s, Wills had taken a studio, No. 15, at 76 Fulham Road. These were (and still are) known as the Avenue Studios, a row of fifteen individual studios formed from the earlier foundry and workshops of the

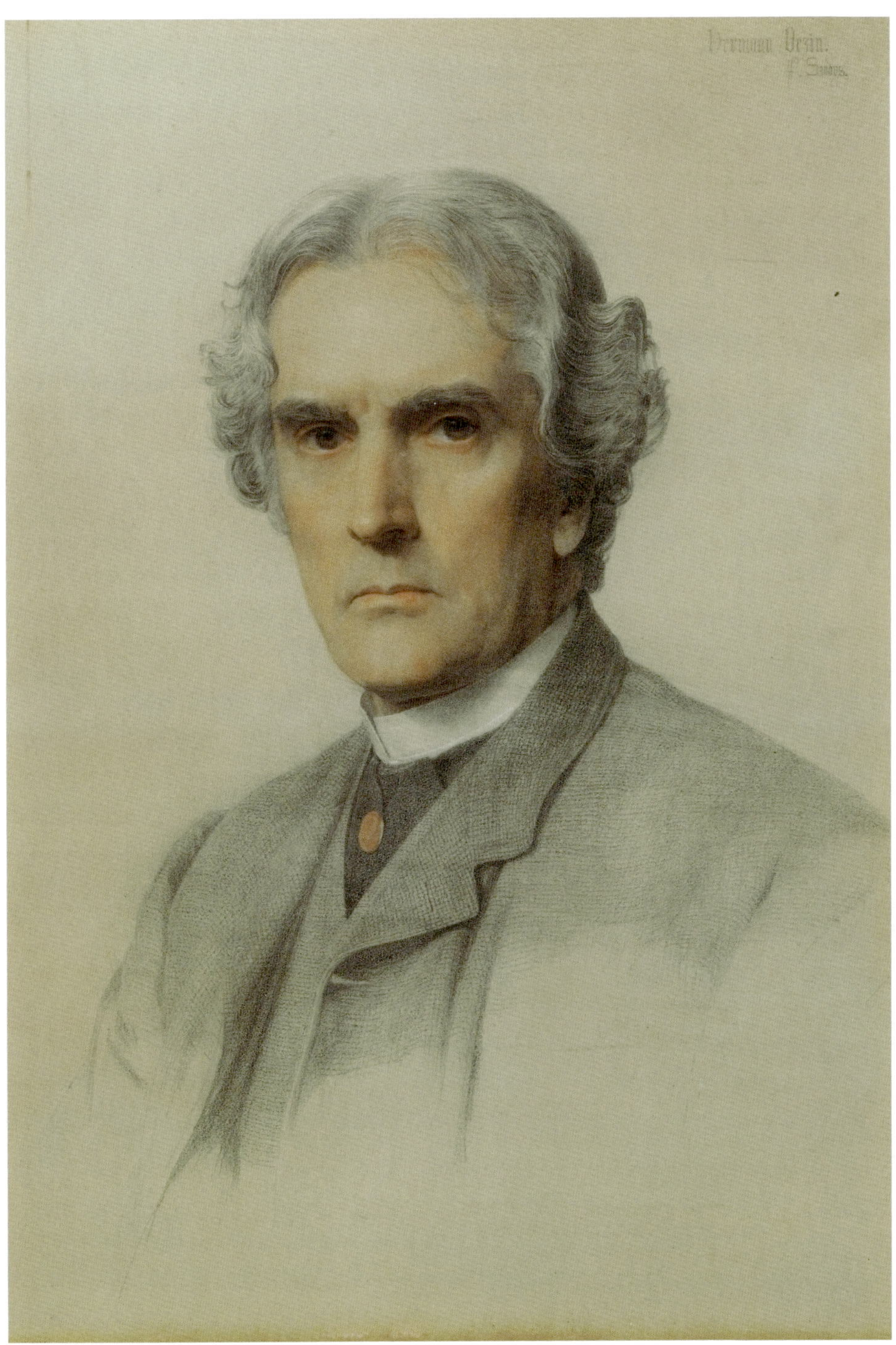

Hermann Vezin (1829-1910). Chalk drawing. Early 1880s. An actor from Philadelphia domiciled in Britain. He was considered to be the most intellectual and scholarly actor of his generation.

sculptor Baron Carlo Marochetti, after his death in 1867. The benevolent Wills soon became the centre of an entourage of friends and hangers-on from the theatrical, literary and, art world. The biography by his brother, Freeman Wills, reveals how life went on at No. 15: 'Among those who made common property of that studio was a disciple of the pre-Raphaelite school, a sharp-featured rather picturesque artist, who had been secretary to a celebrated painter.'[84] This refers to Henry Treffry Dunn (1838–1899) who worked as a studio assistant for Rossetti from 1867 until 1881, when Rossetti's illness and retirement to Birchington ended their association. Dunn had been a friend of Wills since the days when both were studying at Heatherley's art school.[85] Dunn, brought his easel and painting materials and set himself up in Wills's studio. By now an alcoholic, he evidently was becoming as burdensome to Wills's establishment as a cuckoo in the nest.

Prior to the advent of Dunn, Wills's life, according to his brother was: 'bright and vigorous, and my brother had troops of friends to draw him out of his studio in the evenings. … The convivial party used to break up in the small hours and walk home in the moonlight across London on their several ways. It might be Vezin with Dante Rossetti walking in front, Wills with Sandys bringing up the rear. Sandys, the clever draughtsman, takes it into his head that his friend Wills, as being entitled to the honours of a dramatist, should walk in front of Vezin, a mere actor. Wills adopts the idea, and striding forward, with mild dignity, keeps in front of Vezin. Presently, however, having maintained this order of going long enough to protect the rights of dramatic authorship, they roll back together in a hansom [cab], Vezin and he, the rest of the way to the studio, lulled to sleep by the motion. The playfully assumed dignity is forgotten by the time they arrive at the Avenue, Fulham Road; but it was characteristic that, when a little convivial, a lingering boyishness appeared.'[86]

In the later 1880s, perhaps for reasons of economy, Wills moved along the Fulham Road to another studio adjacent to Walham Green railway station, at number 454A, where Whistler also had a studio.[87]

Back in 1881, in early March, Sandys was embarking on the series of 'bust' portraits of Alexander Macmillan's stable of authors. These portrait commissions should have sustained Sandys for the decade of the 1880s but evidentially they did not. As they accumulated and were uniformly framed, they came to enhance the Macmillan publishing offices in St Martin's Street, and some were engraved for frontispieces to the sitters' works as published by Macmillan.

The first sitter to Sandys was John Morley (1838–1923). The young Morley had been taken on by Macmillan as reader and literary adviser, but by the eighties he was a busy and influential author and Liberal politician. We know the date when Sandys was working on the portrait from a letter, dated 3rd March 1881, from George Meredith to Sandys. Both Morley and Sandys were friends of Meredith, and Meredith wrote that he planned to call at Morley's house when Sandys would be at work on the portrait, and to invite him down to Box Hill for a visit, hoping that he would bring their friend Wills with him.[88]

In April 1881, at the time of the census, Sandys was listed as staying at Macmillan's house, Knapdale, in Upper Tooting, perhaps working on the double portrait of Macmillan himself with his young son John Victor (b.1877). Sandys had recently finished a double portrait of two of Arthur Flower's children, Ethel Daisy and her younger brother, Hugh Duncombe Flower, which was dated March 1881. Another portrait dated 1881 was of Mrs Margaret Oliphant (1828–1897) commissioned by her friend George Lillie Craik (1837–1905) who was Macmillan's business partner. Craik evidently admired the work that Sandys was doing for Macmillan and decided to commission portraits for himself.

Sandys came to Mrs Oliphant's home at Windsor in July, when she wrote on the 15th (to her publisher, Blackwood): 'I am entirely taken off work by the dreadful business of sitting for my portrait, which Mr Craik has asked me to do for him. The artist Mr Sandys, who has just finished a very fine head of Matthew Arnold, is here, living in my house, and taking a great deal out of me.'[89] She wrote to Craik soon after, on 17th July: 'Mr Sandys's work is going on admirably. He is making a most beautiful drawing, the most wonderful piece of workmanship I ever saw. He applauds me as a sitter, and intends, I hear, that this should be the best drawing he ever made. The likeness everybody seems to consider very satisfactory. To me it becomes very touching from the fact that every day it is more and more like my mother, of whom I have no good likeness.' She wrote again on 21st July: 'I have been in town today. Mr Sandys gave me a holiday, as the picture is just done – only an hour or two's work required about the dress. The drawing is quite beautiful. It seems to me much more dignified and imposing than I ever was, or could be, but barring this size and grandeur, which Mr Sandys seems to me to give all the heads he draws, it is considered an admirable likeness, as well as the most beautiful piece of work I ever saw. I believe he intends to take it up to town to-morrow, and I hope you will allow me to have it photographed for the benefit of my immediate friends. I am sure your kind heart will be a little troubled about me. Don't be so. I am sure my enforced idleness under Mr Sandys was the thing that drove me to despair, and I shall be better when I am at work again.'[90]

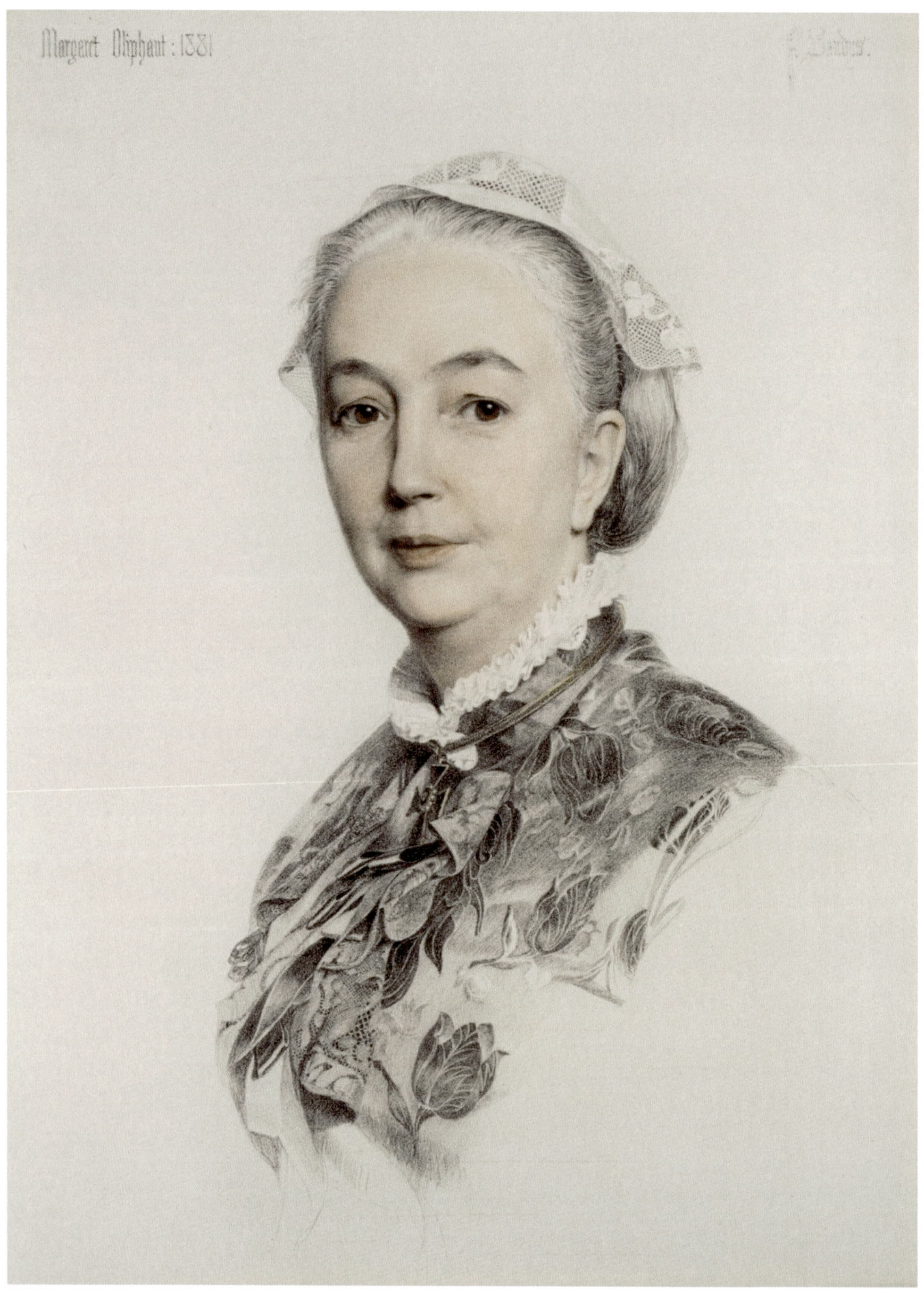

Mrs Margaret Oliphant (1828-1897). Chalk drawing. 1881. She became a professional writer after the death of her husband. The portrait was commissioned by her friend George Lillie Craik who was a partner in the publishing house of Macmillan & Co.

The editor of her biography, Mrs Coghill, makes the comment: 'Unfortunately this drawing, though no doubt a fine piece of workmanship, is not a good likeness. Possibly the mood of depression so unusual to the bright nature of his subject reacted on the artist.'[91] Another comment about the length and tedium of sitting for Sandys was made by Mrs Stirling in her memoir of her sister: 'Mrs Oliphant was then sitting to Mr Sandys for a chalk portrait. I remember how she grumbled at the length and number of hours this talented and perhaps over-conscientious draughtsman required her to sit. She declared that he hypnotised her, he stared at her so long and so minutely.'[92]

Nevertheless, after the portrait was done, she wrote to the man who commissioned it: 'Entreat Mrs Craik in my name to come and bear me company in Mr Sandys's gallery. I don't think it is quite proper that I should be there alone. He is a dreadful tyrant, it is true, but it is only once in a way. I do hope she will be persuaded to sit. I feel sure he would make a beautiful piece of work of her.' Sandys did portray Craik himself in 1882, but nothing by him of Mrs Craik (the author Dinah Mulock) is known.[93] Both the portraits of Craik and Mrs Oliphant were in Sandys's format for the Macmillan authors and were also framed in the same style (by Foord & Dickinson of Wardour Street).

As we have discovered from Mrs Oliphant's letter to her friend, Sandys had just finished a portrait of Matthew Arnold (1822–1888) for Macmillan in July. Arnold was the distinguished poet and critic, son of Dr Thomas Arnold, the famous headmaster of Rugby School.

By August 1881, Sandys was in a highly distressed state having been turned out of the studio in Spenser Street by his landlord Cyril Flower. He wrote to Flower in his awkward and stilted way: 'You wished me this morg [*sic*] to decline in writing your offer to let me have my easels and paints. I decline your offer. I will with the greatest possible pain also give my consent to the things at Spenser St being sold. I do not wish you to take the trouble to send or have sent a list of things you have already sold. … It would only tend to unsettle and distress me more. But I should be glad if you would say what value you would place on the books, and so enable me, possibly to induce a friend to buy them for me.'[94] Fortunately another commission from Craik came up, and in November Sandys went to 19 Warwick Crescent to work on a portrait of the poet Robert Browning (1812–1889), who was then sixty-nine and at the height of his reputation; indeed the Browning Society had just been founded the month before in October 1881.

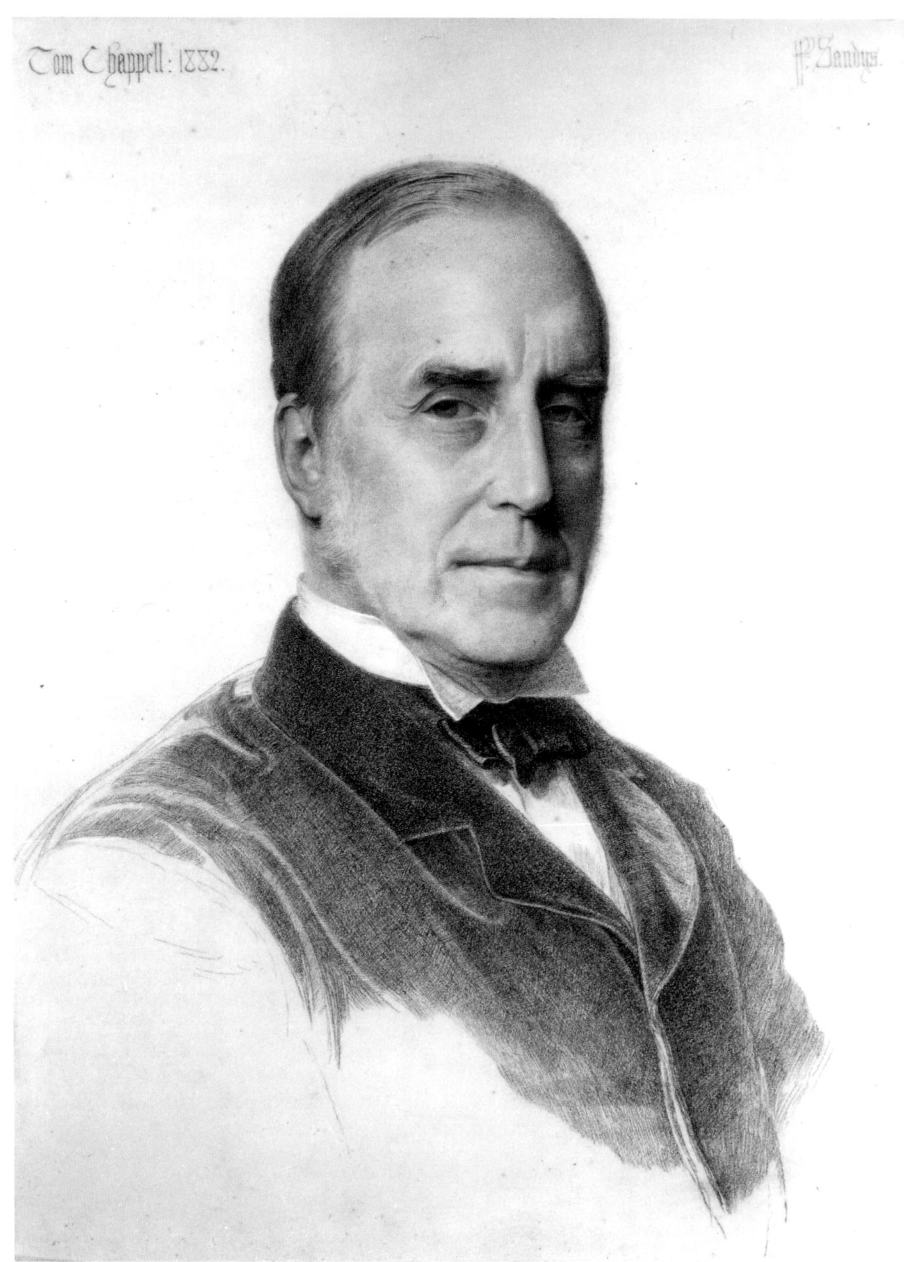

Thomas Patey Chappell (1819-1902). Chalk drawing. May 1882. He was the leading force of the music emporium, founded by his father, at 50 New Bond Street. Besides selling musical instruments and printed music, he was a promoter of concert performances, and was one of the founders of the St James' Hall, initiating there the idea of 'popular concerts'. He was one of the original supporters of the Royal Albert Hall and of the Royal College of Music.

In an article reviewing the many portraits of Robert Browning, for *The Magazine of Art* in 1890, William Michael Rossetti wrote: 'It would be difficult to find a face better drawn or more carefully and delicately realised than this, and yet I do not think that it is among the likenesses which must decidedly convey to the spectator a vivid idea of the actual man. The face seems to be longer than Browning's, and the expression is altogether more sedate and less transitional than his. … Mr Sandys gives us Browning observant as assuredly he was, but not with that sharpness and that volition in observation which were so peculiarly his.'[95] Rossetti identifies so aptly Sandys's typical strengths and failings (which are observable particularly in his portraits of men). This tendency, perhaps, was attributable to his short-sightedness. Although the Browning portrait is dated November 1881, it may have been started earlier in the year before the interval in which Browning habitually departed for Venice, for the summer and autumn.

There is another portrait dated 1881 for Macmillan. This is of Professor Goldwin Smith (1823–1910), the Anglo-Canadian journalist and educator, the opportunity being taken when Smith was in England from July 1881 to June 1882.[96] Sandys probably tackled the portrait in the latter part of 1881.

By November he was living at Maude Grove with the family and again entreating Howell to sell the drawings.[97]

On 8th December 1881 he was writing from 29 Bedford Square, a lodging house in Brighton, where perhaps he was staying to arrange for, or to undertake, another portrait commission.[98] This still remains unexplained.

1882 should have been a financially successful year, given that he completed at least seven well-paid commissions for portraits, three of which were for Macmillan, two, or possibly three, for a new patron found for him by Howell, Samuel Paddon the diamond merchant, and two for an earlier patron, the music entrepreneur Thomas Chappell. However, he continued to be intermittently short of money, having to beg Howell for cash to pay for lodgings, rail fares, and other expenses, and suffering a 'great row … with the little girl' at Maude Grove at the end of July – no doubt over the shortage of money for living expenses.

Four of his portraits for Macmillan and Craik were entered for the RA Summer Exhibition: *Robert Browning*, *James Russell Lowell*, *Goldwin Smith*, and *Matthew Arnold*. The address given in the catalogue was 129 Wardour Street, the address of his framers Foord & Dickinson.

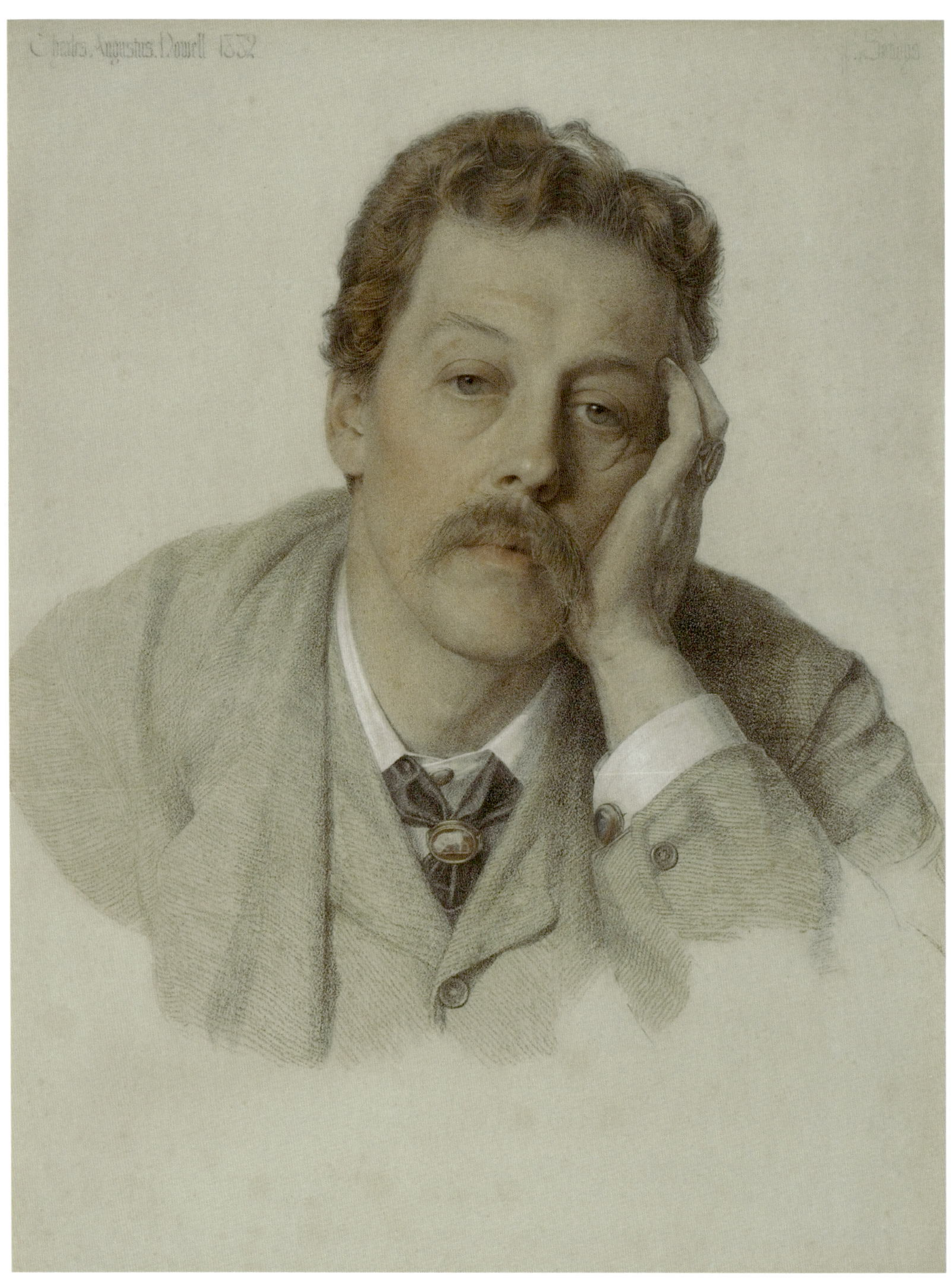

Charles Augustus Howell (1840-1890). Chalk drawing. 1882. A former secretary to Ruskin, he became an intimate in the circle of Rossetti and his friends. Although some distrusted him, he became particularly involved with the unbusinesslike Rossetti and Sandys. This portrait was undoubtedly made to pay a debt either financial or personal to Howell.

He completed an exceptionally fine portrait of Howell himself which is dated 1882, probably the year of its completion, as the intention of starting one had been mentioned by Sandys as early as 1874.[99] Again, this was probably a payment in kind for debts.

The earliest of the portraits dated 1882 was of James Russell Lowell for Macmillan. Lowell (1819–1891), a well-known poet and writer, was then (from 1880 to 1885) American Ambassador to the Court of St James. Little is known about the circumstances of its execution, except in a somewhat peripheral story related many years later by Sandys to Elizabeth Pennell.[100] It seems, probably around this time, that a Mrs Lawrence gave a lunch party which included Lowell, Sandys, and the gregarious Meredith.[101] Lowell was known for his good humour and wit. As Sandys recalled: 'Meredith as usual talked in a loud, vibrant voice. [Lowell] said he had been thinking all through lunch of the Bible. "But why?" countered Sandys. Because, Lowell explained, "In the Bible we read of the still small voice of God."' The Lowell portrait was shown at the Royal Academy in 1882, and therefore must have been completed by March.

In early May he was engaged on portraits of members of the Chappell family of whom he had already made two portrait drawings in 1872 and 1873. He wrote to Howell from their Thames-side villa, the Weir House, Teddington.[102] There are three portraits, all dated 1882, which must have been drawn there at the same time. One of these is of Thomas Chappell himself, and another is of one of his stepdaughters, Marion, who was already married to Henry Joseph Chinnery, but lived at Weir House at this time until 1896 when the Chinnerys moved to Oxfordshire.[103] Sandys complained in his letter to Howell that he was sorry that the commission was for drawings 'because my sitter would have made an especially fine picture'.[104] This referred to the portrait of Miss Emily Chappell, whose family name was 'Girlie'. She was Thomas Chappell's youngest daughter, who married in the following year Thomas Charles Pleydell Calley.[105] During the time Sandys was working on this portrait it is evident that his friend John Brett (1832–1902) had lent him his studio at 38 Harley Street where he hoped to show Mrs Lewis (probably Mrs Arthur Lewis) the portrait of Miss Chappell. In another matter, Sandys writes from there to Mrs Lewis in which he apologises for missing her invitation and hearing about her 'Italian trip', but had to go to Teddington for the Chappell sittings.[106]

John Brett was no doubt away painting in Wales, or later (from 1883) in his yacht *Viking*, which was his annual summer habit of work on his landscapes and seascapes. Brett first became known for his painting of *The Stone Breaker*

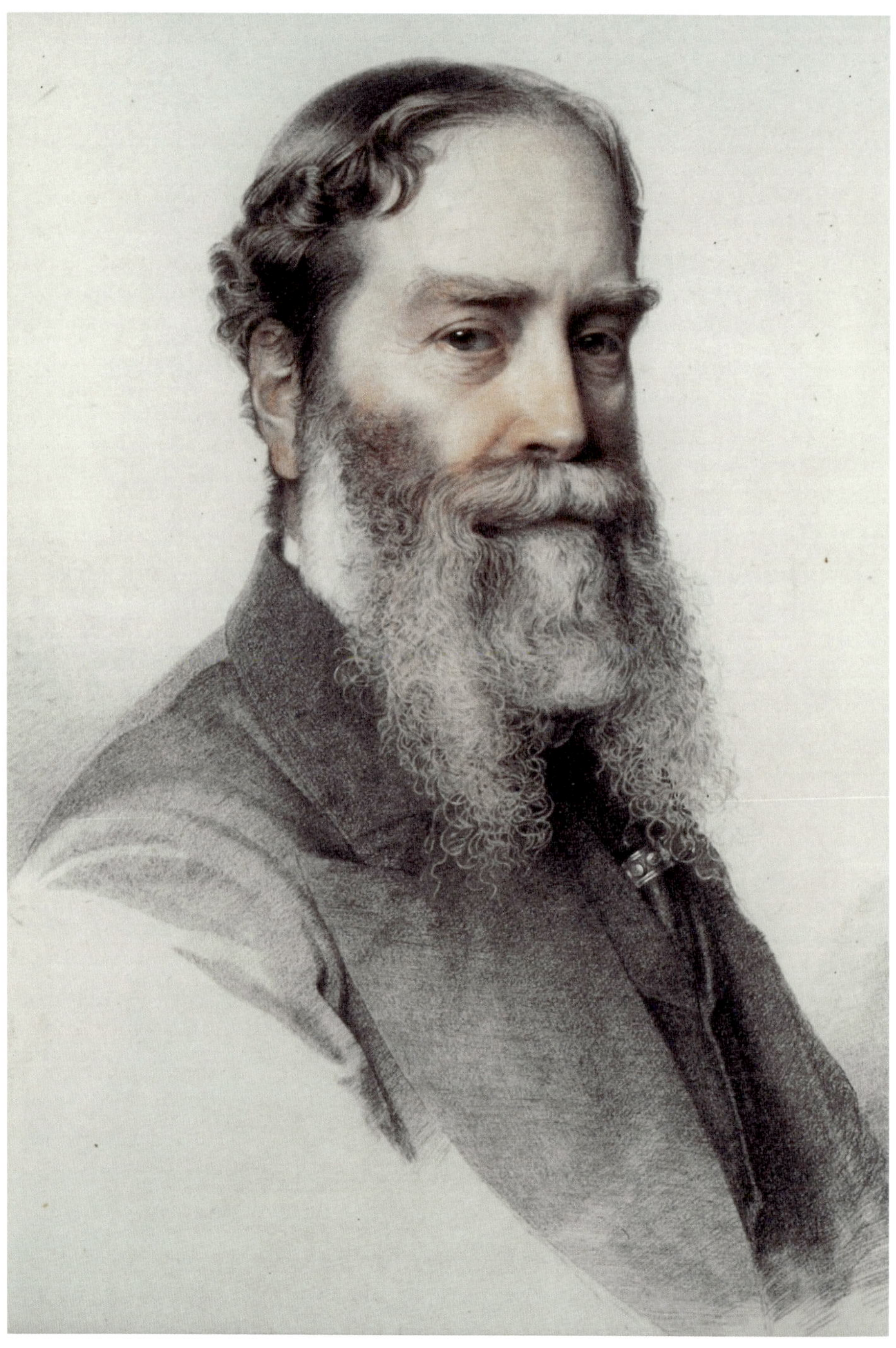

James Russell Lowell (1819-1891). Chalk drawing. 1882. One of the authors published by Alexander Macmillan. It formed a part of the series of eleven authors commissioned from Sandys in the 1880s. Lowell, a poet, was at the time the US ambassador to the Court of St James.

(1856) and was originally a protégé of Ruskin who admired his attention to detailed nature.[107] Although I have failed to find a record of Sandys's and Brett's first meeting, it was no doubt in the '60s. In any case the financially successful Brett seems to have become a sympathetic friend to Sandys. A clue might be that they both lived in similar circumstances with clandestine 'wives' and large families. This factor may have formed the bond.

On 30th May, Sandys was writing from Maude Grove to Howell arranging for a visit to Selsey Bill, near Chichester,[108] where the Howell family had taken a seaside cottage named Old Danner. There we find him writing again to Howell, who was then in London, on 15th June. He was working on a portrait of Rosalind Blanche Howell, Howell's daughter, aged five. 'I am working at little Rosalind's drawing. She sits remarkably well for so wee a little thing – and must be rewarded by rich and rare presents – she has already been promised white rabbits. It is well Jumbo has left the country or I should promise you would bring him down for her.'[109] In the same letter[110] he was beseeching Howell to 'get' for him thirty or, preferably, fifty pounds, to service an existing debt to 'a',[111] until he could finish and be paid for his portrait of the writer J. H. Shorthouse (1834–1903).

According to C.L. Cline, the portrait of Rosalind was to repay a debt to Howell (for which £105 was credited to Sandys by Howell).[112] This was immediately followed by another letter from Selsey Bill dated 19th June. Sandys, in a panic, wrote that he was threatened by 'a' to pay up the same day, else 'the things [will be] catalogued and moved, and sold either Friday (23rd June) or Monday (26th June)'. The 'things' was a reference to the contents of his studio at Spenser Street, which he was about to lose, no doubt a considerable setback for Sandys, who had carefully gathered together suitable furnishings for this studio, as we have already seen.

He added, referring to his portrait of Rosalind: 'I have made it with a quiet wondering expression – just as she sat listening to the stories I have to tell her.' Further on he wrote: 'I shall have quite finished it by Wednesday and ready for you.[113] If you come as you say on Wednesday, there will be quite time for me to finish the drawing carefully by the end of this month, if not long before, as I hope, but I think the drawing will turn out a "snorter" and I am most anxious to finish it … you must bring a box of soldiers: and some green trees for Rosalind. These I have promised as well as the white rabbits, do not forget.' In the same letter he wrote: 'Settle the matter with W. Rossetti positively if you can, one way or other.' This perhaps is related to items in an account rendered to Sandys by Howell, covering the dates 2nd June to 25th August 1882, in which Sandys appeared to have bought a 'brass shield'

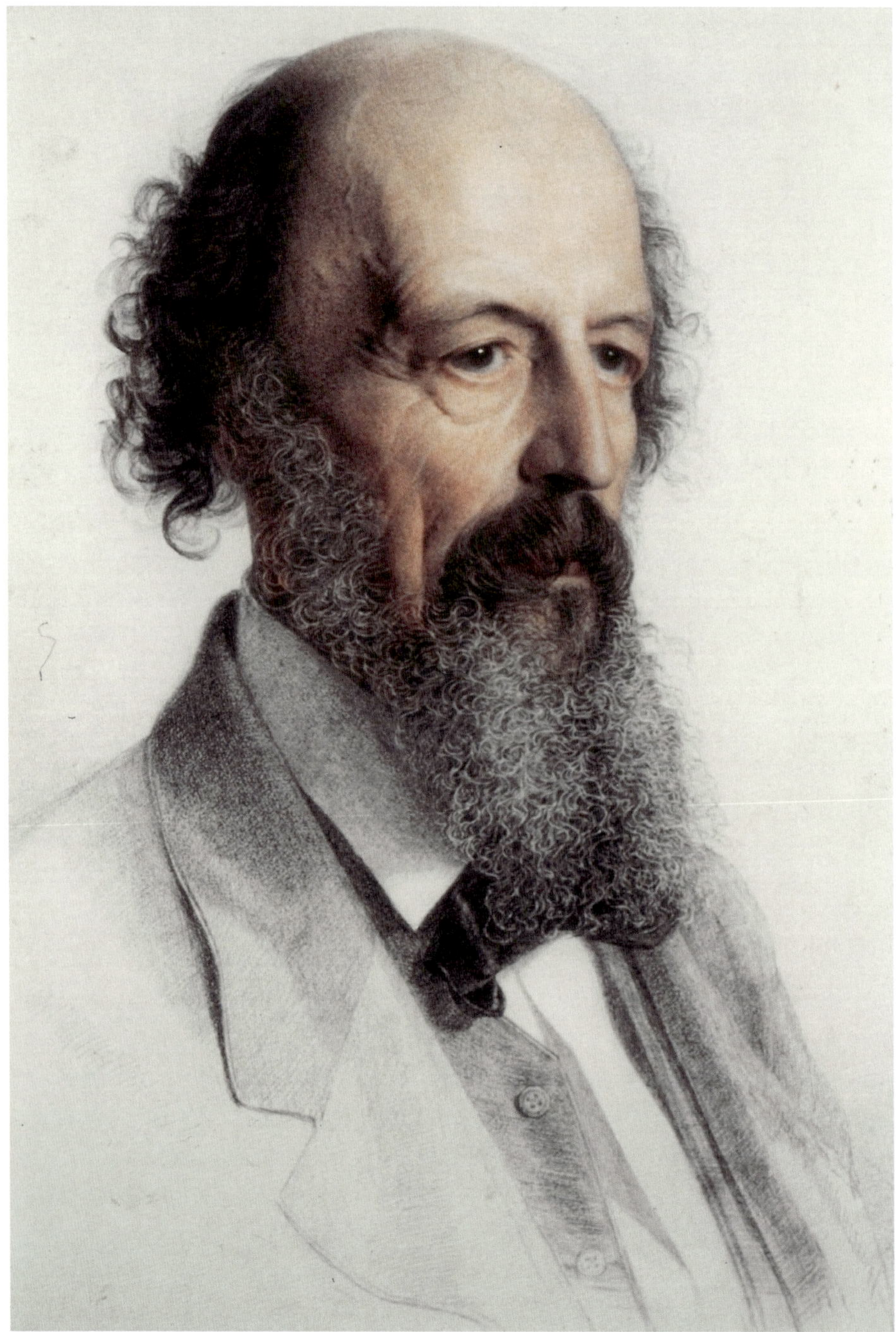

Alfred Tennyson (1809-1892). Chalk drawing. 1884. The Poet Laureate was included in the Macmillan commission. Sandys stayed at Knapdale, Alexander Macmillan's house at Tooting, South London, and commuted to Tennyson's house, Aldworth in Surrey. Tennyson was a reluctant sitter causing Sandys much frustration.

for £12 and a 'marble frame' for £2.10 from the Rossetti sale on the 22nd July.[114] Dante Gabriel Rossetti had died at Birchington in April, and there were several sales following, including household goods from his Chelsea house.

He was back at Maude Grove in July where he was getting ready to leave for Edgbaston to start the portrait of J.H. Shorthouse, but the journey had to be delayed because of a wrongly addressed 'note'. This may have been from Shorthouse to inform Sandys when he would be ready for sittings.[115] There followed 'a great row … with the little girl' which was no doubt again about money. He asked Howell if he could 'pick me up tomorrow Tuesday on your way back from Goodwood'.[116] No doubt Howell followed the horses as did Sandys.

Sandys had already mentioned having to go to *Brummagen* in his letter of 12th May. Shorthouse was another of Macmillan's authors, who had recently published a novel, titled *John Inglesant*, to great acclaim. Shorthouse lived in Edgbaston, Birmingham, and the sittings commenced on 15th August, after the Shorthouses returned home from holidaying in the Lake District. Shorthouse's time for sitting was limited because of a prior arrangement to attend a music festival starting on the 29th.[117] On the afternoon of the 15th, after the sitting, Sandys wrote to Howell: 'Shorthouse is delightful. He is a very little fellow with a head very like a Vandyke head … or perhaps I ought to say a head of Charles I's time. He has neither moustache or beard – and but slight whiskers – rather long. It is a fine head. Very fine and remarkable eyes – and mouth of the most humorous order – in fact his face though full of thought is full of brightness and humour. It is the very nicest Hotel I have ever been in – but it will be accompanied not only with comfort but expense. Do not fail to let me have £10 this week that I may pay my bill on Monday – and send £3 if not more to Maude Grove. It is very cold and raining in torrents. Birmingham seems a most delightful place. It is the very reverse of all I anticipated.'[118]

Sandys's stay was at the Plough and Harrow, Edgbaston. Thereafter followed a series of woeful letters from him to Howell on the matter of his lack of 'coin' to travel anywhere to occupy his afternoons, since Shorthouse would only sit from 9.30 till 1.00. The weather was wet and cold and 'Birmingham itself is quite without interest of any sort. Shorthouse is delightful – and I look forward each morning to the sitting – and [am] thoroughly despondent when it is over. … I suppose I may give up all thought of the Marks commission for the three children. You thought of showing the drawings to Agnew – don't you think it may be done at once – I do not think the frames important – also he might say something about the child and the engraving – My expenses here I am sure are more than £1 a day. That I shall not be able to get away without £12 more at least – try and bugger it up and send to me in a day if possible – and if possible, make it £15. I should not think of taking it off the drawings – but will give it you back with this I have already recd out of the Macmillan checque [*sic*].'[119] The reference to 'engraving' may be that Agnew's were contemplating having a print made from either *St George* or the *Head of St George*. Such a reproduction of the latter did appear in the Supplement to *The Artist*, of January 1897.

Howell, it seems, let him down by sending only £6, Sandys replying that he was grateful, but it would not enable him to pay his hotel bill the next day, Monday 21st August. He wrote: 'I am rather in a state what to do. I cannot finish before Thursday or Friday – possibly Saturday. On Saturday I must be away. Every place is let then for the Festival. Shorthouse sits only from 9.30 till 1 o'clock – the rest of the day I have to myself, but I have been unable to go anywhere. One afternoon I went to Dudley eight miles from this. Today I had intended to have gone to Coventry but this I have been obliged to give up – so that with the wretched wet and cold weather – no coin – nothing to do – I have been devilish blue.'

He next brings up the subject of the possibility of the commission from Murray Marks to draw his three children but accepts that it is unlikely, so that he needs Howell to find 'a portrait or two at once.' Murray Marks was the wealthy art and antiques dealer, whose wife Louisa had been portrayed by Sandys in 1873, and in 1875 Sandys had drawn the family's pug dog Sambo, but no trace of any identifiable portraits of the Marks children has been found.

Sandys acknowledges the receipt of £3 from Howell on Tuesday the 22nd: 'So many thanks for the £3. I shall have to bother for £10 more to get me home. I shall leave here if possible, on Friday, but certain [*sic*] on Saturday. I think I had better decide to finish Mrs. P(addon)'s drawing and go down on Monday evg.' By Thursday morning Sandys is frantic: 'For goodness' sake do not fail me tomorrow. I must give up my rooms on Saturday morg – by 10 o'clock. I cannot wait. Every place is let for the forthcoming festival. I have no choice but to leave. I expect to finish Shorthouse tomorrow.'[120]

With time on his hands in the afternoons, he wrote a letter to his old friend William Weldon in a humble vein, fearing to 'intrude myself into your great troubles, I write now because I cannot remain silent, and now I write I can only say you have no more sincere sympathiser or friend in this world.'[121] This must refer to the legal difficulties Weldon was then having with his estranged wife Georgina Treherne (1837–1914), the then well-known amateur soprano. Still needing the funds to pay his hotel bill and return fare to London, after many entreaties to Howell, Sandys finally received money from him to his great relief on 24th August. He told Howell how difficult it had been to work in such poor light as the almost incessant rain had cast a general gloom over the proceedings.[122] He had complained of this before when he was working in Cyril Flower's house in Wales. The heavily-curtained interiors of Victorian houses must have been a particular problem when he was having to work in his clients' houses instead of in a purpose-built studio. He worked for two more days, completing the portrait on the 26th, and returned to London.

On the 25th or 26th he probably received from Howell his account, mentioned earlier, covering the period between 2nd June and 25th August. It shows that there were five payments to 'Mrs Nevill' totalling £24, and to 'A. Sandys Esq.' two payments totalling £8. Surprisingly, Howell paid a guinea on Sandys's behalf on 29th July for a catalogue of the Hamilton Palace sale.[123] On 4th August he charged Sandys 18/- for a box of cigars,[124] and on the next day sent him £3 for the outward journey to Chiltern Green. This was the railway station nearest to the home of Arthur and Isabel Flower, at The Hyde, near Luton. Presumably, this was to finish his commission to portray the two Flower children in a double portrait. It was dated March 1881, perhaps when it was commenced. The next double portrait of Flower children was not until December 1885.[125]

The Shorthouse portrait done, the sitter wrote to Macmillan on 23rd September: 'We thought [the portrait] a most beautiful work of art, but rather too large, and, as Mr Grove says, too "important".[126] I was very much entertained with Mr Sandys's conversation and company.'[127] Mrs Shorthouse was more revealing later in her book when she wrote: '[Sandys's] work is exquisite, and the upper part of the face perfect in likeness and expression, but, unhappily, the face is made too long – a defect which has characterised some other portraits by this gifted artist.'[128]

Back at Maude Grove, he arranged to travel to Woodlands, Redhill, the residence of Samuel Wreford Paddon (1847–1920), to finish the portrait he had already started of Paddon's wife Rebecca and to tackle the portrait of their baby son Stanley. The commission had come about through Howell who had made himself indispensable to Paddon in furnishing and decorating his houses in Chelsea and Surrey in the latest aesthetic taste. The wealthy Paddon was in the South African diamond business and, no doubt, wished to establish himself in London society.[129] Howell had also introduced Whistler to Paddon, resulting in a commission for a full-length oil portrait of Rebecca Paddon.[130]

Unfortunately, but perhaps inevitably, from this connection there arose another occasion in which Whistler's ire was inflamed enough to prompt him to write another satirical pamphlet *The Paddon Papers: The Owl and the Cabinet* (1882). It was aimed at Howell (The Owl) for his chicanery (as perceived by Whistler). At first Paddon took Howell's side. However subsequently, in 1885, Paddon, having learned more about his transactions with Howell, took him to court and won the case to Howell's considerable financial loss and bankruptcy. These events and the ill-feeling engendered probably put an end to Rebecca Paddon's portrait sittings to Whistler.[131] However, Sandys was not involved in these troubles and completed his portraits of Mrs Paddon and her baby boy Stanley (1881–1963) in 1882, and her little daughter Eva (1880–1969) in 1883.

In September Sandys was engaged in drawing another portrait for Macmillan, of J.R. Green (1837–1883), the historian, at his Kensington Square residence. Green was dying of tuberculosis at the time. (He died in March 1883.) Sandys wrote to Howell on the 12th: 'I shall not be able to finish Green this week – poor fellow he is very bad – and I have had three such dark afternoons I could not see to do anything well – and even that with difficulty – I should think that I shall finish him Tuesday or Wednesday.'[132] This was followed on the 14th by: 'I do not know when I shall finish Green's drawing. Four afternoons have been so dark I have been unable to do anything – this afternoon he was so ill – even had it been light – I do not think he would have been able to sit – and I could have made the best portrait of all.'[133] Sandys did manage to complete the head, but the shoulders and coat are merely suggested. Macmillan had it engraved by G.J. Stodart and published it as the frontispiece to Green's *The Conquest of England* (1883).

Sandys was invited by his friend William Weldon to dinner on Sunday 1st October to meet Joseph Ashby Sterry (*c.*1836–1917), who also became a friend, along with a man named Smart. On the 19th he sent an interesting letter to Howell urging him to place bets on two horses at the Cambridgeshire Handicap at Newmarket (not having the cash to do so himself). He wrote: 'I think the right thing is to put on at once five pounds on Hackness. Ten to one is the price now. When we spoke we could have had eighteen. Hackness soon will be 5 to 1. And five pounds on Peregrine one should get at least 100 to 1 about Peregrine and we will divide the two bets … I have not the money till the end of the week.' Airing his knowledge, he wrote: 'I think Hackness is a first rate chance, but I believe in Peregrine if he is got [*sic*] "fit" and runs – you will quite understand – with 100 to 1 chance there is a great risk, but still if you win there is a good lump to pick up. Hopper I know trains for Peck.[134] I should have mentioned this only you said Rosa knew Peck – and of course whatever is done with these horses is done by order of Peck so that

Hopper really is next to nothing in the matter … a wink from Peck would be worth £1000 on the spot … I am full of hope about Peregrine as he is still being carried on through good steady work – if he goes on well – they will get the money on in a day or two and he will come to comparably short odds … ask Rosa to find out about him day by day for if he goes on – it would be worthwhile putting £20 more on him only be sure to ask Rosa to tell you who is her informant.'[135] Peregrine had won the race in 1881 but it was Hackness that won in 1882.

The next event we know about through correspondence is that the Howell and the Sandys (Neville) families met at the Crystal Palace to celebrate Hugh's seventh birthday on 10th November.[136]

At some point in 1882, presumably in the summer, judging by the sitters' dresses, Sandys produced a double portrait of the two little sisters May and Winnie Gillilan, merely dated 1882. They were the daughters of William and Mary Gillilan who lived at 5 Clarendon Place, just north of Hyde Park. William Gillilan was a retired Lieutenant of the Royal Fusiliers, born in New York in 1845. The Gillilans were an affluent couple, with a household supporting a nurse and six servants. They were to commission further portraits by Sandys in 1885, 1886 and 1887.

Also dated 1882 is Sandys's portrait of George Lillie Craik, Macmillan's partner. In spite of Mrs Oliphant's entreaties that Craik should commission Sandys to make a portrait of his wife, Dinah Mulock, nothing came of it, but perhaps this portrait of himself resulted instead.

Sandys was in the habit of sending a Norfolk turkey to friends before Christmas. The Meredith family were in receipt of one, as we know from a letter of thanks from Marie Meredith on 2nd January 1883.[137]

We know nothing of the circumstances of the commission of an oil portrait dated 1883, now at Rufford Old Hall (National Trust), which may have been begun by Sandys earlier, but which was completed and signed in 1883.[138] This is *Sir Thomas George Fermor-Hesketh* (1849–1924), a half-length portrait of a young man aged thirty-three, seated, in hunting clothes and carrying a whip. He had succeeded his elder brother as 7th Baronet in 1876 and was married in 1880 to a Californian heiress, Miss Florence Sharon. Rufford Old Hall was the ancestral home of the Hesketh family,[139] who had built the magnificent Easton Neston House (completed 1702) at a time of the family's prosperity. The marriage with Lady Florence would bring about another period of prosperity.

On 24th January, he was writing to Howell from Brickhill Manor, Bletchley. He was there to draw the portraits of Sir Philip and Lady Sophia Duncombe-Pauncefort-Duncombe, and found it very cold there. The Duncombes were the parents of Isabel Margaretta Cockayne Pauncefort-Duncombe who had married Arthur Flower in 1873. Sandys was reminding Howell to send £5 to him, but for some unknown reason he did not wish it 'to be part payment either of your drawing or Mrs Paddon's, but will return it to you when I return'. He further wrote: 'Do you think you could manage to let me have the things of Rossetti's in a fortnight[?]'[140] In another letter from Brickhill Manor to Howell on 30th January he wrote: 'I was in a devil of a state for I had to stay with Flower on Saturday [27th] and then to get to Mr Chinnery on Monday [29th] and get back here today. ... The commercial note is splendid – thanks for it. I will send you a Portuguese epitaph in exchange. Yours in great haste.'[141]

Sandys was still at Brickhill Manor when he wrote again on 1st March to Howell, on black-edged paper (his father had died in Norwich on 9th February). Howell had sent him some items of jewellery, one of which he liked and the other he thought overpriced and suggested pawning it. He was planning to return to London on either the 5th or the 6th, and on the 10th to travel to Arthur Flower's house, The Hyde, near Luton.

On 14th March, he was writing to Howell from Maude Grove in a faint and shaky hand: 'I have been in bed almost since I saw you. Not able to go to Norwich. Soon as I can get out will get the money and bring [it to] you. Have not got it – till I go out for it.'[142] One may assume that the journey to Norwich would be to settle his father's affairs and see to his probably ailing mother (she died on 22nd September). Nevertheless, he managed to submit the portraits of Mrs Chinnery and Miss Chappell to the Royal Academy Summer Exhibition which were hung that year. Sandys's address given in the catalogue was that of the framers Foord & Dickinson, who had an arrangement with artists for delivery to the Academy on the required day. Not only these but six of his portraits of authors were shown at the Royal Birmingham Society of Artists in their Spring 1883 Exhibition at the invitation of their secretary Jonathan Pratt. These included *John Morley* (1881), *J. Henry Shorthouse* (1882), *Robert Browning* (1881), *Goldwin Smith* (1881), *James Russell Lowell* (1882), and *Matthew Arnold* (1881). All except *Robert Browning*, which was lent by George Lillie Craik, were lent by Alexander Macmillan.[143]

Among the correspondence between Sandys and Howell is a bill headed 'London 9th April 1883' for £26.10.0. Below is the statement: 'Three months after date pay to myself or my order the sum of twenty-six pounds ten shillings for value received. To Frederick Sandys Esq., 28 Maude Grove, Fulham Road, London.'[144] Signed on the reverse 'H. Chaplin'. This no doubt accounts for the sum that Sandys owed Howell noted in the letter of 14th March.[145]

There is a gap in this correspondence until 8th July when Sandys writes to Howell from 9 St Giles' Hill, Norwich: 'I was telegraphed for on Friday – my mother dying – today she is better – and I think I may get her round for a time – but she may change again as my father did. Now I have not any money. I had arranged to commence Leyland ['s portrait] on Tuesday [10th]. This must stand over for a time – do you think if you mentioned it to him that at such a time, he would advance £150[?] This is what I want – if not £100. This is what I want here to put my mother at ease – at once – by return.'[146]

A week later and still at Norwich, Sandys writes again to Howell: 'I am very sorry to hear of your bad luck it seems by your note.' There is no mention of an advance from Leyland which he had hoped for. Instead, 'you gave me to understand that you arranged the bill, etc. with Chaplin a fortnight since and also to increase the sum. I shall write to Chaplin to say I have heard from you – that you have arranged the bill – unless I have a telegram from you to the contrary'. He wrote that he was planning to leave Norwich on Tuesday the 17th.[147] In spite of being busy recently with portraits for which he must have received good money, it seems that he had found himself in yet another financial crisis.

In another inexplicable letter written from Maude Grove, dated 'Thursday', which may be from August 1883, surprisingly, Sandys entreats Howell to do something to help a man named Molteno.[148] He wrote: 'You said you thought Herman would and could do something for Molteno. I ask him to bring this note to you – if you can help him, I am sure you will. If I had been able to get out, I should have come round to you with him – but I cannot get out. Now if Herman could be induced to do something at once – if only re helping Molteno! A quid or two. I am sure it would be of service to him. Do you think it possible for you and I to get up a subscription for Molteno – so as to raise £25 for him[?] I intended to have talked this matter over with you – but here I am as ill as can be – and so low-spirited. I ought to have been in Norwich with my mother. I give him the last ten shillings I have till I can get out to help him. I doubt very much if he has sixpence in his pocket. If of the slightest convenience to you – let the people sell the chain. I may not be able to get out before Saturday.'[149]

There is a record of another sitter for the Macmillan commissions, whose portrait remained unfinished. This was Sir Garnet Wolseley (1833–1913). The reason for it being unfinished is revealed in a letter to Wolseley from Macmillan: 'What a success Sandys seems to me to have made of your portrait. An artist, like a historian, can present a matter or a man well, when his subject has interesting material. This clearly Sandys found in your face … he is away from London, as I think you are, but when you both return I hope the problem of the coat will be solved.'[150] Unfortunately, nothing more came of it. General Wolseley was a busy man, being called away for duty many times throughout the 1880s.

Thursday 20th September found Sandys in Norwich and writing to Howell: 'I was called down here by telegram a day or two after I met you. My mother was quite expected to die on Saturday last – again on Monday – but it can be a struggle only of a day or two. In this trouble I am compelled to do that which I am most unwilling, but I must depend upon you to send me not less than £20 off the drawings – by Sunday – now oblige me – send more if possible. I know full well you are troubled, but whatever your troubles may be they are nothing when compared to mine at this moment. I am distressed I am compelled to ask this, for I had made up my mind I should not trouble you more.'[151]

Sandys writes again the next day: 'Dear Howell. I write again today – do not fail me. My mother I do not think will live through the day – do not fail.'[152] In fact Mary Ann Sandys died on 22nd September at the family dwelling, 9 Grapes Hill, of 'senile decay', having been nursed by her next-door neighbour Elizabeth Chenery. Her death certificate states that she was seventy-seven which implies a date of birth of 1806. The age given on the certificate is probably accurate; other records give birth dates of 1809 and 1811.

Sandys lost no time in clearing the house on Grapes Hill, first selling to 'Mr Jackson … all the pictures prints and drawings belonging to the late Mr A Sandys' for £22.10.0.[153] The buyer was Frederick Jackson (1830–1912) who was a local amateur artist, antiquarian, and collector. Amongst this collection was a small album in which Anthony Sandys, late in his life (the album itself, from the design of its cover, must date no earlier than 1880), had probably started to mount a miscellany of his son's early work and, to confuse matters, some of his own. This was eventually sold on to a London dealer named Arthur T. Home. Home sold it to Charles Fairfax Murray in 1901 and wrote in a letter to Murray: 'I had [it] last Sept. from Mr Jackson of Bethel Street, Norwich, he bought it at the sale of Mr F. Sandys's father.'[154] Murray gave this album to the Fitzwilliam Museum, Cambridge in 1917.

The description 'all' cannot have been accurate, for 176 lots were later sold on 16th October 1883 by Spelmans, the Norwich auctioneers. The catalogue was titled *The Collection of Pictures and Drawings of the Late Mr Anthony Sandys*. Many of the lots contained a multiplicity of items and included, besides his own, Frederick and Emma's work, work by Cotman, Crome and others of the Norwich School. One lot (82) was an unframed portrait drawing of *Jackson, Sculptor* by F. Sandys, which remains untraced.[155] Sandys and Robert Jackson were Norwich contemporaries, Jackson going on to have a successful career as a jobbing sculptor in London, notably working as chief assistant to the supervising sculptor John Thomas on the sculptures adorning the Palace of Westminster.[156]

Six days after his mother's death, Sandys wrote to Mary from Grapes Hill: 'Dear little Girl, I have been hard at work packing. I think I shall finish by Monday. I have been at it night and day. I have sent you nine large boxes by luggage train, and three smaller and lighter by passenger train. These three I have paid the carriage. The others you will have to pay. You had better clear out some room for the boxes of linen are very heavy and so are the books. I enclose a list of the glass. This has still to come, so has the dinner service. I trust in fact on Monday to send up seven or eight more boxes. Two larger than you have yet.

'I have numbered the labels so do not remove them for I am able to judge what is in [them]. No. 3 is full of things you may or may not find useful at once. I sent you the key. No. 12 are dresses mostly of my sister's – but they require perhaps looking after, badly packed by me. No. 10 also has a dress of my sister's which may be crushed. The other boxes had better remain till I come back. I am so tired of this packing.

'I cannot write anymore. I send you two "quid" to pay for the carriage. I thought I could have paid here.

'With love to all – in haste aff. Fredk Sandys.

'Take care of the list it will save so much trouble. You had better have the heavy boxes in the bottom room. They are dreadful to get up and down stairs.'[157]

These household items and the dresses were probably welcome in the Maude Grove home.

On 30th September, again from Grapes Hill, Sandys wrote to Howell: 'I was much disappointed I did not hear from you this morg with £10 as promised. Depend on it I would not bother you for money unless it was needful. In answer to your telegram I sent the caricature to you. I had a letter from Liberty but no checque [*sic*]. I sent a telegram to him saying you had the caricature. I have written to him by this post. Be sure to send the "tenner". I cannot move without it.'[158] From this it seems likely that among the papers at Grapes Hill, Sandys found an impression of his once sensational caricature of 1857, *A Nightmare*. Arthur Liberty (1843–1917) hearing of it, probably through Howell, apparently wished to buy it. Needless to say, Sandys anxiously awaited payment.

At the end of the year (1883), his affairs were still precarious, but an exchange of letters still shows a certain cordiality between himself and Howell, as fathers of their families. From Maude Grove, Sandys wrote to Howell at Selsea Bill on Christmas Eve (a Monday): 'Many thanks for sending on Sunday. I enclose a "fiver". I have no time to get anything to send. Get something yourself – for yourself – and Kitty and Rosalind – Give them my best wishes for all happiness – and if you are a bit happier for a day or two I shall be. I have only a moment to catch the post – good luck to you.' In a postscript he wrote: 'I did not get the coin till just four o'clock. I have now everything to do – so do not think anything of my sending a present in this form – it is the best I can do with the best of wishes. The sausages were splendid.' The registered envelope was postmarked 'Piccadilly Circus DEC 24 83' and 'CHICHESTER DEC 25 83'.[159]

In February 1884, having completed the portrait of Mrs Paddon, Sandys received 100 guineas in payment from Howell, as the agent.[160]

At some point in 1884, Sandys was working on a portrait of Alfred, Lord Tennyson, at his house at Aldworth, near Haslemere, Surrey, while staying at Knapdale, Macmillan's house in Wandsworth. This was to be another of the portraits of authors commissioned by Macmillan. It must have been a longish daily train journey for him, and he would have liked to stay at Aldworth, as is evident from a letter he wrote to the 'dear little girl': 'Tennyson has not said anything more at present about my staying here.' The letter is revealing about Tennyson in other ways: 'Tennyson cannot endure sitting – tries to get out of it with any and every excuse. This worries me more than I can say. I could make such a fine head. I really think were it not for the money I would give it up rather than run the chance of failing to do what I might and could. I never get more than two hours and a half in the day, and this at intervals. The rest of the time we potter about. Of course this would be nice enough if I had not to work, but it tries my patience more than I know how to bear, and I am more miserable than I can tell you. At this moment I feel I will never do another portrait. … I have written this in the wood waiting for him to sit again!' The letter ends with: 'I shall be home early at Macmillan's this afternoon when I will go at him again about the checque [*sic*]. Give my love to all the children and kiss them all for me. Send me Herman Merivale's play of the *White Pilgrim*.'[161] Despite Sandys's tendency to distort the heads of his sitters (which I attribute to his increasing myopia) characterising the Macmillan commissions and others in the 1880s, the portrait of Tennyson is one of the most true to life and successful.

Sandys's request for a copy of the Herman Merivale play of 1883 (to read) shows his continuing interest in the contemporary theatre. Friendships with playwrights, actors, designers for the theatre, journalists, and critics are evident throughout his adult life. His membership of the Garrick Club brought him many such acquaintances. Merivale (1839–1906) was the son of a senior civil servant, and became a barrister and civil servant himself but, after his father's death in 1874, he gave this up and became a prolific writer of dramas and farces, and wrote one novel.

Another inspired portrait worked on at about this time was that of Richard William Church (1815–1890), Dean of St Paul's from 1871 to 1890. He was a Tractarian, a writer and an intellectual. It is dated 1884 and was part of Macmillan's on-going commission.

While carrying on with these commissions of author-portraits, Sandys evidently fitted into his schedule a portrait of Macmillan's daughter-in-law Margaret Helen, née Lucas (1857–1939). She was married to George Augustin Macmillan (1855–1936) who was the second son and successor to his father in the publishing business.

In August and September 1884, Sandys was in Cromer to make portraits of the Hoare family: the little boy Samuel (1880–1959), later to become a distinguished statesman,[162] and his brother Oliver. Although his correspondence does not mention it, he also completed a portrait of their mother, Katherine Louisa, née Hart Davis (1846–1931) who is remembered as a skilled needlewoman. The Hoares were at their summer residence, The Cliff House, Cromer.

Sandys had just arrived in Cromer on 26th August and wrote to Howell under the letterhead of Hotel de Paris, Cromer. As ever, living from hand-to-mouth, he wrote: 'I recd the "tenner" from Baderstone[163] yesterday and came down here – could not get a bed at the Hotel – have got a beastly little room outside where I am now writing & I go to the Hotel for my meals. It is so bitterly cold I do not know what to do – so I shall give up all notion of a little pleasure here with you – quite apart from the discomfort however. I have another commission for a child – a son of S. Hoare – so that I shall [work?] on the two children – as each one rests I go on with the one who is not resting. I shall try and get the two done by Tuesday [2nd September] or Wednesday next – and get away from this place at once – I never liked it – and who in the world do you think came rushing into my arms – overjoyed to see me – well I cannot tell you. Perhaps I had better – well here it is – Cyril Flower, who is staying at the Hotel with his wife and Lady de Rothschild. They have been very nice this morg – and Cyril has gone a long way out of his way to be kind and civil. What could I do – and what can I do[?] I shall get away as quick as I can. I wish it were tomorrow.' This unexpected encounter must have been the first since they parted on bad terms in 1880. Cyril Flower enjoyed sea-bathing at Cromer and later, in 1897, built a holiday villa, The Pleasaunce,[164] nearby at Overstrand.

Sandys continued: 'The two children are both nice children to do – and it is fortunate getting £200 now instead of £100. Now let me ask you to help me – with fifteen or twenty pounds till these drawings are done. I had to part with five out of the ten to the little girl, so that I had only five to come here with – and I cannot pay my bill. … Let me hear from you as I am anxious – and this weather is wretched, and I have no place to sit but the bedroom – damn the place.'[165]

Sandys was still in Cromer on 27th September, writing to Howell under the letterhead of the Hotel de Paris: 'I have finished my work and shall return to town either tomorrow or Tuesday. It has been a most doleful time. I had to send to Rossi for the desired coin.[166] I did write at once in answer to your telegram for I was not sure till yesterday – [that] I should not have to stay here and draw two more portraits. However yesterday it was settled to postpone them. … It is raining like the devil – and [has] been almost since I have been here.'

Another letter to Howell from Cromer has been preserved, dated 'Monday eveng' (13th October 1884): 'Do you think during the next four or five days you will be having money – so that you could let me have £10 for a week. I am to do two drawings so that I shall have to be here for quite a fortnight longer and I must send money to town – dreadful needs – and Rossi cannot do much. I saw him yesterday terribly low-spirited. It is bitterly cold here and it has rained almost ever since I have been here. After finishing these two Hoares I shall go to the Buxtons to draw one or two little boys. Write to me and say if money will be coming to you. I do not want it for more than the week – till I complete these two drawings of Hoares. He concluded enigmatically "Never mind Papa – get it".'

There exists with a Buxton family descendant a portrait drawing of Anthony Buxton as a little boy, dated 'Septr 1884'.[167]

The last letter from The Hotel de Paris, Cromer, dated in full 'Monday Oct. 20', as if to emphasise that he was still there. He wrote: 'Dear Howell – You have never answered my note. I am at my wit's end.' He next reported having seen some antique silver at Rossi's shop in Norwich, thinking that Howell might want to invest in it. 'Rossi has two beautiful silver vases something this shape [drawing]. One weighs ten ounces – date Queen Anne – capital mark. The other weighs 4 ounces – time of George the First. These two are 30 shillings the ounce. He has a set of castors *[sic]* date 1742 – 15 shillings an ounce – 35 ounces in weight. He has also a tankard with cover lid – beautiful Irish mark – date 1682 weight about 32 ounces – price 30 shillings an ounce. Will any of this lot suit you[?] What horse is to win[?] What has become of Legacy[?] Write.'[168]

There was an invitation from George Meredith, from Box Hill, to stay in November,[169] and in December Sandys sent the Meredith family a Norfolk turkey which arrived on Christmas Eve. Meredith characteristically wrote: '…under [a] chaplet of sausages. We attacked it two days following, drinking to the Lord of Norfolk's health, and wishing him with us. … Our cottage offers few attractions in the pit of winter, but should a mad fit seize you, pray come hither and bite. You know you are always welcome.' Meredith planned to spend a day or two in London at the end of January when he would 'endeavour to call at the Cottage in the Town'.[170]

By the mid-1880s Sandys was in a new abode known as The Cottage, in Holland Park Road. This was a detached purpose-built studio with living accommodation, erected in 1880 together with several other studios, on part of the old Holland House estate which was then rapidly being parcelled off and developed. This was a newly desirable area for an artist to be, where his predecessors in the road were the painters Val Prinsep, Frederic Leighton and W.B. Richmond.[171] Sandys's current finances being what they were, it is difficult to imagine how he was able to take on such an establishment as well as maintain the family at Maude Grove, but probably the recent Norfolk portraits had provided him with some funds, at least for the time being.

Another child, named Edwyn Miles, was born on 11th October, but died at the age of only two weeks, and was interred in the family plot at the Brompton Cemetery.[172]

In early December 1884 he was writing to Howell from 'The Cottage, Holland Park Road'. 'Now do pray like a good fellow get the chairs at once sent to ... [scratched out] ... Maples[173] – I do so need them – I want so much to get my place right by Xmas – which I fear even if I have the chairs at once I shall hardly be able to do. Could you do anything about the Rossetti things[?]'[174] The last letter of 1884 to Howell was written on the 30th: 'I wish you would come and see me here tomorrow (Wednesday) anytime between 12 and 5 o'clock. I intended to write, but I have been so bothered, to say the Turkey was the best I ever tasted, the very best, Sir, in the world.'[175]

Sandys was at The Cottage from 1883 to 1888, but financial difficulties continued, added to by his having to pay the rent of this newly built studio-house. However, he was determined to set up shop in a respectable studio as befitted a professional portrait painter. Mary and family, of course, continued in their lodgings at Maude Grove – a second rent to pay.

In 1885 he produced three portraits, two of Mrs Gillilan, a drawing and an oil painting made from it, and in December, a double portrait drawing of two of the young children of Arthur Flower, Conrad Herbert and Violet. The portraits were perhaps executed at The Hyde or perhaps at their London house at 36 Prince's Gate.

A study of the head of Hugh in red chalk which, seemingly, was intended to be worked up, eventually, as a full-length oil painting, to be titled Samuel, was made in 1885.[176] This was to fulfil the commission from Cyril Flower, made in 1880 with other stipulations, for which he was to receive £12 per week from Flower. Flower was to take the oil painting and Sandys could keep the drawing. It is not known for how long the £12 continued to come from Flower, but in default of the oil painting of Samuel being executed, the drawing went into Flower's collection instead of being retained and sold by Sandys. It was reproduced by the Autotype Company, but in a letter to Howell, he complained that he had not the money to collect the drawing from the Company (in Oxford Street) and asked him to call in and ask them to return it to him. Sandys was also feeling unwell and low-spirited.[177] He wrote again to Howell in April: 'How about the bill for £25 – if you could manage it and divide the plunder it would carry me through this picture – a fortnight will, I am glad to say, see the end of it.'[178]

Aside from portraits, around this time he produced some potboiler 'fancy heads' based on some of his earlier images. Two of these from the 1880s were based on *The Magdalen* of 1862. Since the originals had long since been sold and therefore were out of sight, Sandys would have had to rely on an Autotype print to copy. By the 1880s, the technical advance of photography enabled photographic firms, such as that of the Autotype Company and Frederick Hollyer, to make good quality photographic reproductions of drawings and paintings.[179] Particularly in the case of drawings, these prints were so accurate as to almost fool the eye. Sandys's resort to replication of his earlier works, often with the addition of a spray of foliage or flowers in the background, began to be a frequent practice in his declining years.

Still dependent on Howell, Sandys wrote anxiously to him on 8th April 1885: 'Where are you? You never look me up – or answer a note. I suppose it is no use to ask you to come here tomorrow Thursday, if not send a telegram to say if you will be at 91 S.R. at seven o'clock on Thursday evg – or will you meet me at the Café at that time?'[180] This brief note tells us that Howell was living at 91 Southampton Row, his last abode, and that the Café Royale had begun to be a haunt of Sandys.

The next letter to Howell, on 11th April, Sandys writes: 'Enclosed are the "bills" … I am so bad, I ought not to have come out today.' At the bottom of the letter Howell has written 'Bill for £50 / Do for £25'. On the 28th Sandys was complaining about his backache: 'I am much about the same, I am sorry to say – my back is if anything worse.'[181]

Little is known thereafter until September, when he received a sad letter from his good friend George Meredith to say that his wife was dying. He wrote: 'Write again when you are in the mood. It is a burst of light to hear from a friend.'[182] In October, Sandys wrote to Howell: 'I am so done up today after my walk home so late last night or rather this morg that I am sure that I shall not be able to get to you this afternoon – so pray do not wait in one second.'[183]

At the end of October, we learn of the possibility of an important portrait commission (which never materialised) from a letter dated 30th October 1885, to W.E. Gladstone from James Knowles, the architect and journalist, who wished Gladstone to sit for a portrait by Sandys.[184] Knowles wrote: 'I am wanting to repeat my prayer for the sittings to Sandys which I begged for yesterday.' Knowles was a close associate of Cyril Flower in the development of Victoria Street and parts of Battersea, but in the 1870s he turned his energies to the intellectual side of journalism, firstly as editor of the *Contemporary Review* and, from 1877, as founder and editor of *The Nineteenth Century*. Both were monthly reviews of contemporary matters, literature, the arts and politics, with a Liberal bias. No doubt Gladstone would have been as reluctant to sit as Tennyson was.

Eighteen eighty-six began with another shortage of funds, as evidenced by his letter to Howell written on 16th February (which he wrongly dated to the 17th, but the postmark of the 16th contradicts this). He wrote: 'On Thursday last when I saw you, you gave me hope positive you would try and manage me a "fiver" the following day – do try and manage it tomorrow – and post it to me here registered. I cannot get up to you for two reasons – one you will have but little difficulty in guessing – the other that I am working very hard – for my picture must be finished this day three weeks – and I have most unfortunately had two days – yesterday and today so dark I do not know what my work will be like when a bright day comes and enables me to see it. … Do send tomorrow Wednesday.' The oil portrait being worked on was that of William Gillilan which was shown at the Royal Academy in 1886.[185] It was the last work by Sandys shown there until the retrospective exhibition which was organised after his death. The critic J.M. Gray tells us that it was a life-size portrait.[186] It remains untraced at the time of writing, though we know its appearance almost exactly from the fine chalk portrait, the preliminary work, which appeared on the market in 1981 and was sold to Thomas Agnew.[187]

In a letter from The Cottage dated 4th March, the year not recorded but perhaps it was 1886, Sandys wrote to Hastings, the solicitor: 'I am more vexed than I will say with the contents of your note – When did you give the drawing of the *Medusa* head up to Apps? And why? Please answer me by return. I am placed by this most unfortunate act in a very embarrassing position. At my last interview with you I asked you for the drawing, and you promised me the drawing.' Hastings probably was holding the picture in bond for a loan; Mr Apps may have been a money lender. This letter must have come into the hands of Howell since it is at the John Rylands University Library in the collection of Sandys letters given by Charles Fairfax Murray.[188]

A portrait dated May 1886 is of a boy in a sailor suit, Dion William Palgrave Clayton Calthrop (1878–1937). He was the son of the actor John Clayton and his wife Eve Boucicault. His uncle was the artist Claude Calthrop (1845–1893). Brought up in an artistic-theatrical and fashionable family, he became an artist and playwright himself, and wrote and illustrated books on costume and garden history. In his memoir, *My Own Trumpet* (1935), he recalls: 'I am sitting for my portrait to Frederick Sandys in a studio in Holland Park Road. That also links up with the present, because I have been painted there by Whistler, though the picture is lost or destroyed; drawn there in the same studio by Phil May, and painted there later by George Spencer Watson, the RA.' He continued with an anecdote: 'They were always in debt, Sandys and Whistler, at that time, and I was told only dared to go out on Sundays. Can that be true? Anyhow, I do know that Whistler had painted an imaginative

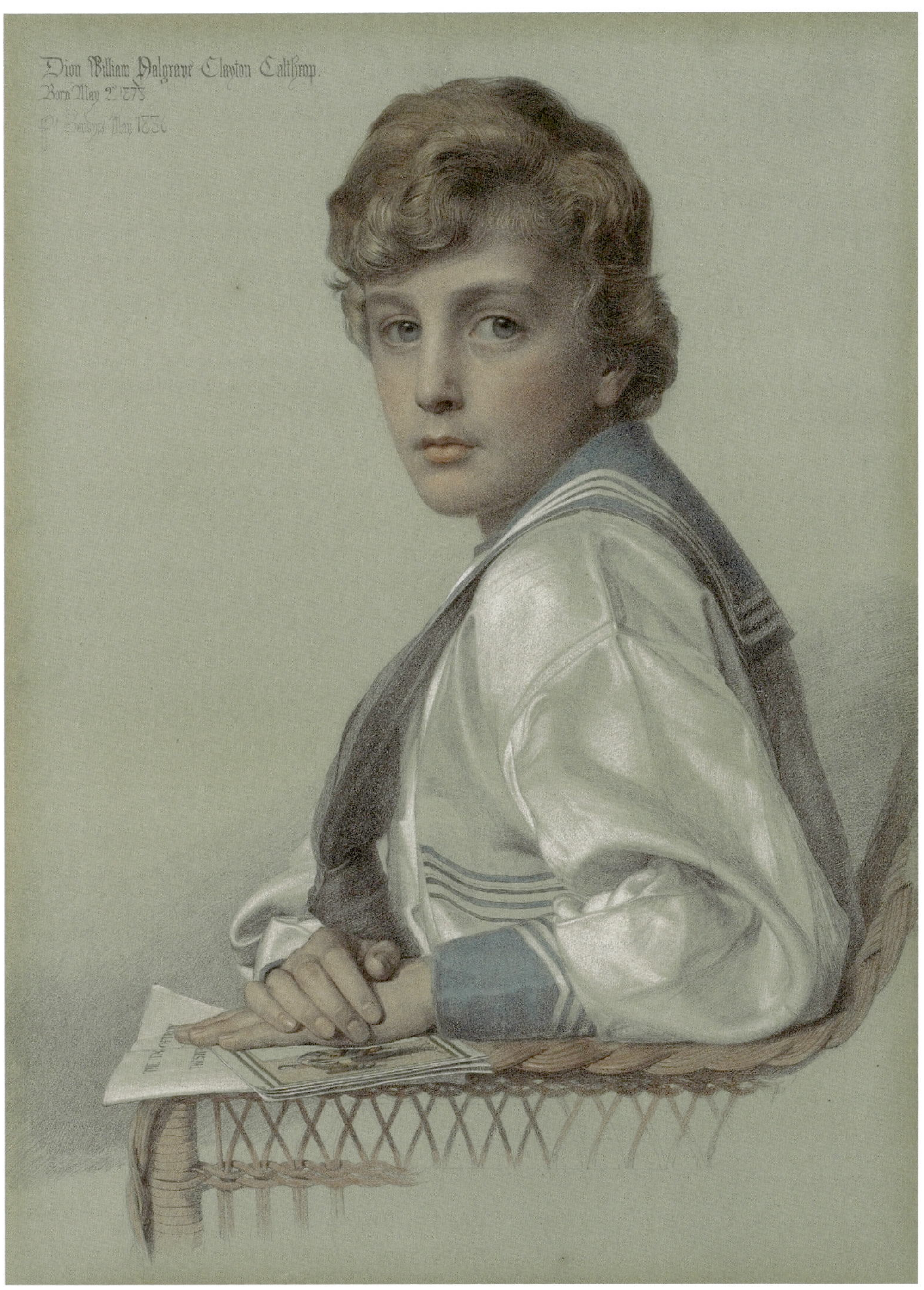

Dion William Palgrave Clayton Calthrop. Chalk drawing. May 1886. The son of John Clayton, the actor, and Eve, the daughter of Dion Boucicault, the dramatist. He studied art in London and Paris.

picture which I have never seen since, and that he dashed into the studio one day – no, not dash, he didn't dash – he came in and said excitedly that he had a rich American coming to see his picture. "But," said Sandys, "what are you going to call it?" "Valparaiso Harbour," Whistler replied. And as such it was sold.'[189] Interesting though it may appear, the letter hardly makes sense and is obviously a garbled second – or third – hand anecdote. Whistler's Valparaiso pictures date from the late 1860s.

Another portrait dated 1886 is of George Andrew Brand (1861–1911) with his little terrier dog. George was the second son of James Brand (1832–1893)[190] of Sanderstead Court, Surrey, formerly of Bedford Hill House, Streatham, where the family were neighbours of the Flower family (and also the Dyce family to whom they were related). The eight portraits of the Brand family by Sandys, of which George Andrew is one, undoubtedly came about through the Flower connection.

He also portrayed Lewis Flower (1856–1902) in 1886. Lewis, known to his friends as Peter, was a younger brother of Cyril Flower. As a young man and somewhat of a playboy in the modern sense, he was an admirer of Margot (Margaret) Tennant (1864–1945), who later married the politician H.H. Asquith and became Countess of Oxford and Asquith. In her novel *Octavia* (1928) one of the central characters is based on him.[191] They were close to marriage, but she turned him down as not being 'serious' enough. He died unmarried.

On 6th December, Sandys's youngest child Gertrude was born.[192] Growing up into a beauty, she was a boon to her father as a model in his late years, and at least twelve drawings of her were produced as she was growing up, the most notable being *Wondertime* of 1900. She married Lionel Crane,[193] the elder son of Walter Crane in 1913, and they had one son, Anthony.

In the 1880s there was a rise in the number of ambitious loan exhibitions being organised in the provinces, as well as Scotland and Wales. Prosperity and civic pride in the large industrial towns had already led to the building of fine town halls, public libraries, municipal museums and art galleries. Local art societies were formed providing a shop window for the increasing number of professional and amateur artists to be found throughout the land.[194] From records of exhibitions, one finds that works by Sandys were shown at the annual Spring Exhibition of the Royal Birmingham Society of Artists in 1883 and, in the same year, at the Huddersfield Fine Art and Industrial Exhibition. In 1886, works by Sandys were shown at the Edinburgh International Exhibition and in Liverpool at the Grand Loan Exhibition. This on-going tendency was given a particular impetus by the celebration of the Queen's Golden Jubilee of 1887. In 1887, he was represented in the Royal Jubilee Exhibition at Manchester and at the Royal Yorkshire Jubilee Exhibition at Saltaire. These were mostly loan exhibitions from local collections, the owners of which were happy to show their status as art collectors. It perhaps brought a wider knowledge of his work but did not earn him much, if anything, of that vital commodity – money.

While still at The Cottage, Sandys wrote to George Craik of Macmillan's, wishing Craik and Alexander Macmillan would come to see two pictures on which he was working. It is only dated 'Tuesday', typically for Sandys.[195] He never seemed aware of the current date, in his unbusinesslike way.

We know of six dated portraits which Sandys must have completed in 1887, and one which has been tentatively given to this year. The dated portrait of William Gillilan's little daughter Christabel, aged four, holding her toy elephant is very appealing. She is dressed in velveteen outdoor clothes and a fur bonnet.[196] Two more dated portraits of members of the Furber family are of Charles Furber and Nellie Furber, perhaps one of Charles's daughters.[197] The portrait of Nellie, aged seventeen, was given to the Birmingham Art Gallery in 1950 by the sitter, who became Mrs William Bramson. Charles Furber (1818–1890) of Holborn and St John's Wood was an auctioneer and surveyor, but nothing is known of a Sandys connection. Sandys also completed portraits of two young aristocrats, descendants of the 4th Earl of Bessborough. The elder of the two was Violet Louisa Ponsonby (1876–1953), aged eleven. Her brother was Richard Arthur Brabazon Ponsonby (1878–1937) who was to pursue a career in the Far East. They were the children of John Henry Ponsonby-Fane and Florence Farquhar of Brympton House, near Yeovil, Somerset. Portraits of aristocrats are a rarity in Sandys's oeuvre. Another portrait dated 1887, titled *Forget Me Not*, suggests that the sitter was perhaps the wife of H.C. Merivale, the author of the successful play of the same title, in which Sandys is known to have been interested.[198]

There is little to tell about Sandys's activities in 1888 except for the production of three portraits and an invitation in May to visit George Meredith at Box Hill, bringing 'Mr Watts'. The latter is undoubtedly Theodore Watts-Dunton, before he annexed his mother's maiden name.[199] Watts-Dunton (1832–1914) was a solicitor, before giving up the law to become a writer and poet. He was welcomed into the Rossetti circle in about 1872 and became a devoted friend and support to both the impractical Rossetti and the wayward and childlike Swinburne, the latter coming to live under Watts's roof in Putney until his death. Although I have found no evidence of any direct communication between

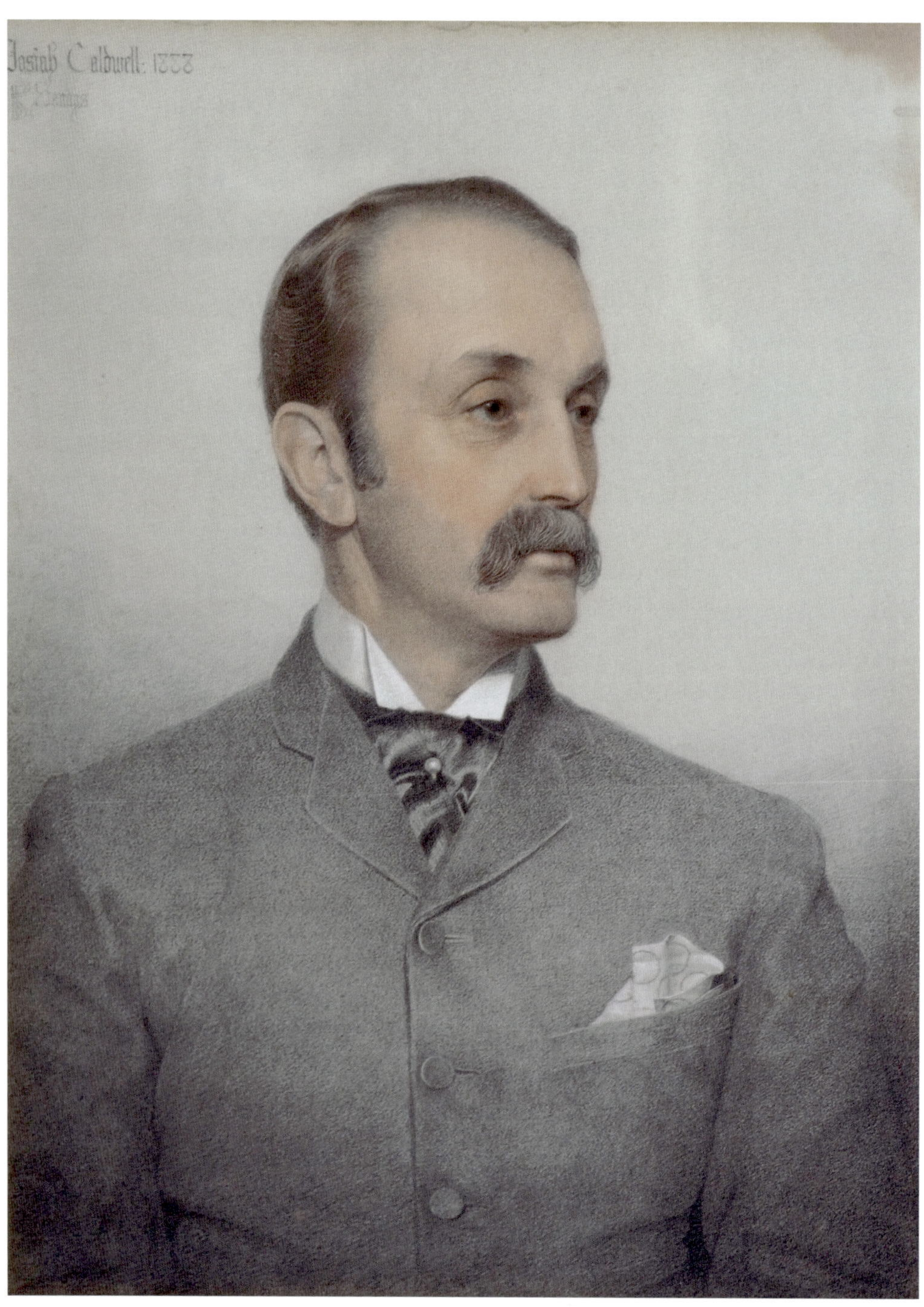

Josiah Caldwell (1837-1896). Chalk drawing. 1888. An American businessman and Abolitionist from Connecticut who brought his family over to England in the 1870s, and remained until his death in 1896. He commissioned Sandys to paint a portrait of his daughter Julia.

Sandys and Watts-Dunton, they certainly knew one another. The occasion in May 1888 when Sandys was invited by George Meredith to bring Watts-Dunton and travel down to Box Hill for lunch was perhaps the beginning of a friendship between Meredith and Watts-Dunton which lasted until Meredith's death in 1909.[200]

Watts-Dunton is best known for his highly romantic novel *Aylwin* which was a best-seller when it was published in 1898. The book's setting in the wilder landscapes of Wales and Norfolk has an interacting cast of gypsies, artists, and poets. His sources of inspiration for this mélange of personae were his artist and poet friends in the Rossetti circle of the 1860s. Rossetti himself can be seen in the character of D'Arcy, and though Cyril Aylwin is a minor character in the story, Watts-Dunton clearly had Sandys in mind. Importantly, the gypsy Sinfi Lovell, who figures throughout the book, was inspired by Keomi, Sandys's lover in the 1860s.

It was George Borrow (1803–1881), whom Sandys had met earlier in his life in Norwich (see pages 20 and 23), who set off this interest in gypsy life by the publication of his autobiographical *Lavengro* (1851). Borrow was a traveller and a linguist. In his wanderings around Europe and Britain he became fascinated by the nomadic gypsy tribes who had lived in Europe, including Britain, for centuries. He published a wordbook of their Anglo-Romany dialect (1874).

Meredith, who was another romantic, had included gypsies in the cast of characters of his *The Adventures of Harry Richmond* (1871), one of whom he actually named 'Keomi'. These stories and the books of Francis Groome (1851–1902), another Romany enthusiast, were the beginnings of a trend from which developed the idea of a picturesque and colourful gypsy life which attracted many artists, poets, and writers in the early twentieth century, and contributed to a fashionable bohemianism taken up by middle-class artists in Britain such as Augustus John, Alfred Munnings and others.

Turning to the conventional side of society, two of Sandys's three portraits dated 1888 were of an American couple, Josiah Caldwell (1837–*c.*1896) and his wife Anita Smith Caldwell (1842–1887). They were wealthy New Englanders: Josiah was a railway entrepreneur and businessman at a time of rapid railway expansion in America, and Anita had been born in Cuba of a Rhode Island family. They lived in Boston and New York City in the early 1870s, but by the late 1870s they had moved to England. By the time of the 1881 census, they had settled in Broadwater Down, an 1860s development of large detached villas near Tunbridge Wells, Kent. There, the two youngest of their six children were born in *c.*1875 and *c.*1879. Anita died in November 1887, but Sandys had presumably already started her portrait in early 1887, finishing it posthumously in 1888 (as dated).

Sandys's friendship with John Brett continued undiminished, and Brett's diary records that Sandys brought Caldwell to the Bretts for dinner in March 1888.[201] Sandys introduced another picture buyer to Brett, as recorded in Brett's Studio Log in April 1888: 'Sketch sold to Mr Gillilan. A friend of Sandys – a new customer.'[202]

By July 1888, Josiah Caldwell, now widowed, had moved the family to a rented country house, Forest Hall, near High Ongar in Essex. We know this because Sandys was commissioned to paint the portrait of the elder of his two daughters, Julia (1870–1933), and the detailed diary he kept while working on this portrait has been preserved by the Sandys family.[203] It follows the pattern of his diary of 1880, described earlier. There may have been other such diaries, but if so, they have disappeared.

This is not a printed diary (as in 1880) but is a plain ruled notebook which Sandys dates himself without recording the year. However, from internal evidence it can be dated to 1889,[204] which enables us to date the portrait of Julia. The diary runs from 29th June when he sets off from Liverpool Street to be met at Chipping Ongar station by Mr Caldwell and taken to Forest Hall where there were several people staying, as Sandys noted. After the arrival of his easel on 1st July, he started work on the preliminary drawing for the portrait. There are pages and pages in which the daily activities at Forest Hall of the family and guests are noted, and one senses the reason that Sandys writes the diary so fully is because he has a great deal of time on his hands and no one to confide in. The diary demolishes the Arkwright family legend[205] that the portrait was undertaken at Easton Lodge, the family home of Lady Warwick,[206] but it is very probable that the Caldwells knew her socially, being neighbours.

Julia 'sat' for him for roughly three-hour periods (sometimes less), irregularly, during the next sixteen days, wearing for the first time the dress in which she was to be portrayed, brought down from the London dressmaker on the 13th. She was a reluctant sitter, and as Sandys relates on the 18th: 'My sitter takes no interest in the work[;] on the contrary [she is] horribly bored by it.' Having decided he had finished the preliminary drawing,[207] he returned to London on Monday 22nd July. He also wrote that he 'engaged a studio – Carlyle Studios in King's Road, Chelsea – a wretched little ill-lighted room'. Not being satisfied with the drawing of the arm and hands, he redrew them from a model (whose name has been thoroughly erased in the diary). He then traced the whole figure in the drawing and transferred it to a canvas, marking in the outline with a mixture of raw umber and Indian red, then laying in the shadows with the same, with the addition of flake white. Then comes a typical wail, 'but being quite unskilled and ignorant did not make the half tints or shadows sufficiently dark'. He continued to narrate his routine, with the details of the several colours and varnishes he used, until the underpainting was completed, which took him to 22nd August. At this point he noted, describing his usual technique: 'I have always first put on a ground of white mixed with copal varnish and into this I painted as above.'[208] He had a preoccupation with fast-drying varnishes and oils, to hasten the drying of the underpainting, before he could add to it.

While still in London, he received an invitation[209] from Meredith to lunch at Box Hill in early August, but the date had to be re-negotiated so that Meredith's daughter 'Riette' could be with them. She was 'rowing on the Thames' at the time, so the date of the lunch would have to be postponed until Sunday 11th August.

Having much spare time at Forest Hall, Sandys wrote letters to his children. Three have been preserved by the family from this time. One was written in mid-July to Winifred, the eldest in the acknowledged family: 'My dear little Winifred, You do not write, and you see I cannot write eight letters, one to each of you, every time.[210] I am constantly wondering what you are doing what all of you are after. I am working as well as I can but I cannot get more than three hours a day for sittings from Miss Caldwell, do what I may. The rest of my time I dawdle about the garden or walk about over the Park and the fields looking at the weeds and trees. The latter are not very picturesque. There are any amount of fine well grown oaks but no good group. No good views it is a flat uninteresting country. The weeds however are very fine indeed, some I should have liked to have drawn if I had the things here to have done them with. The last few days however have been wet and unsettled. Yesterday I played some games of croquet on the wet lawn, but I chiefly like to potter about by myself ... the two Miss Caldwells have gone over to a picnic at Epping Forest this afternoon. They wanted me to go, but I preferred staying, and so you have this note. On Saturday I went over to see a nice little church about five miles from here. The walls of the nave are simply large oak trees sawn in halves and placed on end side by side, the inner side polished with age. This part of the church is supposed to be Anglo Saxon.[211] Give my love around and with a good lot for yourself till I see [you]. Your F.S.' 'F.S.' seems a little absent-minded for a father to end his letter to his daughter.

There are also two letters to his youngest, Gertrude, from this time at Forest Hall: 'My dear little angel Gertrude. I am just off to bed but before going I want to send you a piece of cake that was brought for my tea and you will find in the box another piece of cake which was for my tea yesterday, so this may be a little dry. This I am sure you will give to my boy Guy.[212] That is of course if he has been good. You will also find in a little piece of paper a shilling. You must get your Mother to give you two sixpences for it. One is for good little Gertie. The other for Guy. You will give it to him if he has been very very good and I wonder if you could give him a kiss for me – a good one, both your arms round his neck. I received your note Mildred sent. It was capital, but you ought to have drawn me something on the easel. Could not you draw me Ruth looking at the two sixpences – and Mr Wills[213] singing at the back with his wig on one side of his head, just covering his right eye and is winking with his left. If you cannot draw the wig, Winifred must. If you cannot draw the wink, Mildred will. Now good night. You never wrote to me about going to Greenwich, seeing all sorts of things and ships and eating all the S H R I M P S in Greenwich. Oh you little angel, once more Good Night. Your loving Father.'

Another letter to Gertrude, 'My dear little Angel ...', but dated only 'Thursday' from Forest Hall, must have been written in the summer, because he asks: 'Have you been to the Exhibition again I wonder. Have you been riding in a mail cart?' A Spanish exhibition, opening in June 1889, was being presented at Earl's Court. The exhibition ground would have been within walking distance for the family.

After the break, the return to Forest Hall was on Saturday 24th August, bringing down a potted myrtle bush acquired from Veitch the nurseryman – a very large one, which may be seen in the background of the finished portrait. He was without his sitter for another month (until 24th September), so worked on the foliage with which he surrounded the figure, sprays of rose leaves which he selected from the garden with more shrubs sent down from Veitch's nursery. He wrote about the materials he used as he carried on painting. Besides raw umber and Indian red and Davis's and Roberson's White, which were employed for the drawing-in of the figure, and for the darker-toned areas he used ivory black, blue black, amber white, yellow ochre, raw sienna, burnt sienna, burnt umber, Prussian blue, permanent blue, aureolin, yellow madder, Naples yellow, 'crome [*sic*] green', terre verte, light red, scarlet vermilion, crimson madder, and viridian, variously mixed with copal varnish or spike oil. He appears to have spent more time on the foliage than the rest of the painting.

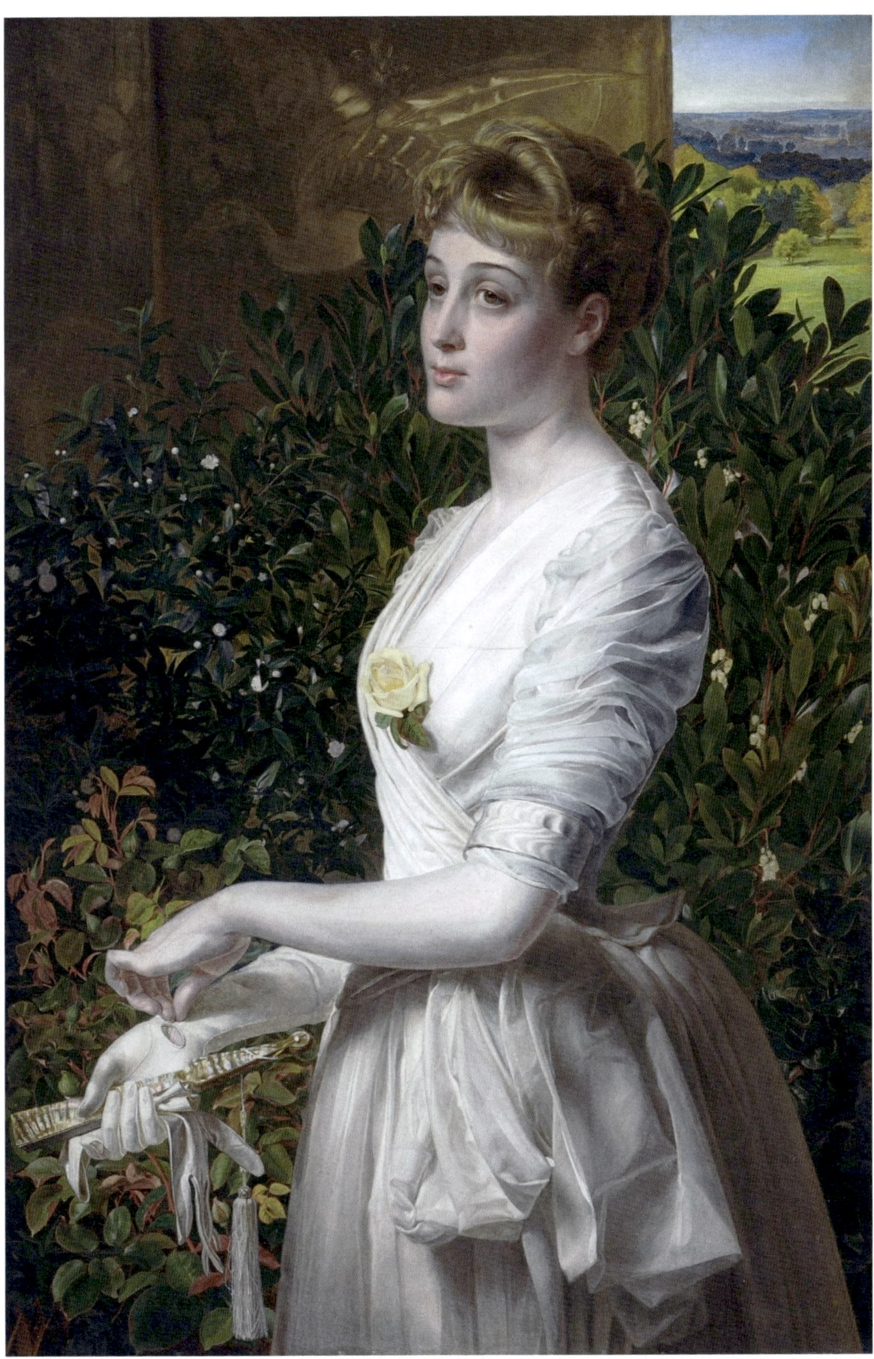

Julia Caldwell (1870-1933). Oil on canvas. August-December 1889. Julia was the eldest daughter of Josiah Caldwell and his wife Anita Smith Caldwell, from New England. The portrait was painted while the family was residing at Forest Hall, Ongar, Essex. Julia eventually married Loftus Joseph Wigram Arkwright in 1894, a descendant of Sir Richard Arkwright the early industrialist.

In writing while painting and glazing some of this foliage, he revealed his usual self-doubts: 'I have not painted with sufficient body, nor have I painted with sufficient strength or power. This I think I can correct in the glazing, only with extra time or labour – but I am without experience!!! And [at] my time of life when most men's work is done, mine [is] to commence. How delighted I should be to be able to do it. I must.'

On the 24th, the sitter posed briefly in the newly made ball gown with a fresh yellow rosebud pinned to her bodice. A few weeks later, on 17th October, he complained: 'All my work has been done in a hurry on this picture' and '[I am] longing to paint a picture for myself in my own way, and calmly, no worry.'

A happier day was spent on 31st August: 'The result of my week's work fairly good, remembering it is four years since I had a brush in my hand.'[214] From 1st September to 6th December, he interrupts the narrative with two pages of self-critical comments on his technique such as: 'The background I have chosen is not only a mistake. It is lunacy – simple. I have now been at work a month and not half the background finished,' and 'the tints which I had thought strong and even so beyond nature, I find tame and poor – have more reliance on my eye and think less of the future, so I feel at this moment, for whilst painting I thought my colour not so vivid as nature, but more becoming to a modest picture. Which view shall I find to be the right one [?]' Later, on 10th November: 'My picture in the frame proves I should not tremble at force – for what I had thought forcible is quite tame. I felt I had not the force of nature, but thought I was painting to the advantage of the picture and the general effect – a grand mistake.' On 29th November, Sandys also wrote: 'The more I work, the deeper the conviction that I fear force – and reality. This is most marked in my distance – it seemed to me absurdly forced as I paint now – it is washy, and must be strengthened.' On 6th December: 'Bewildered on returning to the Myrtle to complete it – to find out how little I have realised as I had believed at the time, the variety and colour of the leaves. I almost doubt if it can be done in the system I have adopted – if it can – what experience must be required!!! I cannot avoid working in too cold a tone – even for truth.'[215]

Much of November was spent on the area behind the foliage: a gold-coloured Japanese or Chinese embroidered silk screen and a distant view out of a window (a favourite device of his which can be seen in earlier portraits).[216] However, it was giving him some anxiety: '14th… I should have gone over my preparation with raw umber and perhaps a little aureolin mixed with it. I am in a mess and now must muddle out of it.' And on the 15th: '… painted the sky, mixing Naples yellow and white with pure ultramarine; for the lower part terre verte and white – made in this a grand fiasco. My thoughts seem to have left me at the time, after pondering over this sky and [illeg.], and now to blunder. This blunder and the blunder of the gold background will give me great trouble. …'[217]

Meanwhile, he distractedly pondered over an idea for a future subject: '"The Return of the Dove to the Ark" … I think I might make a good subject of this without the labour of an elaborate background.'[218] Understandably, the generally poor light at that time of year was the subject of his frequent complaint. For instance, on the morning of 24th November: '[I] did a little work on the arbutus but it became so dark I could only mess about, had to stop at 12.30. At 1 it became lighter but only for a few minutes – then for the rest of the day all was darkness … to my room 10.15 – blowing a gale. To bed most sad from my position. It is heart breaking – from what?' After a long day's work on the 29th, he mused: 'If I could but get my neck free for a time,[219] I believe still I might paint some pictures that both as paintings and as subjects might live.'[220]

In early December, Sandys fussed over the various parts of the background foliage and although Julia and her sister returned from town on the 5th, it was not until the 9th that he got a two-hour sitting from her and he 'worked on the eye [and] eyebrow farthest away, and nose'. 'He had been sent a copy of *Pen and Ink Drawing*,[221] a book by an American Pennell – a beautifully got up book – a present from Macmillan.' This he spent a few evenings reading, after which he snorted to his diary, 'the man knows nothing of his subject'.[222]

On the 10th, 12th, 13th, 15th, 16th, 17th, 18th, 19th, and 21st he got sittings from the young woman, each averaging between two and three hours. Halfway through his note on 21st December, four pages of the diary have been removed which must have covered the completion of the painting and his return to London (probably on the 23rd). One wonders what details these pages might have revealed. It is known that his daughter Winifred, particularly, was later to remove anything in the family papers which she thought might cause embarrassment to the family or cause the family name to be defamed in any way. In 1910 she attempted to sell the 1880 diary (with her excisions) to Samuel Bancroft Jr, the American collector, but he turned it down.

This 1889 diary shows that Sandys did not develop his paintings as a balanced whole, adjusting as he progressed, but they were drawn and laid out, and fixed from the beginning to the end, with the final stages spent in adjusting relative

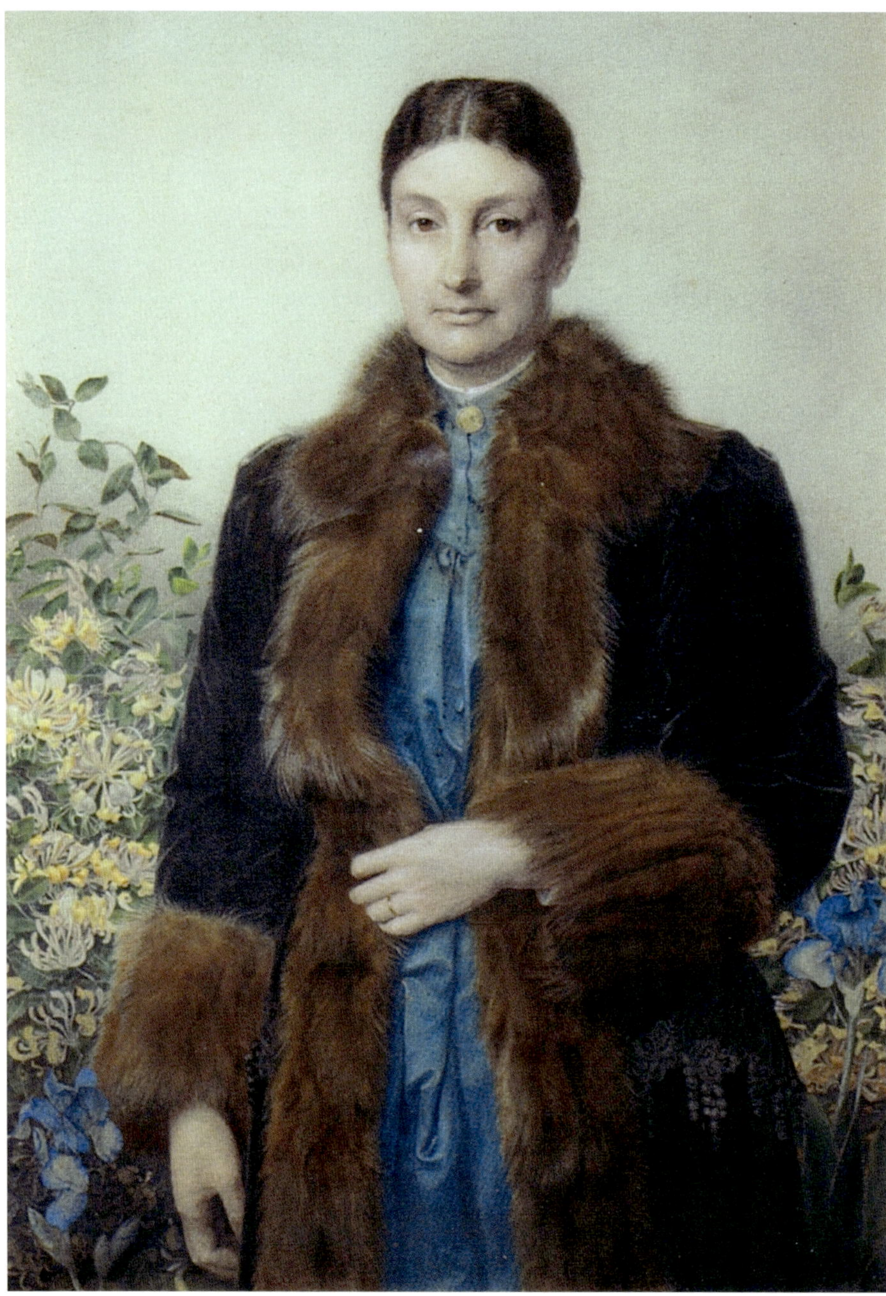

Mary Ann, Lady Quilter (1843-1927). Chalk drawing. Late 1880s. The wife of Sir William Cuthbert Quilter, a man of many parts: politician, stockbroker, farmer and art collector. He built Bawdsey Manor, Suffolk, in the county where the family originated. She was the mother of Harry Quilter, the art critic, and Roger Quilter, the composer. Although the medium of the portrait is coloured chalks, it comes near to the completeness and finish of an oil painting.

colours and the tonal values of light and shade. This 'old master technique' worked for the likes of Holbein,[223] whom Sandys so greatly admired, but this anachronistic technique led to Sandys's portraits having a wooden, ikon-like appearance, successful in his earlier portraits but in the instance of the *Julia Caldwell* portrait, a failure. Moreover, styles and fashions in painting had moved on considerably by the 1880s and 1890s.

These last sittings were concerned with small portions of the face and neck, and to adjusting the tones in the poor and frustratingly changeable conditions of light. On the 18th he exclaimed: 'This is a damp, dismal, dark, foggy, God forsaken country. I, after my work is completed, will never come to it again.' The portrait had taken five months to complete.

To return to 1888, Sandys was also at work on two portrait drawings of young men, one dated and titled, but the other undated and untitled, yet there is every indication of their being brothers and being worked on, or very near, at the same time.[224] One is of James Harvey Brand and the other, one would guess, is his brother Wilfred John who was ten years younger. They were the sons of James Brand (1832–1893), the wealthy City merchant with China and East India Company connections, who lived at Bedford Hill House, Streatham. These two young Brands appear to have been the last members of this family to have been portrayed by Sandys, judging from the nine portraits that I have traced.

About this time, Sandys produced a very fine undated portrait drawing of Mary Ann, née Bevington, (1842–1927) the wife of Cuthbert William Quilter (1841–1911) who was a highly successful stockbroker and art collector.[225] His art collection was well-known and was shared between his town house at 74 South Audley Street and his Suffolk country estate at Bawdsey Manor (which he built in 1886). He possessed Sandys's *Miranda* (*c.*1868) which he probably bought from Agnew's in the 1890s,[226] and sold when he was drastically 'down-sizing' in 1909. This was explained in a letter from Lockett Agnew to his American client Samuel Bancroft Jr, referring to a painting by Rossetti in the Quilter collection which Bancroft was anxious to acquire, but was wondering why it was being sold: 'I don't think Sir Cuthbert Quilter has been dabbling in anything which has involved him in much loss. His family marrying, and dispersing, he found his house in South Audley Street much too large for him and sold it. I have been storing his pictures in the "Pantechnicon" [227] for twelve months, and as his country house is full, he determined to sell: I really think that is the only reason.'[228] Quilter later bought Sandys's drawing *Nepenthe* (1892).[229]

Besides the portrait of Quilter's wife, Sandys around this time completed another family portrait, a double portrait of their two daughters Maude and Nora.[230]

It must have been after he had left The Cottage in the late 1880s, that his close friendship with W.G. Wills becomes more evident from the reminiscences of the artist Edwin Ward (1859–1933) who wrote: 'Later on in a room near Walham Green, Wills and Dunn were joined by another man of rare genius, Frederick Sandys, who though perhaps a little soured by disappointment, unlike his two old cronies, preserved to the last a scrupulous regard for his personal appearance.[231] Tall and distinguished, he was always dressed in well-cut clothes, resplendent in highly varnished footwear, his shapely hands and spotless linen beyond reproach. Two men of rare genius marooned and forgotten away in the wilds of Walham Green – both cultured gentlemen, accustomed to the best the world could offer, ending their days uncomplainingly amid drab and sordid surroundings, with poor old Dunn acting as factotum, shuffling out at intervals to forage for food and beer when funds permitted.' Although they no longer exist, there once were studios and workshops adjacent to Walham Green station (now renamed Fulham Broadway) on an irregular strip of land adjoining the railway line and station.

[1] His pictures were listed in the catalogue as: *Portrait of Mrs Cyril Flower* (257); *Portrait of Cyril Flower Esq.* (258); *Portrait of Mrs William Brand* (259); *Proud Maisie* (265); *Proserpine* (266); *Lethe* (287); *Study for an Oil Picture* (460).

[2] London, RA, 1880, 1233.

[3] London, RA, 1880, 1289, *Ethel and Mabel*. It is undated, but it was probably completed in 1879 or early 1880.

[4] Letter from F.S. to Mary dated Friday (11th June, 1880). Sandys Family Archive. Maude Grove was renamed Fernshaw Road in 1892.

[5] The Royal Aquarium was built between 1875–1876 on a three-acre site in Tothill Street, Westminster. It had a large glass-roofed hall for concerts, exhibitions, theatrical and other spectacular performances. It had a winter garden, fish tanks and a restaurant. It was demolished in 1902. The site is now occupied by Westminster Central Hall.

[6] Godwin diary for 1880. London, V&A, Archive of Art and Design.

[7] Archibald Stuart Wortley (1849–1905), a wealthy artist, had commissioned a double house with two studios in Tite Street from Godwin in 1878, for himself and his friend Carlo Pellegrini (1839–1889).

[8] Godwin diary for 1880. London, V&A, Archive of Art and Design.

[9] Recorded in the Roberson account books from 1880 to 1881. University of Cambridge, Hamilton Kerr Institute.

[10] Sandys Family Archive. It might have found a resting place in Wilmington, Delaware, USA, if Samuel Bancroft, the collector of Pre-Raphaelite art, had bought it from Winifred Sandys. She offered to sell it to him in a letter of 14th December 1910 (Delaware Art Museum, Bancroft Archive). There are noticeable excisions in it, probably by Winifred.

[11] Manchester, Rylands. op. cit., 1279/69-84.

[12] Recorded in the black and white image in Esther Wood's monograph of 1896, p. 49. The wolfskin also appears in the 1871 portrait of the Norwich dignitary J.H. Tillett.

[13] Godwin's 1880 diary records that he wrote to Sandys on 10th February but does not note the subject. London, V&A, Archive of Art and Design.

[14] Sandys's 1880 diary, Saturday 14th February. Sandys Family Archive.

[15] Frederick Weekes (1833–1920), artist, was the friend and partner of the architect William Burges. He was the son of the portrait sculptor Henry Weekes (1807–1877).

[16] Theodore Allingham, the lawyer, we have noted before. Salade or Salet = helm, or helmet.

[17] Godwin Papers. Two letters from Weekes to Godwin: nd October? (1880), and 4th October (1880). It would seem that the sword was still missing. London, V&A, Archive of Art and Design.

[18] Birmingham, CM&AG. 853'06, 854'06.

[19] Probably the artist George Hamilton Barrable (fl. 1873–1890).

[20] Deduced from the 1881 and 1891 census returns for 28 Maude Grove. The birth date is from a family birthday book in the Sandys Family Archive.

[21] Winifred aged 9; Mildred aged 7 1/2; Hugh aged just 5; Maud Mary nearly 4; Constance aged just 2; joined in April 1880 by Ruth.

[22] This represents the foster care of Frederick and Mary's two eldest children, Cissily aged about 11, and Dorothy aged about 10 in 1880.

[23] Manchester, Rylands. op. cit., 1279/69,72. Sandys to Howell, dated Monday (14th June 1880), and Sandys to Howell, dated Friday (25th June 1880). One assumes that Sandys was planning to work directly on the copper plate, out of doors.

[24] These were described in a letter of 21st June as '*Study for Faustine* – the other at the moment I cannot remember the name … one is more complete than the other. He suggested £100 for the two. Manchester, Rylands. op. cit., 1279/70.

[25] Manchester, Rylands. op. cit., 1279/69. For George Webb, see n. 532.

[26] Letter from F.S. to Howell, 24th June 1880. Manchester, Rylands, op. cit., 1279/71.

[27] Letter from F.S. to Howell, 28th June 1880. Manchester, Rylands op. cit., 1279/73.

[28] F.S. to Howell, 21 June 1880. Manchester, Rylands, op. cit., 1279/70.

[29] Sandys's 1880 Diary. Sandys Family Archive. The brothers George and William Webb, solicitors, of Clerkenwell were sympathetic to artists. One of the Webbs was a creditor of Sandys, and was known also to E.W. Godwin, for the latter noted in his diary on 21st March, 1882 (London, V&A, Archive of Art and Design. Godwin 1882 diary), that Sandys had paid a debt to Webb. This was the last mention of Sandys in Godwin's diaries. Significantly, in his previous note referring to Sandys, on 28th January 1882, Godwin wrote that he had sent a registered letter to Sandys. See also below on 15th October 1880. Godwin was later to recommend the Webbs to Oscar Wilde (H. Montgomery Hyde, "Oscar Wilde and his architect" in *Architectural Review*, 109, March 1951, p. 176). The Webbs also acted for Whistler. Sandys's 1880 Diary. Sandys Family Archive.

[30] Godwin must have had them on loan. These are the untitled *Alcestis and Penelope*. He suggested £250 for them. Sandys to Howell dated 'Saturday' (10th July 1880). Manchester, Rylands. op. cit., 1279/75.

[31] These must be the studies made at Fairlight in May 1870, which must have been bought at this time by his friend William Weldon (III, *The Artist Special Winter Number*, 1896, unpag.).

[32] Letter from F.S. to Howell, 21st June 1880. Manchester, Rylands op. cit., 1279/1279/70. *Faustine* appears to have been bought by John Dye of Norwich. *Antigone* was bought by Theodore Rossi of Norwich and sold on to Edward Trafford of Wroxham Hall, Norfolk.

[33] Letter from F.S. to Howell dated Friday (25th June 1880). Manchester, Rylands. op. cit., 1279/72. Benjamin remains unknown.

[34] Letter from F.S. to Howell, 2nd July (1880). Manchester, Rylands, op. cit., Eng.Ms. 1279/74.

[35] Note in Howell's writing 'Cash advanced to Sandys', dated 8th July 1880. Manchester, Rylands, op. cit., 1279/167.

[36] Letter from F.S. to Howell. Manchester, Rylands, op. cit., 1279/175.

[37] Sandys's last effort of painting in oils had been about five years since – possibly he was thinking of the portrait of *Mrs Temple Soanes* of 1875–79.

[38] Letter from F.S. to Howell, dated 'Sunday Augt 8. 1880'. Sandys was addressing his letters to 'Fulham House', probably meaning Chaldon House, Fulham. Howell at this time was about to leave or had left Chaldon House, ahead of its demolition. Manchester, Rylands, op. cit., 1279/77.

[39] Sandys's only known portrait of Howell is a drawing dated 1882 (Ashmolean Museum). Perhaps it was already started some two or three years earlier?

[40] F.S. to Howell, dated 'Saturday' (10th July). Manchester, Rylands, op. cit., 1279/175.

[41] Sandys's 1880 Diary. Sandys Family Archive.

[42] Letter from F.S. to Howell, 'Thursday Evg' (30th July 1880). Manchester, Rylands. op. cit., 1279/76.

[43] Sandys's 1880 Diary. Sandys Family Archive.

[44] Sandys's 1880 Diary. Sandys Family Archive.

[45] Sandys's 1880 Diary, Wednesday 11th August. Sandys Family Archive,

[46] Letter from F.S. to Howell, dated 'Sunday Augst 8 1880'. Manchester, Rylands. op. cit., 1279/77. A locket, stockings, and a necktie arrived from Howell on about the 26th, acknowledged by Sandys in a letter of August 27th. Manchester, Rylands, op. cit., 1279/79.

[47] Constance Battersea, *Reminiscences*, (1922).

[48] Letter from F.S. to Howell. Manchester, Rylands, op. cit., 1279/77 and 78.

[49] Mrs Frost, the housekeeper at the Spenser Street studio. Sandys's Diary for 1880. Sandys Family Archive.

[50] Sandys's diary entry on Saturday 14th August 1880. Sandys Family Archive.

[51] George Meredith had commented on this when they went on walks together in the 1860s.

[52] Letter from F.S. to Howell, dated 8th August 1880. Manchester, Rylands. op. cit., 1279/77,78.

[53] Sandys's diary entry on Thursday 26th August 1880. Sandys Family Archive. The oil sketch has not been identified.

[54] Sandys's diary entries from Saturday August 28th to Tuesday 31st August 1880. Sandys Family Archive.

[55] Letter from F.S. to Howell, Sunday 29th August (1880). Manchester, Rylands, op. cit., 1279/80.

[56] Letter from F.S. to Howell. Manchester, Rylands, op. cit., 1279/82. Rosalind Blanche Catherine Howell (b.1877). Her portrait was

tackled in June 1882.

[57] Letter from F.S. to Howell. Manchester, Rylands, op. cit., 1279/84.

[58] Sandys's diary entries from Wednesday 1st September to Saturday 11th September 1880. Sandys Family Archive.

[59] John Jones, born *c.*1839 in Hull. He was the eldest son and second eldest child of Justice and Rosanna Jones. He stayed on in Hull and became a baker.

[60] Sandys's diary entry for Monday 13th September 1880. Sandys Family Archive.

[61] Letter from F.S. to Howell dated 29th September 1880. Manchester, Rylands. op. cit., 1279/83.

[62] Possibly Arthur Jermy Jephson (1859–1908), an adventurer with a Norfolk family connection.

[63] Alfred Gardiner Hastings, solicitor, of Nelson, Son & Hastings, proctors and solicitors, at 18 Bennet's Hill, Doctors' Commons. Law List 1880, and City of London Directory 1880.

[64] Sandys's diary entries from Monday 4th October to Thursday 7th October 1880. Sandys Family Archive.

[65] Sandys's diary entry for Friday 8th October 1880. Sandys Family Archive.

[66] William Quiller Orchardson (1832–1910). Scottish artist, who moved to London in 1863. Known for his conversation pieces and portraits.

[67] Perhaps one of these people was the local Liberal Party agent? Cyril Flower retained his constituency until 1885, when the passing of the Redistribution Bill abolished it.

[68] Sandys's diary entry for Monday 11th October 1880. Sandys Family Archive.

[69] George Webb, op. cit., n. 441. He was known also to E.W. Godwin, as his name appears in Godwin's diaries of 1877 and 1882, when Godwin reported that Sandys had paid the debt to him on 21st March. It was to Webb that Sandys shipped his drawing and painting (untraced) of the *Head of Medusa*, probably as security for a debt.

[70] Sandys's diary entry for Tuesday 19th October 1880. Sandys Family Archive.

[71] I cannot identify Woodruffe. Mrs Parfitt perhaps was the housekeeper at Ffrwdgrech.

[72] Sandys's diary entry for Wednesday 20th October 1880. Sandys Family Archive.

[73] From accounts noted at the back of Sandys's 1880 diary. Sandys Family Archive.

[74] This perhaps refers to designs in 1878 for an overmantel and a colour scheme for Sandys at Spenser Street. Susan Weber Soros, (ed.) *E.W. Godwin. Aesthetic Movement Architect and Designer.* (1999), p. 370.

[75] Letter from F.S. to Rossetti, (6th November 1880). Vancouver, University of British Columbia. Library, Special Collections.

[76] The falling-out between Rossetti and Sandys was in 1869. However, they were on cordial terms again in

July 1873 during the illness of 'the little girl'. Rossetti invited Sandys to Kelmscott Manor in June 1874, but the visit did not come about. They probably met again in 1874, but by 1880, Rossetti had virtually withdrawn from social life, seeing few friends, and had already started on the mental and physical decline which ended in his death in April 1882.

[77] Surely this is untrue! What does Sandys mean by this?

[78] Letter from Rossetti to F.S., Sunday (7th November 1880). W.E. Fredeman (ed.), The Correspondence of D.G. Rossetti, the Last Decade, vol.ix (1880–82). Cambridge, 2010. p. 303. Letter no. 80.344.

[79] Esther Wood, *A Consideration of the Art of Frederick Sandys, Special Winter Number of The Artist.* (Constable, London, 1896) p. 50. Unfortunately the illustration is black and white.

[80] After Cyril Flower, the cartoon drawing seems to have gone into the collection of William Gillilan and was sold at his death at Christie's in 1925.

[81] Birmingham CM&AG, 853, 854'06.

[82] This photograph was at the Maas Gallery in the early 1970s. The dedication was clearly not by Sandys. The original drawing was reproduced, in sanguine, as a supplement to *The Artist*, January 1897, opp. p. 1.

[83] George Webb. op. cit., n. 570.

[84] Freeman Wills, *W.G. Wills, Dramatist and Painter* (1898), p. 89.

[85] Gale Pedrick. *Life with Rossetti* (1964), p. 28. Their Heatherley days must have been in the early 1860s.

[86] Freeman Wills, ibid., p. 90.

[87] See p. 171.

[88] Letter from George Meredith to F. S.:, dated 3rd March 1881. C.L. Cline (ed), *The Collected Letters of George Meredith*, (1970). Letter 267.

[89] *Autobiography and Letters of Mrs M.O. Oliphant.* (ed.) Mrs Harry Coghill (1899), p. 297.

[90] Ibid. Mrs Harry Coghill. p. 298.

[91] Ibid. Mrs Harry Coghill, p. 298.

[92] A.M.W. Stirling, *A Painter of Dreams* (1916), p. 337. Her sister was Evelyn De Morgan. The portrait of Mrs Oliphant is now in the collection of the National Portrait Gallery.

[93] Mrs Craik (Dinah Maria Mulock, 1826–1887) a successful author, is best known for her novel *John Halifax, Gentleman* (1856). Hubert von Herkomer painted a fine portrait of her in the year of her death.

[94] Letter from F.S. to Flower, dated 'Wednesday night, August 24 1881'. Former collection of Prof. Allen Staley, New York, now at Getty Research Institute, Los Angeles.

[95] W.M. Rossetti, 'Portraits of Robert Browning', in *The Magazine of Art*, vol. 13, 1890. pp. 249–250.

[96] Elisabeth Wallace, *Goldwin Smith: Victorian Liberal* (1957), p. 89. Sandys's portrait is illustrated on p. 117.

[97] Letter from F.S. to Howell, dated by Howell to 30th November 1881. Manchester, Rylands. op. cit., 1279/85.

[98] Letter from F.S. to Howell, dated by Howell to 8th December 1881. Manchester, Rylands, op. cit., 1279/86.

[99] Letter from F.S. to Howell, dated by Howell to 1st February (1874). Manchester, Rylands, op. cit., 1279/57.

[100] E.R. and J. Pennell, *The Whistler Journal*, (1921), p. 25.

[101] Mrs Lawrence was the American, Catherine Sumner, who had become the wife of Charles Napier Lawrence (1855–1927) in 1881. Sandys was to portray them both in 1898. Later on, she was especially helpful to Sandys's daughter Gertrude at her marriage to Lionel Crane in 1913.

[102] Letter from F.S. to Howell, dated 12th May 1882 by Howell. Manchester, Rylands, 1279/87.

[103] The Chinnerys moved in 1896 to Oxfordshire, first to Bucknall Manor, then Fringford Manor. Henry Chinnery, a wealthy stockbroker, was a keen sportsman, and hunted in Buckinghamshire with Lord Rothschild. They had two children, Ellis Haldane Chinnery (1874–1957), and Dorothy Marion Chinnery (1878–1961).

[104] Letter dated 12th May 1882 by Howell. Manchester, Rylands, 1279/87.

[105] Thomas Charles Pleydell Calley (1856–1932) of Burderop Park, Swindon, was a distinguished professional soldier, ending his military career as Commander of the 1st Life Guards (1902–1906). After leaving the army he became Unionist MP for Wiltshire in 1910. Their only child, Miss J.M. Calley, died at Burderop Park in 1974.

[106] Letter from F.S. to Mrs Lewis dated 'Tuesday' (1882), from 38 Harley Street. Author's collection.

[107] Brett's *Stone Breaker* (1856), at the Walker Art Gallery, Liverpool, is greatly in contrast to Henry Wallis's contemporary picture with the same title. Brett's figure being of a healthy young boy; Wallis depicted a tragic figure of a worn-out man apparently either dead or dying, in the road, as his task.

[108] Letter from F.S. to Howell. Manchester, Rylands, 1279/88.

[109] Jumbo, an African elephant, was a great attraction at the London Zoo, arriving there in 1865. He was bought in 1882 by P.T. Barnum and shipped to North America, where he died in 1885 after a railway accident.

[110] Letter from F.S. to Howell dated 15th June 1882. Manchester, Rylands op. cit., 1279/90.

[111] The person 'a' is undoubtedly Frederic Arthur of Motcomb Street, the provider of furniture for the studio at Spenser Street. He was listed in the bankruptcy papers of 1876. The Shorthouse portrait is dated August 1882. See letter of 19th June 1882.

[112] C.L. Cline, *The Owl and the Rossettis*, (1978), p. 16.

[113] Letter from F.S. to Howell, Monday 19th June (1882). Manchester, Rylands, op. cit., 1279/91.

[114] Listed in Howell's manuscript account, dated 25th August 1882,

sent to Sandys. Manchester, Rylands, op. cit., 1279/172.

[115] J. Henry Shorthouse, Lansdowne, Edgbaston, to Sandys, 23rd July 1882. Manchester, Rylands, op. cit., 1279/162.

[116] Letter from F.S. to Howell, 24th July 1882. Manchester, Rylands, op. cit., 1279/92.

[117] J. Henry Shorthouse, Lansdowne, Edgbaston, to Sandys, 23rd July 1882. Manchester, Rylands, op. cit., 1279/162.

[118] Letter from F.S. to Howell, Tuesday 15th August (1882). Manchester, Rylands, op. cit., 1279/93.

[119] Letter from F.S. to Howell, dated Sunday (20th August 1882). Manchester, Rylands, op. cit., 1279/94.

[120] Letter from F.S. to Howell, 'Thursday morg', dated by Howell to 24th August 1882. Manchester, Rylands, op. cit., 1279/96.

[121] Author's collection. Dated 23rd August (1882), which was a Wednesday.

[122] Letter from F.S. to Howell dated Thursday night (received by Howell and dated 25th August 1882). Manchester, Rylands, op. cit., 1279/97.

[123] This famous sale of paintings and *objets d'art* from Hamilton Palace took place in June and July 1882 and took 17 days.

[124] This was evidently sent to his friend Weldon in sympathy at the time of Weldon's marital tribulations. Weldon's letter of thanks, dated 27th September 1882, was sent from Pangbourne where he moored his houseboat on the Thames. Sandys Family Archive.

[125] The portraits of this family were: *Philip Arthur and Mary Isabel* (June 1877), *Arthur Flower* (July 1877), *Isabel Flower* (July 1877), *Ethel Daisy and Hugh Duncombe* (March 1881), *Conrad Herbert and Violet* (December 1885).

[126] This was, undoubtedly, George Grove (1820–1900), the founding editor of *Grove's Dictionary of Music and Musicians.*

[127] *The Life and Letters of J.H. Shorthouse,* (ed.) Sarah Shorthouse, (1905), pp. 168–9.

[128] *The Life and Letters of J.H. Shorthouse,* ibid., p. 177

[129] E.R. and J. Pennell. *The Whistler Journal,* (1921), p. 61, and author's correspondence with J.R. Somerset-Paddon in 1978.

[130] Sold in 1932 in the USA by Major Cecil Paddon (1875–1962), Rebecca's eldest son and Samuel's stepson. *The Catalog of American Portraits* identifies it to be at the Ackland Art Museum, Chapel Hill, North Carolina, where it has no attribution.

[131] C.L. Cline, (ed.), *The Owl and the Rossettis*, 1978, pp. 24–25.

[132] Letter from F.S. at Maude Grove to Howell at the Paddon house, Redlands. 12th September (1882). Manchester, Rylands, op. cit., 1279/99.

[133] Letter from F.S. at Maude Grove to Howell at the Paddon house,

Redlands. 14th September (1882). Manchester, Rylands, op. cit., 1279/100.

[134] Robert Peck (1845–1899), a well-known trainer of racehorses.

[135] *Rosa*: Rosa Corder (see p. 154), Letter from Sandys to Howell (18th October 1882). Manchester, Rylands, op. cit., 1279/103.

[136] Hugh's birthday was 2nd June, as recorded by Mrs Walter Crane in a family Birthday Book. This and so many of the other family records seem to be unreliable in such personal details.

[137] C.L. Cline. *Collected Letters of George Meredith* (1970). No. 768.

[138] No preliminary drawing has come to light, but at the Grosvenor Gallery Summer Exhibition of 1879, a *Portrait of Sir Thomas G.F. Hesketh*, Bart. (no. 153) was shown, which probably was this preliminary drawing.

[139] The family, having ceased living there, gave Rufford Old Hall to the National Trust in 1942. This portrait was hung originally at Easton Neston until the latter was sold by the family in 2005 and the contents sold at auction. It was purchased by the National Trust by private treaty with funds from the V&A Purchase Grant Fund. It now hangs at Rufford Old Hall.

[140] Letter from F.S. to Howell, dated 'Wednesday' (24th January 1883). Manchester, Rylands, op. cit., 1279/104.

[141] Letter from Sandys to Howell, dated 'Tuesday evg' (30th January 1883). Henry Chinnery and his wife Marion lived at Weir Bank, Teddington. Sandys may have been there to finish her portrait. Manchester, Rylands, op. cit., 1279/105. The Portuguese epitaph remains a mystery, but probably refers to Howell.

[142] Letter from F.S. to Howell, dated 'Wednesday' (14th March 1883). Manchester, Rylands, op. cit., 1279/107. His father died on 9th February, so Sandys would have missed the funeral.

[143] I am indebted to Stephen Wildman for this information from the archives of the RBSA.

[144] Manchester, Rylands, op. cit., 1279/175.

[145] H. Chaplin was probably a money lender.

[146] Letter from F.S. to Howell, dated 'Sunday' (8th July 1883). Manchester, Rylands, op. cit., 1279/108.

[147] Letter from F.S. to Howell, Sunday (15th July 1883). Manchester, Rylands, op. cit., 1279/109.

[148] This could refer to a descendant of George Anthony Molteno or his son James Anthony who were of the family of printsellers in Pall Mall in the 1780s until about 1837 when the latter was bankrupted. Several of their descendants emigrated. Pall Mall was then a centre of bookshops, engravers, printers and printsellers. Refs: *London Gazette* and Molteno family website.

[149] Letter from F.S. to Howell at 91 Southampton Row, Russell Square (where Howell had moved in 1878). Manchester, Rylands, op. cit., 1279/101.

[150] Charles Graves, *Life and Letters of Alexander Macmillan* (1910), p. 372.

[151] Letter from F.S. to Howell (Thursday 20th September 1883). Manchester, Rylands, op. cit., 1279/110.

[152] Letter from F.S. to Howell (written Friday 21st September 1883, received by Howell on Monday 24th September, Manchester, Rylands, op. cit., 1279/111.

[153] Receipt for £22.10.0. Dated Norwich 23rd September 1883. 'Received from Mr Jackson by Frederick Sandys'. Norwich, Castle Museum, Art Dept. Archives.

[154] Letter preserved with the Album No. 865. Cambridge, Fitzwilliam Museum, Prints and Drawings Dept.

[155] Messrs. Spelman, at the Bazaar Rooms, Norwich. *Catalogue of the Collection of Pictures and Drawings of the late Mr. Anthony Sandys.* 16th October 1883.

[156] Robert Jackson (*c.*1824–*c.*1905). Owing to the early death of John Thomas in 1862, it is likely that Jackson's work lies undetected within the Thomas oeuvre. Frederick Jackson of Bethel Street, Norwich was perhaps related to the sculptor.

[157] Sandys to the 'little girl', dated 28th September 1883. Sandys Family Archive.

[158] Letter from F.S. to Howell, 30th September (1883). Manchester, Rylands, op. cit., 1279/112.

[159] Letter from F.S. to Howell. Manchester, Rylands, op. cit., 1279/114.

[160] Receipt signed by Frederick Sandys, dated 20th February 1884. Manchester, Rylands, op. cit., 1279/176.

[161] Letter written in pencil on black-bordered paper with an 1882 watermark. Dated Wednesday. The portrait is dated 1884. Sandys Family Archive.

[162] Samuel John Gurney Hoare was created 1st Viscount Templewood in 1944.

[163] Unidentified.

[164] Assisted by the young architect Edwin Lutyens.

[165] Letter from F.S. to Howell, Tuesday (26th August 1884). Manchester, Rylands, op. cit., 1279/118.

[166] Theodore Rossi (1831–1914), the Norwich art and antiques dealer, long known to Sandys. Rossi lent him money on several occasions.

[167] Anthony Buxton (1881–1970), the son of Edward North Buxton (1840–1924) of Knighton House, Essex. His widowed grandmother, Catherine Gurney Buxton (1814–1911) lived at Colne House near Cromer.

[168] Letter from F.S. to Howell, 20th October (1884). Manchester, Rylands, op. cit., 1279/121.

[169] Letter headed, 'Box Hill. November 8th, 1884' from Meredith to Sandys. Published in Cline, (1979), letter no. 873. Delaware Art Museum, Bancroft Archive.

[170] Letter headed 'Box Hill. December 31, 1884' from Meredith to Sandys. This is the first clue that Sandys had moved to a new address. Published in Cline, No. 875. University of Texas at Austin, HRC.

[171] Giles Walkley, *Artists' Houses in London*, 1764–1914, 1994, p. 269.

[172] Brompton Cemetery records. The interment was authorised by Mrs Mary Neville Sandys on behalf of her husband Frederick Neville Sandys, by letter dated 27th October 1884.

[173] Maple & Co., the well-known furniture business of Tottenham Court Road (1841–*c.*1997) must have had extensive workshops which could recondition as well as manufacture pieces.

[174] Letter from F.S. to Howell, dated 'Wednesday' (10th December 1884). Manchester, Rylands, op. cit., 1279/122. 'Rossetti things' must refer to the sale of Rossetti's household goods, in which Sandys was interested, and asked Howell to bid for some items (T.G. Wharton, Martin & Co. *Contents of Residence of Dante Gabriel Rossetti.* ... 5th 7th July 1882).

[175] Letter from F.S. to Howell, dated 'Tuesday Evg' (30th December 1884). Manchester, Rylands, op. cit., 1279/123.

[176] Dated 1885 in Wood (opp. p. 24).

[177] Letter from F.S. to Howell, from The Cottage, dated 24th March (1885), and dated 30th March (1885). Manchester, Rylands, op. cit., 1279/130.

[178] Letter from F.S. to Howell, from The Cottage, dated Thursday (9th April 1885). Manchester, Rylands, op. cit., 1279/131.

[179] The Autotype Company, based on an invention of Joseph Swan, was active from 1868 to the 1920s. Its address from 1883 to 1892 was at 74 New Oxford Street. Frederick Hollyer, of Pembroke Square, Kensington, also began photographing works of art as reproductions in the 1870s.

[180] Letter from F.S. at The Cottage, to Howell, dated 'Wednesday evg.' (8th April 1885). Manchester, Rylands, op. cit., 1279/132.

[181] Letter from F.S. at The Cottage, to Howell, dated Monday (28th April 1885). Manchester, Rylands, op. cit., 1279/134.

[182] Letter from Meredith at Box Hill, 8th September 1885, to Sandys (sold to Samuel Bancroft Jr by Winifred Sandys). Wilmington, Delaware Art Museum, Bancroft Archive. Cline, Letters of George Meredith, vol.2. Letter no. 921

[183] Letter from F.S. to Howell, dated Tuesday 6th October (1885). Manchester, Rylands, op. cit., 1279/135.

[184] Letter dated 30th October 1885 from James Knowles to W.E. Gladstone. This reference kindly brought to my notice by Dr Priscilla Metcalf. BM Add.Ms. 44232, folio 28.

[185] No. 1083 in the RA catalogue.

[186] J.M.Gray, 'Frederick Sandys and the woodcut designers of thirty years ago' in *Century Guild Hobby Horse*, 3, October 1888, p. 154.

[187] Sotheby's, 10th November 1981, lot 77, bought by Thomas Agnew for £2,400. Presently untraced.

[188] Letter from F.S. to Hastings, dated 4th March (1886?). Manchester, Rylands, op. cit., no. 1279/145.

[189] Dion Clayton Calthrop, *My own Trumpet, being the Story of my Life* (1935), pp. 27–29.

[190] Sandys portrayed him in 1880.

[191] Oxford DNB (2004), by Eleanor Brock.

[192] Gertrude's birth certificate shows that she was born at 28 Maude Grove on 6th December 1886, registered as Gertrude Sandys, but her mother was registered as Mary Neville. No father's name appears.

[193] Lionel Francis Crane (1876–1942) became an architect. I am indebted to their son Anthony Crane (1916–2008), for unstinting help, and for a valued friendship.

[194] Largely the result of art schools being set up in industrial towns and cities from the 1840s onward (a government [i.e., Board of Trade] initiative to improve the quality of design in manufactured articles). It was an important stimulus to the visual arts in general.

[195] Letter from F.S. to Craik from The Cottage, Holland Park Road, Kensington, W. Dated 'Tuesday'. Author's collection.

[196] This portrait is illustrated in *The Artist*, Special Winter Number (1896), p. 55.

[197] Birmingham, Art Dept. records. This gives Nellie's birth date as *c.* 1870. Robin Furber, a descendant of Charles, wrote to the author in 1999, that Charles Furber fathered 22 children.

[198] See p. 227.

[199] Watts added his mother's maiden name in 1896 to clarify his identity.

[200] They were both members of the Omar Khayyam Club which might also account for their friendship.

[201] Brett's Pocket Diary, 1888. 11th March. Kindly communicated by Charles Brett, 8th June 2010.

[202] Brett's Studio Log, 7th April 1888. Ibid.

[203] Sandys's 1889 Diary. Sandys Family Archive.

[204] Sandys's 17th July entry notes that when Caldwell came home from London he '…told me of a fresh Whitechapel murder which occurred last night. …' (Alice McKenzie, a prostitute, was found with her throat cut in Castle Alley, Whitechapel on 17th July 1889).

[205] Julia Caldwell married Loftus Joseph William Arkwright in June 1894.

[206] Frances Evelyn Greville, popularly known as 'Daisy', married in 1881 Lord Brooke, later the 5th Earl of Warwick (1893).

[207] This preliminary drawing remains in the possession of Julia's great grandson.

[208] Sandys's 1889 Diary. Sandys Family Archive.

[209] Letter of 2nd August (Friday), 1889, from Meredith to Sandys. Yale University, Beinecke Rare Book and Manuscript Library.

[210] The eight acknowledged, surviving, children would have been Winifred, Mildred, Hugh, Maude, Constance, Ruth, Guy, and Gertrude.

[211] This church at Greenstead in Essex still exists.

[212] Guy Edwin was born in May 1882.

[213] A contemporary photograph shows W.G. Wills clearly to be wearing an ill-fitting wig.

[214] This must refer to the Gillilan portrait commission of 1885.

[215] Sandys's 1889 Diary. Sandys Family Archive.

[216] It was, as he noted, the view out of his bedroom window at Forest Hall.

[217] Sandys's 1889 Diary. Sandys Family Archive.

[218] Had he remembered, subconsciously perhaps, Millais's *Return of the Dove to the Ark* which stood out at the RA Exhibition of 1851? It is thought that Millais omitted any background details in this picture to have it ready for the sending-in day of the exhibition.

[219] This must refer to his debts.

[220] Sandys's 1889 Diary. Sandys Family Archive.

[221] Joseph Pennell, *Pen Drawing and Pen Draughtsmen, Their work and their methods. A study of the art today with technical suggestions.* (1889).

[222] Sandys's 1889 Diary. Sandys Family Archive.

[223] Hans Holbein, the Younger (1497–1543).

[224] They came on the market at the same time: Sotheby's Belgravia, 9th April 1980, lots 58 and 59.

[225] He was the son of William Quilter. He became Liberal MP for Sudbury from 1885–1906, and was created 1st Bt. in 1897. Harry Quilter the critic was his brother, and his son was the composer Roger Quilter.

[226] See Elzea, *Frederick Sandys, a Catalogue Raisonné.* 2001, no. 2.A.107. Footnote 7.

[227] Pantechnicon: An early 19th century London warehouse for furniture sales and storage. Their novel removal vans, emblazoned with the name, led to its adoption as a new word in the language.

[228] Letter from Lockett Agnew to Samuel Bancroft Jr, dated 19th July 1909. Delaware Art Museum Library, Bancroft Archive. The Pantechnicon, Motcomb Street, Belgravia, is a large Greek Revival building of 1830. In spite of a disastrous fire in 1874, it became a storage facility. The name became attached also to the removal vans associated with it.

[229] See *Catalogue Raisonné*, no. 5.5. This probably remained at Bawdsey Manor, since it was not sold by Christie's until 1936, when the Manor was sold to the Air Ministry.

[230] *Catalogue Raisonné*, no. 5.43a.

[231] Edwin A. Ward, *Recollections of a Savage* (1925), pp. 106–107. W.G. Wills died on December 13th 1891, and Treffry Dunn in 1899. They had known each other since their student days at Heatherley's art school.

opposite: *Miss Doris Catto.* detail. see page 268

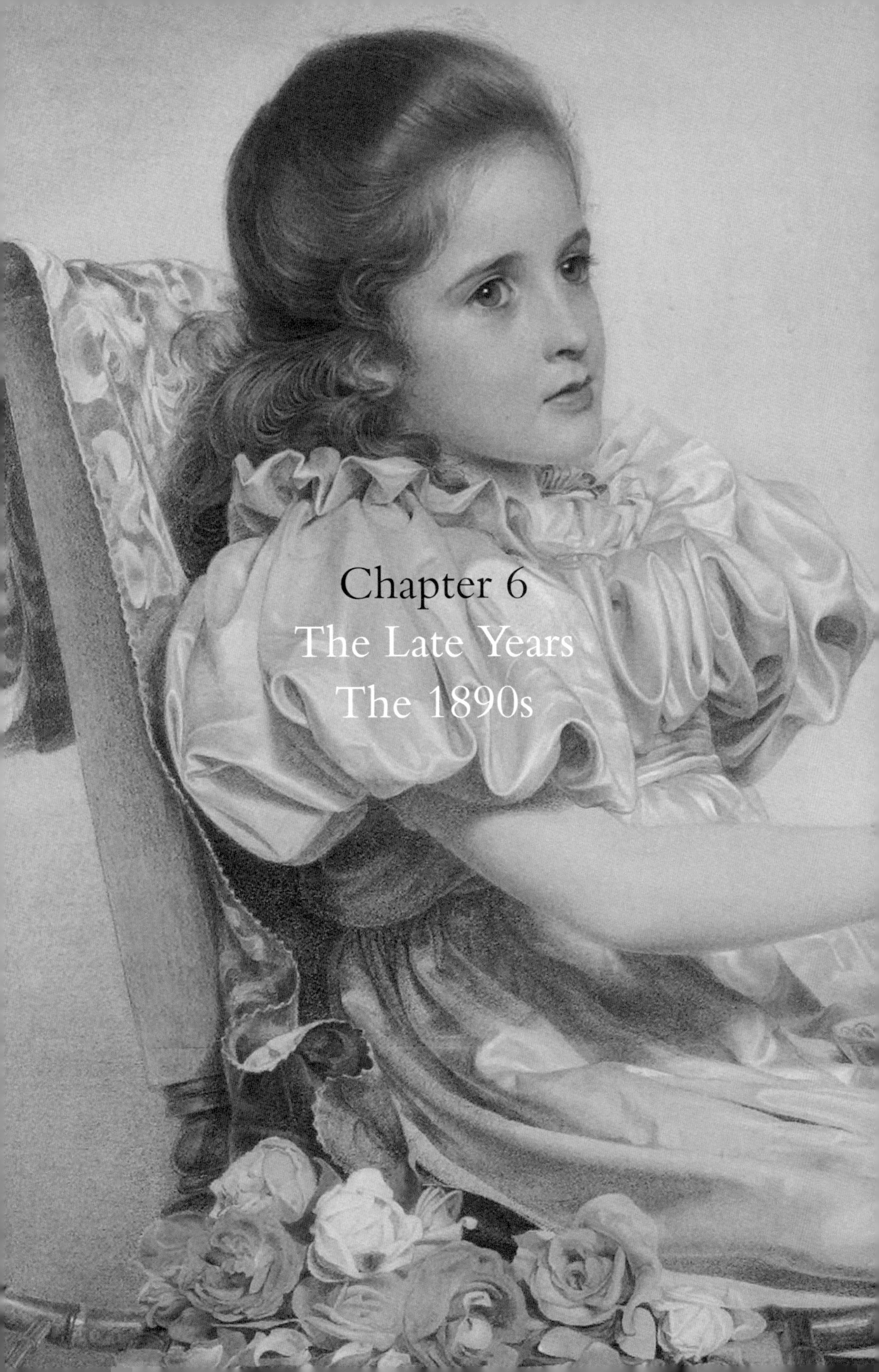

Chapter 6
The Late Years
The 1890s

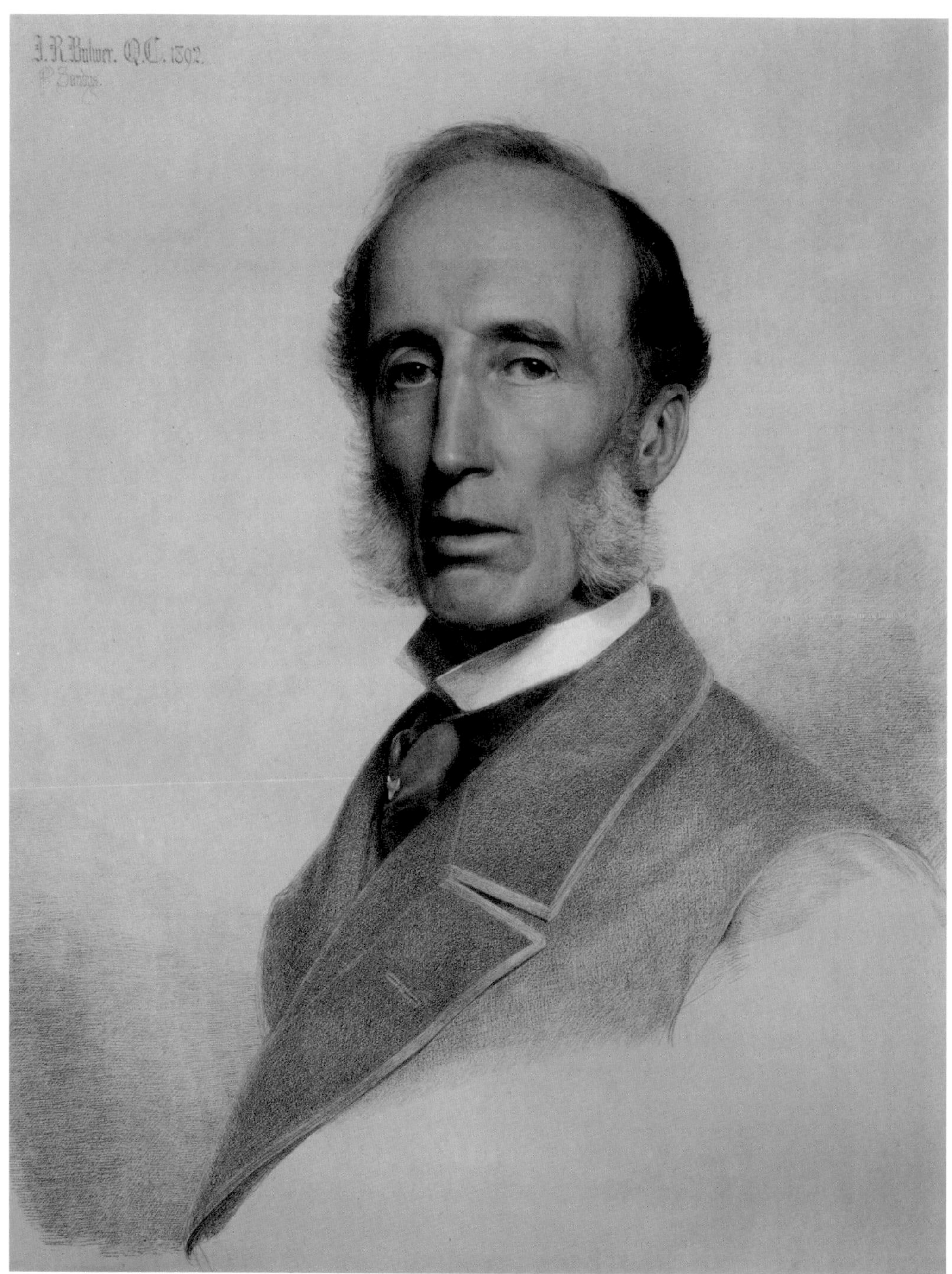

James Redfoord Bulwer (1820–1899). Chalk drawing. 1892. The eldest son of the Rev. James Bulwer, Sandys's early patron. J.R. Bulwer became a lawyer and a Conservative Member of Parliament and remained friendly with Sandys until his death in 1899. This drawing was preliminary to a three-quarter length oil portrait.

Eighteen ninety was a lean year for Sandys. Only one commissioned portrait dated 1890 appears in the records.[1] This is of George Meredith's daughter, Marie Eveleen (1871–1951), often referred to by her father as Mariette or Riette. It was probably commissioned by Jean Palmer, who was a favourite friend of Meredith's, or by Meredith for Jean Palmer.[2]

Also in 1890, Sandys drew a head of his daughter Mildred in his usual style of head and shoulders facing to the left with flowers in the background.[3] Dated but untitled, it surfaced in 1931 at Rodman's gallery in Belfast, and its earlier history is not known.[4] Funds must have been very low, as Sandys was driven to ask his erstwhile friend Swinburne for a loan, but it was firmly refused.[5] His friend and agent Howell, after a long illness, died in April 1890, which would have been a major blow to Sandys.[6]

1891 does not seem to have offered much relief, as only one portrait commission can be traced. It was to portray the two children from the second marriage of Alexander Macmillan: Mary (*c.*1873–1960) and John Victor Macmillan (1877–1956). They were aged about eighteen and fifteen at the time. John Victor later became Bishop of Guildford.

The census of 1891 reveals that at 28 Maude Grove there were two households. Listed first was that of Martha Stevens (the 'lodging housekeeper') which included her grandson and her lodger, who was a dressmaker. The second, in the larger of the two households, was that of Frederick and Mary Neville and their eight children ranging from Winifred, the eldest, aged twenty, to Gertrude, the youngest, aged four. It seems to have been the only time in which the whole family was living at one address, except at the very end of Sandys's life, when he joined Mary and the family who had moved to Hogarth Road, Earl's Court.

An insight into Sandys's friendships at this time is the announcement of a funeral on 17th November 1891 at which Sandys was listed as one of the mourners.[7] It was the funeral of Lewis Strange Wingfield (1842–1891) the youngest son of the 6th Viscount Powerscourt, an Irish peer. Lewis Wingfield was an extraordinary and restless man who had achieved much in his short life: actor, writer, painter, traveller, theatre costume designer, and pioneer of 'dress reform' for women. Other mourners, besides the Wingfield family, were Sandys's friends Joseph Knight, William Weldon, and Joseph Ashby-Sterry.

In April 1892 his old friend George Meredith, mildly rebuking him for not appearing for lunch on Sunday the 3rd, through missing the train to Dorking, wrote that he was to be expected on the 10th: 'If you set your mind to catch the train instead of missing it, and resolutely determine that you arrive before dinner is a dish of bones and the bottle a corkless vacancy.' Furthermore, he wrote that Riette, his daughter, had reported that 'you are bearing the look of your age handsomely'.

Meredith regretted that now he scarcely visited the Garrick Club but four times a year and that the Club seemed to have lost its 'levity'. Furthermore, 'Ashby Sterry looks ready to burst out if there were inducement. But Lowry Whittle parades, and all become Lowries in the shadow of him'.[8]

Sandys produced another 'fancy picture' in 1892, which he titled *Nepenthe*, inscribing the title in Greek letters on a scroll. This time, to create this drawing, he copied the head from his full-length picture *Lethe* of the early 1870s, for which his sister Emma had been the model, adding poppy flowers and indications of a distant landscape taken from a study he had made in 1870. This was bought by Sir Cuthbert Quilter and then, after Quilter's death, by Sir Jeremiah Colman, the orchid-growing relative of the Norwich Colmans. *Lethe* was owned by Lord Battersea, who normally hung it at his Overstrand summer home, The Pleasaunce, but it was lent to the 1892 'Fine Art Loan Exhibition' and shown at Easter at St Jude's schoolhouse in Whitechapel.[9]

Another picture, probably from this date, titled *Jealousy*, shows the head of his eldest daughter Winifred who was about twenty at the time. The subject comes from an anonymous poem inscribed in a scroll at lower right: 'Jealous girls these sometimes were/While they lived or lasted here/Turned to flowers, still they be/Yellow marked for jealousy.' The background is filled with a flat decorative scene with a crescent moon, a winged archer, two hearts impaled with an arrow within a glowing nimbus, and a distant ghostly castle. The foreground is filled with daffodils and the scroll with the text. What prompted this elaborate subject is a mystery. Perhaps the lines were by Winifred herself who was beginning to dabble in writing poetry.

These late confections might be called Symbolist in style, and since several were illustrated in the art periodicals and were exhibited in the 1900s in London, where they could be seen more widely, one might say that they contributed to this turn-of-the-century movement.

A letter from Sandys to Eliza Brightwen (1830–1906) at The Grove, Stanmore, shows that he visited her in November 1892 when she offered to give him one of her chrysanthemums to draw. He must have been staying with the Donaldsons at Lymes Holme, Great Stanmore, which was the neighbouring estate to The Grove and within walking distance. He wrote: 'Yesterday you

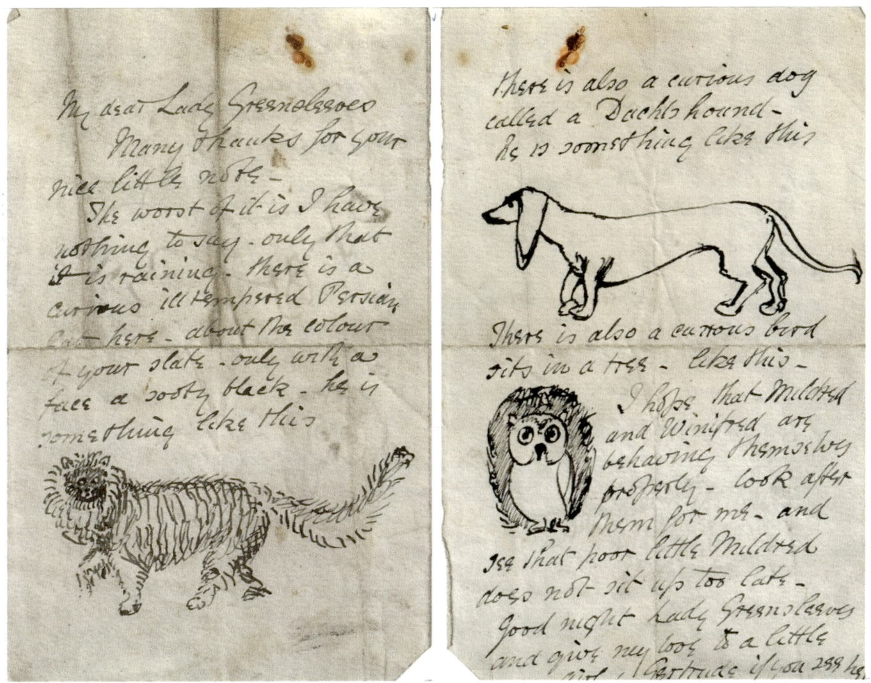

My dear Lady Greensleeves
Many thanks for your
nice little note –
The worst of it is I have
nothing to say – only that
it is raining – there is a
curious ill tempered Persian
Cat here – about the colour
of your slate – only with a
face a sooty black – he is
something like this

There is also a curious dog
called a Dachshound –
he is something like this

There is also a curious bird
sits in a tree – like this –
I hope that Mildred
and Winifred are
behaving themselves
properly – look after
them for me – and
see that poor little Mildred
does not sit up too late –
Good night Lady Greensleeves
and give my love to a little
[illegible] Gertrude if you see her.

Letter, undated but *c.*1892, from Sandys to his youngest daughter Gertrude written from Lymes Holme, George Donaldson's house.

were kind enough to offer me that magnificent chrysanthemum to draw. I should be most grateful if you could do so now. I hope it would travel up to town with me this afternoon, without harm or injury. I have sent a large box that it may be carefully brought. Might I ask for a piece of the foliage, this seemed to me equally fine as the flower.'[10]

Mrs Brightwen in her memoir[11] recalled this visit: 'November 24th. I had a very interesting visit from an artist – Frederick Sandys, a white-haired old man who knew my husband's family and all the past generations. How we did talk of old days! Mr Sandys remembered hearing Mrs Opie (wife of the painter) sing at Earlham, where Joseph John Gurney lived, and it was in his lifetime too. We made a tour of the rooms to see the various pictures; the drawings by old masters specially interested him, and to my surprise he liked the museum and lingering long over all the cases talking and asking questions.[12] I am often surprised at the little things which will give pleasure to others. He admired the shape of some seed capsules, so when I had given him a copy of my book, I ventured to offer him a pincushion made out of a poppy head, stuck with pins and tied with blue ribbon, value about twopence! He seemed as pleased as if I had presented him with an "old master"!'

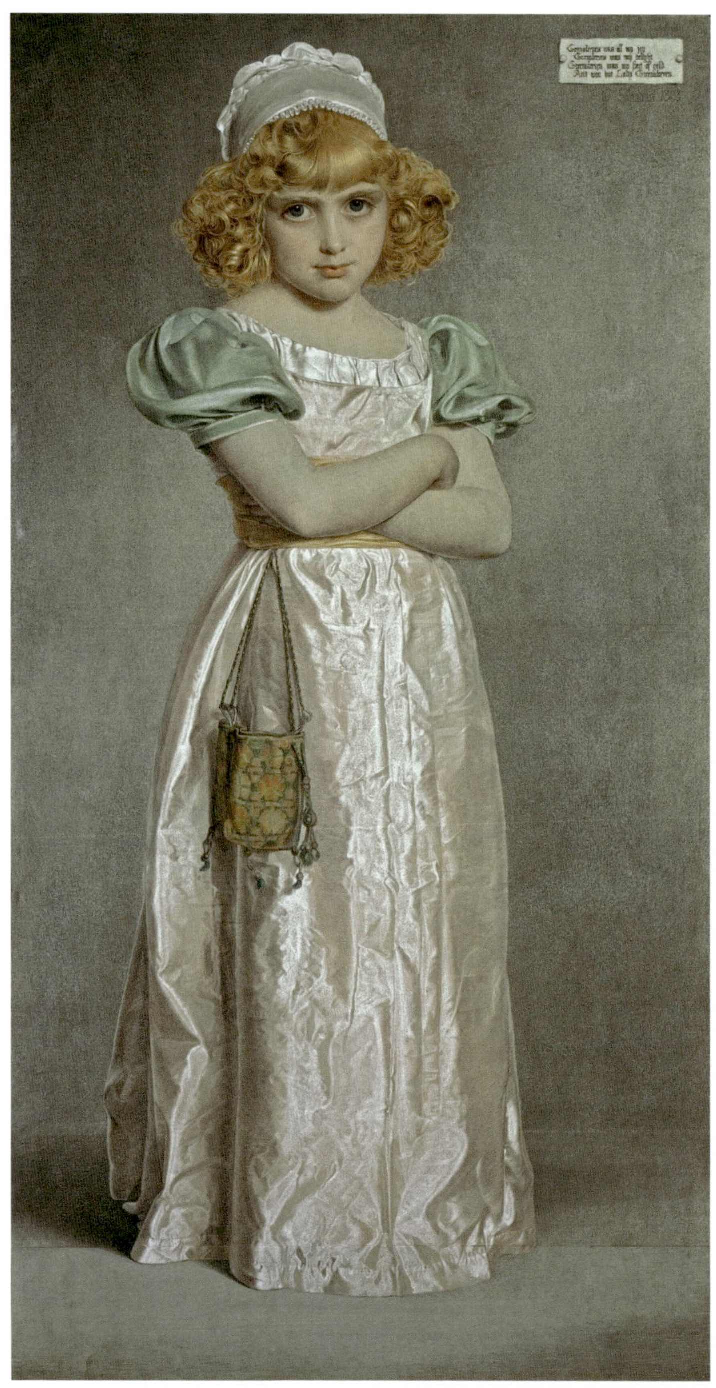

My Lady Greensleeves. Chalk drawing. 1892-1893. The inspirational model was Sandys's daughter Gertrude who was six at the time. It repeats his earlier idea of 1880 when he portrayed his son Hugh at a similar age in pseudo-historical costume. She later married Lionel Crane, Walter Crane's eldest son.

Sandys wrote several letters to his youngest daughter Gertrude from Lymes Holme: 'My dear little Lady Greensleeves … if I had been able to come home this evening[,] I do not suppose you would be up. That would have been a nice kettle of fish indeed. What should I have done without you to look after those beautiful slippers of mine[?] ... I hope no one has been wearing them. I expect you to look after them when I am away. You can wear them if you like, but no one else. … Give my love to Guy. I hope he has learnt his new piece of Poetry. Goodbye just one kiss for you and one for Guy and just give one to Ruth. Your affcy.' (Drawings of a pig and an owl followed the letter.)[13] From this letter, we know that he had already started on the large drawing of *My Lady Greensleeves*. In fact, Donaldson was to show it in December 1892 in his Bond Street gallery to great acclaim, even though it was unfinished. It was shown with another unfinished work, *The Fates*, which has not been identified. *Selene (or Queen of the Night)* was also shown.[14]

In another undated letter he wrote: 'My dear Lady Greensleeves. Many thanks for your nice little note. The worst of it is I have nothing to say – only that it is raining. There is a curious ill-tempered Persian cat here – about the colour of your slate – only with a face a sooty black – he is something like this [drawings follow]. There is also dog called a Dachts hound – he is something like this [more drawings follow] … I hope that Mildred and Winifred are behaving themselves properly – look after them for me – and see that poor little Mildred does not sit up too late. Good night Lady Greensleeves and give my love to a little girl – Gertrude if you see her.' He was besotted with his youngest child, Gertrude, and she provided fresh inspiration for him in his late work.

Another loving letter to Gertrude was written from Lymes Holme: 'My dear little Greensleeves, So you have not got rid of your cold yet, what do you mean[?] Why you are worse than a little chicken and more trouble? The gentleman where I have been has seventeen little chickens. They picked their way out last Wednesday and Thursday. They are the tiniest little darlings you ever saw. They were a lot of trouble. The eggs were put into a box and kept so hot for about twenty day[s] and then first one and then another gave a little peck with his little beak inside the shell and then another and the shell broke and then out came one little chick and then another and another till they were all out. They were then wrapped up in Flannel put into a basket and put in the front of [the] fire – and very funny they looked all huddled together. Give my love to Ruth and Constance and to Guy. Goodbye your aff … Father.'[15]

My Lady Greensleeves (begun in 1891, dated 1893) is one of the finest works of Sandys's later years (he was sixty-three in 1892). Gertrude, his youngest child, who was six years old at the time, was turning into a beauty. As noted, twelve years earlier, he had worked on a comparable picture, but in oils, with his son Hugh for a model.

It is more than possible that Sandys was inspired by Holbein's full length portrait of *Christina of Denmark* (*c*.1538) which was shown to the public in London, firstly on loan from the Duke of Norfolk to the National Gallery from 1880 to 1909, and lent out from there to various exhibitions including the Royal Academy in 1880, the New Gallery in 1890, and to the Grafton Gallery in 1894. It was finally bought for the National Gallery in 1909.[16]

An interesting detail in *Greensleeves* is the embroidered purse hanging from her waist. A watercolour of two early seventeenth century embroidered purses was originally in James Bulwer's Grangerised *Norfolk Collection* (recording various antiquities to be found in Norfolk, see p. 48). It was listed there as *Anne Boleyn's Bag*. This watercolour has been attributed to Sandys in the past, but it may have been by Bulwer himself.[17] At any rate, Sandys was familiar with it.

The whole of the *Norfolk Collection* (watercolours, drawings and prints) was inherited after James Bulwer's death in 1879 by Bulwer's eldest son, and Sandys's friend, James Redfoord Bulwer (1820–1899). We know from letters that, in the 1890s, Sandys was reacquainting himself with the Collection around the time when he was carrying out his portrait of J.R. Bulwer. This may have been the opportunity to notice the watercolour of the purse for this detail in *Greensleeves* as the purse is almost identical to it. Around this time he was in the habit of spending Sundays with Bulwer at his chambers at the Inner Temple, helping him with his watercolour painting and designing flower beds for him for the Temple Gardens.[18]

As already noted, *Greensleeves* was shown in an unfinished state at George Donaldson's gallery in New Bond Street in December 1892. When finished it had evidently been bought by Francis Prange,[19] the manager of the newly opened Grafton Galleries, for he was the lender when it was shown there in 1895 in the exhibition, titled Fair Children. It was sold soon after to the collector James S. Budgett of Stoke Park, Guildford.

Also in 1892, Sandys portrayed Edward Grey (1862–1933) the young Liberal politician before he achieved prominence.[20] Cyril Flower may have led to this political connection, of which we know little about. The whereabouts of this fine and unusually animated chalk portrait still remains obscure.

Jealousy. Chalk drawing. Early 1890s. A Symbolist work showing that Sandys was aware of the new movement in art. His daughter Winifred was the sitter.

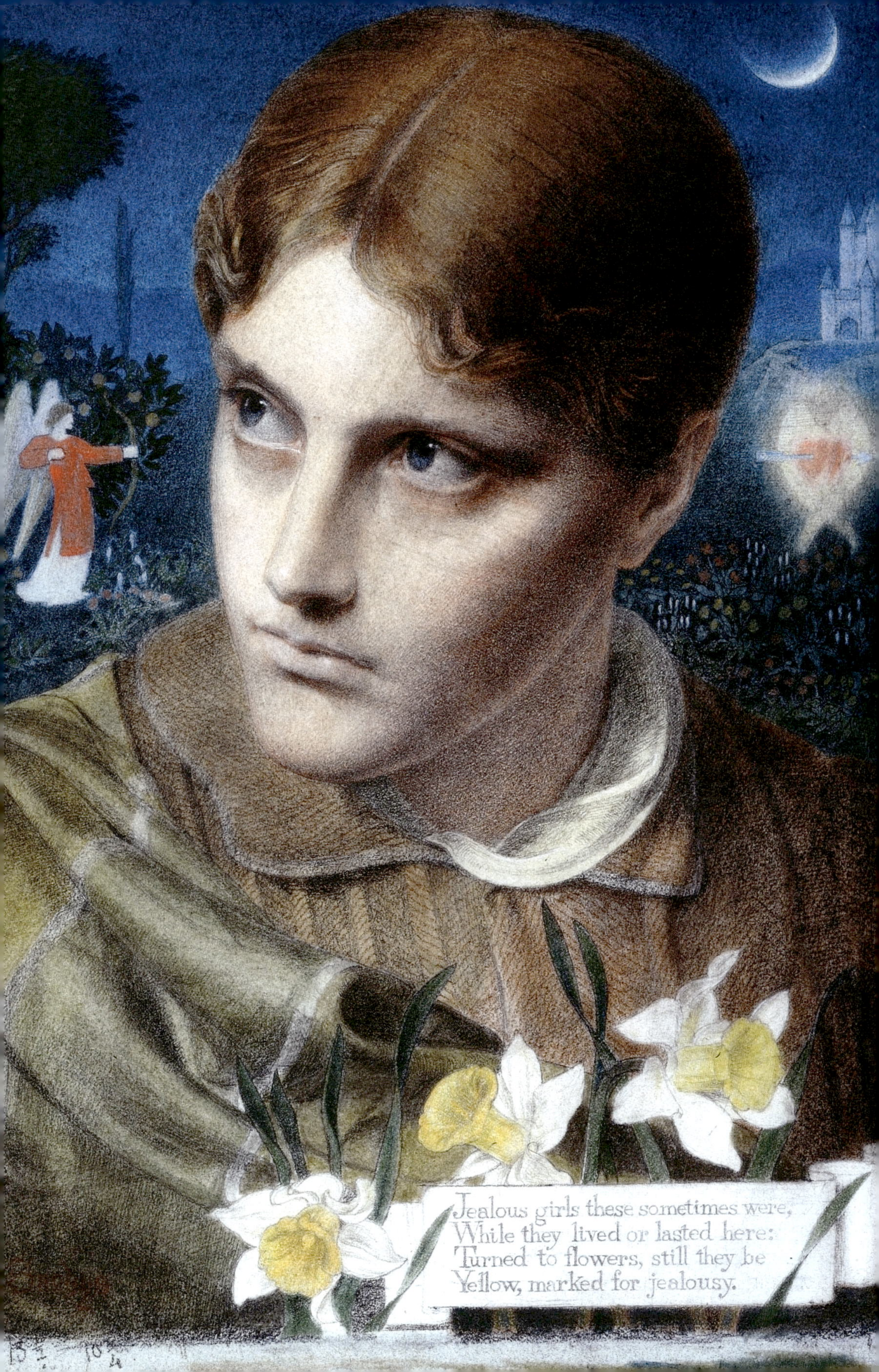
Jealous girls these sometimes were,
While they lived or lasted here:
Turned to flowers, still they be
Yellow, marked for jealousy.

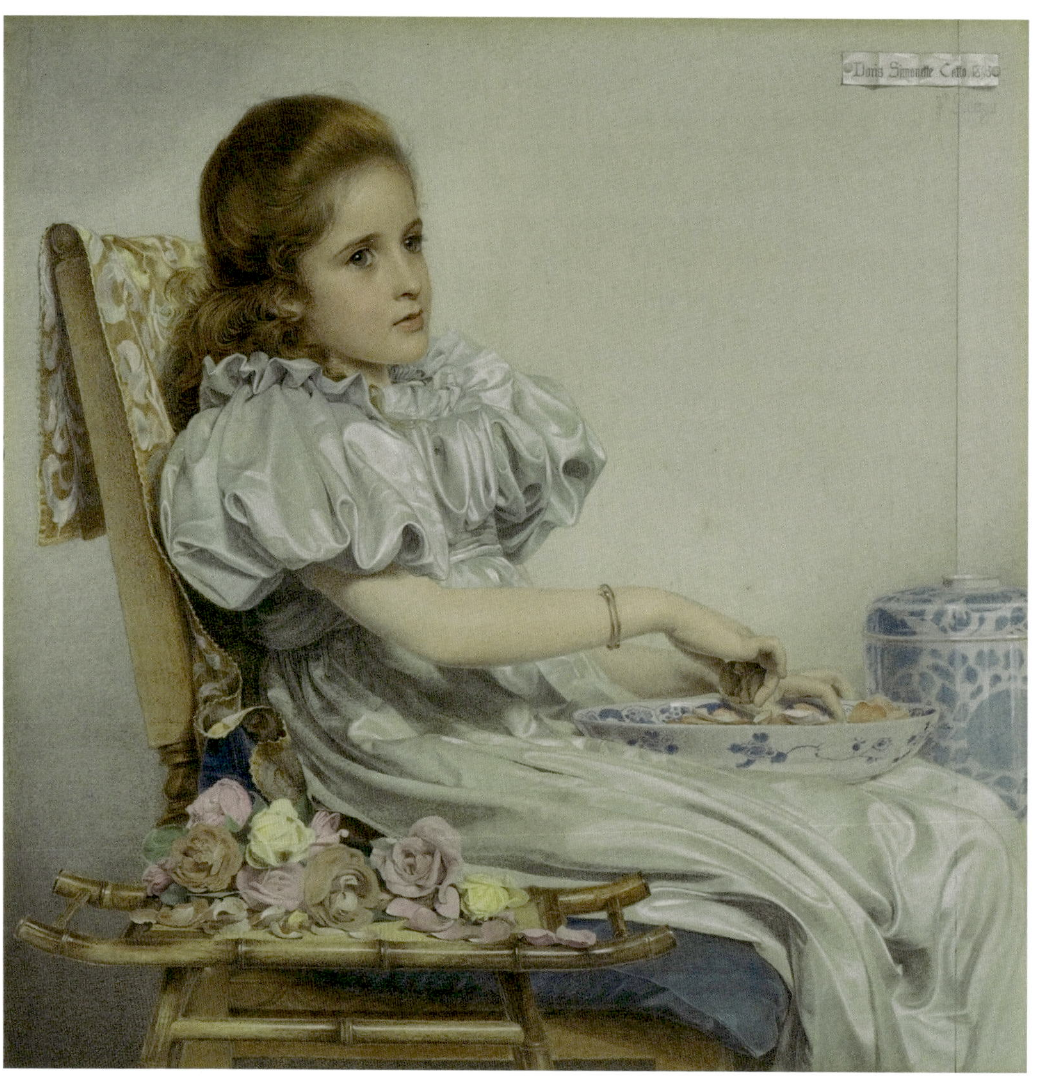

Miss Doris Catto. Chalk drawing, *c*.1893. She was the daughter of a wealthy Australian sheep farmer. It was shown at the New Gallery in 1894.

Referring to the *J.R. Bulwer* portrait, it was perhaps, personally for Sandys, a more interesting portrait to work on. The preliminary chalk drawing was begun in 1892, culminating in the oil painting derived from it which is dated 1894. The latter hangs in the Great Hall of the Temple but it is impossible to see as it is hung so high. In fact, it contains several interesting details. It shows, three-quarter length, an upright elderly man with grey side-whiskers holding a walking stick and gloves as if just departing for a walk. Behind him, on a table, is a blue and white Chinese porcelain jar. On the wall behind him is a framed picture, its glass reflecting the scene through a window in the opposite wall of the room, of City roof-tops and the dome of St Paul's Cathedral. The pose of the figure recalls the 1858 portrait which Sandys made of Bulwer's father. This late portrait, made when Sandys was sixty-five, was painted as meticulously as ever, showing that his style was unchanged over the years, unaffected by the developments in painting styles and new techniques occurring in his lifetime.

J.R. Bulwer had risen high in the world of law and politics. He was Conservative MP for Ipswich between 1874 and 1880, and for Cambridgeshire between 1881 and 1885. He was editor of the Common Law series of the *Law Reports* (1866–1886) and was Treasurer of the Inner Temple from 1880. He was Master in Lunacy at the time of the portrait. It was he who had Sandys illustrate with etchings his climb of Mont Blanc for *Extracts from My Journal* published privately in Norwich in 1853.[21] In his youth, Bulwer was a pioneer Alpine climber and was justly proud of his exploits. Like his father, he was an amateur watercolourist, but less talented.[22]

It appears that in the nineties, as noted, Sandys was in the habit of spending time with Bulwer at his chambers at the Temple. A letter from Sandys has been preserved at the National Portrait Gallery recounting this period in his life: 'For many years, indeed up to this last year, I used to go frequently on the Sunday and work on his watercolour paintings, putting in figures, etc. assisting in designing beds for his flowers in Temple Gardens.'[23] In this letter, the circumstances of how the portrait came about were explained: 'One afternoon after being terribly misled by a friend, and wanting fifty pounds, I went to Mr Bulwer and made an offer to paint his portrait for £150, £50 to be paid to me then, and £10 each week till the picture was completed. To my surprise he told me that he could not afford it, that he had sustained a great loss – either £8000 or £18000, I think the latter, that he had only just completed the payment, etc. I waited with him chatting until he went to his dinner. He gave me a lift in his cab to Suffolk [Street] leaving him on the steps of his club. He asked me in and said I will have the portrait, but I cannot pay

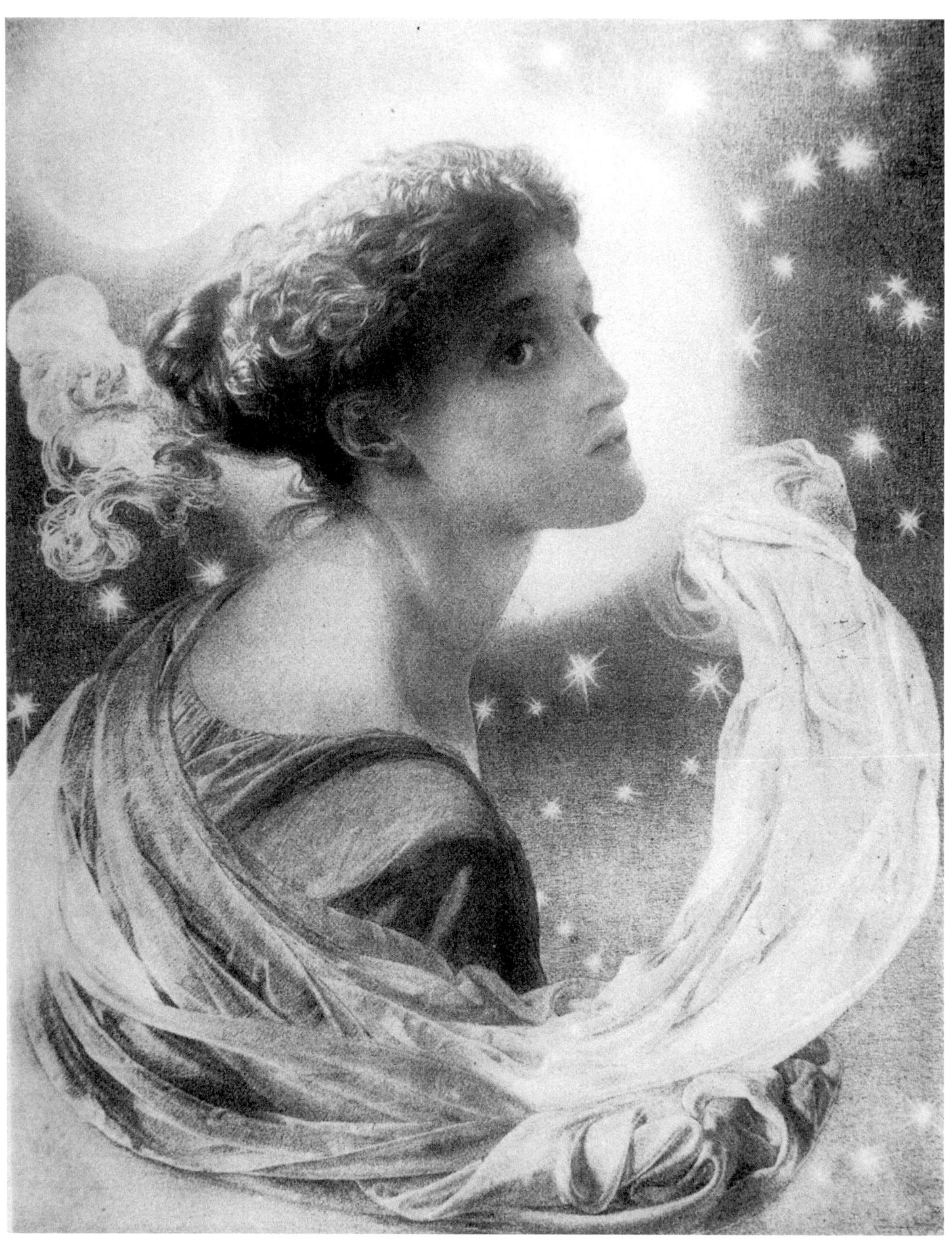

Selene. Chalk drawing. 1894. The Greek mythological Goddess of the Moon. The sitter was his daughter Winifred.

fifty down, so I had £10 each week – till £150. The chalk drawing I gave him – as I think he wished to give it to his little niece to whom he was much attached.'[24] Sandys's debt was undoubtedly due to a betting loss.

This portrait contains many allusions to J.R. Bulwer's life and its associations. On the wall behind the figure is dimly seen a framed watercolour which can be recognised as *Cliffs on the North-East Side of Point Lorenzo, Madeira*, a subject which had been painted by Bulwer's father in the 1820s and was subsequently copied by his father's friend John Sell Cotman.[25]

Sandys evidently brought his daughters along to the Inner Temple at the time he was painting the portrait. There exists a letter from Winifred Sandys to Harold Hartley in which she wrote: 'Many many years ago, when my father was painting Judge Bulwer's portrait, he got permission to take us to his rooms in the Temple.'[26] According to her, Bulwer was away hunting in Yorkshire at the time. The main substance of her letter is her disappointment in not being able to see the Rev. James Bulwer's *Norfolk Collection*. Hartley was involved in trying to sell this at the time of the letter. After a period of years the collection was sold in a much depleted state to Russell J. Colman who bequeathed it to Norwich Castle Museum in 1946.

At this time, during the 1890s, an interest was growing in the wood-engraved magazine illustrations of the 1860s, which by now had acquired a historical dimension. The family magazines in which they had appeared – *The Cornhill, Once a Week*, and *Good Words*, etc. – had been consigned to the attics of the original subscribers, and it was a younger generation who discovered them and saw their qualities anew. Two influential books were published in 1889: *Pen Drawing and Pen Draughtsmen* by Joseph Pennell,[27] and *Of the Decorative Illustration of Books* by Walter Crane. Meanwhile Charles Fairfax Murray was quietly amassing a collection of the graphic works of Sandys and the Pre-Raphaelites including their work as illustrators. He showed four wood-engraved illustrations by Sandys from the 1860s at the fourth of the Arts and Crafts Exhibition Society's exhibitions at the New Gallery in Regent Street in 1893.[28] By the time of Gleeson White's great compendium *English Illustration: The Sixties* (1897), the 'Sixties' had become a subject for collectors (as he suggested in his first chapter titled The New Appreciation and the New Collector). Reproductive wood-engraved illustrations for magazines and books had been increasingly supplanted by new technology, namely photographic process blocks, since the early 1880s.

Two fine portrait drawings were undertaken in 1893: *Mrs Emma Elizabeth Catto* in December, and her daughter Doris probably at about the same time.

The portrait of the young Doris Catto was shown at the Society of Portrait Painters exhibition in October 1894, attracting interest and critical praise.[29]

The Catto family were from Bridgewater, Victoria, Australia, where John Catto was described in 1903 as a 'grazier'.[30] He seems to have been wealthy enough to visit England frequently. Possibly the discovery of gold in the 1850s at Ballarat, Victoria, had contributed to his prosperity. He and Emma Elizabeth were in London in 1887, when Doris was born and her birth registered. The family of three can also be found there in the 1911 census for St Marylebone. It seems strange that the portrait of Emma Elizabeth was sold at Christie's as early as 1913[31] since her daughter Doris, who seems to have settled in London, died fifty years later in 1964.[32]

Another of Sandys's chalk pictures, from 1893, was *Helen of Troy* which is known from the catalogue of the Sandys retrospective exhibition at the Royal Academy in 1905 when it was lent by his patron William Gillilan.[33] It was undoubtedly based on the head of one of the Sandys daughters.

The year ended with his old friend George Meredith wishing Sandys to undertake for him a potential gift for Jean Palmer (Mrs Walter Palmer): 'Would it be possible for you – at your leisure – for a sum to suit my small purse, to sketch a duplicate of the Bhanavar with her Serpents, that you did for Chapman? – a sweet lady, a friend of Riette's, whom I adore, as you would, admires it: and I should like to present a copy from the master's hand. Payment, if you undertake it, you must submit to. Only I can't give much – say, £15. Please answer.'[34] The book illustration that Meredith wanted Sandys to copy was his frontispiece for Meredith's oriental story, *The Shaving of Shagpat*, the second edition, published by Chapman and Hall in 1865. In the book it was published as a monochrome steel engraving by John Saddler (1813–1892). Sandys's colourful watercolour version must have been made from the engraving since Sandys no longer had his design for the original. As a copy of this sort, it is unique in his work.[35]

In spite of these several commissions, there is evidence that Sandys was hard-up at this time. In 1893, he wrote to Charles William Sherborn (1831–1912), the engraver: 'Will you let me ask for the balance of 6/s which with the 4/s you let me have on Saturday will make me indebted to you 10/s. I am so sorry I should have to bother you. I will return it during the week. I feel very seedy yesterday and today. I do not know what can be wrong with me. I return the *Dante* with my best thanks.' The letter is written in pencil and is undated, but on the back of the letter Sherborn has noted 'Monday May 30 1893 – 10' and 'Friday Augt 18. 93 – 5'.[36] There were other such letters to

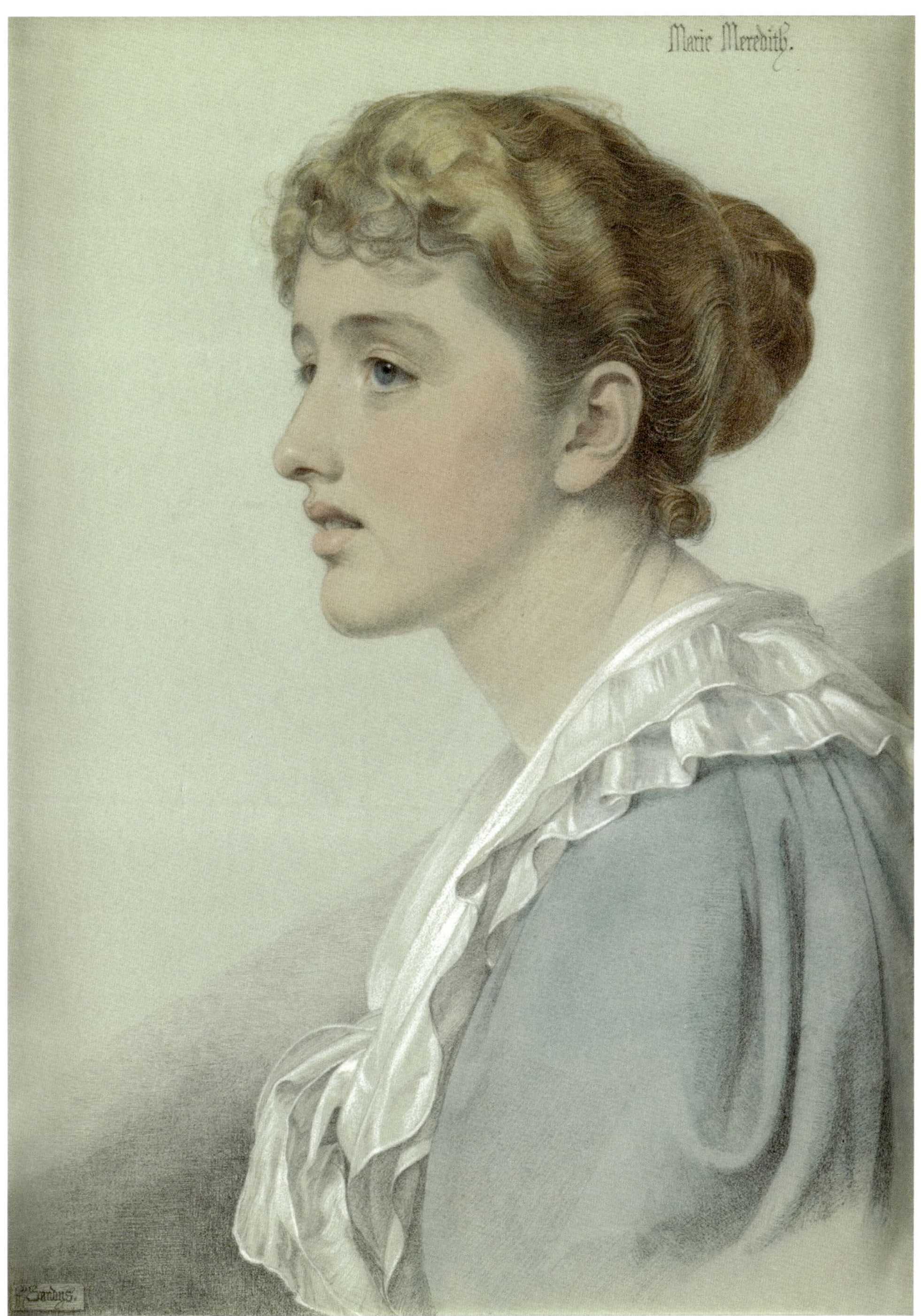

Marie Meredith. Chalk drawing. 1894-1895. George Meredith's daughter, commissioned by her father to commemorate her marriage in 1894.

him in 1897. Sherborn, who had engraved Sandys's 1861 portrait of James Anderson Rose for Rose himself in 1890, lived in Finborough Road which was within easy walking distance of Maude Grove.[37] The pencilled note was probably delivered by one of the Sandys children.

At Christie's in 1891, Sandys's early picture *Mary Magdalen* of *c.*1859 came on the market after James Anderson Rose's death in 1890 and was bought by Charles Fairfax Murray (who was then associated with Agnew's).[38] Murray sold it to his American client Samuel Bancroft Jr in December 1894. This was priced £76, compared to £146 for Rossetti's *Water Willow*, which Bancroft bought at the same time. It was the first of Sandys's paintings to cross the Atlantic and he probably knew about this, though Murray seems to have kept his distance somewhat from him. All the same, it must have pleased him that his name was getting more widely known. Also, in 1894 there were good showings at The Society of Portrait Painters in October when five of his portraits were shown, and at The Grafton Gallery's Fair Women summer exhibition in 1894 when *Medea* (1866–1868) and *Helen* (*c.*1867) were shown.

Around 1894 to 1896 there is evidence that Sandys had the use of a studio at 6 Clareville Grove Studios, Kensington, where several studios had been added to the houses which had been built in an 1840s development of small villas.[39]

In February 1894 Sandys was to be found in a nursing home, Netley House, Henrietta Street, with a broken humerus of his right arm. His letter to an unknown party was written for him perhaps by one of the nurses. He asks if the recipient would visit him there and mentions a Mr Morrison as being apprised of his present condition.[40] John Brett, in a letter to F.G. Stephens, described the accident as: '…on the night of the 2nd of January when the roads were all covered with ice, he got out of a "bus" and slipping up broke his right arm near the shoulder. I do not know whether he is a personal friend of yours but I am sure you will be grieved to hear of such an accident to so great an artist, He has been in bed for a month and very nearly died. Fortunately, he is in the hand[s] of Mr Nunn a very first rate surgeon and is well cared for at the delightful hospital of Miss Mason in Henrietta Street.'[41]

Sandys must have recovered sufficiently to be working again in June on a portrait. Meredith's daughter, Marie Eveleen, tenderly nicknamed by him as 'Dearie', was about to become the second wife of a wealthy neighbour and widower, Henry Parkman Sturgis, when Meredith commissioned a portrait, perhaps as a wedding present. Progress was slow and there is a letter from Meredith to Sandys written in December: 'I have bidden the Dearie march to the finish of her portrait, and she has vowed over again that she wished to

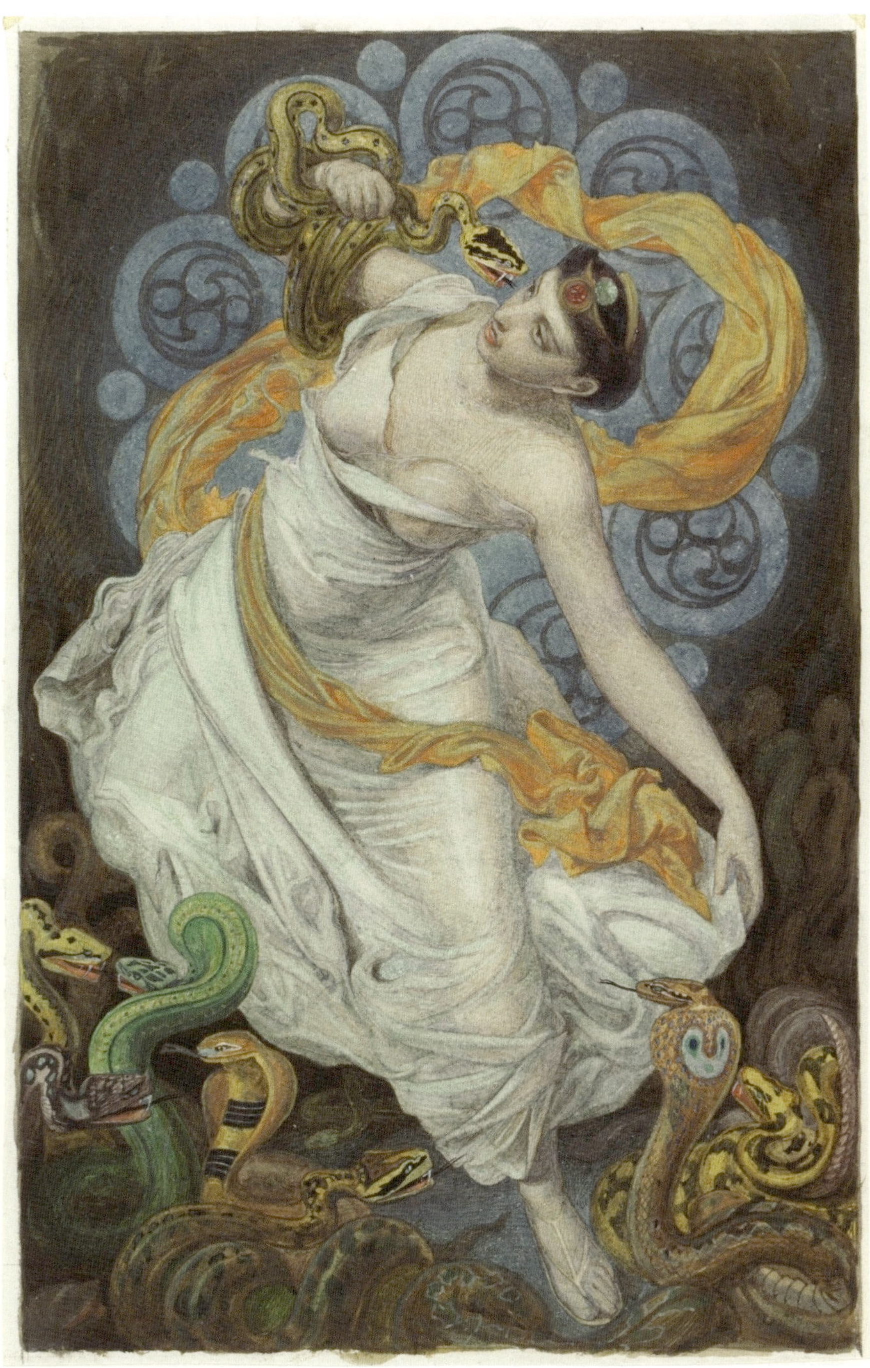

Bhanavar Among the Serpents of Lake Keratis. Watercolour. 1894. A unique decorative watercolour by Sandys. It was based upon the monochrome engraved frontispiece which he drew for the second edition of George Meredith's fanciful novel in Arabian Nights' style, *The Shaving of Shagpat* (1865).

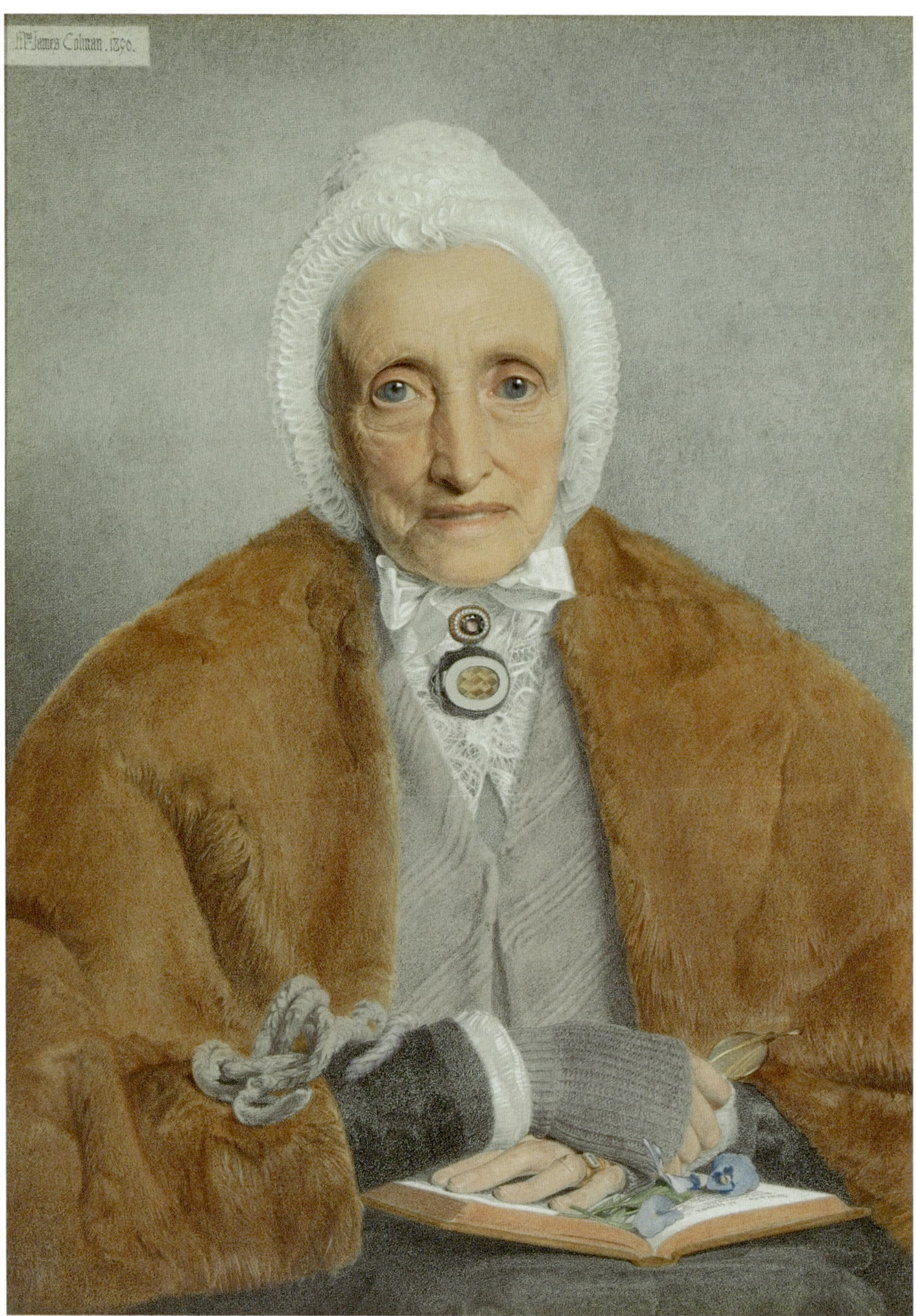

Mary Burlingham Colman (1805-1898). Chalk drawing. 1896-1897. Perhaps Sandys's finest portrait drawing. The sitter was the mother of Jeremiah James Colman, the virtual founder of the fortunes of Colman's, flour and mustard millers of Norwich.

and would. Your call will compel her. She has had visitings and receivings to do since her marriage.'[42]

It is in October 1894 that we find Joseph Pennell first met Sandys. He had written about his work in his book on illustration, *Pen Drawing and Pen Draughtsmen* (1889), and found him 'a curious beggar – but most amusing'.[43] Whistler was to make an unforgettable comment about the encounter in 1895 in a letter to his wife Beatrix: 'Joseph [Pennell] has a mania for discovering – and now he has discovered Sandys! And he proposes to wipe the eye of Van Eyck with this large Briton!'[44]

Pennell and his wife Elizabeth, who were both from Philadelphia, after having firmly established themselves in the London world of art and journalism since their arrival in 1884, decided to set up an after-dinner 'open house' in their Buckingham Street apartment on Thursday evenings. This was partly to keep their days clear for their own work – Joseph was an active illustrator and both were journalists – and no doubt partly to keep abreast of events in the London art world through gossip. They already knew Whistler after Joseph had called on him, as a fellow-American, at his studio in Tite Street soon after they had arrived in London.

At the New Gallery in 1895, Sandys's *Portrait of Mrs Jane Lewis* of 1864 was shown at the Society of Portrait Painters' Annual Exhibition, eliciting high praise from a newspaper correspondent in October:[45] 'Among Englishmen the man who most interests me is hardly known as a painter. Indeed, to the shame of the younger generation, he is hardly now known at all. This is Frederick Sandys. I have no hesitation in saying that this year, if it should so happen that any of the leading French and German artists or critics would come over to see the show of the Society of Portrait Painters, the fame of Frederick Sandys would be spread throughout Europe. … Nor have I any hesitation in saying that if his picture (No. 6), the *Portrait of Mrs Lewis* was placed by the side of the Van Eyck in the National Gallery, it would hold its own, and in some ways throw the Old Master completely in the shade.' The writer continued for a total of eleven inches of a close-set column in praise of the picture, ending: 'Still I am certain that, in the near future, the world will discover that there was, at the time, another painter quite as great as any of the Pre-Raphaelites at work among them, though he never signed the mystic letters after his name.'[46]

Sandys was still living in lodgings at 34 Addison Gardens in 1895 (the family being at Maude Grove) but was using a studio at 296 King's Road. This was where he worked on the chalk drawing *Cassandra*, with his eldest daughter

Winifred as model. He wrote from there to Graham Robertson:[47] 'I have just completed a chalk drawing of a head of *Cassandra*. She is shrieking out her prophesies – supposed to be on the walls of Troy – her hair and drapery blown in front of her. It [is] very dramatic, and I do not hesitate to say it is the best thing I have ever done. … Would you care to see it? If so when would you come to a studio I have for the present at 296 Kings Road Chelsea – they are called Carlyle Studios, Carlyle Square just at the bottom of Church Street. I am anxious to sell the drawing at once. I may say now the price is sixty guineas. Did I not wish to sell it at once I would not sell it for less than one hundred – so much do I believe in the drawing, and I think you as an artist will agree with me so far.'[48]

Unfortunately, Robertson did not succumb. It was later shown in early 1904 at the Leicester Galleries from where it was bought by the entrepreneur Harold Hartley (1851–1943) who became a great admirer of Sandys in his later life. He wrote in his autobiography *Eighty-Eight, Not Out* (1939): 'Frederick Sandys impressed me more than any other as a unique personality. I had the privilege of knowing him intimately during the latter portion of his life. He seemed to have known all his contemporary celebrities. He was the most entertaining talker I ever met.'[49]

In the later nineties Sandys was often seen in the company of younger artists such as Aubrey Beardsley (1872–1898) at the Café Royal in Regent Street, as chronicled by Robert Ross,[50] and William Rothenstein.[51]

Around this time, Sandys probably produced a very fine 'fancy picture', unfortunately not dated. This was *Daffodils* taken from one of his daughters, which repeated an old familiar format of his – a figure behind a ledge on which she rests her hands. On the face of the ledge is a tablet inscribed with a short poem likening the transience of spring flowers with human life. This may have been from the pen of Winifred, of whose poetic efforts Sandys was proud.

Graham Robertson left a vivid picture of Sandys at this time in his reminiscences, *Time Was* (1931): 'In appearance he was like a Duke from Stageland, tall and thin, handsome in a way that now recalled Don Quixote, now Mephistopheles, and with the courtly manners of the (stage) grand seigneur. His stately calm and incorrigible Bohemianism formed the subject of a Hundred Merry Tales in which Rossetti and Whistler used to delight, and many of which the latter related to me. One in particular I remember. Sandys was, as usual, in pecuniary difficulties, and several of his friends had assembled at Rossetti's house to discuss the raising of a sum that would enable him to emigrate. Sandys, during the conference, lounged on a sofa, apparently taking not the faintest interest in the whole affair, but when his would-be benefactors had departed, he slowly sat up. "Whistler," he said, in deep, meditative tones, "if I got that money to go away with – I could stay here!"' [52]

'A strange wayward man, neither able nor wishful to obtain cheap popularity, his name and works are but little known, yet, amongst a brilliant company, he was one of the most highly gifted. Towards the end of his life there was a slight falling-off in his work; his fancy heads became pretty instead of beautiful and his portraits began to coincide rather too much with the sitter's own idea of him or herself, but he left record of his genius in a few magnificent subject pictures, a brilliant series of black and white drawings and two portraits of old ladies, *Mrs Anderson Rose* and *Mrs Lewis*, which will certainly take their place among the highest achievements of modern art.'[53]

Another of his earlier paintings, *Gentle Spring* of 1863–1865, was shown in May 1895 at the Goupil Gallery in Regent Street. This exhibition, titled A Connoisseur's Treasures, showed the collection of Alexander Constantine Ionides who had died in 1890. His son Alexander A. Ionides died soon after in 1898, and *Gentle Spring* was eventually sold at Christie's in 1902.[54]

At the Grafton Galleries' Fair Children exhibition in 1895, *My Lady Greensleeves*, now finished, was shown by the gallery manager Francis Prange. Prange must have acquired it from Sandys, and so it seems that the dealers were bringing him out of the relative obscurity into which his name and reputation had sunk.

A portrait executed in 1895 was commissioned by his old patron Alexander Macmillan, who died the next year. It was of his daughter Olive, who was now Mrs Norman Maclehose.

Joseph Pennell was another who helped bring the elderly Sandys out of semi-obscurity by recognising him as a significant illustrator. He was active in drawing attention to the subject by his writings and by organising exhibitions which often included Sandys's works. He founded the Society of Illustrators in 1893 which functioned as an exhibiting society for their work.[55] He included Sandys's work in *A London Garland*, a picture book and anthology of poetry edited by W.E. Henley (1849–1903), a friend of the Pennells, published by Macmillan's for the Society of Illustrators in 1895. For this, Pennell acquired an unfinished drawing on an uncut woodblock by Sandys. It was titled *The Spirit of the Storm*, and was reproduced by photo-engraving for the first time.[56]

His wife Elizabeth, who closely collaborated with all her husband's activities, acted as amanuensis and recorder of their life in London. They encountered Sandys in 1898 probably when Joseph was organising the Loan Collection of Lithographs at the South Kensington Museum in which he was showing Sandys's *A Nightmare* of 1857, which must have been quite a rare curiosity by this time. Sandys took to dropping in at their flat at Buckingham Street at tea-time and staying long hours reminiscing about his past, no doubt encouraged by Elizabeth who recorded them from memory and published them in the Pennells' books about Whistler.[57] They are a valuable source about Sandys in old age.

Through George Meredith's correspondence with Jean Palmer we know that a portrait of her was planned in December 1895, when Meredith jokingly warned her of Sandys's habitually slow method of work: 'Avec ses 3 sittings, et encore 3! Ce sera toujours 3! Diviser les Reines de leurs sujets, voila son jeu et sa joie.'[58] Despite the warning, we read that shortly afterwards 'Queen Jean' (or 'Lady Jean') summoned Meredith to London to view her portrait at the New Gallery on 25th April 1896,[59] 'three and a half months in incubation'.[60]

An earlier work, *Lethe* (1874), lent by Cyril Flower, was shown at a loan exhibition at the Art Gallery of the City of London in 1896.[61] The Director of the Gallery, Alfred Temple, had instituted loan exhibitions to vary the normal diet of the permanent collection, as part of his strategy to shift the art-going public's interest eastwards.

The *Jean Palmer* portrait led to her husband Walter sitting for Sandys, and then perhaps a year or so later their daughter Gladys. The latter two portraits, unsigned and undated, were never finished.

Gladys (later Gladys Brooke, the wife of Bertram Brooke the Tuan Muda of Sarawak) wrote in her autobiography describing Sandys when he was working on her portrait: 'I remember the tall old man; his strength impressed itself on me as soon as he entered the room, yet his hands shook so constantly that while he worked he had to steady his right hand by holding it firmly against his board. He charged a thousand pounds each for his pictures, but in spite of these vast earnings he never had a penny to his name … [afterwards] Sandys disappeared, and the two portraits with him. For many months we could not get in touch with him or find any trace of the pictures (we learned later that he had pawned them). One day, however, an old four-wheeler drove up to the house, and in it was my portrait and my father's. The old cabby lifted them out and carried them up into the hall; he set them down against the wall, demanded his two and sixpence, and left the house.'[62]

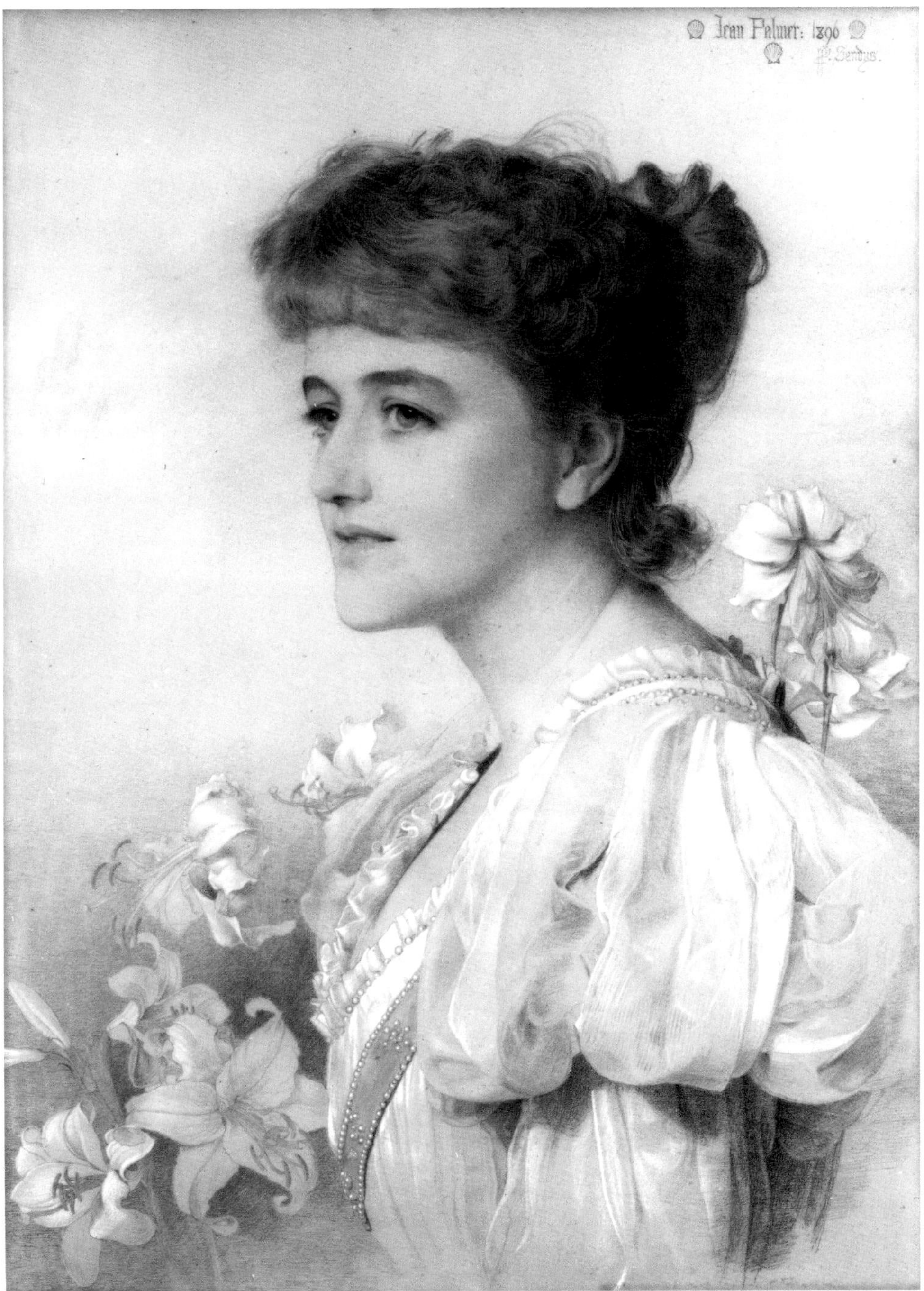

Jean Palmer (*c.*1860-1899). Chalk drawing. 1896. Married in 1882 to Walter Palmer, one of the sons of the founder of the Reading biscuit manufacturers. Her musical salons were well-known in 'Society' at the time. George Meredith was one of her admirers.

There is a letter from Sandys dated 24th April (1896) to the master wood engraver Joseph Swain,[63] addressed to the *Punch* magazine offices at Bouverie Street (Swain was manager of the *Punch* engraving department). He begs for an impression from the woodblock of his old illustration for George Meredith's poem *The Old Chartist*, which Swain had engraved in 1862, to give to 'a lady – a great friend of mine, of Meredith also'. The lady, no doubt, was Mrs Palmer.

Around this time, in early spring, Whistler, with whom Sandys had resumed his friendship after many years, replied to a letter (untraced) from Sandys, writing that he was moving to Hampstead in search of fresh air for his ailing wife, Beatrix, who was to die of cancer on 10th May. Like Whistler, Sandys had known her since the 1870s when she was married to her first husband, E.W. Godwin. Whistler had just taken a studio at 8 Fitzroy Street and was hoping that Sandys 'would come up some afternoon' and talk about the past over a cigarette.[64]

In May, three of his daughters, Gertrude, Winifred and Connie, were staying at the invitation of a Mrs and Miss Coombe at Bexhill-on-Sea in Sussex. Sandys wrote from Addison Gardens to Gertie on the 6th, a long and entertaining letter: 'My dear little Gertie. Little I call you but that seems wrong now – you must be getting a big strong, red-cheeked, rosy girl – out for long walks by day – on the beach – up to your ancles [*sic*] in sand and water before breakfast talking walking and chatting with shrimpers looking into their shrimp nets and larking about with shrimps, young crabs, starfish and I suppose looking abroad for a mermaid. But I suppose you have not met one. Should you see one would you be sure to ask her if I were to come to Bexhill if she would mind sitting to me quite still in a nice little pool – for me to paint her tail and fins if she has any. I would not trouble her to sit for the face. I think I could do one from you now.

'So you have heard the Cuckoo, and the Nightingale and the Lark, but I suppose you have not yet found a nest with eggs or little ones in – with your sharp little eyes – you ought. When you see a lark mounting up in the sky higher and higher, you may be sure he is almost immediately over his nest which is in the grass on the ground – in fact his nest is very little more than a little hole scraped in the ground. There is very little furniture in it. He sings to please his mate and the little ones.

Study of a woman's head. Chalk drawing. *c.*1899. An uncompleted late drawing. It was stated by Constance Sandys that the model was her sister Mildred.

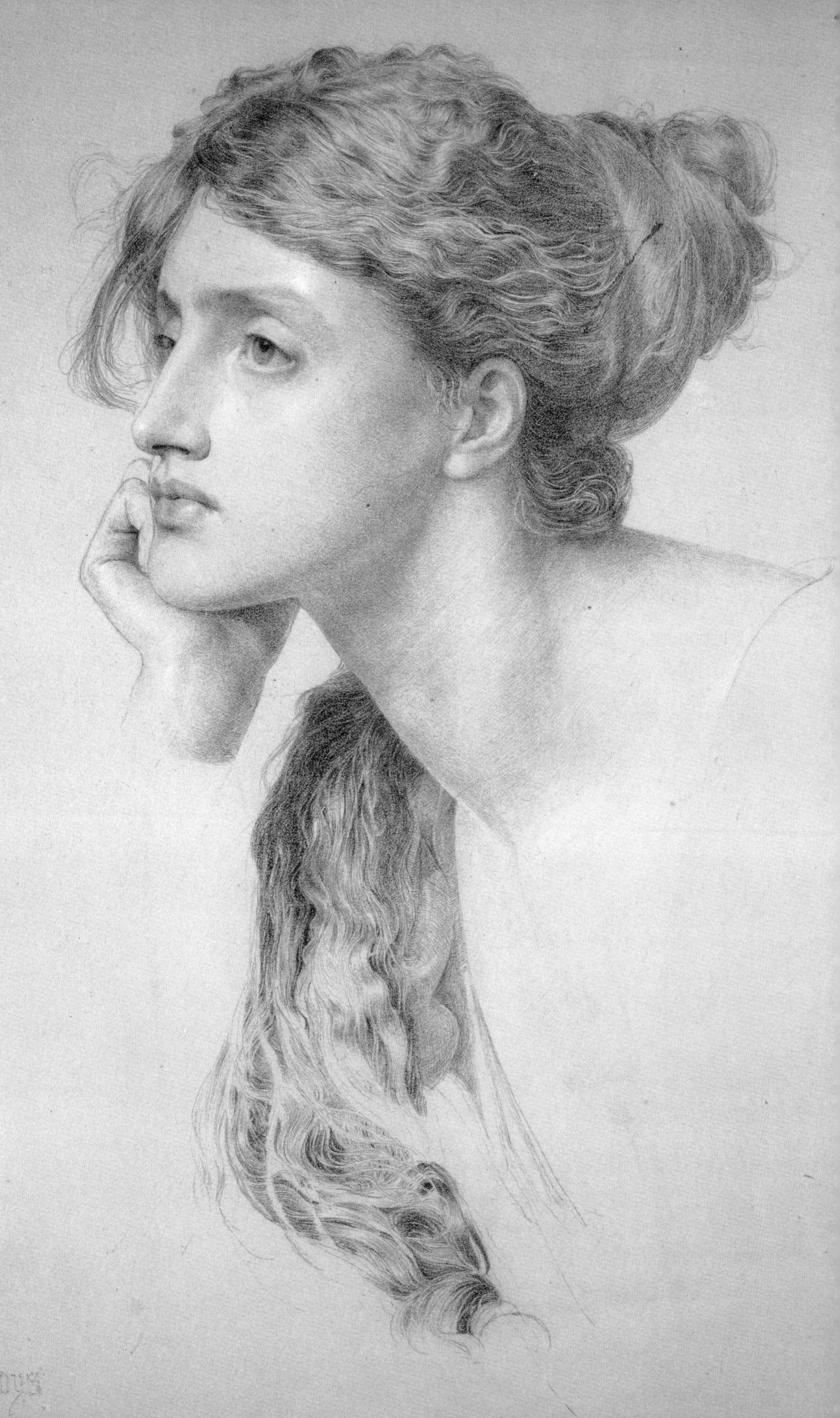

'As you go along the lanes the fences by the side are full of nests of the Hedge Sparrow, Chaffinch, Thrush and Blackbird – you might peep into the nest and see it full of little ones with enormous mouths wide open always – you might take one egg out of a nest but the others you must leave or the mother would be full of grief.

'I suppose you have not seen the Grifon [*sic*] and the Turtle dancing about on the beach in the evening – or the Walrus and the Carpenter eating oysters.[65]

'Now Good bye – with my best love to you and Winifred and Connie – and my best and kindest regards to Mrs and Miss Coombe. What can I do or say to thank them for their great kindness to you all. Your aff. Father. F.S.'[66]

On 23rd September, again from 34 Addison Gardens, he wrote to George Macmillan, who, on the death of his father, Alexander, in January 1896, succeeded him as head of the publishing business. In this letter Sandys was making a concentrated effort to get more work to pay his debts.

'Dear Mr Macmillan, I want to induce you to have three of your distinguished authors drawn. I will do them now at once or at any time that will be convenient. To be drawn in London.

'I will draw them for 50 guineas each – making 150 guineas for the three. I am making this reduction as it would be such a favour and help to have one hundred now.

'I have had an almost incredible series of disappointments this year. I have had commissions for the following portraits – all postponed for one reason or another[:]

Mr Walter Palmer
Lord Delawar's [*sic*] Child
Mr Dreyfus
Mrs Dreyfus
Hugh Hoare's Son
Honble Marsey Mainwaring's Daughter
one of George Meredith for Messrs Constable.

'Meredith could only sit for a sketch to be done in two hours – this I refused – his head being far too fine not to do well. It was for a frontispiece to their new edition of Meredith's work. I think you will say I was right when you see the sketch Sargent has made since.

'I had also commissions from Mrs Rutson, Captain Rawson, Mr Hurst and Mrs Cave. These however I think have fallen through.

'I have also one of a Grandchild of J.J. Colman of Norwich but unfortunately the child has an attack of Influenza and it may be a month before I do it.

'Meanwhile I am prevented proceeding with an oil painting I have in hand.[67]

'I have named this small sum of 150 guineas because it would be of such inconceivable benefit to go on with my painting, and I stand in great fear of losing the few things – easels etc I have in my Studio unless I pay £25 tomorrow.

'Do let me hope you will consider this matter and I trust favourably to me and so render me indeed a great service. Believe me, yours faithfully, Fredk Sandys.

'I will call tomorrow about twelve oclock.'[68]

Of the portraits mentioned the chalk portrait of Walter Palmer had been completed; an oil portrait was commissioned later in *c.*1900 (but may have been started earlier).

Mrs Rutson's daughter, Margaret, was portrayed soon after this time in a pastel by Paul Helleu (1859–1927), who as a younger and more fashionable artist, may have been preferred.[69] However, the Colman family in Norwich came up trumps with commissions for two portraits: the little boy Geoffrey Russell Rees Colman, aged four-and-a-half, dated December 1896 (he had recently recovered from the flu), and his great-grandmother Mrs James Colman (1805–1898). They cost £105 and £210, paid for by Jeremiah James Colman in December 1896.[70]

Although Mrs James Colman had misgivings about her portrait being a success, I believe that it joins the ranks of Sandys's finest portraits. While working on it, Sandys was staying at the Maid's Head Inn in Norwich. From there he wrote to his daughter Maud (now aged twenty): 'I cannot get my drawing of the old lady done before Tuesday, work as I may, so that I cannot get back before Wednesday but it may be Thursday.' He continued: 'Tell Winifred I want her to go to Barbe's in Regent Street and get me a pencil of red chalk and send it to me so I have it by return post – she knows the sort I mean, thick red in cedar.'[71] Evidently Maud had written to say that she wanted a new skirt, to which he replied: 'I am sorry you have not a nice fine skirt. I suppose you would like a nice pink muslin one with little white daisies all over it – but you cannot have it, but I send you ten shillings. I fancy you can get a nice skirt suitable for the weather we are having [it was December]. You can get the enclosed postal order changed[;] take 10 shillings for yourself and give 10 shillings to Hugh.'[72]

There is a reference to a portrait of Hugh Hoare's son which was postponed in 1896, but it may not have been executed, as it has not come to light.[73] Hugh Edward Hoare (1854–1929) was Liberal MP for West Cambridge from 1892 to 1895. He had two sons, Percival (b.1888) and Evelyn (b.1889), both of whom were killed in World War I.

A sighting of Cyril Flower and Sandys walking along the cliffs at Cromer or at nearby Overstrand, probably from the late 1880s or 1890, is worth mentioning. It comes from *The Wheel of Life* (1897) by the poet and journalist Clement Scott (1841–1904). 'I chanced to meet on the "grass of the cliff" Cyril Flower, now Lord Battersea, walking with his old and attached friend, Frederick Sandys, the artist genius, who, with the greatest gift given to man, never worked hard enough at his divine art.'[74] It shows the disappointment generally felt by those who were aware of Sandys's character.

Late in 1896, the first monograph on Sandys was published by *The Artist* as their first Special Winter Number. The editor was Wallace L. Crowdy for Archibald Constable & Co. The author was Esther Wood, an art journalist of the day. In his introduction, Crowdy explained the 'genesis' of the work:

'Some years ago three men were standing in the entrance to the Café Royal, and by their striking appearance attracted the attention of passers-by. These three men were Cyril Flower, Frederick Sandys, and Reginald Upcher – all three intimately associated with the county of Norfolk.[75] Shortly after this it was my pleasure to become well-acquainted with the last of these, and through him the enthusiasm of admiration for the work of Frederick Sandys has long possessed me.'

He continued by outlining the several preceding articles about Sandys and his work: in 1884, 1888, 1889, and 1895, by J.M. Gray and Joseph Pennell, all of which he stated were inaccurate. Though Crowdy implied that the new undertaking, which apparently took six months to put together and had the assistance and cooperation of Sandys himself,[76] would be as correct as could be. In fact, it contains many inaccuracies, perhaps showing that the author Esther Wood was unable to get enough attention from Sandys throughout the process of interviewing, writing, and editing. The trouble was that Sandys had secrets to keep and probably also had a failing memory by this time.

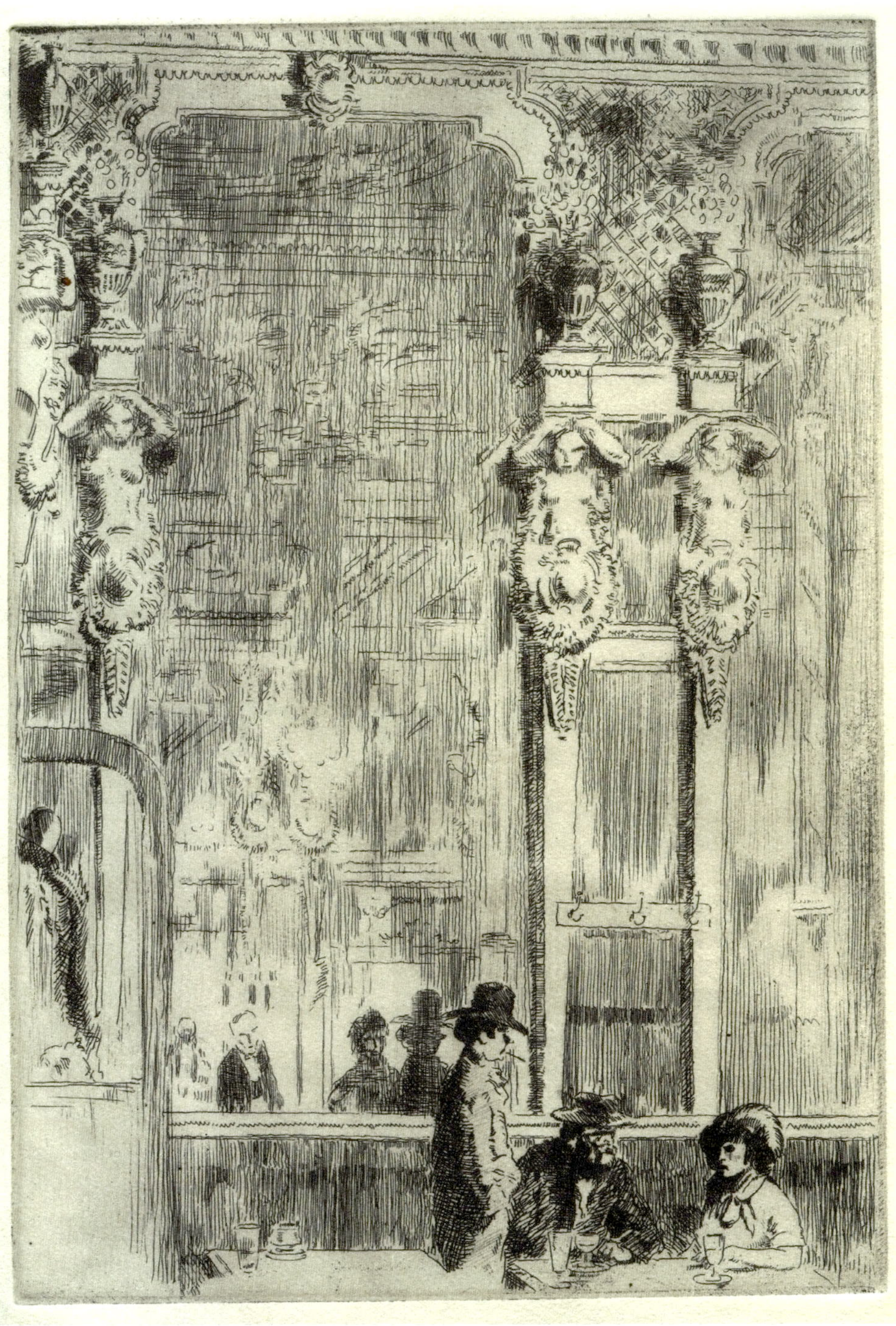

The Domino Room of the Café Royal 1920. Etching by Frederick Carter (1883-1967). One of Sandys's haunts late in life, the scene is as he would have known it.

However, this was the first piece of writing to cover all of his life and work, not only the illustrations which had inspired Gray and Pennell to write about him. Moreover, many of the original owners of Sandys's works were still alive, as indeed were some of his friends. As Charles Fairfax Murray wrote: 'There is, as you say, no good account of Sandys and there's never likely to be one. He won't supply much information about himself, but the inaccuracies of Gray's article which were so terrible that he was obliged to correct them. Still the information he gives is very meagre. I suppose I know more about him than any outsider, but it's a difficult subject to handle, the more so that he has several children.'[77]

Inadequate as the reproductions in this monograph appear to us today, they were technically advanced at the time. There are two photogravures printed in sepia, one credited to the Autotype Company and the other to the Swan Electric Engraving Company. The majority are half-tone block monochrome prints by William H. Ward & Co.[78]

In spite of the gushing style of Esther Wood's text, which sometimes degenerates into sheer nonsense, and in spite of the errors, the book does usefully illustrate five works by Sandys which have since disappeared from sight. Of these, most importantly, is *St George for Merrie England* which he had produced for Cyril Flower. She also mentions other missing works, some of which have not yet surfaced to this day, and whose appearance can only be guessed.[79]

In conclusion, Wood gently berates Sandys with: 'Rossetti himself was not a more desultory or prodigal worker … [and] it is a matter of marvel and regret that the nett result of finished masterpieces should be proportionately small. … Among the group of great artists with whom the name of Frederick Sandys will ever be associated, none have brought more original genius to bear upon their tasks, or fulfilled them with less regard to accepted codes and habits of discipline. But the wise critic, knowing the futility and unreason of quarrelling with those temperamental conditions which so often beset genius, will be content to estimate on their own splendid merits the finished works that have issued from a master-hand and a golden age of art.'[80]

[1] Christie's 6th March 1911 (73), vendor C.W. Carey, bought by Huggins for £5.0.0. Untraced. The 1911 sale contained as lot 75 Sandys's watercolour *Bhanavar the Beautiful* commissioned by George Meredith as a gift for her.

[2] Jean Palmer died in 1909 and her husband Walter Palmer died in 1910.

[3] Mildred Emma was born in December 1872 so would be about 18 in 1890.

[4] It was bought from the Gallery by the Ulster Museum, Belfast.

[5] Letter from Swinburne to Sandys, dated 1st December 1890. Cecil Y. Lang, *The Swinburne Letters*, (1959–62). vol. 6, no. 1550A.

[6] Cline, (ed.) *The Owl and the Rossettis* (1978). p. 27.

[7] *The Morning Post*, 17th November 1891. Joseph Knight wrote the entry for Lewis Strange Wingfield in the DNB.

[8] Letter from Meredith to Sandys, dated 7th April 1892. Yale University Library. Joseph Ashby Sterry (1836?–1917) artist, poet, journalist, and novelist, was a friend and supporter of Sandys and was of a lively disposition. James Lowry Whittle (b.1840) was a barrister and journalist. He was a writer on political subjects.

[9] These annual free loan exhibitions, organised as charity fundraisers by Canon Samuel Barnet the vicar of St Jude's Church, were the predecessors of the Whitechapel Art Gallery initiative (1901).

[10] Letter from Sandys to Mrs Brightwen, dated Friday (25th November 1892). J.A. Symington Collection, Rutgers University Library.

[11] Eliza Brightwen, *The Life and Thoughts of a Naturalist*, (ed.) W.H. Chesson (1909), pp. 107–108.

[12] After her husband's death in 1883, she converted the billiard room at The Grove into a 'museum'.

[13] Sandys Family Archive.

[14] Anon. report in *The Daily Graphic*, 19th December 1892. Sandys Family Archive.

[15] Sandys Family Archive.

[16] Michael Levey, *National Gallery, The German School*, 1959. pp. 54–57.

[17] A group of six items from the *Norfolk Collection* came up for sale at Christie's on 12th October 1971, lot 88, which included this watercolour. The vendor was Mr R. Berry, and it was bought by the Colnaghi gallery. Watercolours in the *Norfolk Collection* are not signed, as they were considered merely illustrative.

[18] Letter from Frederick Sandys to anon. (executor of J.R. Bulwer?) from 31 Cheniston Gardens, 20th December (1899). National Portrait Gallery Archives.

[19] Francis Gerard Prange (b.*c.*1843). The Grafton Gallery was at 8 Grafton Street (off Bond Street).

[20] This portrait is illustrated opposite p. 30 in Grey of Falloden, *Twenty-Five Years*, 1892–1916, vol. 1, (1925). It was shown in 1896 at the New Gallery, Summer Exhibition, as no. 373.

[21] See p. 23.

[22] The author, in a visit in the 1980s to the Print Room of the National Gallery, Washington DC, in a group

of unidentified watercolours, several attributable to J.R. Bulwer.

[23] Letter from Sandys to anon (probably J.R. Bulwer's executor) dated 'Wednesday Decr. 20th' (1899). Bulwer died 4th March 1899. National Portrait Gallery Archive.

[24] This preliminary chalk drawing has descended in the Bulwer family and is now in Vancouver.

[25] The Bulwer original is in the V&A Museum collection, bequeathed by Sydney D. Kitson, P.31-1939. The Cotman copy is in the Vancouver Art Gallery, the gift of Mrs H.A. Bulwer in 1961.

[26] Typed letter from Winifred Sandys to Harold Hartley dated 9th December 1920, in Colman Collection records, Art Department, Norwich Castle Museum.

[27] Which Sandys had scorned, when he was given a copy by Alexander Macmillan (see p. 258).

[28] These four designs for illustration, *Life's Journey, If, The Little Mourner,* and *Jacques de Caumont* are now in the Birmingham Art Gallery Collection.

[29] New Gallery, Fourth Exhibition of the Society of Portrait Painters, 1894, no. 107.

[30] Electoral Roll for 1903, State of Victoria, Division of Grampian, Bridgewater, Mimsie Station.

[31] Christie's 21st July 1913, lot 28, bought by Port for £1! It was later with the Walker Gallery.

[32] She eventually died in Wandsworth, South London in 1964. Death Index for 1916–2007.

[33] RA Winter Exhibition 1905, *Exhibition of Works by the late G.F. Watts and the late Frederick Sandys,* no.265. Lent by William Gillilan Esq.

[34] Letter from Meredith to Sandys from Box Hill, 28th December 1893. Bancroft Archive, Delaware Art Museum Library.

[35] Now in the V&A Museum. Gift of R.G. Searight, 1987 (SD.9.11).

[36] Undated note (1893) from Sandys to Sherborn, a copy of which was kindly sent to me by the late Derek Sherborn.

[37] As well as that of his wife Emily Winter Rose, also of 1861. James Anderson Rose was himself an avid collector of historical engraved portraits, and this engraved portrait of Rose was intended for the frontispiece of *A Collection of Engraved Portraits (Further Selection) exhibited by the late James Anderson Rose.* London, 1894. Instead, a photograph of Rose was substituted.

[38] Christie's 5th May 1891, lot 156, sold to C.F. Murray for £27.6.0.

[39] Information supplied by B. Curle, Local Studies Librarian, Royal Borough of Kensington and Chelsea. Letter of 14th October 1981.

[40] Washington. Library of Congress, Manuscript Division. Pennell Collection.

[41] Letter from John Brett to F.G. Stephens dated '2 Feb.'94' from Daisyfield, Putney. Bodleian Library, Oxford, Special Collections. MS. Don.e.81.

[42] Letter from Meredith to Sandys dated 17th December 1894. Delaware Art Museum Library, Bancroft Archive. Cline, Letter no. 1596.

[43] Letter from Joseph Pennell to J. McNeill Whistler, dated 10th February 1894. Glasgow University Library, MS Whistler, P 212.

[44] Letter from. J. McNeill Whistler to Beatrix Whistler, Dated (from postmark) 28th October 1895. Glasgow University Library, MS Whistler W 624.

[45] This cutting was preserved by the Sandys family but lacks any date or newspaper reference. Sandys Family Archive.

[46] Those letters were 'PRB'. The anonymous correspondent may have been Joseph Pennell.

[47] Walford Graham Robertson (1866–1948), wealthy artist, author and collector, a young dandy in 1890s London.

[48] Letter from Sandys to Graham Robertson, dated 1st March (1895). Henry E. Huntington Library, San Marino, California.

[49] *Eighty-Eight, Not Out* (1939) p. 240.

[50] *Dictionary of National Biography*, Second Supplement, 1912.

[51] William Rothenstein, *Men and Memories* (1935), p. 259.

[52] This is a version of the story of the derivation of Sandys's nickname '£500', in which Rossetti suggested £500 might be raised for Sandys to emigrate to America; Sandys replied that if he had £500, he would not need to go.

[53] W. Graham Robertson, *Time Was* (1931), pp. 91–92.

[54] Christie's, 15th March 1902 (32). Sold to the dealer Thomas McLean. Ashmolean Museum, Oxford. A372. Gift by Robert Langton Douglas in 1921 in memory of his son.

[55] A.S. Hartrick. *A Painter's Pilgrimage Through Fifty Years*. 1939, p. 115.

[56] This woodblock was from the 1860s but the drawing on it was never finished and it was discarded. Pennell probably acquired it from Sandys. Pennell had it photographically reproduced by Carl Hentschel for *The London Garland*, and sold it in 1901 to the Art Gallery of South Australia, Adelaide.

[57] Elizabeth R, and Joseph Pennell, *The Life of James McNeill Whistler*, 2 vols. (1908). *The Whistler Journal* (1921).

[58] Letter from Meredith to Mrs Walter Palmer, dated 16th December 1895. C.L. Cline, *Collected Letters of George Meredith*, vol. 3 (1970). Letter no. 1664.

[59] New Gallery, *Ninth Summer Exhibition*, No. 370. Mrs Walter Palmer.

[60] Letter: Meredith to Alice Meynell, dated 24th April 1896. University of Texas at Austin. Cline, *The Collected Letters of George Meredith*, no. 1689, vol. 3 (1970).

[61] The Guildhall Art Gallery.

[60] *Relations and Complications, Being the Recollections of H.H. The Dayang Muda of Sarawak* (1929). This was ghost-written by the American writer Kay Boyle (1902–1992) who confessed later that the contents were decidedly sketchy owing to her having to work with vague and inadequate information.

[63] Letter from Sandys to Swain, dated 24th April (*c.*1896), from 34 Addison Gardens. Boston, Museum of Fine Art, Hartley Collection. Harold

Hartley had bought the Swain Collection from Joseph Swain's son J.B. Swain.

[64] Letter from Whistler to Sandys, nd. (Probably April 1896) from The Savoy Hotel. This letter was sold by Winifred Sandys, on behalf of Mildred Sandys, to Elizabeth Pennell for £1.0.0., 16th November 1909. Washington, Library of Congress, Manuscript Division. LC 1/469-0471.

[65] Referring to Lewis Carroll's companion stories, *Alice's Adventure in Wonderland* (1865) *and Through the Looking-Glass* and *What Alice Found There* (1871).

[66] Letter from Sandys to Gertrude Sandys, dated Wednesday, 6th May (1896). Sandys Family Archive.

[67] Possibly the oil portrait of Walter Palmer of *c.*1900. It was probably based on the chalk portrait. Untraced.

[68] Letter from Sandys to (George) Macmillan, dated Septr 23rd (1896). University of Reading Library. Macmillan Collection, no. 18/272.

[69] National Trust, Nunnington Hall, Yorkshire. No.979746.

[70] The cheques are dated 9th December and 22nd December 1896. Colman Collection, Norfolk County Record Office.

[71] Lechertier Barbe & Co. were long-established suppliers of artists' materials at 60 Regent Street at this time. They moved to 95 Jermyn Street in 1898 and closed in 1970.

[72] Letter from Sandys to Maud, dated 15th December (1896). Collection of Ruth Edwards, grand-daughter of Maud.

[73] Letter from Sandys to (George) Macmillan, 23rd September 1896, from 34 Addison Gardens. University of Reading Library. Macmillan Collection. 18/272.

[74] This quotation is from an undated and unidentified press-cutting in the Sandys Family Archive.

[75] Reginald Upcher (1841–1898) was a garden designer. The family home of the Upchers was Sheringham Hall, Norfolk.

[76] He stated that the introduction to Sandys came about through Will Meredith, George's son.

[77] Letter from Charles Fairfax Murray to Samuel Bancroft Jr, dated 27th December 1897. R. Elzea, *Delaware Art Museum, Occasional Paper No.2,* (February 1980), Letter no. 79.

[78] W.H. Ward was one of the sons of Marcus Ward, the founder of the famous Belfast lithographic printers and stationers. He had left Belfast to manage the London branch, and became involved in the new photographic reproduction processes.

[79] Missing works (including those mentioned by Wood) are *Judith and Holofernes*, ink drawing, and *Judith*, oil, 1864. *Portrait of Mrs George Meredith*, chalk drawing, 1864. *Mrs William Morris*, oil. 1870. *Mrs Crabbe as Cleopatra*, medium unknown, 1873–76. *Mischief*, chalk drawing, 1875. *Mrs Temple Soanes*, oil portrait, *c.*1878. *Samuel*, chalk drawing, 1885. *Portrait of Christabel Gillilan*, chalk drawing, 1887.

[80] A Consideration of the Art of Frederick Sandys (by Esther Wood). *Special Winter Number of The Artist*, vol. 18 (November 1896) pp. 62–63.

opposite: *Helen Brown*. detail. see page 323

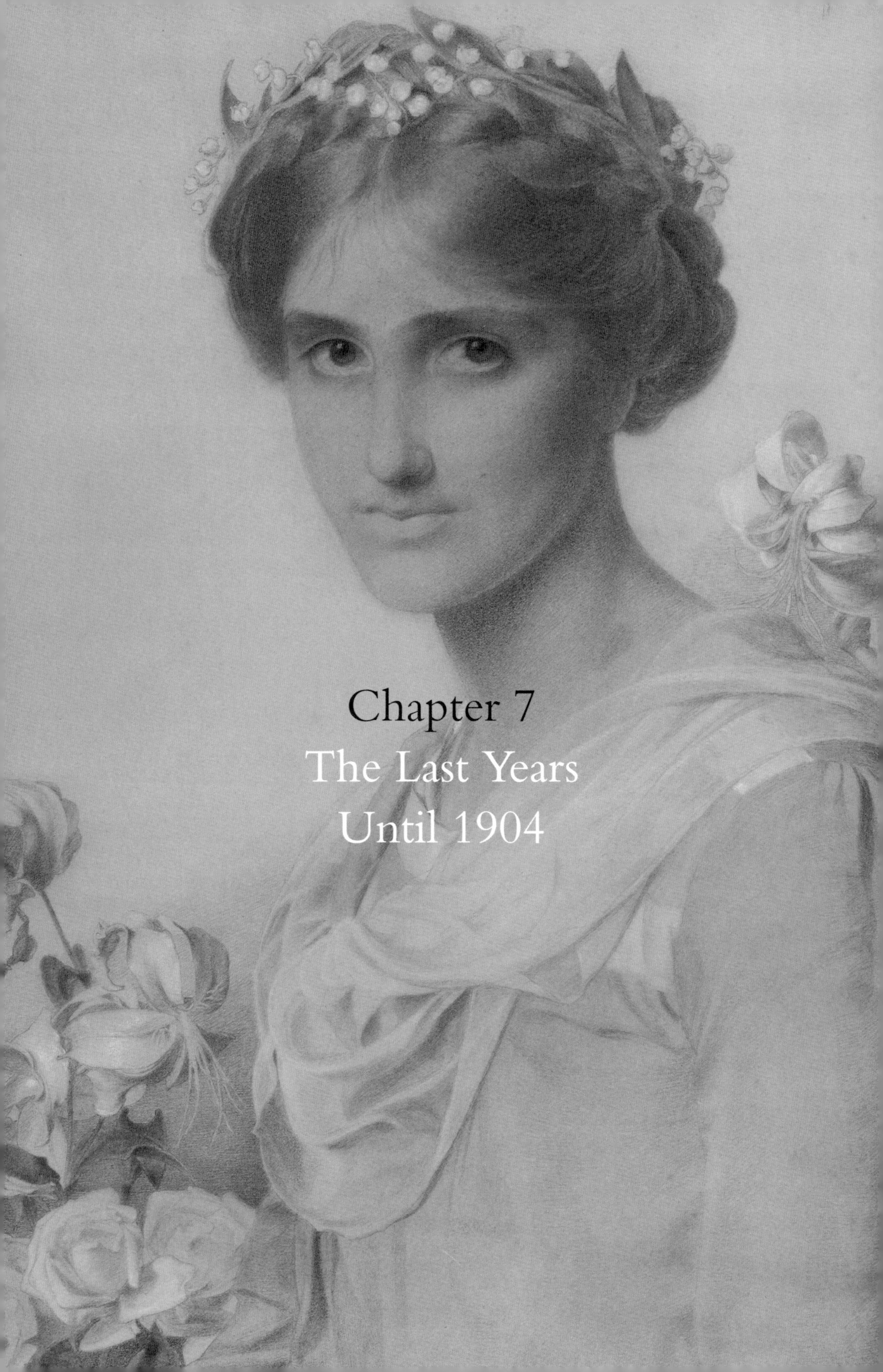

Chapter 7
The Last Years Until 1904

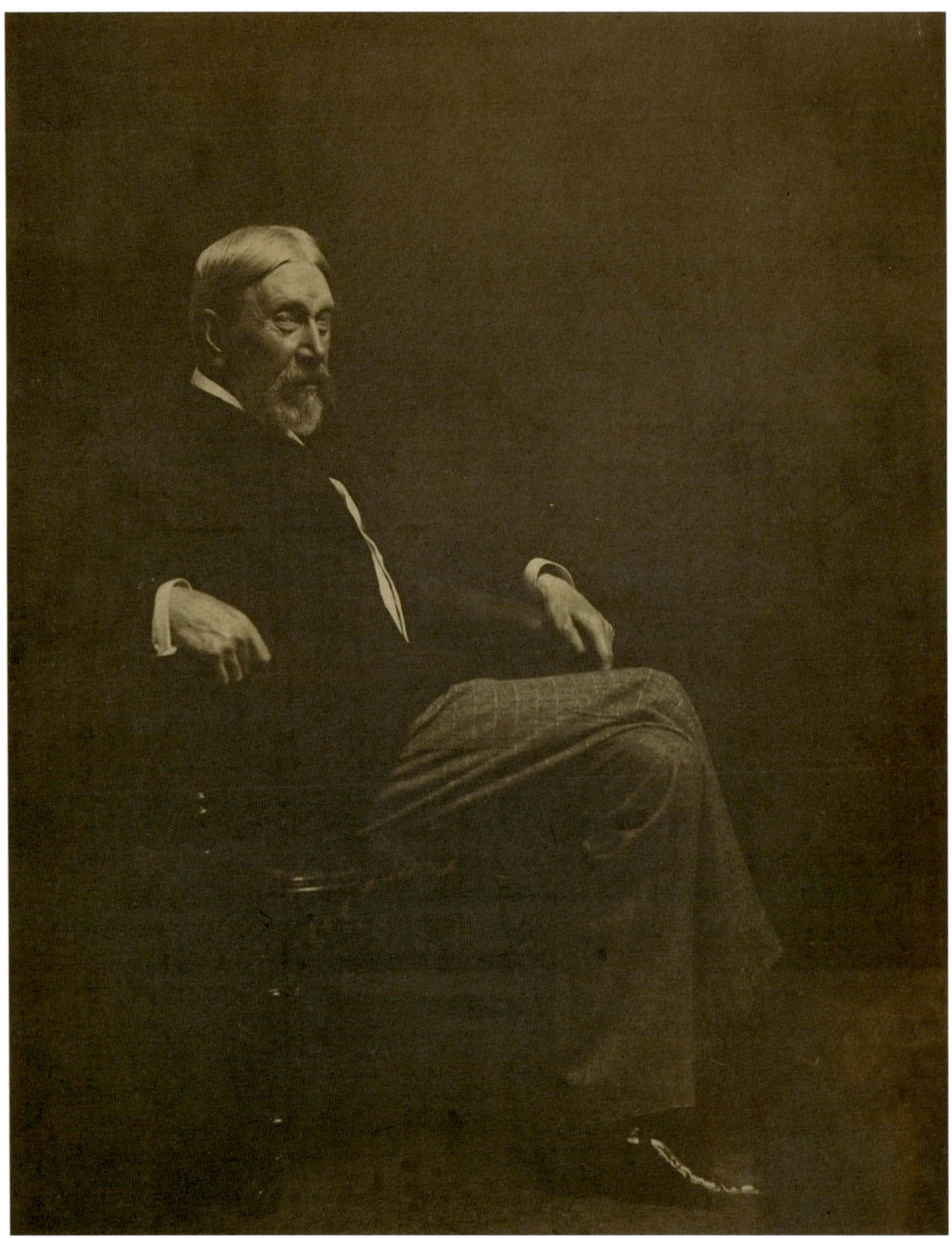

Frederick Sandys in about 1900. The photograph undoubtedly was taken by his friend Percy Wood.

In the unceasing need for money to live on, in the 1890s Sandys entered a period of making copies, or 'versions', of his own work. Such copies can be seen in the 1896, or later drawing *The Weeping Magdalen* (or *Tears, Idle Tears*). Sandys probably made this by copying the Autotype sepia reproduction that appears in the Esther Wood book[1] of his painting *The Magdalen* of 1862, adding a spray of Passiflora – a pot-boiler indeed! As his daughters grew into young women, they were pressed into service as models for further 'fancy head' drawings; thus, we see Winifred figuring in several that date from around this time such as *May* and *Daffodils*, garnished with appropriate flora. One titled *Winifred*, which was illustrated in *The Studio*[2] and is dated 1896, takes the exact pose of his *Miranda* of *c.*1868, together with the flowing hair. Another 'fancy head', of 1898, was drawn from Mildred and, although at first untitled, was bought by William Gilillan and was given the title *Poppies* in the Gilillan sale in 1925. *Iris* was from Winifred and, although dated 1898, was never finished.[3]

The artist Edwin Ward (1859–1935), another witness to Sandys's late years, wrote in his *Recollections of a Savage:* 'He was usually to be found towards the last at the "Punch Bowl Club" where he held his court surrounded by a crowd of admirers enthralled by his stories. Here he could sip his grog in peace and comfort, the cost being defrayed by his audience, and when in the small hours the party separated, the trifling sum for his cab was pressed into his hand without loss of dignity to the lion of the evening. His was a proud spirit which even in his penniless condition had failed entirely to break, and to the last he produced those wonderful drawings which had brought him enduring fame but had failed to provide a sufficiency of means to enable him to spend his declining years in reasonable comfort.'[4]

The founder of this small club was Percy Wood (1860–1904), a sculptor, and a habitual gambler, who became a close friend. Sometime in 1897 Sandys embarked on a portrait of Wood titled *Rah-rih-wah-gas-da*, dressed as a Mohawk Indian chief. Sittings were held at the Club's rooms at 79 Wells Street (which were taken over by the London Sketch Club[5] after the demise of the Punch Bowl Club following Wood's early death). Progress was slow on the portrait, 'owing to the sitter being of rather a restless disposition [it] took four years to complete,' and it was not until 1901 that it was finished and signed.[6] Percy Wood was the son and assistant of the sculptor Marshall Wood (1820–1882), who had been working in Canada, having been commissioned to produce a memorial to the Mohawk Indian chief Joseph Brant (1743–1807), a collaborator with the British colonists, which was unveiled in 1886 in Brantford, Ontario. In recognition of the work he did, the Mohawk tribe honoured the younger Wood by making him a Mohawk chief, of which he was rather proud. Wood also attempted to set himself up as a portrait photographer in London and took a series of fine portraits of Sandys around this time.

A souvenir of a happy time at the Punch Bowl Club is recalled in a printed announcement of their '20th House Dinner' of 23rd February 1900, at which 'Bro. Fredk. Sandys [was] in the Chair'. The Brethren enjoyed a remarkable meal, with a menu well worth quoting at length:

'Soup made from the Tails of Oxen, then a Sir-Loin with Horseradish Sauce, Potatoes in their Jackets and Green Garden Stuffs, then for a change to either an Irish Stew made from the Loins of Southdowns, or a jug made from the pavid Hare, with the usual Red-Currant Jelly, winding up with Jumbles and Gingerbread. Cheese and Bath Olivers, moistened with Nut-Brown Ale and Punch. Nota Bene there will be a special Brew of Punch for our toasting, prepared from a recipe courteously supplied by Mr George Birch FSA, to whom we are also indebted for this delightful drawing.'[7]

There were two portrait commissions which we know about in 1897: a drawing of Adele Donaldson, which must have been done in the spring, for she wears a wreath of forget-me-nots and is surrounded by apple blossom. Another, possibly from later in the year, which is only known through a letter Sandys wrote from Ford Castle in Northumberland to 'Dear little Gertrude', dated only 'Saturday night'. He writes about going to the village shop to buy a postcard of Ford Castle to send her, and about his new friend 'Rover': 'He insisted on walking with me and the Parson.'[8] The sitter for the portrait drawing is unknown, but was probably either Henry, 6th Marquess of Waterford (1875–1911), or his bride, Lady Beatrix Frances Fitzmaurice (1877–1953), who were married on 16th October 1897.

In early August Sandys writes to Charles Fairfax Murray from 34 Addison Gardens, apologising for not recognising him in passing in Bond Street: 'I am short sighted I think you know – the other day when I met you in Bond Street. It was only after a few minutes had passed I recalled you. I wanted to see you. I turned back but you had either got into a bus or turned in [to] some shop. Could you come and see me tomorrow – any time you will[,] if you will wire to me to the above address[.] I should be glad[,] before 10.30[,] but I want you to come to a studio I have at 296 Kings Road, Chelsea. Carlyle Studio – near Carlyle Square.'[9]

Another letter probably connected with Sandys's short-sightedness is addressed from 122 Regent Street to Gertrude: 'Ducketty Wuckety Duck. I rec'd your really long letter, but I can only write you half a short note. But I am quite weighed down by my gigantic indebtedness to you so enclose you a postal order for 10 shillings – better than nothing – will send you the rest shortly. The other 10 shillings is for Mildred and please give her a good bang from me – you know where. Give my love to all and with a tiny bit [to] you. I remain your obliged and very humble servant F.S.' The Regent Street address was that of Negretti & Zambra, opticians, and the letter must date from 1896 or 1897 when Gertrude was ten or eleven.[10]

He wrote again in August to Murray from 34 Addison Gardens: 'I have a chalk drawing of a head – life size – most carefully worked and highly finished. Will you come round to me tomorrow morning (Thursday) at any time between 10.30 and 12 o'clock[?] You might buy it or possibly sell it for me – and so render me a great favour and service. I should like to have kept the drawing myself, but I am very cornered.' On the reverse, he wrote: 'I ought to have £40 or £50 but I will sell it for anything to have … [the cash].'[11]

This was followed by: 'I am much obliged by your note and beg to thank you. I wrote to you having a chalk drawing of a head – the size of life which I was anxious to sell. I fancy you said some years back you would like one or two. I thought it possible you might care to buy this one – or possibly you will know someone who would. And to sell it at once. I ask but a small price – 30 guineas otherwise I should want 60. It has not been seen. I have been too unwell to attend to anything. I took it to Mr J. Davis, 5 Albemarle St – this 5 doors from Piccadilly. His office is on the first floor. On his office door is the name of Mr Knight solicitor. Mr Davis will allow anyone to see it. I should be glad if you would call.'[12]

The drawing which he was hoping to sell was probably one of the two large drawings from the late 1870s which were borrowed for a while by Godwin, probably the one entitled *Penelope* whose early provenance is unknown. Presumably, Sandys raised some money from Davis, leaving it with him for security.

The drawing did not sell, and at the end of August, on the 27th, he was still in need of cash. He wrote to his friend, the engraver, Charles Sherborn pathetically: 'I was promised a little money today, but I have of course been disappointed. Do let me ask you to lend me ten shillings or a sovereign, which I will faithfully return you sometime next week – soon as I receive the money still due on this portrait. I could have had it finished last week had it not being [*sic*] for want of cash to go on with. Now I am stopped for want of both black and brown chalk. I have got a drawing of a head – a capital drawing the size of life – which I ought to get 50 or 60 gns for, but I will sell for 30 gns. I had a man coming to see it last Friday week. He did not come. I waited till Saturday afternoon. I then had to "pop" it for a "fiver". On the Monday he came. I then had not the drawing. You will see this by the enclosed agreement – which please return. I want to try and get it by some good luck in the next day or two. Do lend me a sovereign if you can. I will also do my best to return you some if not all of what I owe you now.'[13] To sweeten the request, he enclosed a voucher for hospitality at the 'Old Welcome Club' at the Earl's Court show ground.

This voucher reveals that he had already met Harold Hartley, the undoubted source, of the voucher who knew and admired Sandys's 1860s illustration work, and was later to help the impoverished family after Sandys's death by buying drawings and studies for illustration still remaining with them.[14] Hartley was the entrepreneur behind a series of spectacular exhibitions, first at Olympia from 1891 to 1892, then at Earl's Court from 1895. In 1897 the exhibition was titled The Victorian Era, to celebrate the Queen's Diamond Jubilee, and was the third in which Hartley was involved as an organiser at the Earl's Court exhibition site.

A few days later, Sandys wrote again to Sherborn from his lodgings in Addison Gardens: 'Tuesday. My dear Sherborn, I send you two photos. They are very fine photos I think. I want dreadfully badly six shillings to enable [me] to go on working and finishing my drawing, and send away by Friday. Now I will either sell the photos to you for six shillings. The price to me is ten. Or, which I should so much prefer, if you will lend me the six shillings till I am paid for the drawing, I shall be delighted to present you with the photos.' The letter was annotated by Sherborn 'August 31st, 1897. 10/-.'[15]

Another soliciting letter, probably from around this time, was written to Edward Burne-Jones, which we know only from Burne-Jones's reply: 'I am sorry for your troubles. I was engaged when your messenger came & have only now read your letter & send the £15 you ask for – I hope it will be of service & be in time, and I will not forget about portraits if ever I am asked.'[16]

When the International Society of Sculptors, Painters and Gravers was formed in December 1897, largely on the initiatives of Joseph Pennell and Whistler, Sandys was elected a member, probably as a courtesy as an elder practitioner. In 1899 he was placed on the executive committee as a further gesture of respect. Whistler, almost as elderly as Sandys, was in place as President, but the main organisers were Pennell and his fellow American Francis Howard, a journalist, who were the active committee members. Harold Hartley was co-opted as an adviser. As a new exhibiting society with a deliberately international outreach, it got off to a good start, and lasted annually until 1925 (though much diminished by the 1914–1918 war). Their dinners were held at the Café Royal where Sandys would be present.[17]

Two Sandys works from private collections were lent to the first show in 1898: the impressive oil portrait of *Mrs Jane Brand* (1874) and the chalk portrait of *Cristabel Gillilan* (1887).[18] At the fifth exhibition, six months after Sandys's death, six of his works were shown by the lenders Harold Hartley and Walter Palmer.[19]

These are the years when Sandys, as a survivor from the Pre-Raphaelite heyday (Rossetti had died in 1882, Brown in 1893, Millais in 1896, and Burne-Jones in June 1898), assumed somewhat of a reputation as an authority on the period for the younger generation of artists and bohemians. In memoirs of the time, he was noticed as a habitué of the Café Royal in Regent Street, holding forth to his juniors, or anyone who would offer him a drink or a coffee. As Joseph Comyns Carr (1849–1916), the art and drama critic wrote: 'Sandys remained to the last a remarkable talker, keenly critical, and on occasion warmly appreciative. There was a period during his later life when he might be found almost any afternoon in the lower room of the Café Royal, and there, over a cigar and a cup of coffee, he would gossip freely of those earlier days during his association with Rossetti, always taking care, as it seemed to me, to let it be understood that when his own association with any one of the men of that time had ceased, they had ceased to be afterwards very interesting or notable.

Comyns Carr continued: 'I remember Whistler used to give some very humorous imitations of incidents that occurred in Sandys's studio, and he was particularly happy in the reproduction of a scene between the painter and his father – real or fanciful I cannot pretend to say – in which something of the haughty reticence and reserve exhibited on both sides was very entertainingly reproduced.'[20]

Robert Ross[21] recalled Sandys being seen at the Café Royal in the company of Aubrey Beardsley,[22] Will Rothenstein,[23] and other young artists. It may have been there where Sandys met Robert Ponsonby Staples, the eccentric Irish artist who was active in London around the turn of the century and was often to be found at the Café Royal. Around 1899 to 1900 he made a profile portrait in pastels of Sandys 'while at work' which he offered to the National Portrait Gallery in 1930.[24] It was turned down by the then Assistant Director Henry M. Hake and returned (it is now untraced). Ponsonby Staples wrote in

1930: 'Sandys may be a bit forgotten, but I remember the reverence shown to him by Alfred Gilbert, the sculptor, on my introduction one evening.'[25]

In her recollections of 1898, we start to read much about Sandys in Elizabeth Pennell's *The Whistler Journal* (1921), in particular after he visited the Pennell's London apartment in Buckingham Street on 3rd October. She wrote: 'Sandys came early in the afternoon, a little after two. J [Joseph Pennell] had to leave almost at lunch for a Committee Meeting at South Kensington for the Lithograph show. But Sandys stayed on until half past six and talked steadily the whole afternoon. It was like listening to, instead of reading, a book of memoirs. He told one story after another, so that it would be hopeless to try and remember them all (more's the pity). J's connection with the coming exhibition of Lithographs at South Kensington and the fact that Sandys'[s] *Nightmare* ... is to be shown, started him talking about it.[26] He thought our impression was one of ten printed on India paper, but, looking at it more closely, he found it was not.[27] He hardly knew whether it could be called a lithograph. It was done partly with a brush, partly with a pen, on zinc with some sort of ink brought to him by a man who patented the method. It was out five days after the Academy opened [the Royal Academy of 1857][28] and three hundred were sold the first week and then the man disappeared with the plate and has never been heard of since.'[29]

She continued, re-telling the story about how he snatched a likeness of Rossetti for the caricature by calling on him in Chatham Place to ask if he could see his paintings. Of the figures he caricatured, Rossetti became his friend, Millais (whom Sandys already knew) seemed non-committal, Holman Hunt was indignant, but Ruskin's father was 'furious' and wanted to prosecute the perpetrator of the cartoon – who was of course unknown at the time since the print was anonymous. He tackled George Smith, the publisher (of Smith & Elder), and offered £500 if the artist could be named. Nothing seems to have come of this.

Another of Sandys's stories of his early days which Elizabeth Pennell recorded was about Millais. He thought that he was 'as beautiful as a god in his youth'. He also told her about the winning of the Silver Medal of the Society of Arts. *The Society of Arts Premium Lists, 1846-53*, in fact, state that in the 1846–1847 session that the Silver Isis Medal was conferred on him.

This led to further memories: '[Sandys] tried to reunite Millais and Rossetti, who did not see each other because Rossetti was hurt at Millais not having suggested his name for the Royal Academy when there was the chance. Sandys asked Rossetti to dinner, saying Millais was to be there, and Rossetti would not come. Then Sandys asked him without telling him, and Rossetti came, and the two were friends again at once. Millais begged to be asked to the studio to see Rossetti's pictures and asked Rossetti to come and see his children – he had some very pretty children, he said. But Rossetti never went and never asked Millais to come to him and so they lost sight of each other again[30] – [furthermore] Rossetti was cruelly represented by William Michael Rossetti, Sandys thought, for he was really the most abstemious of men – knew so little of wine that, having tasted a "bishop" of ordinary claret warmed with spices, wanted to make one of fine old Madeira worth about two or three pounds a bottle that someone had given him. Sandys was shocked and would not allow it.' My thought is that this story illustrates rather more Rossetti's extravagance than his ignorance.

Following this is a most interesting anecdote of an outing in about 1861: 'Sandys went once with Rossetti, Swinburne and Meredith to Hampton Court, and between Waterloo and Hampton Court Station each one of the three wrote a poem. He remembered Swinburne's in particular because it was *Faustine*[31] written to see how many rhymes he could find to the name.'[32]

Meredith, as we have noted, was a faithful friend of Sandys. Elizabeth Pennell further recorded from her conversations with Sandys: '[He was] loud in praise of Meredith as a brilliant talker', but as she continued, Sandys showed an unexpected insight into Meredith's character: 'He was wonderful though at the expense of his friends. Often had three or four friends dining with him on Sunday and, if the humour seized him, would select one of the company and dissect him for the benefit of the others … this lost him many friends, [and] was the reason for his quarrel with Rossetti.'[33] This is borne out by Rossetti's biographer who wrote that, after Meredith's original agreement to share the Cheyne Walk house with the Rossetti brothers and Swinburne, he irritated Gabriel Rossetti so much at breakfast one day (in the summer of 1863) that he threw a cup of tea at Meredith – and Meredith departed![34]

Elizabeth Pennell also recorded Sandys's opinion of Ruskin's marital behaviour thus: 'Ruskin treated Lady Millais when she was Mrs Ruskin abominably. He was not brutal, he never reproved her. But he kept a diary, and every Monday morning he had her up before him and read her a list of all her misdemeanours for every day in the past week.'[35] This is ironic after what we know about Sandys's own behaviour towards his first (and only legal) wife Georgiana (see p. 26, 38).

Later on, in July 1903, when Mrs Pennell was talking to the illustrator A.S. Hartrick (1864–1950), he had a Sandys story (which must have come from

Whistler originally): 'Whistler at Sandys' studio met Sandys' father [this must have been sometime before 1883, as Anthony Sandys died that year].[36] Sandys asked the old gentleman, "Will you have a glass of port father?" "Well, Fred, I don't mind if I do!" And Sandys searched elaborately in a cupboard, "Strange there does not seem to be any port, will you have some brandy, father?" "Well, Fred, I don't mind if I do!" Another search pursued then: "Strange, I can't find the brandy. Will gin do father?" "Why, yes, Fred", and Sandys called the slavey, "Run and get a penn'orth of gin" Then the father, as elaborately, got out a cigar case with two cigars in it, offered it to Whistler who refused, then to Sandys who took one. The old gentleman put the case back in his pocket, elaborately, got out his knife and handed it to Sandys, "Do you know which end to cut off, Fred?"'[37]

Alas, owing to his peculiar Micawber-like quality, combining dignity with impecuniosity, but perhaps not with Micawber's perennial optimism, I am afraid Sandys was often open to ridicule. In truth, he was his father's son, even to the touch of dandyism in keeping up appearances.

In the 1890s the Pennells established after-dinner 'at home' evenings on Thursday nights, at their apartment in Buckingham Street, providing them with much useful art world gossip. However, Elizabeth wrote in her *Nights*[38] that Sandys: 'Seemed to prefer the evenings when we were alone, to my surprise, for the homage he received when he did come on Thursday must have been pleasant. Drawings of his hung prominently in our rooms, J. then hunting the salesrooms for the originals of the Sixties as industriously as the barrows and shops for their reproductions. And so to the man who prefers fame to reach him during his lifetime, surely it should have been an agreeable experience to sit, or to be enthroned as it were, in so friendly an atmosphere, with some of his own finest work on the wall behind him for background, and surrounded by a worshipping group asking nothing better than to be allowed to sit at his feet and listen to his every word – which was a sacrifice for his worshippers in Buckingham Street who rejoiced in the sound of their own voices as did most of the company. But the Nineties are not more wonderful and stimulating to the young men of today who look back to them so admiringly, than the Sixties were to us whom they kept up into the small hours of many a Friday morning, inexhaustible as a subject of our talk, and Sandys, standing for the Sixties and all we found in them so admirable, could command any sacrifice.'

'We looked upon the "men of the Sixties" as masters, among them giving to Sandys a leading place. If he was not any longer doing the work for which we took off our hat to him, he certainly looked the leader – tall, handsome, dignified, just enough of a stoop in his shoulders to become his age, his dress irreproachable, the white waistcoat immaculate, pale yellow hair parted in the middle and beautifully brushed, beard not patriarchal exactly but eminently correct and well cared for, manners princely. It was clear that he liked the role of master and his voice was in keeping with the part. But he was a master who presided at his best over a small audience, and, no doubt knowing it, he avoided our Thursdays.

'He was also a master given to small gossip. We heard from him less of art, its aims and ideals, its mediums and methods, than of the sayings and doings of the Pre-Raphaelites who were his friends and contemporaries. The name of "Gabriel" was ever in his mouth. It was Rossetti whom he most loved – or love is not the word, less of affection revealed in his memories than a sense of injury, as if it had somehow been the fault of "Gabriel" and the others that he had not come off as well as they, though of all "Gabriel" had been the most active in seeing him through the tight places he so successfully got himself into. This, no doubt, was the reason Rossetti felt entitled to a little laugh now and then over Sandys's difficulties. Sandys was a man who needed to be seen through tight places until the end, as we had occasion to know by the urgent note he sent us on a Saturday night, more than once, from the Café Royal, his favourite in his later years, where a variety of unavoidable accidents, with a curious faculty for repeating themselves, would keep him prisoner until his friends came to his relief.

'He was full of anecdote, which was quite in the order of things, the Sixties having supplied anecdote for a whole library of books and magazines. Could I tell Sandys's stories with Sandys's voice I should be tempted to repeat them yet once again, though many were told us also by Whistler, and these J. [Joseph] and I have recorded in the *Life*. Whistler told them better, with more truth because with more gaiety and joy in their absurdity. And yet, the solemnity of Sandys added a personal flavour, gave them a character nobody else could give. I have not forgotten how he turned into a parable the tale of the cross-eyed maid in the Morris shop in Red Lion Square, whose eyes were knocked straight by a shock the company of Morris, Marshall and Faulkner administered deliberately, and then were shocked crooked again by a shock they had not provided for or against. And, as Sandys recalled them, the strange beasts in "Gabriel's" house and garden might have been let loose from out of the Apocalypse. But Sandys's voice has been stilled forever and the anecdotes have been published oftener, I do believe, than any others in the world's rich store of clichés.'

It was at the Pennells's apartment that Sandys first met Walter Crane, as the latter related in his *Reminiscences*.[39] He gave praise to Sandys's draughtsmanship and imagination, besides commenting that: 'He had a strange penetrating gaze, and a somewhat sarcastic way of speaking.' Neither could then have foreseen that their children, Lionel Crane and Gertrude Sandys, would fall in love and marry some six years later in 1913 (apparently with parental disfavour on both sides).

In 1898 Sandys executed two portraits. They were of the Hon. Charles Napier Lawrence (1855–1927), created Lord Lawrence of Kingsgate in 1923, and his American wife Catherine, née Sumner, (d.1934). Lawrence was a son of the great 'Lawrence of the Punjab' who was Viceroy of India from 1864 to 1869. He was a businessman and railway executive who evidently had an interest in art. He had two early oils by Sandys: *Oriana* (1861), which was sold to him by Charles Fairfax Murray in the early 1900s, and *La Belle Ysoude* (or *Ysolde*) of 1862. Lawrence bought the latter from Agnew's in 1920. Both were originally in the Clabburn collection. He also owned Burne-Jones's *The Depths of the Sea*. Lady Lawrence was later to take an interest in Sandys's daughters, as we know from letters from Winifred Sandys to Samuel Bancroft Jr in 1913. She was helpful with arrangements for the clandestine marriage of Gertrude Sandys to Lionel Crane[40] and was witness, together with Winifred, to the nuptials at St Mary Abbot's Church, Kensington, on 2nd August 1913.

Sandys had a letter from his friend John Brett on New Year's Day 1899 thanking him for the 'magnificent turkey', which he had sent, and invited him, Winifred, and Mildred to dinner on 3rd January. Sandys certainly had a good Norfolk source for turkeys, for Christmas turkey gifts to particular friends feature often enough in his correspondence to establish it as a regularity. How he could afford to do this, though, is the question, as he was bankrupted in 1899. It is also to be noted that only two daughters were invited by Brett. Mary presumably had to stay at home and cook for the rest of the brood who were too young to be included. Incidentally, a clue that John Brett was unwell by 1899 is the state of his handwriting in this letter.[41] Brett died in December 1900.

The only known portrait by Sandys with an 1899 date was a half-length of Olive Slaughter (b.1887) the only daughter of Sir William Capel Slaughter (1857–1917), a notable solicitor specialising in business law (Slaughter and May of 18 Austin Friars, E.C.). Olive is surrounded by spring flowers, indicating the time of year of the sittings. Almost certainly the commission came through the Lawrences.[42] Olive married Jack Sanders, who was acquainted with Edgar Wallace (1875–1932), the author of the best-selling *Sanders of the River* (1911). It was said that the author used his name for the title.[43]

Also dated 1899 is a female head, and another undated replica of it. Both are unfinished to various degrees. The more complete one was bought at Christie's by Harold Hartley[44] and was illustrated in *The Studio* in October 1904 as owned by him. The weaker version remained with the family until it was sold by Constance Sandys for £30 to the Victoria and Albert Museum in 1921. The sitter was Mildred Sandys, as attested by Constance.[45]

Other related unfinished works are an untitled full-length female nude figure drawing, measuring just over four feet, which probably would have had 'classical' drapery added to it,[46] and another of the head only, which has been given the title *Persephone*.[47] Such unfinished works must have been a result of Sandys's frequent ill-health at this time. Two letters exist that were written to the Pennells, one dated 21st March 1900 and the other probably from a little earlier. Sandys wrote to Joseph Pennell asking for a loan of £4 or £5. He wrote: 'I have had this shocking Influenza and have been in bed more or less for six weeks. Although I am now better, I am left so weak I can hardly get about. … My son brings this. I should have come myself, but I am too tired to do so.'[48] The other letter is to Elizabeth Pennell from Winifred Sandys; she wrote: 'My father asks me to write and thank you for your letter and kind remembrance of him, but he is not at all well.' She also thanks her for putting forward one of her poems to the editor of *The Century*, an American magazine (it was not accepted).[49]

Although at a low ebb physically, a cheerful thought came to Sandys, as his old friend George Meredith related in a letter to Leslie Stephen, in which he was concerned with Stephen's ill-health at the time: 'You will not be like Sandys, the artist, who to my condolence, replied – "Never was so happy in my life!" – Bailiffs had been after him for thirty years, and in bed he lay smiling.'[50]

Sandys had eventually mustered all of his energies by the spring, enlivened with the prospect of a commissioned portrait. This was to be of the wife and two young sons of Henry Edmund Christy of Lordington, Emsworth, Sussex, and it is dated 1900.[51] He wrote several letters to Gertrude (now fourteen) from Lordington, one dated: 'Monday night … I wish you were here with me – to hear the cuckoo crying out from wood to wood. To see all the little birds all busy feeding all their little ones. Some flycatchers chasing flies in the most wonderful way to take home to the little gaping mouths, little I say. I ought to say large. These little boys are rather troublesome sitters. I do not know what to do with them. What can you recommend? The whip? I have not anything to say only that Mr Christy has in the field adjoining his lawn about 500 young pheasants, some a day old and some a week old. Most absurd little things … give my love to the black beetles and mind you do not stamp on one. Your loving old Pap – Ask Guy to send me at once two of the reproductions he has of the head of the big boy – as *Samuel* – and one of the *Medea* I want.'[52]

Another from Lordington, dated 'Saturday night': 'My dear little Gertrude. You write one tiny little note and you write no more. Surely you have something to say – or am I quite forgotten. Tell Guy to write and let me know all he has been doing and how Wood is and how the Punch Bowl goes on.[53] … I am drawing two very nice little boys – but they are shocking – terrible bad sitters – I do not know what to do with them. Cannot you tell me what to do – this afternoon the eldest Stephen his name is – but he is called Stephie – would not sit at all – would turn the back of his head. I promised him toys – the chalk I had sent down, but no use, he would keep his back to me. I was nearly mad. Yesterday he sat fairly well. What am I to do I ask you[?]

'I have been working very hard from 10 or 10.30 to seven and after. This evening I did not leave off till the gong went to dress for dinner at 7.30 so I feel extra good – a sort of old worn out but charming angel – I ought to have used a large A for angel but you will forgive that.

'There's such a lot of birds here singing away all day long. A Green Woodpecker has a nest somewhere near my bedroom window – where I do not quite know but I see them constantly flying out to a tree just opposite for some insects for the young one I suspect. There are in the Park over five hundred little pheasants just out of their shells hatched by a lot of old hens (chickens). This rain is, Mr Christy says, unfortunate for them, if they get out of the coops away from the hens into the long grass they will be drowned – fancy being drowned in wet grass. No one answers my notes but I hope you will. Tell me everything you can think of. Mrs Christy is so nice. She is the daughter of a great Admiral[.] Her brother is at the Cape and has won the Victoria Cross. He is a great gunner. I must go to bed now for it is just twelve o'clock and I am always called at 7.30 and get up and have my breakfast at 8.40. With my very best love, yours lovingly F.S.'

Both boys died at the Western Front in 1916, Stephen in July, and Basil in October. This group portrait must have been a poignant reminder to the family.

In April 1900, Mrs Barstow, the sitter for a portrait in the mid-to late 1860s (it is one of Sandys's finest), wrote to him, asking that he come to Shenley

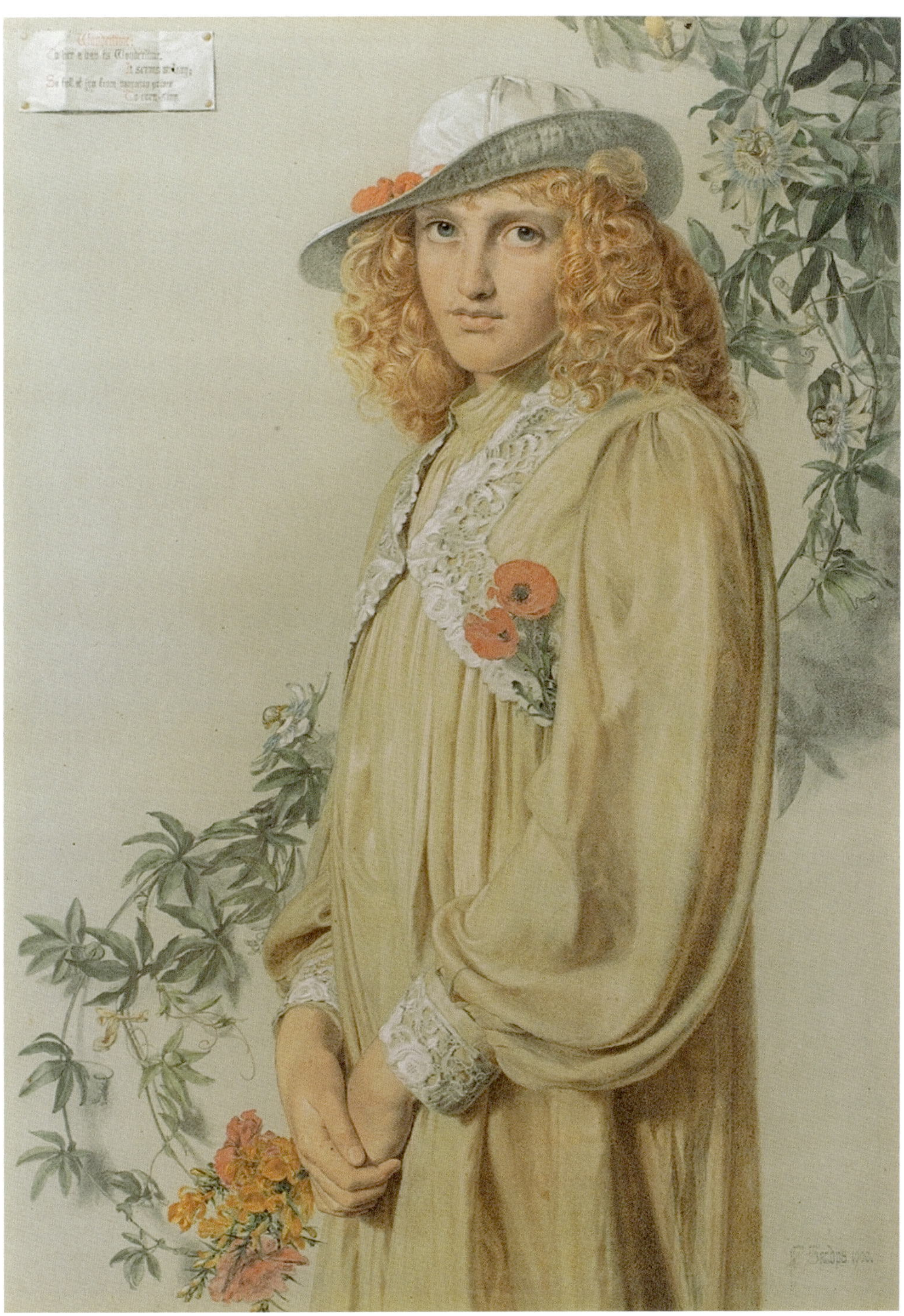

Wondertime. Chalk drawing. 1900. In fact a portrait of his youngest child, Gertrude.

in Hertfordshire, where she was now living, to sign her unfinished portrait.[54] This picture had suffered from an earlier episode of financial difficulty when Sandys was occupying his painting room at 47 Leicester Square. The Barstows had removed it lest it be carried away by bailiffs. The portrait remains unfinished and unsigned to this day.

Wondertime was not a commissioned portrait but an inspired one of Gertrude at this time. This and *The Red Cap,* also of 1900, mark the appearance of Gertrude, aged fourteen, as a more frequent model now that she was growing up. *Wondertime* was shown at the Leicester Galleries between February and March 1904, after which it was in the hands of Lawrie and Co. of 159 New Bond Street (a gallery lasting from 1893 to October 1904, when the partnership was dissolved).[55] It was sold at Christie's in January 1905 for £42 to a Mr Heldemann. *The Red Cap* was 'bought from the artist' by the Scottish collector William Connal but was sold a few years later in 1908.[56] Also in 1900, Sandys was reported to have begun an oil portrait of Walter Palmer, the work interrupted by the General Election of 1900, on account of Palmer's involvement.[57] Palmer was elected Conservative member for Salisbury. Perhaps circumstances prevented the resumption of work on the portrait as it has not been traced, finished or unfinished.

In the second half of the 1890s and early 1900s, several Sandys children appear to have had seaside holidays at Pevensey Bay in East Sussex. Sandys would sometimes stay nearby to visit them, at a small boarding house named Harold Lodge in the village of Pevensey. There is a faded snapshot showing Sandys and his daughter Gertrude standing together on a beach, no doubt at Pevensey Bay, which must have been taken around 1901.[58] The 1901 census shows that six of the children were staying at Kilmarnock in Marine Terrace, Pevensey Bay: Mildred (aged twenty-four), Maude (twenty-two), Constance (twenty), Ruth (eighteen), and Gertrude (twelve), all under the supervision of Guy (seventeen), as 'Head'. They were listed as 'living on own means'.

A letter from Sandys is undated but perhaps written in early August 1900 to: 'My dear little Gertrude. First[,] before I forget[,] tell Winifred she is to buy you a pair of boots at once either in Pevensey or Eastbourne. Next write and tell me all you are doing. I am glad Guy threw a stone at the jellyfish even if it did not hit it. It must have been a great lark for seeing the tents all blown about – but why did not you go to Eastbourne to see the wreck[?] Give my love all round and a kiss – two for you[.] With love Yours F.S.'[59] The wreck may have been the two-masted ship *Caroline* carrying coals from Goole which was driven ashore at Eastbourne during a storm in early August 1900.

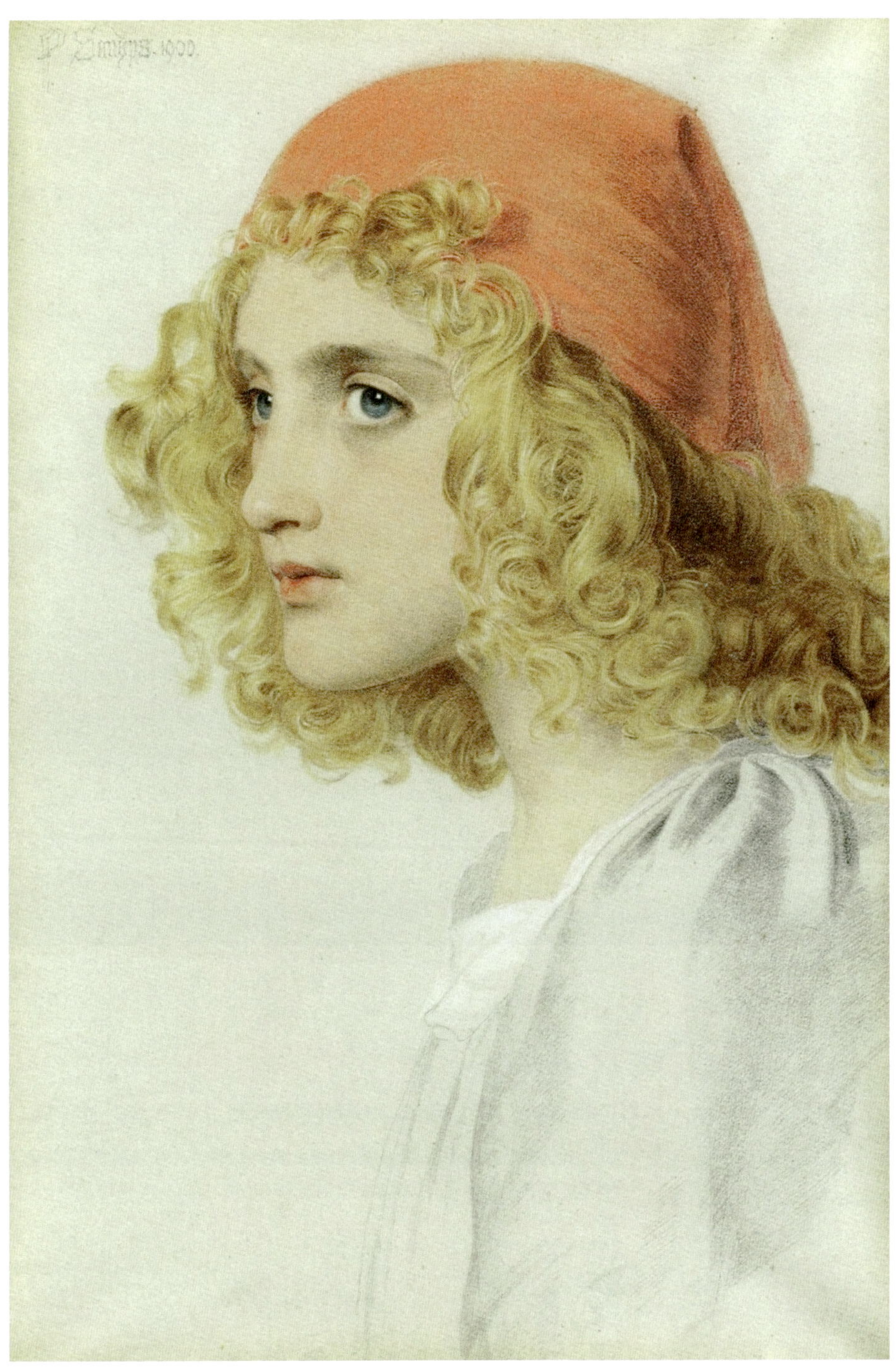

The Red Cap. Chalk drawing. 1900. Gertrude was the model.

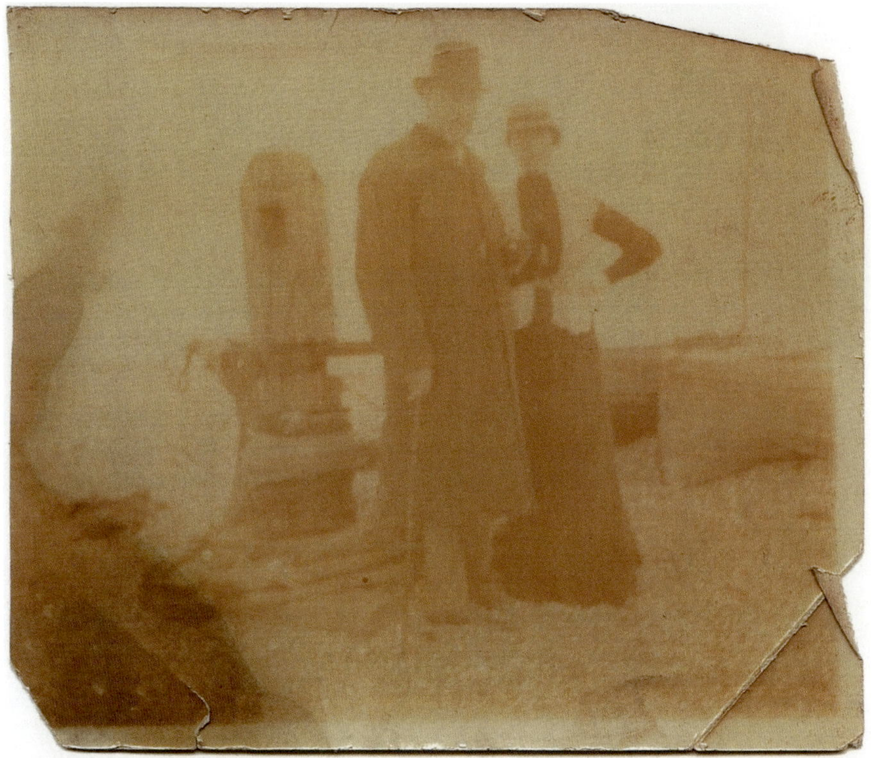

Sandys and Gertrude, his youngest child, a snapshot taken on the beach undoubtedly at Pevensey Bay. *c.*1900.

Val Prinsep and his wife Florence, née Leyland, started buying property at Pevensey Bay in the early 1890s, now that they had a young family (their three sons were born in 1886, 1888, and 1894); Val also built himself a summer studio there. Was it then a coincidence that Sandys's children holidayed at Pevensey Bay too? Sandys had known Val Prinsep since the open house Sundays at Little Holland House, the home of Val's parents. Sandys was there, for instance in 1862 in mid-July, which we know from George du Maurier's letter to his mother (see pp. 76-77). He had also been a neighbour of Prinsep in Holland Park Road in the mid-1880s. However, any such Pevensey connection remains unsubstantiated.

There is a poignant undated letter to Mary headed: 'Wednesday – 5.30' to 'Dear little Girl – That you are having a most horrible time goes without saying – even here we are beginning to feel it. How you are getting on for food and how Guy get[s] on plagues me. Not receiving a telegram from you makes me feel certain you have not succeeded in your effort to get even £30, and what you really want is £200 to go on with. And I seem helpless to advise. One piece of good news I have to send you – although it does not help us in this immediate need – I have drawn a head of Gertrude the size of life infinitely better than the *Wondertime*.[60] I should entirely finish it on Saturday. I should not sell it for less than 60 gns – so when the time comes there is so much more. I have never done such a good or beautiful head – if one had paid for the last frame I should at once order one. Gertrude has sat so well. If no money turns up by the morning's post[,] I do not know how we shall pull through the day. I do hope something will. [I have four pence left – deleted]. I feel very much for your forlorn state in London – what can be done[?] I have only time to catch the post – Yours aff. F.S.'[61]

The head of Gertrude to which he refers is very likely *The Red Cap*, which is one of the best of his late works in chalk.

In the 1901 census the rest of the family, Mary, Winifred, Hugh, and Sandys himself, were listed as being at 279 Colherne Road, near the Brompton Cemetery. The 'Head' of the inhabitants listed there was Margaret Ann Briers, 'Boarding House Keeper'. There were four other boarders and two servants. Hugh, listed as twenty-five years old, was by this time a mining engineer. He was incorrectly listed as being born at Norwich (he was actually born in Belgravia when Sandys had the studio house at Spenser Street).

In June 1901 we learn that Sandys had an accident to his left eye, as he explained in a letter to Lord Wolseley, a possible future sitter: 'I had the misfortune in striking a wax match to splash some of the burning sulphur into my left eye [but] I am very thankful to say the eye is quite itself again.' He goes on to respond to what must have been an enquiry about a portrait: 'My price for chalk drawing similar to the one I made of your Lordship is one hundred guineas. I do so hope one of these times I may have the honour of painting your portrait, thus having more opportunity of doing justice to you.'[62]

Also in 1901, he drew portraits of Mrs Elizabeth Wylie and her daughter Miss Barbara Wylie. Barbara Wylie (1862–1954) was a close friend of Emmeline Pankhurst and was one of the 'militant' suffragettes who were imprisoned.[63]

As he had been paid for these two portraits, perhaps a celebration was made possible: 18th November 1901, finds Sandys 'At Home' at 32 Earl's Court Gardens at 7 o'clock according to a formal invitation card ('Full Dress') sent to 'Miss Gertrude Sandys'.[64] Since Gertrude's birthday was 4th December, it may have been intended as a party for her.

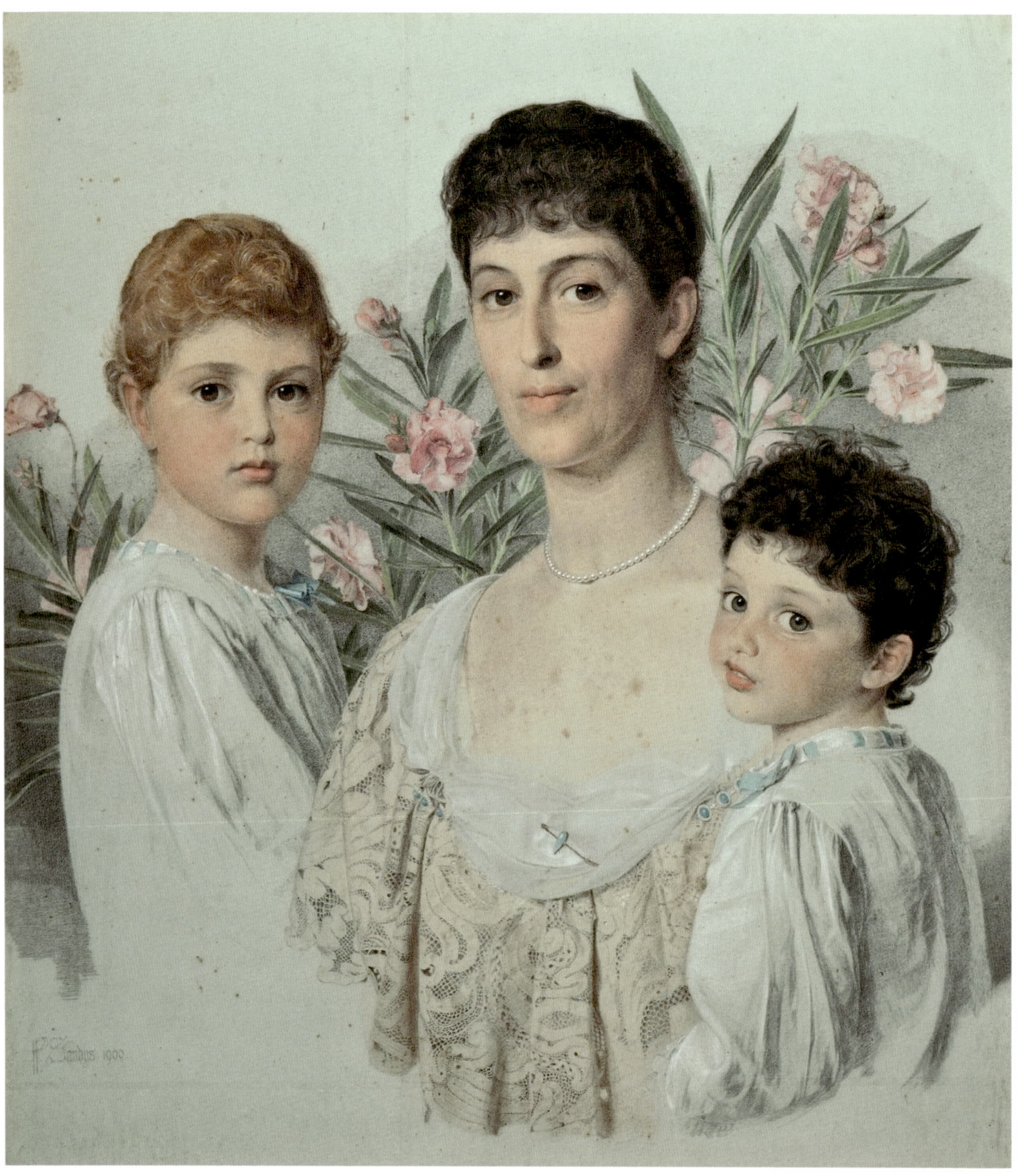

Mrs Henry Edmund Christy and her two sons, Stephen and Basil. Chalk drawing. 1900. A fine example of his late portrait work.

One of his more successful late works was *The White Mayde of Avenel* for which daughter Mildred sat. The principal version is a half-length figure wrapped in white draperies which fly in the wind to the left and right of her head. In a letter to Samuel Bancroft Jr in 1908, Winifred Sandys wrote: 'The subject is taken from Sir Walter Scott's novel *The Monastery*.'[65]

Sandys made at least three undated replicas of the head only of this subject, of varying quality, two of which were bought by his supporters Harold Hartley and William Gillilan. Another work, dated 1902, he titled *Peace and War* and used it in drawings of two opposing half-figures of Connie and Gertrude. Connie, the frowning one, representing 'War', and Gertrude, 'Peace', whose head was copied from *The Laurel Wreath* of 1902.[66]

Also, in 1902 Sandys decided to make a new version of his well-known *Proud Maisie* of the late 1860s (which had been inspired by the young Mary Emma Jones). This time the model was daughter Gertrude, his new inspiration, and William Gillilan bought it to add to his collection.[67] It was later bought by the National Gallery of Canada from Colnaghi's in 1925. Sandys made two more replicas of this in 1903.

Nearing the end of his life and in ill health, Sandys was working as hard as possible, and in 1903 produced about eight large chalk drawings. Firstly, as a wedding present, he drew a pair of portraits of his son Hugh and his new wife Alice Mary.[68] They were married at her local parish church, St Luke's, Paddington on 3rd June 1903. Hugh's portrait shows that he had become a handsome young man with a large light brown moustache in the fashion of the day. By 1903 he was a Mining Engineer, having most probably studied at the Royal School of Mines (then housed, between 1872 and 1913, in the Huxley Building at South Kensington).[69] They had no children. Travel records show him as visiting South America and Africa on business, and Montreal (perhaps to see his brother Guy who had emigrated there). Alice Mary died in 1950, and Hugh in 1953 by drowning in Spain – suspected as a suicide by his nephew Anthony Crane who had to travel to Seville to identify his body.

From the Hartley correspondence we find him sending Sandys money for several purchases and requesting a photographic portrait. Sandys's replies state that he had promised to sit for Hollyer and to Dallmeyer,[70] others which had been taken by amateurs he considered failures.[71] At the time Hartley was deeply involved with the exhibitions at Earl's Court, and he sent Sandys and the family free tickets to the exhibitions and the 'Welcome Club' on the site.

Sandys's association with the art dealer Ernest Brown (*c.*1853–1915), judging by correspondence,[72] began about 1900 when Brown was working for the Fine Art Society, the Bond Street gallery where Brown had been since the 1870s. Brown was in charge of organising and mounting exhibitions, as well as with the publication of etchings. This was during the so-called 'Etching Revival'.

Ernest Brown was a kind and compassionate man, as demonstrated by the following recollection by his son, Oliver Brown (1885–1956): 'My father had met him coming out of a bar in the North End Road.[73] … He was shocked by his poor and shabby condition, so unlike the Sandys he had known. He brought him to our house, the first of many visits when he would stay for hours, never stopping his reminiscent talk of the time when he lived with Rossetti and when Swinburne and Meredith had been his friends. On other visits I recall that he was immaculately dressed. Sandys was a handsome and distinguished-looking figure even in his old age. He had four unmarried grown-up daughters when we knew him and life was not easy for them. He had managed to quarrel with his old friends and patrons. The most notable of them, Cyril Flower (afterwards Lord Battersea), had given him many generous commissions some twenty-five years before, but they had not been on speaking terms for years until they met again in the [Leicester] Galleries during the Sandys exhibition.' The exhibition had been organised by Brown during February and March 1904.[74]

In one of his many letters to Brown, Sandys discusses the completion of a drawing which Brown seems to have been interested in acquiring: he could not complete it until he could pay the model, implying that he needed an advance. Since the model was no doubt one of his daughters, it may have been a stratagem to obtain some much-needed cash. At the same time, he said that he had a 'finished sketch … for an oil painting' and would sell it for 15 guineas.[75]

While still at the Fine Art Society, Brown had received another letter from a distressed Sandys:[76] 'I have been very uncomfortable and most unwell – so I have been able to work but little. I have three heads here unfinished – two you have seen. Two to you when finished would be £15 each – and one £10. I want you to let me have £1.10 tonight or as much as you can tonight, the rest tomorrow when I will call at Bond Street. I cannot walk or I should have called at Bond Street today. I send you thirteen photographs to keep till I complete or repay you.[77] The photos average to me 5 shillings each. I do not mean this as the prices they would fetch. I simply send them as a proof of good faith. I shall be here tomorrow morning if you are able to call – but pray send me as much as you can, if not the £1.10. I must get into town tomorrow morning and I cannot walk. If I could have had three pounds I could have finished these drawings two months since.'

There are seven letters or notes from Sandys to Brown headed 32 Earl's Court Gardens, variously dated 'Monday evening', 'Friday' and, 'Wednesday evening' etc., which must date between 1901 and 1903 when Sandys was at that address. Excerpts from these include: 'I want you to lend me £1 this evening. I ought to have received some [money] today. However I was disappointed and shall now have I fear to wait till after Ascott [*sic*]. ...'[78] And 'will you call on me here on Sunday next between 3 and 4.30. I shall be glad if you will. I want you to see your drawing ... I have been hoping for some time you would call. ... Will you call on me on your way into town tomorrow (Wednesday) morning[?] I have a little drawing which I call *Highland Mary*[79]... I have put some very good drapery round the head of the *White Lady of Avenel* I have a little more to do to the face – which I shall do tomorrow.[80] I want you to call here tomorrow morning (Thursday), look at your drawing and give me the balance which is very small. For I have I am sorry to say to dine out tomorrow night ... also I want to send two of my daughters down to Pevensey by 2 o'clock train tomorrow.'[81] Also 'I am awfully disappointed you did not come this morning, still more so that you did not come this evening or wire. Now be sure to come tomorrow morning and oblige'.[82]

In 1903, Ernest Brown moved from Bond Street to Leicester Square to manage a newly founded gallery, the Leicester Galleries, in partnership with the brothers Wilfred and Cecil Phillips. Although Leicester Square was a less prestigious location for an art gallery than Bond Street, being surrounded by music halls and places of entertainment, it did contain the auctioneers Puttick and Simpson, housed in Sir Joshua Reynolds's old house and studio and, importantly, the editorial offices of the new art periodical *The Studio*. Even though it remained somewhat of an outpost, the gallery's good reputation helped maintain a leading position for more than sixty years.

A 1903 letter to Brown is revealing. It is the first to be headed 5 Hogarth Road, where Mary and the family had been living for about a year and Sandys had evidently moved in with them: 'I am compelled to ask you again to let me have £1.10 today. I shall have a drawing finished on Thursday if you will call on Thursday evening or Friday morning. I should have had it finished before but I had to turn out of the place in Earls Court Gardens – and at present I am here till I can find another, my old landlady and her husband have taken a tailors shop in Duke Street by South Kensington Station.[83] And they had made me so comfortable. I shall never find so comfortable a couple again. I hope you will oblige me for I have a very important matter on hand tomorrow.'[84] It is astonishing, but revealing of his habitual lifestyle, that he was still intending to seek further lodgings separate from his family. The earliest surviving dated letter written by Sandys from the Hogarth Road address was to Harold Hartley on 24th June 1903.[85] He was to die there a year later.

Probably late in 1903, Ernest Brown commissioned a portrait of his daughter Helen (Nellie), who was then sixteen. There is a series of letters from Sandys to Brown written in the course of working on the portrait. Sandys asked if he could be paid in instalments after each sitting (held at his request at the Brown family house at 82 Edith Road, Chelsea).[86] Brown kept these letters and had them bound together in an album. They make interesting, if pathetic, reading.[87]

Ernest's son, Oliver Brown, who was seventeen at the time, wrote about this in his memoir: 'After his lunch he used to say to my mother, "Is there perhaps a letter waiting for me?" There was always an envelope on the mantelpiece addressed to him containing the modest sum which was his daily payment for the work he had done to the elaborate drawing. He was tired and worn out and some days he added very little.

'One day he arrived in a cab on a bitterly cold morning. My mother said: "Where is your overcoat, Mr Sandys?" "Pawned my overcoat for the magnificent sum of three shillings", replied Sandys. Later in the day my mother ventured: "Could not one or two of your daughters get some work to do?" whereupon Sandys with a note of indignation answered: "I hope I can keep my own daughters!" On another occasion I recall Sandys coming in with a completed drawing which he wanted to show and probably sell to my father. It was quite a small parcel, but he had hired a messenger boy to carry it.'[88]

Among the letters there is also an anxiously underlined note to Brown: 'You must really let me have £5 this evening.'[89] Another speaks of his portrait of Nellie: 'I am sorry I cannot have the drawing finished before Thursday afternoon late. I have worked early and late of course, today has been dreadful. I like it better than any head I have done – and I must finish it thoroughly. Meantime I am ill for want of money. It is just a fortnight since I went out.'[90]

Sandys throughout his life often complained about poor light, due to short hours of daylight or dark days because of bad weather, and sometimes unsuitable premises: 'I have done all I can do today to the drawing. I must

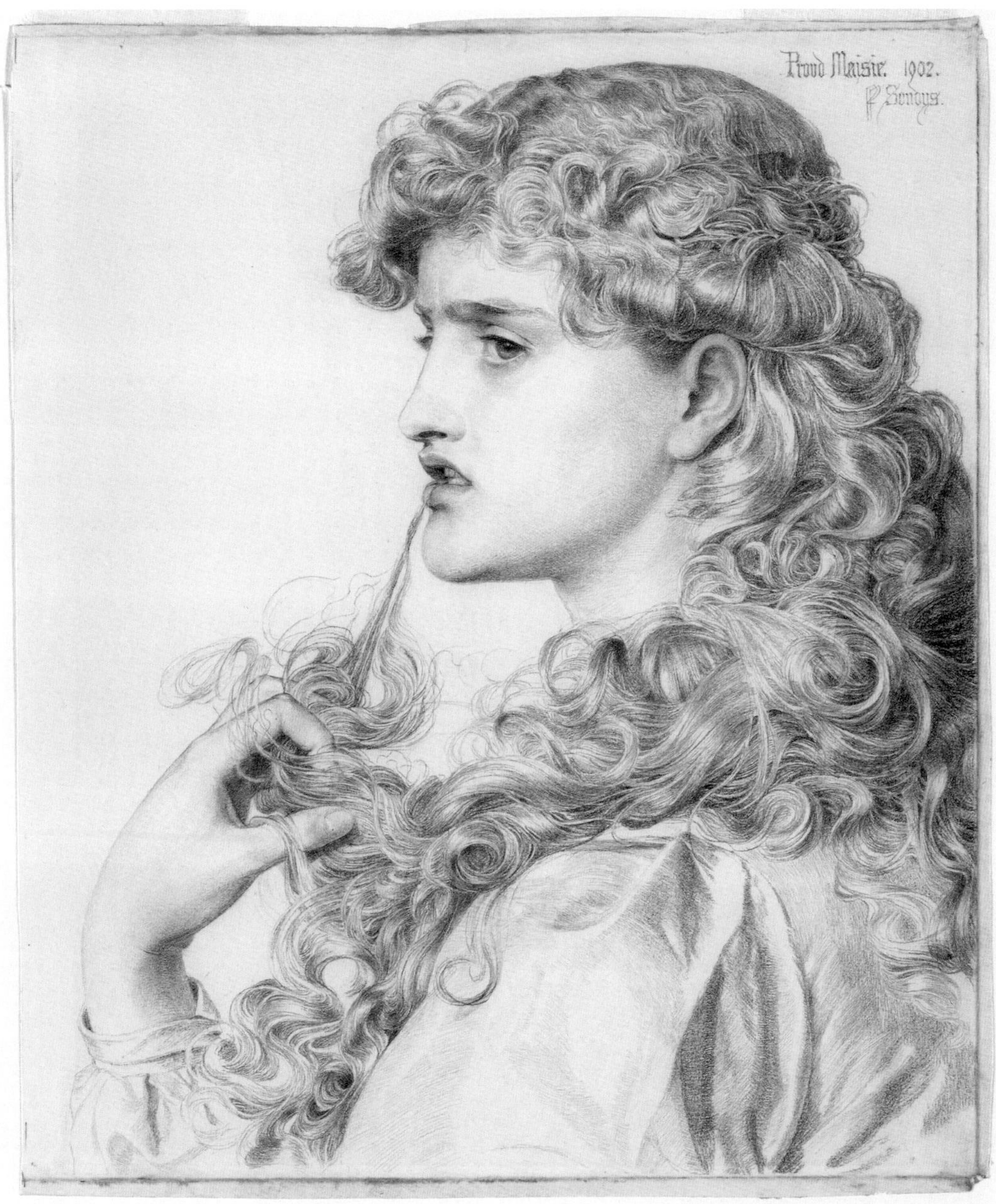

Proud Maisie. Chalk drawing. 1902. The last by date in the succession of his well-known 'Proud Maisie' subjects, but drawn afresh from his daughter Gertrude.

have a long day on Sunday when I hope to have as fine a day as today although it came over very dark at the end … now do send the rest of the money by my daughter. I do so want to go out.'[91]

In another letter, written about this time also: 'I should come up to you but it is a bright day, the first for ten days – and I am at work on the drawing. I am unwilling but I must ask you for at least £2.10 or more. I must get some pencils[,] red chalk[,] pink[,] and white. I must get red and white roses. I want also Swinburne's Poems with St Dorothy in … my daughter will get the chalk I must have and bring back with her.'[92] A letter written in pencil using Leicester Galleries headed notepaper was probably written on or after a visit to the Galleries. Finding Brown was out he wrote: 'I am glad you like the drawing. I wanted to see you but as I cannot, I write. I want you to let me have £5 more on the drawing. This will enable me to finish the drawing during the next week. I bother you now, as I do not want to run about tomorrow. You can send it down by Oliver.'[93]

Ernest Brown did not waste time before organising an exhibition to celebrate the elderly artist and help him financially. Accordingly, the Leicester Galleries put on an exhibition titled Exhibition of Drawings by Frederick Sandys and Other Eminent Artists running in February and March 1904. Although it was not purely a Sandys retrospective, it had a strong showing of his work, amounting to twenty-two items including one oil portrait (which was ex-catalogue). The rest of the exhibition included studies and minor works by Frederick Shields, W.B. Richmond, D.G. Rossetti, Simeon Solomon, H.J. Stock, and Burne-Jones. The catalogue was prefaced by the art critic F.G. Stephens (1828–1907), virtually Sandys's contemporary, who titled it *The Higher Art, an Appreciation of Drawings.*

Stephens wrote: 'It has been truly said of Mr Sandys'[s] art, of which one part at least was never more fully represented than here, that he never, either in painting proper, or in drawing per se, failed to aim at great achievements in form, so that – however strongly animated by fierce and furious passions his works may be, from the *Oriana* of 1861 and the *Medea* of 1869 to the most recent design which is before us – every subject he has chosen is expressed in lovely shapes and exquisitely delineated. In this respect not even Leighton or Burne-Jones, ardent devotees of beauty as they were, though mostly working in wider fields than Mr Sandys affects, has excelled him.

'Apart from this worship of beauty, neither Leighton nor Burne-Jones ever rose to the delineation of passionate emotion in high keys such as our present subject fears not to excel in. No master of old – not Holbein nor Da Vinci himself –

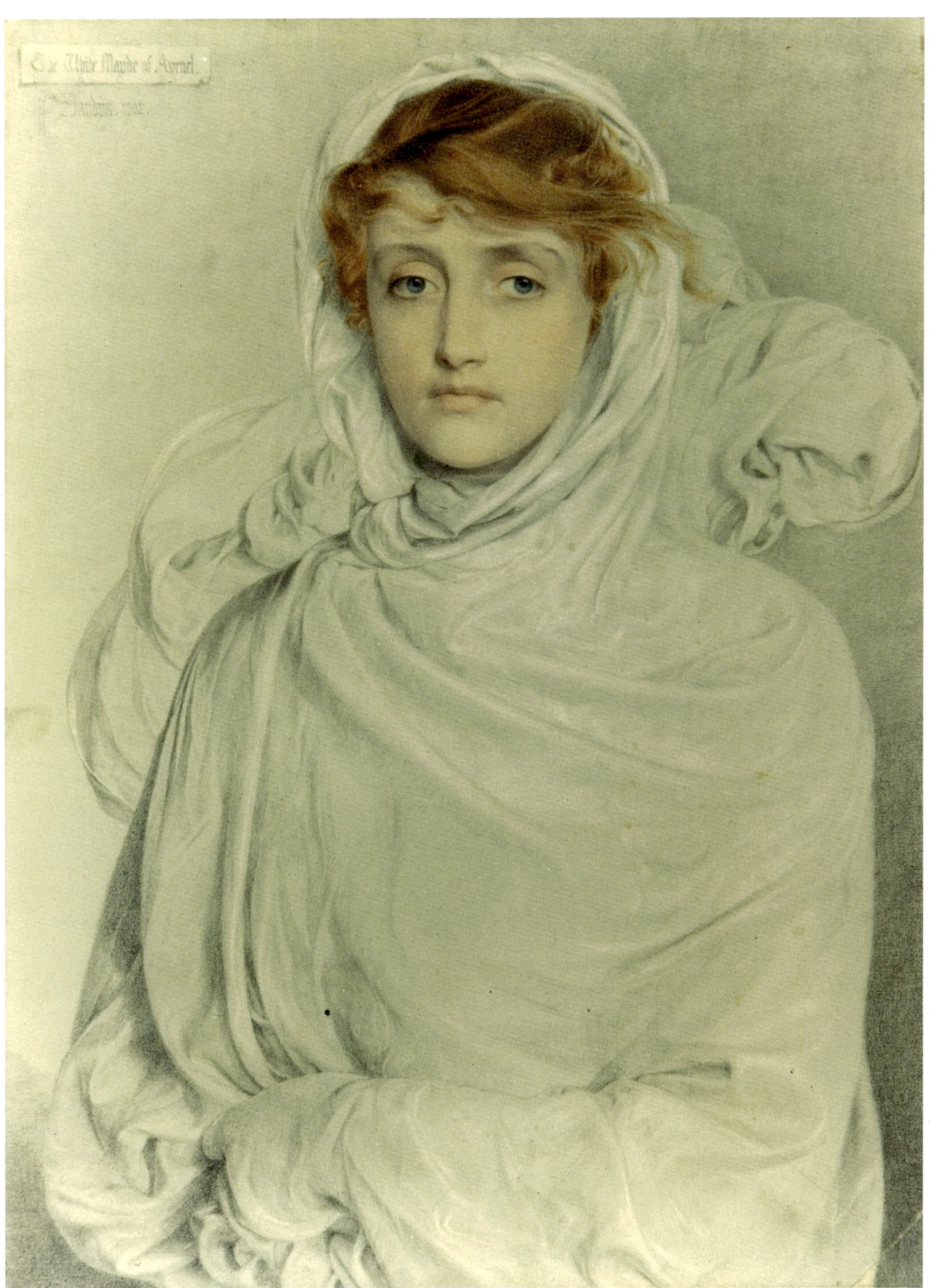

The White Mayde of Avenel. Chalk drawing. 1902. Mildred Sandys was the model.

drew the utmost details of the human form with more faithful and searching hands than Mr Sandys'[s], as is proved in some of the examples we have now in view, witness the lips and eyelids, not less than the golden tresses of *Portia*[94] that enclose her subtly inspired features. Witness again the mass of *Cassandra's* auburn hair which the gale that besets the 'topmost tower of Ilion' where she stands, tortures and shakes as it streams before her, being torn from under the snood of the Trojan virgin. Nor is it only in his works of imagination, such as these aptly represent, that our artist has employed with success, his untiring skill. Among the portraits he has produced, of which that of the late Mrs Anderson Rose is pre-eminent, and from which Rajon made an etched masterpiece, the same skill, knowledge and indomitable care are to be discovered.

'Because he is far more completely represented on this occasion than any of his companions in distinction, and not on account of the comparative importance of any of them, it is proposed in these notes to treat Mr Sandys'[s] contributions first and more at large than those of his neighbours.

'The largest of the former group, being entitled *Lady Greensleeves*, is a charming illustration of the old song to which it owes its title and motto:

'... And who but Lady Greensleeves ...'

'Is that which stands before us in the whole length, nearly life-size figure of a young girl, fresh, pure and alert, with her exquisitely drawn and modelled arms folded before her as she looks earnestly, yet with a soupcon of shy gaiety, out of her eyes like pale sapphires. Her dress of primrose satin, the sheen of which could not be more choicely rendered, is in the taste of Queen Anne's days, witness the white coif that binds her fair hair and the puffed shoulder pieces of pale green, which, to be in keeping in [*sic*] her name, she wears. The charm of the picture affects us deeply by means of the smile – tenderly expressed as it is – that, hardly dimpling the cheeks, hovers about the girl's lips, an element which, except in the face of the *Portia* by the same artist that accompanies *Lady Greensleeves*, is the most happy of his illustrations of that rarest of all faculties in design – power to deal subtly with the transitory and evanescent expressions of beautiful faces.

'Shakespeare's *Portia* never had an apter or a subtler representation than by the fair maiden's form to which we now come as she stands offering flowers to us, and crowned with those virginal white blossoms which are in keeping with the purity of her features and her grave, not sad, looks, as well as with the aspect of one who knows her own will and must needs abide by it, come what may. *Peace and War* embodies, perhaps less subtly than either of the

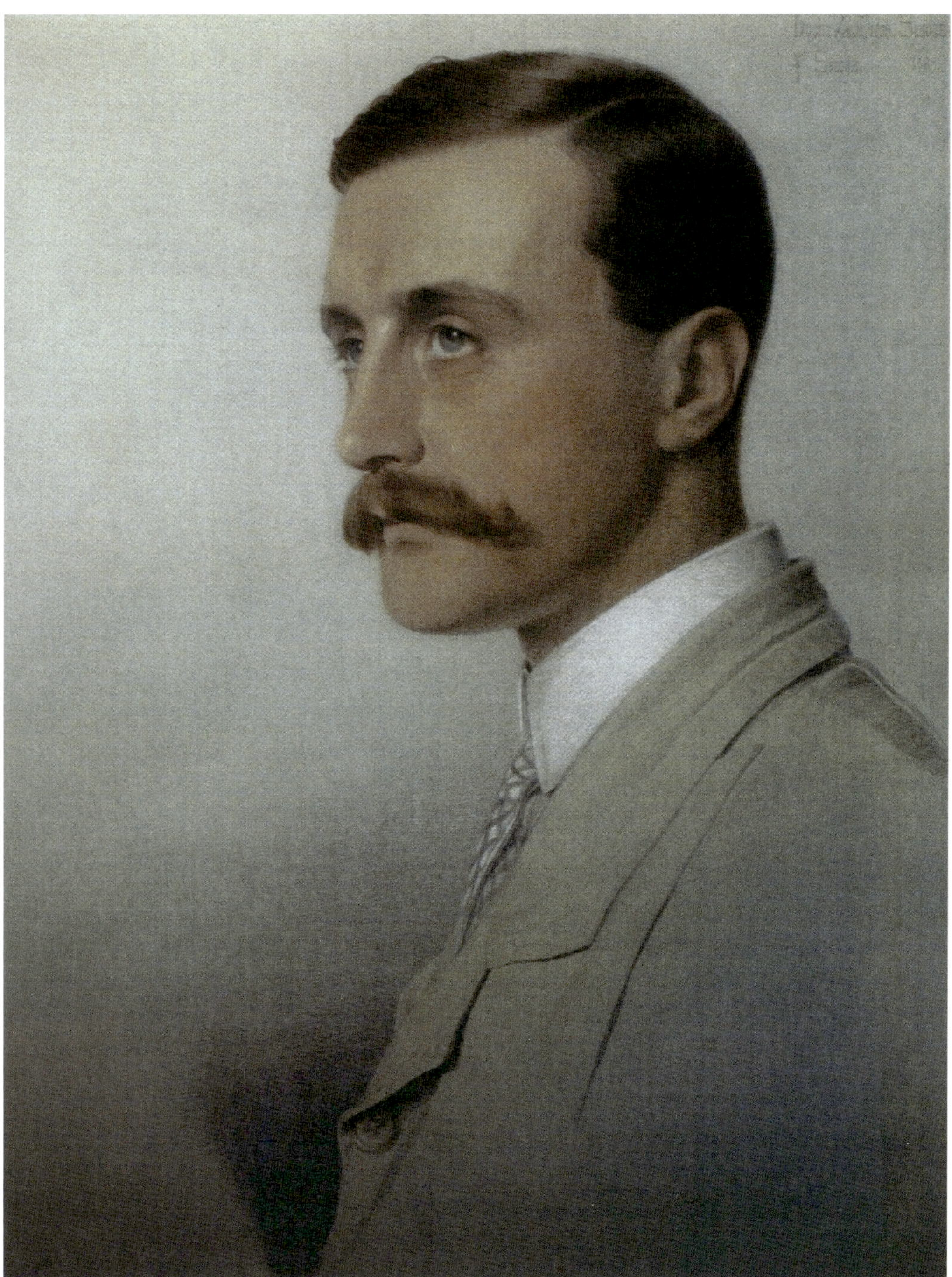

Hugh Sandys. Chalk drawing. 1903. This portrait was a wedding present from Sandys to his son. Hugh was a Mining Engineer in 1903. He and his wife, Alice Mary, had no children, and she died in 1950, and Hugh in 1953 by drowning in Spain.

above, a motive strongly in contrast with theirs. This motive appears in the faces, actions and expressions of two contrasting figures of damsels, who, not without a purpose, closely resemble each other, and yet are diversely moved and differently inspired. *Peace*, holding emblematic lilies, sits at rest, sedate, composed, and partly lost in a day-dream, the nature of which appears as finely and subtly as the like occurs in *Lady Greensleeves* and *Portia*'s faces. *War*, on the other hand, gazes forward with the concentrated wrath which we see in certain Greek masks of bronze and marble that are appropriated to the Furies or the remorseless Fates. She holds symbolical red roses, and in her parted lips no one can fail to see the bitterness of those antique types to which we have referred. It is again right to call attention to the Da Vinci-like drawing of the eyes, results of the most difficult draughtsmanship as those features are, and the mouths on *Peace* and *War*.

'*Cassandra*'s passionate and minatory face and action transport us in a moment from the last-mentioned emblems to the topmost towers of Troy, and they do so with so much force that, while the gale sets her loose tresses streaming, we seem to hear her cries as she runs along the ramparts denouncing death and ruin for her ancestral Ilion. We are impressed by, and shudder while we look at, her wide-open eyes and the pallid hues of her flesh, worn as it is by vigils of Fate-inspired agony. Though not the most terrible of Mr Sandys'[s] readings of antique legends – that distinction is due to his snake-like *Medea*[95] – the face of *Cassandra*, menacing doom, is at least equally powerful and original in art. *Cassandra* and *Medea* combining prove, we think, that if any painter can depict the deadly charm of the beautiful Gorgon with success that fortune is Mr Sandys. *Iris* is very different from any of the above delineations of character and passion. The half-length owes its title to the blue flowers in her hand, while the wreath of darker celandine[96] that binds her hair is in unison with those blossoms. This work is a delicate translation of character and serene beauty into form and colour, and quite another sort of thing from any of the crude and ill-digested outcomings of those "extravagancies of the Velasquez-cult" to which a recent critic has ascribed so much of the "modern" art-craze, that affects ugliness and disdains studies in the higher art.

'*May* a younger maiden than any of the above holds yellow irises and has fine clear-cut and high-bred features, with a very natural expression. *Red-cap*, so-called from her head dress, is unusually pretty, *The White Lady of Avenel* is inspired by that legend to which Scott gave life, and shows, appropriately, the ghost-like and mournful form swaithed [*sic*] in white, and with heavy-lidded eyes, impassive and presageful, comes before us as in a dream. *Proud Maisie*, biting the ends of her long hair and looking sidelong with fiery bitterness, is one of the most original of Mr Sandys'[s] renderings of the character and

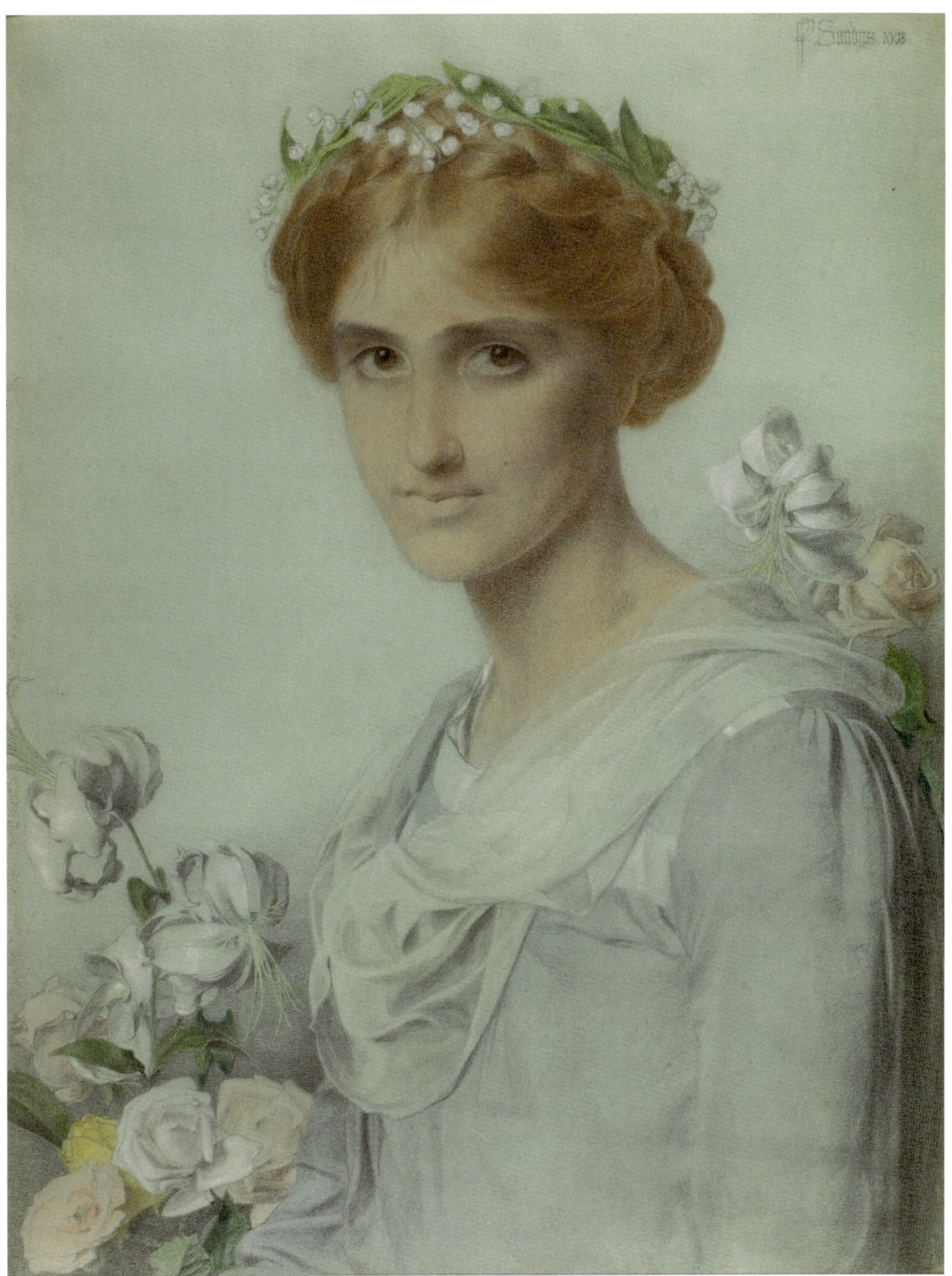

Helen Brown. Chalk drawing, 1903. The daughter of Ernest Brown of the Leicester Galleries.

intense passion of an old dramatic legend. It is better known than some of the above-mentioned examples. These notes on that portion of the distinguish artist's output must, for lack of space and not for want of matter, conclude with a call for attention to his masculine and finely drawn portrait, which has been engraved, of Matthew Arnold's masculine face, and the touching delineation of Tennyson's features in his advanced age, the latest, I think, of the likenesses of the great Laureate.'

This relic of Victorian 'art criticism' by the now elderly Stephens who was, as we say nowadays, 'pulling out all the stops', was surely in sympathy with Sandys's age and failing health. It must have given Sandys and his family a great deal of satisfaction. The exhibition also must have boosted sales. At least six works were sold, some of which were sold to other dealers. George Macmillan, James S. Budgett,[97] and Lord Battersea were lenders of significant earlier works such as *Greensleeves*, *Lethe*, and the *Portrait of Matthew Arnold*. Mrs Arthur Lewis, née Kate Terry, lent the superb oil portrait of her mother-in-law, of 1864.

As Oliver Brown recalled: 'The bulk of our show consisted of his later coloured drawings but they lacked the hard and masterly brilliance of his early drawings and wood-engravings. We had only one oil painting – the very fine portrait of Mrs Jane Lewis only rivalled by his magnificent portrait of another old lady, Mrs Anderson Rose – both dating from the sixties.'

There is evidence that Sandys was assisting Brown in finding exhibits. For instance he reported that (the younger[98]) Mrs Rose declined to lend her portrait on the grounds that she was unwell and that lending it would make her worse by adding to her anxiety about the picture.[99] On the other hand, Mrs Lewis was agreeable, as well as Lord Battersea, to lend.[100]

There are ten more letters in the Takamiya Collection written from 5 Hogarth Road. None are dated except by the day of the week, but they must date from 1903, and a few from early 1904. These continue to reveal Sandys's extreme financial straits:

'Do let me ask you to make it three pounds instead of two. Small as the sum is it will make a very considerable difference to me for the next few days.'

'I am sorry you did not see me yesterday. It was kind of you to bring the Larkspur, but it was too stale and faded to draw from. I shall tomorrow have some quite fresh from Barkers.[101] Now I must ask you to let me have £5 tomorrow morning. This is most important. I have to pay it by 12 o[']clock.

The drawing will be done or nearly so on Sunday [he was writing on Thursday] if you will call between five or six or later. But without this £5 I shall not be able to go on. I shall have to go out and hunt for [*sic*] possibly wasting [two] or three days. I am sorry I am obliged to make this request.' What was he having to hunt for? Perhaps more fresh Larkspur? More probably it was art materials.

'I am going to do that which I would do anything to avoid – I have nearly finished the face of the drawing – two hours would complete it – the hair is nearly also finished. I have only the cap and the dress to do. All could be done by next Sunday [the letter was written on Tuesday night] but I must pay £9 tomorrow by two o[']clock. I have made I am sure the most beautiful face[,] the mouth especially, I have ever done. Come tomorrow morning and see it and let me have the £10 I have still to take on the drawing. Surely I am worth helping so far – and for so small a sum for three or four days. I have been unable to get out or to try and help myself.'[102] Sandys must have been referring to the second version of *The Red Cap* which is dated 1903. The model, as in the 1900 version, was Gertrude, but in any case, Sandys probably based it on a photograph of the 1900 version, because the original had already been purchased by the collector William Connal.[103]

Another letter to Ernest, dated 'Wednesday afternoon' and written on paper embossed with 'Ye Punch Bowle/ 79 Wells Street/ Oxford Street W' (using old notepaper from the now defunct club): 'I am so ashamed of myself. I received the checque [*sic*] quite safely at 12.30 – about the same time I received two letters – which I had to answer at once. These quite put your note out of my head for the time. I have sent you a wire which I trust you will receive in time to save you any anxiety. I have been to Albany Street and seen Mr Dixon himself.[104] He remembers perfectly photographing the drawings for Macmillan but cannot say if the negatives have been preserved. He will look and send me a note at once. I ordered him to print a *Browning*, a *Mrs Oliphant* and a *Green the Historian* at once if he could find the negative. I am very sorry and ashamed I should have neglected to have sent you a line acknowledging the checque [*sic*] at once – particularly after your good nature taking the trouble to send it to me by hand.'

In the last letter in the collection, Sandys wrote: 'I am writing a line on my knees to say how sorry I am I shall be unable to draw on Sunday.[105] I have had a severe chill on the liver, and it is difficult to touch it. It must remain till next Saturday week. I am sorry. I am glad to hear from Macmillan that Roberts has appointed a proximate time to sit.[106] I have been waiting for four years. He agreed to sit before he went to South Africa. I hope to be out for an hour or two tomorrow, and I may try to call.'[107]

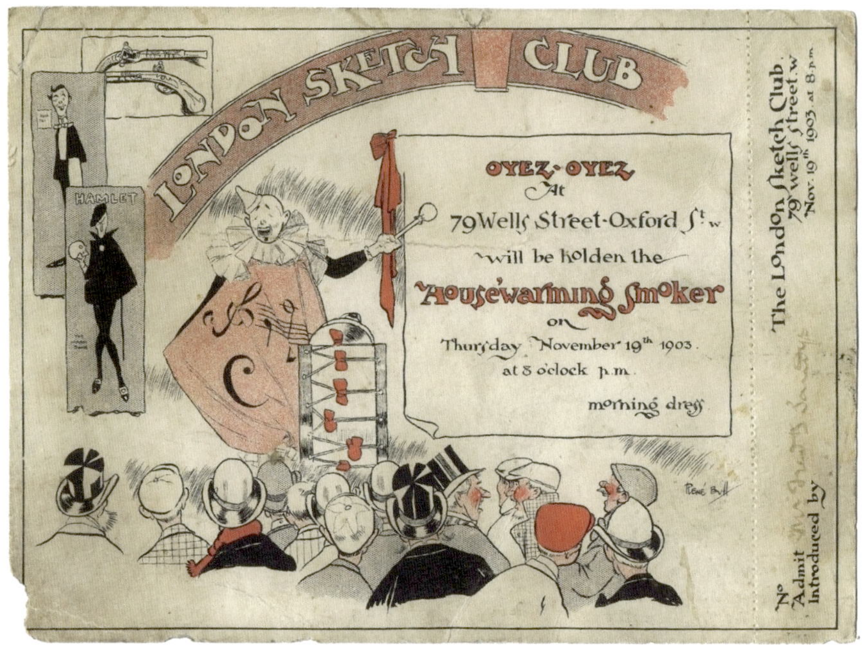

Invitation card to a meeting of the London Sketch Club, 19th November 1903. Designed by René Bull, and addressed to Mr Frederick Sandys. Evidently he did not take up the invitation, probably because he was unwell.

Following this in the Ernest Brown collection is a printed black-bordered card with:

Mrs Frederick Sandys & Family

Return thanks

For kind sympathy with them in their great sorrow

5, Hogarth Road 25th June 1904

Accompanying this is a hand-written note (by Mary): 'The funeral of Frederick Sandys will take place on Thursday at Brompton Cemetary [*sic*] the Corteges leaving Hogarth Road at noon.[108]

A sitting for the Lord Roberts appointment must have occurred because there exists a ghostly image recognisable as Roberts in the Macmillan collection. When it was returned by Roberts to the family after Sandys's death, poor Mary Sandys showed her distress in a letter to George Macmillan: 'I was greatly grieved to see it in such an unfinished state knowing that it was intirely [*sic*] the fault of Lord Roberts. The little that is done only shows what a splendid drawing and likeness it would have been. …' She wanted Macmillan to call to see it and talk to her about it. No doubt Macmillan paid the widow in full, and so this last portrait joined the rest of the Macmillan collection. It was shown in its unfinished state at the Society of Portrait Painters at the New Gallery in October 1904.

Another unfinished late portrait, which appeared in recent years, is that of A.C. Duval (1852–*c.*1923), an engineer and amateur artist. An inscription on the backboard of the portrait of Duval reads 'I, A.C. Duval, sat for this portrait in the autumn of 1903 to Frederick Sandys at his house 5 Hogarth Road … My friend Frederick Sandys died on June 25th, 1904, before he had finished and signed this drawing.'

The death certificate was signed by Dr Howard Stewart.[109] Sandys died of 'congestion of kidneys and liver syncope' and his son Hugh was 'present at the death'. His age was given as seventy-two years, but he was actually seventy-five. A death mask appears to have been made, as recorded in a letter from Constance to the Norwich Castle Museum in 1933. She was offering it for sale for 25 guineas. It was turned down by the curator, and has since disappeared.

[1] Esther Wood (1896).

[2] *The Studio*, vol. 33 (October 1904), p. 16.

[3] *Iris* was offered for sale by Mary Sandys to the V&A Museum in 1905 but it was declined. In 1908 it was offered for sale to Samuel Bancroft Jr, who was not tempted. In 1912 it was offered again to the V&A (as a gift paid for by an anonymous donor), and again declined. It is now at the Art Museum of the Rhode Island School of Design, after passing through several hands in the interval.

[4] Edwin A. Ward, *Recollections of a Savage* (1923), p. 107.

[5] Evidently the London Sketch Club continued to embrace Sandys as a guest, as an unused invitation dated November 1903 remains in the Sandys Family Archive.

[6] *Art Journal* (1905), pp. 81-82, illus. p. 81. Anonymous note 'Frederick Sandys' (by R.E.D. Sketchley). Letter from George Monckton to the Curator, Norwich Art Gallery, dated 25th February 1935. Monckton was hoping to sell it for 250 gns, but it was declined. Norwich Castle Museum, Art Dept. Archives.

[7] Decorative typographic cover of announcement which must have originally included a drawing by Birch (missing). George Henry Birch (1842–1904) was an architect and a curator of Sir John Soane's Museum. Sandys Family Archive.

[8] The Parson mentioned was probably the Rev. Hastings M. Neville who was an amateur watercolourist and author. He wrote *Under a Border Tower* (1897).

[9] Letter from Sandys to Murray. Envelope postmarked AU.6.97, addressed to Fairfax Murray Esq., 17 Shaftesbury Road, Ravenscourt Park, Hammersmith. Manchester, Rylands. Eng.Ms.1279/149.

[10] Letter from Sandys to Gertrude dated 'Wednesday', Sandys Family Archive. Kelly's London Directory 1898 gives Negretti & Zambra, Opticians, at 122 Regent Street. I am grateful to Philip Collins of Barometer World Ltd. for information.

[11] Letter from Sandys to Charles Fairfax Murray, dated Wednesday (August. In pencil '1897' probably dated by C.F.M.). Manchester, Rylands, Eng. Ms.1279/151.

[12] As above. Dated 'Tuesday Evg'. Probably dated by C.F.M. 'Sept. 7. 1897'. Manchester, Rylands. Eng. Ms.1279/150.

[13] Letter from Sandys to C.W. Sherborn (1831–1912), dated by Sherborn to 27th August, 1897. Sherborn made an account note on the top corner of the letter, totalling £2.0.0. Collection of the late Derek Sherborn.

[14] Harold Hartley (1851–1943), a born entrepreneur, was a publisher of trade journals and manufacturer of distilled water, who became an organiser of the large 'popular' exhibitions, first at Olympia with Joseph Lyons, and then at Earl's Court. He formed an important collection of English book and magazine illustrations of the 1860s, stemming from a childhood hobby, which was sold by his descendants to the Museum of Fine Art, Boston in 1955.

[15] Letter from Sandys to C.W. Sherborn. Collection of the late Derek Sherborn.

[16] Letter from Burne-Jones to Sandys. Undated on headed notepaper 'The Grange'. Ian Hodgkins & Co. *Catalogue 92, Spring 1997*, no. 42.

Burne-Jones is known to have had reservations about contact with his old acquaintance, but this was nevertheless a helpful act.

[17] A. Ludovici. *An Artist's Life in London and Paris* (1926), p. 142.

[18] London, Knightsbridge, *Exhibition of International Art*, 1898. Nos. 10 and 265.

[19] London, New Gallery, The 5th Exhibition of the International Society of Sculptors, Painters and Gravers, 1905. Nos. 153 and 154, Portraits of Walter Palmer and Gladys Palmer (lent by Walter Palmer); 160a, *A Nightmare*, 164, *Cassandra*, 165. *Portrait of Alfred Tennyson*, 166, *Winifred* (lent by Harold Hartley).

[20] J. Comyns Carr. *Some Eminent Victorians* (1908), pp. 115–116.

[21] Robert Ross (1869–1918) on Sandys in *Dictionary of National Biography* (1912), pp. 263–265.

[22] This must have been before 1897 when the ailing Beardsley moved to Menton, dying there in March 1898.

[23] William Rothenstein, *Men and Memories* (1932), p. 259.

[24] Letter from R. Ponsonby Staples to H.M. Hake, dated 9th April 1930. London, National Portrait Gallery.

[25] Idem. Letter from R. Ponsonby Staples to H.M. Hake, dated 24th May 1930.

[26] The impression shown at South Kensington was lent by T.R. Way, which had formerly belonged to James Anderson Rose.

[27] The author has not seen any printed-on India paper. Presently traced originals number 14. A reduced facsimile was published in the print collector Richard Fisher's *Catalogue of a Collection of Engravings, Etchings and Woodcuts* (1879), opp. p. 346.

[28] The Royal Academy Summer Exhibition of 1857 opened on 2nd May. It was then still held at Somerset House.

[29] E.R. and J. Pennell. The Whistler Journal (1921), p. 22.

[30] *The Whistler Journal* (1921), p. 23.

[31] Swinburne's poem *Faustine* was first published in *The Spectator* in 1862.

[32] *The Whistler Journal* (1921), p. 24.

[33] *The Whistler Journal* (1921), pp. 24–25.

[34] Oswald Doughty. *Dante Gabriel Rossetti, a Victorian Romantic* (1949), p. 311. However, Whistler had another reason for the departure, as reported by Elizabeth Pennell.

[35] *The Whistler Journal* (1921), p. 25.

[36] The address of the studio probably was No.1 Spenser Street, Victoria, where he resided and worked from 1873 to August 1881.

[37] *The Whistler Journal* (1921), p. 28.

[38] Elizabeth Pennell. *Nights. Rome, Venice, London, Paris* (1916). "Nights in London", pp. 207–209.

[39] Walter Crane, *An Artist's Reminiscences* (1907), p. 326.

[40] Letter from Winifred Sandys to Samuel Bancroft Jr, dated 9th August 1913. Lionel Francis Crane (1876–1943), an architect, was the elder son of Walter Crane. Delaware Art Museum Library, Bancroft Archive.

[41] Collection of Robert B. Simon, New York.

[42] The Hon. Charles Napier Lawrence wrote a tribute to Sir William Slaughter on his death in March 1917.

[43] Letter to the author from the sitter's nephew D.B. Macdonald, dated 14th September 1991.

[44] Christie's, 12th March 1900, lot 31, bought by Hartley for 6gns.

[45] V&A Museum acquisition records, 21/6805. Accession no. E.2292-1921.

[46] It was presented in 1926 to the Birmingham City Art Gallery by Joseph Duveen (856'26). Duveen probably bought it charitably from the family after Sandys's death.

[47] This was sold by Mary Sandys to Sandys's friend from the Punch Bowl Club days, George Monckton (1868–1936), in September 1904.

[48] Letter from Sandys to Joseph Pennell, from 31 Cheniston Gardens. Dated Saturday evening (early 1900). Washington, Library of Congress, Manuscript Division. Pennell Whistler Collection.

[49] Letter from Winifred Sandys to Elizabeth Pennell, from 31 Cheniston Gardens. Dated 31st March 1900. Washington, Library of Congress, Manuscript Division, Pennell Whistler Collection.

[50] Letter from Meredith to Leslie Stephen, 30th December 1902. Cline, The Letters of George Meredith. Letter no. 2136.

[51] Henry Edmund Christy (1865–1931) and his wife Ethel May (née Phipps Hornby). The sons were Stephen (1896–1916) and Basil (1897–1916).

[52] Letter from Sandys to Gertrude from Lordington, dated 'Monday night' (Spring 1900). Sandys Family Archive.

[53] Percy Wood (1860–1904), the founder of the Punch Bowl Club in the 1890s, appears to have known the Sandys family intimately.

[54] Transcripts of a letter from Mary E. Barstow to Sandys, dated 14th April 1900, and Sandys's reply dated 'Good Friday', sent to the author by the late Mrs J.M.O. Barstow.

[55] One of the partners, Arthur J. Sulley, carried on at the same premises, but specialising in Old Master paintings.

[56] Christie's, London, 14th March 1908, lot 25.

[57] Undated, unidentified press cutting from 1900. Sandys Family Archive.

[58] Sandys Family Archive.

[59] Sandys Family Archive.

[60] See pp. 307-308.

[61] The letter probably dates from 1900. Sandys Family Archive.

[62] The portrait of Wolseley, referred to, was commissioned by Alexander Macmillan in 1883. Letter from Sandys to Lord Wolseley, dated 12 June (postmarked 1901), Hove Central Library. Wolseley Papers.

[63] London University, School of Economics, The Women's Library (ZLAC/2). She is listed there on 'the Roll of Honour of Suffragette Prisoners, 1905–1914'.

[64] Printed invitation card with autograph inscription, dated 18th November (1901), Sandys to Gertrude. Sandys Family Archive.

[65] Letter from Winifred Sandys to Samuel Bancroft Jr, dated 28th May 1908, from 5 Hogarth Road. Winifred sold her miniature copy of

this subject to S.B. Jr. Delaware Art Museum, Bancroft Archive.

[66] According to Gertrude's son, Anthony Crane.

[67] Christie's sale of 15th May 1925 after Gillian's death, lists: *St George for Merrie England*, drawing (1880); *Unwinding the Skein*, drawing (*c*.1870); *Poppies*, drawing (1898); *Helen of Troy*, drawing (1893); *Proud Maisie*, drawing (1902); *White Mayde of Avenel* (head only), drawing (*c*.1902). The six family portraits were not in the sale.

[68] Although Sandys titled her portrait *Muriel Alice Sandys*, census and marriage records give her name as 'Alice Mary'. She was the daughter of Henry Elwell Dehane, a 'Collector, Great Western Railway Co.' in 1881, and 'Superintendent Clerk' in 1901.

[69] Now part of the V&A Museum.

[70] Thomas Rudolphus Dallmeyer (1859–1906), successor to his father, the lens designer John Henry Dallmeyer, was at 25 Newman Street, W. Dallmeyer sat for a portrait by Sandys, now lost.

[71] Perhaps Sandys refers to the photos taken by Percy Wood, the sculptor. In fact, these are outstandingly good.

[72] A collection of 35 letters from Sandys was kept by Ernest Brown. He had them mounted and Riviere-bound in a Morocco leather album which is now in the collection of Professor Toshiyuki Takamiya of Tokyo, who generously allowed me access to them.

[73] Part of Fulham, near Hammersmith.

[74] Ernest Brown left the Fine Art Society and formed the partnership Ernest Brown and Phillips in 1903 trading as the Leicester Galleries. *Exhibition, The Memoirs of Oliver Brown*. (ed.) Nicholas Brown (1968), p. 6.

[75] Letter from Sandys to Mr Brown, undated but *c*.1900 (on Fine Art Society headed notepaper). Takamiya Collection, Tokyo.

[76] Letter from Sandys to Mr Brown, dated 'Thursday evening', *c*.1900. Probably delivered by his son Guy. Takamiya Collection.

[77] These were probably mounted reproductive photographs (such as were made by the Autotype Company) which had been made of some of his earlier works.

[78] The Ascot Week races are held in June. This probably refers to a bet which he was hoping would bring in some money.

[79] Unidentified.

[80] The only dated version of this subject is from 1902.

[81] As already noted, there are references to his children lodging at Pevensey Bay in the early 1900s. The 1901 census finds six of them at Kilmarnock.

[82] Letter from Sandys to Ernest Brown, headed as from 32 Earl's Court Gardens. Takamiya Collection, Tokyo.

[83] Probably Bute Street, as there is no Duke Street in South Kensington. Sandys likely misheard it.

[84] Letter from Sandys to Ernest Brown, headed 5 Hogarth Road, dated 'Sunday'. Takamiya Collection, Tokyo.

[85] Boston, Museum of Fine Art. Hartley Collection. Dated to 1903 from the postmarked envelope.

[86] This is at the border of Chelsea and Fulham. The 1901 census found them there (when Brown was still 'Manager Fine Art Society').

[87] Takamiya Collection, Tokyo.

[88] *Exhibition, the Memoirs of Oliver Brown*, Nicholas Brown (ed.) 1968, pp. 17–18.

[89] Note from Sandys to Ernest Brown, dated Wednesday (late 1903?). Takamiya Collection, Tokyo.

[90] Letter from Sandys to Ernest Brown, from 5 Hogarth Road, dated Tuesday night (late 1903?). Takamiya Collection. The portrait was shown from May–October 1904 at the Kunsthistoriche Austellung, Dusseldorf.

[91] Letter from Sandys to Ernest Brown. Not addressed or dated, but late 1903? Takamiya Collection, Tokyo.

[92] Letter from Sandys to Ernest Brown. From 5 Hogarth Road, dated Tuesday (late 1903?). Takamiya Collection, Tokyo.

[93] Letter from Sandys to Ernest Brown, headed 'The Leicester Galleries', undated. Takamiya Collection, Tokyo. Oliver, Ernest's son, became a partner in the Leicester Galleries business in 1914.

[94] This late work, probably with Gertrude as model, has not yet come to light. This is the only evidence of its existence.

[95] Stephens must mean *Medusa* not *Medea*.

[96] He must be mistaken, for celandines are bright yellow.

[97] James Smith Budgett (1823-1906), a wealthy London sugar merchant.

[98] Emily Winter Rose, widow of James Anderson Rose.

[99] The portrait referred to was probably that of *Mrs Susanna Rose* of 1861–1862 (the mother of James Anderson Rose). The owner of this portrait in 1903 would have been Emily Winter Rose, the widow of James Anderson Rose.

[100] Letter from Sandys to Ernest Brown, from 5 Hogarth Road, dated Tuesday (late 1903?). Takamiya Collection, Tokyo.

[101] Barkers department store, Kensington High Street.

[102] Letter from Sandys to Ernest Brown from 5 Hogarth Road, dated 'Tuesday night'. Takamiya Collection, Tokyo.

[103] William Connal Jr, wealthy Scottish ship owner and collector.

[104] Henry Dixon (1820–1893), photographer, 112 Albany Street, NW1. Evidently the 1880s portraits for Macmillan and also for Craik were copied photographically and prints were for sale.

[105] This is referring to the portrait of Nellie (Helen) Brown

[106] General Roberts (1832-1914).

[107] Letter from Sandys to Ernest Brown, from 5 Hogarth Road, dated Friday night. Takamiya Collection, Tokyo.

[108] Takamiya Collection, Tokyo.

[109] He owned a replica of *St Dorothy* (1904) and in the same year he commissioned a portrait of his daughter.

opposite: 5, Hogarth Road, Earl's Court. see page 346

Chapter 8
Afterwards

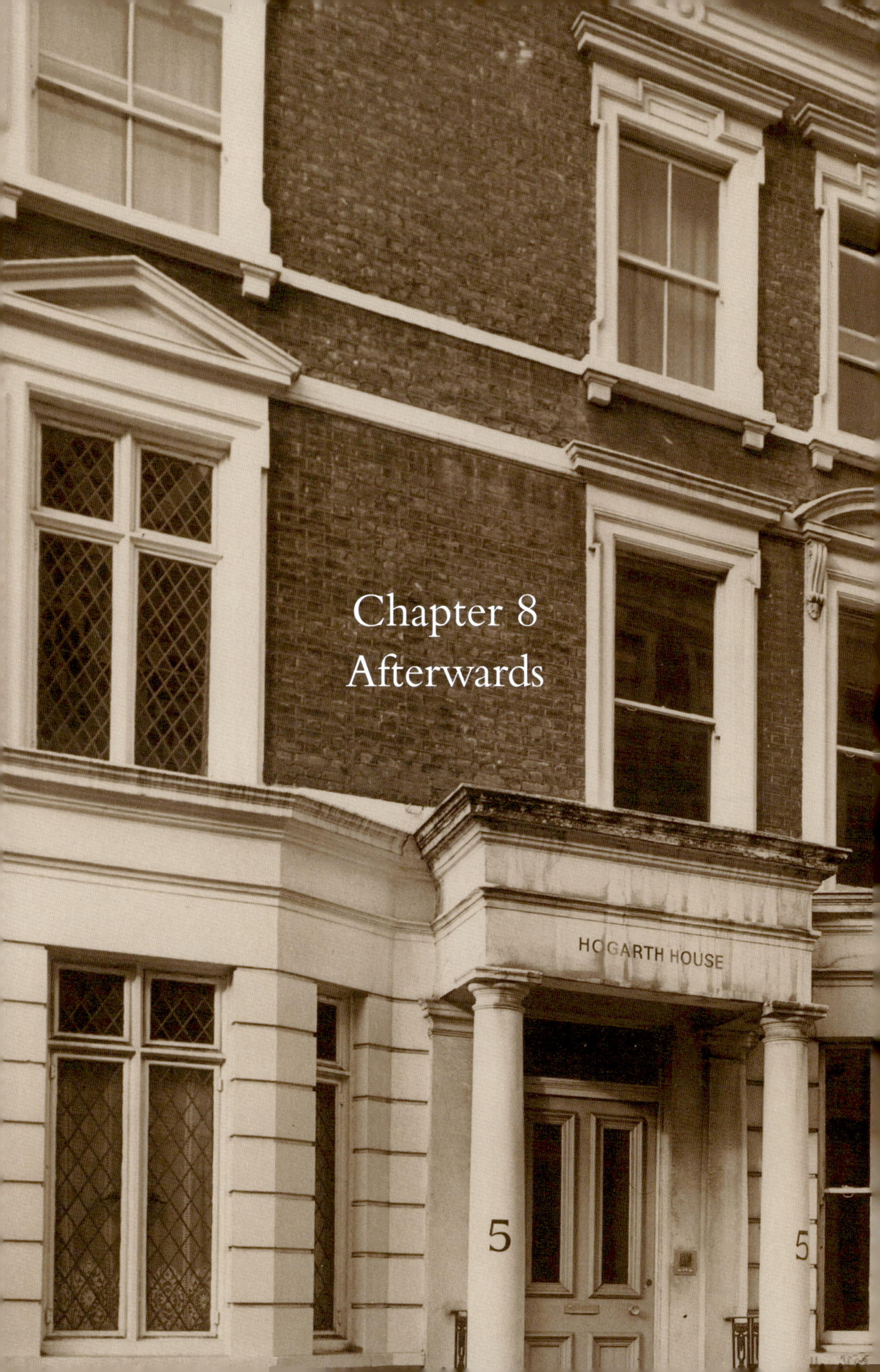

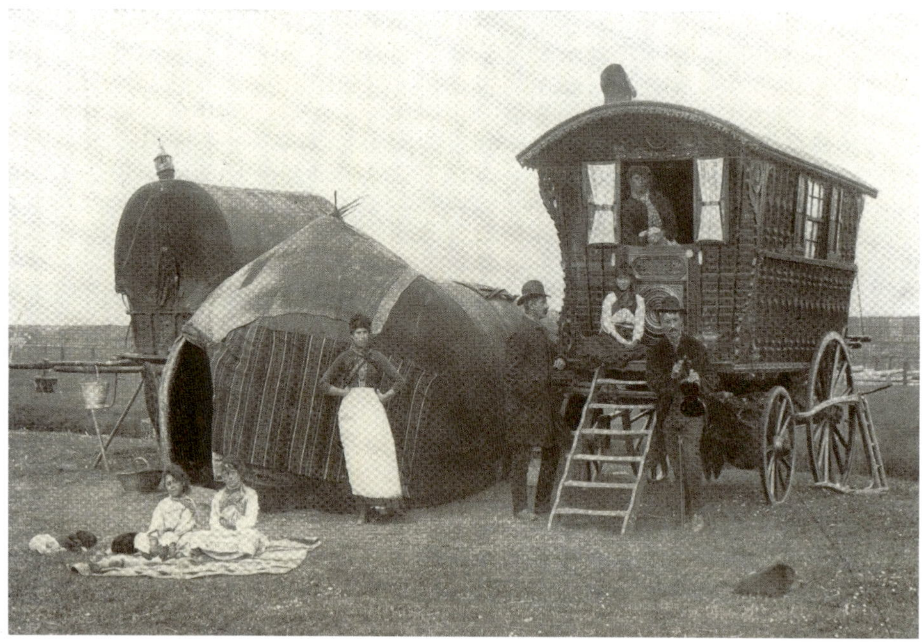

Keomi (now Mrs Bonnett) at the window of her caravan on Epsom Downs taken in the late 1880s. Her husband Charles Bonnett stands in profile to the left of the van. Nellie Bonnett sits at the top of the steps and Frederick Cyril Gray stands to the right of the steps holding a fiddle. Madeline Gray leans in front of the tent. The two children on the ground sheet are probably Florence and Rose Bonnett. Frederick and Madeline Gray were the second and third children of Keomi and Frederick Sandys. From George Hall, *The Gypsy's Parson* (*c.*1915), opp. p. 202.

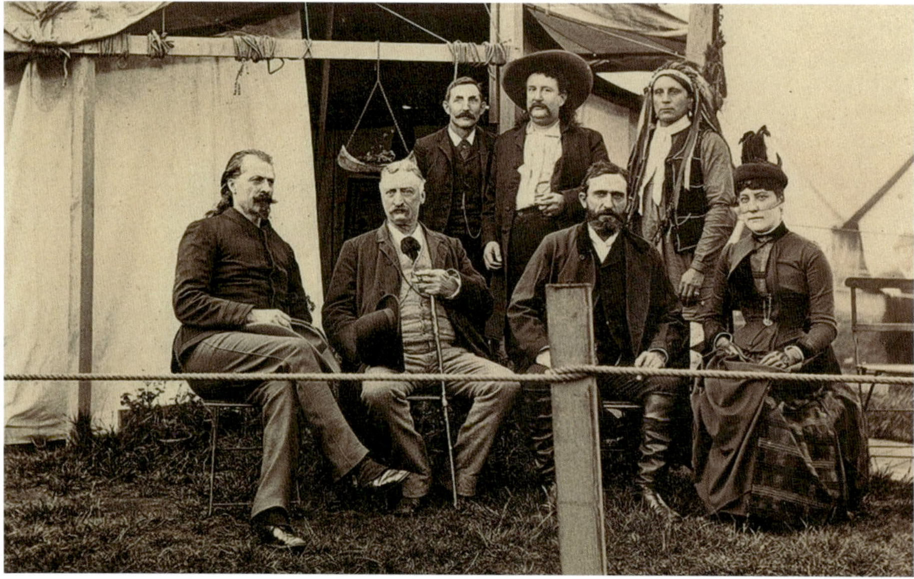

Buffalo Bill (William Cody, 1846-1917) left, and some of his entourage during the first visit to England of his 'Wild West Show' held at the Earl's Court showground in the summer of 1887.

To complete the story of Frederick Sandys's singular life and legacy, my feeling is that besides the history of the products of his eye and hand, an outline note of the lives of his progeny would make a fitting ending.

His first four children were by his beautiful model, the gypsy Keomi Gray (1841–1914), three of whom were born in London. Aethela Maud's birth was registered in January 1864 (after her birth in 1863), her mother was then living at 4 Barrosa Place, Chelsea. Frederick Cyril was registered in June 1865 as being born at 1 Earl's Court Terrace (but Keomi's residence was noted as at 20 Merton Road, Kensington). Madeline Mabel was born in London about 1868, location unknown. Keomi's fourth and last child by Sandys, Henry Herbert, was born around 1869 or 1870 in Norfolk. Thus, it appears that Keomi had returned to her family (the Grays) with her children sometime before Henry Herbert was born. The children took her surname, Gray.

In 1875 Keomi married Charles Bonnett, a well-to-do horse dealer from Yarmouth. Bonnett and Keomi must have joined her family for, on the 1881 census day, the Grays and the Bonnetts were to be found in caravans at Litcham, on the Dereham Road in Norfolk.

Aethela (or Ethel) Maud travelled to the USA in the late 1880s, reputedly pregnant after an affair with 'Buffalo Bill' Cody whose immensely popular and innovatory Wild West Show she had joined in England. I would suppose that Cody, in setting up his show in England, would have contacted gypsy horse-traders, among others, to obtain enough mounts for his shows. After crossing the Atlantic with the Cody entourage at the end of their European tours, she gave birth to a daughter named Maud in Boston, Massachusetts, in about 1889. There she married Arnold Lee an American. She returned to England alone with her daughter in 1891, and in later years ran an antiques shop in Islington. Ethel Maud died close to her gypsy family in Great Yarmouth in 1936.[1]

Frederick Cyril was described as a 'hawker' when he married Laura Smith in 1888. Laura was later known as 'Madame Laura', a palmist working at Yarmouth Pier. A photograph is preserved showing Frederick Cyril and Laura on the steps of their caravan; it probably dates from the time of the 1914–1918 war. He seems to be in army uniform, and she sports a spectacular leopard skin coat. He is wearing riding breeches, showing that he was involved with horses, perhaps in some aspect of procuring mounts for the British Army. He seems rather tall and has a marked facial resemblance to his biological father. The 1911 census noted him as a 'travelling showman providing amusements, etc. for the public'. He and Laura had seven known children. He died in Gorleston, Norfolk, in 1943.

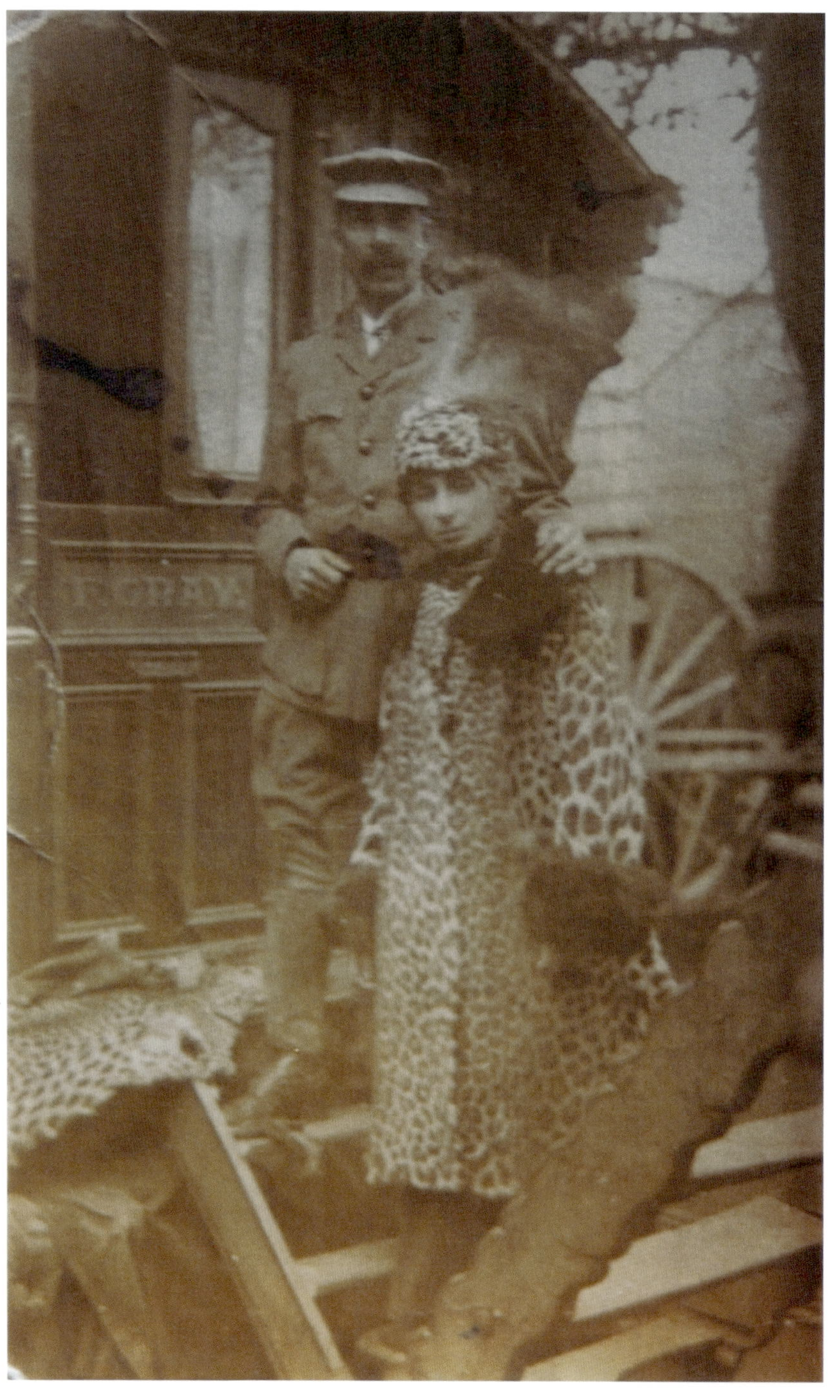

Frederick Cyril Gray and his wife Laura Smith on the steps of their caravan at the time of the First World War. He was the second child of Keomi and Frederick Sandys.

Madeline Mabel married Albert (Albi) Smith, the brother of Laura Smith, in 1890 in Great Yarmouth. Smith was a horse dealer. Madeline became known as 'Madame Cynthia', also a palmist, working at Yarmouth's Pleasure Beach. The couple had seven children. She died in 1966 and was buried at Gorleston. The last of Frederick Sandys and Keomi's children, Henry Herbert, married Begonia Gray in 1894. She was the daughter of Louis (or Lewis) Gray, who was Keomi's brother. They had seven children.

Keomi had three more children with Charles Bonnett: Nellie, Rose and Florence. The young Alfred Munnings (1878–1959) encountered her in Norfolk in the first decade of the twentieth century and painted her handsome daughters Nellie and Charlotte Gray,[2] and later wrote of how he listened to her stories of Sandys, Rossetti and Millais.[3] Keomi's last years were spent in a house in Yarmouth, and she died in 1914 aged seventy-three, which indicates a birth date of *c.*1841. Her grave in Gorleston Cemetery (shared by her husband Charles Bonnett) is surmounted by a fine cruciform monument with a supporting angel, which is touchingly inscribed 'In Loving Memory of our Dear Mother'.

Not to be forgotten, though short-lived, was the first child whom Mary Emma Jones and Sandys had together. The first clue of her existence appeared to me from the record of the purchase of a burial plot in the Brompton Cemetery under the name Neville. The child was named Maura, but she died on Christmas Eve 1868, aged one year, in the house of a baby-minder at Millwall, according to her death certificate. Her death was described as being caused by 'violent shock due to accidental scalding'.

Next came Cecilia (Cissily) and Dorothy (Dora), born in Brompton in 1869 and 1870 respectively. They were fostered, under the name Neville, at 22 Kingsbridge Place (or Street), Poplar, at the same address as the unfortunate Maura. Recorded as living there were Edward Smith and his wife Elizabeth. Edward Smith was a police constable at Millwall.[4] It is not known when the children were moved to Kensington, but they were next fostered by T.J. McManus, of Phillimore Gardens. McManus, a builder by trade, was listed in Sandys's bankruptcy papers in 1876 when he owed him £250 for maintenance arrears for two children. I recognised a link through my conversation with the late Peter Eaton, the antiquarian bookseller. He told me that in the early 1950s he had obtained books and pictures, which had belonged to Frederick Sandys, from an old lady living near Hammersmith. Although he had sold the books by the time of my visit in the 1980s, he still had a fine *Proud Maisie* and a drawing of a female head at his Buckinghamshire house, *Lilies* (which I deemed to be by Emma Sandys).

As previously mentioned, when I discussed this with Anthony Crane, Sandys's grandson, he told me that he had understood that there were two elderly ladies, Dora and Cecilia McManus, living in Hammersmith, who were cousins of some sort. However, on my looking into public records, it appeared in fact that they were his oldest aunts. It remains a mystery why they were 'off-loaded' at such an early stage to a foster family. That they stayed there permanently was undoubtedly due to the fact Sandys and Mary had abandoned them through being unable to provide for their upkeep. The censuses of 1901 and 1911 show that James McManus continued to house and support the two at 112 Brook Green, Hammersmith. Cissily died in 1937, and Dora in 1955, so it must have been Dora who sold the items to Peter Eaton.

The full household of Frederick, Mary, and their eight, acknowledged, living children was last recorded at 28 Maude Grove[5] in the (April) 1891 census under the name of Neville. In April 1901 under the name Sandys, Frederick, Mary, Winifred, and Hugh, had moved to a boarding house at 279 Colherne Road. The other children, Guy, Mildred, Maude, Constance, Ruth, and Gertrude were found living separately by the census taker at that time. The address was Kilmarnock, Pevensey Bay, Sussex. Shifting reasons and day to day necessities are unrecorded and are therefore lost to us after an interval of some 120 years, but at least the core of the family held together as a close unit to the end of their several lives. The family's name change to Sandys seems to have occurred between those two dates [i.e. *c.* 1900].

As one would imagine, family funds must have been shorter than ever after Sandys's death in 1904. Proof of this can be found in the family's correspondence, in their attempts (sometimes fruitlessly) to sell his remaining works, finished or unfinished, to museum curators in Norwich and South Kensington, as well as to private collectors such as Samuel Bancroft in the USA. Large sheets of studies were cut up into smaller units, each one neatly signed with the monogram 'AFS' or 'FS', for which Winifred probably was responsible, being a practical woman.

However, the family had grown up and the children, of necessity, were starting their own independent lives, some marrying and moving away, some earning their own living. The two daughters Winifred and Gertrude (the eldest and the youngest) stayed on with their mother at 5 Hogarth Road, Earl's Court, where they had moved in around 1903.

Winifred Catherine (1871–1944) tried to follow in the footsteps of her beloved father as an artist. She responded to a late nineteenth-century fashion for miniature painting for which she seems to have made a minor reputation.

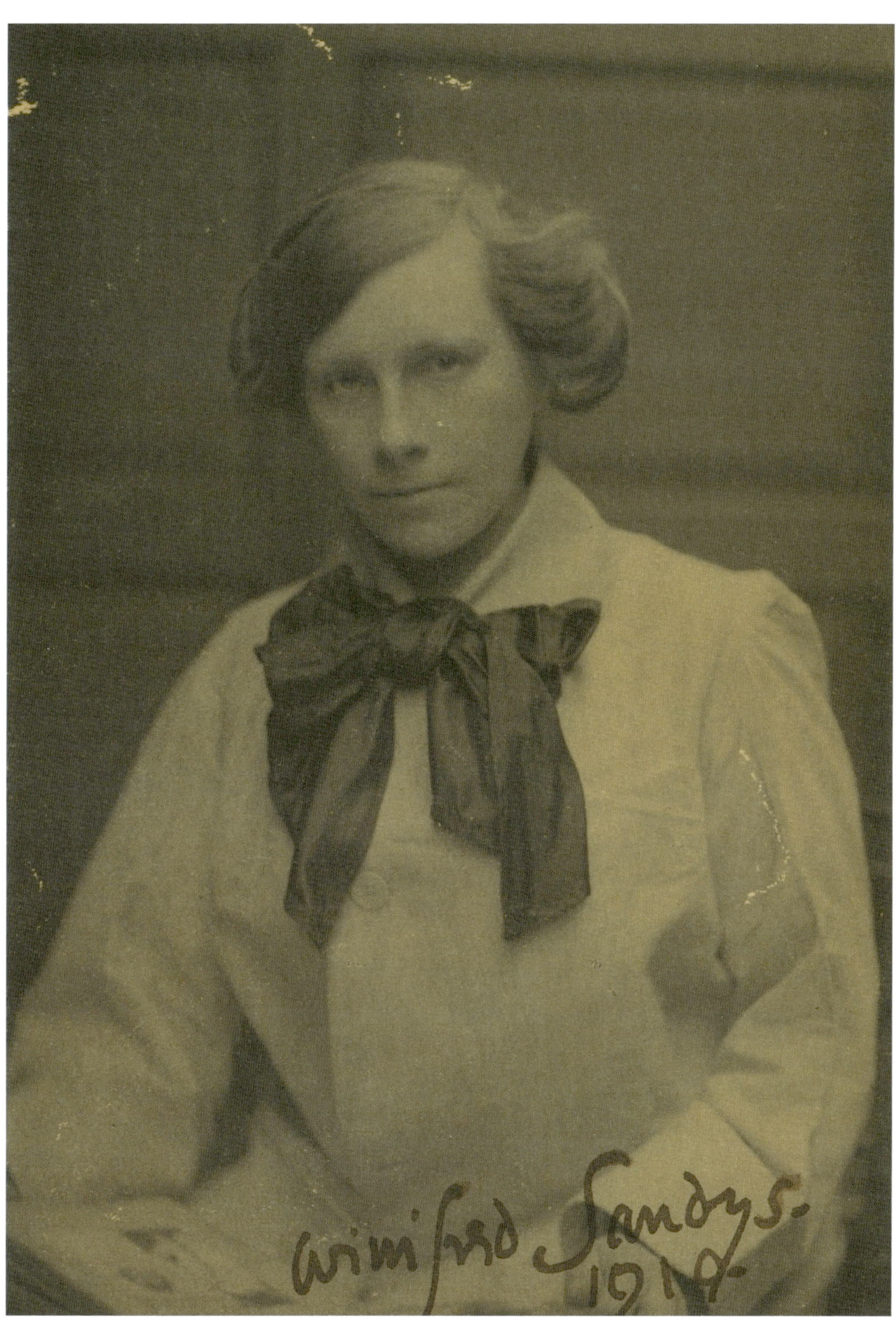

Winifred Sandys in 1919. Photograph sent by her to Samuel Bancroft Jr.

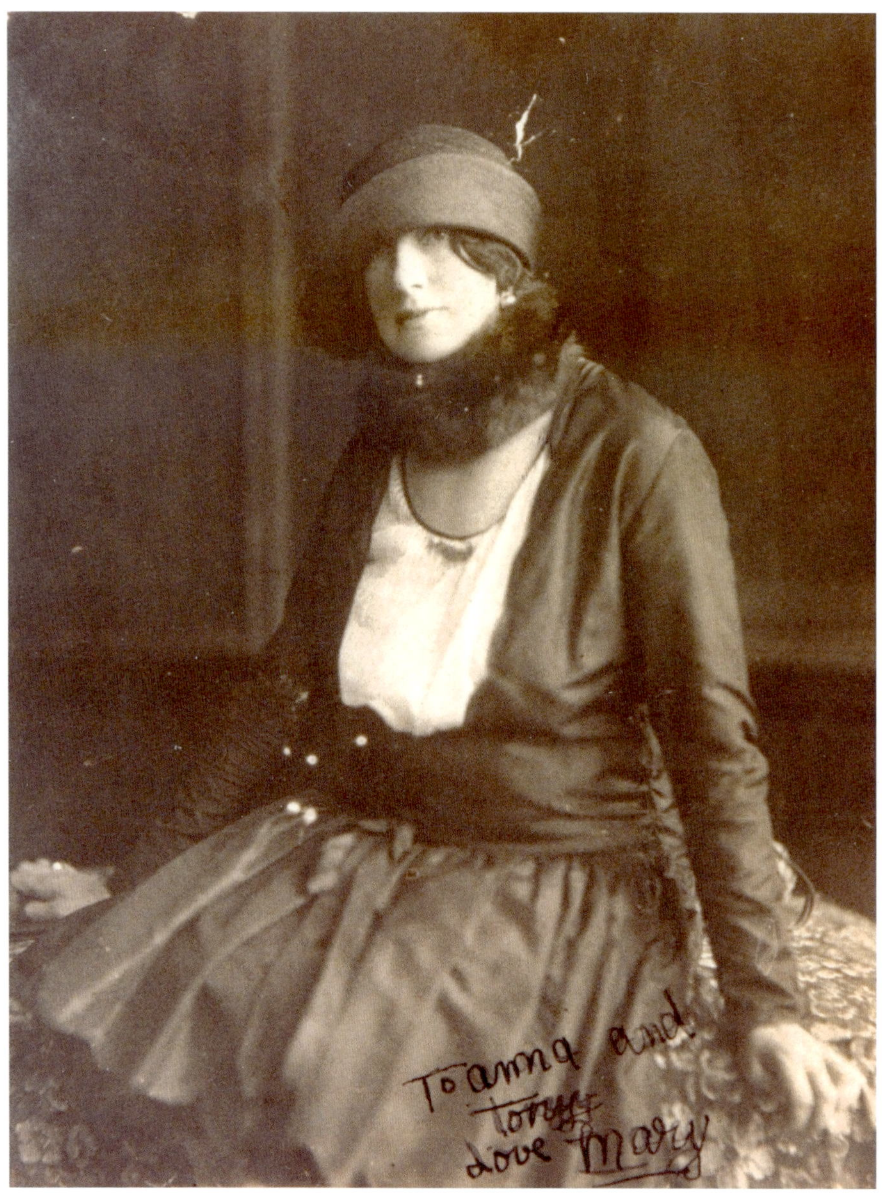

Maude Mary Sandys. Photograph *c.*1920, given by her to Anthony Crane and his first wife Anna.

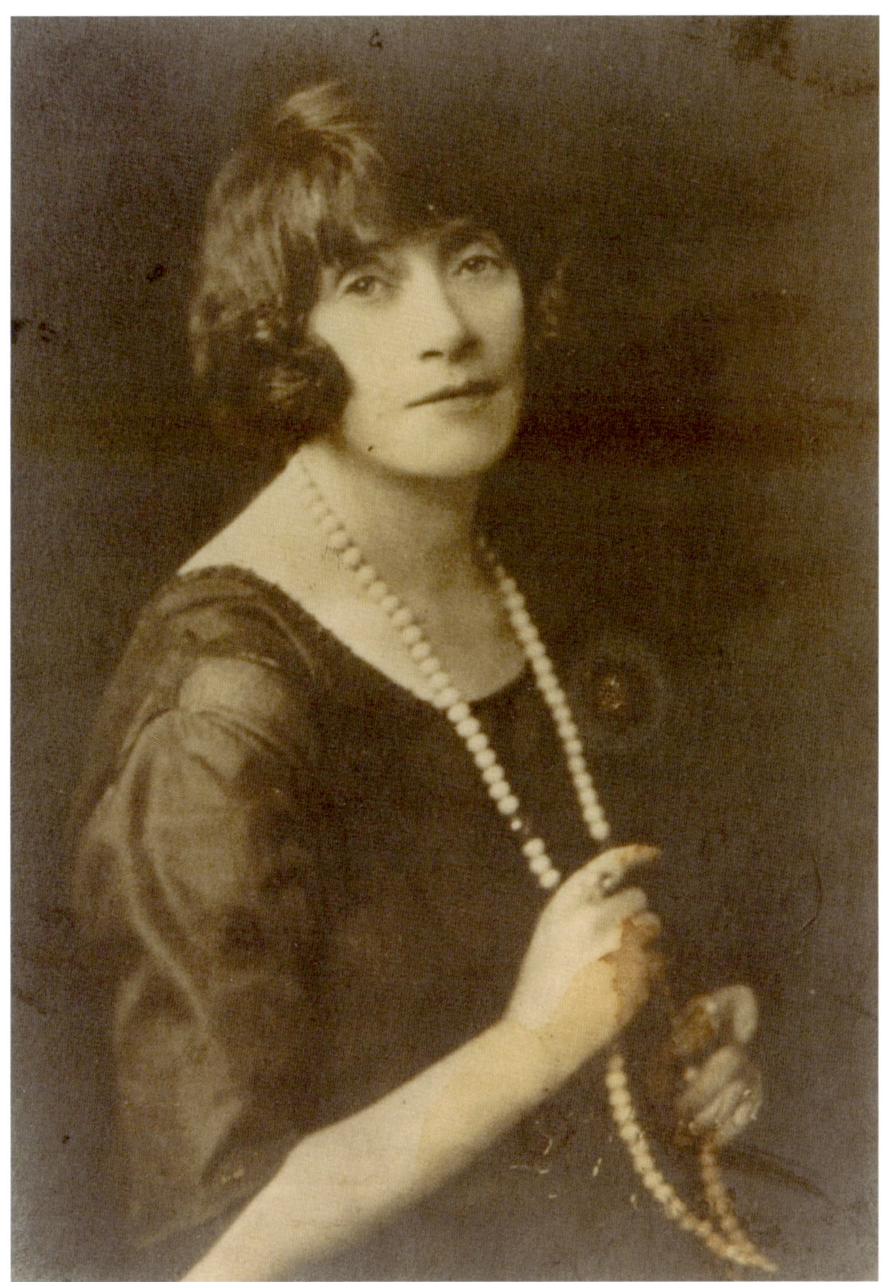

Mildred Sandys in 1920. Photograph taken by Douglas Scott.

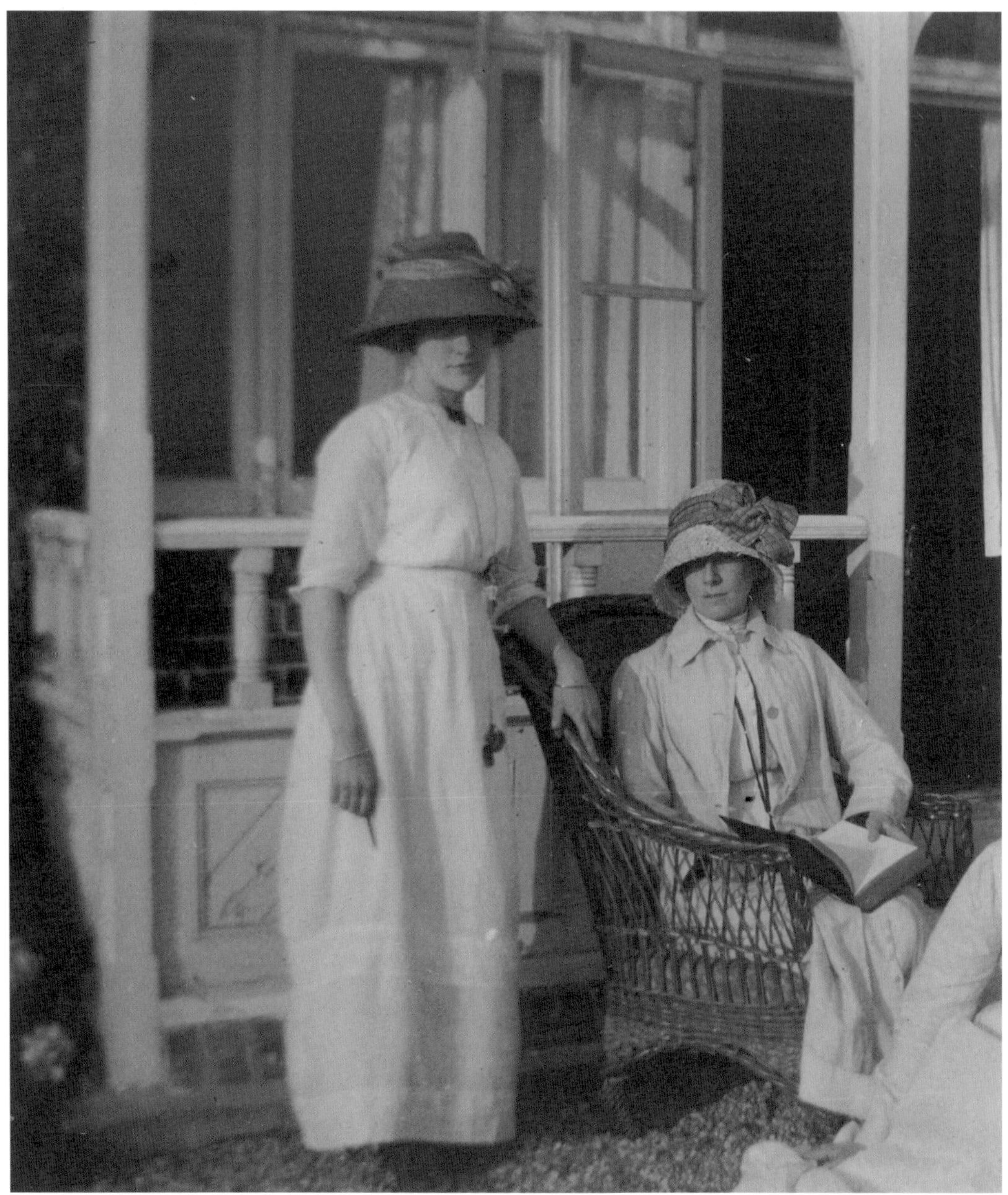

Gertrude and Winifred holidaying at Selsey in 1910, a snapshot sent by Winifred to Samuel Bancroft Jr.

At best she was a careful copyist, usually on a smaller scale, of some of her father's work. She also seems to have been one of the more articulate and practical of the sisters. She was close to her youngest sister, Gertrude, with whom she shared a 'studio' at 10 Aubrey Road, Campden Hill in 1910. As already noted, Winifred attempted to sell her father's diary for 1880 (with its tantalising excisions probably by Winifred herself) to Samuel Bancroft Jr in 1910 for 50 guineas, but he turned it down.[6]

Mildred Emma (1872–1937) appears not to have married. It seems she had aspirations to become a portrait photographer[7] but, according to her nephew Anthony Crane, she became an 'interior decorator' instead. According to her sister Winifred, it was she who posed for her father for *The White Mayde of Avenel*. In 1910 she tried to sell a letter dated 20th May 1869 from George Meredith to Sandys for £10 to Samuel Bancroft Jr, but he was not interested. In 1911 she was living on her own as a boarder at 4 Scarsdale Terrace in Kensington and in 1917 she, with the Soldiers and Sailors Help Society, applied for a patent for 'Improvements in Noah's Arks and like Toys'. This was one of the several charities set up to provide workshops for the employment of disabled ex-combatants resulting from the 1914–1918 war. At Mildred's death in July 1937, she was described as a 'Decorative Artist' formerly living at 45 Manor Street, Chelsea. Her age was given as fifty-nine, but she was in fact sixty-five. She died at 5 Hogarth Road with her sister Constance in attendance.

Through my correspondence, from July 1974 to March 1976, with the late Henry Rossiter (1885–1977), Curator Emeritus of the Prints and Drawings Department of the Museum of Fine Arts, Boston[8] I learned something more about Mildred whom he knew as 'Sandy'. He remembered her as wearing 'earrings made of the strips of ivory from the handle of a fan, about 10" long, and lived in Chelsea'. They evidently had met at the Twenty-One Gallery, which was above Rossiter's flat in the Adelphi, which was owned by Mrs Molly Bernhard-Smith 'who was a long-time friend of Sandy's'.

Sandys's eldest son Hugh Algernon Negus Sandys (1875–1953) became a qualified mining engineer and a member of the Institute of Mining and Metallurgy. He had married Alice Mary (or Muriel) Dehane (*c.*1873/4–1950) in 1903. His father completed a pair of portraits of the couple that year, probably as a wedding present. Hugh made many journeys between 1901 and 1938, to Egypt, Southeast- and West Africa, Spain, Canada, and Argentina as an investigator and agent, sometimes accompanied by Alice. For instance, in June 1929 they travelled on the steamship *Flandria* to Vigo, Spain, and onwards to Buenos Aires. Hugh travelled alone to Montreal (where his brother Guy had settled) in 1928, and again in 1931.[9] Alice died in 1950 in London of heart failure. Hugh died by drowning in Spain in 1953.

In 1923, Maud Mary (1876–1962), with her twelve-year-old son, married Ernest William Hales, a solicitor. Probably in the mid-1930s she wrote from an address in Wimbledon to the Norwich Castle Museum curator offering to sell a caricature of her father by 'Ravenhill'.[10] It was turned down.[11] One hopes that it may reappear. Maud Mary's son, calling himself Peter Anthony Hales, later Sandys (1911–1983), married firstly Alfhild Thanderz in 1936, and then in 1950 Joan Smith with whom he had several children.

Constance (1878–1962) trained as a nurse. In 1933 she was at 5 Hogarth Road when she wrote to the curator at Norwich Museum offering for sale 'a cast of my father[']s (the late Frederick Sandys) head taken after death … as it is necessary for me to part with it … for twenty five guineas for the Museum'. As noted, this was turned down and has since disappeared.[12] She was still at Hogarth Road in 1957 when she was hoping to sell to the National Portrait Gallery, for £15, a pair of miniatures of her father and mother, painted in 1906 by her sister Winifred.[13] According to Anthony Crane, she and Maud lived at Hogarth Road until they died.[14] They sold the leasehold in the 1940s but were given licence to stay on.

Ruth (1880–1941) became a successful graphic artist, influenced by Albert Rutherston. Notably, she was responsible for the house style of Lilley & Skinner's fashionable shoe business, designed a London Transport poster advertising the London Zoo, and produced some very stylish children's book illustrations. According to Anthony Crane, she had rather spectacular 'russet gold locks'.

Guy (1882–1957) was in lodgings at 57 Princes Square in Lambeth in 1910,[15] and was described in the 1911 census as a 'Timber Importer and Merchant's clerk', married to Isabel Brennan. The couple were next living in a four-room apartment at 39D Telferscot Road near Tooting Bec Common. His sister Maud Mary was living with them with her three-month old baby Peter Anthony. In March 1913 Guy and Isabel were on the list of passengers on the SS *Canada* from Liverpool, bound for Montreal, where they settled. After Isabel's death there in 1928, he married Evelyn Mary Price, a widow. He died in Montreal in 1957, leaving a third wife, Mary Wilkes.

The 1911 census also shows Mary with her remaining children, Winifred, Ruth, and Gertrude, at 5 Hogarth Road. Mary was registered there as a ratepayer until 1919, dying there in September 1920. Winifred was listed as

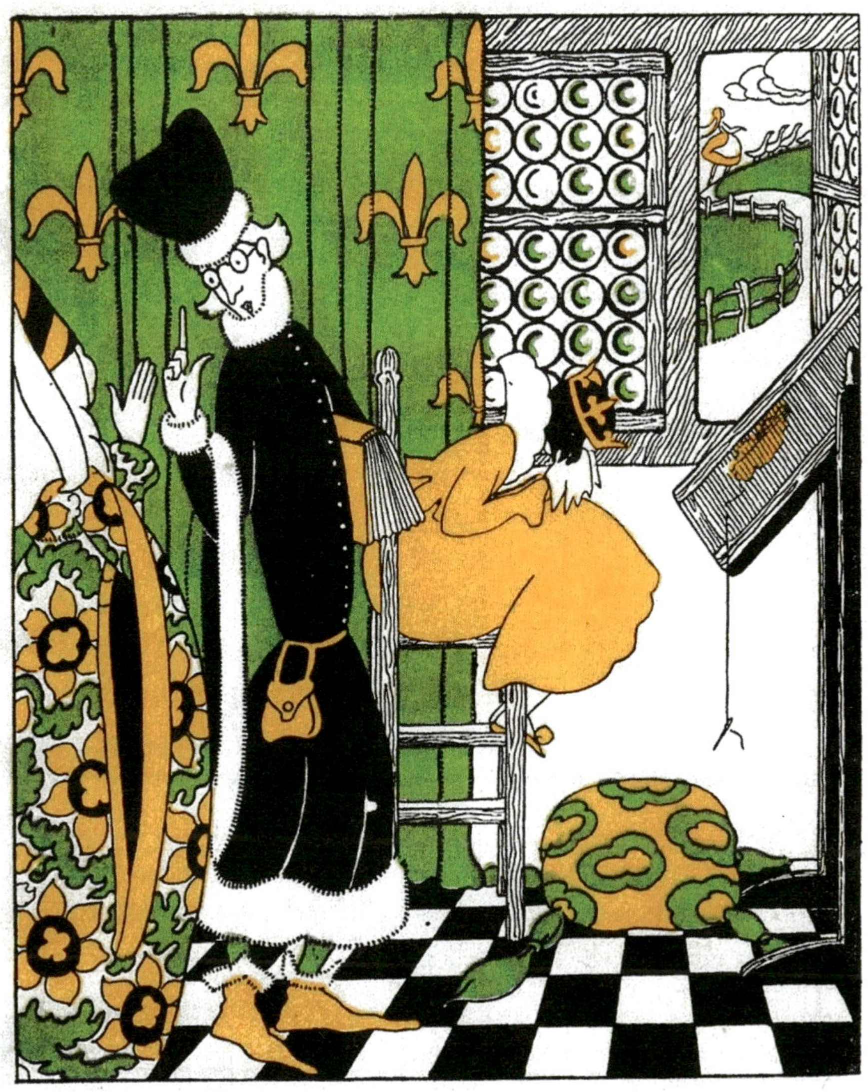

THE DOCTOR SAID SHE MUST GO TO BED AT ONCE

Illustration by Ruth Sandys: 'Princess Matilda and Matilda' in *The Great Book for Children* (1929).

a 'portrait painter', Ruth as a 'black and white artist', and Gertrude, who was then twenty-five years old, was listed as having no occupation. The Hogarth Road dwelling was described as having nine rooms, including the kitchen. Anthony Crane recalled that: 'The main living rooms would be turned over completely to a cottage industry producing, for example, painted powder-puff dolls or stencilled canvas shopping bags or whatever decorative fad was marketable at the moment.'[16]

On 2nd August 1913, Gertrude (1886–1920) and Lionel Crane (1876–1943) were married at St Mary Abbot's Church, Kensington. Lionel Crane was the elder of the two sons of Walter Crane (1845–1915) and Mary Frances Crane, and was an architect working in the 'Arts and Crafts' style. In 1892 Lionel was articled to Reginald Blomfield and attended the Royal Academy Schools from 1897–1900. During these years he travelled widely in Europe. Professionally, he embarked on a short-lived partnership with Detmar Blow which ended in 1905, after which he took on a partnership with William Willan. He was also associated with Harrison Townsend during the building of the Horniman Museum, at Forest Hill, South London, between 1898 and 1901. It appears from a letter from Winifred to Samuel Bancroft Jr that there was opposition to the marriage of Lionel with Gertrude from both mothers. The couple therefore married secretly with the help of the wealthy Lady Catherine Lawrence, the wife of Sir Charles Napier Lawrence, who provided Gertrude's wedding outfit and trousseau and much else besides.[17]

In April 1916 Gertrude gave birth to Anthony, their only child. Sadly, Gertrude died of pneumonia in June 1920, perhaps a late victim of the Spanish flu epidemic. Not long afterwards, in July 1921, Lionel married Winifred, and they brought up Anthony together.

Mary Emma Jones, or 'Mrs Sandys's (earlier referred to as 'Mrs Neville'), died at 5 Hogarth Road in September 1920, leaving her two daughters Ruth (1880–1941) and Constance (1878–1962) still living there.

Anthony Charles Walter Crane (1916–2008) had a successful life as a linguist and translator. In the 1939–1945 war, he served as a Captain in the Intelligence Corps, and was awarded the MBE for his work at Bletchley Park. After the death of his first wife Anna, he married his partner, Angela. He inherited both the Crane family papers and the Sandys family papers, and in his retirement lectured on his two grandfathers, of whom he was very proud.[18]

5 Hogarth Road, Earl's Court (in 1973). Frederick and Mary both died at this address. Here, in 1911, lived Winifred, Ruth and Gertrude, who lived there with their mother until Gertrude's marriage in 1913.

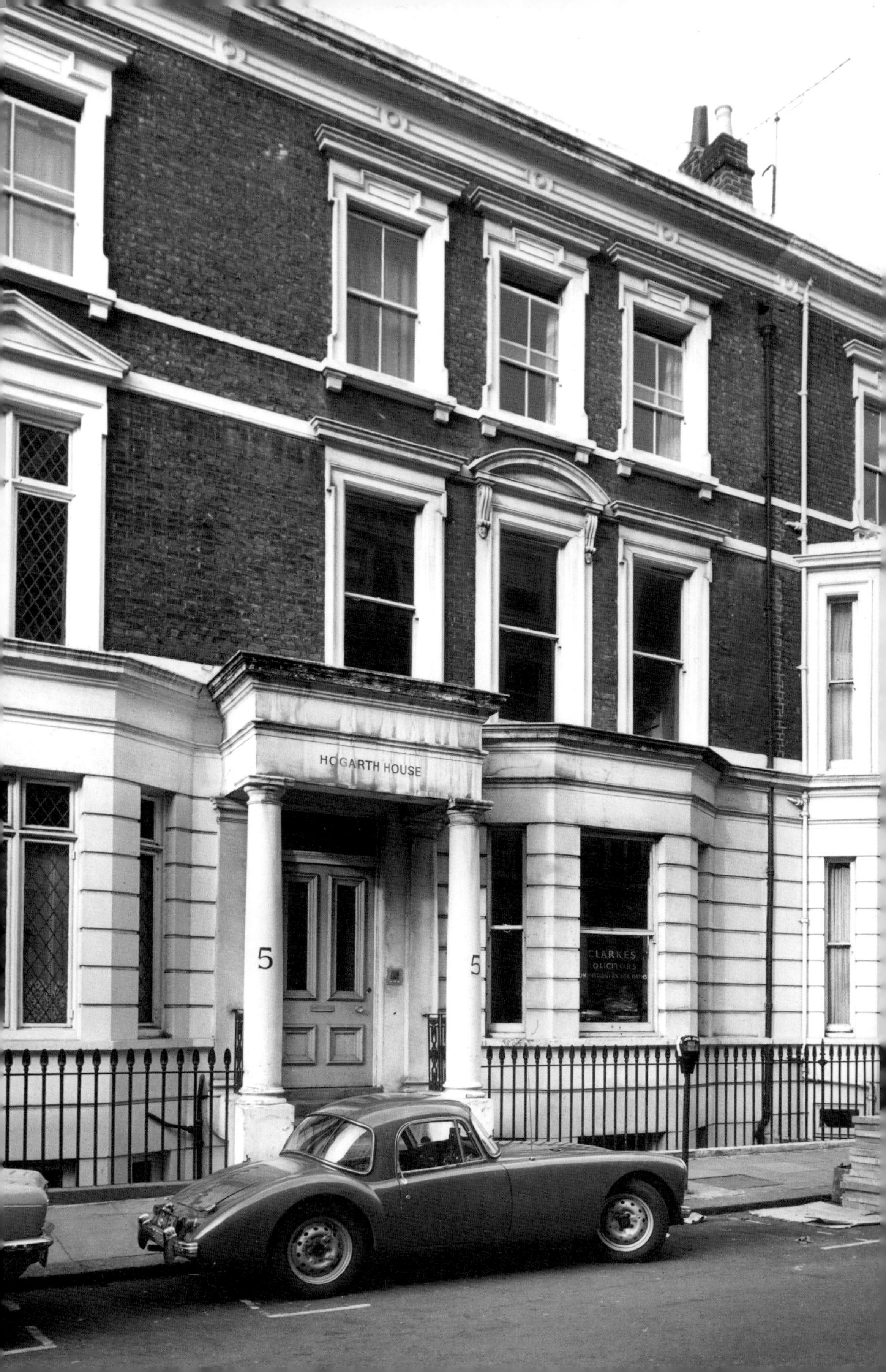
HOGARTH HOUSE
5
5
CLARKES

[1] The information regarding Keomi's family was gleaned from the author's correspondence with Sharon Heppell, Vice-Chair of the Romany and Traveller Family History Society, and editor of their *Journal*. Gypsy family research is unfortunately difficult due to illiteracy and to the irregularities of their way of life. However, Mrs Heppell was extremely helpful to me with information from her research and records.

[2] I am unable to identify Charlotte as one of Keomi's daughters. Munnings must have been mistaken. Rose, born *c.*1879, would be more likely his subject, as she was close in age to her sister Nellie (b. *c.*1877).

[3] Alfred Munnings, *An Artist's Life. (1950-52).* Vol.1, p. 65.

[4] Information from the 1871 census of Poplar, Tower Hamlets.

[5] Maude Grove was renamed Fernshaw Road in 1892.

[6] Letter from Samuel Bancroft Jr to Winifred Sandys, dated 29th December 1910. Delaware Art Museum Library, Bancroft Archive.

[7] Letter from Samuel Bancroft Jr to Winifred Sandys, dated 21st July 1908. Delaware Art Museum Library, Bancroft Archive.

[8] Rossiter had the foresight to buy for Boston the important (Harold) Hartley Collection of British Illustration, from his son Sir Harold Hartley in 1955.

[9] Guy's first wife Isabel died in September 1928. Anon. (Montreal) press cutting. Sandys Family Archive.

[10] Leonard Raven-Hill (1867–1942), artist, illustrator and cartoonist.

[11] Undated letter from Mrs Mary Hales from 3 Thornton Road, Wimbledon. Norwich Castle Museum, Art Department files.

[12] Letter from Constance Sandys to the curator, dated from the curator's reply of September 1933. Norwich Castle Museum, Art Department files.

[13] Correspondence of Constance Sandys with C.K. Adams, July 1957. They were turned down, but a record photograph was taken of them. London, National Portrait Gallery Archives.

[14] Records show that Ruth died at Hogarth Road in 1941, possibly being nursed there by her sister Constance. She had been living in St Margaret's Road, Twickenham.

[15] Electoral Registers, Kennington, Lambeth, 1910.

[16] Brighton Museum and Art Gallery, *Frederick Sandys 1829–1904.* Exhibition catalogue (1974). Essay, "The Pater" by Anthony Crane, p. 14.

[17] Letter from Winifred Sandys to Samuel Bancroft Jr, dated 9th August 1913, from The Studio, 10 Aubrey Road, Campden Hill. Delaware Art Museum Library, Bancroft Archive.

[18] The Walter Crane Archive is to be found in Manchester, divided between the University Library and the Whitworth Art Gallery. The Sandys Family Archive is in London in the Word and Image Department of the Victoria and Albert Museum.

opposite: *Trade card.* detail. see page 110

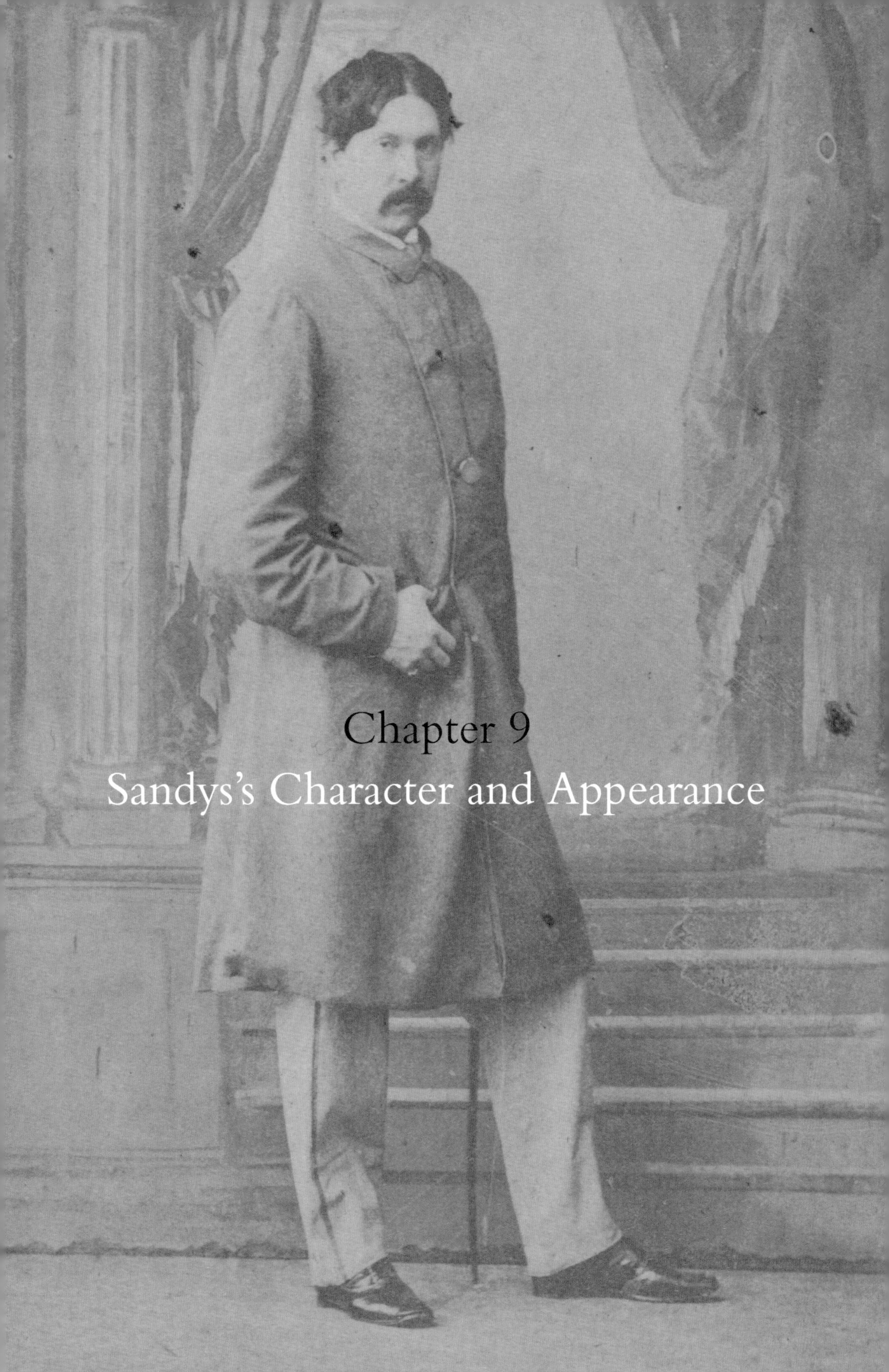

Chapter 9

Sandys's Character and Appearance

Sandys was living at a time when many artists became wealthy. There was a new, educated generation of middle-class art collectors whose money came from industry and the professions. Art collecting became an expression of elite status instead of merely recording one's family in portraits (although portraits were wanted too, luckily for Sandys who became known for being able to produce a good likeness). The newly rich inhabited substantial villas and mansions, and bare walls needed pictures. However, there were two contemporary artists who failed to take full advantage of this favourable turn – both of them eccentric and unbusinesslike: Sandys and Whistler. But unlike Whistler, Sandys had a large and growing family to support. This factor, and a need to keep up appearances when mixing with wealthy clients and cultured society, let alone to participate in a freely convivial life with his bohemian friends, led to a chronic impoverishment of himself and his family. His letters headed with addresses from numerous lodging houses are proof of his having to move on after owing rent. At times, Sandys was so short of cash that he could not afford to pay for the materials that he needed to complete his work. This can be noted from the accounts of suppliers, such as Roberson's, with whom he fell into debt several times.[1] An occasional ploy was to find the current patron to pay the bill for him, deducting the sum from the final payment for the picture.

Another factor contributed to a chaotic budget – betting – a habit of the poorly-off, risking money in the usually futile hope of winning a 'fortune'. Although in Sandys's case he was often lucky. As previously mentioned, there is a story from a chronicler of *The Pink 'Un* (or *The Sporting Times*), which places him as a habitual gambler on the horses:[2] 'In 1876 Sandys wanted to back the treble event on the strength of a dream: *Thunder* for the City, *Petrarch* for the Two Thousand, and *Kisber* for the Derby. He wanted to take £8000 to 10, but being short of the necessary tenner asked Ballyhooley to fund it and go halves in the bet. Ballyhooley either couldn't or wouldn't, so Sandys borrowed a sovereign, and took eight hundred pounds to a sovereign. And when the treble event came off, a broken Irishman kicked a hole in his hat and retired to his native morass.'[3]

In his personal affairs, it seems he had not the self-discipline to bear the financial responsibilities which he brought upon himself by fathering many children. His parental background probably had much to do with this. His parents were from the then poorly educated artisan class, and although Sandys himself had the benefit of a scholarship to the local grammar school, which considerably helped in his educational and social progress, his family were poor, and as is often the case with the poor, it was natural to try and better themselves by whatever means they could. His father Anthony certainly had high aspirations for himself, as well as for his talented son. Strict truthfulness and integrity were not characteristics of either father or son. 'Improving' their name by adding the 'y' was a part of this – it added a hint of aristocratic family connections.

A telling statement comes from Sandys's obituary in *The Times*:[4] '… those who can carry back their memories … will always regard him as the man who might, if he had so chosen, have been among the foremost artists of his time … his work was the result not only of a genuine artistic conception but of prodigious labour; which is perhaps one reason why so few fine pictures by him are in existence. Another cause, we fear, was to be found in a certain irresolution of character, which hindered his productiveness and prevented many very willing patrons from giving him commissions.' The writer added, however, that he should be represented in public collections (which in 1904, he was not). He is still inadequately represented in the National Collection of British Art at the Tate Gallery, but thanks to the perspicacity of Charles Fairfax Murray he is well represented at the Birmingham Art Gallery. He is also well represented at his birthplace, Norwich, in the Castle Museum, where it is due to local patronage, notably that of the Colman family. Unfortunately, in recent years, to Britain's great loss, some of his finest portraits have gone overseas.

G.C. Williamson, the biographer of the nineteenth century dealer Murray Marks, devoted a whole chapter in his book to Sandys, writing: 'Amongst the most wonderful draughtsmen of the '60s and '70s none was more skilful than Frederick Sandys … (his) best work has been compared to the drawings of Dürer and the panels of Van Eyck. … The very able artist of whom this praise is not too high, was at the same time one of the most extraordinary of men … very largely he educated himself. … He was always in difficulties all his life. A borrower at all times, very seldom paying back any of the sums which he borrowed so freely, and yet, strangely inexact and careless and tiresome in his personal habits as he was, his work was invariably marked by scrupulous exactitude, marvellous attention to details, and extraordinary facility, coupled with a wonderful power of rendering every accessory with a perfection almost Pre-Raphaelite in its characteristics.

'Sandys was a man whose personal appearance one can never forget, perhaps helped by the fact that, summer or winter, he always wore a white waistcoat, and invariably appeared in patent leather boots. Many times he was reduced to possessing but two waistcoats, and he would be met wearing one very much soiled, on the way to fetch the other from the laundress. Shortly afterwards he might be seen resplendent in the second waistcoat, which was generally adorned with gilt buttons. It used to be said that he had a set of half a dozen gold buttons and that whatever happened to him nothing would induce him to part with or even pawn these buttons … the buttons were not gold although quite good ones, and very proud he was of them. … Money he was always wanting and was always ready to borrow. "Huh," he would say, on meeting a friend, "lend me fifty pounds; I must have a hundred, cannot you borrow for me five hundred," but he was often content to have the loan – as he expressed it – of a sovereign or even five shillings, but those who made the loan knew perfectly well that there was no expectation of it ever being returned.

'Everybody tried to help him who appreciated his work; everybody tried to keep him straight; nobody, however succeeded, and to those who came into contact with Sandys, as the present writer did on many occasions, he offered a bewildering psychological problem that was past all comprehension.'[5]

Perhaps the most severe assessment of his character came from the artist Frederick Barwell (1831–1922) who knew Sandys from their earliest days in Norwich: 'His acquaintance began to be cultivated by several of the younger men till some of them became alarmed at his efforts to get them to accept bills of exchange, in slang parlance "to help him to fly kites", and to borrow money off some of them. He had the peculiar faculty of making people who could be useful to him to believe that he was a man of extraordinary genius whose ill-fortune had kept him back, and that he only needed encouragement and help to astonish the world. In the long run they found him an expensive protégé, and that it were better to keep clear of him.'

An obituarist in *The Star* wrote: 'It was not only that he was unusually striking in appearance – sometimes I used to think that he could never have been so splendid in his youth as he was in old age – but he had a charm that all whose privilege it was to know him felt very keenly. And he was a wonderful talker. Had he had his Boswell, what a picture we should have of the great days of Pre-Raphaelitism!'[6]

His adoring daughter Winifred wrote: '…he was over six feet in stature and somewhat leonine; there was a greatness about everything he said or did, that one could not sufficiently admire.'[7] A tendency to dandyism is not uncommonly found in those in the circumstances of a financially precarious life. Uppermost is the necessity of 'keeping up appearances' in spite of all difficulties – it affirmed his stance as a gentleman and a superior being. Furthermore, he was more of a 'club man' and 'diner out' than most of his Pre-Raphaelite friends. His companions were artists, journalists, theatrical people, and architects. There was never a 'home fire burning' or a careful household economy – just a room in a lodging house, except on the brief occasions when he had a studio and indulged in employing a housekeeper to look after a short-lived ménage.

Walter Shaw Sparrow (1862–1940) wrote that: 'He was exceedingly vain and proud, yet eager to accept favours which ought to have been humiliating; cool and genial on the surface, persuasive, attractive, yet haughty, wayward, erratic, and easy to irritate. ... The technical virtues that his genius did employ were irrationally different: minute in verification and research, diligently fastidious and thorough, occupying so much time and so much patience that they invited opposition from Sandys himself. Even when the man and his genius went downhill together, the latter remained devotedly painstaking, delicate and appealing, with a dignified disregard for time and its housekeeping expenses.'[8]

Robert Ross (1869–1918) in his *Dictionary of National Biography* entry on Sandys wrote: 'Intemperate and bohemian modes of life seem to have atrophied his powers. He was a constant borrower and a difficult if delightful friend [and] his relations with most of his associates were chequered. ... He was in the habit of giving friends somewhat varied and inconsistent details of his career.'[9]

The eroticism, which especially permeates his earlier works of the 1860s and renders them so attractive, parallels the sexual promiscuity of his real life. He had a keen eye for feminine beauty and seems to have been irresistibly drawn to bed the object of his admiration without thought of consequences.

It seems preposterous that he was petitioning in 1863 for a divorce from his wife Georgiana, whom he married in 1853 when he was twenty-four. In spite of the expense it would entail, he decided to sue her for adultery when he was in truth committing adultery himself with his model Keomi Gray. The result was that his wife turned the tables on him, and in the course of the legal examination, some unpleasant facts were revealed of him having assaulted her. The Court quite rightly ruled in her favour and also charged him with defaulting on the financial support to which she was entitled. It is doubtful, however, that much alimony was ever paid.

He seems to have given little or no attention to his first four children with Keomi, who returned to Norfolk with them, re-joining her own family after the relationship with Sandys ended. All four children no doubt merged easily into the gypsy community. Indeed, they seem to have done well for themselves within that way of life – of entertaining, providing travelling amusement fairs, fortune-telling, and horse-trading. Sandys's half-gypsy children in turn had children, who therefore became Sandys's unacknowledged descendants.

The first three babies which Sandys had with his new love, the actress Mary Emma Jones, were fostered out from birth at Millwall, East London, and after the accidental death of Maura, the first one, the next two were transferred to the family of a builder in Kensington. The arrears of payment of the costs of the latter contributed to Sandys's 1876 bankruptcy. The foster parents, Mr and Mrs McManus, seem to have adopted the two girls, Cecilia and Dorothy, giving them the McManus surname.[10] Cecilia and Dorothy ended their days as spinsters at a house in Hammersmith. The last surviving one, Dorothy, was able to leave a small bequest to a friend when she died in 1955.[11] Anthony Crane, Frederick's grandson, told me that he was dimly aware of these sisters as unspecified distant relatives. In actual fact, as since discovered, they were Anthony Crane's mother Gertrude's eldest sisters.

Altogether it seems that Sandys was bankrupted at least five times in his life: 1859, 1873, 1876–1877, 1883, and 1899. It is a miracle that he stayed out of prison; that being so, settlements must have been made and, somehow or other, deficiencies were paid up.

It is no wonder that his friend, patron, and lawyer James Anderson Rose became exasperated with him: 'Nobody can be more anxious or willing to serve but there are limits to forbearance. The contents of your letter of Friday evening are intolerable after the pain and trouble I have been taking in your affairs. Being so annoyed I have taken 24 hours to think what I should do & I have determined to accept your letter as your decision that you will at once relieve me from all thought or anxiety about you. I shall therefore take no further steps in the matter of your bankruptcy nor will Messrs Harding whose charges I will pay to the present time as I guaranteed them.'[12] Cyril Flower was another exasperated friend, having tried to help Sandys several times.

The Anderson Rose papers concerning the bankruptcy of 1876 reveal that: '[He] … never kept any books nor any accounts and the statement of his affairs must be prepared by an accountant (Mr Sandys is entirely without funds).'[13]

It is not that he was undervalued for his actual work. His work was well known and admired, and he had many wealthy patrons. There is evidence also that he got good prices for his work. One can only assume that he was hopelessly disorganised in his ways, besides being obsessively slow and laborious in the way he worked. Understandably there were periods of extreme demoralisation, and there was the gambling habit.

At the same time, Sandys denigrated earning money, as his daughter Winifred revealed in a letter to Samuel Bancroft Jr: '… the imperativeness of making money, which as father said, is damnable to art.'[14]

In summary, his character worked against his best interest as an outstandingly talented artist.

[1] Roberson's account books at the Hamilton Kerr Institute, University of Cambridge.

[2] J.B. Booth *Old Pink 'Un Days* (1925), p. 137.

[3] 'Ballyhooley' was Robert Martin (1846–1905), an Irishman who was a journalist on the staff of *The Sporting Times* and was also a burlesque song writer. He was related to Sandys's friend W.G. Wills.

[4] *The Times*, 27th June 1904.

[5] G.C. Williamson, *Murray Marks and his Friends.* (1919), pp. 105–112.

[6] Perhaps written by a member of the Upcher family of Norfolk. The initials 'A.U.' under 'Art and Artists. Frederick Sandys's *The Star*, 28th June 1904.

[7] Winifred Sandys to Samuel Bancroft Jr dated 15th July 1908. Delaware Art Museum Library, Bancroft Archive.

[8] Walter Shaw Sparrow, *One of the Real Victorians, A.F.A. Sandys, Artist and Talker*, (1934). Unpublished typescript in the Sandys Family Archive.

[9] Robert Ross, *Dictionary of National Biography*, Vol. 3, (1912), pp. 263–265.

[10] Mr McManus was by trade a builder, of 29 Phillimore Place, Kensington in an area which was being developed at that time. Library of Congress, Manuscript Division, Pennell-Whistler Collection.

[11] Cecilia (1869–1937) and Dorothy (1870–1955).

[12] Library of Congress, Manuscript Division, Pennell-Whistler Collection.

[13] Library of Congress, Manuscript Division, Pennell-Whistler Collection.

[14] Winifred Sandys to Samuel Bancroft Jr, 2nd September 1911. Delaware Art Museum Library, Bancroft Archive.

opposite: *Proud Maisie.* detail. see page 104

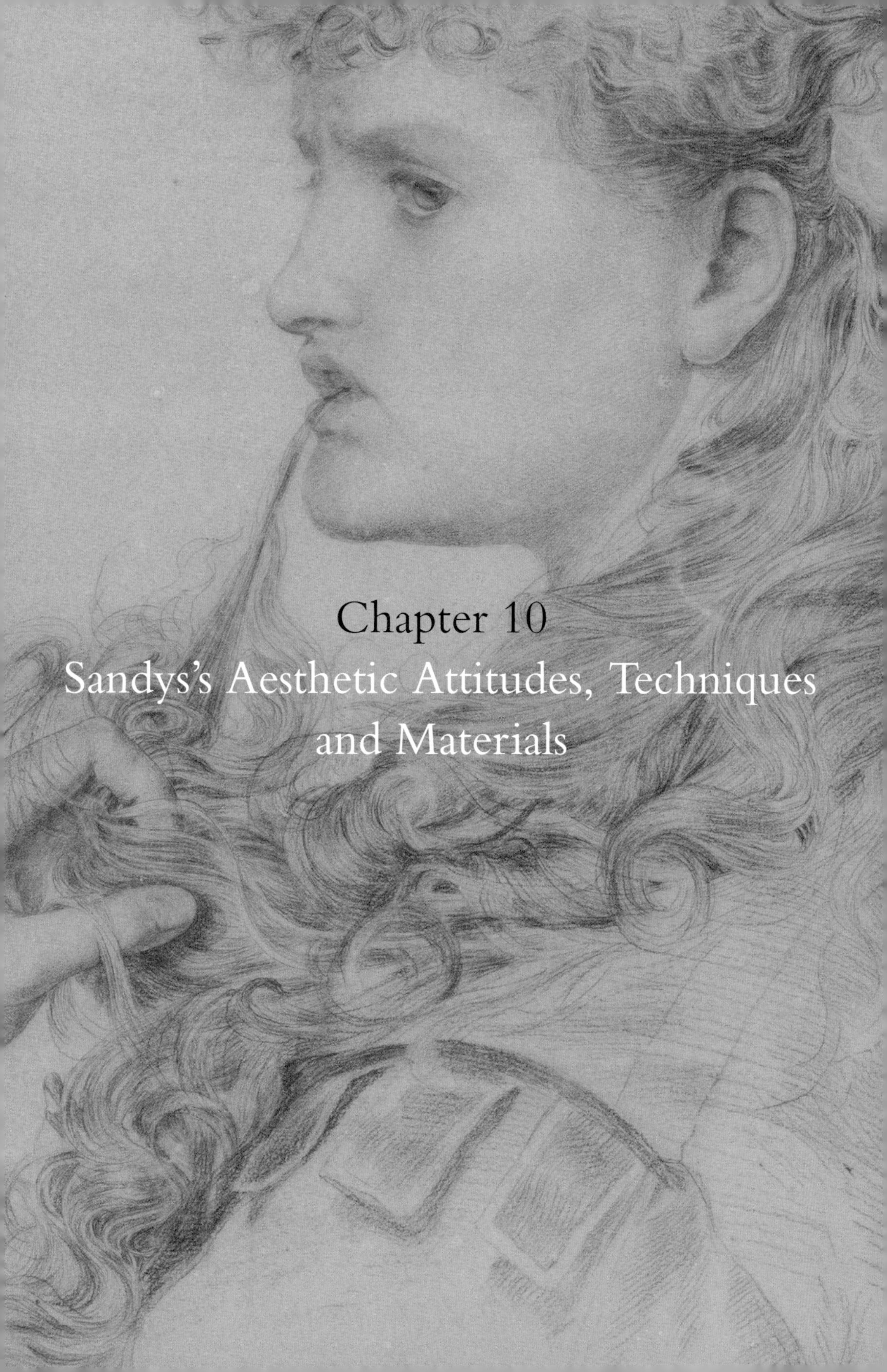

Chapter 10
Sandys's Aesthetic Attitudes, Techniques and Materials

In his earliest paintings, done in Norwich, under the eye of his father, Sandys naturally worked in the prevailing traditional tonal style. Generally, instead of working on a pure white canvas or panel, the artist would first lay down a mid-tone base layer. This can be seen best in an unfinished portrait of his mother (*c.*1849, see p.21). On this base layer, the image would be worked up by adding lighter tones in succession, making the subject stand out in contrast against the mid-toned background, and adding darker tones to complete the tonal range. The aim was to achieve an effect of three-dimensions upon a two-dimensional support. However, by the late 1850s, a change took place in Sandys's work, influenced by the new ideas of the Pre-Raphaelite artists, of laying the colours down on a pure white base ground for maximum lucidity, giving the colours, which were mostly laid on in transparent glazes, great brilliancy. This enamel-like white ground, remaining untouched in this case, can be seen in the unfinished panel painting of *Proud Maisie* (1868, see p. 105). Sandys liked to use a quick-drying medium mixed with his pigments in order to keep his layered applications intact.

Sandys suffered from a lack of a sound academic training, and of opportunities to travel abroad to see the great collections of art in continental Europe. This, with his innate skill in draughtsmanship, might have carried him to much greater heights in his profession. However, he seems to have made the most of what he could see in England, as well as on his important but brief trip in 1862 to the Netherlands with James Anderson Rose, which was apparently the only time he left the British Isles.

Founded in the 1820s, the National Gallery collection was newly housed in the late 1830s in the purpose-built building in Trafalgar Square by the Norwich-born William Wilkins (1778–1839). Therefore, when Sandys first came to London in the late 1840s, the nucleus of the national collection of 'old masters' was conveniently available to him. The National Portrait Gallery was to follow in 1856, housed in Westminster from 1859 to 1872, then in South Kensington and Bethnal Green, before a site was acquired behind the National Gallery, opening in 1896.

In the 1860s there were three major loan exhibitions of national portraits held at the South Kensington Museum, making available to the public arrays of fine paintings by artists such as Memling, Holbein, Clouet, van Dyck, Lely, Reynolds, and Gainsborough.[1] Furthermore, there was a gallery of paintings shown at the International Exhibition of 1862, also at South Kensington – so there was a good deal of inspirational art available to be seen in London in Sandys's lifetime.

The influence of early Northern European painting is clearly to be seen at this time in his portraits in oil, which achieved extraordinarily realistic representations of his subjects. In the technique he developed, he would start with a careful full-scale drawing on paper of the sitter. In this he strove for pin-point accuracy in facial features and pose. He would then trace this outline drawing on to the whitened prepared support, fixing his outlines in dilute sanguine-coloured paint. Then he would proceed to add colours part by part, confining them to the compartments established by his traced drawing. This strict technique was habitual and resulted in a kind of static painting, devoid of energy, movement, and expressive brush-work, which was entirely based on his original drawing. However, in the end result, he could produce an overall balance of colour and tone by adjustments, achieving a three-dimensionality akin to the work of his revered Hans Holbein the Younger. An aesthetic comparison might be made to the work of the older, but contemporary, French artist Jean Auguste Dominique Ingres (1780–1867), in the ability to achieve a smooth but detailed 'finish'. However, the comparison stops there. Ingres was a thoroughly professional master painter, running a studio with assistants. Sandys, by contrast, was a solitary worker with a painstaking and slow technique. This was a real disadvantage as, obviously, it was not an economically viable way of carrying on as a professional artist. Sometimes the end result was an unfinished painting stuck in time for ever. One example of an uncompleted but nevertheless very fine oil portrait is *Mrs Mary Elizabeth Barstow* (*c.*1867, see p. 95), unfinished because the Barstow family, as already explained, had to remove it hastily from Sandys's studio in case of its impoundment by a debt collector.

Since Sandys was chronically short of money, it probably drove him to work on the less laborious (and cheaper to execute) chalk drawings which he could finish relatively fast and, with luck, get a quick financial return. Commissions for oil paintings were rare after the 1870s.

He would always start with the careful drawing on paper, one might say a map of what was before him and, if the customer was not ultimately desirous of an oil portrait, he might take the drawing to a more complete stage. Generally for female sitters, he would fill the surrounding vacant spaces with flowers or foliage. He developed this graphic style increasingly through the 1880s and the 1890s, making some of his chalk portraits virtually equivalent to a finished oil portrait. These portraits came to be much admired. In fact, he seems to have been more at ease when drawing rather than when wielding oil paints with brushes, and the work took much less effort and expense.

Unfortunately, in time, if these chalk portraits have long been exposed to sunlight, the paper support darkens, often disfiguring the work as well as destroying the overall tonal balance. This is often seen in nineteenth century, and earlier, works on paper. By choosing to use tinted papers in later works perhaps was a way of mitigating this problem.

As we have stated, he was an accurate draughtsman of what he saw before him when looking at his subject. In another aspect of Sandys's innate tendencies, if something caught his eye, he might unconsciously repeat his memory of it in one of his compositions.

A device Sandys adopted in some of his oil portraits, ultimately derived from late fifteenth to early sixteenth century portraits both Flemish and Italian, was that of placing a distant landscape, seen through a window behind the sitter. Examples of this can be seen in *Mrs Susanna Rose* (1862), *Julia Caldwell* (1889), and *James Redfoord Bulwer* (1894).

Another device he introduced into several female 'fancy heads' and some oil portraits is a foreground ledge or parapet at the base of the picture, such as in *Vivien* (1863), *Grace Rose* (1866), *Medea* (1866–1868), and *Ysoude* (1870). This was a feature which Rossetti had also used, but which was ultimately derived, from a common element in early Italian, Flemish, and French portraits.

His innovatory use of a two-dimensional decorative but symbolic background, notably seen in his masterful painting, the *Medea* of 1866, anticipated the styles of the later European Symbolist artists.

In my opinion, the best of his oil portraits date from 1860 to 1874: the elderly ladies, *Mrs Susanna Rose* (1861–1862), *Mrs Jane Lewis* (1864), *Anne Susanna Barstow* (1868–1869), and *Mrs Jane Brand* (1874). The best portraits of the younger sitters were *Mrs Hannah Louisa Clabburn* (1860), *Mrs Grace Rose* (1866), and *Mary Elizabeth Barstow* (*c.*1867). Another fine oil subject which is known only from a photograph is *St George for Merrie England* (1880).

As noted in both the oils and the drawings, Sandys loved to include foliage or flowers to fill his undefined 'shallow' backgrounds. His drawing skill was exercised to great advantage, using plants to set off the human figure. His prosperous clients, without exception, would have had some form of plant conservatory attached to their houses, or greenhouses in which to grow prize specimens of flowers. For instance, while staying with the family of his patron George Donaldson to draw a portrait in the 1890s, he visited their neighbour Mrs Eliza Brightwen, the naturalist, at The Grove, Stanmore, and begged her for '... that magnificent chrysanthemum to draw ...' and made arrangements to take it with him back to London. Another time, he asked a fellow artist, the engraver C.W. Sherborn (1831–1912), if he could borrow from him (as he was in a hurry), 'an engraving of a spray of convolvulus or bindweed for a background'.[2] For his oil portrait of Julia Caldwell in 1889, he noted in his diary that shrubs were imported from the James Veitch London nursery and a rose bush from Paul's, the Essex rose breeders, to help him fill the background of his picture.

George Clausen (1852–1944), after seeing the 1905 Memorial Exhibition at the Royal Academy (the concurrent memorial exhibitions of G.F. Watts and Sandys, who both died in 1904) made some very cogent remarks in one of his lectures to students at the Royal Academy. He said: '... a comparison [can be made] between the portraits of Sandys and of Watts in a recent exhibition. Watts's portraits are composed, one element in its relation to another; and this is the true view of nature, which imitative painting (as in the case of Sandys), for all its skill, misses: for a general impression of truth is not produced by adding together all the little truths, but by generalising.'[3] By this, I think Clausen meant that Watts's paintings had achieved an overall unity on the canvas, in contrast to Sandys's copy of what he could see in front of him. However, it cannot be denied that the best of Sandys's portrait work represent a considerable achievement.

As Clausen suggested, Sandys constructed a picture (his illustrations also) by making individual studies which he would fit together to make a whole composition. This piecemeal technique did not allow for much revision nor gave any feeling of movement. His work is all draughtsmanship, and it is the very opposite of 'impressionism'. Nothing went into a picture or tiny illustration without preliminary studies of individual details. His work is in total contrast to many of his contemporaries, notably Whistler, who strove for an instantaneous and overall impression. Whistler was not interested in detail nor in the realistic depiction of textures, which totally occupied Sandys.

A characteristic Sandys practice in the titling of most of his portraits, both drawings and paintings, was his use of a 'Gothic' (or 'black-letter') script. This feature can be traced back to his work on recording Norfolk antiquities for James Bulwer's collection. He had also made copies of examples of such lettering on tombs, medieval memorial 'brasses' and manuscripts. Furthermore, he was familiar with Bulwer's own method of completing each of his sheets before filing them into portfolios, which was to title each subject with red ink in the Gothic script. No doubt Sandys's wealthy patrons appreciated this touch of historicism, which was sometimes augmented by the sitters' family heraldry.

A surprising fact came to the surface after my examination of the records of Roberson's, the supplier of artists' materials:[4] Sandys racked up inordinate expenses by renting, but not returning promptly when finished with, 'lay-figures' from 1853 until as late as 1880.[5] The records also show that he regularly bought prepared panels and canvases for his works in oil, and paper professionally mounted on board or canvas for his chalk drawings, not sparing any expense. After settling one of his bills in 1877, his ledger entry was marked by Roberson's as 'Bankrupt'.

There is no evidence that he employed any studio assistance except, perhaps, in his old age when Winifred, his eldest (acknowledged) daughter, who turned twenty in 1891, showed some talent and a capability to create miniature portraits and miniaturised copies of some of her father's works. She was often sent on errands to buy art supplies for her elderly father.

It is my opinion that after Sandys's death, which left his family in financial straits, it was most likely Winifred who got to work on dividing up sheets of small pencil studies (particularly those he made for illustrations in the 1860s) to sell as individual drawings, adding the initials 'F.S.' by way of authenticating them. Probably also, unfinished drawings which remained in the house would be touched up by her to make them saleable.

In his 1902 article Percy Bate set out clearly Sandys's technique in his later portrait drawings by quoting him: 'In making a chalk portrait I first faintly outline the features, and then, very lightly, with cotton wool, I put on a flat, even tint over the whole face. It is something like a flat wash in watercolours, only there is a little more colour.[6] Then only do I begin to work up the features, with black and an ordinary red chalk only.'[7] By 'red' he meant sanguine-coloured chalk. Not mentioned, but certainly used, was white chalk for highlights especially when using a toned paper support.

Perceptively, Bate went on to write: 'These drawings of his must not be confounded with pastels … [instead] we must seek in the art of older days for something analogous [and] we shall find it in the Drawings of Holbein [and] of Clouet.'[8]

As already noted in his letter to Ernest Brown in late 1903, Sandys preferred to work on prepared paper mounted on board (or stretchers): '… for with a carefully finished drawing I like to have the opportunity of working on [it] when it has been mounted – lest some of the sharpness of the white chalk should have been injured.'[9]

Particularly in his later portrait drawings, there is a tendency to elongate the image vertically – most noticeable in the heads of his sitters (but without any loss of the likeness). This probably was the result of the worsening of his myopia or short-sightedness, which he confessed to, forcing him to stand too close to his subject and to his drawing, thus losing the overall view in which comparative proportions could be better observed.

As it happened, his illustrations pre-dated the invention of photomechanical processes for printing art. Skilled craftsmen were employed who incised the designs on the end-grain of hardwood blocks. Probably through his study of historic engravings, Sandys understood the technique well and drew with the engravers' work in mind. After his death, he was above all remembered for these illustrations. A later generation, coming upon them afresh, recognised their unique aesthetic quality.

He had several faithful patrons who admired his undoubted talent, but his unreliability was an important factor against any success he could have attained as a professional. However, in his career as a whole, there were several bursts of sheer genius, largely in the 1860s, for which one hopes he will continue to be remembered and admired.

[1] Renamed the Victoria and Albert Museum in 1901.

[2] British Library. Add.Ms.42577. f.123. F.S. to Charles Sherborn. Undated but probably of the mid-1890s.

[3] Published as George Clausen, *Aims and Ideals in Art* (1905). Kindly drawn to my attention by Timothy Stevens.

[4] Hamilton Kerr Institute, University of Cambridge. Roberson Archive. Index of Account Holders.

[5] Lay-figures for the use of artists are full sized mannequins (more accurately, like human-sized dolls), either male, female, or child-sized, which could be dressed and posed in the place of a human model.

[6] This technique is akin to 'dozelling', as described in Dyche and Pardon's *New General English Dictionary* (1768).

[7] Percy Bate, "The Late Frederick Sandys: a Retrospect", in *The Studio*, October 1904, p. 15.

[8] Percy Bate, ibid.

[9] F.S. to Ernest Brown dated 'Tuesday afternoon' (late 1903). Takamiya Collection, Tokyo. no. 33.

opposite: *Medea*. detail. see page 101

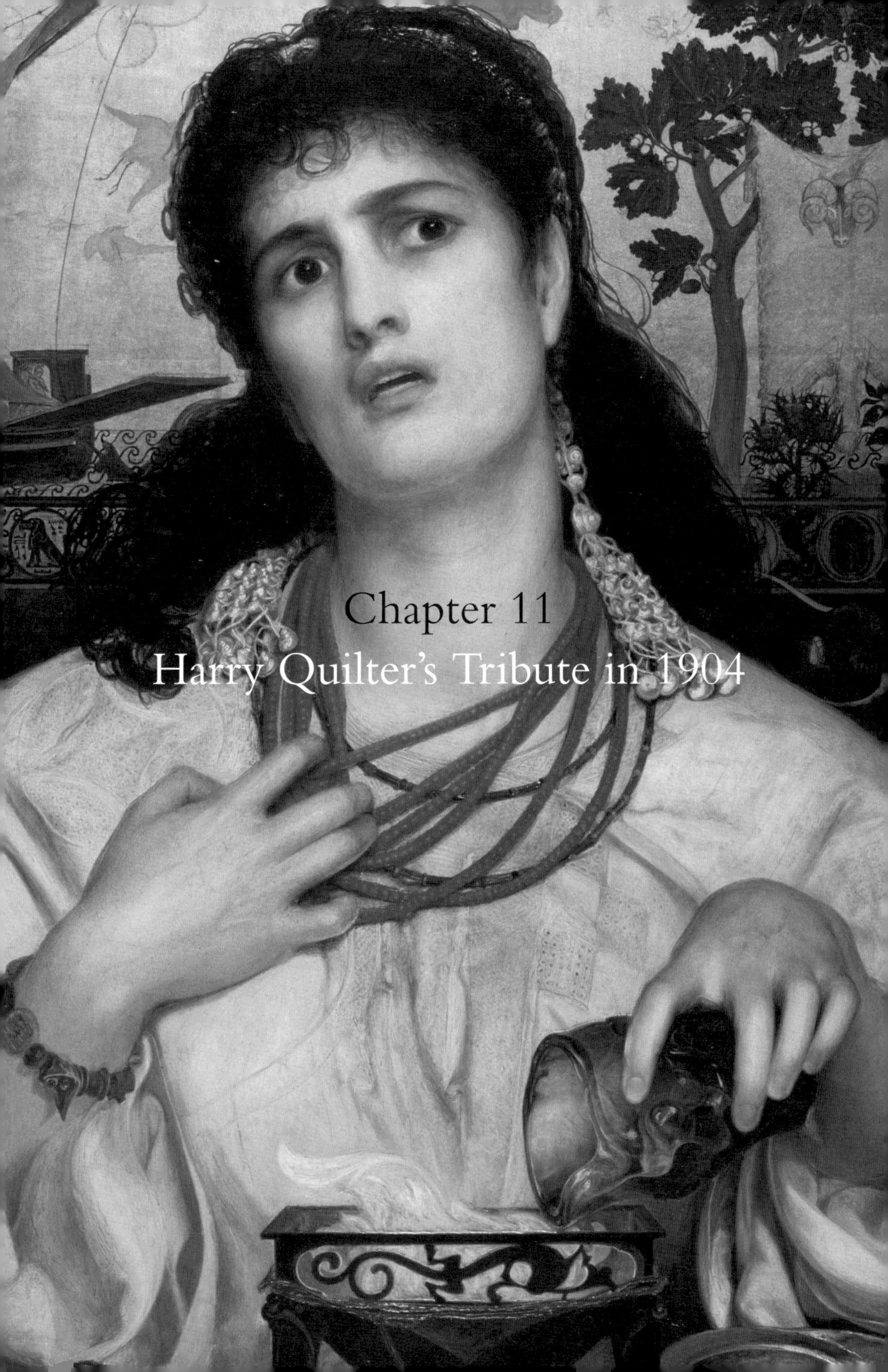

Chapter 11
Harry Quilter's Tribute in 1904

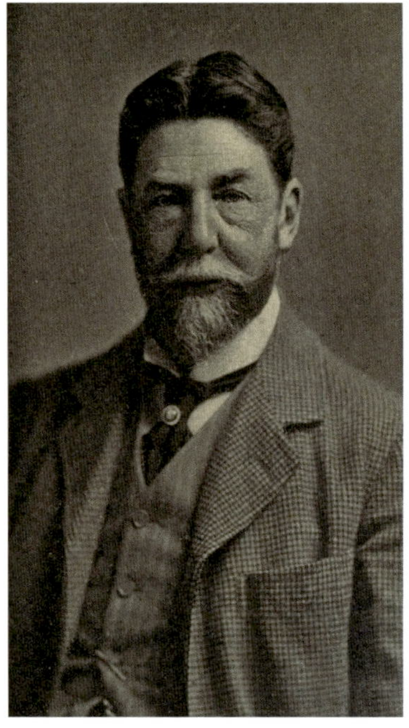

Harry Quilter, 1902, frontispiece in *What's what, a guide for to-day to life as it is and things as they are*, by Harry Quilter, published by Sonnenschein, 1902.

Harry Quilter (1851–1907), a journalist and art critic, was the youngest son of William Quilter (1808–1888) who came to London from Suffolk at the age of seventeen to be articled to a prominent public accountant. William Quilter eventually rose to the top of the profession as founder, and first President of the Institute of Chartered Accountants. He became extremely wealthy and formed a considerable art collection.

Harry, after study and travels, became a journalist. He wrote for *The Academy*, *The Times*, and *The Spectator*, and founded the short-lived *Universal Review*. He praised the early Pre-Raphaelite Movement but was critical of its transition into Aestheticism. He is notable for having purchased Whistler's White House in Chelsea after Whistler was bankrupted, for which thereafter he suffered Whistler's enmity. In this 'Tribute' he was responding to a short obituary in *The Times*, dated 27th June 1904.

A TRIBUTE TO FREDERICK SANDYS.
To the Editor of *The Times*:[1]

Sir, – Will you kindly allow me to endorse most heartily the recommendation which I see was made by *The Times*, that the *Medea* of the late Frederick Sandys (he only died last week, I understand) or some other of that painter's best works – e.g., the portrait of Mrs Lewis – should be acquired by the Chantrey Trustees? The life of this artist was no doubt blameworthy and pitiable in various respects, but in pure artistic achievement his work was in several respects unequalled, and for at least a generation he was a consummately skilful craftsman – who never received either from the critics or the public anything like the recognition he deserved.

In pencil or chalk this technical excellence of handiwork was perhaps most conspicuous, but Sandys was more – far more – than a mere draughtsman; he was a man of that rarest of artistic excellencies – intellectual imaginativeness – he could at once conceive a subject vividly and from the aesthetic point of view, and work it out almost with the precision of a syllogism. To this he joined, in oil colour, a clear brilliance of execution akin to that of the early Flemish painters, and scarcely less complete. With a little encouragement and recognition, and, I fear must be added, a little temperance and self-restraint, he might have been an English Van Eyck.

Far back in my childish years I remember his coming to our house to do a portrait of my mother in that favourite medium of his, black chalk just faintly touched with colour, and, much as I loved the picture then from its sympathy of likeness and delicate rendering of the face dear to me, I honour it even more today for its purely artistic qualities. I do not hesitate to say that this is a perfect piece of portraiture. Well, such portraits as these Sandys did between 1856 and 1876 almost by the dozen, in addition to an enormous quantity of illustrative work and his painting [*sic*] – and I believe the Macmillans possess a whole series of them – of celebrated men and women – Meredith, John Morley, Swinburne, Mrs Oliphant, etc. – which should certainly be in the possession of the nation. Might not some of these possibly be acquired under the Chantrey Bequest? It would be a fitting honour to the artistry of the man whose living it was, of late, almost impossible to help; it would to some very small extent repair the injustice which was perhaps partially responsible for his wasted powers and his pitiable career.

And, might we not go one step further, and so arrange matters with our patrons, connoisseurs, and authorities – Academic and other – that no such neglect and misunderstanding were possible in the future? Is it too much to ask that English painters should try to discover and preserve the genius of their contemporaries, instead of setting an example of neglect and indifference, which the public is only too ready to follow?

Yours obediently,
Harry Quilter
42, Queen's-Gate-Gardens, S.W.

[1] *The Times*, 5th July 1904.

SOURCES

MANUSCRIPTS

Manchester, University of: John Rylands Research Institute and Library.

Sandys Family Archive. Victoria and Albert Museum, Word and Image Department.

Betty Elzea. The Bancroft and Pre-Raphaelite Archives of the Delaware Art Museum.

Betty Elzea. *Frederick Sandys, A Catalogue Raisonné.* (Antique Collectors' Club, Woodbridge, 2001).

Rowland Elzea, (ed.) 'The Correspondence between Samuel Bancroft, Jr and Charles Fairfax Murray, 1892-1916. *Delaware Art Museum Occasional Paper No .2.* February 1980.

Betty O'Looney. Exhibition catalogue. *Frederick Sandys 1829-1904.* Brighton Museum and Art Gallery; Mappin Art Gallery, Sheffield. 1974.

Mary Sandys, (ed.) *Reproductions of Woodcuts by F. Sandys – 1860-1866.* (Carl Hentsche, London, 1910).

Esther Wood. 'A Consideration of the Art of Frederick Sandys'. *The Artist Special Winter Number.* (Constable, London, 1896).

PUBLICATIONS

Marjorie Allthorpe-Guyton. *A Happy Eye: A School of Art in Norwich.* (Jarrold & Sons Ltd., Norwich, 1982).

Frederick Bacon Barwell. Excerpts of ms. memoirs. *Eastern Daily Press,* Norwich, 23 August 1923.

Monica and Nicholas Brown, (eds.) *Exhibition: The Memoirs of Oliver Brown.* (Evelyn, Adams & Mackay, London, 1968).

Dion Clayton Calthrop. *My Own Trumpet.* (Hutchinson & Co. Ltd., London, *c.*1935).

C.L. Cline, (Ed.) *The Letters of George Meredith.* (Oxford University Press, Oxford, 1970).

C.L. Cline, (Ed.) *The Owl and the Rossettis: The Letters of Charles A. Howell and Dante Gabriel, Christina, and William Michael Rossetti.* (University Park, Pennsylvania State University Press, 1978).

Mrs Harry Coghill, (ed.) *The Autobiography and Letters of Mrs M.O.W. Oliphant.* (Brynmill Press Ltd, 1899).

Oswald Doughty and John Robert Wahl, (eds.) *The Letters of Dante Gabriel Rossetti.* (Oxford University Press, Oxford, 1965-1967).

Daphne du Maurier, (ed.) *The Young George du Maurier, a Selection of his Letters 1860-1867.* (Peter Davies, London, 1951).

David B. Elliott. *Charles Fairfax Murray: The Unknown Pre-Raphaelite.* (Oak Knoll Press, New Castle, Delaware, 2000).

John Gielgud. *Early Stages.* (Heinemann Educational, London, 1974).

The Rev. George Hall. *The Gypsy's Parson.* (Sampson Low, Marston & Co., London, 1915).

Harold T. Hartley. *Eighty-Eight Not Out.* (Frederick Muller Ltd., London, 1939).

Carline Mair. *The Chappell Story, 1811-1961.* (Chappell and Co., London, 1961).

A.J. Munnings. *An Artist's Life.* 1878-1959. (Museum Press, London, 1955).

Gail Pedrick. *Life with Rossetti.* (Macdonald, London, 1964).

E.R. and J. Pennell. *The Whistler Journal.* (J.B. Lippincott, Philadelphia, 1921).

Henry H. Roberts. *Memories of Four-Score Years.* 1920.

W. Graham Robertson. *Time Was.* (Hamish Hamilton, 1931).

Elizabeth Robins Pennell. *Nights.* (J.B. Lippincott, Philadelphia, 1916).

Helen Rossetti Angeli. *Pre-Raphaelite Twilight: The Story of Charles Augustus Howell.* (Richards Press, London, 1954).

Mollie Sands. *Robson of the Olympic.* (Society for Theatre Research, London, 1979).

Virginia Surtees, (ed.) *The Diaries of George Price Boyce.* (Real World, Norwich, 1980).

Edwin A. Ward. *Recollections of a Savage.* (H. Jenkins Ltd., London, 1923).

G.C. Williamson. *Murray Marks and his Friends.* (J. Lane Co., London, New York, 1919).

William White. *History, Gazetteer and Directory of Norfolk.* 1845.

See chapter notes for additional information.

ACKNOWLEDGEMENTS

I relied much on the support of my late husband Rowland Elzea at the tentative beginnings of this biography which was often placed on the back burner when household and other practical matters took over. My son Benedict O'Looney has always been supportive and helpful, especially when computer technicalities proved difficult for me. Andrew Wilton has done me an immense service in first reading and editing my imperfect manuscript, after which Debbie Scott put it in good order. My esteemed publisher, Hugh Tempest-Radford of Unicorn Press, has made it into a viable and attractive book. Funding from the Albert Dawson Trust has made it all possible, together with the Paul Mellon Centre which subsidised the illustrations. Overall has been the help and support of Sandys's grandson the late Anthony Crane, who shared his knowledge and memories of his family and gave me access to the family relics and papers, which he bequeathed to me after his death in 2008.

I am also very grateful to the following:

Gretha Arwas
Giorgia Bottinelli
Christian Browning
Ruth Sandys Edwards
Donato Esposito
Susan and Christopher Gale
Julian Hartnoll
Sharon Heppell
Robin Hopkins
Cory Korkow
Dennis Lanigan
Rupert Maas
Maria Renauro
Sir Tim Rice
Anthony Rossi
Christine Shuttleworth
Timothy Stevens
Toshiyuki Takamiya
Mark Taylor
Karen Wilks

INDEX

SURNAMES OF FREDERICK SANDYS'S CHILDREN:

Keomi's four children, I presume, always went by her surname Gray. As for the children of Mary Emma Jones (The Little Girl) Maura must have stuck with Neville, while Cissily and Dorothy probably assumed McManus early on in their foster care home. Winifred, Mildred, Hugh, Maud, Constance, Ruth, Guy, and Gertrude, probably stayed Neville until replaced by Sandys at an unknown date *c.*1900. Edwin, the second to last child, was listed on his death certificate at 14 days old [25.10.1884] as 'son of Mary Sandys'. However, Frederick and Mary and their children are all Neville at the 1891 census. The children at Pevensey are Sandys in the 1901 census. Hugh is Sandys at his wedding in 1903. Our hero Frederick Sandys is clearly Sandys at his death in 1904. The children are all Sandys for the rest of their lives (except the girls who married).

PICTURE CREDITS

a = above, **b** = below, **l** = left, **r** = right

2 Sandys Family Archive
12-13, 26 Yale Center for British Art, Paul Mellon Collection (B1981.25.604)
14 © National Portrait Gallery, London
17 Painters/Alamy Stock Photo
18, 21, 22 © Fitzwilliam Museum / Bridgeman Images
24 Author's Collection
29 from Ibis, British Ornithologists' Union, Jubilee supplement, 1908
33, 41 National Gallery of Canada, Ottawa. Gift of Gwendolen Bulwer, Vancouver, 1961 (9657). Photo NGC
34 © National Portrait Gallery, London
37 Museum of London. Purchased with the assistance of the Art Fund and V&A Purchase Grant Fund. © Museum of London
38 Author's Collection
45 National Museums & Galleries of Wales/Bridgeman Images
47 © The Trustees of the British Museum
50 ©Victoria & Albert Museum, London
53 Courtesy of the Colman family
59, 66 Painters/Alamy Stock Photo
60, 62a, 62b Norwich Castle Museum & Art Gallery (Norfolk Museums Service)
64 Courtesy of Dr. Dennis Lanigan
69 Cleveland Museum of Art. Mr. and Mrs. William H. Marlatt Fund (1979.81)
70 Courtesy of Christian Browning
73 Private collection. Photo © Christie's Images/Bridgeman Images
75 Author's Collection
80 Birmingham Museums (1906P832). Photo by Birmingham Museums Trust, licensed under CC0
83 Ashmolean Museum, Oxford (WA1958.56)
88 Art Gallery of South Australia, Adelaide. Elder Bequest Fund 1901 (01D29)
91 Art Gallery of South Australia, Adelaide. Elder Bequest Fund 1901 (01D30)
92 Yale Center for British Art, Paul Mellon Fund (B1993.20)
95 Photo Jo Winter
101, 365 Birmingham Museums. Presented by the Trustees of the Public Picture Gallery Fund, 1925 (1925P105). Photo by Birmingham Museums Trust, licences under CC0
104, 357 © Victoria and Albert Museum, London
105 Author's Collection
106 © National Maritime Museum, Greenwich, London
108 Norwich Castle Museum & Art Gallery (Norfolk Museums Service)
110l, 349 © The University of Manchester
110r © The University of Manchester
121, 156 The Maas Gallery
122 William Morris Gallery, London Borough of Waltham Forest
124 Museo de Arte de Ponce. The Luis A. Ferré Foundation, Inc. (60.0142)
126 Norwich Castle Museum & Art Gallery (Norfolk Museums Service)
128 from The Artist Special Winter Number, vol. xviii, November 1896
131 Delaware Art Museum. Samuel and Mary R. Bancroft Memorial, 1980 (1980-47)
132 Norwich Castle Museum & Art Gallery (Norfolk Museums Service)
134 Courtesy of the Colman family
136 Private Collection. Photo The Picture Art Collection/Alamy Stock Photo
137 N.M.Rothschild & Sons (NMR 317)
141 Birmingham Museums. Presented by Charles Faifax Murray, 1904 (1904P499). Photo by Birmingham Museums Trust, licences under CC0
150 Private collection
153 © Victoria & Albert Museum, London
165 Courtesy of the late Michael Mott
166 Henry Bedford Lemere photo, Andrew Dickson White Collection. Cornell University Library
168 Author's Collection
185, 241 Private collection
186 Private collection
188 from The Queen's London, a Pictorial Record. Cassell & Co. Ltd. 1896
190 from The Artist Special Winter Number, vol. xviii, November 1896
205 Birmingham Museums. Presented by the Friends of Birmingham Museums & Art Gallery, 1969 (1969P2). Photo by Birmingham Museums Trust, licences under CC0
208 © National Portrait Gallery, London
210 Courtesy of the Arwas Archives
212 © Ashmolean Museum/Bridgeman Images
214, 216 The Macmillan Archive
233 Photo © Christie's Images/Bridgeman Images
236 Courtesy of Ruth Sandys Edwards
244 Courtesy of Timothy Miller
259, 268 Art Renewal Center, N.J., U.S.A. Photo Painters/Alamy Stock Photo
260 Private collection. Photo National Gallery of Canada
263 Sandys Family Archive
264 Wallraf-Richartz Museum, Cologne
267 Tyne & Wear Archives & Museums/Bridgeman Images
270 From The Artist, vol. xviii, November 1896
273 The Maas Gallery
275 © Victoria and Albert Museum, London
276 Courtesy of the Colman family
281 Private collection
283 Museum of Fine Arts, Boston. John H. and Ernestine A. Payne Fund (55.1472). Photo © Museum of Fine Arts, Boston/Bridgeman Images
287 Author's Collection
293, 323 courtesy of Mr and Mrs Christopher Gale
294 Sandys Family Archive
307, 309 Private collection
310 Sandys Family Archive
312 Photo © Christie's Images/Bridgeman Images
317 National Gallery of Canada, Ottawa. Purchased 1925 (3203). Photo NGC
319 University of Dundee Museums
321 courtesy of Ruth Sandys Edwards. Photo Catherine Grillo
326 Sandys Family Archive
333, 347 Photo John Barrow
334a From George Hall, The Gypsy's Parson (*c.*1915), opp. p. 202. (Information thanks to Sharon Heppell of the Romany and Traveller Family History Society)
334b from *True West* magazine
336 Photo and information thanks to Sharon Heppell of the Romany and Traveller Family History Society
339 Samuel and Mary R. Bancroft Pre-Raphaelite Manuscript Collection, Helen Farr Sloan Library and Archives, Delaware Art Museum
340, 341 Sandys Family Archive
342 Samuel and Mary R. Bancroft Pre-Raphaelite Manuscript Collection, Helen Farr Sloan Library and Archives, Delaware Art Museum
345, 366 Private collection